The Montana Vigilantes, 1863–1870

The Montana Vigilantes, 1863–1870

Gold, Guns, and Gallows

Judge Mark C. Dillon

Utah State University Press
Logan

© 2013 by the University Press of Colorado
Published by Utah State University Press

An imprint of University Press of Colorado
5589 Arapahoe Avenue, Suite 206C
Boulder, Colorado 80303

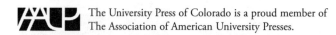 The University Press of Colorado is a proud member of
The Association of American University Presses.

The University Press of Colorado is a cooperative publishing enterprise supported, in part, by Adams
State University, Colorado State University, Fort Lewis College, Metropolitan State University of
Denver, Regis University, University of Colorado, University of Northern Colorado, Utah State
University, and Western State Colorado University.

Cover design by Dan Miller

ISBN: 978-0-87421-919-7 (cloth)
ISBN: 978-0-87421-920-3 (e-book)

Library of Congress Cataloging-in-Publication Data

Dillon, Mark C.
  The Montana vigilantes, 1863–1870 : gold, guns, and gallows / Judge Mark C. Dillon.
    pages cm
  Includes bibliographical references and index.
  ISBN 978-0-87421-919-7 (cloth : alk. paper) — ISBN 978-0-87421-920-3 (ebook : alk. paper)
1. Vigilance committees—Montana—History—19th century. 2. Vigilantes—Montana—History—
19th century. 3. Outlaws—Montana—History—19th century. 4. Criminal justice, Administration
of—Montana—History—19th century. 5. Frontier and pioneer life—Montana. 6. Montana—
History—19th century. I. Title.
  F731.D55 2013
  978.6'01—dc23
                                2013031243

For their generous support of this publication, we gratefully acknowledge the Charles Redd Center for
Western Studies.

Cover photo: Montana Historical Society Research Center Photograph Archives, Helena, Montana

To my wife Michele and our four children, Maura, Monica, Meghan, and Matthew. They represent the inner goodness of the human condition, in sharp contrast to the greed, cruelty, and death described in this narrative.

Contents

Figures

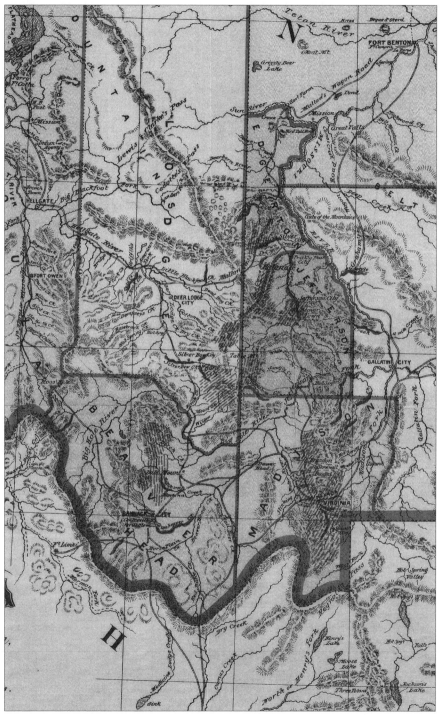

Map of south central Montana drawn in 1865. (Courtesy of the Montana Historical Society, call number B-6.)

Preface

This is a book about history. It involves historical stories of greed, cruelty, politics, chance, crime, and punishment. This book is also about law and due process. The history and law discussed here are subjects so intertwined that it is not possible to discuss one without discussing the other. Vigilantism in Montana in the 1860s and 1870s mixes, in a vibrant way, historical events and their legal overtones.

Writing about the Montana vigilantes poses many challenges, some of which are obvious and some of which may be less so. The most obvious challenge is writing about events that occurred several generations ago. Cases adjudicated in our criminal courts are today so meticulously documented that obtaining information on them is easy, regardless of whether the cases are in state or federal courts and whether they are within appellate- or trial-level jurisdiction. The handling of criminal matters in Montana in the 1860s and 1870s, in both the territory's fledgling court system or at the hands of vigilantes operating outside of an established court system, is not well documented. There is no one alive today who can speak about Montana vigilantism from firsthand knowledge. There are no videotapes or audiotapes that recorded the events in real time. Even black-and-white photographs of the people, places, and things of Montana vigilantism are limited in their number and quality.

Writing about Montana's vigilantism is made even more challenging by the fact that the persons involved did not want contemporaneous evidence of their activities. By definition, they acted outside of any formal or established system of criminal courts. There was never any assurance that vigilante activists would not some day be prosecuted for the roles they played in summarily hanging known and suspected criminals. Some of what has been written was not committed to paper until years after the bloody drama had unfolded, after the risk had safely passed that vigilantes might be criminally prosecuted for their activities.

The best source of information on Montana's vigilantism is the "unofficial" written record left behind by those who lived in the era. The written record includes newspapers articles, nonfiction books, diaries, letters, biographies, and autobiographies that speak to the unique and compelling history of Montana's vigilantism in the latter half of the nineteenth century. The writings of the era connect the land of Montana as it existed in the mid-1800s with the land of Montana today. Only the people living upon the land, and the ways of dealing with serious crime in the region, have changed. The writings from the era, which provide firsthand or, at least, fresh secondhand source information, are perhaps the most reliable historical references that are available today, particularly given the passage of so many years after the events.

Reliance upon the record of events, as written by persons with direct or secondhand knowledge of them, raises a less obvious challenge to contemporary authors of vigilante history. The writers of the record in the late nineteenth century were not necessarily passionless or objective observers of the events. To the contrary, they largely wrote from the standpoint of a bias that was usually sympathetic to the activities of the vigilantes. The writers from the era were either members of a Vigilance Committee themselves or knew and admired other persons who were members. Those who were arrested and hanged by vigilantes did not survive to write their own account of events reflecting their unique viewpoints and biases. The books, newspapers, letters, and diaries of nineteenth-century authors must therefore be examined not just as the treasure troves of information that they are, but must also be examined with a healthy degree of skepticism if ever events are recounted in a way that rings hollow or that are inconsistent with other sources.

The first source to be consulted by any writer examining Montana's vigilante history in the 1860s is Thomas Josiah Dimsdale. He authored an 1866 book that has been reprinted several times called *The Vigilantes of Montana*.[1] Dimsdale was initially a schoolteacher in Virginia City and then became editor of Montana's first newspaper, the *Montana Post*. He was a staunch supporter of the vigilante movement, and although there does not appear to be any irrefutable evidence that he was an actual member of any vigilante organization, at least one historian, R. E. Mather, suggests that he was "[i]n all probability" a member of the movement.[2] He was listed as a vigilante member by M. A. Leeson in the 1885 book *The History of Montana 1739–1885*.[3] In the preface of his book, Dimsdale attests to the accuracy of his account of events, stating that he had "an intimate acquaintance with parties cognizant of the facts related" and felt "certain of the literal truth of the statements contained in [his] history."[4] Dimsdale's claim, that he was acquainted with persons described in the book, suggests that his accounts of events are based upon information obtained first- or secondhand. Nowhere in the book does Dimsdale use the first-person narrative in describing any events he might have observed with his own eyes. Nevertheless, with events that occurred almost 150 years ago, even an account based upon information provided to an author by the actual participants of those events is welcomed source material, and almost the best source available under the circumstances. Dimsdale's account of events should not always be taken as gospel truth, however. He admits, in the same preface, that the vigilantes in Montana were "all honest and impartial men" who admitted "both the wisdom of the course pursued and the salutary effect of the rule of the Vigilantes in the Territory of Montana."[5] Dimsdale is therefore not an objective reporter of events but rather a partisan whose favorable views of vigilantism must, in some ways and at times, color his description of the events in his writings. With that caveat, Dimsdale's book is a necessary starting point in understanding the unusual and compelling events of Montana's vigilantism in the 1860s. Dimsdale's work is more than merely the first among equals.

Many of the chapters in Dimsdale's book were published as part of a periodic series in the *Montana Post* newspaper, of which Dimsdale was editor until his death from tuberculosis on September 22, 1866. The *Montana Post* did not publish contemporary news accounts of any of the vigilante executions at Alder Gulch during the first seven and a half months of 1864, as the newspaper did not publish its first edition until August 17 of that year. By that time, twenty-four persons had already been executed by vigilantes in Bannack and Alder Gulch, starting with Erastus "Red" Yeager and George Brown on January 4, 1864, through and including James Brady on June 15, 1864. Editions of the *Montana Post* contain news articles after 1864 that are not duplicative of Dimsdale's book. This is particularly true of the less notorious vigilante hangings at Alder Gulch and of vigilantism that occurred after Dimsdale's death when additional chapters to his book could no longer be written.

Another period piece of considerable historical importance is that of Nathaniel Langford, titled *Vigilante Days and Ways* and published in 1890.[6] Langford, compared with Dimsdale, was more the wordy intellectual. His accounts of events are, at times, more detailed than Dimsdale's accounts. Sometimes Langford's accounts of events are so strikingly similar to Dimsdale's that one can only assume that he drew portions of them from his predecessor's. Langford was born in 1832 and lived in Montana during the relevant events, from 1862 to 1876.[7] Langford was a man of substance and accomplishment. In 1864 he became a tax collector for the US Internal Revenue Service with his jurisdiction being the newly created territory of Montana.[8] In 1868 outgoing president Andrew Johnson nominated Langford to be governor of Montana Territory, which was subject to approval by the United States Senate. Unfortunately for Langford, the lame-duck Senate refused to act on the nomination, and incoming president Ulysses S. Grant then nominated James M. Ashley to the position.[9] In 1870, Langford was the first superintendent of the Yellowstone Reserve and was part of the movement that eventually led to the creation of Yellowstone National Park.[10] From 1872 to 1876, he was the bank examiner for the western territories.[11]

Langford's work on Montana vigilantism must be taken seriously because there is little question that he was one of the early members of the Alder Gulch Vigilance Committee. His signature does not appear on the original oath of the vigilante organization, dated December 23, 1863, but the names of various prominent members of the Vigilance Committee, such as Wilbur Fisk Sanders, the organization's first president, Paris Pfouts, and the notorious lawman John X. Beidler, do not appear on the document either. In any event, Langford's description of events may be as much an eyewitness account as Dimsdale's but suffers from the fact that *Vigilante Days and Ways* was written twenty-five years after the events it addresses in Bannack and Alder Gulch. Langford, like Dimsdale, is an unabashed supporter and apologist for almost all vigilante deeds, and his writings must therefore be viewed with a degree of knowing suspicion on occasions when the indefensible is defended. Those occasions are identified in this book.

An autobiography of the time that is perhaps overlooked by history is *Reminiscences of Alexander Toponce*. The work was completed in 1920, when Toponce was over eighty years old, and was not published until after his death in 1923. The book is not viewed as central to the events of Bannack and Alder Gulch, as it spans the entirety of Toponce's life, only a portion of which was lived in south central Montana during the relevant period. Nevertheless, Toponce personally knew many of the individuals who shaped the history of south central Montana in the early and mid-1860s. He spent the majority of his time engaged in mercantile activities, in which he was fairly successful, and therefore appears to be an objective observer of events rather than a vigilante actor invested in spinning particular outcomes. He confirms the broad outlines of the major vigilante events.

Edwin Ruthven Purple was a resident of Bannack, Montana, in the early to mid-1860s and witnessed some of the relevant events firsthand. Purple does not appear to have been a member of any vigilante organization, but his writings suggest that he was not particularly sympathetic toward the era's criminals and bullies. Purple wrote *Perilous Passage: A Narrative of the Montana Gold Rush, 1862–1863*. The book parallels the accounts of others about the main historical events of the region during the period. It is a valuable resource in its own way, as it contains certain details about events that are not found in other texts. The book has its limitations, however, as Purple died before his work was complete, and the text that survived him does not include any chapter dealing specifically with the organization and activities of vigilantes at Alder Gulch and Bannack. Purple's writing therefore has not achieved the level of notoriety given to those of Dimsdale and Langford.

Yet another important work was compiled by Lew L. Callaway Jr., *Montana's Righteous Hangmen: The Vigilantes in Action*. Callaway's father, also named Lew L. Callaway, moved with his parents to Virginia City in 1871. Callaway's grandfather was a ranch partner with James Williams, who, as will be seen in this narrative, was a prominent leader of the vigilante movement in Alder Gulch in the mid-1860s. Information contained in Callaway's book may have been sourced, in part, from elder members of his family. Anyone reading the account must question whether, so many years after the fact, James Williams's role in the vigilante movement may have been given greater prominence than it deserved, given the close relationship between the Williams and Callaway families. There is, however, no reason to doubt the accuracy of events described in Callaway's book, as they often mirror the descriptions already provided by Dimsdale, Langford, and others, and as there is little doubt that Williams played a leading role in vigilante activities in 1863, 1864, and 1865. Further, the foreword of Callaway's book is by Professor Merrill G. Burlingame of Montana State College, perhaps the last generation's most respected scholar of Montana's interesting nineteenth-century history.

Francis M. Thompson was likewise proximate to events in Bannack and Virginia City, Montana, for the two and a half years that he lived there in the early 1860s. He personally knew some of the persons that are prominently featured in this narrative, including Governor Sidney Edgerton, Sheriff Henry Plummer, and attorney Wilbur Fisk Sanders.[12] Thompson was not a vigilante, and was certainly no criminal, as he devoted his professional efforts to mining and storekeeping.[13] He was a representative of Beaverhead County in the original territorial legislature that sat in Bannack.[14] Thompson's lack of vigilante credentials cloak his recorded recollections with a measure of objectivity, written after he had returned to New York and his native Massachusetts to live a quiet life as a town clerk, attorney, and probate judge.[15] His recollections are set forth in *Tenderfoot in Montana: Reminiscences of the Gold Rush, the Vigilantes, and the Birth of Montana Territory*.

Granville Stuart is an autobiographer worth noting. Granville and his brother, James, were miners and merchants in Deer Lodge and Virginia City in the late 1850s and 1860s. For more than forty years, Granville Stuart maintained a diary which, later in life, he condensed into book form. His book, *Forty Years on the Frontier*, is actually two books in one. The first, consisting mostly of journal entries, is called *Prospecting for Gold*, which recounts Granville's life and observations from California in 1852 to Virginia City, Montana, in 1864. Notably, Stuart paid tribute to Dimsdale's *Vigilantes of Montana* as "an absolutely correct narrative of the operations of that society."[16] The second book, called *Pioneering in Montana*, chronicles the development of the territory and state of Montana in a predominantly narrative form from 1864 to 1887. Although Stuart was a member of the Alder Gulch vigilantes, he did not play a prominent role in the organization. His diary entries for that time are relevant and nevertheless important to the extent they corroborate some of the events that were written about in more detail by others. The greater significance to Stuart's autobiography is his description of his days as a Montana cattle rancher in the 1880s and the 1884 vigilante movement he led there, called "Stuart's Stranglers." Stuart served as president of the Society of Montana Pioneers in 1886 and 1887 and was president of the Montana Historical Society from 1890 to 1895. His work with the pioneering and historical societies and the writing of *Forty Years on the Frontier* evidences his recognition of and commitment to the preservation of Montana's unique early history. Stuart's autobiography is supplemented by detailed biographical histories, including but not limited to *As Big as the West* by Clyde A. Milner II and Carol A. O'Connor.

Significant detail of the early days of Montana, including the vigilantism of its mining communities, is provided in M. A. Leeson's *History of Montana 1739–1885*, published in 1885. A similar level of historical detail is provided by Frederick Allen's masterful *A Decent Orderly Lynching,* published more recently in 2004.

While most of the published literature is sympathetic to Montana vigilantism or, at least, objective, a revisionist view of the period is provided in the various works of Ruth Mather and F. E. Boswell. Mather's and Boswell's works are must-reads to assure that all relevant and credible viewpoints are considered. They fill a void made by the fact that the persons that were executed by vigilance committees were unable, because of their deaths, to write about their activities and their own points of view.

An examination of Montana's vigilante history also requires a detailed review of original source materials such as diaries, letters, invoices, and newspaper articles written during the period, reminiscences of the period penned by persons with firsthand knowledge of events, and contemporaneous photographs. The Montana Historical Society and the stacks of Montana State University proved to be of enormous assistance as treasure troves of research. Frequently, original source materials corroborate the accounts of events provided by the book authors that were openly sympathetic to the vigilantes, such as Dimsdale, Langford, and others.

Each source that provides first- or secondhand accounts of events is presumed here to be historically accurate unless it conflicts with another source or is implausible, or, at least, questionable on its face. Any source that conflicts with another source or appears implausible or questionable on any point of fact is identified as such in this text or in footnotes.

This book would serve no purpose if it merely marshaled information already set forth in prior publications. The idea for this book originated during a family vacation in Montana, which included horseback riding, whitewater rafting, Yellowstone National Park, a silver mine in Butte, and of course ghost towns along Alder Gulch. I wondered, while touring Virginia City and Nevada City, how the conditions of life and property at the time could have been so dire as to compel law-abiding men to engage in acts of vigilantism against other men, and how different those times and attitudes were compared with what they are today. My curiosity as a lawyer and judge was drawn to the question of how vigilantism was organized and condoned at the time. After all, the people of Montana in the 1860s and 1870s occupied the same land that we occupy today. They enjoyed the same form of democratic government that governs us today, with its separation of powers between executive, legislative, and judicial branches, and its division of powers between the federal government on the one hand and the states and territories on the other. Most significantly, the people who occupied Montana in the 1860s and 1870s were guided by the same federal Constitution, with the same initial fourteen amendments, as guide our government, our rights, and our system of jurisprudence today. Indeed, the Organic Act that created the territory of Montana expressly prohibited the territory's legislature from abridging the rights, privileges, and protections accorded by the US Constitution. Yet, in Montana, there were wide-scale summary hangings of criminals by vigilantes in manners that were contrary to constitutional rights and that are foreign to the concepts of due process known, understood, and accepted by Americans today.

Upon further research, I realized that none of the written accounts of Montana's vigilantism examines the subject through the prism of American *legal* history. A peculiar recognition of the substantive and procedural laws that existed in the western territories in the mid-1800s better informs the factual history of the same period. In my view, an examination of the events of that time cannot be divorced from legal issues that were directly relevant to the behavior of the vigilantes, including the state of criminal justice and law enforcement in the western territories, trial procedures, legislative enactments, territorial politics, and constitutional rights. This book endeavors to fill that void and, for that reason, hopefully contributes to the body of literature that records and analyzes Montana's vigilante past. The historical narrative remains foremost, but analysis of relevant legal issues and their implications is offered to add further context to the events.

Vigilantism has no place in our present society. Its existence in our history is symptomatic of the truly desperate state of affairs that existed in the Civil War era, as chronicled in the pages that follow.

Notes

1. Dimsdale, *Vigilantes of Montana*, iii.
2. Mather, "Was Dimsdale a Vigilante?"
3. Leeson, *History of Montana*, 211.
4. Dimsdale, *Vigilantes of Montana*, iii.
5. Ibid.
6. Langford, *Vigilante Days and Ways*, 7.
7. Ibid.
8. Ibid.
9. Spence, *Territorial Politics*, 11; Allen, *Decent Orderly Lynching*, 362.
10. Langford, *Vigilante Days and Ways*, 7.
11. Ibid.
12. Thompson, *Tenderfoot in Montana*, 3, 146–47, 160.
13. Ibid., 3.
14. Ibid.
15. Ibid., 4.
16. Stuart, *Forty Years on the Frontier*, 2:30–31.

The Montana Vigilantes, 1863–1870

All that Glitters Is Not Gold

Standing under the big sky I feel free.

—Biographical notes of A. B. Guthrie Jr.

The first significant discovery of gold in what is now known as the state of Montana occurred on July 28, 1862, at a spring-fed stream at the Big Hole Basin.[1] Its discoverer, John White, named the stream Grasshopper Creek because of the swarms of grasshoppers that infested the area.[2] Settlers rushed to the area and established the town of Bannack, named after the Bannock Indians that frequented the area for hunting.[3] The spelling of the Bannack municipality with an *ack* instead of an *ock* is not a mistake, as either spelling was considered correct at the time.[4] Within weeks, Bannack's population grew to four or five hundred persons.[5] It marked the beginning of the Montana gold rush,[6] which, while perhaps not as famous as the 1848 gold rush in California, added to the rich and textured history of Montana Territory.[7]

Today, viewing the pristine, undeveloped mountainous regions of Montana can be awe-inspiring. The state displays vast rolling countrysides, snow-capped mountains in July, broad grassy plains, and glinty meandering rivers. Pulitzer Prize–winning author A. B. Gutherie Jr. once sent his publisher some biographical notes that included a quotation from Gutherie's father, "standing under the big sky I feel free."[8] The quote explained the title of Gutherie's 1947 novel, *The Big Sky*,[9] and inspired efforts by the state's Highway Department in 1962 to promote tourism by referring to Montana as "Big Sky Country."[10] Reference to Montana as the land of the "Big Sky" can only truly be understood by being there and visualizing its expanses.

Today, Montana is thinly populated. According to the 2010 census data, its population is 989,415 persons, which equals only 6.8 persons per square mile.[11]

DOI: 10.7330_9780874219203.c001

Figure 1.1. Bannack as it appeared in the 1860s. (Courtesy of the Montana Historical Society, image 940-703.)

Montana's population density ranks forty-eighth among the fifty states.[12] The population of the entire state of Montana is approximately only one-eighth that of the City of New York, which has a population of 8,391,881.[13] The territory's population in the late 1860s was a mere fraction of what it is today.

Away from the automobiles, highways, global positioning devices, cell phones, and other electronic gadgets of modern life, a person's mind can transport itself backward in time to the way things appeared in Montana in the mid- and late 1800s. Montana's undeveloped mountains, streams, and even some of its trees may appear today just as they did 150 years ago. The terrain 150 years ago is cognizable as the same place but at a different time, and was occupied by another generation from our not-too-distant historical past. A significant portion of that generation did not consider itself "American," as Montana was not formed as a territory until May 26, 1864, and was not admitted as a state of the Union until November 8, 1889. In the mid-1860s many inhabitants of present-day Montana were relieved to be away from the death and destruction of the Civil War, while at the same time strongly preferring one side of that conflict over the other.

Montana Territory is known in a variety of geographic, historic, and geologic contexts. Its borders include the near-subsurface volcanic activity, hot springs, and pristine beauty of Yellowstone National Park and Glacier National Park.

The northern Rocky Mountains extend south through Glacier National Park and, in a broken pattern, to Yellowstone National Park in northern Wyoming. Smaller mountain chains run to the west of Montana's Rockies, such as the Cabinet, Mission, Swan, Garnet, Ruby, and Tobacco Root Mountains. Smaller mountain chains also run to the east, such as Little Belt, Big Belt, Snowy, Judith, Absaroka, Beartooth, Big Horn, and Elkhorn Mountains. Montana consists of some of the most rugged, undeveloped, and picturesque real estate of the United States and perhaps of the planet. The land has been carved by massive glaciers that repeatedly advanced and retreated with the changing climate, creating U-shaped valleys that formed lakes from the melted ice. Drainage systems were created, including the Missouri and Yellowstone Rivers.

Topographically, Montana is also situated on the Great Continental Divide, which runs at a roughly northwest-southeast angle at the Idaho border along the Bitterroot and Beaverhead mountain ranges and through Yellowstone National Park; water draining from the east side of the divide flows toward the Atlantic Ocean and water draining from the west side flows toward the Pacific.

Montana was part of Thomas Jefferson's Louisiana Purchase in 1803.[14] Jefferson commissioned a transcontinental exploration of the region by Meriwether Lewis and William Clark, designed to discover its habitats, geography, and routes to the Pacific coast. Three rivers in the region of Montana's earliest gold rush received their names from the Lewis and Clark expedition on July 25, 1805—the Jefferson River, named after President Thomas Jefferson; the Madison River, named after Secretary of State James Madison; and the Gallatin River, named after Secretary of the Treasury Albert Gallatin.[15] The Jefferson, Madison, and Gallatin Rivers converge near Three Forks, Montana, to form the mouth of the Missouri River.

Montana is also the location of famous battles and hardships that involved the United States Cavalry and Native American Indians. Those include General Custer's Last Stand at Little Big Horn on June 25 and 26, 1876,[16] the Trail of Tears, which was undertaken by Chief Joseph and the Nez Perce Indians and which ended in Montana in 1877,[17] and the Battle of the Big Hole with Chief Looking Glass in August of the same year.[18]

And, as primarily relevant here, Montana is a region in which vigilantism took root in gold-mining communities in the mid- and late 1860s and early 1870s.

The presence of gold and silver in south central Montana is related to the region's history of volcanism and geochemistry. The region is part of the North American plate, which, as a result of plate tectonics, is slowly moving westward over a volcanic "hot spot."[19] Because the "hot spot" is stationary, it has generated a string of volcanos on the westward-moving plate, with the oldest volcanos to the west and the youngest to the east. Some are not conical volcanos like those that are familiar today in places such as Hawaii, but are what scientists instead describe as "super massive volcanos" that erupted 2.1 million years ago, and then 1.3 million years ago, and, most recently, 640,000 years ago.[20] What made the volcanos "super massive" was that multiple volcanic vents erupted simultaneously, emptying enough of the magma chamber beneath the surface that the ground collapsed between the volcanos, creating a new erupting caldera as much as 50 miles by 30 miles wide.[21] The energy released from the eruption 2.1 million years ago was 2,500 times greater than the 1980 eruption of Mount St. Helens in the state of Washington.[22] The eruption 1.3 million years ago threw 67 cubic miles of rock and ash over 1,000 square miles.[23] The eruption 640,000 years ago threw 240 cubic miles of rock and ash over 1,700 square miles.[24] Significant geologic activity continues under Yellowstone National Park today, accounting for its geysers, mud pots, slowly changing elevations, and an average of five minor earthquakes each day.[25]

Where Montana's volcanic history leaves off, the science of chemistry begins. The volcanism of the region produced precious metals near the surface of the earth's crust, including but not limited to yellow gold. Gold formed when its elements hardened from the magma during the volcanic cooling processes. Some of the earth's gold is located on or near the earth's gravel-laden surface and can be easily dug and "sluiced" by prospectors.

For 640,000 years, gold had been present near the graveled banks of rivers and streams in south central Montana, waiting to be found by anyone drawn to it. Earlier societies inhabiting the land had no apparent use for the precious metal. Residents of the United States and the American territories in the 1860s were the first persons who did. Indeed, people moved their families, their lives, and all their earthly possessions to be near gold so that they could either prospect for it or provide goods and services to those who prospected for it. Other people moved to the region to steal the gold acquired by the prospectors. Some persons coveted gold to such a degree that they would lie, cheat, and even kill others, if necessary, in order to possess it. In the 1860s the American dollar was backed by both gold and silver, which is why finds of the precious metals in the western territories were important, valuable, and economically necessary. The presence of gold deposits in the western territories played a pivotal role in the federal government's organization of territories and the eventual admission of those territories as states of the Union, including that of Montana.

There was a cohesiveness to western mining communities. Thomas Dimsdale noted the common struggles of western pioneers, that "[t]hose who have slept at the same watch-fire and traversed together many a weary league, sharing hardships and privations, are drawn together by ties which civilization wots not of."[26] Some aspects of the period have been romanticized,[27] with prospectors traveling west to find their fortunes in gold, living among broad-shouldered ranchers, the fur traders, and the common townsfolk in architec-turally distinct wood-framed buildings along a main street. There were rugged mountains and large prairies, herds of buffalo, and Native American Indian tribes in the general vicinity. Always of concern, there were outlaws, murder-ers, coach robbers, gamblers, horse rustlers, counterfeiters, and petty thieves.[28] People traveled everywhere by horse or horse-drawn coaches. Towns would have one or more saloons and a dance hall. Guns of every description were easy to obtain.[29] Most everyone owned a gun, and the guns were always loaded. According to Thomas Dimsdale, disagreements between men were "commonly decided on the spot, by an appeal to brute force, the stab of a knife, or the discharge of a revolver."[30] It was said that the shooting of a man at a barbershop would not interfere with the business of shaving.[31] Shootings were so common that most persons were not particularly bothered by them, except when the violence was perpetrated in furtherance of robberies, or for murders committed in a particularly brutal manner.

Many history books have been written about the development of the min-ing communities in the western frontier in the mid-1800s. They describe a more sober, less romanticized time, as historians are necessarily and professionally guided by hard facts and not by romanticism. They naturally cover the vigilan-tism that took place in Montana in the 1860s, 1870s, and 1880s. Works of fic-tion have also been written using the period as a backdrop, loosely tied to true historical events, and are far too many in number to list here.[32]

Some of the most rugged and gripping continental history emerges from Montana in the mid- and late 1800s. Its factual and legal history is worth exam-ining not just for history's own sake, but for what it says about human nature and our need for well-structured law governing how people are to act in rela-tion to one another. The generation that found itself occupying pristine land in places like Virginia City in 1863–64, Helena in 1865–70, and in the Musselshell Valley in 1884 faced challenges to their lives and property without the benefit of established and effective laws, police, prosecutors, courts, or reliable juries.

The story of Montana presents us with how mankind behaves when there is no effective law in place for resolving disputes, which prompted residents to take the law into their own hands. In some ways, it is frightening. But 150 years ago, people lived it. They lived in an undeveloped region, for the most part scratching out a harsh living without the aid of modern conveniences. They confronted crimes of murder and thievery with a mixture of fear and courage. Fear, that serious crimes would be committed against themselves or their loved ones in the near future. Courage, that honest persons would band together to do something to preempt the crime, or at least punish it after the fact, where no established law enforcement could be of meaningful assistance to them. Today, these concepts seem, and in fact are, foreign to us.

Despite all that has been written of Montana's vigilante period by both historians and writers of fiction, virtually nothing has been written of its vigilantism from a focused legal point of view in books, law reviews, and law journals. Acts of vigilantism cannot be divorced from law and the concept of due process as it existed at the time. The intent of this book is to discuss the Montana vigilantism of the 1860s and 1870s from a distinctly historical-legal perspective, ascertainable from the known facts of the events themselves. The purpose here is not to be judgmental toward any person or group, but to adhere as much as possible to what is historically objective. This book examines the conduct of the vigilantes in the context of the due process norms of the time. It also implicates the role and influence of lawyers and judges who, like their non-lawyer counterparts, shaped the history of the region during the rush to earn fortunes in gold at a time when gold was $20.67 an ounce.

Panning for Nuggets

Montana derived its name from the Spanish word montaña, *which means "mountainous." There had been sentiment for naming the new territory after President Thomas Jefferson, who had acquired the region as part of the Louisiana Purchase of 1803.*[33] *The name of the territory was the subject of debate on the floor of the US House of Representatives, prompting alternative names that reflected Unionist and Confederate preferences.*[34] *In the end, the name Montana was independent of Civil War differences, and it prevailed by a voice vote of the congressmen upon the urging of Representative James M. Ashley (R-OH), who chaired the House Committee on Territories.*[35] *The highest peak in Montana is Granite Peak, which is among the Beartooth Mountains within Custer National Forest and which reaches 12,799 feet above sea level.*[36] *Only the western third and southern tier of the state is actually mountainous and forested. Ironically, despite the territory's name, the majority of the state of Montana is not mountainous at all, and instead consists of foothills and flat grassy plains.*

Notes

1. Allen, *Decent Orderly Lynching*, 6; Pace, *Golden Gulch*, 5; Greever, *Bonanza West*, 216; Cushman, *Montana*, 125. See also Hoggatt, "Western Treasures"; Legends of America, "Montana Legends: Bannack"; Big Hole Tourism Association, "History."
2. Allen, *Decent Orderly Lynching*, 6; Pace, *Golden Gulch*, 5; Greever, *Bonanza West*, 216; Cushman, *Montana*, 125; Hoggatt, "Western Treasures"; Legends of America, "Montana Legends: Bannack"; Big Hole Tourism Association, "History"; Purple, *Perilous Passage*, 125.
3. Purple, *Perilous Passage*, 125; Pace, *Golden Gulch*, 5; Allen, *Decent Orderly Lynching*, 6.

4. Cushman, *Montana*, 55.
5. Allen, *Decent Orderly Lynching*, 6; Legends of America, "Montana Legends: Bannack."
6. Legends of America, "Montana Legends: Bannack."
7. Earlier, smaller discoveries of gold had been made but were not as significant as White's discovery. John Owen and Francois Finlay are credited with discoveries of gold as early as February of 1852 on Mill Creek, west of Fort Owen. Burlingame, *Montana Frontier*.
8. Quoted in Shovers, "From Treasure State to Big Sky."
9. Netstate.com, "State of Montana"; Gutherie, *Big Sky*.
10. Shovers, "From Treasure State to Big Sky."
11. United States Census 2010, "Montana."
12. Ibid.
13. New York City Department of City Planning, "Population."
14. Malone, Roeder, and Lang, *Montana*, 150.
15. Ibid., 35–37.
16. Ibid., 130–31.
17. Ibid., 138–39.
18. Ibid., 136.
19. Breining, *Super Volcano*, 27.
20. Ibid., 17.
21. Ibid., 13–14, 17–18.
22. Ibid., 16.
23. Ibid., 17.
24. Ibid.
25. Ibid., 18–19.
26. Quoted in Fisher and Holmes, *Gold Rushes*, 101.
27. Madison, *Vigilantism*, 29.
28. Wilson, *Outlaw Tales*; Roots, "Are Cops Constitutional?" 685, 714n192, citing the National Commission on the Causes and Prevention of Violence, *Violence in America: Historical and Comparative Perspectives* (June 1969), 97.
29. Jordan, *Frontier Law and Order*, 7.
30. Dimsdale, *Vigilantes of Montana*, 8.
31. Bancroft, *History*, 658, attributing the comment to Dimsdale; Fisher and Holmes, *Gold Rushes*, 324.
32. See, e.g., Harris, *Vigilante's Bride*; Buchanan, *God's Thunderbolt*:; Curry, *Montana Vigilantes*; Taylor, *Roaring in the Wind*.
33. Spence, *Territorial Politics*, 11; Allen, *Decent Orderly Lynching*, 282.
34. Spence, *Territorial Politics*, 11; Allen, *Decent Orderly Lynching*, 282.
35. Spence, *Territorial Politics*, 12; Allen, *Decent Orderly Lynching*, 282.
36. United States Department of Agriculture, Forest Service, "Custer National Forest: Absaroka-Beartooth Wilderness."

2

The Rise and Dominance of the "Fourteen-Mile City" at Alder Gulch

Size and production considered[,] it ranks as the world's richest placer gulch.

—Discovery Monument, Virginia City, Montana

After John White's discovery of gold in Bannack, the influx of prospectors to the area of south central Montana resulted in additional finds of precious metals. On May 26, 1863, gold was discovered in a creek of Alder Gulch in what became Virginia City, Montana,[1] approximately seventy miles east of Bannack.[2] The discovery was made by William Fairweather, who was hoping to find only enough gold to finance a purchase of tobacco.[3]

Fairweather was with a party that included Barney Hughes, Thomas Cover, Henry Rodgers, Henry Edgar, and James "Bill" Sweeney.[4] The men were lucky to be alive, as they had ventured along the Yellowstone River and had been captured and robbed by hostile Crow Indians.[5] Fairweather, who possessed an uncanny ability to handle poisonous snakes, saved his life and the lives of his friends by performing antics with a rattlesnake in the presence of Crow leaders, which resulted in their freedom.[6] The group headed back toward Bannack by crossing the Gallatin and Madison Rivers and camped at an unnamed creek that was surrounded by abundant alder shrubs.[7] There Fairweather found thirty cents of coarse gold in some jutting bedrock and, panning further, earned a quick $1.75.[8] He and the rest of his party then found more gold that day totaling $180.00.[9] Each member of the discovery party staked two 100-foot claims along the gulch, one by the right of discovery and one by "preemption."[10]

Fairweather and his party returned to Bannack to obtain mining supplies and provisions. Such purchases did not go unnoticed in the western

DOI: 10.7330_9780874219203.c002

Figure 2.1. Discovery Monument, marking the site of the
discovery of gold in Virginia City. (Photo by author.)

territorial mining communities, so when the members of the Fairweather
party left Bannack to return to their finds, they were followed by 200 men.[11]
At Beaverhead Rock, which is a significant landmark between Bannack and
Virginia City, the Fairweather party confronted the horde and demanded that
their claims be honored; otherwise they would not show the men the location
of the discovery site.[12] The crowd agreed. The Fairweather Mining District was
organized on June 6, 1863, with Dr. William L. Steele chosen as president,
Henry Edgar as recorder, Dr. G. G. Bissell as its miners' court judge, and Dick
Todd as sheriff.[13] Edgar declined the opportunity to serve as recorder and was
immediately replaced by James Fergus.[14]

The discovery site is today marked by a tall monument along a dirt road[15]
within walking distance of Virginia City's main road, Wallace Street.[16] The
gulch where the discovery was made was called Alder Gulch because of the
abundant alder brush that grew along the banks of the creek.[17] The find was
not only enough to purchase some tobacco, but was of such significance that it
ultimately proved to be one of the richest gold strikes in the American West,[18]

yielding up to $10 million in gold per year.[19] It is estimated that the Alder Gulch had yielded $30 million worth of gold by 1868[20] and $90 million in gold by 1889, equivalent in today's terms to more than $40 billion.[21] The purity of the gold at Alder Gulch was higher than that found to the west in Bannack.[22]

The development of Alder Gulch followed a pattern that had been established fifteen years earlier during the California gold rush. In California a camp would be established at a gold find and a broader mining district would be formed comprising several camps.[23] Mining districts were combined into townships.[24] Mining claims were held under the "land laws" set by the camp or district.[25] Years later, the chairman of the US Senate Committee on Mines and Mining described the system of local laws in the mining districts as a "peculiar genius of the American people for founding empire and order . . . "[26] The tradition formed in California was that the land belonged to all men alike until such time the government said otherwise, so that equality in the ownership of claims was the only legal and immediate conclusion.[27] Land claims were therefore measured out in the mining camps equally for each prospector, as an implicit egalitarianism that placed all men on the same level.[28] Every prospector had an even start regardless of clothes, money, manners, education, family connections, pedigree, prior success, or letters of introduction.[29] Gold was so abundant, and its sources seemed so inexhaustible, that everyone was welcome to take a pick axe and a pan and go to work.[30] The most inexperienced youngster had as much of a chance of finding gold as the most renowned professor of geology.[31] The egalitarianism of mining meant that initially there was little or no theft or disorder in the mining camps.[32] That changed somewhat as gold camps and mining districts grew in size and as competition developed for the prime mining tracts.

Also in California the mining districts were created with set boundaries that included certain defined gulches, divides, flats, and ridges.[33] The wishes of the majority prevailed on matters of importance such as in the election of local district leaders.[34] The mining districts were governed by a presiding officer, a recorder of claims, a sheriff for enforcing security and serving legal documents, and a judge who, with or without jurors, resolved civil disputes between prospectors.[35] There were two forms of civil disputes that miners' courts did not hear—debt collection and minor personal matters between men.[36] Men were expected to settle their financial affairs and petty quarrels among themselves, without involving the mining districts' courts.[37] In 1851 the California legislature specifically authorized each township to select a justice of the peace with authority to try cases worth up to $500, order forcible entries and detainers, and resolve all mining disputes regardless of value.[38] Despite the creation of miners' courts in California, there were sporadic cases in the 1850s of mob rule whereby men were hanged without the benefit of a judge or a jury, usually in instances when a criminal was caught red-handed in the midst of a serious crime.[39]

The traditions of the California gold camps carried over to Montana in the 1860s. Camps sprang up alongside gold finds, and mining districts were organized with officers and miners' court judges. William Fairweather's gold discovery prompted a great influx of new inhabitants to the Alder Gulch area.[40] The optimism of the time was reflected in the acts of a young girl, Mollie Sheehan, who, upon arriving in the Montana Territory with her family by covered wagon, drew her name in the dirt with a stick, and then drove the stick into the ground declaring her "stake."[41] Many of the prospectors that flocked to Alder Gulch were relatively young men, though some were also "old-timers."[42] Some of the persons who prospected for gold in Montana originated from California and brought with them the benefit of their California experiences. At a minimum, the California traditions for organizing gold camps and mining districts were well known and, for the most part, adopted in Montana.

Most of the initial buildings in Virginia City were one-room log cabins with roofs made of poles covered by dirt and sod and with floors of packed earth.[43] By 1864, Virginia City had become the largest mining settlement in the region with a population of approximately 5,000 persons.[44] Another 5,000 persons inhabited other gold camps that sprang up along Alder Gulch,[45] including Summit City, Central City, Nevada City, Pine Grove, Highland City, Beartown, Adobetown, and Junction City.[46] There were other estimates that at its height, in 1864, the population of Virginia City reached as high as 8,000 to 10,000 and that of the greater Alder Gulch area perhaps as high as 15,000.[47] By comparison, the population of Denver at the time was 2,500, Portland 3,000, and Salt Lake City 6,000.[48] Virginia City in Nevada, not to be confused with the one in Montana, had a population of 10,000.[49] The nine mining communities along Alder Gulch became collectively known as the "Fourteen-Mile City."[50] All of these settlements are now ghost towns with the exception of Virginia City, which continues as a thriving, though tourist-driven, incorporated municipality.

Alder Gulch attracted not only miners at the time, but farmers, ranchers, blacksmiths, shopkeepers, carpenters, boot makers, butchers, saloon owners, immigrant Chinese, assayers, prostitutes, and gamblers.[51] As the population of the Alder Gulch region grew, placer miners began using in October 1864 the first water-powered stamp mill, and in December 1865 the first steam mill.[52]

The passions of the Civil War are a backdrop to the gold-prospecting history of Montana in the mid-1860s. The Organic Act that created the territory of Montana expressly prohibited slavery within the territorial borders.[53]

The Montana mining communities attracted Civil War draft dodgers from both the northern and the southern states, though more so from the South.[54] Alexander Toponce wrote of a standing joke that the entire left flank of General Sterling Price's army was living in Cassia County, Idaho.[55] John X. Beidler recounted a story of how he and his friends hauled a long pole to Virginia City on July 3, 1864, to be used for flying a Union flag the next day.[56] Confederate sympathizers cut the pole into six pieces during the night, prompting Beidler and his friends to haul an even longer replacement pole to the site on July 4 for the flying of the flag, until the replacement pole was destroyed by fire that night.[57]

The Civil War backdrop will reappear at times throughout this book. Southerners sympathetic to the Confederacy made up the majority of many of the Montana mining communities.[58] Many of the men who had migrated to Montana had done so to escape conscription into the Confederate Army.[59] Virginia City was originally to be known as Varina City, named in honor of Varina Davis, the wife of Confederate president Jefferson Davis.[60] The majority of the miners who organized the town had come from the South, so when they drew up plans for their 320-acre townsite, they sought to honor the Davis family and the Confederacy with Varina's name.[61] However, a miners' judge who was needed to approve and record the paperwork, Dr. Giles Gaylord Bissell, was a headstrong Connecticut-born Unionist, and he unilaterally changed the town's paperwork to read "Virginia City" as part of the approval process.[62] The city was officially incorporated on June 16, 1863.[63]

Virginia City achieved a number of "firsts" in Montana's territorial history. It was the home of the territory's first newspaper, the *Montana Post*, in 1864.[64] The *Montana Post* was initially published by John Buchanan, who had brought a printing press to the area from St. Louis, Missouri, and the first edition of the paper was issued on August 27, 1864.[65] Its first issue ran 960 copies and cost fifty cents in gold dust per copy.[66] The newspaper was purchased after its first issue by D. W. Tilton and Benjamin R. Dittes.[67] The establishment of a newspaper in August of 1864 was a significant development for Virginia City, as newspapers were the only means of mass communication at that time in the western territories. The *Montana Post*'s editor, Thomas Dimsdale, who had been a schoolteacher by trade, would be heard from through the pages of the newspaper for approximately two years. The *Montana Post* was published in Virginia City until it was moved by its publishers to Helena in early 1868.[68] In the fall of 1866, a Helena newspaper, the *Tri-Weekly Republican*, moved to Virginia City and published until 1867 under the name of the *Tri-Weekly Post*.[69] A third newspaper, the *Montana Democrat*, which was owned by John P. Bruce, published in Virginia City from July 14, 1868, into August of 1869.[70]

Figure 2.2. Thomas Dimsdale. (Courtesy of the
Montana Historical Society, image 941-967.)

Virginia City was the site of the territory's first chartered Masonic lodge in 1864. The first Masonic meeting took place at the Montana Billiards Hall, next to the present-day Fairweather Inn in Virginia City.[71] Masonic lodges had been earlier organized in Bannack and Nevada City, but their charters were apparently lost in the mail, rendering the lodge in Virginia City, which had received its charter from Kansas, the first official Masonic lodge in the territory.[72]

Virginia City was the site of Montana's first professional prize fight on January 2, 1865, between Con Orem, a saloon keeper who was 5 feet 6½ inches and 138 pounds, and Hugh O'Neil, a miner who was 5 feet 8½ inches and 190 pounds.[73] The fight was a bare-knuckled classic. The match continued for 185 one-minute rounds and lasted from before 2:00 p.m. until sunset.[74] The fight ended in a draw.[75]

In 1865 the territorial capital was moved from Bannack to Virginia City,[76] reflecting the growth of the one locale at the expense of the other.[77] Camels

Figure 2.3. Virginia City as it appeared in 1864. (Courtesy of the Montana Historical Society, image 956-061.)

arrived in Virginia City in 1865 for freighting.[78] Virginia City was also the site of the territory's first public school, which opened its doors in 1866.[79]

Virginia City was a vibrant municipality for its time and place. It attracted men and a small number of women from all walks of life. By 1864, commerce in Virginia City included a stationery store, a drugstore, lumberyards, meat markets, a boot shop, dry goods stores, and public bathrooms.[80] It was also the site of grocery shops, two tobacco shops, four livery stables, two brewers, two banks, four hotels, two bakeries, two "Chinese stores," one bowling alley, ten lawyers, five doctors, and seven saloons.[81] The number of lawyers seems relatively high but reflects the litigious nature of mining disputes that developed in the gold camp boomtowns of the western frontier. A proprietor named A. M. Smith opened a photography studio over Con Orem's saloon, which did a booming business.[82] Photography was a sought-after novelty at the time. Another proprietor named Thomas White opened a barber shop where customers could have both a cut and a color.[83] The city attracted culture in the form of a bookstore, a reading room, a theater, educational lectures, and regular organized prize fights.[84] Virginia City inspired the human desire to work hard with the goal of becoming wealthy, particularly, in this case, through prospecting. A Catholic chapel was opened by Father Joseph Giorda in the fall of 1863.[85] A Methodist church was established in late 1864, headed by Pastor A. M. Hough.[86] An Episcopal church was established on December 25, 1865.[87] "Hurdy-gurdy" houses were established where men could drink alcohol, socialize, and dance to music with women in a somewhat respectable fashion.[88] Carolyn Abbott Tyler wrote that hurdy-gurdy houses became "as plentiful as gold dust."[89]

In sharp contrast with culture and religion, there was also a tawdry side to life in the western territories, reflected in a fair amount of gambling, alcoholism, and brothels.[90] Mollie Sheehan, who much later in life shared her reminiscences with her daughter, recalled as a young child seeing "fancy ladies" with painted cheeks and gaudy clothes, smoking cigarettes while walking up and down the streets.[91] Dimsdale observed that "all the temptations to vice are present in full display, with money in abundance to secure the gratification of the desire for novelty and excitement, which is the ruling passion of the mountaineer."[92]

The outward appearance of ordinary life in the western mining frontier generally, and in Virginia City specifically, masked repeated instances of serious robbery and murder tied directly or indirectly to gold wealth, which gave rise to vigilantism. Alexander Toponce remarked that the discovery of gold at Alder Gulch "attracted the greatest aggregation of toughs and criminals that ever got together in the west. They came up the Missouri River on the steamboats by the scores, deserters from the Union and Rebel armies, river pirates and professional gamblers and sharpers."[93] Toponce's sentiments were echoed by Tyler, who wrote in her reminiscences that "[r]oad agents and outsiders became the terror of the country."[94] Crimes such as robbery and murder became frequent occurrences on the trails that led to and from the region.

Black's Law Dictionary defines "vigilantism" as "[t]he act of a citizen who takes the law into his own hands by apprehending and punishing suspected criminals."[95] Vigilantism is not, in historical practice, a first resort but a last resort. Historian Gordon Morris Bakken breaks vigilantism into three separate categories: "regime-control" vigilantism directed at effecting governmental change, "social-group control" vigilantism targeting minority groups, and "crime-control" vigilantism directed against the perpetrators of crimes handled outside of the formal legal system.[96] As will be shown, events in the region of Bannack and Alder Gulch in 1863–64, Helena from 1865 to 1870, and in the Musselshell Valley in 1884 fit Bakken's "crime-control" definition of vigilantism.

Vigilantism in Bannack and Alder Gulch would not have arisen absent the combination of three factors, which, it is argued here, conspired to trigger the Vigilance Committee into formation and action. Whether the Vigilance Committee would have formed in the absence of any one of the three factors can only be the subject of conjecture and surmise. In any event, the three factors present in the territory that collectively led to the formation of vigilance committees, and the "extra-police" and extrajudicial actions it undertook with mortal consequence in many instances, were as follows:

First, no formal, effective, or honest law enforcement mechanisms, either federal or territorial, existed at the time.

Second, there was a rapid creation of wealth as a result of the discovery of significant deposits of gold.

Third, the transport of wealth to and from Bannack and Alder Gulch by horse or stagecoach was not secure, and, years later, cattle wealth on the Montana prairies was also insecure. In a vacuum where there were no effective police, prosecutorial, and judicial authorities, the prospects for robbery and murder were undeterred and uncontained. Vigilance committees formed as a result.

Once vigilantism was established in Bannack and Alder Gulch, it flourished elsewhere in the territory, particularly in and around Helena. There were many instances of vigilantism in Helena, even though the factors that had led to it in Bannack and Alder Gulch were not all present. Vigilantism may have had an easier time taking root in Helena in 1865–70, as its earlier incidences in Bannack and Virginia City may have had the effect of establishing the private means of law enforcement as an "acceptable" practice in Helena's rough-and-tumble mining environment.

Each of the three factors leading to the committee's formation is discussed in successive chapters.

Panning for Nuggets

While the quantity of gold at Bannack and Alder Gulch prompted a rush to the territory of Montana, silver was not found in any great quantity, though in later years copper and aluminum were found in abundance. There is a very limited number of silver mines in the world. The first significant silver mining district in the United States was at the Comstock Lode, which was discovered in Nevada in 1858. Silver mines are primarily limited to the states of Idaho, Montana, Nevada, and Arizona and the countries of Canada, Mexico, Peru, and Chile. Much of the world's silver supply is not obtained from silver mines, but as a by-product of copper, lead, or zinc extracted through modern industrial processes. Silver's value today is due in large measure to its having the highest level of electrical and thermal conductivity of all of the metals as well as an unusually high level of reflectivity. The symbol for silver on the periodic table is Ag, which is short for "argentum."[97] Argentum is the Latin word for silver, derived from the Sanskrit word "argunas," which means "shining." By comparison, the symbol for gold on the periodic table is Au, which is short for the Latin word "aurum," which means "shining dawn."[98] Aurora was the Roman goddess of dawn.

Notes

1. Sievert and Sievert, *Virginia City*, 14; Montana Heritage Commission, "Virginia City: The Discovery"; Allen, *Decent Orderly Lynching*, 94; Greever, *Bonanza West*, 218; Fazio, "How the Civil War Was Won."

2. Alder Creek originates from Bald Mountain, a peak of the Tobacco Root Range, and empties into the Stinking Water River, now known as the Ruby River. The Ruby River discharges into the Beaverhead River. Allen, *Decent Orderly Lynching*, 8–9; Birney, *Vigilantes*, 45. The Stinking Water River was given its name by local Indians as a result of the noxious smell of hot sulphuric springs at various points along the river's valley (see Allen, *Decent Orderly Lynching*, 9; Pace, *Golden Gulch*, 7; Birney, *Vigilantes*, 45), though there is also lore that the river received its name after hundreds of buffalo froze to death during a particularly severe winter, resulting in the presence and odor of rotting carcasses. Birney, *Vigilantes*, 45.

3. Wolle, *Montana Pay Dirt*, 24; Pace, *Golden Gulch*, 11; Allen, *Decent Orderly Lynching*, 9, 94; Birney, *Vigilantes*, 37; Leeson, *History of Montana*, 211; Barsness, *Gold Camp*, 3–4; Montana Heritage Commission, "Virginia City: The Discovery"; Fazio, "How the Civil War Was Won."

4. Thrapp, *Vengeance!*, 113; Birney, *Vigilantes*, 37–38; Sievert and Sievert, *Virginia City*, 14. According to Bill Sweeney, he and Harry Rogers made the initial discovery of gold at Alder Gulch, finding approximately $1.50 in gold within ten minutes, and then $27.00 in gold. James "Bill" Sweeney Reminiscences, 1921, Mont. Hist. Soc., SC-823, folder 1-1, p. 4. However, history decidedly credits Fairweather for the initial gold discovery.

5. Burlingame, *Montana Frontier*, 84.

6. Allen, *Decent Orderly Lynching*, 91–92.

7. Burlingame, *Montana Frontier*, 87; Allen, *Decent Orderly Lynching*, 92.

8. Bancroft, *History*, 628.

9. Wolle, *Montana Pay Dirt*, 24.

10. Ibid.

11. Ibid.

12. Burlingame, *Montana Frontier*, 87; Wolle, *Montana Pay Dirt*, 24.

13. Burlingame, *Montana Frontier*, 96; Wolle, *Montana Pay Dirt*, 24.

14. Burlingame, *Montana Frontier*, 96.

15. This author observed the monument in July of 2010. The side of the monument reads:

    > ON THIS SPOT MAY 26, 1863 GOLD
    > WAS DISCOVERED BY
    > WILLIAM H. FAIRWEATHER
    > HENRY EDGAR THOMAS W. COVER
    > BILL SWEENEY HARRY RODGERS
    > BARNEY HUGHES
    > —
    > THE GULCH WAS NAMED ALDER
    > THE MINING DISTRICT FAIRWEATHER
    > —
    > ON MAY 26, 1864 MONTANA TERRITORY
    > WAS CREATED BY ACT OF CONGRESS
    > APPROVED BY PRESIDENT LINCOLN
    > —
    > ALDER GULCH HAS PRODUCED OVER ONE
    > HUNDRED MILLION DOLLARS IN GOLD
    > —
    > SIZE AND PRODUCTION CONSIDERED IT RANKS
    > AS THE WORLD'S RICHEST PLACER GULCH

16. Wallace Street was named after Idaho Territory's first governor, William M. Wallace, as Montana was a part of Idaho Territory in 1863 (see Allen, *Decent Orderly Lynching*, 101; United States History, "Idaho"); it remains the name of the main thoroughfare of Virginia City to this day.

17. "Narrative of James Sweeney," James "Bill" Sweeney Reminiscences, 1921, Mont. Hist. Soc., SC-823, folder 1-1, p. 4; "Beginning of Alder Gulch," *Fergus County Argus*, July 1, 1903, p. 4, col. 3; Bancroft, *History*, 628; Pace, *Golden Gulch*, 12; Allen, *Decent Orderly Lynching*, 92.

18. It has been estimated that between 1862 and 1876, the territory of Montana produced gold worth $150 million from approximately 500 gulches. It has also been estimated that between 1862 and 1950, Montana produced gold worth $390,647,052 and silver worth $570,765,138. Greever, *Bonanza West*, 215.

19. Allen, *Decent Orderly Lynching*, 9.

20. Greever, *Bonanza West*, 219; Mendenhall, *Gold and Silver Mining*, 5. A $60 million estimate for the same period is set forth in Leeson's *History of Montana*, published in 1885. Leeson, *History of Montana*, 211.

21. Virginia City Chamber of Commerce, "A Brief Virginia City History." Gold has increased in value since the Internet posting.

22. Toponce, *Reminiscence*, 59; Allen, *Decent Orderly Lynching*, 95.

23. Shinn, *Mining Camps*, 5.

24. Ibid.

25. Ibid.

26. Ibid., 8, quoting a report on a bill pending before the Congress in 1866.

27. Ibid., 110.

28. Ibid.

29. Ibid.

30. Ibid.

31. Ibid.

32. Ibid., 118.

33. Ibid., 123.

34. Ibid., 125.

35. Ibid., 125, 183–84.

36. Ibid., 126.

37. Ibid.

38. Ibid., 199.

39. Ibid., 227.

40. Birney, *Vigilantes*, 42.

41. Baumler, *Girl from the Gulches*, 30.

42. Sievert and Sievert, *Virginia City*, 14.

43. Wolle, *Montana Pay Dirt*, 25.

44. Montana Heritage Commission, "Virginia City: The Discovery."

45. Ibid.

46. Callaway, *Montana's Righteous Hangmen*, 103; Langford, *Vigilante Days and Ways*, 136; Virginia City Chamber of Commerce, "A Brief Virginia City History"; see also Barsness, *Gold Camp*, 17.

47. Thrapp, *Vengeance!*, 124; Greever, *Bonanza West*, 219.

48. Cushman, *Montana*, 97.

49. Ibid.

50. Montana Heritage Commission, "Virginia City: The Discovery."

51. Greever, *Bonanza West*, 235.

52. Ibid., 219.

53. Organic Act of the Territory of Montana, Act May 26, 1864, ch. 95, sec. 6, 13 Stat. 85 et seq.

54. Toponce, *Reminiscences*, 61; Rolle, *Road to Virginia City*, xviii.

55. Toponce, *Reminiscences*, 61.

56. Burlingame, *Montana Frontier*, 155.

57. Ibid., 156.

58. Toponce, *Reminiscences*, 62.

59. Bancroft, *History*, 644.

60. Langford, *Vigilante Days*, 127; Toponce, *Reminiscences*, 61; Pace, *Golden Gulch*, 16; Burlingame, *Montana Frontier*, 87; Thrapp, *Vengeance!*, 122; Birney, *Vigilantes*, 42; Montana Heritage Commission, "Virginia City: The Discovery"; Cushman, *Montana*, 96; Peavy and Smith, *Gold Rush Widows*, 150; Virginia City Chamber of Commerce, "A Brief Virginia City History"; Allen, *Decent Orderly Lynching*, 94; Fazio, "How the Civil War Was Won."

61. Milner and O'Connor, *As Big as the West*, 84; Langford, *Vigilante Days*, 127; Barsness, *Gold Camp*, 16; Montana Heritage Commission, "Virginia City: The Discovery"; Virginia City Chamber of Commerce, "A Brief Virginia City History"; Allen, *Decent Orderly Lynching*, 94; Greever, *Bonanza West*, 218.

62. Pace, *Golden Gulch*, 16; Burlingame, *Montana Frontier*, 87; Allen, *Decent Orderly Lynching*, 94; Birney, *Vigilantes*, 42; Cushman, *Montana*, 97; see also Langford, *Vigilante Days*, 127; Virginia City Chamber of Commerce, "A Brief Virginia City History"; Montana Heritage Commission, "Virginia City: The Discovery"; Legends of America, "Montana Legends: Virginia City." According to author Frederick Allen, the Virginia City name caused confusion with a Virginia City in Nevada Territory as well as with a California town of the same name. Allen, *Decent Orderly Lynching*, 94; Fazio, "How the Civil War Was Won."

63. Sievert and Sievert, *Virginia City*, 14.

64. Greever, *Bonanza West*, 232–33; Virginia City Chamber of Commerce, "A Brief Virginia City History."

65. Bancroft, *History*, 652n22; Access Genealogy, "Montana Organization, Boundaries, and Elections," n. 22.

66. Montana Yesterday, "Montana's First Newspaper."

67. Bancroft, *History*, 652n22; Access Genealogy, "Montana Organization, Boundaries, and Elections," n. 22; Allen, *Decent Orderly Lynching*, 300–301. There is disagreement in the sources about whether the newspaper was sold to Tilton and Dittes after the publication of one issue or two.

68. Bancroft, *History*, 652n22; Library of Congress, National Endowment for the Humanities, "About This Newspaper: The *Montana Post*"; Chronicling America, "About the *Montana Post.*"

69. Bancroft, *History*, 652n22; Access Genealogy, "Montana Organization, Boundaries, Elections," n. 2; Leeson, *History of Montana*, 322.

70. Leeson, *History of Montana*, 322; Library of Congress, National Endowment for the Humanities, "About the *Montana Democrat.*"

71. Virginia City Chamber of Commerce, "A Brief Virginia City History"; Ellingsen, "History of Virginia City Masonic Temple." But see Greever, *Bonanza West*, 231–32, which states that the first Masonic lodge was formed in Virginia City in 1868.

72. Leeson, *History of Montana*, 375.

73. John W. Grannis Diaries, 1863–78, Mont. Hist. Soc., SC-301, folder 4-4; Stuart, *Forty Years on the Frontier*, 2:23–24; Howard, *Montana High, Wide, and Handsome*, 49. Grannis describes the prize fight in his diary as having gone 188 rounds, lasting three hours and eight minutes.

74. Howard, *Montana High, Wide, and Handsome*, 49.

75. Ibid.

76. Allen, *Decent Orderly Lynching*, 320; Greever, *Bonanza West*, 229; Leeson, *History of Montana*, 212; Legends of America, "Montana Legends: Virginia City"; Virginia City Chamber of Commerce, "Fun Facts."

77. In 1875 the territorial capital was again moved, to Helena, which had by that time become the more prosperous. Virginia City Chamber of Commerce, "A Brief Virginia City History."

78. Virginia City Chamber of Commerce, "Virginia City Firsts."

79. Virginia City Chamber of Commerce, "A Brief Virginia City History"; Legends of America, "Montana Legends: Virginia City"; Virginia City Chamber of Commerce, "Fun Facts." But see Greever, *Bonanza West*, 234, which states that the first public school opened at Virginia City on March 5, 1878.

80. Peavy and Smith, *Pioneer Women*, 191.

81. Leeson, *History of Montana*, 776–77.

82. Stuart, *Forty Years on the Frontier*, 2:23.

83. Ibid.

84. Peavy and Smith, *Pioneer Women*, 191.

85. Leeson, *History of Montana*, 779; Malone, Roeder, and Lang, *Montana*, 89.

86. Howard, *Montana High, Wide, and Handsome*, 45.

87. Leeson, *History of Montana*, 779.

88. Fisher and Holmes, *Gold Rushes*, 181.

89. Carolyn Abbott Tyler Reminiscences, 1862–65, Mont. Hist. Soc., SC-1430, folder 1-1.

90. Allen, *Decent Orderly Lynching*, 275.

91. Baumler, *Girl from the Gulches*, 32. Mollie Sheehan was a young girl who maintained a diary of her experiences on the western frontier.

92. Dimsdale, *Vigilantes of Montana*, 8.

93. Toponce, *Reminiscences*, 61.

94. Carolyn Abbott Tyler Reminiscences, 1862–65, Mont. Hist. Soc., SC-1430, folder 1-1.

95. Garner, *Black's Law Dictionary*, 1704.

96. Bakken, *Practicing Law in Frontier California*, 99–100.

97. Stwertka, *Guide to the Elements*, 127.

98. Ibid., 180.

3

The First Factor Leading to Vigilantism in the Region
The Absence of Police, Prosecutorial, and Judicial Authority

*Plummer ought to be hung, and . . . if he was at the [San Francisco] Bay
he would be hung before night.*

—Juror Denny, January 1858

Die like a man and don't make such a fuss of it.

—George Ives to Jack Cleveland, late 1862

T
he areas now known as Idaho and Montana, and all but the southwest corner of Wyoming, were originally part of Idaho Territory, which was created by the US Congress on March 3, 1863.[1] Efforts by the Idaho Territorial Legislature in December 1863 to create counties and to appoint public officials, including sheriffs and judges, did not extend to the outlying region of Bannack and Alder Gulch, as there was anticipation that Montana would soon become a separate territory.[2] Alder Gulch was separated from Idaho's territorial capital, Lewiston, by several hundred miles of rough terrain, inaccessible as a result of mountainous snow during part of the year.[3] Montana did not become a separate territory until May 26, 1864.[4] It was by calendrical coincidence that Montana Territory was created on the one-year anniversary of William Fairweather's discovery of gold at Alder Gulch.

Originally, Montana comprised recognized counties.[5] An impetus for the creation of Montana Territory was the recognition that its newly discovered

DOI: 10.7330_9780874219203.c003

gold wealth could help finance the costs of the Civil War.[6] The Organic Act of 1864, which created the territory of Montana, set forth guidelines for the establishment and operation of executive, legislative, and judicial branches of government, including an elected seven-member Territorial Council, an elected thirteen-member Legislative Assembly, and an election for one nonvoting representative to the United States Congress.[7] From May 26, 1864, forward, any governance that had existed in Idaho Territory ceased to have jurisdictional effect in the newly created territory of Montana.[8]

On June 27, 1864, President Lincoln appointed the chief judge of Idaho's Supreme Court, Sidney Edgerton, as Montana's first territorial governor,[9] but several months passed before other territorial and local offices were filled.[10] Governor Edgerton directed the conduct of a territorial census for drawing Council and Assembly election districts, which revealed a territorial population of 15,822 persons.[11] Of that number, roughly two-thirds resided in Madison County, inclusive of Alder Gulch.[12] In the fall of 1865, President Andrew Johnson appointed Thomas Francis Meagher, a hero of the Civil War, as Montana's secretary, and Meagher became the territory's acting governor when Edgerton returned to his native Ohio.[13] More will be written of Governor Meagher later in this narrative. Nathaniel Langford sought an appointment from President Lincoln as Montana's surveyor general, but perhaps because he was a Democrat, he did not get the job.[14]

The first territorial elections were not held in Montana until October 1864, and the legislature did not sit until December of that year.[15] The majority of the elected Assembly was Democratic while the majority of the Council was Republican.[16] The Council would normally have been in Democratic hands, but Governor Edgerton, a Republican, successfully kept Democrats from taking their seats by requiring that the legislators pledge an oath of loyalty to the Union, which certain legislators sympathetic to the Confederacy refused to do.[17] One historian described the interests and motivations of the Bannack legislators as "not so much to govern as to oversee the slicing of the public pie."[18] The territory's first representative to Congress was the 300-pound Democrat Samuel McLean, who defeated a Unionist lawyer, Wilbur Fisk Sanders, for the position.[19] Sanders would be heard from again. In the meantime, there were no federal or territorial police, prosecutors, or courts. The first federal court in the territory, presided over by Chief Justice Hezekiah Hosmer at a dining-room table at the Planters House Hotel in Virginia City, did not convene until December of 1864.[20] There were also no state-based police, prosecutors, jails, or courts,[21] as the territory did not achieve statehood until November 8, 1889.[22] Ground would not be broken for a county courthouse in Virginia City, in Madison County, until 1873.[23] Consequently, during 1863 and 1864, Montana

Figure 3.1. Sydney Edgerton, who holds the distinction of having served in all three branches of government as a congressman from Ohio, chief justice of Idaho, and governor of Montana. (Courtesy of the Montana Historical Society, image 942-075.)

existed in a governmental and law enforcement vacuum. Formal territorial law enforcement simply did not exist, at least not in any meaningful way.

The discovery of gold attracted many honest, sober, and industrious men to the region,[24] ready to dedicate their livelihood to the task of prospecting. However, as described by Paris Pfouts, a Virginia City shopkeeper, in his 1868 autobiography, the region also attracted "roughs" who were "the most depraved and abandoned characters from California, Oregon, Nevada, Idaho, Salt Lake Valley, and not a few from all the western [United] States."[25] Alexander Toponce likewise lamented that the discovery of gold at Alder Gulch "attracted the greatest aggregation of toughs and criminals that ever got together in the west."[26] Granville Stuart wrote as a young man that the "respectable citizens outnumbered the desperados, but having come from all corners of the earth, they were unacquainted and did not know whom to trust. On the other hand, the 'roughs' were organized."[27] The absence of established law enforcement helped breed the conditions that gave rise to vigilantism.[28] In particular, the lack of a credible system for enforcing criminal law provided the otherwise law-abiding citizenry with the justification for, and an acceptance of, private action as a means of protecting personal and property rights.[29] As described by history professor Richard Maxwell Brown, "[v]igilante action was a clear warning to disorderly inhabitants [of the western frontier] that the newness of the settlement would provide no opportunity for erosion of the established values of civilization."[30]

The absence of territorial law enforcement was not helped by the Civil War. President Lincoln and the United States Congress were preoccupied by the war between the Union and the Confederacy. The future of the Union was at stake. The Civil War ultimately cost 620,000 soldiers' lives.[31] The direct economic costs of the Civil War, including governmental expenditures, property destruction, and the loss or diversion of human capital, has been estimated at over $6.6 billion in 1860s dollars.[32] Filling territorial jobs in far-off Montana was understandably low on the list of national priorities.[33]

The citizens of Bannack and Alder Gulch were therefore left to their own devices in 1863–64 for providing law enforcement and for resolving civil and criminal disputes. They did so in three ways: the creation of "miners' courts," the hiring of local sheriffs, and, when sheriffs proved to be corrupt or ineffective, the resort to vigilantism.

Miners' courts were established as a means of adjudicating civil mining claims and other property issues.[34] The concept was borrowed from precedent established during the California gold rush, where even the California legislature recognized the determinations of miners' courts as binding resolutions of property claims.[35] The proceedings of miners' courts were governed by a desire for fair play, particularly in adjudicating disputes over mining claims, and their decisions were final and accepted.[36] Early Montana miners' courts were enlisted to adjudicate criminal matters, as with the trial, conviction, and execution of Peter John Horan for the murder of Lawrence Keeley in 1862.[37] However, consistent with the California experience, miners' courts in Montana often proved to be inadequate for administering criminal justice, as life and property continued to be at extreme risk for persons traveling through the desolate countryside, particularly travelers who were known to be in possession of gold.[38] Paris Pfouts wrote in his autobiography that "[t]here were no laws in force, save such as the miners had adopted in public meetings for their own government, and which were changed or annulled as suited by the exigencies of a case as it arose."[39]

Communities therefore sought to address the problem of criminal justice by creating positions of local sheriffs.[40] The number of robberies and murders of travelers, as well as the presence of "rough sorts" in saloons and way stations, angered the citizenry.[41] A sheriff who was elected to provide a measure of law and order, to be headquartered in Bannack, was Henry Plummer.[42] Plummer was 5 feet 9 inches, 135 pounds, had brown hair and spoke in a low, quiet voice.[43] His demeanor was unassuming. Without anyone knowing it at the time, Sheriff Plummer would become a central motivating protagonist in the history of Montana vigilantism in 1863–64.

The election for sheriff was held on May 24, 1863.[44] Plummer's prospects for election may have benefitted from his reputation of being an excellent gunslinger and someone whose experience and demeanor would enable him to control the criminal element in the region. Indeed, Plummer had a reputation for being a "quick draw," surpassed in the area only by the devilishly handsome Charley Forbes.[45] The election was conducted at a miners' meeting presided over by Walter Booth Dance, which also included the elections of a local judge, B. B. Burchette, and a coroner, J. M. Castner.[46] Plummer won the election over his opponent, Jefferson Durley, with a comfortable majority of the 554 votes that were cast.[47]

Once elected, Sheriff Plummer had authority to appoint deputies for the other municipalities in the area.[48] Plummer did, in fact, appoint a number of deputies that included D. H. Dillingham as chief deputy, and Buck Stinson, Ned Ray, and Jack Gallagher.[49] Some of Plummer's deputies were unsavory characters, but initially the miners paid it no mind so long as they remained free to prospect for gold without interference.[50] On August 25, 1863, Plummer erected gallows in Bannack made of two tall uprights and a crossbeam, which he used for the hanging of Peter John Horan.[51] The gallows remained available for future use, visible from the town's main street 200 yards away.[52] Seventy miles to the east, the miners of Alder Gulch had selected Dick Todd as sheriff, whose jurisdiction extended to the various mining communities of Alder Gulch, including Summit, Highland, Junction, Adobetown, Nevada City, and other smaller settlements.[53] The deputy sheriffs of Nevada City, Junction, and Virginia City, Montana, were Robert Hareford, Adriel Davis, and, for a short time, J. B. "Buzz" Caven, respectively.[54]

The miners of Bannack likely did not know the full background and criminal disposition of their newly elected sheriff, Henry Plummer.[55] Plummer's public life began as an elected city marshal in Nevada City, California, in 1856.[56] While marshal, he was investigated by a coroner's jury, but acquitted of wrongdoing, in the shooting and death of Sheriff W. W. Wright in an apparent "friendly fire" incident between city law enforcement and California vigilantes during the attempted apprehension of certain escaped prisoners.[57] While still a city marshal, during the evening of September 25, 1857, Plummer

Figure 3.2. Sheriff Henry Plummer. (Courtesy of
LegendsOfAmerica.com.)

shot and killed John Vedder at the Hotel de Paris in Nevada City, California.[58]
The incident apparently arose from Vedder's belief that Plummer was romanti-
cally involved with Vedder's wife, an accusation that both Plummer and Lucy
Vedder denied.[59] Plummer was arrested for the crime and held on $8,000 bail.[60]
Plummer's defense was that he acted in self-defense after Vedder had fired
the first shot, but there was no physical evidence corroborating that claim.[61]
Plummer was indicted, tried before a jury, convicted of murder in the second
degree, and sentenced on January 18, 1858, to twelve years of hard labor at San
Quentin prison.[62]

Plummer's twelve-year prison sentence at San Quentin might normally
have removed him from any role as an historic vigilante antagonist. However,
the conviction was appealed to the California Supreme Court and provides
interesting insight into trial processes and procedures of western courts at
the time. Plummer's appeal focused, in large part, upon the alleged bias and

partiality of three trial jurors, Getchel, Denny, and Jameison, who purportedly expressed opinions of Plummer's guilt prior to their impanelment as jurors.[63] Post-trial affidavits acquired from witnesses accused juror Getchel of having stated that "the people of Nevada [City] ought to take Henry Plummer out of jail and hang him."[64] Juror Denny was accused of having stated prior to the trial that "Plummer ought to be hung, and that if he was at the [San Francisco] Bay he would be hung before night."[65] The appellate decision provides no detail about the statements of bias attributed to juror Jameison.[66] The trial court had denied Plummer a new trial when the witnesses' affidavits were produced, but on appeal the California Supreme Court eloquently determined that a new trial was warranted as "[t]he law permits no such malicious sentiments to fill the breasts of those to whose discretion the lives of our people are confided."[67] The California Supreme Court therefore ordered that Henry Plummer receive a new trial on the basis of the prior jurors' partiality that had favored the prosecution.[68]

Plummer's retrial for the murder of John Vedder resulted in another conviction for murder in the second degree, this time ending with a sentence of ten years of hard labor at San Quentin.[69] There was also another appeal to the California Supreme Court, this time focused upon the admissibility of two witnesses' testimonies and the trial court's instructions to the jury.[70] Unlike Plummer's first murder conviction, the second conviction was affirmed on appeal by the California Supreme Court.[71]

Once again, Henry Plummer's role as a potentially historic figure in law enforcement should have been at an end. However, Plummer was wily and politically connected. Through his political connections and by faking or exaggerating serious illness while in prison, Plummer received on August 15, 1859, a pardon for the Vedder murder from California governor John Weller.[72] Plummer was released from San Quentin, a free man.

After briefly returning to law enforcement and then working as a prospector,[73] Plummer was involved on February 13, 1861, in a fight at a brothel with W. J. Muldoon, resulting in Muldoon's death several weeks later from the injuries he sustained in the altercation, though Plummer was not charged with any crime.[74] After the fight he fled Nevada City, California, but returned when it was apparent that no charges would be filed against him. He quickly became embroiled in another brothel fight, this time with William Riley, during which Plummer sustained a slash wound to the scalp and Riley was shot and killed.[75] Plummer was again arrested but escaped from custody three days later by successfully bribing a jailer.[76]

To avoid an arrest warrant that had been issued as a result of the Riley shooting, Plummer fled to Walla Walla in Washington Territory[77] and then to Lewiston in Idaho Territory, where he was involved in an incident that resulted in the shooting death of Pat Ford.[78] Ford had ordered Plummer and his friends to leave a party because of their drunken and disorderly behavior, resulting in the fatal shootout.[79] Plummer is also believed to have been involved in the murder of a saloon owner named Hildebrandt,[80] whom Plummer had robbed of gold.[81] To help avoid capture on his outstanding California arrest warrant, he sent false word back to California newspapers that he had been hanged in Washington Territory.[82]

Plummer traveled farther east to Bannack in what would later become part of Montana Territory, arriving there on November 22, 1862.[83] In Bannack he shot and killed his onetime friend Jack Cleveland, in the presence of witnesses, at a saloon in the Goodrich Hotel on January 14, 1863.[84] The shooting arose out of a disagreement over whether Cleveland had been repaid a debt incurred during a card game by a man named Jeff Perkins.[85] At the time of the murder, Cleveland, Perkins, Plummer, and others were in Bill Goodrich's saloon when the quarrel broke out, and Cleveland used insolent, insulting language without letting up.[86] Losing patience, Plummer said to Cleveland, "I've got tired of this damn nonsense," and shot his gun at Cleveland twice.[87] One of the bullets hit Cleveland in the chest and he fell.[88] Cleveland asked of Plummer, "You wouldn't shoot a man when he's down, would you?"[89] Plummer responded, "No, get up you son of a bitch. I'll shoot you on your feet."[90] Cleveland managed to stand up and was then shot twice more in the face.[91] The gun was shot so close to Cleveland's face that it caused powder burns to Cleveland's skin.[92] Two loyal bystanders, George Ives and Charley Reeves, took Plummer from the saloon and warned that he had made serious trouble for himself.[93] Plummer, perhaps feeling his oats, told everyone in the saloon his name as he left the premises.[94]

Edwin Ruthven Purple came out of his store from across the street as a result of the commotion and heard Cleveland begging that someone shoot him again to put him out of his misery.[95] George Ives, who had returned to the saloon, displayed a shocking lack of sympathy by telling Cleveland to "die like a man and don't make such a fuss of it."[96] Cleveland lingered in agony for four hours in the care of Henry Crawford and Harry Phleger until death finally overtook him.[97]

With further time to think, Plummer feared that Cleveland, during the four hours before his death, might have told Crawford the identity of his shooter and that Crawford would make trouble.[98] In fact, while Cleveland was still alive, Plummer inquired of Crawford what, if anything, Cleveland had said about the incident.[99] Crawford admitted to nothing.[100] It is unclear why Plummer was not equally concerned about information that Cleveland might have imparted to Phleger.

Figure 3.3. The Goodrich Hotel in Bannack, where Henry Plummer shot and killed Jack Cleveland. The original Beaverhead County Courthouse is the brick building to the left. (Courtesy of the Beaverhead County Museum in Dillon, Montana.)

Plummer nevertheless determined that it was in his interest to kill Crawford to eliminate him as a potential trial witness to any dying declaration uttered by Cleveland about the identity of his shooter.[101] On March 6, 1863, the two men were involved in a shootout wherein Plummer was shot in his dominant arm and the bullet, which traveled down the bone, lodged in the wrist and shattered a wrist bone.[102] Plummer was treated for the injury by Dr. Jerome Glick, who recommended that a portion of the arm be amputated.[103] Plummer's friends drew their pistols and pointed them at the doctor, threatening that Glick save Plummer's arm and his life or be killed.[104] Fortunately for Plummer, gangrene or other complications never set in and Plummer kept his arm. The bullet remained in Plummer's wrist for the rest of his life.[105]

Henry Crawford was unharmed in the altercation with Plummer, but fearing for his life, he fled the territory for the safety of Wisconsin.[106] The injury to Plummer's wrist did not help his marksmanship, and, as a result, the best marksman remaining in the region was Charley Forbes.[107]

There is a dispute as to whether Plummer was ever arrested for Cleveland's murder; some historians state that Plummer was never arrested for the offense,[108] while others maintain that he was tried for the crime but acquitted on the basis of self-defense.[109] Edwin Ruthven Purple, who lived in Bannack at the time, recorded in his unfinished book that Plummer was tried for Cleveland's murder at Castner's Hall before Judge Hoyt, with George Copley acting as the prosecuting attorney and H. P. A. Smith and C. W. Rheem acting as the defendant's co-counsel.[110] According to Purple, Plummer testified at the trial that, while he was a marshal in California, he had killed Cleveland's brother while arresting him for a Wells Fargo robbery and that Jack Cleveland followed him to Bannack to exact his revenge.[111] However implausible the defense's story might sound, given the friendship that had actually existed between Plummer and Cleveland, the jury was satisfied that there was insufficient evidence on which to convict Plummer for the murder.[112] The verdict may have been helped by the fact that Cleveland was roundly disliked in Bannack and would not be missed.[113] Purple's account of Plummer's trial contains such detail as to its place, participants, and substance that history should give Purple the benefit of the doubt that Plummer was, in fact, tried for the murder of Jack Cleveland and acquitted of the crime. Moreover, the 1903 remembrances of Aaron T. Ford, archived at the Montana Historical Society, make reference to a trial of Henry Plummer in which George Copley was the prosecuting attorney and C. W. Rheem and H. P. A. Smith were defense counsel and which resulted in Plummer's acquittal.[114] Though Ford's description of the trial is fuzzy on some of its details, it tends to corroborate Purple's account.

The true motive behind Plummer's shooting of Jack Cleveland might conceivably have had nothing to do with money but with love. Plummer and Cleveland were both smitten with a respectable teacher in the area, Eliza "Electa" Bryan.[115] In fact, Cleveland had even proposed marriage to Bryan, though the proposal must not have been accepted.[116] Cleveland's death eliminated a potential rival for Bryan's affections. Henry Plummer and Electa Bryan became engaged by early 1863. Bryan had traveled to Montana with her sister, Martha Jane Vail, and her sister's family.[117] The Vails were upset with Bryan's decision to marry Plummer based primarily upon Plummer's reputation for violent behavior.[118] Plummer's shooting of Jack Cleveland underscored their concerns.[119] The Vails enlisted the support of Francis Thompson to convince Bryan to break the engagement.[120] When Thompson spoke with Bryan, it became clear that she loved Plummer unconditionally, believing him to be a good man in whom she had the utmost faith.[121]

Initially, Thompson succeeded in convincing Bryan that she should return to the eastern United States for the spring and that if she still felt the same way about Plummer by the fall, she could return to Montana to marry him.[122] She packed her bags for the trip but never left the area because the level of the Missouri River had become too low for steamships to pass.[123] On June 2, 1863, Plummer visited Bryan at the Vails' farm and met Francis Thompson for the first time.[124] Thompson was impressed by Plummer and could see the couple's devotion to each other.[125] The marriage was on, delayed only by the time needed for the arrival of Methodist reverend Henry Reed to officiate the ceremony and,

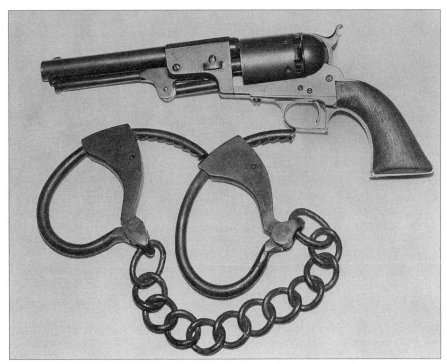

Figure 3.4. Sheriff Henry Plummer's gun and handcuffs. (Courtesy of the Montana Historical Society, image 950-248.)

when it became apparent that Reed could not attend, for a substitute man of the cloth to be arranged.[126]

Plummer married Electa Bryan on June 20, 1863.[127] The ceremony was performed by Father Joseph Minatre, a Jesuit, of St. Peter's Mission, located in Cascade, approximately 140 miles northeast of Bannack.[128] Martha Jane Vail was too distraught to attend her sister's wedding ceremony.[129] Since there was no woman present who could act as a bridesmaid, Francis Thompson tied a white handkerchief around his arm and with good humor served as the bridesmaid pro tempore.[130] The best man was Joseph Swift Jr.[131] After the ceremony, the bridal party enjoyed a wedding breakfast consisting of buffalo hump and corn-meal bread that had been ground in a hand mill, and the happy couple then set out in a four-wheeled wagon for Bannack.[132]

Plummer foreswore saloons and, despite his questionable background, successfully campaigned for sheriff of Bannack in mid-1863 while speaking regretfully of his past associations.[133] He explained to the miners that voted in his election, "Now that I am married and have something to live for, and hold an official position, I will show you that I can be a good man among good men."[134]

Plummer and most of his deputies took advantage of their law enforcement positions to form a broader criminal enterprise, in association with others, in the region of Bannack and Alder Gulch. The chief deputy, D. H. Dillingham, appears to have been an honest man and posed a problem for Plummer and his deputies.[135] However, in choosing other deputies, Plummer selected men who he believed would be adept at playing both sides of the law.[136] Dillingham soon became suspicious of his colleagues and disclosed his suspicions about them to a traveling settler named George Washington Stapleton.[137] Stapleton and another man, Jim Dodge, were moving from Bannack to Virginia City, taking with them a considerable amount of gold dust in the process.[138] Dillingham believed that Stapleton and Dodge had been targeted for robbery by his fellow deputies.[139] Word of Dillingham's warnings to Stapleton reached the ears of road agent conspirators. Apparently, a decision was made that Dillingham needed to be eliminated.[140]

On June 29, 1863, fellow deputy Buck Stinson, Hayes Lyons, and Charley Forbes confronted Dillingham in open public on Wallace Street in Virginia City and killed him.[141] Dillingham had been called out into the street on a ruse.[142] According to author Thomas Dimsdale, three shots were fired at Dillingham in rapid succession, with Lyons's bullet striking Dillingham in the thigh, Forbes's striking him in the chest, and Stinson's aimed too high.[143] Edwin Reuthven Purple attributed the fatal shot to Forbes.[144] Deputy Sheriff Jack Gallagher thereupon "rushed out, as per agreement, and took their pistols," and reloaded them so that no one could tell whose pistol fired the fatal shot.[145] The shooting occurred within the full view of the miners.[146]

Many of the miners wanted to hang the assassins immediately, without any trial.[147] After some heated debate, the majority of residents organized themselves for the purpose of conducting a trial en masse. The question of the accuseds' guilt appeared to be so open-and-shut that John X. Beidler dug the three men's graves before the trial commenced.[148] The trial was presided over by Dr. William L. Steele, assisted by Dr. Giles Gaylord Bissell and Dr. Samuel Rutar.[149] However, the seemingly straightforward set of facts was complicated by the question of which of the three defendants actually fired the fatal shot. Certain witnesses claimed that moments before the murder, Charley Forbes was heard yelling, "Don't shoot! Don't shoot!"[150] Some witnesses believed that Forbes had yelled "Don't shoot!" while simultaneously firing his shot at Dillingham.[151] It was determined, therefore, that the defendants would be split into two trials, with the first being that of Stinson and Lyons, followed by a second trial for Forbes only. At the time, nobody, including Forbes, could have foreseen that the splitting of the trials would have a profound effect on the outcomes of both.

Figure 3.5. Dr. William L. Steele, first president of the Fairweather Mining District and a judge of the miners' court that tried Buck Stinson, Hayes Lyons, and Charley Forbes. (Courtesy of the Montana Historical Society, image 945-091.)

The trials were conducted the next day, but there is no stenographic record of the witnesses' testimonies. Stinson and Lyons were tried and convicted of the murder and were sentenced to be hanged, but Forbes was acquitted in the separate trial held later that same day.[152] Deputy Gallagher, who had taken all three of the suspects' guns immediately after Dillingham's shooting, testified that upon examining Forbes's gun, it had not been fired.[153] Forbes testified in convincing fashion that he had actually tried to prevent Stinson and Lyons from carrying out the murder of Dillingham, that he had yelled "Don't shoot" as the murderous deed was unfolding, and that he never fired his own gun.[154] Speaking generally, Dimsdale wrote that "[n]o matter what may be the proof, if the criminal is well-liked in the community, 'Not Guilty' is almost certain to be the verdict of the jury, despite the efforts of the judge and prosecutor."[155] Speaking of Forbes specifically, Dimsdale attributed Forbes's acquittal to his good looks and education, the fully loaded gun that he claimed was his, and his eloquent appeal to the mass of citizens hearing the evidence.[156] Forbes later boasted, "I talked too well for them to hang me."[157]

Stinson and Lyons were placed into a wagon that was slowly driven toward the execution site.[158] However, the acquittal of Forbes agitated a portion of the crowd in sympathy with Stinson and Lyons, and the members of the public that favored a rescission of the death sentences gained the upper hand. Respectable women in the crowd cried for Stinson and Lyons and pleaded that their lives be spared.[159] "Oh, don't hang the poor boys," screamed one woman hysterically.[160] Aaron T. Ford alleges in his reminiscences that attorney H. P. A. Smith gave $25.00 to each of the women to cry.[161] "Save them," others cried, "Save the poor boys' lives."[162] Smith raised his voice and made a sentimental but lawyerly plea for Stinson's and Lyons's lives.[163] As the death wagon continued its slow and morbid journey toward the execution site, a touching letter by Hayes Lyons to his mother was read to the crowd.[164] Lyons began weeping uncontrollably in the wagon.[165] His letter spoke of a boy's love for his mother, apologized for a crime that had been forced upon him by others, and described the virtuous repentant life he would live if only the good people of his community would give him the opportunity to redeem himself in their eyes.[166] Those who were moved by the tear-jerking document were duped, as Lyons had not composed or even seen the letter—it had been actually written by his friends in a last-ditch effort to curry favor with the public.[167] The letter nevertheless had great impact. "Let's have another vote," yelled someone from the crowd,[168] and despite divided opinion, more than one public revote on Stinson's and Lyons's death sentences were taken, which ultimately resulted in both men being freed later on the same day.[169]

The revotes on the men's death sentences were taken different ways and were somewhat farcical each time. It was initially taken as a voice vote of "ayes" and "nays," and both sides claimed victory.[170] A second revote was taken by forming the crowd into two lines that were counted by monitors. The line that persons formed in favor of the executions required its supporters to walk up a hill while the line of persons in favor of rescinding the death sentences required them to walk down the hill; naturally, some persons were inclined to take the lazier route.[171] Again, both sides claimed victory.[172] The process caused utter confusion and miscommunication, and it was decided that a third revote would be taken. For the third revote, two pairs of men were chosen, and persons favoring execution were to pass through and be counted by one pair of men while those favoring rescission were to pass through the second pair.[173] This method proved unworkable as some persons passed through the monitors several times in order to multiply their votes.[174] Exasperated, Deputy Gallagher, who was of course sympathetic to the defendants, rode his horse into the crowd, and waving a pistol, declared, "Let them go, they're cleared."[175] Hence, the authority of the jury en masse was usurped by Gallagher, and Stinson and Lyons were permitted to live another day. Stinson and Lyons leapt from their death wagon onto the back of a horse belonging to an Indian woman and, while riding past Judge Steele to freedom, said, "Goodbye, Doc."[176]

Meanwhile, the corpse of Deputy Dillingham lay under a sheet upon a gambling table in a nearby wickiup.[177] John X. Beidler remarked of the crowd that "they don't seem to have any tears for the man whom those poor boys murdered."[178] In his writings, Edwin Reuthven Purple was convinced that had more miners been present, the votes would have been different and both Lyons and Stinson would have been hanged.[179]

After the vote was taken that spared Stinson's and Lyons's lives, Beidler placed a sign over their freshly dug graves that read, "Graves to let."[180] In grandiose fashion Lyons stopped his horse and urinated in his grave after the rescission of his sentence as a means of mocking his close brush with death.[181] Members of the crowd who approved of the result went to nearby saloons to toast the men that had escaped their death sentences, while the women discussed their victory over picket fences and on the main street.[182]

After the trial, Forbes purportedly boasted that he had, in fact, fired the shot that proved fatal to Dillingham.[183] Dimsdale recounts that Forbes always had a particular quickness and dexterity at handling a revolver.[184] He had even sewn a scabbard onto his belt, wearing the buckle exactly in the front, so that his right hand could grasp the gun butt, with the forefinger on the trigger and the thumb on the cock with perfect certainty, and he could fire his revolver on a moment's notice.[185] Edwin Reuthven Purple independently acknowledged Forbes's renowned skills as a marksman.[186] Since Forbes was recognized as being a highly accomplished marksman, his better aim at Dillingham's chest, compared to that of Buck Stinson or Hayes Lyons, makes perfect sense. Forbes's shout of "Don't shoot! Don't shoot!" while firing the fatal shot may have been, under this scenario, a clever means of deflecting guilt, which proved successful for Forbes in the long run.

However, the events played out in a manner that placed Forbes's life in further jeopardy after the trial, as he had put his own interests ahead of those of his companions in crime. Forbes had secured for himself a separate trial by claiming that he was innocent of wrongdoing, while also implicating Stinson and Lyons in the Dillingham murder. It is unknown whether Forbes knew of the danger he faced upon his acquittal. Forbes soon left Alder Gulch for good, never to be heard from in Montana again.[187] There is some speculation that Forbes was murdered at Big Hole after his trial by Augustus "Gad" Moore, in vengeance for having "sold out" his comrades in crime.[188]

As an irony peculiar to that area of the federal territory at that time, one of Sheriff Plummer's continuing deputies—Buck Stinson—had become a convicted murderer, but was a free man unpunished for his crime. Dillingham was dead, and his premeditated public murder on Wallace Street, in the presence of witnesses, proved that the criminal justice system in Alder Gulch was not serious or credible. The Dillingham murder, witnessed as it was by onlookers, and the failure of society to hold anyone accountable for the death, symbolized the broken-down state of criminal justice in Alder Gulch at the time. There could only have been a foreboding feeling that Dillingham's unpunished murder meant that there was no justice in Alder Gulch, and that the criminal element operating in the area could continue to commit crime without fear that society would impose any meaningful penalty upon future offenders. Dimsdale reported that "the state of society badly deteriorated, until a man could hardly venture he was safe for a single day . . . Wounded men lay almost unnoticed about the city, and a night or a day without shooting, knifing, or fighting would have been recognized as a small and welcome installment of the millennium."[189] The violent state of society was reflected by a warning to Mollie Sheehan from her stepmother, that she run from errand to errand and not be afraid,[190] presumably to reduce the risk of being caught between Virginia City gunfighters, shot by a stray bullet, or finding herself in the midst of an out-of-control brawl not of her making.

With the election of Henry Plummer as sheriff, the unpunished public murder of Chief Deputy D. H. Dillingham, the absence of effective territorial or federal law enforcement, and the organization of a regional criminal enterprise, as discussed in detail in a later chapter, gold wealth, which was the lifeblood of the mining communities, was insecure and subject to extreme risks. Foxes were guarding the proverbial henhouse at a time when gold was being mined and transported in increasingly significant proportions.

Panning for Nuggets

Montana's official nickname is the Treasure State because of its rich mineral reserves. In addition to gold, copper, and aluminum, Montana is also a source of valuable gemstones such as sapphires and quartz. The state's official motto is "Oro y Plata," which, translated from Spanish, means "gold and silver."

Notes

1. Organic Act of the Territory of Idaho, Mar. 3, 1863, 12 Stat. 808 et seq.; Langford, *Vigilante Days*, 138; Allen, *Decent Orderly Lynching*, 84; Greever, *Bonanza West*, 229.
2. Allen, *Decent Orderly Lynching*, 279.
3. Greever, *Bonanza West*, 229; Sievert and Sievert, *Virginia City*, 20.
4. Organic Act of the Territory of Montana, Act May 26, 1864, ch. 95, sec. 1, 13 Stat. 85 et seq.; see also Pace, *Golden Gulch*, 42; Sievert and Sievert, *Virginia City*, 21; America's Library, "Lincoln Created the Montana Territory"; Graf, *Land of Liberty*, 23; Allen, *Decent Orderly Lynching*, 289.
5. Spence, *Territorial Politics*, 27.
6. Ibid.; Allen, *Decent Orderly Lynching*, 280.
7. Organic Act of the Territory of Montana, Act May 26, 1864, ch. 95, sec. 4, 13 Stat. 85; Sievert and Sievert, *Virginia City*, 21.
8. Allen, *Decent Orderly Lynching*, 296.
9. Sidney Edgerton Family Papers, Mont. Hist. Soc. MC 26, box 1-1, folder 1-1; Spence, *Territorial Politics*, 17. A copy of Edgerton's appointment as governor may be found in the Edgerton Papers, box 1-1, folder 1-2.
10. Allen, *Decent Orderly Lynching*, 296, 299; Greever, *Bonanza West*, 229; Sievert and Sievert, *Virginia City*, 21.
11. Sievert and Sievert, *Virginia City*, 21.
12. Ibid.
13. Wylie, *Irish General*, 232. Sievert and Sievert, *Virginia City*, 23.
14. Spence, *Territorial Politics*, 17.
15. Thrapp, *Vengeance!*, 125; Greever, *Bonanza West*, 229.
16. Sievert and Sievert, *Virginia City*, 22.
17. Spence, *Territorial Politics*, 25.
18. Barsness, *Gold Camp*, 188–89; Spence, *Territorial Politics*, 29.
19. Sievert and Sievert, *Virginia City*, 22; for McLean's weight, see Spence, *Territorial Politics*, 42.
20. Allen, *Decent Orderly Lynching*, 308; Greever, *Bonanza West*, 230. The court did not even publish its opinions until 1868. Greever, *Bonanza West*, 230.
21. Kelley, "Hanging Tree and the Pillory."
22. Enabling Act of the State of Montana, Feb. 22, 1889, 25 Stat. 676; see also Greever, *Bonanza West*, 234; Johnson, Crowley, and McNamee, "Montana"; Brown, *Portraits of the States*, 5.
23. Callaway, *Montana's Righteous Hangmen*, 131.
24. Pfouts, *Four Firsts*, 96.
25. Ibid.
26. Toponce, *Reminiscences*, 61.
27. Stuart, *Forty Years on the Frontier*, 1:237.
28. Hine, "Vigilantism Revisited," 1242–43; McGrath, *Gunfighters, Highwaymen, and Vigilante*, 265 (regarding vigilantism in California); Brown, *Strain of Violence*, 96; Caughey, *Their Majesties the Mob*, 6.
29. Hine, "Vigilantism Revisited," 1242–43; McGrath, *Gunfighters, Highwaymen, and Vigilante*, 265 (regarding vigilantism in California); Brown, *Strain of Violence*, 96; Caughey, *Their Majesties the Mob*, 6; see also Crutchfield, *It Happened in Montana*, 39.
30. Brown, *Strain of Violence*, 97.
31. McPherson, *Battle Cry of Freedom*, 854.
32. Ransom, "Economics of the Civil War."
33. Sievert and Sievert, *Virginia City*, 21.
34. Thompson, *Tenderfoot in Montana*, 21; Allen, *Decent Orderly Lynching*, 10. The Montana Territorial Legislature enacted a law recognizing the customs and practices of miners' courts. Greever, *Bonanza West*, 229–30.

35. Thompson, *Tenderfoot in Montana*, 21, citing, inter alia, Owens, *Riches for All*, 176–201; Shinn, *Mining Camps*; Paul, *California Gold*, 210–39; Ellison, "Mineral Land Question in California," 71–92.

36. Thrapp, *Vengeance!*, 125–26; Pemberton, "Montana's Pioneer Courts," 99. The federal Mining Law of 1872 was later enacted to render mineral deposits part of the public domain and to set federal standards for mining district regulations. The law included a provision that established procedures for processing adverse mining-related claims. Bakken, *Mining Law of 1872*, 9–11.

37. Thompson, *Tenderfoot in Montana*, 179; Pemberton, "Montana's Pioneer Courts," 100.

38. Thompson, *Tenderfoot in Montana*, 22.

39. Pfouts, *Four Firsts*, 95.

40. Morriss, "Private Actors," 128n44. The office of sheriff derives from medieval Europe, where the royal reeve was appointed to maintain order in the shire. With time, the reeves of the shires became known as sheriffs.

41. Allen, *Decent Orderly Lynching*, 163.

42. Pryor, *Lawmen*, 47; Callaway, *Montana's Righteous Hangmen*, 14; Langford, *Vigilante Days*, 114; Allen, *Decent Orderly Lynching*, 88; Birney, *Vigilantes*, 91; Anonymous, *Banditti of the Rocky Mountains*, 69; Greever, *Bonanza West*, 227; Barsness, *Gold Camp*, 26–27; McConnell and Reynolds, *Idaho's Vigilantes*, 18; Cushman, *Montana*, 117. William J. McConnell had been a captain of the Payette, Idaho, vigilantes, a representative of Idaho in the US Senate, and the governor of Idaho from 1893 to 1896. The anonymously authored *Banditti of the Rocky Mountains* is believed to have been written by a Chicago newspaperman named John Lyle Campbell. Allen, *Decent Orderly Lynching*, 317. Plummer's genealogical name may have been spelled with one *m*, but over time use of *mm* became common. For the sake of consistency, the later version is used here.

43. Purple, *Perilous Passage*, 139.

44. Mather and Boswell, *Hanging the Sheriff*, 36; Callaway, *Montana's Righteous Hangmen*, 14; Allen, *Decent Orderly Lynching*, 88; Thrapp, *Vengeance!*, 133; Birney, *Vigilantes*, 91; McConnell and Reynolds, *Idaho's Vigilantes*, 18.

45. Milner and O'Connor, *As Big as the West*, 89; Purple, *Perilous Passage*, 139.

46. Purple, *Perilous Passage*, 186; Callaway, *Montana's Righteous Hangmen*, 14; Allen, *Decent Orderly Lynching*, 88.

47. Purple, *Perilous Passage*, 186; Allen, *Decent Orderly Lynching*, 88; Birney, *Vigilantes*, 91; Mather and Boswell, *Hanging the Sheriff*, 36; see also Callaway, *Montana's Righteous Hangmen*, 15; Cushman, *Montana*, 117.

48. Langford, *Vigilante Days*, 114.

49. Pace, *Golden Gulch*, 29; Callaway, *Montana's Righteous Hangmen*, 15; Allen, *Decent Orderly Lynching*, 89; Thrapp, *Vengeance!*, 133; Birney, *Vigilantes*, 105; Cushman, *Montana*, 117.

50. Thrapp, *Vengeance!*, 134.

51. Langford, *Vigilante Days*, 225; Thompson, *Tenderfoot in Montana*, 179; Anonymous, *Banditti of the Rocky Mountains*, 89; Pace, *Golden Gulch*, 36; Allen, *Decent Orderly Lynching*, 117; Caughey, *Their Majesties the Mob*, 83–84; Ellen Baumler, "Capital Punishment and Executions in Montana," in Bakken, *Invitation to an Execution*, 340.

52. Allen, *Decent Orderly Lynching*, 117.

53. Ibid., 101.

54. Ibid., 173–74. Caven served briefly as a deputy sheriff under Henry Plummer in the summer of 1863, until he moved to Virginia City and became sheriff there in September 1863. Ibid., 174. He did not remain sheriff in Virginia City for long, as he was informed by Plummer that he would live longer if he were to resign his office in Plummer's favor. Clampett, "Vigilantes," 450.

55. Gard, *Frontier Justice*, 169.

56. Pryor, *Lawmen*, 45–46; Allen, *Decent Orderly Lynching*, 28; Dimsdale, *Vigilantes of Montana*, 219; Birney, *Vigilantes*, 63; Anonymous, *Banditti of the Rocky Mountains*, 22; Crutchfield, *It Happened in Montana*, 38.

57. Allen, *Decent Orderly Lynching*, 33–34.

58. Ibid., 41–42; Dimsdale, *Vigilantes of Montana*, 219; Birney, *Vigilantes*, 63; Anonymous, *Banditti of the Rocky Mountains*, 22, 44.

59. Allen, *Decent Orderly Lynching*, 39; see also Cushman, *Montana*, 113.

60. Allen, *Decent Orderly Lynching*, 44.

61. Ibid., 45.

62. Ibid., 42–47; Birney, *Vigilantes*, 63; Barsness, *Gold Camp*, 27.

63. *People v. Plummer*, 9 Cal. 298, 300 (Cal. 1858).

64. Ibid., 300.

65. Ibid.

66. Ibid., 301.

67. Ibid.

68. Ibid. Plummer's second argument on appeal, which was not successful, was that a fair and impartial trial could not be had in his home county owing to the prejudice and feeling there against him. *People v. Plummer*, 9 Cal. 298. The California Supreme Court determined that the venue argument had been waived by Plummer's failure to renew it after his original application to change venue had been postponed by the trial court. The circumstances of juror bias may have contributed to a post-appeal determination by the trial court to move the second trial to a different venue. In any event, the legal proposition set forth in *People v. Plummer*, that a defendant in a capital case may be entitled to a new trial upon a showing of juror partiality, was later expressly overruled by the California Supreme Court in *People v. Fair*, 43 Cal. 137 (Cal. 1874). In *Fair* the court held that section 440 of the state's Criminal Practice Act, in effect by that time, set forth the exclusive grounds for ordering new trials, and that post-verdict evidence of juror bias was not among those recognized in the statute. *People v. Fair*, 43 Cal. 147. See, generally, Bakken and Farrington, *Women Who Kill Men*, 19–39.

69. Allen, *Decent Orderly Lynching*, 48; Birney, *Vigilantes*, 63; Anonymous, *Banditti of the Rocky Mountains*, 22; Cushman, *Montana*, 114; Fisher and Holmes, *Gold Rushes*, 333.

70. *People v. Plummer*, 12 Cal. 256 (Cal. 1859).

71. Ibid.

72. Pryor, *Lawmen*, 46; Pace, *Golden Gulch*, 29; Allen, *Decent Orderly Lynching*, 50; Gard, *Frontier Justice*, 169; Birney, *Vigilantes*, 64; Anonymous, *Banditti of the Rocky Mountains*, 22; Cushman, *Montana*, 114. The illness that was claimed was tuberculosis. Pryor, *Lawmen*, 46.

73. Allen, *Decent Orderly Lynching*, 51–52.

74. Ibid., 52, citing, inter alia, *Nevada Journal*, Feb. 14, 1861.

75. Allen, *Decent Orderly Lynching*, 52–53; Birney, *Vigilantes*, 65, which refers to the shooting victim as Ryder rather than Riley.

76. Allen, *Decent Orderly Lynching*, 53–54; Birney, *Vigilantes*, 64; Cushman, *Montana*, 114; Pryor, *Lawmen*, 46.

77. Crutchfield, *It Happened in Montana*, 38.

78. Bartholomew, *Henry Plummer*, 39–40, 42; Birney, *Vigilantes*, 69; Pryor, *Lawmen*, 47; Allen, *Decent Orderly Lynching*, 55; Gard, *Frontier Justice*, 170; Crutchfield, *It Happened in Montana*, 38.

79. Bartholomew, *Henry Plummer*, 39–40, 42; Birney, *Vigilantes*, 69; Pryor, *Lawmen*, 47; Allen, *Decent Orderly Lynching*, 55; Gard, *Frontier Justice*, 170; Crutchfield, *It Happened in Montana*, 38.

80. McConnell and Reynolds, *Idaho's Vigilantes*, 15; Bartholomew, *Henry Plummer*, 41; Morriss, "Private Actors," 128n43, citing Greever, *Bonanza West*, 261–62.

81. Olsen, "Lawlessness and Vigilantes," 107.

82. Pryor, *Lawmen*, 46; Birney, *Vigilantes*, 64.

83. Allen, *Decent Orderly Lynching*, 70; McConnell and Reynolds, *Idaho's Vigilantes*, 17 (which places the date of Plummer's arrival in Bannack as October of 1862).

84. Pryor, *Lawmen*, 47; Callaway, *Montana's Righteous Hangmen*, 15; Pace, *Golden Gulch*, 27; Allen, *Decent Orderly Lynching*, 74–76; Dimsdale, *Vigilantes of Montana*, 25; Thrapp, *Vengeance!*, 133; Birney, *Vigilantes*, 77–78; Bartholomew, *Henry Plummer*, 7, 43; Greever, *Bonanza West*, 226; McConnell and Reynolds, *Idaho's Vigilantes*, 18; Olsen "Lawlessness and Vigilantes," 111.

85. Langford, *Vigilante Days*, 81; Allen, *Decent Orderly Lynching*, 74.

86. Purple, *Perilous Passage*, 137.

87. Langford, *Vigilante Days*, 81; Purple, *Perilous Passage*, 137; Cushman, *Montana*, 115–16; Birney, *Vigilantes*, 77 (which gives the exact quote as merely "I'm tired of this"); Bartholomew, *Henry Plummer*, 43; Allen, *Decent Orderly Lynching*, 74 (which gives the exact quote as "You son of a bitch, I'm tired of this"). Langford's and Bartholomew's accounts describe one shot hitting Cleveland below the belt.

88. Langford, *Vigilante Days*, 81; Allen, *Decent Orderly Lynching*, 74.

89. Cushman, *Montana*, 116; Purple, *Perilous Passage*, 137; Birney, *Vigilantes*, 77; Allen, *Decent Orderly Lynching*, 74.

90. Langford, *Vigilante Days*, 81; Purple, *Perilous Passage*, 137; Cushman, *Montana*, 116; Birney, *Vigilantes*, 77; Bartholomew, *Henry Plummer*, 43; Allen, *Decent Orderly Lynching*, 74.

91. Langford, *Vigilante Days*, 81; Purple, *Perilous Passage*, 138; Cushman, *Montana*, 116; Birney, *Vigilantes*, 77; Allen, *Decent Orderly Lynching*, 74. Allen's account describes one shot to Cleveland's chest and one to the head.

92. Purple, *Perilous Passage*, 138.

93. Langford, *Vigilante Days*, 81; Allen, *Decent Orderly Lynching*, 74–75.

94. Purple, *Perilous Passage*, 138.

95. Ibid.

96. Ibid.

97. Ibid.; Cushman, *Montana*, 117; Fisher and Holmes, *Gold Rushes*, 333–34.

98. Purple, *Perilous Passage*, 153; Allen, *Decent Orderly Lynching*, 75–76. Allen states that Cleveland lingered for three hours, rather than four, prior to his death.

99. Langford, *Vigilante Days*, 81; Allen, *Decent Orderly Lynching*, 76.

100. Langford, *Vigilante Days*, 81; Allen, *Decent Orderly Lynching*, 76.

101. Purple, *Perilous Passage*, 154; Cushman, *Montana*, 117.

102. Dimsdale, *Vigilantes of Montana*, 39–40; Purple, *Perilous Passage*, 155; Olsen, "Lawlessness and Vigilantes," 115.

103. Buchanan, "Dr. Jerome Glick."

104. Ibid.

105. Dimsdale, *Vigilantes of Montana*, 39–40.

106. Purple, *Perilous Passage*, 158; Cushman, *Montana*, 117.

107. Purple, *Perilous Passage*, 183.

108. Dimsdale, *Vigilantes of Montana*, 27 (which notes that Plummer was never arrested for the murder since shootings, duelings, and outrages were daily occurrences in Bannack at the time); Allen, *Decent Orderly Lynching*, 76.

109. Purple, *Perilous Passage*, 148; Mather and Boswell, *Hanging the Sheriff*, 28–29; Birney, *Vigilantes*, 79–81; Milner and O'Connor, *As Big as the West*, 88.

110. Purple, *Perilous Passage*, 147.

111. Ibid., 147–48.

112. Ibid., 148; Towle, *Vigilante Woman*, 40; see also Fisher and Holmes, *Gold Rushes*, 334.

113. Cushman, *Montana*, 116.

114. Aaron T. Ford Reminiscences, 1903, Mont. Hist. Soc., SC-702, box 1-1, pp. 1–2.

115. Towle, *Vigilante Woman*, 40.

116. Ibid.

117. Thompson, *Tenderfoot in Montana*, 80.

118. Ibid., 150; Allen, *Decent Orderly Lynching*, 65, 95.

119. Allen, *Decent Orderly Lynching*, 95.

120. Thompson, *Tenderfoot in Montana*, 150; Allen, *Decent Orderly Lynching*, 97.

121. Thompson, *Tenderfoot in Montana*, 150–51; Allen, *Decent Orderly Lynching*, 97.

122. Thompson, *Tenderfoot in Montana*, 151; Allen, *Decent Orderly Lynching*, 98.

123. Allen, *Decent Orderly Lynching*, 98.

124. Ibid., 99.

125. Thompson, *Tenderfoot in Montana*, 151; Allen, *Decent Orderly Lynching*, 99.

126. Allen, *Decent Orderly Lynching*, 99; Towle, *Vigilante Woman*, 41.

127. Howard, *Montana High, Wide, and Handsome*, 46; Thompson, *Tenderfoot in Montana*, 141, 152; Langford, *Vigilante Days*, 114; Allen, *Decent Orderly Lynching*, 99; Gard, *Frontier Justice*, 172; Anonymous, *Banditti of the Rocky Mountains*, 63; Cushman, *Montana*, 118; Crutchfield, *It Happened in Montana*, 38.

128. Thompson, *Tenderfoot in Montana*, 141; Allen, *Decent Orderly Lynching*, 99–100. Thompson claims to have personally attended the wedding ceremony. Because no women were present except for the bride, Thompson fulfilled the role of bridesmaid at the request of Father Minatre.

129. Allen, *Decent Orderly Lynching*, 100.

130. Thompson, *Tenderfoot in Montana*, 141; Allen, *Decent Orderly Lynching*, 99–100; Towle, *Vigilante Woman*, 41.

131. Thompson, *Tenderfoot in Montana*, 141.

132. Ibid.; Allen, *Decent Orderly Lynching*, 100; Towle, *Vigilante Woman*, 41–42.

133. Langford, *Vigilante Days*, 114–15.

134. Ibid.; Olsen, "Lawlessness and Vigilantes," 118.

135. Purple, *Perilous Passage*, 186–87; Thrapp, *Vengeance!*, 136.

136. Thrapp, *Vengeance!*, 133.

137. Langford, *Vigilante Days*, 128; Allen, *Decent Orderly Lynching*, 102; Thrapp, *Vengeance!*, 136; Birney, *Vigilantes*, 107; Gard, *Frontier Justice*, 172; see also Dimsdale, *Vigilantes of Montana*, 64; Pace, *Golden Gulch*, 29; Bartholomew, *Henry Plummer*, 9; Anonymous, *Banditti of the Rocky Mountains*, 77–78. Dimsdale identifies the person to whom Dillingham confided as Dodge, who was traveling with Stapleton.

138. Thrapp, *Vengeance!*, 136.

139. Ibid.

140. Hamilton, *From Wilderness to Statehood*, 238.

141. Aaron T. Ford Reminiscences, 1903, Mont. Hist. Soc., SC-702, box 1-1, p. 4; Purple, *Perilous Passage*, 191; Allen, *Decent Orderly Lynching*, 102–4; Thrapp, *Vengeance!*, 136; Sanders and Bertsche, *X. Beidler*, 26; Milner and O'Connor, *As Big as the West*, 87; Gard, *Frontier Justice*, 172; Bartholomew, *Henry Plummer*, 9; Barsness, *Gold Camp*, 33; Greever, *Bonanza West*, 227; see also Thompson, *Tenderfoot in Montana*, 187.

142. Thrapp, *Vengeance!*, 136.

143. Dimsdale, *Vigilantes of Montana*, 65; see also Langford, *Vigilante Days*, 130. Langford recounts the bullet wounds to Dillingham's thigh and chest were inflicted by Lyons and Forbes, but does not describe Stinson's shot.

144. Purple, *Perilous Passage*, 191.

145. Ibid.; see also Thrapp, *Vengeance!*, 136; Hamilton, *From Wilderness to Statehood*, 239.

146. Thrapp, *Vengeance!*, 136.

147. Hamilton, *From Wilderness to Statehood*, 239.

148. M. W. Anderson, "Notes on W. Y. Pemberton's Lecture before the Unity Club at Unitarian Church, May 12, 1868," William Y. Pemberton Papers, 1863–69, Mont. Hist. Soc., SC-629, p. 10; Sanders and Bertsche, *X. Beidler.*, 29; Purple, *Perilous Passage*, 192. According to Dimsdale, graves for Stinson and Lyons were not dug until after they were found guilty of the Dillingham murder. Dimsdale, *Vigilantes of Montana*, 67.

149. Langford, *Vigilante Days*, 128, 131; Dimsdale, *Vigilantes of Montana*, 66; Sanders and Bertsche, *X. Beidler*, 26; Allen, *Decent Orderly Lynching*, 102; Birney, *Vigilantes*, 111.

150. Allen, *Decent Orderly Lynching*, 104.

151. Ibid.

152. Aaron T. Ford Reminiscences, 1903, Mont. Hist. Soc., SC-702, box 1-1, p. 4; Dimsdale, *Vigilantes of Montana*, 67, 70; Langford, *Vigilante Days*, 131–33; Sanders and Bertsche, *X. Beidler*, 27–28; Purple, *Perilous Passage*, 192; Pace, *Golden Gulch*, 30; Allen, *Decent Orderly Lynching*, 105; Thrapp, *Vengeance!*, 136; Birney, *Vigilantes*, 114–15; Gard, *Frontier Justice*, 172; Bartholomew, *Henry Plummer*, 9; Barsness, *Gold Camp*, 34; Greever, *Bonanza West*, 227; Anonymous, *Banditti of the Rocky Mountains*, 82; Hamilton, *From Wilderness to Statehood*, 239; Olsen, "Lawlessness and Vigilantes," 121.

153. Allen, *Decent Orderly Lynching*, 104.

154. Ibid., 105.

155. Dimsdale, *Vigilantes of Montana*, 12.

156. Ibid., 68; Birney, *Vigilantes*, 115.

157. Purple, *Perilous Passage*, 192.

158. Hamilton, *From Wilderness to Statehood*, 240.

159. Purple, *Perilous Passage*, 192; Birney, *Vigilantes*, 118; Allen, *Decent Orderly Lynching*, 106; Hamilton, *From Wilderness to Statehood*, 240.

160. Towle, *Vigilante Woman*, 23.

161. Aaron T. Ford Reminiscences, 1903, Mont. Hist. Soc., SC-702, box 1-1, p. 4.

162. Towle, *Vigilante Woman*, 23.

163. "Notes on W. Y. Pemberton's Lecture," 10.

164. Dimsdale, *Vigilantes of Montana*, 69; Purple, *Perilous Passage*, 192; Hamilton, *From Wilderness to Statehood*, 240.

165. Towle, *Vigilante Woman*, 24.

166. Ibid., 23.

167. Ibid.

168. Ibid., 24.

169. Dimsdale, *Vigilantes of Montana*, 70; Langford, *Vigilante Days*, 133–34; Toponce, *Reminiscences*, 61; Sanders and Bertsche, *X. Beidler*, 29; Allen, *Decent Orderly Lynching*, 106; Thrapp, *Vengeance!*, 137; Birney, *Vigilantes*, 119; Barsness, *Gold Camp*, 35; Greever, *Bonanza West*, 227.

170. Dimsdale, *Vigilantes of Montana*, 69–70; Barsness, *Gold Camp*, 34; Allen, *Decent Orderly Lynching*, 106.

171. Dimsdale, *Vigilantes of Montana*, 70; Sanders and Bertsche, *X. Beidler*, viii; Birney, *Vigilantes*, 118.

172. Barsness, *Gold Camp*, 34.

173. Dimsdale, *Vigilantes of Montana*, 70; Allen, *Decent Orderly Lynching*, 106; Barsness, *Gold Camp*, 34–35; Birney, *Vigilantes*, 118; Hamilton, *From Wilderness to Statehood*, 240.

174. Allen, *Decent Orderly Lynching*, 106; Birney, *Vigilantes*, 123; Greever, *Bonanza West*, 227; Towle, *Vigilante Woman*, 24.

175. Dimsdale, *Vigilantes of Montana*, 70; Barsness, *Gold Camp*, 35; Allen, *Decent Orderly Lynching*, 106; Towle, *Vigilante Woman*, 24; Hamilton, *From Wilderness to Statehood*, 240.

176. Towle, *Vigilante Woman*, 25.

177. Ibid.

178. Birney, *Vigilantes*, 119; Towle, *Vigilante Woman*, 25.
179. Purple, *Perilous Passage*, 192–93.
180. "Notes on W. Y. Pemberton's Lecture ," 10; Sanders, *History of Montana*, 29; Towle, *Vigilante Woman*, 27.
181. Purple, *Perilous Passage*, 193; Allen, *Decent Orderly Lynching*, 107.
182. Towle, *Vigilante Woman*, 25.
183. Dimsdale, *Vigilantes of Montana*, 68.
184. Ibid.
185. Ibid.
186. Purple, *Perilous Passage*, 183.
187. Allen, *Decent Orderly Lynching*, 107; Langford, *Vigilante Days*, 134.
188. Langford, *Vigilante Days*, 134–35; Thompson, *Tenderfoot in Montana*, 187; Callaway, *Montana's Righteous Hangmen*, 21; Mather and Boswell, *Vigilante Victims*, 153.
189. Thrapp, *Vengeance!*, 137.
190. Baumler, *Girl from the Gulches*, 31.

4

The Second Factor Leading to Vigilantism in the Region
The Value of Gold and Silver

The Congress shall have the power to . . . coin money [and] regulate the value thereof.

—US Constitution, art. 1, sec. 8

A second factor explaining the rise of vigilantism in Montana is the central role played by gold in the economies of the United States and its territories in the 1860s and 1870s.

There are 118 elements on the current Periodic Table, some metallic and some not. Of those elements, gold has historically been the premier metal for use as currency. Other metals have been used as currency to some extent. The United States, for instance, has minted silver dollars, and the five-cent nickel is now partially made of its current namesake.[1] Pennies are made partially of copper. Gold, however, exceeds all other metals as a basis for establishing the underlying value of goods and currencies. Gold is the metal that occupies an exalted place in the historical financial consciousness of humankind. The desire to possess gold motivated men in Montana in the 1860s and 1870s to steal and kill for it, just as it motivated vigilantes to execute those who committed gold-related crimes.

But why gold? Why silver? What reason, based on chemistry, history, practicality, tradition, or romanticism, elevates gold and, to a lesser extent, silver as the elements of monetary value that mankind covets more than any others?

Arguably, gold is better suited than all other metals to act as a primary currency or to define currency values. Other solid-state metals are inappropriate for various reasons; either they are hazardous (such as uranium, and arsenic),

DOI: 10.7330_9780874219203.c004

too reactive (such as iron, which rusts), too readily available (aluminum, nickel, copper, to name a few), or too rare to locate in sufficient quantities to make into bars or coins for wide distribution (bismuth and thorium).[2]

The elimination of all gaseous, liquid, harmful, unstable, common, and rare elements leaves only five elements on the Periodic Table that could be "practical" candidates as a currency baseline: gold, silver, platinum, palladium, and rhodium.

Historically, palladium and rhodium have not been viewed as a basis of currency, as the two metals were not even discovered until the nineteenth century: palladium in 1802 by William Hyde Wollaston and rhodium by the same scientist in 1803.[3] Rhodium presents the additional disadvantage of being a mere derivative of platinum ore.[4]

Platinum was not discovered until the sixteenth century by Spanish conquistadors and therefore was never considered as a form of currency during the preceding centuries of human development.[5] Upon its discovery, platinum was not seriously viewed as a currency candidate because its high melting point, at 3,214.4°F,[6] posed too great a challenge during many of the past centuries for melting the metal into coins.[7] Palladium also has a high melting point, at 2,825.6°F.[8] Rhodium has the highest melting point of the five "practical" metals, at 3,567.2°F.[9] The ability to easily forge precious metal into coins is important, as coinage provides a currency with portability, indestructibility, homogeneity, divisibility, and relative currency stability.[10]

Silver is malleable and available in sufficient, but not overabundant, quantities.[11] It has a relatively low melting point, 1,763.47°F, and, as gold's attractive sibling, it is therefore a strong candidate for coinage.[12] However, silver will always be the subject of worldwide industrial demand as it is the most reflective of all of the metals and also the most electrically conductive.[13] Platinum, palladium, and rhodium each have niche industrial uses as well.[14] Silver, platinum, palladium, and rhodium might not be optimally suited as a leading form of currency, since their availabilities and costs might unpredictably fluctuate from year to year based upon the rise or fall of the industrial demands for them.[15] In addition, silver coins, when exposed to air, tarnish,[16] and while tarnish might not be as inconvenient as the rust that forms on iron, it is another reason that silver could be viewed as less than optimal as a primary monetary medium of exchange.

By process of elimination, gold, which primarily has ornamental and investment uses but which serves little industrial purpose, has performed a natural role for much of history as the metal that best sets a stable baseline of value throughout the world. Its melting point is closer to that of silver, at a manageable 1,947.52°F.[17] Also, gold coins do not tarnish or rust.[18] The purity of gold is measured in carats. Pure gold is 24-carat.[19] Softer, less pure gold is 18-carat, meaning that it consists of only 75 percent gold, and 12-carat, which consists of only 50 percent gold.[20]

For these reasons, national currencies have oftentimes been pegged to a "gold standard."[21] A gold standard is defined by three features: (1) the interconvertibility between domestic money and gold at a fixed official price, (2) the freedom of private citizens to import, export, and own gold, and (3) a set of rules fixing a country's quantity of money in circulation to that country's gold reserve.[22]

The US Constitution, article 1, section 8, provides that "The Congress shall have the power to . . . coin money [and] regulate the value thereof." The language of the Constitution gives the federal government a virtual monopoly over the standardization of money and the management of the nation's money supply.[23] Conversely, the individual states were forbidden from coining money, defining the value of coinage, circulating their own money, or recognizing anything but gold and silver as legal tender for the payment of debts.[24] Less clear under the Constitution was whether the federal government had the authority to issue paper money and charter national banks,[25] though eventually both issues were resolved in favor of expanded federal power.

Pursuant to the clear authority set forth in the Constitution in article 1, section 8, the federal government enacted the Coinage Act of 1792, which created a national mint and based the nation's lawful coinage on both gold and silver.[26] The 1792 law created denominations of coins that are familiar today, including dollars, half dollars, quarters, dimes, "half dimes," and cents.[27] The 1792 law also created denominations of coins that are less familiar today, consisting of "eagles" (ten-dollar coins), "half eagles" (five-dollar coins), "quarter eagles" (two-and-a-half-dollar coins), and "half cents" (half a penny).[28] The 1792 statute set forth the amount of gold or silver that the various coins were to contain.[29] Eagles, half eagles, and quarter eagles were to be made of gold.[30] Dollar coins could be made of defined amounts of gold or, alternatively, silver. Half dollars, quarters, dimes, and half dimes were to be made only of silver.[31] The one-cent and half-cent coins were the only pieces of currency to be made of copper, which was a less expensive metal, consistent with their roles as the cheapest of the denominations.[32] Half dimes were not yet known as "nickels," as the nation did not introduce metallic nickel to the five-cent piece until 1886.[33]

A dollar was defined by the Coinage Act of 1792 as 371.25 grains of silver or, alternatively, 24.75 grains of gold.[34] This yielded a statutorily defined silver-to-gold ratio of 15:1.[35] However, increases in silver production in Mexico and South America eventually caused a change in the actual worldwide silver-to-gold ratio, raising the market-priced ratio to 15.5:1.[36] As a result of the market forces, silver became overvalued at the mint, gold became undervalued, and the United States evolved to a de facto silver standard.[37] Further coinage acts were enacted in 1834 and 1837,[38] which statutorily readjusted the United States' bimetallic ratio to 16:1.[39] Discoveries of gold in Russia, Australia, and California in 1848 then conspired to depress the actual market price of gold relative to the 16:1 legal ratio that had been established by the US Congress in 1834.[40] Gold therefore became overvalued at the mint, silver became undervalued, and the country reverted to a de facto gold standard.[41] The Coinage Act of 1837 fixed the price of gold at $20.67 per fine ounce,[42] which prevailed, despite market forces, until 1934.[43] A "fine ounce" is defined as an ounce of a precious metal that is at least 99.5 percent pure.

The statutory 16:1 ratio between the prices of silver and gold during the 1860s[44] established the official price for silver at $1.29 per ounce.[45] Silver was officially demonetized in the United States upon the enactment of the Coinage Act of 1873,[46] which discontinued the minting of silver dollars and tied the national monetary system exclusively to gold.[47] The potential remonetization of silver took center stage in the presidential election of 1896 when William Jennings Bryan, during his acceptance speech at the Democratic National Convention in Chicago, declared that " . . . you shall not crucify mankind upon a cross of gold."[48] However, advocates of silver never gained the upper hand in the US Congress, and silver was never remonetized as a basis for the US dollar.

The nation's monetary policy was affected by the Civil War. President Lincoln, faced with the financial costs of the war, was a monetist. During the early 1860s there was still no central US bank. The only legally recognized money was gold and silver coins and state-chartered bank notes redeemable in an equivalent amount of gold and silver on demand.[49] On February 25, 1862, Lincoln signed into law the Legal Tender Act, which authorized treasury secretary Salmon P. Chase to issue paper money printed in green ink known as "greenbacks."[50] Greenbacks were not redeemable in gold or silver but were backed by the full faith and credit of the federal government, to be redeemable for gold or silver some day in the future.[51] Until that time, federal money had consisted only of coins equal to their face value in gold or silver. Federally issued paper money was a novel concept at the time. The federal government flooded the economy with greenbacks to such an extent that it doubled the national money supply, sparked inflation, and helped Lincoln finance the costs of the war.[52] The National Banking Act of 1863 thereafter created a system of national banks and a uniform national currency.[53] The methods undertaken by Lincoln for financing the Civil War transformed the American banking and monetary system into a decidedly Hamiltonian, rather than a Jeffersonian or Jacksonian, model.[54] Nevertheless, the US government welcomed new supplies of gold and silver such as those found in the western territories, as they helped support the value of the nation's paper currency, officially tied, as it was, to the precious metals.

There were four US presidents after Abraham Lincoln who also made significant decisions that affected the relationship between gold and the American monetary system—Woodrow Wilson, Franklin Delano Roosevelt, Richard Nixon, and Gerald Ford. The presidential decisions are briefly summarized here to illustrate the happy marriage that existed between gold and money in the 1860s, compared with their slow and painful divorce from one another that developed in the twentieth century.

On December 23, 1913, President Woodrow Wilson signed into law the Federal Reserve Act, which created a Federal Reserve Board and regional reserve banks responsible for managing the nation's money supply and the federal government's reserves of gold and silver.[55] The United States declared its entrance into World War I by votes of the US Senate and US House of Representatives on April 2 and April 4, 1917, during Wilson's second term in office.[56] A war traditionally increases the spending of the federal government, and World War I was no exception to that general rule. President Wilson signed the Trading with the Enemy Act on October 6, 1917, which, in section 5, vested the president with the authority to forbid the sale of American gold and silver to all foreign buyers.[57] Wilson exercised the authority that had been granted to him.[58] The purpose of prohibiting foreign sales was to preserve the United States' gold and silver supply relative to the nation's paper money supply, which had been expanded by the Federal Reserve as a means of financing the costs of World War I.[59]

The United States remained on a true gold standard until at least April 5, 1933. On that date, early in the administration of President Franklin Delano Roosevelt, the federal government required that all persons with gold coins and gold certificates in denominations of $100 or more surrender them to the US Treasury by May 1, 1933, in exchange for the long-standing price of $20.67 per ounce.[60] The government accumulated a total of $770 million in gold coins and certificates as a result.[61] On January 30, 1934, the federal government enacted the Gold Reserve Act, which outlawed most private possession of gold and increased gold's legal price per ounce from $20.67 to $35.00.[62] As a result of the Gold Reserve Act, the federal government unilaterally increased the value of its gold holdings by 69.33 percent in one day. The increase in the value of the government's gold assets was deliberate, as it allowed the government to further inflate the paper money supply in a Keynesian attempt to pull the nation from its economic depression. From that point forward, the US gold standard became more of a theory than a fact.[63] In July of 1944, forty-four Allied nations from around the world signed the Bretton Woods agreement that created a World Bank and an International Monetary Fund, which were believed to be necessary for the post–World War II development of national economies and which tied the global price of gold to the US dollar.[64]

The US government maintained the legal price of gold at $35.00 per ounce until August 15, 1971, when President Richard Nixon announced that the government would no longer exchange gold for any fixed value.[65] This was the last step in the nation's complete abandonment of a gold standard, and which caused the US dollar to join the ranks of true "fiat" currencies backed by nothing other than faith and confidence in the US government.

On December 31, 1974, President Gerald Ford signed an executive order that permitted Americans to again privately own gold bullion.[66] The executive order converted the precious metal into what has essentially become an investment vehicle, particularly as a hedge against inflation and against declining dollar values relative to other currencies. Just as the United States never returned to a bimetallic standard after the demonetization of silver, the nation never returned to the gold standard either.

Thus, in 1863 and 1864, at a time when gold was the preferred precious metal over silver, its official price was fixed by the US government at $20.67 per ounce.[67] Gold was crucial to the United States as a basis of its currency exchange, unlike the monetary system that developed in the twentieth century that incrementally removed gold from any central role in the American economy. Gold was the lifeblood of the western mining communities. Gold was the focal point of commerce, carried in small sacks and dispensed by most persons in a way that was second nature. Gold was central to the lives of people on a daily basis, similar to how wallets, dollar bills, and credit cards are routinely used by persons today. Prospecting for gold was therefore a necessary, important, and visible profession in the 1860s, far more so than it is today. Bannack, Virginia City and its neighboring mining camps, and, later, Helena were "company towns" where the company consisted of the prospectors of gold.

The gold discovered at Bannack and Alder Gulch was of high quality, particularly that found at Alder Gulch.[68] The fixed price for gold and silver presumed a fine purity, so precious metals of lesser purity were sold for less.[69] While coins and greenbacks were freely exchanged in the states, gold was the primary form of currency exchanged in the western mining communities such as those of Montana in the 1860s. Storekeepers in the western mining communities did not use cash registers in the sale of their products, as the cash register would not even be invented until 1878 by James Ritty.[70] Rather, merchants in the territorial West kept scales on their sales counters, as most everyone paid their bills with gold nuggets, gold flakes, or gold dust that would be weighed for determining value.[71] Vendors needed to use care and training that gold dust not be confused or diluted with copper, brass, or bronze.[72]

The importance of gold and silver to the economy of the United States and its territories was factored into their prices. Gold's official price of $20.67 per ounce was enough of an incentive for miners to prospect for it in Montana and other territories by mining, panning, and "sluicing." Of course, the value of a dollar in 1863–64 must be viewed in the context of the relative economics of the time. The official $20.67 price of gold per ounce in 1863 is equivalent to $370.00 per ounce in 2012 dollars, accounting for straight adjustments of the consumer price index during the interim period.[73] Other methods for comparing 1863 commodity values with today's values, such as the "average American earnings value" and the "labor value," render a $20.67 ounce of gold equal to $4,270 per ounce and $5,690 per ounce, respectively, in 2012 terms.[74] Accordingly, in relative terms, while gold may or may not be a more valuable commodity today than it was in the mid-1860s depending on the method used to compare its worth, it nevertheless represented great value as the premier precious metal of the time.

Relatively speaking, the cost of living in the mining communities was high. Goods brought to the miners required considerable freighting over great distances, which had the effect of adding to their retail costs.[75] The high cost of living in the western territories provided an even greater incentive for miners to be productive in their efforts. An example of the high costs in Virginia City is provided by Alexander Toponce, who wrote that while in Brigham City, Utah, in 1866, he saw a 600-pound dressed hog that he purchased for six cents per pound. Although his wagon was already laden with tools and food, he hauled the meat in freezing weather to Virginia City, where he sold it for a dollar per pound, representing a considerable markup in price.[76]

Much of the world's gold is extracted from small nuggets attached to rocks and minerals and in the form of small flakes and dust.[77] Gold in south central Montana was not found upon the ground surface itself, but was close enough to the surface as to be accessible by shoveling.[78] Prospectors at Alder Gulch limited their claims to manageable 100-foot sections along the surface of the gulch.[79] The initial discoverers of gold at Alder Gulch allowed themselves 200-foot sections fronting the stream.[80] The sectioning of surface claims gave rise to the term "placer mining."[81] Anyone could dig for gold without any need of initial wealth or special skills.[82] Gold from Alder Gulch was heavier and more pure than that obtained from other Montana placer mines.[83] The number of prospectors who made large fortunes from placer mining was limited.[84] Some prospectors, known as "leasers," took portions of a claim in exchange for paying a percentage of their discoveries to the stakeholder.[85]

Panning for gold in the gulch accounted for little production.[86] Instead, prospectors operated by digging through the gravel along the banks of the gulch.[87] Gold is typically found in veins that must to be separated from the rock and gravel around them.[88] To do so, prospectors built twelve-foot sluice boxes made of yellow pine, through which the water of the gulch would flow.[89] Nails were scarce, so carpenters cut the wood planks for the sluice boxes with great precision.[90] "Riffles" were raised, perpendicular strips inside the sluice boxes that clotted the gravel, and the "bail" was the water current that pulsed over the riffles.[91] Gravel was shoveled into the sluice boxes, and the force of the running water at the riffles separated heavier elements, such as gold, from lighter elements, such as sand and clay, that continued downstream. At the end of each day, prospectors used a tin scraper to scrape even the tiniest particles of gold dust from their sluice boxes.[92] Prospecting was not a profession for weaklings. However, no particular training was required to join the profession. The tools used by prospectors—a sluice box, a pickaxe, a shovel, a scraper, and a container to hold gold nuggets, flakes, or dust—were simple, limited in number, and relatively inexpensive.

The success of the sluice-box system depended on two separate but related factors favoring the prospector. First, the sluices needed to be on a downward angle of at least seven inches per 12-foot box.[93] Fortunately, below Virginia City, Alder Gulch dropped 100 feet per mile for eight miles.[94] It was therefore an ideal area for placer mining. Second, there needed to be water flowing at a rate of at least 120 feet per minute.[95] A four-inch angular descent of the sluice box was minimally adequate if accompanied by sufficient water velocity.[96] The sluice boxes typically enabled prospectors to wash seventy-five cubic yards of gravel per day.[97] The process was several times more efficient than panning for gold.[98] Sluice boxes would periodically need to be cleaned of debris. The work was backbreaking, involving highly intensive manual labor, particularly in the shoveling of the gravel, and was performed in hot and cold temperatures as the seasons changed. Prospectors spent hours each day digging, shoveling, and standing in the water of the stream in the gulch. Prospectors were understandably angry if, after a year of physical labor, their hard-earned gold profits were stolen from them by criminals.

Mining claims were initially staked out in 200-foot increments, and then 100-foot increments that straddled both sides of the gulch.[99] At one point in 1863, miners who had emigrated from British Columbia to the region convinced the miners of Alder Gulch to divide the claims into 100-foot stakes on each bank of the gulch, separated at the middle of the stream.[100] The division was consistent with the methodology already in use in California.[101] The division allowed for twice as many claims but with each claim half the size.[102] Alexander Toponce, who was prospecting at Alder Gulch at the time, lamented the fact that the division cost him half of his claim.[103]

After the conclusion of the Civil War, Montana attracted investment money and "war profits" from the eastern United States, which enabled some miners to find gold more efficiently.[104] Innovations that were capitalized included hydraulic mining techniques that washed the banks of the gulches by powering water through high-pressure hoses and nozzles.[105] Such techniques, though limited at the time, enabled one or two miners to achieve in one hour what normally took scores of miners an entire day.[106]

The amount of gold that was mined in Montana during the period was staggering given the manpower required and the absence of modern technology. As already noted, mining at Alder Gulch grew to yield well over an estimated $10 million in peak years, measured in the dollars of the time, and an approximate total of $90 million during the boom years of 1863 through 1889.[107] In today's dollars, the numbers are even more staggering. Settlers came to the area with high expectations of making fortunes. Some of them struck it rich. Most did not. In his reminiscences, Laurence Abraham Fenner wrote that "[w]ith the great majority [of prospectors], it was a short struggle and the fight was given up, and they either went back to the States disheartened or found an early grave."[108]

The presence of gold explains the interest of the US government in creating Montana Territory on May 26, 1864, and to recognize Montana as the forty-first state on November 8, 1889. Indeed, Sidney Edgerton, who would become Montana's first territorial governor, traveled to Washington, DC, to lobby for the creation of the territory, and during the trip he displayed gold nuggets to President Lincoln and members of Congress to visually underscore his arguments.[109]

While gold may have been the motivating factor behind the US government's interest in forming Montana Territory, the value of gold was a significant motivating factor to the many individuals who moved their livelihoods to the region. The profit motive was the same for the prospectors who labored throughout the year to mine the gold, as it was for the criminals who gravitated to the region to steal gold wealth from them. The prospectors had honest intentions. The criminals, of course, did not. In recognizing that the profit motive of the prospectors was as strong as that of the criminals, it is understandable that both the absence of formal law enforcement and the value placed upon gold provided corresponding motivations for criminals to steal gold wherever, whenever, and however they could. As will be shown in the next chapter, the trails leading in and out of the region provided the criminal element with their best opportunities for committing their crimes.

Panning for Nuggets

The first Catholic mass in Virginia City was held on All Saint's Day, on November 1, 1863.[110] The mass was celebrated by Father Joseph Giorda, a Jesuit priest who was unfamiliar with the cost of goods and services in the area and the value of gold dust used to pay for them.[111] *During the mass, Father Giorda received contributions of gold dust from the members of the congregation that had gathered.*[112] *After the mass, he sought to pay the fees of the stable that had housed his team of horses for two days. He was shocked by the $40.00 bill for the horses' room and board and said that he did not have enough money to pay it. When asked to examine the gold dust that had been donated to him during the mass, he was relieved to be informed that his congregants had been quite generous, as the amount and weight of the dust was worth several hundred dollars.*[113]

Notes

1. United States Mint, "Nickel."
2. Elements Database, "Periodic Table: Uranium"; Webelements, "Arsenic"; Elements Database, "Periodic Table: Iron"; Life's Little Mysteries Staff, "Why Did Gold Become the Best Element for Money?"; Benson, *Periodic Table*, "Aluminum"; Ibid., "Nickel"; Ibid., "Copper"; Israel Science and Technology Homepage, "List of Periodic Table Elements."
3. Stillwater Palladium, *Palladium, Metal of the 21st Century*, "History of Palladium Part 3"; Benson, *Periodic Table*, "Palladium"; Bentor, *Periodic Table*, "Rhodium."
4. Gray, *Elements*, 111.
5. BuyCoin.com, "Platinum Coin History"; Benson, *Periodic Table*, "Platinum."
6. Benson, *Periodic Table*, "Platinum." While the cited materials identify melting points of various metals in Celsius, the temperatures have been converted into Fahrenheit for the reader.
7. BuyCoin.com, "Platinum Coin History"; Butler, "Bernanke Defends QE II"; Life's Little Mysteries Staff, "Why Did Gold Become the Best Element for Money?"
8. Bentor, *Periodic Table*, "Palladium."
9. Ibid., "Rhodium."
10. Skousen, *Economics of a Pure Gold Standard*, 11.
11. Benson, *Periodic Table*, "Silver"
12. Bentor, *Periodic Table*, "Silver."
13. Gray, *Elements*, 115.
14. Ibid., 111, 113, 179.
15. The best example of price fluctuations might be that of rhodium from January 2004 to December 2008. Between January 2004 and mid-2008, the price of rhodium rose by an astonishing 2,100% and then, during the last half of 2008, crashed by 92.4%; Ibid., 111.
16. Ibid., 115; Stwertka, *Guide to the Elements*, 128.
17. Bentor, *Periodic Table*, "Gold."
18. Gray, *Elements*, 181.
19. Stwertka, *Guide to the Elements*, 180.
20. Ibid.
21. England, for instance, had a long and loyal history with the gold standard between 1717 and 1931. France followed a bimetallic gold/silver standard from the Middle Ages until 1878, and a gold standard until 1914. Bayoumi, Eichengreen, and Taylor, *Modern Perspectives*, 65–71, 77–78.
22. Eichengreen, *Gold Standard*, 3–4.
23. Hurst, *Legal History of Money*, 10–12.
24. Ibid., 8–9.
25. Ibid., 13.

26. Acts of the Second Congress, Sess. Laws 1792, ch. 16, secs. 1, 9, 16.

27. Ibid., ch. 16, sec. 9.

28. Ibid.

29. Hurst, *Legal History of Money*, 32.

30. Eagles were discontinued in 1933 (see CoinResource, "United States Coins History and Mint Information"), but in 1986, the US Mint resumed striking $20.00 gold eagles and silver eagles, which are primarily used today for commemorative and investment purposes. United States Mint, "American Eagles"; Golden Eagle Coins, "American Gold Eagles" and "Silver American Eagles."

31. Acts of the Second Congress, Sess. Law 1792, ch. 16, sec. 9. Pennies were made of copper until 1982 when the mint changed their composition to primarily zinc.

32. Ibid.

33. Acts of the Second Congress, Sess. Law 1792, ch. 16, sec. 9; Bayoumi, Eichengreen, and Taylor, *Modern Perspectives*, 71. The Coin Site, "1866–83 Nickel Five Cents Shield."

34. Acts of the Second Congress, Sess. Law 1792, ch. 16, sec. 9.

35. Ibid., sec. 11.

36. Eichengreen, *Gold Standard*, 4–5; Bayoumi, Eichengreen, and Taylor, *Modern Perspectives*, 71.

37. Eichengreen, *Gold Standard*, 5; Bayoumi, Eichengreen, and Taylor, *Modern Perspectives*, 71. The imbalance between the official silver-to-gold ratio and the market force prices caused citizens to sell their silver to the US Mint for coinage while selling their gold abroad, where the price was higher than it was in the United States. Eichengreen, *Gold Standard*, 5.

38. Acts of the Twenty-Third Congress, Sess. Law 1834, ch. 96; Acts of the Twenty-Fourth Congress, Sess. II, Sess. Law 1837, ch. 3; see also Eichengreen, *Gold Standard*, 5.

39. Bayoumi, Eichengreen, and Taylor, *Modern Perspectives*, 71.

40. Eichengreen, *Gold Standard*, 5.

41. Bayoumi, Eichengreen, and Taylor, *Modern Perspectives*, 71; Eichengreen, *Gold Standard*, 5. By 1851, a silver dollar was worth $1.04 in the open market, prompting citizens to use gold coins rather than silver coins in their transactions. Eichengreen, *Gold Standard*, 5. The 16:1 ratio is widely considered today to reflect the relative amount of gold and silver available on the planet, that for every 16 ounces of silver, there is one ounce of gold. The investment community therefore reports the gold/silver ratio backwards, as the preeminent position of gold over silver should be reported as 1:16 rather than 16:1. David Morgan, author of the monthly *Morgan Report*, does not adopt the generally accepted natural 16:1 ratio of silver to gold. Financial Sense, "Silver Still Consolidating."

42. Acts of the Twenty-Fourth Congress, Sess. II, P.L. 24, 5 Stat. 136.

43. P.L. 737, 48 Stat. 337; Bayoumi, Eichengreen, and Taylor, *Modern Perspectives*, 72.

44. Officer and Williamson, "Price of Gold" (using the website's gold/silver price ratio calculator).

45. The official prices for gold and silver were not necessarily the same as the actual "market prices," as gold sold in New York for as much as $30.02 an ounce in 1863 and for $42.03 an ounce in 1864, with the price of silver subject to roughly the same silver/gold ratio. Ibid. (using website calculator for each year). The rise in gold and silver prices at the time likely reflected inflationary pressures and the shortage of the metals caused by the financial demands of the Civil War. Funda-Mental, "History Behind the Nickel Coin." In Montana during the mid-1860s gold could be bought at various times for between $18.50 an ounce (see Toponce, *Reminiscences*, 59) and $20.25 an ounce (see Cushman, *Montana*, 140), either of which were slight discounts off of the official government price. Any disparity between gold's official price and the actual prices in Montana and New York might reflect premiums and discounts dictated by the market, based upon the metal's availability in each area. Even more specifically, any difference between the Montana and New York

prices might have been influenced by the economic law of supply and demand. Montana, where the price was lower, had an immediate and continuing source of supply while New York, where the price was higher, had no ready self-provided supply of the precious metals.

46. P.L. 4231, 17 Stat. 424; Bayoumi, Eichengreen, and Taylor, *Modern Perspectives*, 75.

47. Drabelle, *Silver Mines*, xv.

48. Blum et al., *National Experience*, 486. Republicans sympathetic to the coinage of silver formed the National Silver Republican Party, which endorsed Bryan for the presidency. Bryan lost the popular vote and the election to William McKinley, with an Electoral College vote of 271 to 176. Ibid., 487, 488.

49. DiLorenzo, *Real Lincoln*, 251–52.

50. Ibid., 252; Act of February 25, 1862, ch. 33, secs. 3, 5, 12 Stat. 345, 346.

51. DiLorenzo, *Real Lincoln*, 252. Ironically, when Salmon P. Chase later became chief justice of the United States, he was among a minority of justices who ruled that the issuance of greenbacks was unconstitutional. Legal Tender Cases, 79 U.S. 457, 570 (1870) (Chase, in dissent).

52. DiLorenzo, *Real Lincoln*, 253; Wahl, "Give Lincoln Credit," 718.

53. National Banking Act, ch. 58, 12 Stat. 665. A second National Banking Act was enacted in 1864 to correct certain technical problems. Act of June 3, 1864, ch. 106, 13 Stat. 99.

54. Wahl, "Give Lincoln Credit," 707–8.

55. Federal Reserve Act of 1913, 12 U.S.C. ch. 3; "Affixes His Signature at 6:02 P.M., Using Four Gold Pens," *New York Times*, Dec. 24, 1913, p. 1, col. 1.

56. Blum et al., *National Experience*, 558.

57. Trading with the Enemy Act, 40 Stat. 411, 415, sec. 5(a) and (b). Violations of presidential decrees under the act subjected the violator to up to ten years in prison and/or a $10,000 fine. Ibid., 40 Stat. 411, 425, sec. 14.

58. Ryan, *How the Gold Standard Works*, 32.

59. Ibid.,

60. Executive Order 6102—Forbidding the Hoarding of Gold Coin, Gold Bullion, and Gold Certificates within the Continental United States; Ryan, *How the Gold Standard Works*, 34.

61. Israel, *Major Presidential Decisions*, 106.

62. P.L. 737, 48 Stat. 337; Ryan, *How the Gold Standard Works*, 34.

63. Israel, *Major Presidential Decisions*, 106.

64. Ryan, *How the Gold Standard Works*, 34.

65. Ibid., 43; Schlichter, "Forty Years of Paper Money."

66. Executive Order 11825—Revocation of Executive Orders Pertaining to the Regulation of the Acquisition of, Holding of, or Other Transactions in Gold.

67. Officer and Williamson, "Price of Gold," (using website calculator for each year).

68. Toponce, *Reminiscences*, 59; Cushman, *Montana*, 140.

69. Cushman, *Montana*, 140.

70. NCR Retirement Fellowship, "James Ritty."

71. Toponce, *Reminiscences*, 59.

72. Cushman, *Montana*, 148.

73. Williamson, "Seven Ways to Compute the Relative Value of a U.S. Dollar Amount." There are of course various methods available for comparing cost values over time. The CPI is the recommended method for comparing the cost of commodities during different times (see MeasuringWorth, "Choosing the Best Indicator").

74. Williamson, "Seven Ways to Compute the Relative Value of the U.S. Dollar Amount" (using website calculator).

75. Guice, *Rocky Mountain Bench*, 40; Shinn, *Mining Camps*, 139 (as to the same effect in California mining districts).

76. Fisher and Holmes, *Gold Rushes*, 134.

77. Ryan, *How the Gold Standard Works*, 23.
78. Cushman, *Montana*, 351; Malone, Roeder, and Lang, *Montana*, 68.
79. Thrapp, *Vengeance!*, 114; Cushman, *Montana*, 153.
80. James "Bill" Sweeney Reminiscences, 1921," Mont. Hist. Soc., Collection No. 823, p. 5.
81. Malone, Roeder, and Lang, *Montana*, 68.
82. Ibid.
83. Toponce, *Reminiscences*, 58–59; Thrapp, *Vengeance!*, 121.
84. Cushman, *Montana*, 151.
85. Ibid.
86. Ibid.
87. Ibid., 153.
88. Oracle ThinkQuest, "Placer Mining."
89. Cushman, *Montana*, 153.
90. Ibid., 160.
91. Ibid.
92. Baumler, *Girl from the Gulches*, 36.
93. Cushman, *Montana*, 153.
94. Ibid.
95. Ibid., 159.
96. Ibid., 153.
97. Ibid., 159.
98. Ralph, "Basic Placer Mining for Gold."
99. Toponce, *Reminiscences*, 58; Thrapp, *Vengeance!*, 114.
100. Toponce, *Reminiscences*, 58; Thrapp, *Vengeance!*, 114.
101. Toponce, *Reminiscences*, 58.
102. Thrapp, *Vengeance!*, 114.
103. Toponce, *Reminiscences*, 58.
104. Safford, *Mechanics of Optimism*, 27.
105. Ibid., 19.
106. Ibid.
107. Leeson, *History of Montana*, 223.
108. Laurence Abraham Fenner Reminiscences, 1898, Mont. Hist. Soc., SC-686, box 1-1, folder 1-1.
109. Doyle, *Journeys*, 137.
110. Baumler, *Girl from the Gulches*, 35.
111. Ibid.
112. Ibid.; Allen, *Decent Orderly Lynching*, 112.
113. Baumler, *Girl from the Gulches*, 36; Allen, *Decent Orderly Lynching*, 112.

5

The Third Factor Leading to Vigilantism in the Region
The Insecure Means of Transporting Wealth

Oh, for God's sake, don't kill me! You can have all the money I've got.

–Bill Bunton, October 26, 1863

T he criminal enterprise that allegedly operated under the auspices of Sheriff Plummer, and which is described below, primarily targeted travelers leaving the region with gold and gold-related wealth.

The transportation of wealth to and from south central Montana could not be accomplished in 1863–64 by planes or automobiles, yet to be invented. Even railroads had not yet reached the area, as the charter for the Northern Pacific Railroad was not signed by President Lincoln until July 2, 1864, and the main line connecting Lake Superior to Puget Sound was not completed until 1883.[1] Construction of the Utah & Northern Railroad, which headed north to Dillon, Montana,[2] and then linked with the Northern Pacific Railroad at Butte, was not launched until 1873 and was not completed until 1883.[3] Unlike today, there was no electronic means for transferring money between bank accounts. Travelers of the time therefore relied primarily upon horses and slow-moving horse-drawn stagecoaches as a means of transporting themselves, and their wealth, over a limited number of known trails connecting the greater Northwest with established locales such as Salt Lake City to the south, San Francisco to the west, and points east in Minnesota.[4] The trails included the Bozeman Trail, the Bridger Trail, the Oregon Trail, the Mullan Road, the Montana Trail, the Nez Perce Trail, the Corinne Road, and the Northern Overland Route.[5]

DOI: 10.7330_9780874219203.c005

The Mullan Road ran between Fort Benton, in what is now Montana, to Dalles, Oregon.[6] It was named after Lieutenant John Mullan, who conducted its initial exploration and construction.[7] The road's construction began in 1850s and was not completed until 1862.[8] Its initial purpose was to aid surveys for an anticipated Pacific-bound railroad.[9] It was a significant route into Montana Territory from the Pacific Northwest.[10]

The Oregon Trail was a major trail connecting points in Missouri to Oregon Territory.[11] There was a marked increase in the use of the Oregon Trail in 1849 and 1850 as part of the California gold rush,[12] and then by emigrants in the early 1860s fleeing the Civil War that was being fought in the eastern United States.[13] Prospectors traveling to the gold discoveries at Bannack and Alder Gulch followed the Oregon Trail as far east or west as Fort Bridger, and then turned north into Montana.[14]

There were two main trails that headed north from there to Montana. One was the Bozeman Trail, forged by John Bozeman, which cut to the east of the Big Horn Mountains to what would become Fort C. F. Smith and then west to Virginia City and beyond.[15] The second was the Bridger Trail, which cut to the west of the Big Horn range toward Virginia City.[16] Each trail had its advantages and disadvantages.

The Bozeman Trail was not as direct as the Bridger Trail. The significance of the Bozeman Trail was more than the trail itself, as its opening triggered more than a decade of warfare between the federal government and Native American Indians of the northern plains.[17] Travelers on the trail were subject to skirmishes with the Sioux Indians.[18] The Sioux and their allies, the Northern Cheyenne and the Northern Arapaho, were protective of the bountiful hunting grounds that were guaranteed to them by the 1851 Fort Laramie Treaty.[19] There was no military presence on the Bozeman Trail in 1863 and 1864,[20] as Fort C. F. Smith was not established until 1866.[21] However, the Bozeman Trail had plentiful resources that were required for wagon trains, including fish, berries, antelope, deer, buffalo, and fowl.[22] The Bozeman Trail was ultimately discontinued under the terms of the 1868 Fort Laramie Treaty.[23] The man who blazed the Bozeman Trail, John Bozeman, was honored by the designation of Bozeman, Montana, with his namesake.[24]

The Bridger Trail was the more direct route into Montana and was not subject to Indian attacks,[25] but it offered inadequate grazing and potable water necessary to sustain the animals needed to pull the wagons.[26] Blazed by Jim Bridger,[27] the Bridger Trail funneled approximately 25 percent of Virginia City's population to the region during the 1864 trail season.[28] The wagon trains that used the trail were sizable. Ten separate trains used the trail between May and September 1864.[29] The largest single train left for Virginia City on

Figure 5.1. John Bozeman, who blazed the Bozeman
Trail. (Courtesy of the Montana Historical Society,
image 941-362.)

June 10, 1864, consisting of 129 wagons transporting 350 to 450 people.[30]
The smallest of the wagon trains left for Virginia City in May consisting of 10
wagons.[31]

There were other options for travelers who did not require use of the
Bozeman or Bridger Trails. From the south, travelers used the Corinne Road,
which ran from Corinne, Utah, into Montana.[32] Jesuit missionary Father Pierre-
Jean de Smet said that the route received so much travel that "not a blade of
grass can shoot up on account of the continual passing."[33]

There was also a more northerly route that extended across Dakota Territory
and entered Montana at Fort Union and the Missouri River.[34]

Anyone unwilling to use the trails to south central Montana could venture into the region by other means. Travelers could ride a steamboat up the
Missouri River to Fort Benton, take the Mullan Road westward, and turn south
to the mining communities of Alder Gulch.[35]

More locally, there was a single seventy-mile stagecoach route that connected Bannack and Virginia City, which avoided smaller mountains by running roughly parallel to the Stinking Water River, which is now known as the Ruby River, and the Beaverhead River.[36] The local trail became the site of numerous stagecoach robberies and murders in 1863 and 1864. The seventy-mile journey between Virginia City and Bannack was particularly prone to crimes perpetrated by "road agents."[37] The route's streams, canyons, mountain passes, ledges, thickets, and valleys afforded thieves the advantage of concealment, surprise attacks, and planned getaways.[38] There was a particular increase in the number of travelers to and from the region in the late fall of 1863. Mining was difficult, if not impossible, during the months of winter, as frozen ground was not conducive to digging and cold or frozen streams were not conducive to sluicing. Many prospectors, particularly those who had already earned some fortune during the earlier months, preferred to leave the area temporarily and perhaps see relatives and friends elsewhere rather than to remain idle in Bannack or Alder Gulch during the icy months of winter.[39]

There were two main stagecoach lines that ran between Bannack and Alder Gulch, Peabody & Caldwell's and A. J. Oliver's.[40] Riders and coaches traveling from the area would change horses and rest at various designated ranches, including the Rattlesnake Ranch outside Bannack,[41] which was owned by conspirators Bill Bunton and Frank Parish and which served as the road agents' primary headquarters.[42] A stop at the Rattlesnake Ranch was unavoidable for travelers.[43] Ranches at the time played a role similar to that played by rest stations along modern interstate highways, where the traveler can eat a meal, service the vehicle, and rest before the next leg of the trip.

The criminal syndicate worked in the following manner: spies at local businesses, acting on behalf of Sheriff Plummer and the road agents, would learn when persons were planning to travel with valuables such as gold from Bannack or the other communities of Alder Gulch.[44] The term "road agents" was a euphemism for "indolent opportunism."[45] Spies provided information about travelers from their placements at businesses and horse ranches.[46] A private mark would be made identifying the traveler or the traveler's stagecoach as a target for robbery.[47] In one noted instance, Sheriff Plummer personally placed a colored scarf around the neck of an intended victim to mark him for a robbery.[48] Information about the traveler would be passed on to other conspirators. The road agents established points of rendezvous and would send word of a targeted traveler by means of horseback from point to point.[49] Road agents recognized one another by use of a certain sailor's knot in their ties.[50] The secret password they used among themselves was "I am Innocent."[51] They would select the location of ambush, and according to Dimsdale, each road agent would usually be armed with a pair of revolvers, a double-barreled shotgun, and a knife or dagger.[52] They would disguise themselves with masks.[53] Blankets would cover their horses except for the horses' heads, legs, and tails so that the road agents could not later be identified by the horses they rode.[54] The road agents would approach their victims with guns leveled, disarm the victims, search for or be given demanded valuables, and then ride off.[55] Safe houses were located at the Rattlesnake Ranch, Robert Dempsey's Cottonwood Ranch, and Peter Daley's "Robbers' Roost."[56] Murdered victims would sometimes be stripped of their clothes and thrust head first into "wolf holes" so that it would appear as if the deaths were caused by Native American Indians.[57] Sheriff Henry Plummer and his deputies, Ned Ray, Buck Stinson, and Jack Gallagher, would assure that no serious investigation would be undertaken of the crimes.[58] If a victim of road agents reported a trail robbery at Bannack, conspirator George Hilderman's job was to learn whether any of the road agents were identified by name, and if so, the victim would then be murdered to assure further silence.[59] The conspirators divided the stolen wealth among themselves, and their enterprise was apparently profitable.

Many travelers were robbed at gunpoint. Still others that left for "the States" were never heard from again and were presumed killed.[60] With the increased travel in the fall of 1863, criminal activity against travelers spiraled, and it prompted fear and anger among the miners who were being physically intimidated and who were losing up to a year's worth of hard-earned gold profits.[61] While the precise number of travelers killed by the road agents may never be truly known, Langford places the number at 102.[62] Dimsdale uses the same number, 102, based upon the "discoveries of the bodies of the victims, the confessions of the murderers before execution, and other reliable information sent to the [Vigilance] Committee," but "scores" of other persons had been murdered and buried whose remains were never discovered.[63] This rate of murder, if accurate, coupled with the rate of nonlethal highway robbery, was significant given the limited population of the region at the time, and even more significant as a percentage of only those persons who traveled at the relevant times and places. If the number of murders was a mere estimate, then it might be expected to have been a rounder number, such as an even 100, or 110. Nevertheless, author Frederick Allen questions the reliability of the number of murders on the ground that it appears to have evolved from a "consensus" in the community at the time,[64] and authors Mather and Boswell deem the count to be exaggerated.[65]

The incidents of robberies and murders, whatever their exact number, eventually became high enough to prompt action in response. Discussions about the possible formation of a vigilante force at Alder Gulch began in the fall of 1863 as a consequence of these escalated events.[66] Some of the more notable crimes committed by road agents are summarized here.

The Robbery of Peabody & Caldwell's Stagecoach

Records from the era recount the details of the more notorious crimes committed by the road agents. Many of them were violent, compelling, and downright harrowing. One involved the robbery of a Peabody & Caldwell stagecoach on October 26, 1863. Its driver was William Rumsey.[67] Passengers initially included men named Mattison, Percival, and Wilkinson.[68] Another traveler named "Bummer Dan" McFadden was leaving the region with his hard-earned gold wealth, which was ironic, as "Bummer Dan" had a reputation for being a lazy moocher who "bummed" food and drink from others during his earliest days in Bannack.[69] Before long in the region, McFadden had reaped the rewards of two lucrative mining claims and was ready by the winter of 1863 to leave the region with his profits.[70] To outsmart thieves who might have heard of his planned departure, McFadden left Virginia City on foot and then caught the Peabody & Caldwell stagecoach at Bob Dempsey's ranch along the route from Virginia City.[71] He had sold his gold dust for approximately $2,000 and concealed the money in buckskin purses in a shoulder bag and within a belt hidden cleverly under his clothing.[72] The stagecoach was traveling westward from Virginia City to Bannack, which could ordinarily be accomplished in a single, long day.[73]

The stagecoach was delayed in the morning because of snow.[74] It therefore did not reach the Rattlesnake Ranch until dusk on October 25, 1863.[75] The Rattlesnake Ranch was a station stop where there was to be a change of horses and where the passengers could take a brief rest from their travels.[76] However, on this occasion, a team of fresh horses could not be found, and the party was required to spend the night at the ranch, where they imbibed alcohol with one of the ranch owners, Bill Bunton.[77] The following morning, still in need of steeds, two old horses were placed on the team from worn-down stock, which had the inevitable effect of slowing down the stagecoach for the leg of the day's trip from the Rattlesnake Ranch to Bannack.[78] Rumsey's arm was overtired from the previous day's whipping, so it was arranged that Bunton would accompany the party to Bannack in order to whip the horses while Rumsey drove them.[79] The weather was cold and blustery.[80] Wilkinson left the ranch separately with his friend, Bob Zachary,[81] who weeks later would be hanged as a road agent. In any event, the team of old horses weakened and slowed while on the trail to Bannack.[82]

After the horses slowed from fatigue, two hooded road agents appeared on the trail, each armed with a shotgun.[83] They demanded in broken Irish that everyone in the Peabody & Caldwell stagecoach put their hands in the air.[84]

According to Dimsdale and Langford, Bunton responded by yelling theatrically, "Oh, for God's sake, don't kill me! You can have all the money I've got."[85] Dimsdale described Bunton's theatrics as "stool-pitching," to help the robbers by setting an example for the others.[86]

Rumsey, Bunton, and the passengers were forced off the stagecoach, disarmed, and robbed of whatever money was on their persons.[87] "Bummer Dan" McFadden appears to have been the main target of the road agents,[88] as one of the robbers said to him, "You are the man we are after."[89] The passengers were threatened several times by the armed robbers to do as they were ordered or they would be shot.[90] All of the money that McFadden had hidden under his clothing, at various locations on his body, was found and turned over to the road agents.[91] The hooded thieves' last words before riding off were a threat that if they ever heard from the passengers, they would be killed.[92] The robbery yielded $2,800.[93]

As the stagecoach arrived in Bannack, Percival saw Frank Parish confer with the local sheriff, Henry Plummer.[94] Parish was the co-owner of the Rattlesnake Ranch with Bill Bunton.[95] Percival believed he recognized Parish's horse and accoutrements as one of the horses used by the robbers during the crime.[96] McFadden and Percival believed they knew the identities of the hooded road agents, but were astute enough to not divulge their suspicions to anyone, not even Sheriff Plummer, lest they be murdered to assure their silence.[97] According to Dimsdale and Leeson, they privately believed the thieves to be Frank Parish and George Ives.[98] According to Langford, they believed the thieves to be Frank Parish and Bob Zachary,[99] who had earlier left the stagecoach party at the Rattlesnake Ranch. Bill Bunton's transparent behavior at the site of the robbery raised suspicions about his own complicity in the episode.[100] These suspicions of alleged involvement in the robbery of the Peabody & Caldwell stagecoach would, within a matter of weeks, come back to haunt the criminals involved.

The Robbery of A. J. Oliver's Stagecoach

Whereas the passengers of the Peabody & Caldwell stagecoach were astute enough to remain silent about who they believed their robbers to be, Leroy Southmayd, who was robbed on November 22, 1863, was not so astute.[101] Looked upon charitably, Southmayd might have been fearless. Looked upon uncharitably, he was downright foolish.

Southmayd was a prospector who took an A. J. Oliver & Company stagecoach from Virginia City, through Bannack, en route to Salt Lake City.[102] The departure of the stagecoach was observed by Jem "Old Tex" Crowell, who seemed to be paying too much interest in the travelers and their cargo.[103] The coach passengers were observed by George Ives at the rest stop at Lorrain's Ranch near the Stinking Water River.[104] The stagecoach was surveilled as it moved along the trail toward Bannack by "Whiskey Bill" Graves and Bob Zachary.[105] It spent a night at Point of Rocks, and the robbery occurred the following morning at 11:00 a.m.[106]

The robbery itself followed the usual script. After leaving Lorrain's Ranch, three horsemen who had been riding quietly ahead suddenly wheeled their horses, readied their shotguns, and galloped back to Southmayd's stagecoach.[107] One road agent kept his shotgun aimed at Southmayd.[108] A second road agent kept his shotgun aimed at the stagecoach driver, Tom Caldwell.[109] The third road agent kept his shotgun aimed at two passengers, Captain Moore and a discharged driver named Billy.[110] At gunpoint, the road agents ordered the passengers of Southmayd's party to dismount from the coach with their hands raised in the air.[111] Southmayd was relieved of $400 worth of gold dust, Captain Moore was robbed of $100 in US Treasury notes, lesser amounts were taken from Billy, and several pouches were taken from Caldwell.[112] During the holdup, Southmayd positively recognized the road agents, despite their disguises, as George Ives, "Whiskey Bill" Graves, and Bob Zachary,[113] but kept that information to himself at that time. The victims of the robbery were given the usual warning against talking promiscuously about the crime.[114]

When the stagecoach arrived at Bannack, Southmayd informed Sheriff Plummer that his assailants were Ives, Graves, and Zachary.[115] He did so against the well-intentioned advice of Dr. Gaylord Bissell and George Crisman.[116] Bissell and Crisman were certain that Southmayd would be killed for his revelation, with Bissell telling Southmayd that his life was "not worth a cent."[117]

Upon his return to Virginia City, George Ives, while intoxicated at a brothel, purportedly declared himself the "Bamboo Chief" that had robbed Tom Caldwell and the Southmayd party.[118]

Southmayd changed his travel plans and, after spending three days unmolested in Bannack, embarked on a return journey to Virginia City.[119] Ominously, Deputy Sheriffs Buck Stinson and Ned Ray also chose to travel in the same coach to Virginia City, along with Southmayd, Caldwell, and a sixteen-year-old boy.[120] Southmayd was urged not to go, as it was apparent to all that Stinson and Ray intended to kill him.[121] Southmayd was defiant, saying, "I've got to go. Let me have my shotgun and I'll take my chances with the road agents."[122] Southmayd was undeterred, and he, Caldwell, and the boy then each armed themselves with shotguns for protection.[123]

The daytime ride toward Virginia City was uneventful. At suppertime, the stagecoach arrived at the Cold Spring Station, where the trail crossed the Stinking Water River.[124] There, at the station, were two of the three road agents that Southmayd had earlier identified as his robbers, "Whiskey Bill" Graves and

Bob Zachary, along with a third man, Aleck Carter.[125] Each was armed with a gun, a pistol, and a knife.[126] But at that time there was no confrontation, and the travelers joined the road agents inside the ranch house for dinner, again without incident.[127] Zachary was drunk, or was at least pretending to be.[128] When dinner ended, and by prearrangement, Southmayd and the sixteen-year-old boy mounted the stagecoach so that Southmayd was seated behind Stinson and the boy behind Ray, with their shotguns on their laps at the ready.[129] It was nearing nightfall.[130] Shortly after the stagecoach left the Cold Spring Station with fresh horses, Graves, Zachary, and Carter rode up toward the coach, wheeled their horses, and called "Halt!"[131] At that moment, Southmayd leveled his shotgun at Carter, Caldwell aimed his shotgun at Graves, and the boy aimed his shotgun at Zachary.[132] Carter protested that they only wanted to offer the travelers a drink of whiskey.[133] The offer made little sense, as all of the men had just consumed a round of drinks courtesy of the proprietor of the station.[134] Southmayd and Caldwell suspected that the whiskey bottle was poisoned, so they only allowed the bottle to touch their lips without actually drinking from it.[135] If the road agents had planned to attack Southmayd and Caldwell at that time, their plan was aborted. The stagecoach moved on toward Virginia City without incident, but with Southmayd and the boy strategically seated so as to keep Stinson and Ray under close watch.

At the next station stop, which was Lorrain's Ranch, Caldwell and Southmayd discussed their options, which included fleeing into the brush.[136] Caldwell convinced Southmayd that they could defend themselves if need be.[137] Their conversation was overheard by Stinson, who then assured Southmayd and Caldwell on his "honor" and on his "life" that they would have a safe trip to Virginia City.[138] Stinson and Ray could not allow the others to escape through the brush, as the result would be to bring the wrath of Virginia City upon them and their road agent colleagues.[139]

During the entire last leg of the trip to Virginia City, Stinson and Ray sang in a loud voice, which was the signal to other road agents that they not launch an attack.[140] In the end, the unusual courage of Leroy Southmayd and Tom Caldwell in making the trip to Virginia City with Buck Stinson and Ned Ray is what appears to have saved their lives.

The Attempted Robberies of Conrad Kohrs

One person who managed to avoid being robbed by road agents was Conrad Kohrs, who later in life achieved phenomenal success as a cattle rancher and who served in Montana's territorial and state legislatures. Kohrs, though German, had immigrated to the United States from Denmark at the age of 15.[141] He was working in Deer Lodge as a butcher in 1863 when he was twenty-eight years old.[142] Late that year, while traveling with canteens filled with gold dust, which was needed to purchase cattle, he encountered Sheriff Plummer during a trip to Bannack, who asked Kohrs where he was headed.[143] Kohrs was not candid about his itinerary because it was understood that when traveling with gold dust, the fewer persons who knew of your plans, the better. Kohrs believed that Plummer suspected he was returning to Deer Lodge.[144] A day or two later, Kohrs met parties of friends on a secondary trail at the north side of Silver Bow Creek near a point called "The Hump."[145] Kohrs's friends included John Grant, Leon Cannell, Louis DeMar, L. R. Maillet, a man named Normandin, a mountaineer nicknamed "Old Caribou," and a man from Oregon named Bissell.[146] The group was approached by George Ives and "Dutch John" Wagner, who were traveling from Deer Lodge to Virginia City.[147] Kohrs believed that Ives and Wagner had been dispatched to Deer Lodge to rob him, but they did not initially find him, as Kohrs had outwitted them by staying off the main wagon trail that connected Bannack and Deer Lodge.[148] Ives and Wagner went on their way.

At 10:00 p.m. that evening, Bissell reported that two men were prowling around the camp and feared that the men would steal his horses.[149] Most of the others in the group, who were playing cards, dismissed Bissell's concerns.[150] At midnight, when the card game broke up, George Ives and "Dutch John" Wagner were found armed with weapons within fifty yards of the camp.[151] Outnumbered and detected, Ives and Wagner ran off.[152] There was no reason for Ives and Wagner to be there in the first place, and had their intentions been honorable, there was not necessarily any reason for them to run off. Kohrs and his friends concluded that Ives and Wagner had intended to rob them of their possessions.[153] To prevent any further robbery attempt, four men armed with doubled-barreled shotguns stood watch at the camp through the remainder of the evening.[154]

A few days later, Kohrs was traveling from Virginia City on a horse named Grey Billy.[155] At Camp Creek he met Jim Spencer, who warned Kohrs that Ives and Wagner were in the area and, Spencer surmised, were after Kohrs.[156] Kohrs was carrying approximately $5,000 in gold dust at the time.[157] Spencer described Ives's horse as a large bald-faced sorrel and Wagner's horse as brown.[158] After leaving Camp Creek and reaching the Continental Divide, Kohrs observed two riders gaining on him that seemed to match Spencer's descriptions.[159] The chase to Deer Lodge began. Kohrs threw off anything that added weight to his horse, such as his blanket, overcoat, pistol, and belt, and managed to save himself only by having the faster horse.[160] Grey Billy was so pushed to the limit of its endurance that it was permanently "ruined by [the] hard and fast ride."[161]

Figure 5.2. Conrad Kohrs. (Courtesy of the Montana Historical Society, image 943-353.)

The Attempted Robbery of Moody's Stagecoach

Another notable attempted robbery and attempted murder was of the passengers and crew of Moody's stagecoach. It was known by that name as it was organized by the freighter Milton S. Moody.[162] The three-wagon caravan with a string of packhorses was bound for Salt Lake City from Virginia City during the first week of December 1863 carrying seven passengers, among them John Bozeman, who had blazed the Bozeman Trail, and Melanchthon "Lank" Forbes, a wealthy miner.[163] The additional passengers were John McCormick, M. V. Jones, William Sloan, John S. Rockfellow, and Henry Branson.[164] There was $80,000.00 worth of gold dust hidden in canteens contained within the freight.[165] There were also $1,500 in US Treasury notes hidden in a sack.[166]

The day before the attempted robbery, the group was in the Black Tail Deer Canyon, and while decamped for breakfast, they heard one man in the brush say to another man, "You take my revolver and I'll take yours, and you come right on after me." Every man in the Moody party grabbed his revolver and cocked it. "Dutch John" Wagner and Steve Marshland then rode their horses into the camp, shotguns in hand, only to see that the several travelers were already aiming guns at them as they came into sight.[167] Any plan to rob the Moody party was immediately suspended. For reasons unexplained, neither Wagner nor Marshland were wearing masks.[168] William Sloan knew Marshland personally, and the two men exchanged pleasantries.[169] Wagner and Marshland explained that they were in the area looking for lost horses.[170] The encounter ended without incident.

However, two days later, two masked men attempted an actual robbery of the Moody stagecoach. The incident occurred on top of the Continental Divide, at Rock Creek between the Red Rock Valley and Junction City.[171] The masked road agents were believed to be Marshland and Wagner, as the members of the Moody party had seen them in the area acting suspiciously just two days before.[172] The two masked robbers, on horses, jumped out of the brush in front of the moving wagons and, with their shotguns aimed at the wagon drivers, ordered them to halt.[173] The wagon train stopped. The man believed to be Wagner remained on his horse, covering the drivers with his shotgun. The man believed to be Marshland dismounted his horse and searched the drivers and wagons.[174] The search of Moody, one of the drivers, failed to reveal $100 hidden in a shirt pocket and a revolver hidden in the leg of his boot.[175] A wad of tobacco was appropriated from a driver named Kit Erskine.[176] The robber cut open a sack in one of the wagons and found $1,500 in treasury notes but did not examine the gold-laden canteens.[177] The last wagon of the caravan contained a sick man named Kennedy, who was being tended to by Lank Forbes.[178] As the man believed to be Marshland climbed onto the back of the last wagon and drew back its curtain, Forbes fired his gun, striking the masked robber in the chest.[179] The man screamed, fell to his knees on the back of the wagon, then fell to the ground, and, regaining his footing, ran off into the woods.[180] The gunshot spooked the horse mounted by the man believed to be Wagner, and as the horse reared, the robber fired multiple shots at the stagecoach drivers, missing their heads by inches.[181] In the confusion, Moody reached into his boot, grabbed his hidden revolver, and fired three rapid-succession shots at the robber, with one bullet striking the man in the shoulder as he retreated.[182] The robbers, though wounded, each escaped in different directions without having stolen any of the wagon train's most prized cargo, the gold- laden canteens.[183] Moody later reflected that since the assailants had been wounded, they probably could have been captured if he or members of his party had given immediate chase.[184]

The two assailants, believed to be Wagner and Marshland, were marked by the bullet wounds that they had each sustained in the altercation. They would remain on the run for several weeks and will be heard from again in this narrative.

The Magruder Trail Murders

Lloyd Magruder had come to Virginia City from Elk City, Idaho, in the fall of 1863 with a wagon train of dry goods.[185] He sold his entire inventory within three weeks and cleared a profit of $12,000.[186] While there, Magruder entertained the idea of running for Congress.[187] Also, while in Virginia City, he befriended "Doc" Howard and Howard's associates, Chris Lowrie, Jem Romaine, and Billy Page.[188] Howard was an actual physician, but breaking with what would be expected of someone bound to a Hippocratic Oath, he preferred to invest his efforts in serious and lethal crimes instead.[189]

On October 5, 1863, Magruder left the region for Idaho, taking with him his season's profits.[190] To deceive road agents, he had written his wife to say that he did not intend to leave for Idaho for another two weeks, until October 20.[191] He hired "Doc" Howard, Chris Lowrie, Jem Romaine, and William Page as guards to accompany him on the trip in exchange for a payment to each of them of $200.[192] Unbeknown to Magruder, his new companions, Howard, Lowrie, and Romaine, each had a history of robberies and were escaped convicts from a California penitentiary.[193] Before the group left for Idaho, four miners and pioneers named Charley Allen, Robert Chalmers, Horace Chalmers, and William Phillips arranged to join Magruder's party.[194] Another traveler, L. O. Holt, had originally intended to accompany the party to Idaho but changed his plans at the last minute and left for Idaho at a later time.[195] The wagon train set out westward toward the Bitter Root Mountains in the direction of Idaho.[196]

At 10:00 p.m. on the eighth day of travel, after the travelers had decamped for the night, Lowrie picked up an axe, saying that he would need it to make some firewood.[197] By this time, the travelers had already crossed the territorial border into Idaho. Lowrie and Magruder left to watch the herd so that the other members of the party could retire to sleep.[198] While sitting with Magruder at a fire, Lowrie stood with his axe, muttered something about putting wood on the fire, and then swung the axe into Magruder's head, killing him.[199] Howard immediately appeared, took the axe from Lowrie, and swung it at Magruder's body several more times.[200] Lowrie and Howard then walked to where the others were sleeping, and Lowrie used the axe to kill the Chalmers brothers.[201] Romaine killed Phillips by stabbing him in the abdomen with a bowie knife.[202] Charley Allen sat up from his sleep, having been awakened by the noise, only to be shot in the back of the head from a shotgun discharged by Howard.[203]

William Page did not go on the trip intending to commit any crime, but he was told of the criminal plan earlier in the day and was called upon after the fact to help dispose of the bodies.[204] According to Nathaniel Langford, Lowrie described the killings at the scene as a "grand success."[205] The bodies of the victims were wrapped in blankets and cast 800 feet into a canyon with the expectation that they would be devoured by wolves.[206] Most of the items belonging to the victims were burned, and any other scraps were thrown over the same precipice.[207] Most of the animals that belonged to the murdered men were slaughtered.[208] Howard chose to keep one particularly fast horse and saddle that had belonged to Magruder.[209] The murderers did their work wearing moccasins to make it appear that Indians were the culprits.[210] An approaching storm covered any remaining evidence of the crimes under two feet of snow.[211]

Howard, Lowrie, Romaine, and Page intended to use the US Mint in San Francisco to melt their stolen gold dust into coins and then travel with the gold to New York.[212] The weather remained unusually snowy on their way to San Francisco, and facing starvation, they went to Lewiston as the only place where they could replenish their provisions.[213] There they acted too suspiciously by keeping their coats turned up about their faces, with broad-brimmed hats pulled low to their eyes, and they hesitated giving their false names, John Smith, Joseph Smith, Thomas Jones, and James Jones.[214] They were recognized by a stagecoach agent, and suspicions grew that they had something to do with Magruder's failure to arrive in Lewiston as expected.[215]

A friend of Magruder in Lewiston named Hill Beachy became convinced that the men were responsible for Magruder's failure to return, particularly when Magruder's horse and saddle possessed by the men were recognized by an Indian boy named Jack.[216] Many people in Lewiston believed that Beachy was jumping to conclusions, particularly when the letter that Magruder had sent to his wife, Maggie, had arrived explaining a later departure date from Virginia City.[217] The four mysterious travelers left for Portland and then San Francisco. Thereafter, a man from Virginia City arrived in Lewiston and explained that Magruder had actually left earlier than the letter said and that he was traveling in the company of Howard, Lowrie, Romaine, and Page.[218] That information, coupled with the suspicious behavior of the "Smiths" and "Joneses," the recognition of Magruder's horse and saddle, and Magruder's failure to reach Lewiston, prompted Beachy to doggedly pursue the men to San Francisco, where they were arrested and held.[219]

The suspects were imprisoned in San Francisco for four weeks as legal proceedings were commenced to determine whether they would be extradited to Idaho for trial.[220] The outcome of the proceedings was uncertain, as Magruder's body had not been recovered and there was no direct evidence at that time that he had even been murdered.[221] Beachy was forced to hire an attorney to prevent the suspects from receiving a habeas corpus release.[222] Ultimately, San Francisco authorities directed that the suspects be returned to Lewiston, at Beachy's insistence, for trial.[223] As a condition of their extradition, Beachy was required to give a solemn promise, made in open court during the

Figure 5.3. Hill Beachy, who spearheaded the effort to capture the Magruder trail murderers. (Courtesy of the Montana Historical Society, image 940-808.)

habeas corpus proceeding, that the men would not be summarily hanged by vigilantes in Lewiston.[224]

The evidence against Howard, Lowrie, Romaine, and Page was initially flimsy and circumstantial, such as their possession in Lewiston of the horse and saddle that might have belonged to Magruder as well as Magruder's coincidental disappearance.[225] Any testimony by the boy "Jack" identifying Magruder's horse and saddle would be singularly unpersuasive, as the testimony of any Native American Indian was viewed as inherently suspect. The bodies of the Magruder party had not been located. There were no witnesses to any crime.

Hill Beachy remained convinced that Howard, Lowrie, Romaine, and Page were involved in Magruder's disappearance between Virginia City and Lewiston.

While awaiting the men's possible indictment in Lewiston, Beachy sized up the suspects and determined that Page was the weakest of the group.[226] Beachy orchestrated a ruse designed to scare Page into a confession. Four nooses were hung from a beam in a room of the building where the suspects were being confined, with a dry goods box positioned beneath each noose.[227] Howard, Lowrie, and Romaine were each taken from their cell, one at a time an hour apart, and finally, Page was taken from his cell as well.[228] Page was walked past the room with the hanging nooses visible through an open door, prompting Beachy to yell, on cue, "What's the matter with you fellows, I told you to keep that door shut!"[229] Beachy slammed the door and, turning to Page, said, "You shouldn't have been allowed to see that, Bill."[230] In another room where there was a table, paper, pens, and ink, Beachy told Page that each of his three colleagues had confessed to the Magruder murders and would soon be hanged, and that Page's only hope of not being executed was to confess to whatever he knew and to act as a witness for the prosecution.[231] Page was tricked into believing that Howard, Lowrie, and Romaine had confessed their crimes, even though they had actually done nothing of the sort. Page was shaken. He told the entire story from the time the Magruder party left Virginia City until the time the survivors were arrested in San Francisco.[232] He not only provided direct evidence of the crime through his admissions, but his information was corroborated by the presence of abandoned gear at Cottonwood Creek, which Page told authorities in Lewiston they could find there.[233]

Page provided the evidence that was needed to indict the others and also testified at their trial for the prosecution.[234] Additional witnesses placed Howard, Lowrie, Romaine, and Page together in a party of nine before the crime, while other witnesses identified them as a party of four in Lewiston seeking a stagecoach for their trip to the Pacific coast.[235] Trial evidence included the defendants' possession of Magruder's horse and saddle and evidence of the carnage that was discovered at the crime scene that had been identified by Page.[236] L. O. Holt, who fortuitously did not accompany the Magruder party to Idaho, was able to identify certain mules that the defendants had brought to Lewiston and a piece of cloth that Magruder had used to bundle gold dust that was recovered from the San Francisco Mint.[237]

Howard, Lowrie and Romaine were each convicted of the murders by a jury under the legal processes of Idaho Territory and were hanged for their crimes in Lewiston on March 4, 1864.[238] Lowrie and Romaine admitted their complicity in the murders after their trial and prior to their hangings, but Howard admitted nothing to the bitter end.[239] Beachy received $17,000 in gold coins from the US government, which had earlier been deposited by the robbers at the San Francisco Mint, and he gave the money to Magruder's widow, Maggie.[240] The

Figure 5.4. Anton Holter, who narrowly avoided death during a trail robbery on December 8, 1863. (Courtesy of the Montana Historical Society, image 942-816.)

murder of the Magruder party was not avenged by vigilantism but illustrates the danger that persons faced while traveling on the region's trails with valuables such as gold and the reality that some travelers departed from Montana mining communities never to be seen alive again.

The Robbery and Attempted Murder of Anton Holter

Another incident involved Anton Holter, who was driving two yoke of oxen to Virginia City for sale on December 8, 1863.[241] En route, he encountered two hooded robbers at Ramshorn Creek demanding money.[242] He believed the hooded thieves to be George Ives and Aleck Carter. Holter could produce only ten dollars and had to convince Ives that he was in possession of no other money or valuables.[243] The thieves cursed at Holter and belittled him for travel-ing with so little money.[244] Holter was ordered to ride away, and as he began doing so, one of the thieves, presumably Ives, aimed a pistol at Holter's head and fired a shot.[245] Holter saw what was happening out of the corner of his eye and immediately ducked.[246] The bullet whizzed through Holter's hat and literally grazed his scalp.[247] The gunman aimed to fire another shot, but the gun misfired, allowing Holter to escape with his life by running away on foot.[248] Holter fled for home "blessing his cap-maker."[249]

The Robbery of Henry Tilden

On November 13, 1863, a teenager named Henry Tilden was dispatched by Wilbur Fisk Sanders and Idaho's chief justice, Sidney Edgerton, to Horse Prairie for the purpose of corralling some scattered cattle that Sanders and Edgerton jointly owned.[250] Tilden was the son of a family friend of both Sanders and Edgerton.[251] The next evening, while riding a horse alone from Horse Prairie toward Bannack, Tilden encountered three masked horsemen who produced revolvers and sternly ordered him to dismount the horse and raise his hands.[252] Tilden complied. Tilden recognized the leader of the men, who held a gun to his head, as Henry Plummer.[253] The men searched Tilden's pockets but found nothing of much value.[254] The amount of money in Tilden's pockets ranged from as much as ten dollars, according to Thomas Dimsdale, to as little as a dollar or two, according to Francis Thompson.[255] An account of the events by Hattie Sanders, the wife of Wilbur Fisk Sanders, states that Tilden's pockets contained nothing but a comb and a picture of a girl.[256] Finding little or nothing of value, the men allowed Tilden to ride away with the warning that if he ever told anyone of what had occurred, they "would blow off the top of his head."[257]

Tilden rode off in such a fright that he crashed his horse into a mining ditch, fell from the saddle, and was rendered unconscious.[258] When he came to in the snow, he continued his frantic ride toward the homes of Wilbur Fisk Sanders and Sidney Edgerton, yelling for help at the top of his lungs.[259] Upon reaching the Sanders's home at Yankee Flat, Tilden breathlessly told Hattie Sanders of the holdup and specifically identified Henry Plummer as one of the assailants.[260] Wilbur Fisk Sanders was not home at the time. Hattie Sanders retrieved Judge Edgerton from a nearby house and the story was related again.[261]

Tilden remained steadfast in his story, explaining to Judge Edgerton that during the incident, he recognized Plummer's revolver and the red lining of Plummer's overcoat.[262] Tilden had delivered the gun to Plummer only two days earlier at the express office where the boy worked.[263] The overcoat that Plummer wore with its red lining was unique.[264] Edgerton was initially doubtful of young Tilden's claim. The robbery had occurred at dusk, in a snowstorm, the men were wearing masks, and the assailants could have been anyone.[265] However, out of an abundance of caution, Judge Edgerton instructed Tilden not to tell anyone that Plummer was involved, lest he be killed by his assailants.[266] When Wilbur Fisk Sanders later heard of Tilden's claims, he was also initially skeptical of the boy's account.[267] Edgerton and Sanders did not think that Tilden was at all dishonest, but they questioned whether he might have simply been mistaken. At the time, few if any people had reason to doubt the integrity of Sheriff Henry Plummer. In Edgerton's view, the stop and frisk of Henry Tilden might have been nothing more than a precautionary measure undertaken on a snowy night by the men involved, coupled with the overly active imagination of a fifteen-year-old boy.[268]

The same evening, Nathaniel Langford and Samuel T. Hauser were intending to travel the same trail in the opposite direction, bound for the United States with several Mormon freighters for part of the journey and with a considerable amount of gold dust in their possession.[269] Their gold dust was no secret, as a day earlier, at the bar of Goodrich's Hotel, Langford gave the sack of gold dust to Plummer for safekeeping. He believed that the sheriff could not steal it since its transfer had been witnessed by a number of respectable citizens and that the gold would therefore be safer with Plummer than with Langford himself.[270] The following morning, prior to Langford's and Hauser's departure, Plummer dutifully returned the sack containing the gold dust and, at the same time, presented Hauser with a red woolen scarf.[271] "You will find it useful these cold nights," Plummer said.[272] The scarf may have actually been intended to help identify Hauser as a target for robbery after nightfall.[273] To complicate matters, Langford believed that he had been under surveillance for two days by Plummer's deputies, Buck Stinson and Ned Ray.[274]

During the same day of Langford's and Hauser's planned departure from Bannack, there was a report that a deposit of silver ore had been found near the Rattlesnake Ranch.[275] Wilbur Fisk Sanders learned of the find from Samuel McLean while the two men were in Bannack.[276] Ironically, Sanders and McLean, both lawyers, would later run against each other to be the nonvoting representative of Montana Territory in the US House of Representatives. Sheriff Plummer had particular knowledge judging the quality of silver ore as a result of his earlier life experiences in California, and he was requested to go to the Rattlesnake area to examine it.[277] A group of lawyers including Sanders, Edgerton, and McLean were concerned that Plummer might organize a mining district in a way that would cut them and others out of the silver claims they hoped to stake there.[278] Plummer left Bannack that day in the northward direction toward Rattlesnake.[279] Plummer downplayed his interest in the silver discovery by stating that his true reason for going to Rattlesnake was to seize the horses of Frank Parish, who was gravely ill at the ranch.[280] Plummer explained that if Parish died, his Indian wife might take all of the horses that belonged to Parish, Bunton & Company and deliver them to her tribe west of the mountains near Fort Lemhi.[281]

Perhaps there was some question about whether Plummer was leaving for the Rattlesnake Ranch to organize a mining district or, alternatively, to secure Parish's horses.[282] The securing of Parish's horses might have been viewed suspiciously, as a convenient cover story to obscure his true mining-related purpose for hastily leaving Bannack for Rattlesnake. Sanders decided that it was in his best interest, and in the best interests of his friends, for him to follow Plummer to Rattlesnake. Upon making arrangements for the trip, Sanders found most of the horse stables in Bannack empty from the stampede of prospectors to Rattlesnake earlier in the day, and he could therefore only rent an uncooperative mule of such small size that his feet almost reached the ground while upon it.[283] The sight of Sanders upon the mule must have been quite comical as he rode from Bannack in pursuit of Sheriff Plummer and the new silver lode to the north.

Meanwhile, Plummer, once out of sight, abandoned the route to Rattlesnake and doubled back southward toward Horse Prairie.[284] All persons, except perhaps for Plummer's closest associates, believed that the sheriff was headed for Rattlesnake either to secure Frank Parish's horses or, for the more suspicious, to help form a mining district. In fact, Plummer obviously pursued neither task upon changing course for Horse Prairie, which Sanders would sadly discover upon his arrival at the Rattlesnake Ranch later that evening. Both reasons for Plummer's trip to the Rattlesnake Ranch were diversions from his true apparent plan, which involved his presence along the twelve-mile trail between Bannack and Horse Prairie during the same evening that Nathaniel Langford and Samuel T. Hauser would be traveling with their valuable gold dust.

Dimsdale wrote that when the Langford-Hauser party left Bannack the evening of November 14, they knew nothing of the earlier incident involving Henry Tilden.[285] Langford's own account, however, reveals that he and his party learned of the robbery of Tilden at 7:00 p.m., just as they were preparing to leave Bannack for Horse Prairie.[286] Undeterred, Langford and Hauser each loaded their guns with twelve revolver shots and kept the guns cocked during their journey to Horse Prairie.[287]

If Plummer and his associates had been lying in wait for Langford and Hauser, knowing of the valuable gold dust that they possessed, it is unclear why they would have bothered with a robbery of Henry Tilden. After all, Tilden had been a single rider traveling at the time of his stop in a direction that was opposite of that which was already publicly known and anticipated for Langford and Hauser.

In any event, Langford, Hauser, and the Mormon freighters traveled unmolested until they reached camp later in the evening, as if the road agents had been caught off guard by their timing on the trail. During the evening, according to both Dimsdale and Langford, the road agents might have concluded that Tilden had arrived in Bannack in time to warn the travelers that robbers were on the trail, causing Langford and Hauser to cancel their departures.[288] Alternatively, the road agents might have concluded that word of Tilden's robbery would prompt the formation of a search party for the robbers, causing them to lie low.[289] Yet alternatively, the road agents' plans might have merely been thrown off by the timing of Langford's and Hauser's departure from Bannack, which was originally scheduled for 5:00 p.m. that evening but which did not actually occur until two hours later.[290] In any event, Henry Plummer appeared in Bannack during the evening looking for Langford, and when he was informed that Langford and Hauser had already left for Horse Prairie, Plummer immediately left in pursuit.[291] Clearly, Plummer was not at the silver strike near the Rattlesnake Ranch and was no longer particularly concerned about Frank Parish's horses.

Langford reported that later in the evening while his traveling party was camped, he was unable to sleep, so he walked the perimeter of the camp with a double-barreled shotgun.[292] During his walk, Langford observed four masked men lurking nearby who realized that Langford had them in his gun sights and who rode off after being spotted.[293] The language of Langford's writings suggests that he did not immediately know the identities of the masked men. According to Langford, the four men were "afterwards ascertained" as Henry Plummer, George Ives, Buck Stinson, and Ned Ray.[294] The source and reliability of that identifying information is uncertain. Notably, Langford claimed that his traveling party had been stalked on the Horse Prairie Trail by four men, whereas Henry Tilden claimed to have been accosted by only three.

Something odd happened during the same evening. Wilbur Fisk Sanders had arrived at the Rattlesnake Ranch, despite the reluctance and slowness of his mule, and, after eating a late dinner, retired to bed for the night. Jack Gallagher, who had been one of Sheriff Plummer's deputies, arrived at the Rattlesnake Ranch at midnight demanding food and drink and insisting that he trade his worn-out horse for a fresh one.[295] The commotion awoke Sanders from his sleep. Sanders was still seeking Plummer in connection with the silver deposits that had been discovered in the area.[296] Sanders was not yet aware of any of the allegations made by Henry Tilden, as he had left Bannack hours before Tilden's purported robbery occurred. Sanders asked Gallagher if he knew where Plummer was, which was an innocent enough question under the circumstances.[297] Gallagher reacted to the question violently by pulling his pistol, aiming it at Sanders's head, and threatening to shoot.[298] Sanders might not have initially known what to make of Gallagher's response, but he seized a shotgun from a nearby bar and aimed it at Gallagher, ready to fire.[299] Gallagher opened his overcoat and dared Sanders to shoot him.[300] The incident was defused by others who were present, including Erastus "Red" Yeager and Bill Bunton, and ultimately Gallagher and Sanders made amends over a drink at the bar.[301] The curious aspect of the event was Gallagher's overreaction to Sanders's simple inquiry of Plummer's whereabouts. It was as if Gallagher, who was close to Plummer, had information to hide. If Plummer's plan for the evening had been to rob Langford and Hauser of their gold dust on the trail to Horse Prairie, Gallagher's conduct may have betrayed his knowledge that the sheriff of Bannack was up to no good. Of course, any such insight is purely conjectural.

In the days that followed, news of the robbery of Henry Tilden spread through the Bannack grapevine, though the news did not include any information about the identities of the specific thieves involved.[302] Plummer's involvement, if true, was kept as a closely held secret by those who knew Tilden well. Two or three days after the event, Sheriff Plummer approached Tilden at the express office where he worked and asked him if he could identify the persons involved in the crime.[303] Tilden was frightened by the inquiry, but adhering to the advice he had received from the adults that he trusted, he lied to Plummer and said that he had no idea who the men were that robbed him.[304] Every night thereafter, when Tilden's workday was over, he ran the entire distance to his boarding house in fear.[305] For the next two months, nothing more would become of young Henry Tilden's insistence, uttered in private, that Henry Plummer had menaced him with a gun on the trail from Horse Prairie.

The identities of the road agent conspirators operating in the region of Bannack and Alder Gulch were, of course, secret through most of 1863. Carelessness by the road agents allowed some of the victims and intended victims of robbery to know, or figure out, some of the road agents' identities. Nathaniel Langford, for instance, described how his own travel party, after leaving Bannack for Horse Prairie, had been stalked by four persons he believed to be Henry Plummer, George Ives, Buck Stinson, and Ned Ray.[306] Leon Southmayd believed that he knew the identities of the men who had robbed him on the A. J. Oliver & Company stagecoach—George Ives, "Whiskey Bill" Graves, and Bob Zachary. Likewise, Conrad Kohrs held suspicions about Henry Plummer, George Ives, and "Dutch John" Wagner. By the very end of 1863, ugly rumors and innuendo circulated in the region about Sheriff Plummer, George Ives, "Whiskey Bill" Graves, Bob Zachary, Aleck Carter, Bill Bunton, and Plummer's deputy sheriffs, Buck Stinson, Ned Ray, and, for a while, Jack Gallagher.

Granville Stuart wrote in his diary an entry on November 30, 1863, that foreshadowed events that were to come: "There has [sic] been several robberies on the road between [Virginia City] and Bannack seventy miles away and few people are living between the two camps. There is certainly an organized band of highway men about here and something will have to be done soon to protect life and property."[307]

Of all the various trail robberies that occurred in 1863, the alleged robbery of Henry Tilden appeared to be the least important of them all. The Tilden incident did not involve gruesome murders and death, as with the killing of the members of the Magruder party. The incident did not come within inches of a killing, as with the shooting attempt against Anton Holter. The incident did not involve an actual theft of significant valuables, as with the robbery of "Bummer Dan" McFadden and others traveling on the ill-fated Peabody & Caldwell stagecoach and of Leroy Southmayd on the equally ill-fated A. J. Oliver & Company stagecoach. The Tilden incident, if true, did not even rise to the level of importance of the apparent robbery attempts against Conrad Kohrs, as Kohrs was traveling on each occasion with significant amounts of gold dust for the purchase of cattle. Henry Tilden was not killed, injured, or robbed of money beyond token amounts, if that. The claims of a teenager fifteen or sixteen years old did not even seem credible to many of the adults who listened to his story and who feared that he might merely have been displaying an overactive imagination.

Nevertheless, the alleged robbery of Henry Tilden in mid-November 1863 preceded other events that sparked rumors about Sheriff Plummer and others, including but not necessarily limited to those involving Leon Southmayd and the A. J. Oliver & Company stagecoach, the violent attempted robbery of Moody's stagecoach, and the robbery and shooting at Anton Holter. Ironically, within two months' time, the allegations raised by young Henry Tilden would prove to be the most significant of them all. As will be shown, his terror on November 14, 1863, whether real or mistaken, would directly lead to the vigilante deaths of various men in Bannack.

The absence of effective law enforcement, the value of gold, and the insecurity of trails leading to and from the region were providing combined incentives for prospectors and other citizens to take the law into their own hands. It was in this climate of robberies, murders, and suspicion, shortly after the killing of D. H. Dillingham and the trials of Hayes Lyons, Buck Stinson, and Charley Forbes, that the body of a young man named Nick Tiebolt would be discovered. Events in the region of Alder Gulch and Bannack were about to take a dramatic turn.

Panning for Nuggets

There is a public misconception over the phrase "riding shotgun." One might believe that "riding shotgun" in the front passenger seat of a motor vehicle, to the right of the driver, originates from the old American West, when an armed law enforcement officer would sit next to a stagecoach driver to provide protection for traveling people and goods. In reality, there is no evidence that the phrase "riding shotgun" was ever used during the 1800s, and it bears no relationship to historic events in the western territories. The phrase appears to have been popularized by Hollywood in a 1939 movie called Stagecoach, *in which actor George Bancroft played the role of Marshal Curly Wilcox. Marshal Wilcox provided protection to stagecoaches in various scenes of the movie, and in one of those scenes he said, "I'm going to Lordsburg with Buck. I'm gonna ride shotgun."*[308]

Notes

1. Northern Pacific Railway Association, "Brief Introduction"; Northern Pacific Railway Historical Association, "Home."
2. Sievert and Sievert, *Virginia City*, 18. The railroad did not reach Dillon until October 5, 1880.
3. Greever, *Bonanza West*, 225; see also MendonUtah.Net, "Utah Northern Railroad."
4. Allen, *Decent Orderly Lynching*, 61; see also Fisher and Holmes, *Gold Rushes*, 116.
5. Allen, *Decent Orderly Lynching*, 61; Greever, *Bonanza West*, 223–24; Holmes, *Montana*, 105–6; Hamilton, *From Wilderness to Statehood*, 133.
6. Thompson, *Tenderfoot in Montana*, 79; Greever, *Bonanza West*, 224.
7. Burlingame, *Montana Frontier*, 128–29.
8. Ibid.; Mullan, *Report on the Construction of a Military Road*.
9. Thompson, *Tenderfoot in Montana*, 79.
10. Burlingame, *Montana Frontier*, 84.
11. Olson, *Oregon Trail*, 6–7; Uschan, *Oregon Trail*, 4.
12. Dary, *Oregon Trail*, 206, 239.
13. Ibid., 289.
14. Ibid., 292; see also Barsness, *Gold Camp*, 14.
15. See, generally, Dary, *Oregon Trail*, 206, 239; Burlingame, *Montana Frontier*, 132.
16. Lowe, *Bridger Trail*, 23; Johnson, *Bloody Bozeman*, 110; Greever, *Bonanza West*, 224.
17. Doyle, *Journeys*, 1.
18. Johnson, *Bloody Bozeman*, 110; Burlingame, *Montana Frontier*, 132; Sievert and Sievert, *Virginia City*, 17. A peace treaty had been reached with the Sioux Indians permitting use of the Bozeman Trail, but it did not bind hostile factions of the Sioux and Cheyenne tribes. The trail was therefore protected by three strategically placed forts, Fort Reno and Fort Kearney in present-day Wyoming and Fort C. F. Smith in south central Montana. Crutchfield, *It Happened in Montana*, 35.
19. Lowe, *Bridger Trail*, 21–22; Fort Laramie Treaty of September 17, 1851, 11 Stat. 749 (1851). The treaty was signed between the United States and the Cheyenne, Sioux, Arapaho, Navajo, Crow, Shoshone, Assiniboine, Mandan, Hidatsa, and Arikara Indian nations.
20. Lowe, *Bridger Trail*, 149.
21. Ibid., 178.
22. Burlingame, *Montana Frontier*, 132; Lowe, *Bridger Trail*, 179.
23. Lowe, *Bridger Trail*, 22; Sievert and Sievert, *Virginia City*, 11.
24. Montana History, "Bozeman."
25. Lowe, *Bridger Trail*, 21.
26. Johnson, *Bloody Bozeman*, 129.
27. Burlingame, *Montana Frontier*, 132–33; Lowe, *Bridger Trail*, 22; Sievert and Sievert, *Virginia City*, 17.

28. Lowe, *Bridger Trail*, 22.

29. Ibid., 94.

30. Ibid.

31. Ibid.

32. Holmes, *Montana*, 105–6.

33. Ibid.

34. Ibid., 106; Hamilton, *From Wilderness to Statehood*, 148.

35. Sievert and Sievert, *Virginia City*, 17; Holmes, *Montana*, 105; Hamilton, *From Wilderness to Statehood*, 144.

36. Allen, *Decent Orderly Lynching*, 156. The Stinking Water River in Montana is known today as the Ruby River.

37. Allen, *Decent Orderly Lynching*, 8; Birney, *Vigilantes*, 46; Langford, *Vigilante Days*, 143. Violent crime on the western overland routes was not the norm, but it did on occasion occur. Reid, *Law for the Elephants*, 355. The incidence of violence in Montana in 1863 and 1864 exceeded the western norm.

38. Langford, *Vigilante Days*, 143; Reid, *Law for the Elephants*, 355. It was safer for road agents to target travelers on the trails between Bannack and Virginia City than to rob miners near settled communities, as any road agents who were caught could have been quickly tried by miners' courts. Morriss, "Private Actors," 128n47.

39. Morriss, "Private Actors," 128n47; see also Thompson, *Tenderfoot in Montana*, 159; Pace, *Golden Gulch*, 32.

40. Allen, *Decent Orderly Lynching*, 112; Callaway, *Montana's Righteous Hangmen*, 20; Birney, *Vigilantes*, 47. A. J. Oliver was the first of the two stagecoach lines. By July of 1863, the company ran three coaches a week from Bannack to Salt Lake City, Utah, which was a four-day trip. Pace, *Golden Gulch*, 31; see also Greever, *Bonanza West*, 225.

41. Langford, *Vigilante Days*, 143.

42. Allen, *Decent Orderly Lynching*, 138; Dimsdale, *Vigilantes of Montana*, 22; Sievert and Sievert, *Virginia City*, 15.

43. Langford, *Vigilante Days*, 145.

44. Ibid., 140, 142; Morriss, "Private Actors," 128.

45. Cushman, *Montana*, 105.

46. Morriss, "Private Actors," 128n46.

47. Langford, *Vigilante Days*, 143; Gard, *Frontier Justice*, 171; Barsness, *Gold Camp*, 28; Morriss, "Private Actors," 128n46.

48. Langford, *Vigilante Days*, 161; Birney, *Vigilantes*, 169–70; Morriss, "Private Actors," 128n46.

49. Langford, *Vigilante Days*, 161; Birney, *Vigilantes*, 169–70; Morriss, "Private Actors," 128n46.

50. Langford, *Vigilante Days*, 195; Leeson, *History of Montana*, 289; Burlingame, *Montana Frontier*, 98; Gard, *Frontier Justice*, 171; Anonymous, *Banditti of the Rocky Mountains*, 79, 123 (which identifies the knot specifically as a "cordon knot").

51. Burlingame, *Montana Frontier*, 98; Gard, *Frontier Justice*, 171; Birney, *Vigilantes*, 124; Bartholomew, *Henry Plummer*, 16.

52. Dimsdale, *Vigilantes of Montana*, 20; Carolyn Abbott Tyler Reminiscences, 1862–65, Mont. Hist. Soc., SC-1430, folder 1-1; Birney, 135.

53. Dimsdale, *Vigilantes of Montana*, 20; Carolyn Abbott Tyler Reminiscences, 1862–65, Mont. Hist. Soc., SC-1430, folder 1-1; Birney, 135.

54. Langford, *Vigilante Days*, 151; Allen, *Decent Orderly Lynching*, 157.

55. Ibid.

56. Gard, *Frontier Justice*, 171.

57. Carolyn Abbott Tyler Reminiscences, 1862–65, Mont. Hist. Soc., SC 1430, folder 1-1.

58. Allen, *Decent Orderly Lynching*, 161.

59. Dimsdale, *Vigilantes of Montana*, 60.

60. Pace, *Golden Gulch*, 32.
61. Allen, *Decent Orderly Lynching*, 163.
62. Langford, *Vigilante Days*, 113.
63. Dimsdale, *Vigilantes of Montana*, 22; see also Bartholomew, *Henry Plummer*, 6, 45; Greever, *Bonanza West*, 226; Fisher and Holmes, *Gold Rushes*, 333, estimating the number at 100, with other additional atrocities that were committed but unrecorded.
64. Allen, *Decent Orderly Lynching*, 255–56.
65. Mather and Boswell, *Hanging the Sheriff*, 100.
66. Ibid., 164.
67. Dimsdale, *Vigilantes of Montana*, 55; Langford, *Vigilante Days*, 144; Purple, *Perilous Passage*, 195; Allen, *Decent Orderly Lynching*, 137.
68. Dimsdale, *Vigilantes of Montana*, 55. Langford identifies the passengers as "Madison" rather than "Mattison" and "Percy" rather than "Percival," along with Wilkinson and McFadden. Langford, *Vigilante Days*, 144.
69. Allen, *Decent Orderly Lynching*, 137.
70. Ibid.
71. Dimsdale, *Vigilantes of Montana*, 55; Leeson, *History of Montana*, 268; Allen, *Decent Orderly Lynching*, 137.
72. Langford, *Vigilante Days*, 144.
73. Ibid.
74. Allen, *Decent Orderly Lynching*, 137.
75. Dimsdale, *Vigilantes of Montana*, 55; Allen, *Decent Orderly Lynching*, 138.
76. Dimsdale, *Vigilantes of Montana*, 55; Langford, *Vigilante Days*, 144–45.
77. Dimsdale, *Vigilantes of Montana*, 56; Langford, *Vigilante Days*, 145; Allen, *Decent Orderly Lynching*, 138–39.
78. Dimsdale, *Vigilantes of Montana*, 56–57; Allen, *Decent Orderly Lynching*, 139.
79. Dimsdale, *Vigilantes of Montana*, 57.
80. Langford, *Vigilante Days*, 145; Birney, *Vigilantes*, 131.
81. Dimsdale, *Vigilantes of Montana*, 56; Langford, *Vigilante Days*, 145.
82. Dimsdale, *Vigilantes of Montana*, 57.
83. Ibid.; Langford, *Vigilante Days*, 145; Leeson, *History of Montana*, 268; Allen, *Decent Orderly Lynching*, 139.
84. Dimsdale, *Vigilantes of Montana*, 57–58; Langford, *Vigilante Days*, 146.
85. Dimsdale, *Vigilantes of Montana*, 57–58; Langford, *Vigilante Days*, 146; Birney, *Vigilantes*, 131; Stuart, *Forty Years on the Frontier*, 1:260. The wording attributed to Bunton by Langford and Birney is slightly different, but identical in meaning.
86. Dimsdale, *Vigilantes of Montana*, 57–58.
87. Ibid., 58–60; Langford, *Vigilante Days*, 146–48; Purple, *Perilous Passage*, 195; Leeson, *History of Montana*, 268–70; Stuart, *Forty Years on the Frontier*, 1:260.
88. Allen, *Decent Orderly Lynching*, 139.
89. Hamilton, *From Wilderness to Statehood*, 242.
90. Dimsdale, *Vigilantes of Montana*, 59–60.
91. Ibid.; Birney, *Vigilantes*, 132–33; Stuart, *Forty Years on the Frontier*, 1:260; Wolle, *Montana Pay Dirt*, 26; Hamilton, *From Wilderness to Statehood*, 242.
92. Dimsdale, *Vigilantes of Montana*, 60; Birney, *Vigilantes*, 133.
93. Dimsdale, *Vigilantes of Montana*, 55–60; Langford, *Vigilante Days*, 144–48; Birney, *Vigilantes*, 133; Allen, *Decent Orderly Lynching*, 137–40. Allen's account quantifies the stolen amount from McFadden alone as $2,500, based on a diary entry by Granville Stuart who, at the time, lived in Virginia City. Allen, *Decent Orderly Lynching*, 139.
94. Langford, *Vigilante Days*, 149.
95. Allen, *Decent Orderly Lynching*, 138.

96. Langford, *Vigilante Days*, 149.
97. Dimsdale, *Vigilantes of Montana*, 60–61; Birney, *Vigilantes*, 133–34.
98. Dimsdale, *Vigilantes of Montana*, 61; Leeson, *History of Montana*, 270; see also Birney, *Vigilantes*, 133–34.
99. Langford, *Vigilante Days*, 148.
100. Allen, *Decent Orderly Lynching*, 139–40.
101. Birney, *Vigilantes*, 134.
102. Allen, *Decent Orderly Lynching*, 155.
103. Dimsdale, *Vigilantes of Montana*, 72; Langford, *Vigilante Days*, 150; Allen, *Decent Orderly Lynching*, 155.
104. Allen, *Decent Orderly Lynching*, 155.
105. Dimsdale, *Vigilantes of Montana*, 72; Langford, *Vigilante Days*, 151.
106. Birney, *Vigilantes*, 134.
107. Langford, *Vigilante Days*, 151; Birney, *Vigilantes*, 134; Allen, *Decent Orderly Lynching*, 157.
108. Dimsdale, *Vigilantes of Montana*, 72; Langford, *Vigilante Days*, 151.
109. Dimsdale, *Vigilantes of Montana*, 72; Langford, *Vigilante Days*, 151.
110. Dimsdale, *Vigilantes of Montana*, 72; Langford, *Vigilante Days*, 151.
111. Langford, *Vigilante Days*, 151–52; Leeson, *History of Montana*, 276; Birney, *Vigilantes*, 136; Allen, *Decent Orderly Lynching*, 157.
112. Dimsdale, *Vigilantes of Montana*, 74; Langford, *Vigilante Days*, 151–52; Leeson, *History of Montana*, 276; Allen, *Decent Orderly Lynching*, 157.
113. Langford, *Vigilante Days*, 153; Leeson, *History of Montana*, 276; Birney, *Vigilantes*, 136; Allen, *Decent Orderly Lynching*, 157.
114. Birney, *Vigilantes*, 136.
115. Langford, *Vigilante Days*, 153; Allen, *Decent Orderly Lynching*, 159.
116. Langford, *Vigilante Days*, 153; Birney, *Vigilantes*, 136.
117. Dimsdale, *Vigilantes of Montana*, 75; Langford, *Vigilante Days*, 153; Allen, *Decent Orderly Lynching*, 159.
118. Dimsdale, *Vigilantes of Montana*, 75–76; Langford, *Vigilante Days*, 154. Langford cryptically referred to the brothel as one of Virginia City's "fancy establishments."
119. Dimsdale, *Vigilantes of Montana*, 76; Allen, *Decent Orderly Lynching*, 159.
120. Dimsdale, *Vigilantes of Montana*, 76; Langford, *Vigilante Days*, 154; Allen, *Decent Orderly Lynching*, 154.
121. Dimsdale, *Vigilantes of Montana*, 76; Langford, *Vigilante Days*, 154; Birney, *Vigilantes*, 137.
122. Birney, *Vigilantes*, 137.
123. Dimsdale, *Vigilantes of Montana*, 76; Langford, *Vigilante Days*, 154; Birney, *Vigilantes*, 137; Allen, *Decent Orderly Lynching*, 159.
124. Dimsdale, *Vigilantes of Montana*, 76; Langford, *Vigilante Days*, 154; Allen, *Decent Orderly Lynching*, 159.
125. Dimsdale, *Vigilantes of Montana*, 76; Langford, *Vigilante Days*, 154; Allen, *Decent Orderly Lynching*, 159–60.
126. Langford, *Vigilante Days*, 154.
127. Ibid., 155; Birney, *Vigilantes*, 137; Allen, *Decent Orderly Lynching*, 160.
128. Dimsdale, *Vigilantes of Montana*, 76; Birney, *Vigilantes*, 138; Allen, *Decent Orderly Lynching*, 160.
129. Dimsdale, *Vigilantes of Montana*, 77; Langford, *Vigilante Days*, 155; Birney, *Vigilantes*, 138.
130. Langford, *Vigilante Days*, 155.
131. Dimsdale, *Vigilantes of Montana*, 77; Langford, *Vigilante Days*, 155; Birney, *Vigilantes*, 138; Allen, *Decent Orderly Lynching*, 160.
132. Dimsdale, *Vigilantes of Montana*, 77; Langford, *Vigilante Days*, 155; Leeson, *History of Montana*, 276; Allen, *Decent Orderly Lynching*, 160.

133. Dimsdale, *Vigilantes of Montana*, 77; Langford, *Vigilante Days*, 155; Birney, *Vigilantes*, 139; Allen, *Decent Orderly Lynching*, 160.

134. Langford, *Vigilante Days*, 155.

135. Dimsdale, *Vigilantes of Montana*, 77; Langford, *Vigilante Days*, 155: Allen, *Decent Orderly Lynching*, 160.

136. Dimsdale, *Vigilantes of Montana*, 77; Langford, *Vigilante Days*, 156: Allen, *Decent Orderly Lynching*, 160.

137. Allen, *Decent Orderly Lynching*, 160.

138. Dimsdale, *Vigilantes of Montana*, 77–78; Langford, *Vigilante Days*, 156; Leeson, *History of Montana*, 276; Birney, *Vigilantes*, 140; Allen, *Decent Orderly Lynching*, 160–61.

139. Langford, *Vigilante Days*, 156.

140. Dimsdale, *Vigilantes of Montana*, 78; Langford, *Vigilante Days*, 156; Birney, *Vigilantes*, 140–41; Allen, *Decent Orderly Lynching*, 161.

141. Kohrs, *Conrad Kohrs*, 1.

142. Ibid., 26.

143. Ibid., 28.

144. Ibid., 29.

145. Ibid.

146. Ibid.

147. Ibid.

148. Ibid.

149. Ibid.

150. Ibid.

151. Ibid.

152. Ibid.

153. Ibid.

154. Ibid., 29–30.

155. Ibid., 30.

156. Ibid., 31.

157. Ibid., 30.

158. Ibid., 31.

159. Ibid.

160. Ibid.

161. Ibid.

162. Dimsdale, *Vigilantes of Montana*, 50; Allen, *Decent Orderly Lynching*, 161.

163. Langford, *Vigilante Days*, 172; Allen, *Decent Orderly Lynching*, 161; Cushman, *Montana*, 105–6; Doyle, *Journeys*, 62.

164. Dimsdale, *Vigilantes of Montana*, 50; Langford, *Vigilante Days*, 172; Leeson, *History of Montana*, 289. Langford identifies passenger Jones's initials as M. T. rather than M. V. Leeson identifies the value of the cargo as $75,000 rather than $80,000.

165. Allen, *Decent Orderly Lynching*, 161; Johnson, *Bloody Bozeman*, 91; Birney, *Vigilantes*, 174 (listing the value of the cargo as $75,000).

166. Langford, *Vigilante Days*, 172.

167. Dimsdale, *Vigilantes of Montana*, 51; Langford, *Vigilante Days*, 173; Birney, *Vigilantes*, 174.

168. Birney, *Vigilantes*, 176.

169. Dimsdale, *Vigilantes of Montana*, 51; Langford, *Vigilante Days*, 173.

170. Dimsdale, *Vigilantes of Montana*, 51; Langford, *Vigilante Days*, 173; Allen, *Decent Orderly Lynching*, 161; Johnson, *Bloody Bozeman*, 91.

171. Dimsdale, *Vigilantes of Montana*, 53; Langford, *Vigilante Days*, 173–74; Allen, *Decent Orderly Lynching*, 161; Cushman, *Montana*, 106.

172. Leeson, *History of Montana*, 289.

173. Dimsdale, *Vigilantes of Montana*, 52. Langford, *Vigilante Days*, 174.
174. Dimsdale, *Vigilantes of Montana*, 53; Langford, *Vigilante Days*, 174.
175. Dimsdale, *Vigilantes of Montana*, 52; Langford, *Vigilante Days*, 174.
176. Dimsdale, *Vigilantes of Montana*, 52.
177. Ibid., 53; Langford, *Vigilante Days*, 174; Allen, *Decent Orderly Lynching*, 162.
178. Dimsdale, *Vigilantes of Montana*, 53.
179. Ibid.; Langford, *Vigilante Days*, 174; Allen, *Decent Orderly Lynching*, 162; Birney, *Vigilantes*, 177–78; Johnson, *Bloody Bozeman*, 91.
180. Dimsdale, *Vigilantes of Montana*, 53; Langford, *Vigilante Days*, 174; Allen, *Decent Orderly Lynching*, 162.
181. Dimsdale, *Vigilantes of Montana*, 53; Langford, *Vigilante Days*, 174; Allen, *Decent Orderly Lynching*, 162.
182. Dimsdale, *Vigilantes of Montana*, 53; Langford, *Vigilante Days*, 174; Allen, *Decent Orderly Lynching*, 162; Birney, *Vigilantes*, 177–78; Cushman, *Montana*, 106; Johnson, *Bloody Bozeman*, 91.
183. Cushman, *Montana*, 106; Birney, *Vigilantes*, 178.
184. Allen, *Decent Orderly Lynching*, 162.
185. Ibid., 133.
186. Ibid.
187. Dimsdale, *Vigilantes of Montana*, 105; Allen, *Decent Orderly Lynching*, 134.
188. Leeson, *History of Montana*, 271. Nathaniel Langford identifies Lowrie as "Chris Lowry." See Langford, *Vigilante Days*, 197. Frederick Allen refers to the same man as "Chris Lowrie." See Allen, *Decent Orderly Lynching*, 238. The Lowrie spelling will be adopted here as Leeson's work was written closest to the events.
189. Langford, *Vigilante Days*, 198; Find A Grave, "Hill Beachy."
190. Allen, *Decent Orderly Lynching*, 133.
191. Langford, *Vigilante Days*, 199; Birney, *Vigilantes*, 145.
192. Langford, *Vigilante Days*, 198.
193. Ibid.
194. Ibid.; Thompson, *Tenderfoot in Montana*, 155.
195. Allen, *Decent Orderly Lynching*, 241.
196. Langford, *Vigilante Days*, 199.
197. Ibid., 200; Thompson, *Tenderfoot in Montana*, 155.
198. Langford, *Vigilante Days*, 200–201.
199. Ibid., 201; Leeson, *History of Montana*, 271; Birney, *Vigilantes*, 149; Fisher and Holmes, *Gold Rushes*, 333; Allen, *Decent Orderly Lynching*, 138.
200. Langford, *Vigilante Days*, 201.
201. Ibid.; Birney, *Vigilantes*, 149; Fisher and Holmes, *Gold Rushes*, 333.
202. Langford, *Vigilante Days*, 201; Thompson, *Tenderfoot in Montana*, 155; Birney, *Vigilantes*, 149.
203. Langford, *Vigilante Days*, 201; Birney, *Vigilantes*, 149–50; Allen, *Decent Orderly Lynching*, 139.
204. Langford, *Vigilante Days*, 200–201; Thompson, *Tenderfoot in Montana*, 155–56.
205. Langford, *Vigilante Days*, 201.
206. Ibid.; Birney, *Vigilantes*, 150.
207. Langford, *Vigilante Days*, 201; Thompson, *Tenderfoot in Montana*, 156; Birney, *Vigilantes*, 150.
208. Langford, *Vigilante Days*, 202; Thompson, *Tenderfoot in Montana*, 155; Birney, *Vigilantes*, 150.
209. Birney, *Vigilantes*, 150.
210. Allen, *Decent Orderly Lynching*, 239.
211. Langford, *Vigilante Days*, 201–2.
212. Ibid., 211.
213. Birney, *Vigilantes*, 151; Thompson, *Tenderfoot in Montana*, 156; Fisher and Holmes, *Gold Rushes*, 333.

214. Langford, *Vigilante Days*, 203; Birney, *Vigilantes*, 152.

215. Langford, *Vigilante Days*, 203–4; Thompson, *Tenderfoot in Montana*, 155; Allen, *Decent Orderly Lynching*, 139.

216. Langford, *Vigilante Days*, 206–7; Thompson, *Tenderfoot in Montana*, 156.

217. Langford, *Vigilante Days*, 204; Birney, *Vigilantes*, 153.

218. Birney, *Vigilantes*, 153.

219. Langford, *Vigilante Days*, 212; Thompson, *Tenderfoot in Montana*, 156–57; Fisher and Holmes, *Gold Rushes*, 333; Allen, *Decent Orderly Lynching*, 236–37; Olsen, "Lawlessness and Vigilantes in America," 156.

220. Langford, *Vigilante Days*, 212; Thompson, *Tenderfoot in Montana*, 156–57.

221. Allen, *Decent Orderly Lynching*, 236.

222. Ibid., 236–37.

223. Langford, *Vigilante Days*, 212; Thompson, *Tenderfoot in Montana*, 156; Allen, *Decent Orderly Lynching*, 236–37; Olsen, "Lawlessness and Vigilantes," 156.

224. Allen, *Decent Orderly Lynching*, 237.

225. Langford, *Vigilante Days*, 206–7; Thompson, *Tenderfoot in Montana*, 157; Birney, *Vigilantes*, 156.

226. Birney, *Vigilantes*, 156.

227. Langford, *Vigilante Days*, 213; Birney, *Vigilantes*, 156.

228. Langford, *Vigilante Days*, 213–14; Birney, *Vigilantes*, 156.

229. Birney, *Vigilantes*, 156.

230. Ibid.

231. Langford, *Vigilante Days*, 213–14; Thompson, *Tenderfoot in Montana*, 156; Birney, *Vigilantes*, 157–58; Allen, *Decent Orderly Lynching*, 238.

232. Birney, *Vigilantes*, 157.

233. Allen, *Decent Orderly Lynching*, 239.

234. Langford, *Vigilante Days*, 215; Leeson, *History of Montana*, 271; Thompson, *Tenderfoot in Montana*, 157; Birney, *Vigilantes*, 158; Fisher and Holmes, *Gold Rushes*, 333.

235. Allen, *Decent Orderly Lynching*, 239.

236. Thompson, *Tenderfoot in Montana*, 157; Allen, *Decent Orderly Lynching*, 239–40. It is unclear whether the Indian boy, Jack, testified as to his identification of Magruder's horse and saddle in the defendants' possession at Lewiston. Idaho's Criminal Practice Act of 1864 does not appear to contain any prohibition of Indian testimony against whites in court proceedings. Even if Jack's testimony was elicited at the trial, it may have been given little evidentiary value.

237. Allen, *Decent Orderly Lynching*, 241.

238. Langford, *Vigilante Days*, 201; Thompson, *Tenderfoot in Montana*, 157; Birney, *Vigilantes*, 158; Fisher and Holmes, *Gold Rushes*, 333; Olsen, "Lawlessness and Vigilantes," 156.

239. Langford, *Vigilante Days*, 215; Birney, *Vigilantes*, 158.

240. Langford, *Vigilante Days*, 215–16; Thompson, *Tenderfoot in Montana*, 158; Birney, *Vigilantes*, 158.

241. Langford, *Vigilante Days*, 177; Allen, *Decent Orderly Lynching*, 162.

242. Langford, *Vigilante Days*, 177; Gard, *Frontier Justice*, 175; Allen, *Decent Orderly Lynching*, 163.

243. Langford, *Vigilante Days*, 177; Allen, *Decent Orderly Lynching*, 163.

244. Allen, *Decent Orderly Lynching*, 163; Cushman, *Montana*, 109.

245. Langford, *Vigilante Days*, 177; Gard, *Frontier Justice*, 175; Allen, *Decent Orderly Lynching*, 163; Cushman, *Montana*, 109; Olsen, "Lawlessness and Vigilantes," 133.

246. Langford, *Vigilante Days*, 177–78; Allen, *Decent Orderly Lynching*, 163.

247. Langford, *Vigilante Days*, 177–78; Allen, *Decent Orderly Lynching*, 163; Cushman, *Montana*, 109.

248. Langford, *Vigilante Days*, 178; Barsness, *Gold Camp*, 31; Allen, *Decent Orderly Lynching*, 163.

249. Barsness, *Gold Camp*, 31.

250. Langford, *Vigilante Days*, 169; Thompson, *Tenderfoot in Montana*, 272; Allen, *Decent Orderly Lynching*, 148.

251. Allen, *Decent Orderly Lynching*, 148.

252. Langford, *Vigilante Days*, 169–70; Thompson, *Tenderfoot in Montana*, 162; Leeson, *History of Montana*, 275–76.

253. Langford, *Vigilante Days*, 170; Gard, *Frontier Justice*, 750.

254. Langford, *Vigilante Days*, 170; Mather and Boswell, *Hanging the Sheriff*, 69–70.

255. Compare Dimsdale, *Vigilantes of Montana*, 48, with Thompson, *Tenderfoot in Montana*, 162.

256. Mather and Boswell, *Hanging the Sheriff*, 69–70, 102–3 (quoting an account by Hattie Sanders).

257. Langford, *Vigilante Days*, 170.

258. Ibid.; Thompson, *Tenderfoot in Montana*, 162; Allen, *Decent Orderly Lynching*, 148.

259. Allen, *Decent Orderly Lynching*, 148.

260. Dimsdale, *Vigilantes of Montana*, 47; Langford, *Vigilante Days*, 170; Thompson, *Tenderfoot in Montana*, 162; Leeson, *History of Montana*, 276; Gard, *Frontier Justice*, 750; Allen, *Decent Orderly Lynching*, 148.

261. Langford, *Vigilante Days*, 170.

262. Mather and Boswell, *Hanging the Sheriff*, 70; Allen, *Decent Orderly Lynching*, 148.

263. Mather and Boswell, *Hanging the Sheriff*, 107.

264. Ibid.

265. Allen, *Decent Orderly Lynching*, 148.

266. Langford, *Vigilante Days*, 170; Thompson, *Tenderfoot in Montana*, 162; Leeson, *History of Montana*, 276; Mather and Boswell, *Hanging the Sheriff*, 70; Allen, *Decent Orderly Lynching*, 148.

267. Helen Sanders, *History of Montana*, 192–93, cited in Mather and Boswell, "First Witness for the Prosecution"; Leeson, *History of Montana*, 276.

268. Mather and Boswell, *Hanging the Sheriff*, 105.

269. Dimsdale, *Vigilantes of Montana*, 46; Allen, *Decent Orderly Lynching*, 141.

270. Langford, *Vigilante Days*, 158; Thompson, *Tenderfoot in Montana*, 163–64; Mather and Boswell, *Hanging the Sheriff*, 69; Allen, *Decent Orderly Lynching*, 141–42.

271. Dimsdale, *Vigilantes of Montana*, 47; Thompson, *Tenderfoot in Montana*, 164; Allen, *Decent Orderly Lynching*, 142.

272. Dimsdale, *Vigilantes of Montana*, 47 ("useful on the journey these cold nights"); Langford, *Vigilante Days*, 159; Thompson, *Tenderfoot in Montana*, 164.

273. Allen, *Decent Orderly Lynching*, 142.

274. Ibid., 141.

275. Langford, *Vigilante Days*, 159.

276. Allen, *Decent Orderly Lynching*, 144.

277. Langford, *Vigilante Days*, 159.

278. Allen, *Decent Orderly Lynching*, 145.

279. Langford, *Vigilante Days*, 159.

280. Ibid., 165.

281. Ibid.; Allen, *Decent Orderly Lynching*, 143.

282. Allen says that Nathaniel Langford's account of these events is suspect, as Langford's writing gives contradictory information about whether Henry Plummer initially headed toward Rattlesnake to secure Frank Parish's horses or to stake mining claims. Allen, *Decent Orderly Lynching*, 142–43. However, the two versions might be consistent with each other if Plummer gave different cover stories to different persons at different times of the day. If

the Sanders group was debating the true reason for Plummer's departure from Bannack, their attention would not have been on the security of the trail between Bannack and Horse Prairie.

283. Ibid., 146.

284. Langford, *Vigilante Days*, 159.

285. Dimsdale, *Vigilantes of Montana*, 47.

286. Langford, *Vigilante Days*, 159.

287. Dimsdale, *Vigilantes of Montana*, 47; Allen, *Decent Orderly Lynching*, 142.

288. Dimsdale, *Vigilantes of Montana*, 47–48; Langford, *Vigilante Days*, 159.

289. Dimsdale, *Vigilantes of Montana*, 48.

290. Ibid.; Langford, *Vigilante Days*, 159; Thompson, *Tenderfoot in Montana*, 164.

291. Dimsdale, *Vigilantes of Montana*, 48; Langford, *Vigilante Days*, 159.

292. Dimsdale, *Vigilantes of Montana*, 48; Langford, *Vigilante Days*, 159; Thompson, *Tenderfoot in Montana*, 165.

293. Dimsdale, *Vigilantes of Montana*, 48–49; Langford, *Vigilante Days*, 160–61; Thompson, *Tenderfoot in Montana*, 165; Allen, *Decent Orderly Lynching*, 142.

294. Langford, *Vigilante Days*, 160–61; see also Dimsdale, *Vigilantes of Montana*, 49; Allen, *Decent Orderly Lynching*, 142.

295. Thompson, *Tenderfoot in Montana*, 166; Allen, *Decent Orderly Lynching*, 148–49.

296. Allen, *Decent Orderly Lynching*, 144.

297. Thompson, *Tenderfoot in Montana*, 166; Allen, *Decent Orderly Lynching*, 149.

298. Thompson, *Tenderfoot in Montana*, 166; Allen, *Decent Orderly Lynching*, 149.

299. Thompson, *Tenderfoot in Montana*, 166; Allen, *Decent Orderly Lynching*, 149–50.

300. Allen, *Decent Orderly Lynching*, 150.

301. Ibid.

302. Gard, *Frontier Justice*, 173.

303. Langford, *Vigilante Days*, 170; Mather and Boswell, *Hanging the Sheriff*, 70; Allen, *Decent Orderly Lynching*, 151.

304. Langford, *Vigilante Days*, 170; Mather and Boswell, *Hanging the Sheriff*, 70; Allen, *Decent Orderly Lynching*, 151.

305. Mather and Boswell, *Hanging the Sheriff*, 70.

306. Langford, *Vigilante Days*, 160–61.

307. Stuart, *Forty Years on the Frontier*, 1:262.

308. Martin, "Riding Shotgun."

6

The Murder of Nicholas Tiebolt and the Trial and Execution of George Ives

Sanders! Ask him how long he gave the Dutchman!

—John X. Beidler, December 21, 1863

S ometimes in history a singular event serves as a catalyst for other significant events that follow.[1] Vigilantism in the region of Alder Gulch traces its
specific origin to the discovery by William Palmer of a dead male body in
early December 1863 as Palmer was outdoors hunting grouse near the Stinking
Water River.[2] The body was discovered when Palmer retrieved a grouse that he
had killed from some brush.[3] Palmer's inspection of the frozen body revealed
that the deceased had been shot above the left eye and then dragged by a lariat
around his neck.[4] By all appearances, the victim had been dragged into the brush
while still alive, as evidenced by the presence of sagebrush clenched in the victim's hands.[5] Palmer sought assistance at a nearby hut, known in those days as a
wickiup, where he met "Long John" Franck and George Hilderman, neither of
whom were willing to be of help.[6] Indeed, Franck and Hilderman told Palmer
to "go to Hell."[7] Franck was known as "Long John" because of his tall height.[8]

Without assistance, Palmer loaded the partially decomposed body into
his wagon and ventured to Nevada City, where the victim was identified as a
popular young orphaned Dutchman named Nicholas Tiebolt.[9] Earlier Tiebolt
had been sent by William "Old Man" Clark to retrieve certain mules that
Clark had purchased. The mules had been pasturing at a livestock ranch, and
Tiebolt left for the ranch with a buckskin pouch containing gold dust but then

DOI: 10.7330_9780874219203.c006

disappeared.[10] Tiebolt's body, though disfigured and unsightly, was identified by a knife that had been given to him two years earlier by Tom Baume and found in the deceased's pocket.[11]

The townsfolk were angered and disturbed by the crime. By all accounts, Tiebolt was a likable and popular young man. Palmer explained that Franck and Hilderman had refused to help with the body, and people noted that both men worked at the ranch to which Tiebolt had been traveling.[12] The ranch was owned by George Ives.[13]

A posse was formed to investigate the murder.[14] It included James Williams, John X. Beidler, Elkanah "Elk" Morse, George Burtschey, Henry Clark, Nelson Story, H. K. Harvey, Thomas Baume, Frank Angevine, and others.[15] John X. Beidler, known in the region simply as "X,"[16] will be heard from more than once later in this narrative. The total size of the posse was approximately twenty-five men.[17] "Long John" Franck and George Hilderman were the prime suspects sought by the posse.[18]

After finding no one at the site where Tiebolt's body had been found, the posse rode to Ives's ranch, where they arrested Franck.[19] One of the missing mules was discovered at the ranch.[20]

James Williams, who was the de facto head of the posse from having provided many of its horses, saddles, and bridles,[21] interrogated Franck with both prodding and coercive threats of execution.[22] Franck admitted that Tiebolt had been robbed of his gold dust and shot to death by George Ives, who was hiding in a nearby hut.[23] Franck explained that he did not help bring Tiebolt's body to Nevada City because he was afraid to be involved.[24] Ives was arrested, followed by Hilderman,[25] and the suspects were brought back to Nevada City, Montana, for trial.[26] Nevada City had been chosen by the posse as the place for the trial, after some internal debate, as it was the mining community that was closest to where Tiebolt's body was found.[27] The prisoners were transported to Nevada City while bound in chains.[28] During the trek to Nevada City, and despite the chains, Ives tricked his captors into a horse race during which he almost succeeded in making an escape into the mountains near Biven's Gulch.[29]

Franck agreed to testify against Ives,[30] and in exchange for that cooperation he would not be tried as a defendant in Tiebolt's murder. Ives and Hilderman were tried separately, with the Ives trial the first of the two.[31] Incredibly, in determining how Ives and Hilderman were to be tried, speeches were made for and against whether to even allow the defendants to have the assistance of counsel.[32] The attorneys who were present were indignant that anyone would propose barring a defendant from exercising a right secured by the Constitution.[33] Ultimately, a decision was made that the participation of attorneys would be permitted at the trial. [34]

An attorney in the area, Wilbur Fisk Sanders, a Unionist,[35] agreed to act as prosecutor,[36] assisted by layman Charles S. Bagg, a miner who was a known Southern sympathizer believed to have credibility with many of the trial spectators.[37] Sanders was the nephew of Idaho chief judge Sydney Edgerton.[38] In agreeing to prosecute Ives, Sanders placed his life at great physical risk.[39] Sanders later wrote that he had "made up my mind that I would push the case with the utmost vigor, and if the guilt of the accused were certain that the retribution should be swift and absolutely remorseless."[40]

Ives was represented by five compensated attorneys, James M. Thurmond, John D. Ritchie, H. P. A. Smith,[41] Colonel Wood, and Alexander Davis.[42] H. P. A. Smith was particularly vocal in his support of the Confederacy. He "would go through our streets flourishing a revolver, swearing that he would shoot any damn s——b—— that would say he was a Lincoln man or an abolitionist."[43]

The trial was presided over by Don Byam of Nevada City, a doctor who had served on various miners' courts,[44] and Judge Wilson from the Junction mining district.[45]

Meanwhile, George "Clubfoot" Lane left on a speedy horse for Bannack to inform Sheriff Plummer of the defendants' arrests and to ask Plummer and a posse to proceed to Nevada City to take protective charge of Ives and Hilderman.[46]

Two Schuttler wagons were drawn side by side as an outdoor makeshift courtroom on the main street of Nevada City, for the judges on one and the witnesses on the other.[47] A court reporter named William Y. Pemberton was given a desk and chair near the wagons, but unfortunately the written record of the trial is not preserved.[48] He was assisted in the task by W. H. Patten.[49] At times during the trial, Pemberton took his trial notes while wearing gloves because of the chilly air.[50] The absence of a written, contemporaneous record of Ives's trial is unfortunate, as it would likely provide the most accurate and complete firsthand description of the events that transpired and would be of great historical value. Absent official stenographic notes, an original source summary of the trial was later written by Wilbur Fisk Sanders,[51] but it might lack the objectivity and candor of a contemporaneous record. Rounding out the trial setting, a bonfire was lit nearby for spectators to warm themselves in the chilly December air.[52] Benches were borrowed from a nearby hurdy-gurdy hall and were placed in a semicircle around the fire, facing the wagons.[53] The skies were clear, and there was some snow on the ground, but the cold was not particularly biting.[54] James Williams, who had been involved in the capture of Ives and Hilderman, deployed approximately fifty armed men around the perimeter of the trial,[55] outnumbering whatever "official" law enforcement was also provided by the local sheriffs, Adriel Davis of Junction and Robert Hereford of Nevada City.[56]

Figure 6.1. Dr. Don Byam, the presiding judge at the murder trial of George Ives. (Courtesy of the Montana Historical Society, image 941-358.)

Sheriff Plummer remained in Bannack, perhaps too cautious to get involved in the unfolding events.[57]

Unlike trials today, where judges are unquestionably in charge of determining matters of law and procedure, there was much public debate over whether Ives's verdict should be by a unanimous jury of six or twelve persons subject to the "reasonable doubt" standard or by the public acting as a jury en masse.[58] The issue was compromised by using two twelve-member jury panels, one from Nevada City and one from Junction, which would render a single "advisory" verdict, with the full assembly of spectators then having the final say on the issue of guilt or acquittal.[59]

At one point during the debate, the sheriff of Virginia City, J. B. "Buzz" Caven, argued from atop a wagon that the jury should be expanded to thirty-six jurors to include twelve from Virginia City.[60] Caven even held in his hand a piece of paper listing the names of the twelve additional jurors that he proposed adding to the group.[61] For a variety of reasons, persons sympathetic to Ives's prosecution were apoplectic at the thought of there being twelve additional jurors from Virginia City. First, an increase in the size of the jury from twenty-four men to thirty-six men appeared to be too unwieldy.[62] Second, there was an innate distrust of Virginia City jurors in the wake of the farcical results that had been reached there in the Dillingham murder case.[63] Third, Caven had briefly served as a deputy of Henry Plummer in Bannack during the summer of 1863, before moving to Virginia City and becoming its sheriff in September of the same year.[64] Caven's proposal was perceived as an effort to pack the jury with persons sympathetic to George Ives and Sheriff Plummer. The fact that Caven had already assembled his handpicked list of Virginia City jurors may have fed the perception that he was attempting to influence the trial's outcome.

Caven's proposal was a test of Wilbur Fisk Sanders's resolve. Sanders forcefully spoke out against the proposal, arguing that residents of Nevada City and Junction deserved to be jurors at the trial, given their proximity to the crime scene, but that residents of Virginia City did not.[65] During the public debate between Caven and Sanders, the two men became so animated about the proposed jurors and so uncompromising in their resolve that their remarks turned personal, and it appeared from their words that their personal conflict could only be resolved by means of a duel that would be conducted after the conclusion of the trial.[66] In the end, Sanders's argument prevailed with the majority of the crowd,[67] and no duel ever materialized between the sheriff and the prosecutor.

The trial began late in the day on Saturday, December 19, 1863, and ended two days later.[68] Upward of 1,500 people were in attendance.[69] The size of the crowd may be attributable to a combination of Tiebolt's popularity, the merciless manner in which he was killed, and the entertainment value of the proceeding itself. The continuation of the trial on Sunday, December 20, which many area residents treated as a day of rest, also likely contributed to the large size of the crowd. Among the spectators was a miner named John W. Grannis. Grannis maintained a personal ledger that he primarily used to record the value of the gold that he sluiced on given days. He heard the news that prisoners were arrested in the death of Tiebolt and described "a very large crowd of miners present."[70] Spectators gathered in the street, on doorsteps, and on rooftops, clamoring for positions from which to watch the proceedings.

Charles S. Bagg delivered the opening statement for the prosecution,[71] perhaps a sign that the prosecution sought to make a connection with the crowd whose Civil War sympathies were largely with the Confederacy and not with the Union.

After opening statements, the prosecution presented the testimonies of William Palmer and "Long John" Franck.[72] Palmer testified about his discovery

Figure 6.2. J. B. "Buzz" Caven, sheriff of Virginia City.
(Courtesy of the Montana Historical Society, image
941-487.)

of Tiebolt's body in all of its gruesome detail and about the curious refusal of
Hilderman and Franck to help him return the corpse to Nevada City.[73] Sanders's
written trial summary states that although Palmer "was rigidly cross-examined
and severely badgered, his testimony remained unshaken."[74] Palmer's testimony
must have had the effect of riveting the participants upon the seriousness of the
matter at hand and set the stage for Franck's testimony that was to follow.

"Long John" Franck testified that Tiebolt had arrived at the ranch to acquire
two mules and that, in making payment, he revealed his pouch containing hundreds of dollars worth of gold dust.[75] Franck described how after Tiebold had
left the ranch, Ives tossed a gold coin to determine who would pursue him for
the gold dust and the two mules.[76] As a matter of kismet, the coin toss designated Ives to do the job himself, so he loaded his revolver, rode from the area
on a horse, and returned a while later with the gold and the mules.[77] From the

witness stand, Franck quoted Ives as saying after the murder, "When I told the Dutchman I was going to kill him, he asked for time to pray, and I told him to kneel down then. He did so and I shot him through the head just as he commenced his prayer."[78] Franck further quoted Ives as saying that since it did not seem right to shoot Tiebolt in the back, he shot him in the forehead instead.[79] Such testimony, if true, was corroborated by the location of the bullet wound found on the corpse.

The cross-examination of Franck by the defense attorneys was brutal. Franck was accused through cross-examination of being willing to "peach on his pals" in order to save himself from an execution that he richly deserved for his own criminal activity.[80] The defense sought to impeach the veracity of the prosecution's key witness by suggesting that Franck's testimony was crafted to cover up his own murderous misdeed by implicating Ives in the crime instead.

The trial also included debate and rulings over exceptions to the rule against hearsay, the admissibility of unsworn statements, and evidence of Ives's alleged collateral crimes.[81] Dimsdale wrote that the trial evidence was not confined to the Tiebolt murder, but included other evidence he cryptically described as "damaging to the reputations and dangerous to the existence of some of his friends."[82] Dimsdale notwithstanding, the historical record is unclear as to whether Judges Byam and Wilson allowed at the trial evidence of Ives's own alleged collateral crimes and, if so, the extent to which such information was admitted as evidence. Persons who believed that they had been victimized in some way by Ives at least came forward and offered to testify against him as to those matters.[83] Witnesses included stagecoach drivers who identified Ives as having had a role in trailside holdups.[84] The later narrative by William Fisk Sanders states that an unnamed witness had testified that, during the preceding autumn, Ives was observed in the Snake River Valley on horseback, wearing an overcoat and a cape, with a sawed-off double-barreled shotgun, at a time when there were many robberies in the area.[85] In other words, Ives had been observed dressed and armed as a road agent. Sanders also mentions that trial testimony had included evidence of Ives's complicity in half a dozen murders, the trail robberies of "Bummer Dan" McFadden and Leroy Southmayd, and other robberies along the road leading to Salt Lake City.[86] Sanders conceded in his trial summary that the witness's testimony "may not have been very relevant to the question of whether Ives committed the [Tiebolt] murder, but he was on trial generally and the proof was quite conclusive that his record in the Snake River Valley would not bear examination."[87] Sanders's account is the best proof available that Ives's alleged criminal activities, independent of the Tiebolt murder, were admitted into evidence at the trial for consideration by the advisory juries and the assembled crowd.

In December of 1863, Conrad Kohrs, who had been an intended robbery victim of George Ives and "Dutch John" Wagner earlier in the year, heard that Ives had been arrested for a crime and was being tried for it in Nevada City.[88] While he may have been tempted to see the trial, he did not travel to Nevada City to do so.[89] Kohrs's stories about Ives's criminal activities could not therefore have been among those presented during Ives's trial but were probably typical of those that were told by others either on or off the official trial record.

Author Frederick Allen writes that during the trial, gossip of Ives's involvement in unrelated crimes may have circulated throughout the same crowd of spectators that ultimately voted on the question of guilt and could have influenced the outcome of the trial.[90] Those unrelated crimes could have included the robbery of Leroy Southmayd in late November of 1863, the robbery and attempted murder of Anton Holter on December 8, 1863, and the robbery of "Bummer Dan" McFadden and the Peabody & Caldwell stagecoach on October 26, 1863. If so, Ives's prior criminal conduct, whether formally admitted into evidence at the trial or not, reduced his chances of being acquitted of the murder of Nicholas Tiebolt. Unfortunately, neither Dimsdale nor almost all other raconteurs of the Ives trial specified what other information, outside of the Tiebolt murder itself, was actually admitted as evidence.

As a general rule today, evidence of unrelated, collateral crimes is not admissible in evidence against a defendant at a criminal proceeding, on the ground that the commission of other crimes or bad acts does not mean that the defendant committed the offense for which he is presently charged.[91] In other words, even if Ives was involved in various alleged trail robberies, evidence of those robberies does not mean, in and of itself, that Ives committed the robbery and murder of Nicholas Tiebolt. The prejudice caused to a defendant by evidence of collateral matters is believed to often outweigh the probative value of that evidence. There are exceptions to the general rule, such as when those other crimes relate in the current case to the defendant's motive, intent, identity, lack of mistake, and the existence of a common criminal plan or scheme.[92] In addition, prior crimes and bad acts are sometimes admissible against a criminal defendant if the earlier conduct speaks to the defendant's lack of honesty or willingness to place his own interests above those of others.[93] Rulings over the admissibility or inadmissibility of a defendant's prior crimes and other bad acts at trial are therefore complicated and require a balancing of competing factors by the trial judge. Such rulings were rendered more complicated for judges of the western frontier, who were often without formal training in the law and equipped with no law books in the back hills of rural Montana in 1863.[94]

In the end, it might not have mattered for Ives whether evidence of his earlier alleged crimes was formally admitted in his trial. At a minimum, rumors of

Ives's prior criminal behavior at least circulated throughout the crowd of specta-tors,[95] the same people who would ultimately decide the question of Ives's guilt or acquittal en masse. It is therefore likely that the spectators heard one way or another of Ives's alleged robberies of Anton Holter, Leroy Southmayd and the A. J. Oliver stagecoach, and "Bummer Dan" McFadden and the Peabody & Caldwell stagecoach. Any rumors circulating through the crowd of spectators could have been quite damning, as the information would not have been sub-ject to any evidentiary filter, cross-examination, or attorney arguments.

In his written reminiscences, James "Bill" Sweeney, one of the members of the original party that discovered gold at Alder Gulch, placed George Ives and Buck Stinson in the general vicinity of the Tiebolt robbery and murder and saw them afterward elated over the $500 that they got "from that fellow."[96] History does not record whether Sweeney testified to that information at Ives's trial. It is also unknown whether Sweeney's reminiscences, written decades after the crime, embellished his own proximity to the events of the day.

The prosecution rested its case.

Ives did not testify on his own behalf.[97] Ives's decision not to testify was likely made upon the advice of his counsel.

Two alibi witnesses were called by the defense, George Brown and "Whiskey Bill" Graves.[98] Their testimonies were largely ineffectual and were undermined by their uncertainties over the date on which Tiebolt was murdered and by inconsistencies within their versions of events.[99] Dimsdale described the alibi testimonies as having "failed altogether."[100] And while Dimsdale acknowledged that Ives's attorneys mixed their brow-beating and insolence with displays of eloquence and learning, he also wrote that "not the rhetoric of Blair, the learn-ing of Coke, the metaphysics of Alexander, the wit of Jerrold, or the odor of Oberlin, could dull the perceptions of those hearty Mountaineers" while Ives's alibi evidence was being presented.[101]

The evidentiary portion of the trial came to an end sometime on Monday, December 21, 1863. Whatever value the trial provided the residents of Alder Gulch, both as a societal necessity and as entertainment, Judge Byam directed that the presentation of evidence and attorney summations be completed by 3:00 p.m. so that the jury could deliberate its verdict the same day, as people needed to return soon to their usual daily activities.[102] The deadline was appar-ently a product of popular demand by the miners.[103]

Closing arguments were made by John D. Ritchie and James M. Thurmond for the defense and by William Fisk Sanders for the prosecution.[104] Ives's law-yers argued that Franck was the true murderer.[105] Ritchie appealed to the softer side of human nature, noting that Tiebolt could not be brought back to life and that the circumstances of his death were uncertain.[106] Thurmond, who had steeled himself with alcohol prior to his summation, pleaded for Ives's acquit-tal.[107] Sanders's summation, however, stole the show. Later in life, William Y. Pemberton, the stenographer at the trial, described Sanders's summation as "the most powerful [he] had ever heard," asserting the people's right to live on earth without fear.[108] Pemberton lamented that persons who did not hear Sanders's closing statement at the Ives trial "never heard the best effort in the lifetime of this gifted man."[109]

Judge Byam invited the jurors to deliberate, but contrary to what is man-datory and routine today, he did not give the jurors any formal charge on the law.[110] Charging the jury on the law might not have mattered if Dimsdale was correct that "[j]uries do not ordinarily bother themselves about the lengthy instruction they hear read by the court. They simply consider whether the deed is a crime against the Mountain Code."[111]

The juries deliberated in an unfinished log building nearby, and after less than half an hour, they returned an advisory verdict finding Ives guilty by a vote of 23 to 1.[112] The sole vote for acquittal was from Henry Spivay, who explained that guilt beyond a reasonable doubt had not been proven to his satisfaction but who may have instead voted for acquittal "for prudential reasons" having to do with his particular fear of retribution.[113]

Collections maintained by the Montana Historical Society include the papers of William Y. Pemberton. Ives and Pemberton had known each other from earlier interactions, and Pemberton went into the trial believing Ives inno-cent of the charge.[114] Pemberton and his assistant, W. H. Patten, were seated in the corner of the jury room and were available to the jurors in the event there were any questions about the trial testimony.[115] There was one ballot to be discussed and voted upon by the jurors—whether George Ives was guilty of murder as charged.[116] Pemberton therefore knew of the advisory verdict when he, Patten, and the jurors returned to the proceeding for its announcement. According to Pemberton's papers, Ives asked Pemberton as the jury was return-ing whether he would be hanged. Pemberton was not authorized to reveal the advisory verdict to him, merely saying, "It's bad enough." Surmising his fate, Ives asked Pemberton for a knife. Pemberton asked, "What do you want with it?" Ives replied, "I want to cut my throat." Pemberton refused to lend Ives his knife, so Ives made a further plea, "If you are [a friend of mine], go get me some poison. I don't want to be hung like a dog." Further conversation between Pemberton and Ives was cut off as the juries' advisory verdict was then announced to the crowd: "Guilty."[117]

Sanders quickly moved that the advisory verdict be adopted by the jury as a whole, which was opposed by attorneys Thurmond and Wood, and when Judge Byam put the question to the crowd, the voice vote of the crowd was

Figure 6.3. Wilbur Fisk Sanders, who vowed that if George Ives was convicted of murder, "retribution should be swift and absolutely remorseless." (Courtesy of the Montana Historical Society, image 944-848.)

decidedly for finding Ives guilty.[118] Ives's friends did not appear to comprehend the significance and speed of what was happening.[119] With momentum in his favor, Sanders immediately moved that the jury as a whole vote to impose a sentence of death by hanging, which Judge Byam put to the crowd.[120] In moving for a death sentence, Sanders was keeping a promise that he had made to himself before the beginning of the trial that if Ives were found guilty, his retribution would be swift and remorseless. With Ives's life at stake, his supporters became more vocal than they had been in opposition to the earlier question of whether the crowd should adopt the advisory juries' recommendation of guilt.[121]

However, the clear majority of the voice vote on the issue of Ives's sentence decidedly favored his hanging.[122] Ives's attorneys had little or no opportunity to object or otherwise react.[123] They had no opportunity to argue to the crowd for a sentence less than death.

After the crowd had quieted, Ives personally asked of Sanders that his execution be postponed until the following morning, claiming that he had a mother and a sister in the United States[124] and that he wished for an opportunity to write them a farewell letter and to make a will.[125] It is noteworthy that Ives's request was not addressed to Judge Byam, who should presumably have been in charge of such matters, but to the prosecutor, Sanders. Any delay of the sentence might have provided Ives and his supporters with an occasion to engineer his escape from custody. The adjournment request, not unreasonable, might ordinarily have been granted. However, John X. Beidler, who was short in height but tall in stature,[126] yelled from the crowd at the crucial moment, "Sanders! Ask him how long he gave the Dutchman!"[127]

Beidler's place in western frontier history was assured by the substance and timing of his remark at the Ives trial. The remark galvanized the crowd's anger over the merciless death of Nicholas Tiebolt by Ives's shooting of him in the forehead as Tiebolt commenced a prayer to God, and allowed Sanders to deny the requested postponement.[128] Ives was given an opportunity to write to his mother while the site for his hanging was being scouted.[129]

Sanders made a further motion that Ives's possessions be confiscated and sold for the proceeds to pay his board and the armed guards and for the remainder to be sent to Ives's mother and sisters.[130] Sanders's motion was hotly debated, with some persons arguing that it was outrageous to take a man's life and to use his assets to pay for the cost of his own trial and execution.[131] The debate became so heated at one point that Sanders reached for his Colt and fired a bullet into the floor of the wagon where he was standing.[132] Attorney John D. Ritchie, thinking that Sanders had opened fire on members of the crowd, grabbed Sanders by the coat, and the two men were pulled apart by James Williams and some of his guards.[133] Sanders's explanation years after the fact, that he had merely been test-firing his weapon in case it was needed,[134] rings hollow under the circumstances.

Within the hour, Sheriff Hareford of Nevada City and Sheriff Davis of Junction, who had been dispatched to locate a suitable location for Ives's hanging, returned to report that they could not find any.[135] Perhaps they were attempting to stall the execution, for reasons unknown, though Davis, at least always sided with swift and sure law enforcement. Hareford and Davis were reprimanded by Judge Byam for their failure.[136] Someone in the crowd remarked that any location for the hanging would do.[137] Someone else then suggested

Figure 6.4. John X. Beidler. (Courtesy of the Montana Historical Society, image 940-844.)

using an unfinished building near the trial by placing one end of a long pole against its wall and the other end of the pole over a crossbeam, with a hangman's noose dangled from the upper end.[138] The suggestion was accepted, and a forty-foot log was carried to the building and a rope was obtained.

An attempt was made by Ives's supporters to attack Hilderman where he was being held in a nearby store, to hang him in retribution for having testified against Ives at the trial, but the attempt to seize Hilderman was thwarted by force of arms.[139]

Ives was brought to the place of his execution. Twice, the length of the rope needed to be adjusted as it was hung from the pole at a length that was too long.[140] Two hundred guards armed with double-barreled shotguns prevented Ives's supporters from attempting to rescue their friend.[141] At the location for Ives's hanging, an empty dry goods box was placed upon a barrel under the noose.[142] Sheriff Hareford adjusted the rope around Ives's neck.[143] Friends of Ives were weeping while others in the crowd yelled, "Hang him!"[144] Ives's protector, Sheriff Plummer, had never arrived and was nowhere to be seen.

Ives's last words at the improvised gallows were, "I am innocent of this crime. Aleck Carter killed the Dutchman."[145] Attorney James Thurmond argued that the crowd was hanging an innocent man.[146] He yelled to the assembled crowd, "Think of his poor mother. Think of sending her word that a lawless band of men in the West hanged her son."[147] Thurmond's final plea was to no avail. An order was given that was a tradition at hangings in the western territories: "Men, do your duty!"[148] The dry goods box was kicked out from beneath Ives's feet and he died at the end of the noose.

Ives's death was the first meaningful blow against the criminal element organized in Alder Gulch.[149] Years later William Y. Pemberton described the conviction and sentence as "a great and everlasting victory; for the first time life and property were rendered safe and secure in these mountains."[150]

The evening that Ives was executed, Pemberton overheard three men on a Nevada City street conspiring to take another man behind a building to kill him.[151] One of the three men said, "Yonder he stands," and another of them called the man over to them.[152] The intended victim was none other than Wilbur Fisk Sanders.[153] As Sanders passed, Pemberton warned him that the three men intended to kill him and advised Sanders not to go behind the building.[154] Fearless, Sanders met the three men, who then crossed the street and strolled together toward the rear of a building.[155] Pemberton then heard a gunshot and ran behind the building, expecting to see Sanders dead.[156] Instead, Pemberton saw the three men running away, as Sanders had pulled his pistol first and fired a warning shot that apparently saved his life.[157]

Ives's final statement, implicating Aleck Carter as Tiebolt's murderer, has given historians much to ponder, as Carter was one of Ives's companions, was present when Ives was arrested, was suspected in other crimes, and had fled the area during Ives's trial.[158] Moreover, Ives professed his innocence only to "this" crime, perhaps suggesting guilt on others.[159] Interestingly, the words "I am innocent" were, as the vigilantes later learned, the code phrase used by members of the road agent gang,[160] perhaps suggesting that Ives remained loyal to his fellow conspirators to his last moments. Ives's use of the phrase "I am innocent" moments before his hanging might have been intended as a coded request to fellow conspirators that they stage a last-minute rescue attempt for him. On the other hand, Ives's statement identifying Carter as Tiebolt's murderer was inconsistent with the tenor of the trial defense, premised, as it was, on Franck's alleged guilt for the murder. Nevertheless, history records that Ives was hanged in front of a large crowd,[161] and any attempts that fellow road agents might have made to save him from the noose had been deterred by Williams's armed cordon as the execution was prepared and carried out.[162]

A separate trial was conducted of George Hilderman the following morning, on Tuesday, December 22, 1863.[163] Hilderman's defense was crafted primarily by H. P. A. Smith and was both subtle and clever.[164] The defense conceded that Hilderman had known of Tiebolt's murder and had helped conceal the stolen mules after the fact.[165] In essence, the defense was that Hilderman was too afraid to report his knowledge to anyone, lest he be killed in retribution.[166] This defense struck a responsive chord with those present. After the hanging of George Ives, many people spoke more freely among themselves about their knowledge of criminal activities that they had previously kept to themselves—as Dimsdale described it, "under circumstances rendering silence a seeming necessity."[167] To underscore the point, the defense called as a witness Dr. Jerome Glick, who admitted that on various occasions he had provided medical treatment to wounded persons that he believed had committed robberies, but he knew better than to reveal his suspicions to anyone.[168] The defense was subtle—that if smart and capable men such as medical doctors were intimidated into silence by the ruthlessness of the region's criminal element, Hilderman could not be faulted for not being forthcoming about Tiebolt's death and the whereabouts of the mules. The trial defense of Hilderman was effective to the extent that it likely saved his life.

Hilderman was convicted but was not sentenced to death.[169] When he learned that his life was spared, Hilderman dropped to his knees and said, "My God, is it so?" After his conviction, Hilderman made a full confession that confirmed the previous testimony of "Long John" Franck about the murder of Nicholas Tiebolt.[170] Hilderman knew of the circumstances of the Tiebolt murder and had concealed the stolen mules, but Sanders viewed him as merely a hapless imbecile whose silence was a result of threats received from Ives.[171] Instead of being hanged, Hilderman was required to leave the territory within ten days and never to return, upon the threat of execution; in fact, he thereafter fled the territory and was never seen in the region again.[172]

For a considerable time after the Ives and Hilderman trials, Wilbur Fisk Sanders lived under the protection of an armed guard.[173] Sanders needed guards in the event that he would be targeted for retribution. The need for armed guards was also an indication that the battle against the criminal element in Alder Gulch was far from over.

Was George Ives truly guilty of the crime for which he was convicted and hanged? The 1863 trial of Ives included no evidence of the kinds typical today that connect defendants to crimes such as DNA evidence, fiber evidence, fingerprint evidence, blood-splatter evidence, other inculpatory physical evidence, videos or other photographic evidence, lineup or photographic identifications, or even an inculpatory statement uttered to law enforcement personnel by the accused. There had been no autopsy performed on Tiebolt's body. There were no direct eyewitnesses to the murder itself. Indeed, there was no physical evidence whatsoever connecting Ives directly to the Tiebolt murder. The testimony of George Hilderman that Ives had committed the murder was not yet elicited, as Hilderman's trial was not conducted until after Ives had already been executed. The evidence against Ives, based upon the historical accounts of the trial, consisted of the following.

First, there was the testimony by "Long John" Franck of Ives's coin flip to determine who would pursue and rob Tiebolt of his gold, and Ives's statement to Franck shortly after the murder by which he acknowledged that he had robbed and killed Tiebolt by shooting him in the forehead. At first blush, Franck's testimony about Ives's statement would appear to be inadmissible hearsay evidence, as it recounted an out-of-court statement by a third person offered for the truth of the matter asserted.[174] However, a party's admission to the criminal conduct that is the subject of the case may always be introduced as evidence-in-chief, as a recognized exception to the rule against hearsay.[175] Here Ives's statements to Franck, if uttered, were unambiguous admissions of wrongdoing. Franck's testimony of Ives's statements was likely the single most key piece of evidence presented by the prosecution during the Ives trial.

Second, Ives's inculpatory statement to Franck shortly after the murder was corroborated by, and consistent with, the proximity of Tiebolt's body to Ives's ranch, the location of the bullet wound on Tiebolt's forehead, and the presence at the ranch of at least one of the mules. The jury was within its rights to deem Franck's testimony as credible, if it so chose.[176]

Third, the location of the killing circumstantially placed Ives near the scene of the crime, but such evidence does not necessarily identify Ives as the individual culprit who pulled the trigger.[177] The mere presence of an individual at or near a crime scene, by itself, is insufficient, at least under current Montana law, to sustain a finding of guilt.[178]

Fourth, the presence of one of Tiebolt's mules at Ives's ranch is also circumstantial in nature,[179] but it is not particularly compelling as there was no issue that Tiebolt had been killed in the general vicinity by *someone*.

Fifth, if testified to, there was the alleged flight by Ives on horseback from his captors while en route to Nevada City. If there is sufficient evidence that a crime has been committed by someone, a defendant's flight may be considered as some evidence of his consciousness of guilt.[180]

Sixth, there was the odd unwillingness of Franck and Hilderman to assist with Tiebolt's body when they were initially approached by William Palmer. This evidence may have suggested that Franck had something to hide at that time, as a potential accessory after the fact or as an obstructor of justice.[181] It explained Franck's behavior when he was first approached by Palmer and, in the end, may have strengthened the jury's assessment of Franck's trial testimony.

Seventh, the trier of fact would have been within its rights to disbelieve Ives's alibi witnesses or conclude their time line as inapplicable if it were so inclined.[182] The testimonies of the alibi witnesses in this instance were apparently perceived as being less than persuasive or credible.[183] Weak or contrived alibi witness testimony could have had the effect of actually detracting from Ives's defense overall.

Eighth, as already noted, the historical record is unclear whether, and to what extent, the prosecution was permitted to introduce evidence of other bad acts and crimes that George Ives had allegedly committed prior to any murder of Nicholas Tiebolt. According to Dimsdale, Ives was suspected in the robbery of Peabody & Caldwell's stagecoach that was perpetrated on October 26, 1863.[184] According to Langford, Ives was also suspected in the robbery and attempted murder of Anton Holter on December 8, 1863.[185] Under common law, there is no particular prohibition against the introduction of evidence against a defendant of his other, prior bad acts and criminal activities. Statutory law and the rules of evidence have in more recent decades developed to exclude evidence at trial of the defendant's prior bad acts and crimes, subject to certain exceptions. For instance, under Montana's current rules, evidence of a person's bad character is not admissible for the purpose of proving that the alleged crime is in conformity with that bad character.[186] Evidence of other, prior crimes is also generally not admissible,[187] to assure that the jury will not penalize the defendant or prejudge him for the other conduct instead of the particular crime that is the subject of the trial.[188] Specifically, in murder trials in Montana today, evidence of a defendant's prior violent acts and reputation for violence is inadmissible.[189] However, the general rule does not apply if the defendant places his own character at issue during a trial.[190] The general rule excluding the evidence also does not apply if the prior conduct or crime "transactionally" relates to the crime that is the subject of the trial,[191] such as where the prior conduct is relevant to proving the defendant's motive, opportunity, intent, preparation, plan, knowledge, identity, or the absence of mistake or accident.[192]

Since the common law did not require the exclusion of evidence of George Ives's prior bad acts or criminal activities, Ives's alleged involvement in the robberies of the Peabody & Caldwell stagecoach, of Anton Holter, of "Bummer Dan" McFadden and the Moody's stagecoach party, and of perhaps other victims could conceivably have been part of the trial. At a minimum, there appears to have been legal argument to the trial judges as to whether to allow such evidence, and it is unknown whether such argument was openly made in the presence of the advisory jurors and spectators, or whether those arguments were instead made at "side bar" beyond the earshot of advisory jurors and en masse jurors.

If evidence of the Peabody & Caldwell, Anton Holter, or Moody's stagecoach robberies was introduced against George Ives during his Nevada City trial, it may arguably have been permissible under the looser trial rules and procedures that were in effect in the western territories at the time. However, since the modus operandi of the Tiebolt robbery and murder appears to be very dissimilar to that of the Peabody & Caldwell, Anton Holter, and Moody's stagecoach robberies, it is highly unlikely that proof of Ives's involvement in those other crimes would be admissible as evidence if a similar trial for the Tiebolt murder were conducted in a courtroom today. Any involvement by George Ives in those other crimes sheds no evidentiary light upon whether he killed Nicholas Tiebolt, in terms of Ives's motive, opportunity, intent, preparation, plan, knowledge, identity, or the absence of mistake or accident to explain the death. With the benefit of historical hindsight, the jury's conviction of George Ives is better supported if it did not rely upon evidence of bad character or prior uncharged crimes and if it instead relied upon the testimony of "Long John" Franck and any reasonable inferences that could be drawn from the other evidence as a whole.

The factual and evidentiary issues that arose make the trial of George Ives one of the most fascinating criminal trials ever held in the United States and its territories. It is a shame that William Y. Pemberton's contemporaneous notes of the proceedings have not survived for historical and legal analysis today.

The trial of George Ives had its winners and its losers. Ives lost not only the trial but his life. The conviction and execution of Ives was also a loss for Sheriff Plummer and the criminal syndicate that operated in the region, as it signified a new willingness and determination by the general citizenry to deal once and for all with the violent crime that plagued them. The sense of failure that might have clouded the conclusion of the trials of Buck Stinson, Hayes Lyons, and Charley Forbes for the killing of D. H. Dillingham was exorcized by the conviction and execution of George Ives.

Some of the attorneys who defended Ives and Hilderman were also losers, at least in the longer term. Passions were high over the trial. Today society maintains a healthy respect for defendants' rights to fair trials with the representation of counsel and for the attorneys who represent even the most loathsome of criminals. In 1863 the attorneys representing George Ives were perceived as being part of the crime problem at Alder Gulch. They received ridicule and threats from the members of the vigilante group that would form. A month later, after five vigilante executions in Virginia City on January 14, 1864, H. P. A. Smith and James M. Thurmond publicly decried the absence of lawful procedure, where the persons who were executed had no rights to legal representation, public trials, juries of their peers, or defenses. Both lawyers were ordered to leave the territory or face death.[193]

Attorney Alexander Davis was also disturbed by the growing absence of lawful procedure in Alder Gulch, but he displayed greater stoicism and diplomacy than some of his other lawyer colleagues. He voiced his criticisms to the members of the future Vigilance Committee quietly rather than publicly and earned the grudging respect of the vigilantes when he resisted threats of banishment that had been directed his way.[194] The respect that people felt for Davis led to his stint, in the spring of 1864, as judge of the short-lived "People's Court," to be discussed in a later chapter of this narrative.

Among the clear winners from the Ives trial was the prosecutor, Wilbur Fisk Sanders, who built a stellar career in law and politics from the notoriety he earned during the Ives case. The day of the Ives trial, he was headed toward a duel with Sheriff J. B. "Buzz" Caven, fired his pistol after Ives's conviction during heated debate over what to do with Ives's assets, and saved himself from a murder attempt by firing his gun behind a building shortly after Ives was hanged. Rather than being viewed as a man of temper and unpredictability, the incidents molded his reputation throughout the territory as a man of bravery, determination, and competence, which served him well in the decades that followed. Conrad Kohrs said in his autobiography, "I think Sanders should be paid the highest compliment for having the courage to take the stand for the people and prosecute these desperadoes, for his action virtually made his life unsafe so long as one of the gang survived."[195] Sanders would become chairman of the Montana Republican Party and hold office in both the territorial legislature and the US Senate.[196]

Another winner that emerged from the trial was "Long John" Franck. Franck successfully testified for the prosecution in exchange for not being charged in the Tiebolt murder or for even being an accessory to the crime.[197] Had Ives been acquitted at trial, it is conceivable that "Long John" Franck would have faced retribution from road agents, perhaps with deadly consequence.

A final winner of note was George Hilderman. Unlike Franck, Hilderman did not have the advantage of any deal that protected him from criminal prosecution. He was charged in the murder of Nicholas Tiebolt, and upon the conviction and execution of Ives, Hilderman's prospects must have appeared quite bleak. The prosecutor, Wilbur Fisk Sanders, made no willing compromises during the trial of Ives, not even in permitting a few hours of delay in carrying out Ives's execution. With Hilderman, Sanders's attitude was quite different. As noted, Sanders believed that Hilderman was merely a weak and foolish man. If Hilderman did not pull the trigger on Tiebolt and failed to come forward with information about the crime out of fear, his banishment from the territory might have been the most just result that could be expected from the rough frontier justice that prevailed at the time. Hilderman entered his Nevada City trial facing death by hanging but left Nevada City with his life. Moreover, had he not been banished from the territory, he might have been executed by vigilantes the following year, when more evidence of road agents' activities came to light.

History can debate whether, on the evidence produced against George Ives, a rational trier of fact could have reached the conclusion that he was guilty beyond a reasonable doubt of the robbery and murder of Nicholas Tiebolt and whether any such conviction could have withstood a meaningful appeal to an appellate court.[198] Surely, many people involved in the events had no doubt of Ives's culpability in the Tiebolt murder and in other, uncharged crimes. If Hilderman's postconviction confession was truthful, then history can be satisfied that the verdict convicting George Ives of the murder of Nicholas Tieboldt was correct. Yet, in a trial where the verdict is determined by the instantaneous voice vote of a large crowd of spectators, history can only wonder how much or how little deliberation actually occurred in the weighing and evaluating of the various forms of evidence offered by the prosecution, some of which was convincing and some perhaps not. The advisory jurors might have weighed the trial evidence, but the spectators en masse, who rendered the final verdict of guilt and voted to impose a sentence of death, did so immediately and without the benefit of any meaningful group deliberation. The amount of process that was due to defendants in 1863–64 was limited, and considerably less than that required by the standards of today.

Leading citizens in Alder Gulch were emboldened by the conviction and execution of George Ives to take further steps against the criminal element in the region.

Figure 6.5. Marker indicating the site of George Ives's trial, Route 287, Nevada City. (Photo by author.)

Panning for Nuggets

The site of George Ives's trial is identified by a historical marker. It is located along-side Route 287, which is the main street of Nevada City, Montana.

Notes

1. Perhaps the most well-worn example of this historical concept is the assassination of Arch-duke Ferdinand being viewed as the event triggering the outbreak of World War I.
2. Langford, *Vigilante Days*, 178; Thompson, *Tenderfoot in Montana*, 169; Allen, *Decent Orderly Lynching*, 3; Johnson, *Bloody Bozeman*, 92; Callaway, *Montana's Righteous Hang-men*, 23; Birney, *Vigilantes*, 180; Barsness, *Gold Camp*, 37; Gard, *Frontier Justice*, 175; Aaron T. Ford Reminiscences, 1903, Mont. Hist. Soc., SC-702, box 1-1, p. 5.

3. Langford, *Vigilante Days*, 179; Thompson, *Tenderfoot in Montana*, 169; Allen, *Decent Orderly Lynching*, 3; Olsen, "Lawlessness and Vigilantes," 134.

4. Thompson, *Tenderfoot in Montana*, 179; Pace, *Golden Gulch*, 33; Allen, *Decent Orderly Lynching*, 3; Callaway, *Montana's Righteous Hangmen*, 23; Sanders, *History of Montana*, 38; Thrapp, *Vengeance!*, 145; Mather and Boswell, *Hanging the Sheriff*, 77; Olsen, "Lawlessness and Vigilantes," 135.

5. Thompson, *Tenderfoot in Montana*, 169; Thrapp, *Vengeance!*, 145; Birney, *Vigilantes*, 180; Johnson, *Bloody Bozeman*, 92; Olsen, "Lawlessness and Vigilantes," 134–35.

6. Langford, *Vigilante Days*, 178–79; Allen, *Decent Orderly Lynching*, 4; Sanders and Bertsche, *X. Beidler*, 48; Johnson, *Bloody Bozeman*, 92; Callaway, *Montana's Righteous Hangmen*, 24; Barsness, *Gold Camp*, 37. A wickiup is made by placing cross poles on four upright posts and covering them with brush; they were not uncommon in Montana. Bancroft, *History*, 640.

7. Birney, *Vigilantes*, 181.

8. "Trial and Execution of George Ives," Wilbur Fisk Sanders Papers, Mont. Hist. Soc., MC-53, box 5, folder 5-1, p. 2.

9. Birney, *Vigilantes*, 181; Barsness, *Gold Camp*, 37; Aaron T. Ford Reminiscences, 1903, Mont. Hist. Soc., SC-702, box 1-1, p. 5. The spelling of the victim varies in various historical texts, sometimes appearing as Tiebalt, Tbalt, Thibault, and Tiebolt. Cf. Johnson, *Bloody Bozeman*, 92, with Allen, *Decent Orderly Lynching*, 4. Thompson and Allen identify the victim as German, not Dutch. Thompson, *Tenderfoot in Montana*, 168; Allen, *Decent Orderly Lynching*, 4.

10. Sanders, *History of Montana*, 38; Allen, *Decent Orderly Lynching*, 4; Mather and Boswell, *Hanging the Sheriff*, 77; Bartholomew, *Henry Plummer*, 9–10.

11. Dimsdale, *Vigilantes of Montana*, 83; Allen, *Decent Orderly Lynching*, 4.

12. Allen, *Decent Orderly Lynching*, 9–10.

13. Ibid., 11.

14. Langford, *Vigilante Days*, 179; Sanders and Bertsche, *X. Beidler*, 39; Barsness, *Gold Camp*, 38; Cushman, *Montana*, 111; James S. Brisbin, "Biographical Sketch of Wilbur Fisk Sanders['] Involvement with Vigilantes," Wilbur Fisk Sanders Papers, Mont. Hist. Soc., MC-53, box 1, folder 1-1, p. 16 (hereafter cited as "Biographical Sketch"). See also Thompson, *Tenderfoot in Montana*, 169; Johnson, *Bloody Bozeman*, 92; Allen, *Decent Orderly Lynching*, 11. Brisbin, Thompson, and Johnson describe the posse as consisting of twenty-five men, while Allen sets the number at one dozen.

15. Sanders and Bertsche, *X. Beidler*, 49.

16. Bancroft, *History*, 659n28; Sanders and Bertsche, *X. Beidler*, 157.

17. Thrapp, *Vengeance!*, 146.

18. Allen, *Decent Orderly Lynching*, 10, 11.

19. Langford, *Vigilante Days*, 180; Allen, *Decent Orderly Lynching*, 15.

20. Langford, *Vigilante Days*, 180; Dimsdale, *Vigilantes of Montana*, 84; Birney, *Vigilantes*, 184; Johnson, *Bloody Bozeman*, 15. Johnson, however, writes that the mule was found at the wikiup. Johnson, *Bloody Bozeman*, 92.

21. Allen, *Decent Orderly Lynching*, 11; Callaway, *Montana's Righteous Hangmen*, 24; Birney, *Vigilantes*, 181.

22. Allen, *Decent Orderly Lynching*, 15.

23. Langford, *Vigilante Days*, 181–82; Dimsdale, *Vigilantes of Montana*, 85; Thompson, *Tenderfoot in Montana*, 169–70; Allen, *Decent Orderly Lynching*, 15; Callaway, *Montana's Righteous Hangmen*, 26; Thrapp, *Vengeance!*, 147; Birney, *Vigilantes*, 185; Anonymous, *Banditti of the Rocky Mountains*, 103; Aaron T. Ford Reminiscences, 1903, SC-702, box 1-1, p. 5.

24. Brisbin, "Biographical Sketch," 16.

25. Ibid. According to Aaron T. Ford, writing in 1903, Hilderman (incorrectly referred to in Ford's document as Hilderbrant) was a champion in pie-eating contests and was called the "Great American Pie Eater." Once Hilderman made a bet that he could bite through ten pies at once. A man slipped a tin pie plate between the pies, causing Hilderman to lose the bet. Aaron T. Ford Reminiscences, 1903, Mont. Hist. Soc., SC 702, box 1-1, p. 5; see also Thrapp, *Vengeance!*, 145; Sanders and Bertsche, *X. Beidler*, 49; Fisher and Holmes, *Gold Rushes*, 335; Wolle, *Montana Pay Dirt*, 28.

26. "Trial and Execution of George Ives," 1; Thompson, *Tenderfoot in Montana*, 170; Pace, *Golden Gulch*, 33; Barsness, *Gold Camp*, 38; Greever, *Bonanza West*, 227.

27. "Trial and Execution of George Ives," 1; Thompson, *Tenderfoot in Montana*, 170; Pace, *Golden Gulch*, 33; Barsness, *Gold Camp*, 38; Greever, *Bonanza West*, 227.

28. Brisbin, "Biographical Sketch," 16.

29. Langford, *Vigilante Days*, 234; Dimsdale, *Vigilantes of Montana*, 86–87; Callaway, *Montana's Righteous Hangmen*, 27–30; Sanders, *History of Montana*, 49; Birney, *Vigilantes*, 187–88; Gard, *Frontier Justice*, 175.

30. Allen, *Decent Orderly Lynching*, 173.

31. Langford, *Vigilante Days*, 184; Allen, *Decent Orderly Lynching*, 177.

32. "Trial and Execution of George Ives," 2.

33. Ibid.

34. Sanders and Bertsche, *X. Beidler*, 57.

35. Sanders served the Union cause at the outbreak of the Civil War by enlisting in the Ohio Volunteer Infantry before moving west.

36. See Wilbur Fisk Sanders Papers, Mont. Hist. Soc. MC-53, box 5, folder 5-1; Langford, *Vigilante Days*, 184; Thompson, *Tenderfoot in Montana*, 170; Bancroft, *History*, 640; Pemberton, "Montana's Pioneer Courts," 100; Pace, *Golden Gulch*, 34; Allen, *Decent Orderly Lynching*, 169–70; Callaway, *Montana's Righteous Hangmen*, 31; Mather and Boswell, *Hanging the Sheriff*, 77–78; Barsness, *Gold Camp*, 38–39; Greever, *Bonanza West*, 227; Hamilton, *From Wilderness to Statehood*, 246.

37. Bancroft, *History*, 640; Burlingame, *Montana Frontier*, 152; Pemberton, "Montana's Pioneer Courts," 100; Pace, *Golden Gulch*, 34; Allen, *Decent Orderly Lynching*, 177; Mather and Boswell, *Hanging the Sheriff*, 77–78; Barsness, *Gold Camp*, 39; Greever, *Bonanza West*, 227; Hamilton, *From Wilderness to Statehood*, 246; see also Sanders and Bertsche, *X. Beidler*, 59–60.

38. Allen, *Decent Orderly Lynching*, 126.

39. Aaron T. Ford Reminiscences, 1903, Mont. Hist. Soc., SC-702, box 1-1, p. 6.

40. Birney, *Vigilantes*, 193.

41. Dimsdale, *Vigilantes of Montana*, 91; Thompson, *Tenderfoot in Montana*, 170; Bancroft, *History*, 640; Pemberton, "Montana's Pioneer Courts," 100; Allen, *Decent Orderly Lynching*, 169; see also Langford, *Vigilante Days*, 184.

42. "Trial and Execution of George Ives," 2; Dimsdale, *Vigilantes of Montana*, 91; Thompson, *Tenderfoot in Montana*, 170; Bancroft, *History*, 640; Sanders and Bertsche, *X. Beidler*, 55; Allen, *Decent Orderly Lynching*, 173; see also Langford, *Vigilante Days*, 184.

43. Andrew J. Smith to Jno. Potter, March 26, 1867, Mont. Hist. Soc., SC-877.

44. Pemberton, "Montana's Pioneer Courts," 100; Bakken, *Invitation to an Execution*, 340; Allen, *Decent Orderly Lynching*, 171; Callaway, *Montana's Righteous Hangmen*, 31; Sanders, *History of Montana*, 55; Thrapp, *Vengeance!*, 148; Bartholomew, *Henry Plummer*, 12; Barsness, *Gold Camp*, 39; Hamilton, *From Wilderness to Statehood*, 247.

45. "Trial and Execution of George Ives," 2; Bancroft, *History*, 640; Allen, *Decent Orderly Lynching*, 176; Barsness, *Gold Camp*, 39.

46. "Trial and Execution of George Ives," 3; Sanders and Bertsche, *X. Beidler*, 62; Birney, *Vigilantes*, 195; Hamilton, *From Wilderness to Statehood*, 246; Olsen, "Lawlessness and Vigilantes," 137.

47. "Trial and Execution of George Ives," 2; Bakken, *Invitation to an Execution*, 340; Allen, *Decent Orderly Lynching*, 176; Pemberton, "Montana's Pioneer Courts," 100; Sanders and Bertsche, *X. Beidler*, 60; Birney, *Vigilantes*, 195; Barsness, *Gold Camp*, 39; Greever, *Bonanza West*, 227; Hamilton, *From Wilderness to Statehood*, 247.

48. Pemberton, "Montana's Pioneer Courts," 100; Bakken, *Invitation to an Execution*, 340; Allen, *Decent Orderly Lynching*, 176; Sanders and Bertsche, *X. Beidler*, 60; Greever, *Bonanza West*, 227; Hamilton, *From Wilderness to Statehood*, 247.

49. Pemberton, "Montana's Pioneer Courts," 100; Allen, *Decent Orderly Lynching*, 177.

50. M. W. Anderson, "Notes on W. Y. Pemberton's Lecture before the Unity Club at Unitarian Church, May 12, 1868," William Y. Pemberton Papers, 1863–69, Mont. Hist. Soc., SC-629, 12.

51. "Trial and Execution of George Ives." Of course, the account of the trial by Sanders puts the prosecution's case in its best light.

52. Ibid., p. 2; Pemberton, "Montana's Pioneer Courts," 100; Bakken, *Invitation to an Execution*, 340; Sanders and Bertsche, *X. Beidler*, 60; Birney, *Vigilantes*, 195; Allen, *Decent Orderly Lynching*, 176.

53. Hamilton, *From Wilderness to Statehood*, 247–48; "Trial and Execution of George Ives," 2; Pemberton, "Montana's Pioneer Courts," 100; Sanders and Bertsche, *X. Beidler*, 60; Birney, *Vigilantes*, 195; Allen, *Decent Orderly Lynching*, 176.

54. "Trial and Execution of George Ives," 2; Pemberton, "Montana's Pioneer Courts," 100; Sanders and Bertsche, *X. Beidler*, 60; Birney, *Vigilantes*, 195; Allen, *Decent Orderly Lynching*, 176.

55. Allen, *Decent Orderly Lynching*, 178; Greever, *Bonanza West*, 227; Callaway, *Montana's Righteous Hangmen*, 31 (which places the number of armed men at 100); Barsness, *Gold Camp*, 40.

56. Allen, *Decent Orderly Lynching*, 173–74.

57. Ibid., 184; Barsness, *Gold Camp*, 41.

58. Allen, *Decent Orderly Lynching*, 173.

59. Dimsdale, *Vigilantes of Montana*, 91; Pemberton, "Montana's Pioneer Courts," 100; Sanders and Bertsche, *X. Beidler*, 60; Allen, *Decent Orderly Lynching*, 173; Birney, *Vigilantes*, 195; Milner and O'Connor, *As Big as the West*, 90; Barsness, *Gold Camp*, 39; Greever, *Bonanza West*, 227; Olsen, "Lawlessness and Vigilantes," 139.

60. Allen, *Decent Orderly Lynching*, 174.

61. Ibid.

62. Ibid.

63. Hamilton, *From Wilderness to Statehood*, 246.

64. Allen, *Decent Orderly Lynching*, 174.

65. Ibid.

66. Ibid.

67. Ibid., 174–75.

68. Langford, *Vigilante Days*, 185; Allen, *Decent Orderly Lynching*, 179; Thrapp, *Vengeance!*, 148; Birney, *Vigilantes*, 197; Johnson, *Bloody Bozeman*, 92; Callaway, *Montana's Righteous Hangmen*, 31; Mather and Boswell, *Hanging the Sheriff*, 78; Gard, *Frontier Justice*, 175.

69. Johnson, *Bloody Bozeman*, 92; Allen, *Decent Orderly Lynching*, 177; Birney, *Vigilantes*, 196 (sets the number at 1,000 to 1,500 persons); Milner and O'Connor, *As Big as the West*, 90 (between 1,000 and 1,500 persons); Sanders and Bertsche, *X. Beidler*, 60 (between 1,000 and 1,500 persons); Barsness, *Gold Camp*, 39; Mather and Boswell, *Hanging the Sheriff*, 77 (1,000 persons).

70. John W. Grannis Diaries, 1863–78, Mont. Hist. Soc., SC-301, folder 4-4.

71. "Trial and Execution of George Ives," 4; Allen, *Decent Orderly Lynching*, 178; Allen, *Decent Orderly Lynching*, 178.

72. "Trial and Execution of George Ives," 2; Allen, *Decent Orderly Lynching*, 179–80; Sanders, *History of Montana*, 61, 64; Greever, *Bonanza West*, 227. Palmer and Franck were likely not the only witnesses for the prosecution but were probably the two of most note.

73. "Trial and Execution of George Ives," 2; Sanders and Bertsche, *X. Beidler*, 61; Allen, *Decent Orderly Lynching*, 179.

74. "Trial and Execution of George Ives," 2.

75. Ibid.; Allen, *Decent Orderly Lynching*, 180; Sanders and Bertsche, *X. Beidler*, 64; Mather and Boswell, *Hanging the Sheriff*, 78; Birney, *Vigilantes*, 198; Anonymous, *Banditti of the Rocky Mountains*, 101; Hamilton, *From Wilderness to Statehood*, 248; Olsen, "Lawlessness and Vigilantes," 140.

76. Allen, *Decent Orderly Lynching*, 180; Sanders and Bertsche, *X. Beidler*, 64; Mather and Boswell, *Hanging the Sheriff*, 78; Anonymous, *Banditti of the Rocky Mountains*, 101.

77. "Trial and Execution of George Ives," 2; Allen, *Decent Orderly Lynching*, 180; Sanders and Bertsche, *X. Beidler*, 64; Mather and Boswell, *Hanging the Sheriff*, 78; Birney, *Vigilantes*, 199; Anonymous, *Banditti of the Rocky Mountains*, 101.

78. Langford, *Vigilante Days*, 185; Thompson, *Tenderfoot in Montana*, 170; see also Thrapp, *Vengeance!*, 148.

79. Langford, *Vigilante Days*, 185; Thompson, *Tenderfoot in Montana*, 170; Thrapp, *Vengeance!*, 148; see also Barsness, *Gold Camp*, 41.

80. Allen, *Decent Orderly Lynching*, 180–81.

81. Ibid., 182; Greever, *Bonanza West*, 227. According to Sanders, the trial included evidence that Ives had been engaged in other acts of theft and murder. Sanders and Bertsche, *X. Beidler*, 66–67.

82. Dimsdale, *Vigilantes of Montana*, 92.

83. Sanders and Bertsche, *X. Beidler*, 63.

84. Hamilton, *From Wilderness to Statehood*, 248.

85. "Trial and Execution of George Ives," 3.

86. Sanders and Bertsche, *X. Beidler*, 66.

87. Ibid. The loose standards of evidence and procedure were not unusual during trials conducted on the western mining frontier. Reid, *Policing the Elephant*, 128.

88. Kohrs, 34.

89. Ibid.

90. Allen, *Decent Orderly Lynching*, 181.

91. Prince, *Richardson on Evidence*, sec. 170; Mont. Rules of Evidence 404(b).

92. Prince, *Richardson on Evidence*, secs. 171, 172, 178, 179, 180; Mont. Rules of Evidence 404(b).

93. Prince, *Richardson on Evidence*, sec. 183; Mont. Rules of Evidence 404(b).

94. The absence of law books was a problem throughout the western territories during the time. Bakken, *Practicing Law in Frontier California*, 26–30.

95. Sanders and Bertsche, *X. Beidler*, 61–62; Allen, *Decent Orderly Lynching*, 181.

96. James "Bill" Sweeney Reminiscences, 1921, Mont. Hist. Soc., Collection No. 823, p. 5.

97. Allen, *Decent Orderly Lynching*, 182; Sanders and Bertsche, *X. Beidler*, 68; Birney, *Vigilantes*, 202.

98. Dimsdale, *Vigilantes of Montana*, 91; Birney, *Vigilantes*, 199.

99. Langford, *Vigilante Days*, 185; Allen, *Decent Orderly Lynching*, 182; Thrapp, *Vengeance!*, 148–49; Birney, *Vigilantes*, 199; Barsness, *Gold Camp*, 41.

100. Dimsdale, *Vigilantes of Montana*, 91.

101. Ibid., 91–92.

102. John W. Grannis Diaries, 1863–78, Mont. Hist. Soc., SC-301, folder 1-1; Dimsdale, *Vigilantes of Montana*, 91; Allen, *Decent Orderly Lynching*, 186.

103. Dimsdale, *Vigilantes of Montana*, 91; Allen, *Decent Orderly Lynching*, 186.

104. Allen, *Decent Orderly Lynching*, 186.

105. Ibid., 193.

106. Sanders and Bertsche, *X. Beidler*, 68.

107. Ibid., 68–69.

108. Anderson," "Notes on W. Y. Pemberton's Lecture," 12.

109. Pemberton, "Montana's Pioneer Courts," 103.

110. Birney, *Vigilantes*, 202.

111. Dimsdale, 12–13.

112. "Trial and Execution of George Ives," 4–5; John W. Grannis Diaries, 1863–78, Mont. Hist. Soc., SC-301, folder 4-4; Langford, *Vigilante Days*, 186; Dimsdale, *Vigilantes of Montana*, 93; Thompson, *Tenderfoot in Montana*, 171; Allen, *Decent Orderly Lynching*, 187; Sanders and Bertsche, *X. Beidler*, 70; Mather and Boswell, *Hanging the Sheriff*, 78–79; Birney, *Vigilantes*, 203; Callaway, *Montana's Righteous Hangmen*, 34; Milner and O'Connor, *As Big as the West*, 90; Bartholomew, *Henry Plummer*, 11–12; Barsness, *Gold Camp*, 41; Greever, *Bonanza West*, 228; Hamilton, *From Wilderness to Statehood*, 249.

113. Sanders and Bertsche, *X. Beidler*, 70; Callaway, *Montana's Righteous Hangmen*, 34; Barsness, *Gold Camp*, 41–42; see also Thrapp, *Vengeance!*, 148–49.

114. Allen, *Decent Orderly Lynching*, 178.

115. Pemberton, "Montana's Pioneer Courts," 101; Donovan, *Hanging around the Big Sky*, book 2, 25.

116. Pemberton, "Montana's Pioneer Courts," 101.

117. William Y. Pemberton Papers, 1863–69, Mont. Hist. Soc. SC-629, box 1-1, p. 93.

118. "Trial and Execution of George Ives," 5; Dimsdale, *Vigilantes of Montana*, 93; Langford, *Vigilante Days*, 186; Thompson, *Tenderfoot in Montana*, 171; Allen, *Decent Orderly Lynching*, 187; Sanders and Bertsche, *X. Beidler*, 71; Mather and Boswell, *Hanging the Sheriff*, 79; Birney, *Vigilantes*, 203–4; Callaway, *Montana's Righteous Hangmen*, 34; Barsness, *Gold Camp*, 42; Gard, *Frontier Justice*, 175; Hamilton, *From Wilderness to Statehood*, 249.

119. "Trial and Execution of George Ives," 5.

120. Ibid.; Dimsdale, *Vigilantes of Montana*, 94; Langford, *Vigilante Days*, 186; Sanders, *History of Montana*, 71; Bancroft, *History*, 640; Allen, *Decent Orderly Lynching*, 187; Birney, *Vigilantes*, 204; Gard, *Frontier Justice*, 175; Bartholomew, *Henry Plummer*, 12; Barsness, *Gold Camp*, 42; Greever, *Bonanza West*, 228; Aaron T. Ford Reminiscences, 1903, Mont. Hist. Soc., SC-702, box 1-1, p. 5.

121. "Trial and Execution of George Ives," 5.

122. Ibid.; Dimsdale, *Vigilantes of Montana*, 94; Langford, *Vigilante Days*, 186; Thompson, *Tenderfoot in Montana*, 171; Sanders and Bertsche, *X. Beidler*, 71; Allen, *Decent Orderly Lynching*, 187; Birney, *Vigilantes*, 204; Callaway, *Montana's Righteous Hangmen*, 34; Barsness, *Gold Camp*, 42; Greever, *Bonanza West*, 228; Hamilton, *From Wilderness to Statehood*, 249.

123. Dimsdale, *Vigilantes of Montana*, 94; Allen, *Decent Orderly Lynching*, 187; Callaway, *Montana's Righteous Hangmen*, 34.

124. Dimsdale, *Vigilantes of Montana*, 94; Allen, *Decent Orderly Lynching*, 188; Sanders and Bertsche, *X. Beidler*, 72; Mather and Boswell, *Hanging the Sheriff*, 79; Birney, *Vigilantes*, 205; Callaway, *Montana's Righteous Hangmen*, 34; Bartholomew, *Henry Plummer*, 12; Hamilton, *From Wilderness to Statehood*, 249.

125. "Trial and Execution of George Ives," 5; Thompson, *Tenderfoot in Montana*, 171; Birney, *Vigilantes*, 205; Barsness, *Gold Camp*, 42; Cushman, *Montana*, 111; see also Milner and O'Connor, *As Big as the West*, 90.

126. Sanders and Bertsche, *X. Beidler*, xiii; Birney, *Vigilantes*, 223.

127. "Trial and Execution of George Ives," 5; Dimsdale, *Vigilantes of Montana*, 95; Thompson, *Tenderfoot in Montana*, 171; Sanders and Bertsche, *X. Beidler*, 72; Allen, *Decent Orderly Lynching*, 190; Mather and Boswell, *Hanging the Sheriff*, 79; Birney, *Vigilantes*, 205;

Callaway, *Montana's Righteous Hangmen*, 34; Milner and O'Connor, *As Big as the West*, 90; Barsness, *Gold Camp*, 42; Cushman, *Montana*, 112; Gard, *Frontier Justice*, 175; Fisher and Holmes, *Gold Rushes*, 335; Bartholomew, *Henry Plummer*, 13; Hamilton, *From Wilderness to Statehood*, 249; Olsen, "Lawlessness and Vigilantes," 141; Convis, *Frontier Vigilantes*, 17.

128. Dimsdale, *Vigilantes of Montana*, 95; Thompson, *Tenderfoot in Montana*, 171; Sanders and Bertsche, *X. Beidler*, 72–73; Allen, *Decent Orderly Lynching*, 190; Callaway, *Montana's Righteous Hangmen*, 34.

129. "Trial and Execution of George Ives," 5–6; Aaron T. Ford Reminiscences, 1903, Mont. Hist. Soc., SC-702, box 1-1, p. 5.

130. "Trial and Execution of George Ives," 6.

131. Ibid.

132. Ibid.

133. Allen, *Decent Orderly Lynching*, 191.

134. Ibid.

135. "Trial and Execution of George Ives," 6; Allen, *Decent Orderly Lynching*, 191; Olsen, "Lawlessness and Vigilantes," 142.

136. "Trial and Execution of George Ives," 6.

137. Allen, *Decent Orderly Lynching*, 191; Olsen, "Lawlessness and Vigilantes," 142.

138. "Trial and Execution of George Ives," 6–7; Dimsdale, *Vigilantes of Montana*, 97; Langford, *Vigilante Days*, 187; Bakken, *Invitation to an Execution*, 340; Sanders and Bertsche, *X. Beidler*, 75; Allen, *Decent Orderly Lynching*, 191; Birney, *Vigilantes*, 208; Callaway, *Montana's Righteous Hangmen*, 35–36; Hamilton, *From Wilderness to Statehood*, 249.

139. "Trial and Execution of George Ives," 7; Allen, *Decent Orderly Lynching*, 191.

140. Donovan, *Hanging around the Big Sky*, book 2, 25.

141. "Trial and Execution of George Ives," 7; Toponce, *Reminiscences*, 72.

142. "Trial and Execution of George Ives," 7; Allen, *Decent Orderly Lynching*, 191.

143. "Trial and Execution of George Ives," 7.

144. Allen, *Decent Orderly Lynching*, 191.

145. Dimsdale, *Vigilantes of Montana*, 98; Thompson, *Tenderfoot in Montana*, 172; Allen, *Decent Orderly Lynching*, 191; Birney, *Vigilantes*, 209; Milner and O'Connor, *As Big as the West*, 91; Barsness, *Gold Camp*, 42. Sanders's written trial summary quotes Ives's last words as "I am not guilty of this murder," with the accent on "this." "Trial and Execution of George Ives," 7.

146. Donovan, *Hanging around the Big Sky*, book 2, 25.

147. Ibid.

148. Langford, *Vigilante Days*, 147; Birney, *Vigilantes*, 209; Donovan, *Hanging around the Big Sky*, book 2, 26; Allen, *Decent Orderly Lynching*, 227.

149. Burlingame, *Montana Frontier*, 99.

150. Pemberton, "Montana's Pioneer Courts," 102.

151. Ibid.

152. Ibid.

153. Ibid.

154. Ibid.

155. Pemberton, "Montana's Pioneer Courts," 103.

156. Ibid.

157. Ibid. Pemberton also explained that the pistol had discharged while Sanders was still in the process of removing it from his overcoat, which set a portion of the coat on fire.

158. Allen, *Decent Orderly Lynching*, 193.

159. Dimsdale, *Vigilantes of Montana*, 98.

160. Langford, *Vigilante Days*, 195; Thompson, *Tenderfoot in Montana*, 175; Pace, *Golden Gulch*, 31; Allen, *Decent Orderly Lynching*, 215; Barsness, *Gold Camp*, 28; Gard, *Frontier Justice*, 171; Pryor, *Lawmen*, 48.

161. Dimsdale, *Vigilantes of Montana*, 99; Langford, *Vigilante Days*, 187; Sanders and Bertsche, *X. Beidler*, 76; Allen, *Decent Orderly Lynching*, 192; Thrapp, *Vengeance!*, 149; Johnson, *Bloody Bozeman*, 93; Bartholomew, *Henry Plummer*, 13–14.

162. Langford, *Vigilante Days*, 187; Callaway, *Montana's Righteous Hangmen*, 36; Olsen, "Lawlessness and Vigilantes," 143.

163. Johnson, *Bloody Bozeman*, 93; Barsness, *Gold Camp*, 44.

164. Dimsdale, *Vigilantes of Montana*, 101; Allen, *Decent Orderly Lynching*, 194.

165. Dimsdale, *Vigilantes of Montana*, 101.

166. Allen, *Decent Orderly Lynching*, 194.

167. Dimsdale, *Vigilantes of Montana*, 101.

168. Ibid.; Allen, *Decent Orderly Lynching*, 194; see also Leeson, *History of Montana*, 286.

169. Dimsdale, *Vigilantes of Montana*, 102; Langford, *Vigilante Days*, 190; Thompson, *Tenderfoot in Montana*, 172; Sanders, *History of Montana*, 78; Johnson, *Bloody Bozeman*, 93; Barsness, *Gold Camp*, 44; John W. Grannis Diaries, 1863–78, Mont. Hist. Soc., SC-301, folder 4-4. Hilderman was later believed to have been part of the road agents gang, and had he not fled the territory as soon as he did, Langford believed that Hilderman would have been hanged. Langford, *Vigilante Days*, 189. Allen writes that Hilderman was never actually convicted of anything, as Sanders determined Hilderman to be "a weak and foolish man" and exercised prosecutorial discretion not to proceed with the trial. Allen, *Decent Orderly Lynching*, 194.

170. Thompson, *Tenderfoot in Montana*, 172–73.

171. Dimsdale, *Vigilantes of Montana*, 101; Langford, *Vigilante Days*, 190; Leeson, *History of Montana*, 286; Thompson, *Tenderfoot in Montana*, 172; Allen, *Decent Orderly Lynching*, 192; Thrapp, *Vengeance!*, 150.

172. Leeson, *History of Montana*, 286; Johnson, *Bloody Bozeman*, 93; Thompson, *Tenderfoot in Montana*, 172; Sanders and Bertsche, *X. Beidler*, 78; Allen, *Decent Orderly Lynching*, 194–95; Thrapp, *Vengeance!*, 150; Greever, *Bonanza West*, 228; Leeson, *History of Montana*, 286; Milner and O'Connor, *As Big as the West*, 91; Hamilton, *From Wilderness to Statehood*, 250.

173. Allen, *Decent Orderly Lynching*, 193.

174. Prince, *Richardson on Evidence*, sec. 200; Mont. Code Ann. Rule 801(c); Mont. Code Ann. Rule 802; *In Re* A.N., 298 Mont. 237, 251 (2000).

175. Prince, *Richardson on Evidence*, sec. 209; Mont. Code Ann. Rule 801(d)(2), Commission Comments to June 1990 Amendment; *Smith v. Smith*, 276 Mont. 434, 441 (1996); *State v. Dolan*, 190 Mont. 195, 202 (1980). Current Montana law mirrors the Federal Rules of Evidence. Cf. Fed. Rule Evid. 804(b) with Mont. Code Ann. Rule 804(b). While party admissions fall outside of the definition of hearsay, there are also standard exceptions to the rule against hearsay by which statements may be admitted as evidence. Mont. Code Ann. Rule 804(b)(1) through (5); Mont. Code Ann. Rule 807. One arguable hearsay exception, as recognized by current Montana law, is when the statement is transactionally part of the crime itself, or closely associated with the crime either just before or after its occurrence. Mont. Code Ann. 26-1-103 (1947); *State v. Brasda*, 319 Mont. 146, 150–51 (2003), denial of post-conviction relief affirmed, 337 Mont. 533 (2007); *State v. Hansen*, 296 Mont. 282, 305 (1999); *State v. Maier*, 293 Mont. 403, 411 (1999), denial of habeas corpus affirmed, 58 Fed.Appx. 259 (2003), denial of post-conviction relief affirmed, 316 Mont. 181 (2003); *State v. Beavers*, 296 Mont. 340, 351 (1999). Here Franck's testimony described Ives's flip of a coin to determine who would pursue Tiebolt immediately prior to the murder, and Ives's description immediately upon his return to the ranch of Tiebolt's shooting. Accordingly, even if Ives's statements were not admissible in evidence as an admission, some or all of the utterances would arguably be admissible as transactionally part of the crime itself. Another hearsay exception, which could also be applicable for admitting into evidence Ives's statements to Franck, is the "statement against penal interest." A statement against

penal interest is defined as a "statement that A) a reasonable person in the declarant's position would have made only if the declarant believed it to be true because, when made, it expose[s] the declarant to civil or criminal liability; and B) is supported by corroborating circumstances that clearly indicate its trustworthiness, if it is offered in a criminal case as one that tends to expose the declarant to criminal liability." Mont. Code Ann. Rule 804(b)(3). The admissibility of the hearsay statement is grounded in its trustworthiness, based upon the declarant's perception, memory, and credibility. *State v. Mizenko*, 330 Mont. 299, 372 (2006), cert. denied, 549 U.S. 810 (2006); *State v. McCord*, 251 Mont. 317, 322 (1992); *State v. Allison*, 122 Mont. 120, 144 (1948). While this hearsay exception requires that the declarant not be available to testify at the trial (see *State v. McCord*, 251 Mont. at 322; *MacDonald v. Protestant Episcopal Church in Dioceses of Montana*, 150 Mont 332, 335 (1967); Prince, *Richardson on Evidence*, secs. 257–58). Ives was "unavailable" to the extent that he could not lawfully be compelled to testify because of his constitutional privilege against self-incrimination. Prince, *Richardson on Evidence*, sec. 258 (citing *People v. Brown*, 26 N.Y. 88, 93).

176. *State v. Ahto*, 290 Mont. 338 (1998) (injuries treated by physician consistent with victim's statement of what had happened); *State v. Arlington*, 265 Mont. 127, 144 (1994) (injuries consistent with victim's statements).

177. Montana's current definition of circumstantial evidence is set forth in Mont. Code Ann. 26-1-102(1) (1983). It defines circumstantial as evidence as "that which tends to establish a fact by proving another and which, though true, does not of itself conclusively establish that fact but affords an inference or presumption of its existence"; see, generally, *State v. Morrisey*, 351 Mont. 144, 178 (1999). Under Montana law today, criminal convictions may be rendered entirely upon circumstantial evidence. *State v. Field*, 328 Mont. 26, 30 (2005); *State v. Vukasin*, 317 Mont. 204, 210 2003); *State v. Landis*, 308 Mont. 354, 362 (2002); *State v. Hall*, 297 Mont. 111, 117 (1999); *State v. Southern*, 294 Mont. 225, 250 (1999); *State v. Lancione*, 288 Mont. 228, 236 (1998); *State v. Buckingham*, 240 Mont. 252, 260 (1989).

178. *State v. Southern*, 294 Mont. at 250; *State v. Johnson*, 267 Mont. 474, 481 (1994); *State ex rel Murphy v. McKinnon*, 171 Mont. 120, 125 (1976).

179. Mont. Code Ann. 26-1-102(1) (1983).

180. Under Montana law today, flight is not sufficient in and of itself to establish a defendant's guilt, but if a crime has in fact been committed by someone, the defendant's flight may be considered by the trier of fact in light of all other evidence in determining the question of guilt or innocence. *State v. Ahmed*, 278 Mont. 200, 213 (1996), cert. denied, 519 U.S. 1082 (1997), grant of habeas corpus reversed, 18 Fed.Appx. 585 (9th Cir. 2001), cert. denied, 535 U.S. 1102 (2002); *State v. Twoteeth*, 219 Mont. 101, 109 (1985); *State v. Hardy*, 185 Mont. 130, 136 (1980); *State v. Gone*, 179 Mont. 271, 277 (1978).

181. Under Montana law today, a witness who did not participate in the planning and execution of a crime, but who assisted the perpetrator after the commission of the crime, is not an accomplice to that crime, and the witness's testimony is admissible at trial as corroborative evidence. *State v. Gonyea*, 225 Mont. 56, 59–60 (1987). However, under current Montana law, a person commits the crime of obstructing justice by purposefully assisting or concealing either an offender or evidence that, if not concealed, might lead to the discovery or apprehension of that offender. Mont. Code Ann. 45-7-303(2)(e) (2009); *State v. Stucker*, 293 Mont. 123, 127–28 (1999).

182. *State v. Maxwell*, 198 Mont. 498, 504 (1982) (finding that the jury could have credited alibi witnesses while still finding the defendant guilty based on time line evidence), denial of habeas corpus reversed, 198 F.3d 254 (9th Cir. 1999).

183. Langford, *Vigilante Days*, 185; Allen, *Decent Orderly Lynching*, 182; Birney, *Vigilantes*, 199.

184. Dimsdale, *Vigilantes of Montana*, 61.

185. Langford, *Vigilante Days*, 177; see also Allen, *Decent Orderly Lynching*, 163.

186. Mont. Rules of Evidence 404(a).
187. Mont. Rules of Evidence 404(b).
188. *State v. Sage*, 357 Mont. 99, 108 (2010); Prince, *Richardson on Evidence*, sec. 170.
189. *State v. Montgomery*, 327 Mont. 138, 143 (2005).
190. Mont. Rules of Evidence 404(a)(1).
191. *State v. Sage*, 357 Mont. 110–11; *State v. McLaughlin*, 351 Mont. 282, 286 (2009); *State v. Mackrill*, 345 Mont. 469, 483–84 (2008).
192. Mont. Rules of Evidence 404(b).
193. Allen, *Decent Orderly Lynching*, 250; Thrapp, *Vengeance!*, 150 (as to H. P. A. Smith).
194. Allen, *Decent Orderly Lynching*, 251.
195. Kohrs, *Conrad Kohrs*, 34.
196. Bakken, *Invitation to an Execution*, 340.
197. Thrapp, *Vengeance!*, 150.
198. Under current Montana law, the standard of appellate review in determining the sufficiency of evidence is whether, viewing the trial evidence in the light most favorable to the prosecution, a rational trier of fact could have found the essential elements of the crime beyond a reasonable doubt., e.g., *State v. Hausauer*, 335 Mont. 137, 142 (2006); *State v. DeWitt*, 324 Mont. 39, 46 (2004); *State v. Vakasin*, 317 Mont. at 209; *State v. Davis*, 300 Mont. 458, 462 (2000); *State v. Weitzel*, 299 Mont. 192, 197 (2000); *State v. Hegg*, 288 Mont. 254, 257 (1998); *State v. Lyons*, 254 Mont. 360, 363 (1992).

7

Formation of the
Vigilance Committee

We the undersigned uniting ourselves in a party for the laudable purpos [sic]
of arresting thievs [sic] & murderers & recovering stollen [sic] property
do pledge ourselves upon our sacred honor each to all others.

—Vigilante Oath, December 23, 1863

The concept of vigilantism in 1863–64 was not new to the American western frontier. Professor Richard Maxwell Brown has identified 326 vigilante movements throughout the long arc of American history.[1] According to Brown, two-thirds of the vigilante movements were in the American West and accounted for five-sevenths of the persons killed by vigilantism.[2] There were 81 "large" vigilante movements, 49 of which occurred between 1850 and 1879 during the period of Civil War violence and the tensions associated with the settlement of the western frontier.[3] Montana was the most significant vigilante territory, with three particularly notable movements, one of which is the vigilantism that arose in Bannack and Alder Gulch in late 1863 and in 1864.[4] Thereafter, vigilantism spread northward to Helena in the period from 1865 to 1870. The third notable vigilante group known as Stuart's Stranglers, discussed in a later chapter, was led by Granville Stuart in the Musselshell Valley region of Montana in 1884. By then, the construction of railroads enabled Montana to become an exporter of livestock and livestock products to the United States. Cattle had become Montana's "new gold." The vigilantism of Stuart's Stranglers was directed against horse and cattle thieves that threatened the ranchers' profitability.[5]

The Vigilance Committee at Alder Gulch was patterned after that which had existed two decades earlier in San Francisco, California.[6] Indeed,

DOI: 10.7330_9780874219203.c007

circumstances in Alder Gulch bore certain loose similarities to those that had existed in San Francisco in the 1850s. San Francisco, like Alder Gulch, had experienced a rapid growth in population as a result of a gold rush.[7] A reliable judicial system was lacking, and the state's Court of Sessions met only once every two months at the county seat.[8] The absence of jails meant that San Francisco defendants could not be held, so defendants were expected to attend their trials on their own and at their own expense, which resulted in many criminals escaping justice.[9] Conditions bred a rapid increase in crime.[10] Criminals gained entrance to San Francisco from the British penal settlements in Australia, organized their gang, known as the Sydney Ducks,[11] and made friends of corrupt court officials, attorneys, police, and politicians.[12] Arson was the crime of greatest concern, as San Francisco was a city built of wood, and arson allowed easy follow-up looting by thieves.[13] Often enough, criminal cases were not tried, defendants were let go, judges refused to render convictions, and juries acted as if they were tainted.[14]

The response to the lawlessness in San Francisco led to the formation of a Committee of Vigilance on June 8, 1851. It ultimately claimed 700 members,[15] with much of the work directed by an Executive Committee that comprised 20 core members.[16] The organization was governed by a written constitution.[17] Vigilante membership was secret, as many of its activities were undertaken outside of the established law.[18] Once formed, the organization set about capturing and dispensing its brand of justice to criminals outside of the formal mechanisms of law enforcement.[19]

The organization and activities of the San Francisco Committee of Vigilance established precedent that was later followed in Montana. The rash of trail robberies and murders committed in the fall of 1863 led to some informal discussions between Wilbur Fisk Sanders and Paris Pfouts, in November of that year, about the need for a vigilance committee.[20] The two men trusted one another by virtue of their mutual Masonic affiliation and their belief that the general public would support vigilante efforts.[21] The idea of a vigilance committee therefore did not originate with the Ives trial, as it had already been percolating in the minds of some of the opinion leaders of Alder Gulch. However, the Ives trial acted as a catalyst that turned mere talk of a vigilance committee into action.

With the conviction and execution of George Ives, the reader may wonder why leading citizens of Alder Gulch felt any need for any vigilance committee. After all, the jury system "worked" in bringing to justice a criminal that twenty-three jurors and the public at large found to be guilty of a heinous crime, and the punishment that was imposed was swift and certain. Arguably, the residents of Alder Gulch had finally determined to stand up to the criminal element that threatened their peaceful mining-community existence, by using the orderly mechanisms of a public trial to try defendants with judges, attorneys, the presentation and cross-examination of evidence, and deliberative jurors. In one sense, the trials of George Ives and George Hilderman could have been hailed as a crowning achievement for the "enlightened" communities of Alder Gulch, consistent with the forward-looking culture that included their barber shops, photography studio, reading rooms, prizefights, bowling alley, public restrooms, dance halls, and theaters.

The formation of a vigilance committee at Alder Gulch in late December of 1863 may be attributable to a continuing distrust of juries by the leading citizens and opinion leaders of the region, *despite* the conviction and execution of George Ives. The open-air murder of Deputy Sheriff D. H. Dillingham and the farcical trials of Buck Stinson, Hayes Lyons, and Charley Forbes that followed were still fresh in everyone's minds, having occurred only weeks earlier in the same year. The prosecutors of George Ives had no confidence or certainty that the murder of Nicholas Tiebolt would be avenged in a manner any more satisfying than that of Dillingham. A Virginia City jury composed of Ives's friends, or the intervention of Sheriff Plummer in the proceedings, or less convincing testimony from "Long John" Franck, or more convincing testimony from Ives's two alibi witnesses might have been all that was necessary for the Ives trial to have concluded with an entirely different result. Professor J. W. Smurr of Montana State University attributes the Vigilance Committee to an imbedded distrust of juries in the absence of an established and credible system of courts.[22]

The Vigilance Committee was formed of leading men from Virginia City and, to a lesser extent, nearby Nevada City and the other mining communities of Alder Gulch.[23] An initial meeting to discuss the formation of the committee was attended by Wilbur Fisk Sanders, Major Alvin W. Brockie, John Nye, Captain Nick D. Wall, and Paris Pfouts.[24] Another man, John S. Lott, would have attended the meeting except that he was one of the advisory jurors in the Ives trial.[25] The initial meeting was conducted during the evening of December 20, 1863, in the back room of the Nye and Kenna dry goods store in Virginia City.[26] The timing of the meeting was significant. It was the night before the final day of the Ives trial, when the attorneys were expected to deliver their summations and the advisory jurors and jury en masse were expected to deliver their verdicts. The participants in the meeting did not know whether the Ives trial would result in a verdict of guilt or whether, even if guilty, any punishment would be imposed commensurate with the crime. No doubt the recent trials of Buck Stinson, Hayes Lyons, and Charley Forbes, where each was believed to have escaped justice, increased the level of nervousness, and the participants at the meeting in the Nye and Kenna store wished to guard against a repeat of those trials' incredible outcomes.

There could also have even been a more sinister agenda to the meeting of Sanders, Brockie, Nye, Wall, and Pfouts the evening before the Ives verdict. Conceivably, the men might have met to discuss a vigilante punishment for George Ives, in the event the trial were to result in his acquittal or in an unsatisfying sentence. For this, there is no particular evidence. However, discussion of what to do in the event of Ives's acquittal would not have been farfetched given the timing of the meeting, the frustration of the participants with crime in the region, and the tempers stoked by the murder of Nicholas Tiebolt and the trial of George Ives.

The identities of the members of the Vigilance Committee were to be held secret.[27] Dimsdale revealed the identity of only Beidler, and even then merely by the nickname of "X."[28] The identities of the members of the Vigilance Committee needed to be protected at the time to save the members from potential criminal prosecution for their deeds in any federal courts that might be established in the territory of Montana. The identities of the members emerged only in the later writings of those with knowledge of these events, published at a time when criminal prosecutions were no longer an issue.

The five men who met to discuss the need for a vigilance committee the evening before the Ives verdict extended invitations to other men to join their fledgling organization, and its membership grew quickly and considerably from there. Oaths were given to early members of the organization at J. M. Fox's home, which stood on land alongside Wallace Street and was later used for a Masonic temple.[29] The archives of the Montana Historical Society contain the original written oath signed by twenty-four early members of the Vigilance Committee, officially formed at Virginia City and Nevada City on December 23, 1863.[30] The oath is believed to have been drafted by John S. Lott.[31] The original oath was signed and dated two days after Ives's execution, suggesting the speed at which men of Alder Gulch, committed to a means of law and order, jump-started the organization.

Some of the signatures upon the oath document are difficult to decipher, but research conducted for the Montana Historical Society has identified virtually all of the original signatories. The original twenty-four signers of the oath were J. H. Balch, Thomas Baume, Charles Beehrer, William H. Brown Jr., John Brown Jr., Charles Brown, William Clark, J. S. Daddow, Alex Gillon Jr., Joseph Hinckley, Enoch Hodson, Hans J. Holst, Anton Holter, Nelson Kellock, C. F. Keyes, Luther Leebold, W. C. Maxwell, Elkanah "Elk" Morse, William Palmer, S. J. Ross, A. D. Smith, John Triff, M. S. Warner, and James Williams.[32]

Additional early members of the Vigilance Committee, whose signatures do not appear on the original oath document, have been identified as Charles S. Bagg, John X. Beidler, John Creighton, Adriel B. Davis, E. P. Eaton,

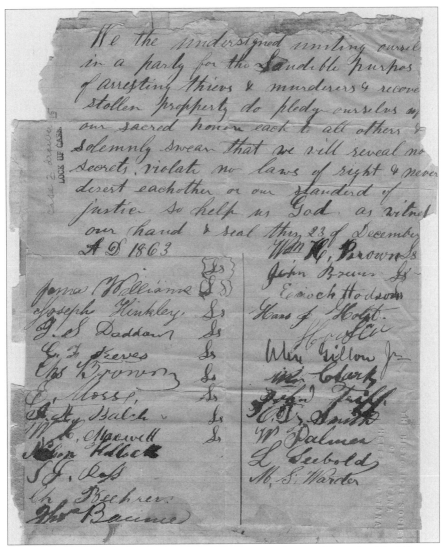

Figure 7.1. Copy of the original Vigilance Committee oath, signed December 23, 1863. (Courtesy of the Montana Historical Society Research Center, Vigilantes Records, SC-953.)

Benjamin Ezekial, Jeremiah M. Fox, John Fetherstun, George Gohn, George W. Harrison, Robert Hareford, Neil M. Howie, George Irvin II, D. J. Jones, Harry King, Richard McLaren, J. S. Rockfellow, William Roe, J. W. Russell, Leroy Southmayd, and of course the original five organizers, Wilbur Fisk Sanders, Alvin W. Brockie, John Nye, Nick D. Wall, and Paris Pfouts.[33]

M. A. Leeson's *History of Montana 1739–1885*, published in 1885, lists several additional members of the Vigilance Committee whose signatures are not contained on the original oath. Leeson's membership list is not limited to the earliest members and, as will be shown, includes the name of at least one person who did not arrive in Montana Territory until mid-1865. The Leeson list includes Ed Hibbert, Henry Crawford, J. M. Castner, Dr. Giles Gaylord Bissell, O. J. Rockwell, Captain Higgins, D. O'Leary, Robert Dempsey, William Rheem, George Copley, Judge Hoyt, Smith Ball, Robert C. Knox, A. Godfrey, Harry Flegger, J. B. "Buzz" Caven, Frank Ray, Lewis LeGrau, Matt Carroll, Samuel T. Hauser, Milton S. Moody, John McCormick, Billy Sloan, John Bozeman, Henry Branson, M. V. Jones, Frank Woody, John Murphy, Tom Connor, Mattison, Wilkinson, "Bummer Dan" McFadden, Bill Sweeney, James Dodge, Dr. William L. Steele, E. R. Cutter, Dr. Samuel Rutar, Jim Brown, Captain Moore, J. C. Guy, George Burtschey, Hedges, Ellis, Colonel Wood, John D. Ritchie, W. H. Patton, William Y. Pemberton, Judge Byam, McK. Dennee, Hill Beechy, Tom Reilly, Melanchthon "Lank" Forbes, Jack Temple, Jemmy Allen, Charley Eaton, Dan Harding, Barney "Baron" O'Keefe, Barney Hughes, John McGrath, James Stuart, Charles J. Curtis, Stephen Reynolds, Judge B. B. Burchette, Major Hutchinson, Ed House, Dr. Palmer, S. M. Hall, G. French, A. F. Edwards, Edward Porter, C. C. Fanner,[34] Andrew O'Connell, S. Kayser, Judge N. J. Bond, Jack Edwards, Judge Lawrence, A. S. Parker, A. J. McCausland, David Dinan, L. F. Carpenter, W. L. Myers, Charles Parks, J. J. Heally, Nelson Story, Chief Judge Ezekiah Hosmer, Judge Lyman Munson, Nathaniel P. Langford, and Thomas Dimsdale.[35] Tom Cover, one of the gold discoverers at Alder Gulch, was also a member.[36]

Many of the names of members of the early Vigilance Committee are already familiar to the reader, and many had been exposed in one way or another to the problem of crime in the region. Barney Hughes, Bill Sweeney, and Tom Cover were among the five original prospectors who discovered gold at Alder Gulch. J. M. Castner was the individual who was elected coroner at the same miner's meeting where Henry Plummer was elected sheriff in Bannack. Dr. William Steele, Dr. Samuel Rutar, and Dr. Giles Gaylord Bissell collectively presided at the murder trials of Buck Stinson, Hayes Lyons, and Charley Forbes for the killing of Chief Deputy Sheriff D. H. Dillingham. Thomas Baume was the individual who gave the knife to Nicholas Tiebolt by which Tiebolt's decayed body was identified when it was transported to Nevada City. William Clark is "Old Man" Clark, who sent Tiebolt to George Ives's ranch to retrieve the mules that he had purchased. William Palmer, also an early vigilante, discovered Tiebolt's body. James Williams was a rancher and the de facto leader of the posse that investigated the Tiebolt murder and arrested George Ives and George Hilderman for the crime. Elkanah "Elk" Morse and George Burtschey were also members of the posse that arrested Ives and Hilderman. John X. Beidler was a member of the same posse and shouted the penultimate phrase "Sanders! Ask him how long he gave the Dutchman!" when the determination was made that Ives's execution be carried out immediately after his trial. As will be seen, "X" Beidler would also play a role in vigilante events in Helena later in the decade. Wilbur Fisk Sanders and Charles S. Bagg were the prosecutors at the Ives trial. John D. Ritchie was one of the five retained attorneys that defended George Ives, and Dr. Don Byam was one of two judges who presided at the trial. William Y. Pemberton was the court stenographer at the trial and would play a future role in Helena trials and in the Montana judiciary. Robert Hereford had been sheriff of Nevada City, responsible for guarding Ives and Hilderman during their trials. Buzz Caven and Adriel Davis had been sheriffs in Virginia City and Junction City, respectively. "Bummer Dan" McFadden, Percival, and Wilkinson were passengers who were robbed while traveling on the Peabody & Caldwell stagecoach on October 26, 1863. Leroy Southmayd and Captain Moore had been robbed of money and treasury bills by road agents in late November 1863 while en route to Bannack from Virginia City. Anton Holter had also been robbed and shot at by road agents on December 8, 1863, and barely escaped the gunfire with his life.[37] Milton S. Moody headed the three-wagon stagecoach that was targeted for robbery in the Red Rock Canyon while en route to Salt Lake City in December of 1863. Melanchthon "Lank" Forbes, Neil Howie, J. S. Rockfellow, Billy Sloan, and John Bozeman, who blazed the trail that bore his name, had been passengers on Moody's stagecoach. John Nye, J. W. Russell, and Paris Pfouts were each store owners in Virginia City and dependent, perhaps, upon the safe transport of provisions to Virginia City for sale in their stores.

M. A. Leeson's extensive list of vigilante members also includes Nathaniel P. Langford and Thomas J. Dimsdale. Both men wrote books detailing Montana's vigilantism. Langford's membership in the organization has never been an issue. Dimsdale's membership, however, had been disguised by him at the time, perhaps to maintain some semblance of journalistic independence given his future role as editor of the *Montana Post* newspaper. If Dimsdale was an actual vigilante, as M. A. Leeson indicates in his 1885 writing, then Leeson confirms a thesis by author-historians Ruth Mather and F. E. Boswell that Dimsdale was a formal member of the Vigilance Committee and that he may have authored his famous book to help insulate the vigilantes from any potential federal prosecutions.[38] Membership in the organization would have been entirely consistent with Dimsdale's unabashed views that favored the vigilance movement.

Leeson's list of vigilantes is perhaps *too* expansive. One name that appears on his list, but on no other list, is that of Hill Beachy. The reader met Hill Beachy in connection with his successful efforts to arrest individuals responsible for the gruesome murders of the Magruder party, traveling from Virginia City to Lewiston, Idaho, in October of 1863. What makes Beachy's inclusion on Leeson's list noteworthy is that Beachy spent his life and career as a freighter in Idaho, Nevada, and California, but not in Montana. While Beachy played a role in fighting crime from his native Idaho, the inclusion of Beachy's name among the members of the Alder Gulch vigilantes suggests that Leeson took certain liberties in composing his list.

Some of the members of the early Vigilance Committee have not yet been introduced to the reader but will be seen later in this narrative. They include John Fetherstun, who would be involved in the arrest of road agent "Dutch John" Wagner and who, as a future deputy US marshal, would give protective custody to James Daniels when Daniels was captured by Helena vigilantes and hanged; Smith Ball and George Copley, who would be involved in the circumstances of the future vigilante execution of "Greaser Joe" Pizanthia; Barney "Baron" O'Keefe, who would house road agent Bob Zachary at the time of Zachary's arrest and execution; Chief Judge Hezekiah Hosmer and Associate Judge Lyman Munson, who would be appointed to their territorial judgeships by President Lincoln in 1864 and 1865; Jeremiah M. Fox, who would be the only person sued in a civil court for his membership in the vigilante organization; Stephen Reynolds, who would preside as the judge during the citizens' murder trial of John Keene in Helena in 1865; Dr. Palmer, who would be a witness at the Keene trial; Nelson Story, who, later in life, would lead the first cattle drive from Texas to Montana, become the first millionaire in Bozeman, Montana, and endow the Agricultural College of the state of Montana in 1893;[39] and James Stuart, the brother of Granville Stuart who two decades later would revive vigilantism by leading Stuart's Stranglers in the Musselshell Valley.

The reported vigilante membership of Chief Judge Hezekiah Hosmer and Associate Judge Lyman Munson, and of miners' court judges Dr. Don Byam, Dr. William L. Steele, and Dr. Samuel Rutar, seems particularly misplaced and inappropriate by today's standards. Judges today are required to scrupulously avoid political activities while in office. Judges at all criminal and civil proceedings must remain fair and impartial arbiters of the facts and legal principles at issue in the cases they hear. Drs. Steel and Rutar had assisted in the judging of the trials of Buck Stinson, Hayes Lyons, and Charley Forbes for the killing of D. H. Dillingham, and Dr. Byam had presided over the trials of George Ives and George Hilderman for the killing of Nicholas Tiebolt. Miners' courts had been enlisted to hear criminal matters in Alder Gulch, including the trials of Ives and Hilderman. The territorial courts, when they were finally organized in Virginia City in late 1864 and in Helena in mid-1865, would adjudicate many criminal matters. The membership of any judge in a vigilante organization easily calls into question the impartiality of the jurist and conflicts with the ground rules of justice that judges were expected to enforce. Notably, Judge Munson, who is named as a vigilante member by Leeson, did not arrive in Montana Territory to assume his duties until July of 1865, which means that the Leeson list of vigilante members is not limited to persons who joined the organization in late 1863 or even 1864, and necessarily includes persons who could not have enlisted until as late as 1865. As will be shown, Justice Hosmer publicly used his authority at the court as a bulwark against vigilantism at Adler Gulch. Leeson's inclusion of Justices Hosmer and Munson as members of vigilante organizations appears to be in error and necessarily calls into question the accuracy of other names on the same list.

Early vigilante membership reveals no discernible socioeconomic pattern. The early members of the Vigilance Committee represented a cross section of the general population of Alder Gulch, including at least one rancher, farmer, lawyer, blacksmith, freighter, brewer,[40] and coroner and multiple prospectors, shopkeepers, miners' court judges, and law enforcement officials. All shared an apparent commitment to forging a society governed by some measure of law and order or, at least, by a measure more certain and reliable than the status quo.

The oath of the Vigilance Committee signed by its earliest members reads:

> We the undersigned uniting ourselves in a party for the laudable purpos [*sic*] of arresting thievs [*sic*] & murderers & recovering stollen [*sic*] property do pledge ourselves upon our sacred honor each to all others & solemnly swear that we will reveal no secrets, violate no laws of right & never desert each other or our standard of justice so help us God as witness our hand & seal this 23 of December ad 1863.[41]

The oath is particularly significant, both factually and legally, as it limits the united purpose of the organization to the arrest of thieves and murderers and to the recovery of stolen property. The document does not reveal any vision that it apply to other societal matters, for example, resolving alleged assaults at saloons or punishing crimes of recklessness, drunkenness, or disorderly conduct. Indeed, the specific intent of the document was to exclude petty crimes from the scope of vigilante activities.[42] The document establishes that the Vigilance Committee formed not more than two days after the execution of George Ives, suggesting the view of its members that Ives's execution was not an end, but a beginning, of the efforts to rid the region of road agents. The ceremonial and legalistic manner in which the organization was formed, including the oath of its membership and the adoption of bylaws (discussed below), also suggests that the vigilantes did not intend to conduct themselves as an unruly mob but as a "righteous" and disciplined organization.

The Vigilance Committee adopted bylaws that established an organizational president, an executive officer, a treasurer, an executive committee, captains, and lieutenants. The full text of the bylaws is set forth in Appendix B. The bylaws, unlike the oath, contain no misspellings and appear to have been written with the organization and legalese of an attorney.[43] One account suggests that the bylaws were written by a nameless clerk who was employed by J. E. McClurg, who patterned the document after the constitution of the San Francisco Vigilance Committee, with which he was familiar.[44] It is also plausible that Wilbur Fisk Sanders, an attorney involved with the Vigilance Committee from its inception, drafted the bylaws or at least assisted in doing so.

The president of the Vigilance Committee was Paris S. Pfouts, a shopkeeper in Virginia City who later penned an autobiography.[45] In his autobiography, Pfouts claims that he was elected president of the committee during a meeting at which he was absent.[46] Other officers included James Williams as executive officer in charge of criminal investigations, John S. Lott as treasurer, and Wilbur Fisk Sanders as prosecuting attorney.[47] Although there does not appear to be any surviving list of captains or lieutenants,[48] John S. Lott is believed to have been a captain of a vigilante company.[49]

The responsibilities of each vigilante officer were defined in the organization's bylaws.[50] Captains and lieutenants were to oversee the investigation of suspected criminals and to arrest such persons upon the collection of sufficient proof.[51] Upon the arrest of a suspect, the matter was to be given over to the Executive Committee of the organization for disposition.[52] The Executive Committee, consisting of seventeen members, was vested with the authority to try criminals arrested by the organization.[53] The organization was to operate in secret.[54] Death was the only sentence that the bylaws authorized be imposed upon a person convicted of wrongdoing.[55] Vigilante movements typically impose the punishment of death, as their unofficial character prevents them from using more traditional methods of punishment such as imprisonment at a jail or the imposition of fines.[56] Decisions by the Executive Committee were final,[57] without any mechanism or opportunity for a reargument or an appeal. The bylaws authorized the seizure of property possessed by an executed criminal to pay for execution and funeral expenses and to satisfy outstanding debts to the decedent's creditors.[58]

The Vigilance Committee's president, Paris Pfouts, wrote that he "selected with great care an executive committee, to decide upon guilt or innocence of the accused persons, and appointed Captains of companies, investing them with power to administer the obligation of the Committee to such as were willing to unite themselves with the organization."[59] If Pfouts is to be believed—and there may be no discernible reason to doubt him on this point—positions of authority within the Vigilance Committee were not filled without deliberation that matched appropriate appointees to specified positions of responsibility.

Figure 7.2. Paris Pfouts, first president of the Alder Gulch Vigilance Committee. (Courtesy of the Montana Historical Society, image 944-366.)

The bylaws of the Vigilance Committee are instructive in several respects beyond their legalistic formalities. Its provisions assured that membership in the organization's Executive Committee would be geographically distributed among the various mining communities of Alder Gulch, though the center of the organization's gravity, with the greatest number of members and its president, was clearly Virginia City.[60] Incoming members of vigilante companies were to be "men of integrity living in their midst," underscoring the self-righteousness of the founding members.[61] The organization's founders must have anticipated the growth of its membership, as bylaw language required companies of more than fifty members to be split into two separate companies.[62] Pfouts claimed in his autobiography that the Vigilance Committee ultimately enrolled 1,000 members.[63]

The Masons may have been a factor in the growth of the Vigilance Committee in Alder Gulch and in the trust that its early members had for one another.[64] A Masonic lodge was established in Virginia City in 1864.[65] Many early members of the Vigilance Committee were Masons.[66] Paris Pfouts was the first Master of the Virginia City Lodge, which he organized at approximately the same time that he helped organize the Vigilance Committee.[67] Wilbur Fisk Sanders, James Williams, Thomas Baume, Neil Howie, and Thomas Dimsdale were also Masons.[68] Adriel Davis joined a Masonic lodge that was officially chartered in Nevada City on January 29, 1866.[69] The fraternal bond of the Masons paralleled the bond of trust that needed to exist among members of the Vigilance Committee, and in some instances, the bonds of one may have helped the other. Records maintained by Virginia City Lodge 1, AF&AM, contain several references to vigilante activities.[70] The Masonic records say that membership in the Vigilance Committee spread to all of the mining communities in the area and that within days of the committee's creation, more than 1,000 men took the vigilante oath, a portion of them Masons.[71] The reported number of men that took the vigilante oath is consistent with that also claimed by Paris Pfouts. The Vigilance Committee was nevertheless a separate organization and by no means an arm of the Masonic Lodge. By the time Paris Pfouts left Montana in 1867 for St. Louis, he had become High Priest and Captain of Hosts of the Royal Arch Masons Chapter, Prelate of the Knights Templar, and Conductor of the Council of Royal and Select Masters.[72]

The original membership of the vigilante organization appears to reflect no names of Asian origin. This perhaps reflects the fact that Asians in Alder Gulch were a segregated community treated, in many respects, as second class.

The Vigilance Committee's bylaws also provided no role for women, as vigilantism at Alder Gulch and Bannack was decidedly male-on-male.[73] Women represented a much smaller percentage of the population than men in frontier mining communities.[74] Nevertheless, women may have been intentionally excluded from the Vigilance Committee, as their purported crying at the trial of Charley Forbes, after the murder of D. H. Dillingham, was blamed for contributing to Forbes's acquittal and, ultimately, the rescission of the death sentences that had been voted upon Buck Stinson and Hayes Lyons for the same crime. Dimsdale acknowledges the role of women in his 1866 book as "sisters, mothers, nurses, friends, sweethearts and wives, . . . the salt of the earth, the sheer anchor of society, and the humanizing and purifying element in humanity."[75] But reflecting the norm of frontier mining communities at the time, Dimsdale dismissed any role of women in vigilante activities, stating that "[s]uch sights are unfit for them to behold, and in rough and masculine business of every kind, women should bear no part."[76]

Word that a vigilance committee had been formed spread throughout Alder Gulch.[77] Now it became time for its members to take action.

Panning for Nuggets

John S. Lott, as treasurer of the Alder Gulch Vigilance Committee, maintained meticulous written records of the organization's receipts and expenses. The Montana Historical Society maintains a copy of sixteen pages of financial accounting records for 1864 that identify donations to the organization by donor, date, and amount, and payments by payee, date, and amount.[78] The account was known as "the ferreting fund," perhaps referring to the organization's mission of ferreting out criminals in Alder Gulch. While financial records were usually specific and seemingly accurate, in one case a receipt was received from "Somebody" for $25.00.[79]

Notes

1. Brown, *Strain of Violence*, 101.
2. Ibid., 102.
3. Ibid.
4. Ibid.
5. Ibid., 101; see also Abrahams, *Vigilant Citizens*, 12; Allen, *Decent Orderly Lynching*, 358; Milner and O'Connor, *As Big as the West*, 220–48. Despite the group's name, persons were not strangled as a means of execution but were instead shot or hanged. Allen, *Decent Orderly Lynching*, 358. See, generally, Phillips, *Forty Years*.
6. Mather and Boswell, *Hanging the Sheriff*, 80; Gard, *Frontier Justice*, 167; Birney, *Vigilantes*, 211–12.
7. Valentine, *Vigilante Justice*, 20 (as to San Francisco).
8. Valentine, *Vigilante Justice*, 27–28.
9. Ibid., 28; see also Gard, *Frontier Justice*, 153.
10. Valentine, *Vigilante Justice*, 29.
11. Abrahams, *Vigilant Citizens*, 58; Gard, *Frontier Justice*, 154.
12. Valentine, *Vigilante Justice*, 42; Gard, *Frontier Justice*, 154.
13. Boessenecker, *Gold Dust*, 34–35.
14. Ibid.
15. Ibid., 35; Greever, *Bonanza West*, 79; see also Abrahams, *Vigilant Citizens*, 59 (setting the number of members at 500).
16. Greever, *Bonanza West*, 79; Abrahams, *Vigilant Citizens*, 59.
17. Bancroft, *Popular Tribunals*, 36:210; Abrahams, *Vigilant Citizens*, 58. The constitution of the San Francisco Committee of Vigilance, dated June 9, 1851, reads, in part: "WHEREAS, It has become apparent to the citizens of San Francisco that there is no security for life and property, either under the regulations of society as it at present exists, or under the law as now administered; therefore, the citizens whose names are hereunto attached do unite themselves into an association for the maintenance of the peace and good order of society, and the preservation of the lives and property of the citizens of San Francisco, and do bind ourselves, each unto the other, to do and perform every lawful act for the maintenance of law and order, and to sustain the laws when faithfully and properly administered; but

we are determined that no thief, burglar, incendiary or assassin shall escape punishment, either by the quibbles of the law, the insecurity of prisons, the carelessness or corruption of the police, or the laxity of those who pretend to administer justice"; Bancroft, *Popular Tribunals*, 36:211; Abrahams, *Vigilant Citizens*, 59–60.

18. Abrahams, *Vigilant Citizens*, 59.

19. Two days after the formation the San Francisco Vigilance Committee, John Jenkins was caught stealing a safe, and the citizens turned him over to the vigilantes instead of the authorities. Bancroft, *Popular Tribunals*, 36:230; Boessenecker, *Gold Dust*, 35; Gard, *Frontier Justice*, 155; see also Greever, *Bonanza West*, 79. Jenkins was summarily tried without the benefit of defense counsel and then hanged from a beam of the US Custom House before 2,000 spectators in Portsmouth Square. Bancroft, *Popular Tribunals*, 36:230, 236–37; Boessenecker, *Gold Dust*, 35; see also Gard, *Frontier Justice*, 155–56; Greever, *Bonanza West*, 79. The vigilantes then captured and hanged a notorious outlaw, James Stuart, on July 11, 1851. Bancroft, *Popular Tribunals*, 36:297; Boessenecker, *Gold Dust*, 35; Gard, *Frontier Justice*, 157–58. In August of 1851, the vigilantes convicted Samuel Whittaker and Robert McKenzie of robbery, burglary, and arson, and sentenced them to be hanged. Valentine, *Vigilante Justice*, 74. California governor John McDougal issued a proclamation against the vigilantes (see Valentine, *Vigilante Justice*, 75; Greever, *Bonanza West*, 79), and on August 20, 1851, Whittaker and McKenzie were taken into police custody by Sheriff Hayes pursuant to writs of habeas corpus. Valentine, *Vigilante Justice*, 76; Gard, *Frontier Justice*, 159–60; see also Greever, *Bonanza West*, 79. Two days later, thirty-six vigilantes led by Captain J. W. Cartwright appeared at the San Francisco jail, seized Whittaker and McKenzie as their prisoners, and summarily hanged them. Bancroft, *Popular Tribunals*, 36:353, 365; Valentine, *Vigilante Justice*, 77; Gard, *Frontier Justice*, 160 (identifying the number of vigilantes involved in the raid as twenty-nine). The San Francisco Vigilance Committee was inactive from then until 1856, when it was revived with 8,000 members organized along military lines into fifty companies. Boessenecker, *Gold Dust*, 36; Greever, *Bonanza West*, 79. The revival was prompted by the shooting death of US marshal William Richardson at the hands of a gambler, Charles Cora, over a personal matter (see Boessenecker, *Gold Dust*, 36; Valentine, *Vigilante Justice*, 100; Gard, *Frontier Justice*, 161; Greever, *Bonanza West*, 79) and by the hung jury that later resulted at Cora's trial. Boessenecker, *Gold Dust*, 36; Allen, *Decent Orderly Lynching*, 30; Gard, *Frontier Justice*, 162; Greever, *Bonanza West*, 79. At roughly the same time, the editor of the *Daily Evening Bulletin*, James King of William, was shot to death by James B. Casey, a member of the Board of Supervisors who was angered over a newspaper story revealing that Casey had once been imprisoned at Sing Sing Prison. Boessenecker, *Gold Dust*, 36; Valentine, *Vigilante Justice*, 101, 107–8; Allen, *Decent Orderly Lynching*, 30; Gard, *Frontier Justice*, 162–63; Greever, *Bonanza West*, 79. The revived Vigilance Committee was headed by a thirty-nine-member Executive Committee. Greever, *Bonanza West*, 79. The vigilantes seized both Cora and Casey (see Valentine, *Vigilante Justice*, 126; Allen, *Decent Orderly Lynching*, 30; Gard, *Frontier Justice*, 164), gave them trials (see Bancroft, *Popular Tribunals*, 37:226; Valentine, *Vigilante Justice*, 131; Gard, *Frontier Justice*, 164–65; Greever, *Bonanza West*, 80), and hanged them on May 23, 1856, at Fort Gunnybags on Sacramento Street in the presence of 3,000 persons. Bancroft, *Popular Tribunals*, 37:237; Valentine, *Vigilante Justice*, 133–34; Greever, *Bonanza West*, 80; Caughey, *Their Majesties the Mob*, 3; see also Boessenecker, *Gold Dust*, 36 (noting the date of execution as May 22, 1856); Fisher and Holmes, *Gold Rushes*, 327–28; and Allen, *Decent Orderly Lynching*, 30 (execution date of May 22, 1856); Gard, *Frontier Justice*, 165. The execution date of May 23, 1856, seems the more plausible date of the two, as the funeral of James King of William was scheduled for May 22 and the vigilantes wished to avoid executing Casey on the same day. Valentine, *Vigilante Justice*, 131–33. In any event, on July 29, 1856, the vigilantes hanged two additional murderers, Joseph Hetherington and

Philander Brace. Bancroft, *Popular Tribunals*, 37:499; Boessenecker, *Gold Dust*, 37; Gard, *Frontier Justice*, 166. The San Francisco Vigilance Committee was nationally reputed for holding trials, providing counsel to persons accused of wrongdoing, punishing criminals, exposing corruption, and for voluntarily disbanding when it deemed its work completed. Boessenecker, *Gold Dust*, 37.

20. "Origin of the Vigilance Committee," Wilbur Fisk Sanders Papers, Mont. Hist. Soc., MC-53, box 5, folder 5-2.

21. Ibid.

22. Smurr, "Some Afterthoughts on the Vigilantes."

23. Dimsdale, *Vigilantes of Montana*, 104; see also Pace, *Golden Gulch*, 35; Clampett, "Vigilantes," 451.

24. Pfouts, *Four Firsts*, 98; Birney, *Vigilantes*, 216; Allen, *Decent Orderly Lynching*, 193; Thrapp, *Vengeance!*, 150; see also Mather and Boswell, *Hanging the Sheriff*, 80; "Trial and Execution of George Ives," Wilbur Fisk Sanders Papers, Mont. Hist. Soc., MC-53, box 5, folder 5-1, p. 8.

25. Thrapp, *Vengeance!*, 150.

26. Allen, *Decent Orderly Lynching*, 182–83.

27. "Trial and Execution of George Ives," 8; Pfouts, *Four Firsts*, 98; Birney, *Vigilantes*, 221; Gard, *Frontier Justice*, 176–77; Bakken, *Invitation to an Execution*, 340; Birney, *Vigilantes*, 217.

28. Birney, *Vigilantes*, 221.

29. Hamilton, *From Wilderness to Statehood*, 252.

30. Vigilantes Records (Virginia City), 1863–84, Mont. Hist. Soc., SC-953, folder 1-2; Langford, *Vigilante Days*, 6; Callaway, *Montana's Righteous Hangmen*, 45; Allen, *Decent Orderly Lynching*, 195; Birney, *Vigilantes*, 215; Abrahams, *Vigilant Citizens*, 63; see also Bakken, *Invitation to an Execution*, 340.

31. Thrapp, *Vengeance!*, 150.

32. See attachment to correspondence of Merrill G. Burlingame to Dave Walter, reference librarian of the Montana Historical Society, dated March 28, 1979; Birney, *Vigilantes*, 222. The Burlingame correspondence refers to Balch by the initials J. H., whereas Birney refers to the initials as I. H.

33. Ibid. Burlingame's list identifies a William Roe, while Birney identifies a William T. Morrow, likely the same person. Birney identifies three additional names not on Burlingame's list, Augustus F. Graeter and Nelson Story.

34. Leeson actually uses the surname of Farmer. This text adopts the surname of Fanner, as the same individual later appears as a member of the jury at the trial of John Keene in Helena and is identified in a contemporaneous newspaper article by the surname of Fanner. The contemporaneous account may be more reliable than Leeson's, written over two decades after the fact.

35. Leeson, *History of Montana*, 265–66. Leeson's list includes a "Dr. Biddle" which, given the similarity of spelling, is likely a reference to Dr. Giles Gaylord Bissell.

36. Thrapp, *Vengeance!*, 152.

37. Allen, *Decent Orderly Lynching*, 162–63.

38. Mather, "Was Dimsdale a Vigilante?"

39. Malone, Roeder, and Lang, *Montana*, 148; Gail Schontzler, "Nelson Story—Hero, Scoundrel Legend," *Bozeman Daily Chronicle*, http://www.bozemandailychronicle.com/100/news makers/article_89773f86-268b-11e0-aca5-001cc4c002e0.html (accessed Mar. 15, 2012).

40. Vigilantes Records (Virginia City), 1863–84, Mont. Hist. Soc., SC-953, folder 1-2; Allen, *Decent Orderly Lynching*, 207.

41. Vigilantes Records (Virginia City), 1863–84, Mont. Hist. Soc., SC-953, folder 1-2.

42. Thrapp, *Vengeance!*, 150.

43. See Appendix B, para. 1; Johnson, *Bloody Bozeman*, 94; Gard, *Frontier Justice*, 178; see also Abrahams, *Vigilant Citizens*, 63; Birney, *Vigilantes*, 218–21; Hamilton, *From Wilderness to Statehood*, 252.

44. Birney, *Vigilantes*, 218.

45. Sanders and Bertsche, *X. Beidler*, 80; Callaway, *Montana's Righteous Hangmen*, 49; Allen, *Decent Orderly Lynching*, 198, 298; Birney, *Vigilantes*, 223; Sievert and Sievert, *Virginia City*, 27; Pfouts, *Four Firsts*.

46. Pfouts, *Four Firsts*, 99; Birney, *Vigilantes*, 217–18.

47. Burlingame, *Montana Frontier*, 99; Birney, *Vigilantes*, 223.

48. Thrapp, *Vengeance!*, 154.

49. Ibid., 150.

50. Callaway, 46, 48–49; Birney, *Vigilantes*, 218–21.

51. Appendix B, para. 10; Callaway, *Montana's Righteous Hangmen*, 49.

52. Appendix B, para. 10; Callaway, *Montana's Righteous Hangmen*, 49.

53. Appendix B, para. 8; Callaway, *Montana's Righteous Hangmen*, 48; Abrahams, *Vigilant Citizens*, 63; see also Allen, *Decent Orderly Lynching*, 197.

54. Birney, *Vigilantes*, 221; Allen, *Decent Orderly Lynching*, 197; Thrapp, *Vengeance!*, 150; Barsness, *Gold Camp*, 45.

55. Appendix B, para. 11; Callaway, *Montana's Righteous Hangmen*, 49; see also Allen, *Decent Orderly Lynching*, 197; Abrahams, *Vigilant Citizens*, 63; Gard, *Frontier Justice*, 178; Hamilton, *From Wilderness to Statehood*, 252.

56. Caughey, *Their Majesties the Mob*, 13.

57. Appendix B, para. 10; Callaway, *Montana's Righteous Hangmen*, 49; see also Allen, *Decent Orderly Lynching*, 197.

58. Appendix B, para. 12; Callaway, *Montana's Righteous Hangmen*, 49.

59. Pfouts, *Four Firsts*, 99; Thrapp, *Vengeance!*, 153.

60. Appendix B, para. 7.

61. Ibid., para. 9.

62. Ibid.

63. Pfouts, *Four Firsts*, 99.

64. Cushman, *Montana*, 119; Thrapp, *Vengeance!*, 151.

65. Virginia City Chamber of Commerce, "A Brief Virginia City History"; Ellingsen, "History of Virginia City Masonic Temple."

66. Abrahams, *Vigilant Citizens*, 69.

67. "Vigilante Code Written by Masons," *Montana Standard*, Mar. 16, 1975.

68. Leeson, *History of Montana*, 780; Allen, *Decent Orderly Lynching*, 184; "Vigilante Code Written by Masons," *Montana Standard*, Mar. 16, 1975.

69. Leeson, *History of Montana*, 780.

70. "Vigilante Code Written by Masons," *Montana Standard*, Mar. 16, 1975.

71. Ibid.

72. Ibid.

73. Abrahams, *Vigilant Citizens*, 138.

74. Ibid.

75. Dimsdale, *Vigilantes of Montana*, 69.

76. Ibid.

77. "Trial and Execution of George Ives," 7–8; Allen, *Decent Orderly Lynching*, 250.

78. Vigilantes Records (Virginia City), 1863–84, Mont. Hist. Soc., SC-953, folder 1-2.

79. Ibid.

8

The Hanging Spree Begins

Now men, as a last favor, let me beg that you will give me a good drop.

Sheriff Henry Plummer, January 10, 1864

With the Vigilance Committee's procedures and staffing in place, its founding members set about the boots-on-the-ground work of investigating, arresting, and executing members of the road agent syndicate. Its initial posse of eight men[1] sought out persons that were the known colleagues of George Ives, specifically Aleck Carter, "Whiskey Bill" Graves, and Bill Bunton.[2] The posse's leader was the same James Williams who had earlier helped investigate the death of Nicholas Tiebolt and who had obtained incriminatory evidence from "Long John" Franck against George Ives. John X. Beidler was also a posse member.[3]

The posse's initial destination was the Rattlesnake Ranch, which was jointly owned by Bill Bunton and Frank Parish.[4] The trip took five wintery days on horseback during which the posse ate only fatty bacon and flapjacks.[5] The Rattlesnake Ranch was deserted when the vigilantes arrived, but they found a note there that read, "Git up and dust and lay low for black ducks."[6] "Git" was a word unique to the lexicon of the American West, meaning "scram."[7] "Git up and dust" was a phrase denoting the same concept, but more emphatically.[8] The note was rightly interpreted as a warning to road agents that vigilantes were approaching, and it was believed that suspects who had been at the ranch had fled.[9]

The vigilantes then found Erastus "Red" Yeager and George Brown in the Stinking Water Valley, not far from the Rattlesnake Ranch.[10] Brown had been one of two alibi witnesses who testified on behalf of the defense at the trial of George Ives. Yeager was employed by Bill Bunton and Frank Parish at the Rattlesnake Ranch where he worked as a cook and a barkeeper.[11] The handwriting on the warning note was determined to be that of Brown's, and it also was determined that the courier of the note to the ranch had been Yeager.[12] Upon questioning, Yeager and Brown made certain statements inconsistent with one another.[13] The vigilantes placed Yeager and Brown under arrest, and preparations were made for the two prisoners to be transported to Virginia City. In fact, the posse took Yeager and Brown a significant portion of the distance to Virginia City, whereupon they decamped for the evening at Lorrain's Ranch. While there, members of the posse engaged in a vigorous late-night debate about whether the two prisoners were road agent conspirators deserving death, and Yeager and Brown were awakened from their sleep for further interrogation.[14] Sensing his doom, Yeager then gave the posse a confession of his, and others', guilt in the road agent gang.[15]

Yeager's confession was singularly significant. It identified the members of a tightly knit highway robbery band and its members' respective assignments.[16] Sheriff Henry Plummer was identified as the leader of the group, with Bill Bunton second in command.[17] George Brown was secretary.[18] Hayes Lyons and William Hunter were "telegraph men" and "roadsters" who passed signals to other road agents.[19] Horse thieves and roadsters, who performed actual hold-ups, were Deputy Sheriff Buck Stinson, Sam Bunton, Cyrus Skinner, George Shears, Frank Parish, Stephen Marshland, "Dutch John" Wagner, Aleck Carter, "Whiskey Bill" Graves, Johnny Cooper, "Greaser Joe" Pizanthia, Bob Zachary, Boone Helm, George "Clubfoot" Lane, Gad Moore, and the late George Ives.[20] Deputy Sheriff Ned Ray was the council-room keeper in Bannack.[21] Nathaniel Langford's recitation of Yeager's list of road agents included Billy Terwiliger, though Terwiliger's name was absent from the list described in the writings of Dimsdale and Beidler.[22] "Doc" Howard and his associates, Chris Lowrie, Jim Romaine, and Billy Page, who had traveled with Lloyd Magruder at the time of his murder, were also named by Dimsdale,[23] though their names were absent from the list recounted by Langford.[24] "Fences" disposed of stolen goods.[25] The secret code word of the organization was "Innocent."[26] Robbery victims were to be murdered if doing so was necessary to secure their plunder.[27] According to Nathaniel P. Langford, the road agent conspirators were bound by oath to perform whatever services were required of them in furtherance of their crimes, and their divulgence of any secrets of the organization under any circumstances was punishable by immediate death.[28] According to one author, the divulgence of road agent secrets was specifically punishable by disembowelment and the slitting of one's throat from ear to ear.[29] Undoubtedly, the road agent syndicate relied upon information about travelers received from livery stable workers, hotel clerks, tradesmen, and others familiar with who was traveling where, when, and with what.[30]

Most of the names on Yeager's list were of men who originated from American states or territories that were sympathetic to the Union during the Civil War, though there is no evidence that road agents were deliberately chosen from among the ranks of Union sympathizers. Sheriff Plummer was born in Maine,[31] and, although elected as a Democrat, his preference for the Union was never concealed.[32] Ives was from Wisconsin, Gallagher, Ray, and Wagner were from New York State, Stinson was from Indiana, Brown was from Minnesota, and Zachary was from Illinois.[33] Yeager was originally from Iowa.[34] Lyons was from Nebraska.[35] The exceptions from southern states were Boone Helm, who had immigrated to Montana from Kentucky,[36] and Aleck Carter, who had immigrated from Virginia.[37]

Confession in hand, the posse did not deliver Yeager and Brown to Virginia City, in apparent violation of the bylaws requiring that prisoners be transported to Virginia City for trial by the Executive Committee. Rather, based on Yeager's confession, James Williams's posse overwhelmingly voted both prisoners guilty of being members of the road agent gang and determined the appropriate sentence for them to be death.[38] Of course, Williams's posse did not violate the Vigilance Committee's bylaws if the organization had delegated him the authority to act at his own discretion, without the need to transport prisoners to Virginia City.[39] However, there is no hard evidence that Williams was given carte blanche by the organization's Executive Committee to summarily execute prisoners without returning them to Virginia City. The reason for Yeager's and Brown's execution by the posse, short of transporting the prisoners the full distance to Virginia City, may have been concern over the danger of being ambushed by road agents while en route to Virginia City.[40]

Yeager and Brown were hanged from the boughs of two cottonwood trees at Lorrain's Ranch in the Stinking Water Valley a short time after Yeager's confession.[41] Stools were used to elevate the condemned men off of the ground.[42] Brown begged for his life for the sake of his wife and children in Minnesota.[43] Yeager's last words were, "Goodbye, boys. God bless you. You are on a good undertaking."[44] The two corpses were left hanging from the nooses for several days to serve as examples that road agents would be punished by death.[45] Yeager's body wore a label that said, "Red! Road Agent and Messenger," while Brown's body wore a label that said, "Brown! Corresponding Secretary."[46] The labeling of a criminal and his crime became a common practice in the American western frontier.

In an evidentiary sense, the summary hangings of Yeager and Brown were unfortunate. It provided no opportunity for the vigilante posse to take Yeager's information and independently confirm its accuracy or completeness. The list would prove crucial to further vigilante activities in 1864, and its worth would be debated by historians decades later. For its part, the posse must have assessed

Figure 8.1. James Williams. (Courtesy of the Montana Historical
Society, image 945-626.)

Yeager's list as credible to have summarily hanged the two men for their alleged
membership in the region's criminal enterprise and to do so without need of
further corroborative evidence.

Yeager's list of road agent conspirators provided Williams's posse with the
evidence they needed on which to immediately pursue additional defendants.
Yeager's confession confirmed suspicions that had already been circulating
about Sheriff Plummer in the region.[47] The vigilante posse wished to direct its
attention to the southwest, toward Bannack, where the biggest potential prize,
Sheriff Plummer, maintained his residence. However, because Bannack was
outside of Alder Gulch, at least some members of the vigilante posse needed to
return first to Virginia City for further consultations and instructions.[48]

In the meantime, "Dutch John" Wagner survived the gunshot that he
received to his chest during the attempted robbery of Moody's stagecoach.
After the attempted robbery, he made his way to Bannack, where he sought
refuge and advice from Sheriff Plummer.[49] Plummer advised Wagner to leave

the territory.[50] The bullet wound to Wagner's chest was damning evidence of his complicity in the Moody's robbery, were he ever to be caught. By early January 1864, Wagner, taking Sheriff Plummer's advice, stole a horse and traveled through Horse Prairie to the trail that led south toward Salt Lake City, away from Bannack.[51]

While vigilantes traveled from the site of Yeager's and Brown's execution toward Virginia City for further instructions, Captain Wall and Ben Peabody, who were not part of the vigilante posse, recognized Wagner on the Salt Lake trail and alerted John Fetherstun of the development.[52] By coincidence, Wagner had encountered vigilante member John X. Beidler on the trail the previous day, where they discussed the execution of George Ives and the attempted robbery of the Moody's stagecoach, but Beidler failed to recognize Wagner or associate him in any way with the Moody's crime.[53] This failure on Beidler's part was uncharacteristic for him, as he proved himself on many other occasions to be extraordinarily streetwise. In any event, when Wagner was recognized the following day, Wall, Peabody, and Fetherstun were unable to agree on whether to capture and hang Wagner summarily or to capture and transport him to Bannack.[54] At the time, none of the men involved in the capture of Wagner had any reason to necessarily doubt the honesty of Bannack's sheriff, Henry Plummer. Wall and Peabody, who preferred taking Wagner to Bannack, consulted with Neil Howie, who rode off and singlehandedly arrested Wagner at gunpoint for his participation in the attempted robbery of the Moody stagecoach.[55] It was, for Wagner, an instance of being in the wrong place at the wrong time. He was already suspected of being involved in the attempted robbery of Moody's stagecoach, and as his captors would soon learn, his name was also included on Yeager's list of road agents.

Wagner's fingers were blackened from frostbite that he had suffered during his travels and were tightly bandaged.[56] Temperatures were bitter cold in January of 1864, reaching as low as thirty-five degrees below zero.[57] Wagner vehemently denied to his captors any involvement in the Moody's robbery.[58] During questioning he was stripped of his shirt, and an examination of his shoulder revealed evidence of a bullet wound consistent with accounts of Moody's witnesses that one of the masked assailants had been shot in that part of the body.[59] Wagner explained that the bullet wound to the shoulder had been accidentally self-inflicted when he fell asleep by a fire, rolled into the flames, and ignited a cap and ball from his own pistol.[60] The explanation was not credible, as his body exhibited no sign of burn marks and a man would need to be utterly consumed by flames before a cap would explode from the heat.[61] Howie decided to take Wagner to Bannack, telling Wagner that he could try to prove his innocence there.[62] Wagner was taken into custody on January 6,

1864, prior to when any vigilante posse would catch up with Sheriff Plummer, Buck Stinson, and Ned Ray.[63]

Howie and Fetherstun kept Wagner under their guard for three days and three nights of travel, arriving near Bannack on January 9, 1864.[64] Wagner once made an unsuccessful attempt at an escape.[65] Fetherstun held Wagner for an additional night in the Sears Hotel.[66] Howie left Fetherstun and Wagner in order to report Wagner's capture to the law enforcement authorities in Bannack.[67] The person Howie informed of Wagner's capture was none other than Sheriff Plummer.[68] Had Howie been a member of the posse at the Rattlesnake Ranch and Lorrain's Ranch, he would have known that Sheriff Plummer had been implicated by Yeager as the head of the road agent syndicate and would also have known not to report Wagner's capture to Plummer. According to Howie, Plummer expressed dismay that people could be hanged without law or evidence and demanded that he be given custody of Wagner.[69] For whatever reason, Howie did not then fully trust Plummer and insisted on retaining custody of the prisoner until a people's tribunal could decide how to proceed.[70]

Meanwhile, Fetherstun became concerned that his strong, six-foot-tall prisoner might again attempt an escape.[71] Fetherstun therefore brought Wagner to Durant's saloon in Bannack in the hope of finding Howie there. While there, Deputy Sheriffs Buck Stinson and Ned Ray entered the saloon and took an interest in Wagner, shaking hands with him. A dozen other men also entered the saloon and took an interest in the prisoner, but unbeknown to Fetherstun, the dozen men were vigilantes from Virginia City as well as trusted local Bannack residents who had been enlisted to assist with the vigilante enterprise.[72] The dozen men arrested Wagner and took him to a nearby cabin, followed by Fetherstun and, ultimately, Howie.[73] The vigilantes were satisfied that Fetherstun and Howie were on the side of the law and shared with them their suspicions about Plummer, Stinson, and Ray.[74]

While in the custody of the vigilantes, Wagner was questioned extensively about his alleged involvement in the Moody's stagecoach robbery, his shoulder wound, and his knowledge of any criminal activities undertaken by Sheriff Plummer.[75] He corroborated certain aspects of Yeager's confession but continued to deny any involvement in the Moody's robbery.[76] Howie and Fetherstun were given custody of Wagner for another night, where they held him at a cabin on the Yankee Flat.[77]

By the evening of January 9, 1864, additional vigilantes from Virginia City reached Bannack bearing a letter subordinating themselves to the authority of Bannack vigilantes.[78] The letter contained an "order" for the execution of Sheriff Plummer and Deputy Sheriffs Stinson and Ray.[79] The Virginia City contingent was led by John S. Lott,[80] who is believed to be the person who penned the

Virginia City vigilante oath but who did not, for whatever reason, sign the document himself.[81] Lott gathered a discreet group of Bannack residents that he believed he could trust and outlined the evidence against Plummer, Stinson, and Ray.[82] The evidence that was discussed included, but was not limited to, Yeager's list of road agents members. Attorney Wilbur Fisk Sanders and Idaho chief judge Sidney Edgerton were among the Bannack participants.[83] Edgerton would become Montana's first governor within half a year.[84] The initial meeting to organize vigilantes in Bannack, at Ben Peabody's residence, was inconclusive, as opinion was divided over whether the sheriff, while perhaps the subject of suspicion and rumor, was the mastermind of the far-reaching criminal enterprise described by Yeager.[85] While the deputy sheriffs, Stinson and Ray, were not particularly popular, Sheriff Plummer was a popular figure in the region. With opinion divided among the participants of the meeting, there was no consensus favoring the arrest and execution of Henry Plummer.

The men who were convinced of Sheriff Plummer's leadership of the criminal enterprise operating in the region did not accept defeat, as they had one further potential trick up their sleeves. By happenstance, there lived in the immediate area a teenager who was a family friend of the Sanderses and the Edgertons—young Henry Tilden. The reader will recall that Tilden claimed that he had been accosted on the trail from Horse Prairie the evening of November 14, 1863, by three men that included Henry Plummer; that Plummer held a gun to Tilden's head while others searched his pockets for valuables; and that Tilden was threatened with death if he revealed the details of the incident to others. Tilden was summoned by the vigilantes. In the early morning hours of January 10, 1864, the discreet group of Bannack and Virginia City residents were assembled for a second time, in this instance to hear directly from Tilden about his experience on the trail from Horse Prairie the previous November. Tilden remained steadfast, as he always had with trusted friends, that on November 14, 1863, Sheriff Plummer and two other men had robbed him at gunpoint.[86] No doubt he discussed his identification of the gun that Tilden had delivered to Plummer two days earlier and the red lining of Plummer's overcoat, which was unique. Some persons in the group might have been bothered by the fact that the youth had kept his identification of Plummer secret for so many weeks.[87] But Sanders and Edgerton were present at the meeting to corroborate that Tilden's account of events matched the account he had given to them the previous November, including the identification of Plummer as one of Tilden's assailants. Sanders and Edgerton could also explain that they had strongly counseled Tilden not to disclose his identification of Plummer to anyone. Moreover, there was no apparent evidence from the night Tilden was robbed that Plummer had ever arrived at the Rattlesnake Ranch to evaluate the silver discovery there or to take custody of Frank Parish's horses. Wilbur Fisk Sanders was at the Rattlesnake Ranch the evening that Tilden was accosted, and he knew from his personal observations and his violent encounter with Jack Gallagher that Plummer was not present. Plummer's presence at Rattlesnake the previous November 14 would have given the sheriff an irrefutable alibi that he was not on the Horse Prairie Trail at the time Tilden claimed he was robbed, but the alibi evidence simply did not exist.

In mid-November of 1863, Tilden's account of his ordeal had seemed doubtful to the adults involved. By January of 1864, Tilden's previously questionable account was ultimately judged to be quite plausible to those who had assembled to discuss the mounting evidence against Henry Plummer and his activities. Tilden's information was consistent with Yeager's confession. Whether Tilden's story was true or exaggerated, it, Yeager's list, and any other evidence or innuendo discussed at the second Bannack meeting were enough to gain the assent of those assembled to hang the sheriff of Bannack, along with Deputy Sheriffs Stinson and Ray.[88]

The decision to arrest and execute Plummer, Stinson, and Ray may have been influenced by the identities of the men present at the Bannack meetings. While Wilbur Fisk Sanders had not yet fully established his reputation for lawyerly oratory and personal courage, Sidney Edgerton was cloaked with the persuasive authority that accompanied his position as chief judge of the Idaho Supreme Court. Indeed, Edgerton was described as "a man of unusual intellect, pleasing personality, and notable oratorical ability."[89] He would be appointed governor of the new Montana Territory later in the year. Edgerton's ultimate belief in the honesty and accuracy of Tilden, and in the criminal guilt of Plummer, Stinson, and Ray, may have been a weighty factor in the group's deliberations.

Dawn was fast approaching. Quick action was required. Sanders and Lott swore in several Bannack vigilantes on the morning of January 10, 1864, and a plan of action was organized.[90] Plummer was arrested without incident at the home of his sister-in-law on the same day by a party led by John Lott.[91] Stinson was arrested at the home of his friend, Toland, by a party led by William Roe.[92] Ned Ray was arrested while sleeping at a Bannack saloon.[93]

The three prisoners were marched under an armed guard across the footbridge of Grasshopper Creek to the gallows at the edge of town where Plummer had earlier hanged the criminal, Peter John Horan.[94] John X. Beidler was among the guards.[95] Stinson and Ray uttered curses along the way,[96] though Plummer, for the early part of the death walk, maintained his composure, begged for his life, and argued that he was innocent of any wrongdoing.[97] As the parties came closer to the gallows, Plummer's bargaining became more desperate. He offered to leave the territory; he requested a jury trial; he asked for time to set-tle his financial affairs; he asked to see his sister-in-law; and he offered for the executioners to cut off his ears, cut out his tongue, and strip him naked in the freezing night.[98] Plummer may have tried to bribe his captors with the promise of giving them a fortune in gold dust that he had buried within a hundred yards of a corner corral post at Robber's Roost.[99] Finally, Plummer said he was too wicked to die.[100] None of Plummer's entreaties received a sympathetic or favorable response. This would not be the last time that a person condemned to death by the vigilantes would make a last-ditch effort to bargain for his life, and, as it will be shown, others did as well. On all such occasions, any negotia-tion by a prisoner to save his life proved fruitless.

The hangings had been planned so hastily that upon reaching the gallows, the vigilantes realized that they had not brought a dry goods box for a drop and only had enough rope to hang one man.[101] Henry Tilden was dispatched to Sidney Edgerton's home to retrieve more rope, and the executions were delayed.[102]

Ned Ray was the first of the three to be hanged.[103] Ray's mistress, Madam Hall, wept in the crowd and had to be physically restrained from rushing to the prisoner as his execution was being prepared.[104] Hall was forcibly returned to her cabin.[105] Rope was eventually thrown over the crossbeam of the gallows. Ray continued his curses as the noose was placed about his neck.[106] Ray's hang-ing was not without complication, as he managed to place his hand between the noose and his neck, and he slowly strangled to death over the course of several agonizing minutes.[107] An entry in the *Helena Independent* published on March 24, 1886, says there was no "drop" at all, as the noose was placed around Ray's neck and the rope was then pulled upward, lifting the prisoner off his feet.[108] A hanging by hoisting a prisoner into the air is known as "the Naval method." Ray's body was hoisted into the air with such force that, according to the newspaper account, the gallows almost tipped over.[109] To keep the gallows from falling over, Ray was lowered back onto his feet as he complained, as if divorced from reality, "Hold on, damn it, you are choking me!" Ray's body was then pulled up more evenly the second time and it eventually resulted in his death.[110] If the *Helena Independent* account is accurate, it explains Ray's slow strangulation.

Buck Stinson was hanged next.[111] As he was about to be hoisted from the ground, he offered to confess, but Plummer persuaded him from doing so, saying, "We've done enough already, twice over, to send us to Hell."[112] One account states that Stinson had asked for a drop but was instead hoisted off the ground.[113] However, according to Dimsdale, the knot slipped under Stinson's chin and Stinson "was some minutes dying."[114] The slipping of the

Figure 8.2. The remains of Henry Plummer's scaffold. A replica of the scaffold was later built at the site. (Courtesy of the Montana Historical Society, image 940-708.)

knot would be of no consequence unless the mechanics of Stinson's hanging involved a "drop" that failed to immediately break his neck. Perhaps after the slow strangulation of Ned Ray, the executioners decided upon a quicker and more humane death for Buck Stinson with a drop, but even Stinson's execution did not go as planned if the knot under his chin slipped from position.

Figure 8.3. Burial site of Sheriff Henry Plummer. (Courtesy of the Montana Historical Society, image 950-247.)

It then became Plummer's turn to die. He dropped to his knees to pray.[115] "Give a man time to pray," he said.[116] A man in the crowd responded, "Certainly, but do your praying from up there," referring to the gallows.[117] Upon standing, Plummer removed his necktie and gave it to a young friend who had boarded with him, to remember him by.[118] Plummer's last words were reported to be a request to his executioners: "Now men, as a last favor, let me beg that you will give me a good drop."[119] The last request makes sense, as the executions of Ray and Stinson, which Plummer had closely witnessed, had both been slow, gruesome, and apparently botched. The noose was adjusted around Plummer's neck. The executioners then physically lifted his torso into the air as high as possible to provide for a sudden drop in satisfaction of Plummer's last request.[120] Plummer died without complication. The execution of Henry Plummer is perhaps the most noteworthy of all of the vigilante executions in 1864, as he was an elected law enforcement officer whose defined duties specifically included the arrest of lawbreakers engaged in crimes against persons and property.

Later that day, Buck Stinson's wife went to the temporary morgue where her husband's body was located to recover her husband's gold wedding band. Stinson's body had been left on the gallows for so long that his hand was frozen stiff, which required Mrs. Stinson to cut off her husband's fingers in order to remove the ring.[121]

The death of Sheriff Plummer was believed to have had a salutary effect. One observer remarked that "after Plummer was hung, life and property were [so] safe . . . that a man might lay a sack of gold dust down on the sidewalk and it would lie there 'til the buckskin rotted off, before anyone touched it."[122]

Henry Plummer's arrest and execution illustrates the disconnect between the accused's probable guilt on the one hand and a lack of vigilante due process on the other. As noted by one author, "Plummer, by the context of his career, deserved what he got, but the charges set forth would never have stood up in court. Aside from hearsay inflated in the passage of time, no actual proof exists that Plummer profited by a dollar from road agents, or planned a robbery."[123] The statement is correct only if Henry Tilden is to be disbelieved.

There was of course more work to be done while the vigilante posse was in Bannack. "Greaser Joe" Pizanthia's name was on Yeager's list, and his log cabin was not far from Bannack. Pizanthia was Mexican. His nickname, "Greaser," reflects the racial prejudices that existed at the time. On January 11, 1864, a vigilante posse approached Pizanthia's cabin, knocked on the front door, and ordered Pizanthia to surrender.[124] Pizanthia must have realized the gravity of the situation and was determined not to be taken prisoner without a fight. His wife and children fled to the safety of a neighbor's cabin. When Pizanthia failed to surrender, Smith Ball and George Copley stormed the cabin through the front door.[125] Pizanthia, anticipating the assault, opened fire and shot Ball in the hip and Copley in the chest.[126] The reader may recall that Copley had been the trial prosecutor of Henry Plummer for the murder of Jack Cleveland, prior to Plummer's election as sheriff in Bannack. Both wounded men fell back from the entrance of the cabin after they were shot and were carried to a nearby hotel.[127] Copley died of the wound after ten hours of suffering.[128] Ball, as will be shown, was able to return to the scene.

A shooting standoff developed between Pizanthia in the cabin and the vigilante posse that had taken safe positions outside. Francis Thompson, whose store was in the vicinity, reported that several errant bullets came through his door and window and he was forced to seek safety behind his log walls.[129] The vigilantes, having witnessed the shootings of Ball and Copley, decided to use more caution and to acquire more firepower. A group of vigilantes asked Idaho chief judge Sidney Edgerton if they could use a mountain howitzer that he kept at his home nearby, and Edgerton readily agreed.[130] The howitzer was carried to Pizanthia's cabin and was propped up on a large wooden box that was taken from Thompson's store.[131] Dimsdale described the howitzer as being positioned within five rods of the cabin,[132] which is a distance of 82.5 feet. The howitzer was fired into the cabin three times. The first two shells had little effect as their fuses were not properly cut and the range was short, but the third shell exploded the cabin's chimney, knocked down the front door, and buried Pizanthia under building debris.[133] The cabin was quickly stormed. Pizanthia's legs were tied with rope, he was dragged from the cabin badly injured, and perhaps by prearrangement, Smith Ball avenged his hip wound by firing all the bullets from his revolver into Pizanthia's vital organs while he lay on the ground.[134] Other men of the vigilante posse set fire to the cabin.[135] Pizanthia's body was then hung on a pole by the neck using a clothesline, a hundred gunshots were fired by the vigilantes into the elevated corpse, and when the body was taken down, it was burned in the fire until no trace of it remained.[136]

The next day, when the fire had cooled, persons were observed panning the ashes for any gold or valuables that might have been in the cabin or on Pizanthia's person.[137]

Fresh from the vengeance that had been extracted upon Pizanthia, the vigilantes immediately turned their attention back to "Dutch John" Wagner, who was still being held under guard. For the vigilantes, who typically performed their tasks quickly and efficiently, it was uncharacteristic for a prisoner's fate to be postponed while the posse performed other business. Wagner was the only alleged member of the road agent gang in 1864 who was held while the vigilantes arrested and executed other persons. History might speculate why this was the case. One plausible explanation may be that the vigilante posse that had initially arrived in Bannack was spread out and that those involved in the questioning of Wagner were not authorized to unilaterally determine Wagner's guilt or to hang him for his crimes. The vigilante bylaws, after all, required that prisoners be turned over to the Executive Committee of the organization for disposition. Under this scenario, it might make sense that Wagner was merely detained pending the arrival of higher-ranking vigilante leaders. However, this explanation does not necessarily explain why, after the execution of Plummer, Stinson, and Ray, the vigilantes next sought to arrest Pizanthia rather than turning their next attention to Wagner, who was already in custody.

A second explanation might be that the events involving Plummer, Stinson, Ray, and then Pizanthia simply took their own course at their own speed before vigilante attention could fully and finally turn to Wagner, who at all times was held securely under guard.[138] In other words, since Wagner was already in custody, the vigilante posse could turn its attention to the capture of Pizanthia, who was not yet in custody.

A third potential explanation, which could be in addition to either of the other explanations, is that Wagner was kept alive in the hope that he would provide incriminating evidence that could be used in the arrests of Plummer, Stinson, Ray, and others. Such an explanation is plausible. After all, despite rumors that Plummer was corrupt, despite the information from Yeager that Plummer was the titular head of the road agent gang that operated in the region, and despite the accusations of Henry Tilden against Plummer, there might have been a certain reluctance on the part of some of the vigilante membership to accept the fact that an elected sheriff was perverting his law enforcement responsibilities for the sake of enriching himself at the expense of others. Plummer's role as a sheriff may have bestowed upon him the benefit of that doubt. Vigilantes, emboldened to execute lesser criminals, might have been more reluctant to act against an elected sheriff absent satisfactory, objective proof of the man's criminal guilt. In other words, it is plausible that the vigilantes, hailing from Alder Gulch, wanted to act more cautiously in arresting and executing the elected sheriff of Bannack, a full seventy miles west of Alder Gulch. Inculpatory evidence from Wagner would have helped alleviate those concerns, requiring that he be kept alive at least for another day until events could more fully play out.

Unfortunately for the vigilantes, Wagner initially refused to incriminate Sheriff Plummer in any unlawful activities.[139] He did not confess to his own misdeeds until after he was informed that he would be hanged, and while admitting his complicity in the attempted robbery of Moody's stagecoach, he implicated his partner, Steve Marshland, in the same endeavor.[140] Any admissions that he uttered were made after Plummer, Stinson, Ray, and Pizanthia were already dead.

Wagner was most cooperative and respectful while held as a prisoner and until the time of his death.[141] The evidence of his criminality appeared to be solid. He had been seen in the vicinity of the attempted robbery of Moody's stagecoach prior to the event. One of the assailants had been shot in the shoulder, and Wagner's shoulder showed the markings of a bullet wound. Wagner's name was on Yeager's detailed list of road agents. And ultimately he confessed to his own crime.

On the evening of January 11, 1864, the Vigilante Committee met, unanimously voted Wagner guilty, and determined that the only appropriate penalty for him was death.[142] Wagner was informed that he was to be hanged within the hour. Wagner was taken aback when informed of his sentence. He pleaded for his life, offering instead that the vigilantes cut off his arms and legs in exchange for letting him go.[143] When all negotiation failed, he requested that he be permitted the opportunity to write to his mother in New

York.[144] Because of his frostbitten hands, Wagner initially dictated his letter to a Dutchman who was able to write the mother in her native language.[145] When the read-back was not to Wagner's satisfaction, he penned another draft of the letter using his own crippled, unbandaged hands.[146] According to Dimsdale, Wagner explained in the letter that he had fallen in with bad men and participated in the robbery of a wagon, was captured, and would die in a few minutes, a sentence that he described as just.[147] The posse escorted Wagner to an unfinished building where the dead bodies of Plummer, Stinson, and Ray were already laid out.[148] The unfinished building later became the B. B. Burchette Hotel.[149] At some point before the execution he made a statement corroborating Yeager's confession.[150] When Wagner saw Plummer's body, he said, "This is the man who got me into all this trouble. Had I never seen him I might have lived an honest man."[151] In an indirect way, Wagner may have implicated Plummer in misdeeds after all.

Wagner requested and was given a chance to pray.[152] He then stood atop a barrel, his neck noosed by a rope that had been thrown over a crossbeam of the second story, and the barrel was quickly withdrawn from underfoot.[153]

Wagner's body remained hanging on the noose into the next day, two feet off the floor.[154] People came to view the corpse, spinning the body on the rope in order to locate the bullet wound in his shoulder, as if a novelty to observe.[155]

With its work done in Bannack, the vigilance posse, which was comprised primarily of men from Virginia City and Nevada City, made the seventy-mile trek eastward to their organization's center. Time was of the essence to quickly capture additional road agents before the criminal element would learn of the turn of events and flee the territory.

Panning for Nuggets

In Bannack a few weeks after Sheriff Plummer's execution, Dr. Jerome Glick wished to recover the bullet that had lodged in Plummer's wrist from when he was shot by Henry Crawford. One evening, he dug into Plummer's grave, severed the arm, and then temporarily hid it in a snowbank while he attended a dance that was being held within a short distance from the gravesite. During the dance, a dog entered the ballroom dragging the severed arm.[156] While the incident caused considerable disruption to the dance, Dr. Glick later took the arm to his office and removed the bullet that proved to be compatible with the caliber of Crawford's gun.[157] Years before any episode of CSI *would air on television, the bullet retrieved by Dr. Glick was observed to be "brightened" by its constant friction with Plummer's wrist joint.[158]*

Notes

1. Allen, *Decent Orderly Lynching*, 210. One text identifies the size of the initial posse as consisting of twenty-four men. Gard, *Frontier Justice*, 177.
2. Dimsdale, *Vigilantes of Montana*, 109; see also Milner and O'Connor, *As Big as the West*, 92; Cushman, *Montana*, 118.
3. Sanders and Bertsche, *X. Beidler*, 84–85; Allen, *Decent Orderly Lynching*, 210.
4. Dimsdale, *Vigilantes of Montana*, 110; Langford, *Vigilante Days*, 192; Allen, *Decent Orderly Lynching*, 210.
5. Donovan, *Hanging around the Big Sky*, book 2, 52.
6. Johnson, *Bloody Bozeman*, 97; Barsness, *Gold Camp*, 45; Thrapp, *Vengeance!*, 156; see also Allen, *Decent Orderly Lynching*, 211; Birney, *Vigilantes*, 228–29 (some referring to the word "get" rather than "git.").
7. Fisher and Holmes, *Gold Rushes*, 160.
8. Ibid.
9. Langford, *Vigilante Days*, 192; Gard, *Frontier Justice*, 177.
10. Dimsdale, *Vigilantes of Montana*, 11; Langford, *Vigilante Days*, 192; Allen, *Decent Orderly Lynching*, 210–11; Mather and Boswell, *Hanging the Sheriff*, 81; Barsness, *Gold Camp*, 46; Gard, *Frontier Justice*, 177; Leeson, *History of Montana*, 289. George Brown had been one of the two alibi witnesses that had earlier testified at the trial of George Ives. Milner and O'Connor, *As Big as the West*, 92.
11. Allen, *Decent Orderly Lynching*, 138.
12. Ibid.
13. Langford, *Vigilante Days*, 193; Dimsdale, *Vigilantes of Montana*, 113.
14. Langford, *Vigilante Days*, 194; Allen, *Decent Orderly Lynching*, 211; Birney, *Vigilantes*, 230; Greever, *Bonanza West*, 228; Olsen, "Lawlessness and Vigilantes," 157; Allen, *A Decent Orderly Lynching*, 212–13.
15. Langford, *Vigilante Days*, 194–95; Dimsdale, *Vigilantes of Montana*, 114–15; Sanders, *History of Montana*, 85; Pace, *Golden Gulch*, 35; Burlingame, *Montana Frontier*, 99; Allen, *Decent Orderly Lynching*, 211; Birney, *Vigilantes*, 233; Bartholomew, *Henry Plummer*, 16; Greever, *Bonanza West*, 228; Leeson, *History of Montana*, 289; Hamilton, *From Wilderness to Statehood*, 255; Olsen, "Lawlessness and Vigilantes," 159–60.
16. Mather and Boswell, *Hanging the Sheriff*, 82; Thrapp, *Vengeance!*, 156; Milner and O'Connor, *As Big as the West*, 92; Johnson, *Bloody Bozeman*, 98.
17. Langford, *Vigilante Days*, 195; Allen, *Decent Orderly Lynching*, 213–14; Birney, *Vigilantes*, 233; Thompson, *Tenderfoot in Montana*, 175; Sanders, *History of Montana*, 85; Callaway, *Montana's Righteous Hangmen*, 60; see also Pfouts, *Four Firsts*, 99; Milner and O'Connor, *As Big as the West*, 92; Bartholomew, *Henry Plummer*, 39; Leeson, *History of Montana*, 289.
18. Langford, *Vigilante Days*, 195; Callaway, *Montana's Righteous Hangmen*, 60.
19. Langford, *Vigilante Days*, 195; Thompson, *Tenderfoot in Montana*, 175; Callaway, *Montana's Righteous Hangmen*, 60.
20. Dimsdale, *Vigilantes of Montana*, 21; Langford, *Vigilante Days*, 195; Thompson, *Tenderfoot in Montana*, 175; Sanders, *History of Montana*, 85; Allen, *Decent Orderly Lynching*, 214–15; Birney, *Vigilantes*, 234; Callaway, *Montana's Righteous Hangmen*, 60. "Mexican" Frank Pizanthia's first name is sometimes given as Joe or "Greaser." Billy Terwiliger's surname is sometimes spelled "Terwilliger" in the literature. "Dutch" John Wagner's surname is spelled by Thomas Dimsdale as "Wagoner." Wagner was not, in fact, of Dutch origin, but was from Deutschland (Germany), which prospectors in the region mistook for "Dutch"; Allen, *Decent Orderly Lynching*, 161. Hayes Lyons's first name is spelled by Dimsdale as "Haze." George Lowrie's name is spelled by Dimsdale and Langford as "Lowry." These variations, though minor, suggest the limits of accurate record keeping at the time and perhaps the

limited educations of some of the persons involved. George Lane was nicknamed "Club-foot" as a result of a deformity in his right foot. Allen, *Decent Orderly Lynching*, 167.

21. Langford, *Vigilante Days*, 195; Callaway, *Montana's Righteous Hangmen*, 60.
22. Cf. Langford, *Vigilante Days*, 195, with Dimsdale, *Vigilantes of Montana*, 21, and Sanders, *History of Montana*, 85.
23. Dimsdale, *Vigilantes of Montana*, 115; Allen, *Decent Orderly Lynching*, 215.
24. Cf. Dimsdale, *Vigilantes of Montana*, 115, with Langford, *Vigilante Days*, 195.
25. Donovan, *Hanging around the Big Sky*, book 2, 53.
26. Langford, *Vigilante Days*, 195; Gard, *Frontier Justice*, 171; Bartholomew, *Henry Plummer*, 16; Greever, *Bonanza West*, 228; Leeson, *History of Montana*, 289; Barsness, *Gold Camp*, 28; Donovan, *Hanging around the Big Sky*, book 2, 53.
27. Langford, *Vigilante Days*, 195; Thompson, *Tenderfoot in Montana*, 175.
28. Langford, *Vigilante Days*, 195.
29. Anonymous, *Banditti of the Rocky Mountains*, 123.
30. Burlingame, *Montana Frontier*, 98; Thrapp, *Vengeance!*, 135.
31. Thrapp, *Vengeance!*, 132n1, 171.
32. Allen, *Decent Orderly Lynching*, 116; see also Langford, *Vigilante Days*, 227.
33. Thrapp, *Vengeance!*, 171; Mather and Boswell, *Vigilante Victims*, 42.
34. Thrapp, *Vengeance!*, 131, 171; Mather and Boswell, *Vigilante Victims*, 22.
35. Thrapp, *Vengeance!*, 171.
36. Ibid.
37. Mather and Boswell, *Vigilante Victims*, 135.
38. Langford, *Vigilante Days*, 194; Dimsdale, *Vigilantes of Montana*, 113; Thompson, *Tenderfoot in Montana*, 174; Mather and Boswell, *Hanging the Sheriff*, 81; Barsness, *Gold Camp*, 46.
39. Allen, *Decent Orderly Lynching*, 262.
40. Ibid., 213.
41. Langford, *Vigilante Days*, 195–96; Johnson, *Bloody Bozeman*, 98; Bartholomew, *Henry Plummer*, 18; Barsness, *Gold Camp*, 46; Hamilton, *From Wilderness to Statehood*, 252; Dimsdale, *Vigilantes of Montana*, 116; Bakken, *Invitation to an Execution*, 341; Allen, *Decent Orderly Lynching*, 215 (spelling the ranch name "Laurin's" Ranch); Thompson, *Tenderfoot in Montana*, 174; Callaway, *Montana's Righteous Hangmen*, 60.
42. Donovan, *Hanging around the Big Sky*, book 2, 54.
43. Bartholomew, *Henry Plummer*, 17; Donovan, *Hanging around the Big Sky*, book 2, 55.
44. Bartholomew, *Henry Plummer*, 19.
45. Allen, *Decent Orderly Lynching*, 215; Mather and Boswell, *Hanging the Sheriff*, 83.
46. Dimsdale, *Vigilantes of Montana*, 117; Allen, *Decent Orderly Lynching*, 215; Birney, *Vigilantes*, 236; Johnson, *Bloody Bozeman*, 98; Milner and O'Connor, *As Big as the West*, 92; Gard, *Frontier Justice*, 178; Leeson, *History of Montana*, 289.
47. Allen, *Decent Orderly Lynching*, 152; Gard, *Frontier Justice*, 173; Birney, *Vigilantes*, 167.
48. Allen, *Decent Orderly Lynching*, 219.
49. Dimsdale, *Vigilantes of Montana*, 118; Langford, *Vigilante Days*, 217.
50. Leeson, *History of Montana*, 286.
51. Dimsdale, *Vigilantes of Montana*, 118; Langford, *Vigilante Days*, 217.
52. Langford, *Vigilante Days*, 218.
53. Langford, *Vigilante Days*, 217–18; Allen, *Decent Orderly Lynching*, 220; Cushman, *Montana*, 106–7.
54. Langford, *Vigilante Days*, 218.
55. Dimsdale, *Vigilantes of Montana*, 120–21; Langford, *Vigilante Days*, 219–20; Birney, *Vigilantes*, 245; Allen, *Decent Orderly Lynching*, 220.
56. Dimsdale, *Vigilantes of Montana*, 134; Allen, *Decent Orderly Lynching*, 243.
57. Langford, *Vigilante Days*, 221.

58. Dimsdale, *Vigilantes of Montana*, 121–22; Langford, *Vigilante Days*, 220; Allen, *Decent Orderly Lynching*, 220.
59. Dimsdale, *Vigilantes of Montana*, 217; Allen, *Decent Orderly Lynching*, 162, 220.
60. Allen, *Decent Orderly Lynching*, 220.
61. Ibid.
62. Langford, *Vigilante Days*, 220; Allen, *Decent Orderly Lynching*, 221.
63. Allen, *Decent Orderly Lynching*, 221.
64. Ibid.; Olsen, "Lawlessness and Vigilantes," 161.
65. Dimsdale, *Vigilantes of Montana*, 122–23.
66. Ibid., 133; Langford, *Vigilante Days*, 222.
67. Dimsdale, *Vigilantes of Montana*, 123; Allen, *Decent Orderly Lynching*, 221.
68. Allen, *Decent Orderly Lynching*, 221.
69. Dimsdale, *Vigilantes of Montana*, 123; Langford, *Vigilante Days*, 222; Allen, *Decent Orderly Lynching*, 221.
70. Langford, *Vigilante Days*, 222; Birney, *Vigilantes*, 245; Allen, *Decent Orderly Lynching*, 221.
71. Allen, *Decent Orderly Lynching*, 223.
72. Dimsdale, *Vigilantes of Montana*, 124; Langford, *Vigilante Days*, 222; Allen, *Decent Orderly Lynching*, 223.
73. Dimsdale, *Vigilantes of Montana*, 124; Allen, *Decent Orderly Lynching*, 223.
74. Dimsdale, *Vigilantes of Montana*, 124; Allen, *Decent Orderly Lynching*, 223.
75. Dimsdale, *Vigilantes of Montana*, 124; Allen, *Decent Orderly Lynching*, 223.
76. Dimsdale, *Vigilantes of Montana*, 125; Langford, *Vigilante Days*, 223.
77. Dimsdale, *Vigilantes of Montana*, 126.
78. Ibid.; Langford, *Vigilante Days*, 224.
79. Dimsdale, *Vigilantes of Montana*, 126; Langford, *Vigilante Days*, 224.
80. Allen, *Decent Orderly Lynching*, 221.
81. Callaway, *Montana's Righteous Hangmen*, 45; Allen, *Decent Orderly Lynching*, 195.
82. Allen, *Decent Orderly Lynching*, 221.
83. Ibid., 224.
84. Edgerton was appointed governor of Montana by President Lincoln on June 22, 1984.
85. Allen, *Decent Orderly Lynching*, 224.
86. Leeson, *History of Montana*, 276; Allen, *Decent Orderly Lynching*, 224.
87. Mather and Boswell, *Vigilante Victims*, 33.
88. Allen, *Decent Orderly Lynching*, 224.
89. Burlingame, *Montana Frontier*, 154.
90. Allen, *Decent Orderly Lynching*, 227.
91. Dimsdale, *Vigilantes of Montana*, 127; Sanders and Bertsche, *X. Beidler*, 92; Birney, *Vigilantes*, 249; Allen, *Decent Orderly Lynching*, 227; Thrapp, *Vengeance!*, 158; Olsen, "Lawlessness and Vigilantes," 161.
92. Dimsdale, *Vigilantes of Montana*, 127; Sanders and Bertsche, *X. Beidler*, 92; Birney, *Vigilantes*, 249.
93. Langford, *Vigilante Days*, 225; Sanders and Bertsche, *X. Beidler*, 92 (referring to the saloon as "a hall."); Birney, *Vigilantes*, 249
94. Allen, *Decent Orderly Lynching*, 227–28; Bartholomew, *Henry Plummer*, 46.
95. Sanders and Bertsche, *X. Beidler*, 92.
96. Dimsdale, *Vigilantes of Montana*, 127–28; Langford, *Vigilante Days*, 225; Allen, *Decent Orderly Lynching*, 228.
97. Langford, *Vigilante Days*, 225; Allen, *Decent Orderly Lynching*, 228.
98. Dimsdale, *Vigilantes of Montana*, 128; Langford, *Vigilante Days*, 225; Allen, *Decent Orderly Lynching*, 228; Fisher and Holmes, *Gold Rushes*, 337 (recounting that Plummer had offered to have his hands and feet cut off in exchange for his life).

99. Fisher and Holmes, *Gold Rushes*, 337; Donovan, *Hanging around the Big Sky*, book 2, 58.

100. Dimsdale, *Vigilantes of Montana*, 128; Langford, *Vigilante Days*, 226; Birney, *Vigilantes*, 252; Fisher and Holmes, *Gold Rushes*, 337.

101. Mather and Boswell, *Vigilante Victims*, 52.

102. Ibid.

103. Dimsdale, *Vigilantes of Montana*, 128; Langford, *Vigilante Days*, 226; Bancroft, *History*, 640; Sanders and Bertsche, *X. Beidler*, 93; Allen, *Decent Orderly Lynching*, 228; Thompson, *Tenderfoot in Montana*, 180; Birney, *Vigilantes*, 252.

104. Allen, *Decent Orderly Lynching*, 228.

105. Mather and Boswell, *Vigilante Victims*, 52.

106. Dimsdale, *Vigilantes of Montana*, 128; Langford, *Vigilante Days*, 226.

107. Dimsdale, *Vigilantes of Montana*, 128; Langford, *Vigilante Days*, 226; Birney, *Vigilantes*, 253; Mather and Boswell, *Vigilante Victims*, 54; Allen, *Decent Orderly Lynching*, 228; Gard, *Frontier Justice*, 179.

108. Sanders and Bertsche, *X. Beidler*, 90, 93; see also Thrapp, *Vengeance!*, 158.

109. Sanders and Bertsche, *X. Beidler*, 90, 93.

110. Ibid.; Mather and Boswell, *Vigilante Victims*, 54.

111. Dimsdale, *Vigilantes of Montana*, 128; Langford, *Vigilante Days*, 226; Bancroft, *History*, 640; Allen, *Decent Orderly Lynching*, 228.

112. Langford, *Vigilante Days*, 226; Thompson, *Tenderfoot in Montana*, 180; Allen, *Decent Orderly Lynching*, 228; Thompson, *Tenderfoot in Montana*, 180.

113. Mather and Boswell, *Vigilante Victims*, 54.

114. Dimsdale, *Vigilantes of Montana*, 128. But see also Sanders and Bertsche, *X. Beidler*, 90, 93 (referencing a description of the hanging in the *Helena Independent* wherein Stinson reportedly died without any struggle).

115. Birney, *Vigilantes*, 253–54.

116. Ibid., 254; Bartholomew, *Henry Plummer*, 20.

117. Birney, *Vigilantes*, 254; Bartholomew, *Henry Plummer*, 20.

118. Dimsdale, *Vigilantes of Montana*, 128; Langford, *Vigilante Days*, 226; Cushman, *Montana*, 119; Birney, *Vigilantes*, 254; Bartholomew, *Henry Plummer*, 46; Gard, *Frontier Justice*, 179; Taylor, *Roaring in the Wind*, 215.

119. Langford, *Vigilante Days*, 226; see also Taylor, *Roaring in the Wind*, 215; Dimsdale, *Vigilantes of Montana*, 128; Thompson, *Tenderfoot in Montana*, 181; Cushman, *Montana*, 119; Birney, *Vigilantes*, 254; Allen, *Decent Orderly Lynching*, 228; Caughey, *Their Majesties the Mob*, 84; Gard, *Frontier Justice*, 179; Olsen, "Lawlessness and Vigilantes," 162; Clampett, "Vigilantes," 451. Author Alton Pryor writes that Plummer's last words were, "Give me two hours and a good horse, and I'll bring back my weight in gold" (Pryor, *Lawmen*, 48), but the statement does not appear to be attributed in other historical texts and is inconsistent with Plummer's claim of innocence.

120. Dimsdale, *Vigilantes of Montana*, 128; Langford, *Vigilante Days*, 226; Thompson, *Tenderfoot in Montana*, 181; Gard, *Frontier Justice*, 179.

121. Mather and Boswell, *Vigilante Victims*, 55.

122. M. W. Anderson, "Notes on W. Y. Pemberton's Lecture before the Unity Club at Unitarian Church, May 12, 1868," William Y. Pemberton Papers, 1863–69, Mont. Hist. Soc., SC-629, p. 13.

123. Cushman, *Montana*, 119.

124. Allen, *Decent Orderly Lynching*, 230.

125. Mather and Boswell, *Vigilante Victims*, 57; Allen, *Decent Orderly Lynching*, 230.

126. Dimsdale, *Vigilantes of Montana*, 130–31; Langford, *Vigilante Days*, 228–29; Leeson, *History of Montana*, 292; Toponce, *Reminiscences*, 72; Sanders and Bertsche, *X. Beidler*, 94 (describing Ball's gunshot wound as to the knee and not the hip); Allen, *Decent Orderly*

Lynching, 230–31; Birney, *Vigilantes*, 258; Milner and O'Connor, *As Big as the West*, 94; Gard, *Frontier Justice*, 180; Leeson, *History of Montana*, 292; Thompson, *Tenderfoot in Montana*, 183; Fisher and Holmes, *Gold Rushes*, 334; Bartholomew, *Henry Plummer*, 21; Taylor, *Roaring in the Wind*, 216; Convis, *Frontier Vigilantes*, 18; see also Johnson, *Bloody Bozeman*, 99.

127. Mather and Boswell, *Vigilante Victims*, 57.

128. Dimsdale, *Vigilantes of Montana*, 130–31; Langford, *Vigilante Days*, 229; Sanders and Bertsche, *X. Beidler*, 94; Thompson, *Tenderfoot in Montana*, 183; Allen, *Decent Orderly Lynching*, 230; Birney, *Vigilantes*, 258; Taylor, *Roaring in the Wind*, 216; Gard, *Frontier Justice*, 180; Aaron T. Ford Reminiscences, 1903, Mont. Hist. Soc., SC-702, box 1-1, p. 6.

129. Thompson, *Tenderfoot in Montana*, 183.

130. Ibid.; Allen, *Decent Orderly Lynching*, 231; Mather and Boswell, *Vigilante Victims*, 57 (stating that use of the howitzer was Edgerton's own idea).

131. Langford, *Vigilante Days*, 229; Thompson, *Tenderfoot in Montana*, 183; Allen, *Decent Orderly Lynching*, 231.

132. Dimsdale, *Vigilantes of Montana*, 131.

133. Dimsdale, *Vigilantes of Montana*, 131; Langford, *Vigilante Days*, 229; Mather and Boswell, *Vigilante Victims*, 57; Allen, *Decent Orderly Lynching*, 231; see also Barsness, *Gold Camp*, 47.

134. Dimsdale, *Vigilantes of Montana*, 131–32; Langford, *Vigilante Days*, 229; Mather and Boswell, *Hanging the Sheriff*, 90; Mather and Boswell, *Vigilante Victims*, 57; Allen, *Decent Orderly Lynching*, 231; Taylor, *Roaring in the Wind*, 217.

135. Mather and Boswell, *Vigilante Victims*, 57; Allen, *Decent Orderly Lynching*, 231.

136. Dimsdale, *Vigilantes of Montana*, 132; Langford, *Vigilante Days*, 229; Sanders and Bertsche, *X. Beidler*, 94; Allen, *Decent Orderly Lynching*, 231; Mather and Boswell, *Hanging the Sheriff*, 90; Thrapp, *Vengeance!*, 158; Birney, *Vigilantes*, 260; Taylor, *Roaring in the Wind*, 217; Johnson, *Bloody Bozeman*, 99; Gard, *Frontier Justice*, 180; Fisher and Holmes, *Gold Rushes*, 334; Bartholomew, *Henry Plummer*, 20; Convis, *Frontier Vigilantes*, 18; Hamilton, *From Wilderness to Statehood*, 256; "A Story of 'Dutch John' Told by Martin Barrett," Alice E. and Martin Barret Reminiscences, Mont. Hist. Soc., SC-400, box 1-1, p. 3; see also Barsness, *Gold Camp*, 47; Olsen, "Lawlessness and Vigilantes," 163.

137. Thompson, *Tenderfoot in Montana*, 183–84; Allen, *Decent Orderly Lynching*, 231; Barsness, *Gold Camp*, 47.

138. Allen, *Decent Orderly Lynching*, 221.

139. Ibid., 224.

140. Dimsdale, *Vigilantes of Montana*, 134–35; Thompson, *Tenderfoot in Montana*, 184; Birney, *Vigilantes*, 261.

141. Allen, *Decent Orderly Lynching*, 242.

142. Dimsdale, *Vigilantes of Montana*, 133–34; Langford, *Vigilante Days*, 231; Allen, *Decent Orderly Lynching*, 242.

143. Dimsdale, *Vigilantes of Montana*, 134; Langford, *Vigilante Days*, 231; Leeson, *History of Montana*, 290; Allen, *Decent Orderly Lynching*, 242.

144. Dimsdale, *Vigilantes of Montana*, 134; Birney, *Vigilantes*, 262; Allen, *Decent Orderly Lynching*, 243. Allen identifies the native language as German, not Dutch.

145. Dimsdale, *Vigilantes of Montana*, 134; Langford, *Vigilante Days*, 231; Allen, *Decent Orderly Lynching*, 243.

146. Dimsdale, *Vigilantes of Montana*, 134; Allen, *Decent Orderly Lynching*, 243.

147. Dimsdale, *Vigilantes of Montana*, 134–35; Langford, *Vigilante Days*, 231–32.

148. Dimsdale, *Vigilantes of Montana*, 135.

149. Purple, *Perilous Passage*, 197.

150. Mather and Boswell, *Hanging the Sheriff*, 114.

151. Purple, *Perilous Passage*, 197.

152. Dimsdale, *Vigilantes of Montana*, 135; Allen, *Decent Orderly Lynching*, 243.

153. Dimsdale, *Vigilantes of Montana*, 135; Purple, *Perilous Passage*, 197; Thompson, *Tenderfoot in Montana*, 185–86; Birney, *Vigilantes*, 263; Gard, *Frontier Justice*, 180.

154. "A Story of 'Dutch John' Told by Martin Barrett," Alice E. and Martin Barret Reminiscences, Mont. Hist. Soc., SC-400, box 1-1, p. 2.

155. Ibid.

156. Fisher and Holmes, *Gold Rushes*, 337; Donovan, *Hanging around the Big Sky*, book 2, 66.

157. Donovan, *Hanging around the Big Sky*, book 2, 66. While one text identifies Dr. Glick by the first name of John, the majority of texts refer to him by the first name of Jerome, as used here. Dimsdale, *Vigilantes of Montana*, 101; Leeson, *History of Montana*, 286; Allen, *Decent Orderly Lynching*, 194.

158. Dimsdale, *Vigilantes of Montana*, 39–40.

9

The Bloody Drama Moves from Bannack to Virginia City

Every man for his principles—hurray for Jeff Davis! Let her rip!

—Boone Helm, January 14, 1864

These are rather tight papers, ain't they boys?

–Aleck Carter, January 25, 1864

January 14, 1864, proved to be the deadliest single day in Montana's vigilante history, as the vigilantes captured five members of Sheriff Plummer's gang and hanged them in an unfinished building at the corner of Wallace and Van Buren Streets in Virginia City.[1] Those specific events were set into motion the evening before, when the vigilante's Executive Committee met and decided upon arresting and hanging six road agents who were believed to be in Virginia City at the time, namely, Frank Parish, Boone Helm, Hayes Lyons, Jack Gallagher, George "Clubfoot" Lane, and Bill Hunter.[2]

Early on the morning of January 14, vigilante parties set off to capture each of the wanted men. Frank Parish was arrested first at a store.[3] Although he initially claimed his innocence from wrongdoing, he later admitted his involvement in horse stealing, cattle rustling, and the robbery of a stagecoach between Bannack and Virginia City.[4]

George "Clubfoot" Lane was employed as a harness maker at the Dance & Stuart store.[5] He was arrested next at the store, expressed his innocence, and asked for a minister.[6] He said, "If you hang me, you hang an innocent man!"[7]

Boone Helm was arrested in front of the Virginia Hotel on Wallace Street.[8] Like the others, he claimed his innocence, comparing himself to "the babe

DOI: 10.7330_9780874219203709

unborn."[9] He swore to his innocence on a Bible that had been brought to him for that purpose.[10] Later he admitted to killing men in Missouri and California and escaping from a jail in Oregon, but denied committing any crimes in Idaho Territory, which included present-day Montana.[11] When asked what he knew about the road agents, he implicated Jack Gallagher.[12]

A team of vigilantes had been dispatched to the Arbor Restaurant to arrest Hayes Lyons, who boarded there.[13] When they searched the premises for Lyons they did not find him, but they did find Jack Gallagher in bed with a shotgun and a revolver.[14] Gallagher was at all times the feistiest man of those arrested in Virginia City that day. "What the hell is this all about!" he demanded.[15] He added, "This is a pretty break I'm getting, ain't it?"[16] Gallagher was secured without incident and brought to where the other road agents were being held.[17] There, upon being informed of his death sentence, Gallagher asked who had "peached" on him. He was told that the informer was Erastus "Red" Yeager, whom Gallagher then cursed with a vengeance.[18] Gallagher held a knife and said, "I'll cut my throat before I let you tie me and hang me!"[19] James Williams ordered Gallagher to drop the knife.[20] Boone Helm told Gallagher, "Don't make a fool of yourself, Jack. There's no sense in bein' afraid to die."[21]

Hayes Lyons had fled into the countryside but was found in a miner's cabin on the west side of Alder Gulch.[22] His arrest was made without incident, as he was eating a meal and had taken off his belt and revolver when confronted by the posse that located him.[23] Lyons told his captors that he had been advised to leave the area two or three days before but had not done so because of his fondness for a woman in the town named Cora.[24] Lyons was returned to Virginia City where he denied being a road agent, but he confessed his involvement in murdering D. H. Dillingham and to knowing some of the men who were road agents.[25]

Bill Hunter, who was also to be arrested on January 14, was the only suspect on the day's list that escaped from Virginia City. He hid in an empty barrel that was standing alongside some full barrels in the cellar of a warehouse.[26] In the dead of night, he crept out of the warehouse and crawled away along a drainage ditch, through a line of pickets that surrounded the town, to freedom.[27]

The five men who were arrested were marched under a heavy vigilante guard to an unfinished, roofless building at the corner of Wallace and Van Buren Streets, which would later become the location of Clayton and Hale's Drug Store.[28] Five ropes were thrown over the main support beam along the roof line and secured at the other end to logs in the rear basement; five boxes were placed on the floor beneath the ropes for use as drops.[29] The prisoners were made to stand on their boxes, and their order, from west to east, was Parish, Helm, Gallagher, Lyons, and Lane.[30] The hands of each were pinioned behind their

Figure 9.1. Site of five vigilante executions on January 14, 1864. The photograph was likely taken in 1896. (Courtesy of the Montana Historical Society, image 956-228.)

backs.[31] A large crowd of spectators formed for the event,[32] by some estimates numbering 6,000 to 8,000 persons,[33] though such estimates might appear exaggerated given their proportion to the total population of Alder Gulch. Armed vigilantes formed columns in front of and behind the condemned men, and a few others armed with pistols took positions in the crowd to guard against any potential rescue attempts.[34]

The hangings occurred one at a time but not in linear order.[35] The hangings did not occur simultaneously for fear that the support beam for the roof could not support five drops at the same time.[36] There were no further confessions.[37] Gallagher's last request, which was granted, was for some whiskey,[38] and his noose had to be loosened to allow for him to drink it.[39] William Y. Pemberton later remarked that Gallagher "took a drink as long as a telegraph pole."[40]

George "Clubfoot" Lane spotted his employer, Walter Booth Dance, in the crowd. He yelled to Dance, "I've known you ever since I came to Virginia [City]. Can't you tell these fellows I'm alright?"[41] Dance yelled back, "There'd be no use in it, George. Personally, I know nothing against you. But I've heard the evidence and that is very strong indeed. Nothing I could say would change matters."[42] Lane responded, "Well then, will you pray for me?"[43] Dance answered, "I'll do that very willingly."[44] Lane remained in good spirits to the end, his last words being, "Good-bye, old fellow—I'm gone."[45] He jumped off his box to speed the process and assure a stronger drop.[46]

Jack Gallagher's last moments were spent crying and cursing, saying, "I hope that forked lightning will strike every strangling ___ of you."[47] Gallagher also reportedly said, "I hope Almighty God will curse every one of you, and that I shall meet you all in the lowest pit of Hell."[48] He was hanged in the middle of a further profane utterance.[49]

Boone Helm maintained his composure to the end. He watched the contortions of Gallagher's body on the noose, knowing that he was next to die.[50] Helm's second-to-last words were "Kick away, old fellow. I'll be in Hell with you in a minute."[51] His last utterance was perhaps the most colorful from all of the persons executed by the vigilantes in the 1860s and 1870s. His last words, in solidarity with the cause of the southern Confederacy, were "Every man for his principles—hurray for Jeff Davis! Let her rip!"[52]

Frank Parish was the next to be hanged. He requested that a handkerchief be tied over his face.[53] John X. Beidler adjusted the rope around Parish's neck, which was followed by Parish's drop.[54] After the hanging, a member of the crowd asked Beidler, "Did you not feel for the poor man as you put the rope round his neck?" Beidler answered, in a display of gallows humor, "Yes! I felt for his left ear!"[55]

Hayes Lyons was the last of the five to be hanged.[56] He requested on three occasions that he be permitted to see his paramour, Cora, but the request was denied in each instance in light of the outcome of the earlier Dillingham murder trial.[57] His final request was that his gold watch, and his dying regards, be conveyed to his paramour.[58]

The young girl Mollie Sheehan, upon sharing her life story with her daughter as an adult, recalled seeing the five corpses hanging from their nooses. She was approximately twelve years old at the time.[59] Sheehan recognized one of the corpses as that of George "Clubfoot" Lane, whom she had known from his work at the Dance & Stuart store.[60] She recognized another as that of Jack Gallagher, who had been among the many members of the Sheehan family's wagon train to Montana in the fall of 1863.[61] Mollie was shaken by the sight of the bodies.[62]

John W. Grannis, a miner who had acted as a guard during the executions, wrote in his diary that he went home "being very well satisfied with the day[']s work."[63] The bodies of the five men remained on their nooses for two hours before being cut down.[64] The five were originally buried at Cemetery Hill overlooking Virginia City,[65] but were later exhumed from among the burial plots of law-abiding persons and removed to nearby Boot Hill. Both Cemetery Hill and Boot Hill are on prime real estate overlooking Virginia City and the scenic vistas beyond. The graves of Lane, Parish, Lyons, Gallagher, and Helm are today conspicuously marked for public viewing.

Figure 9.2. The tombstones at Boot Hill in Virginia City for (*left to right*) Frank Parish, Jack Gallagher, Boone Helm, Hayes Lyons, and George "Clubfoot" Lane. (Photo by author.)

The building where these five executions occurred is preserved at its original location at the intersection of Wallace and Van Buren Streets in Virginia City and is open to the public as a walk-in museum of the events that transpired there.

The *Boise News* of Idaho reported on the developments in Montana in glowing terms. The newspaper wrote, "The San Francisco vigilance committee is entirely eclipsed and overshadowed" by the vigilantes of Montana.[66] It further wrote that "[n]o other vigilance committee in the west equal[s] this Montana one in zeal, singlemindedness of purpose, and ridding the camps of the worst criminals."[67]

Five additional outlaws are believed to have fled the territory at about the time of Ives's earlier conviction and execution. They were J. F. Irwin, Johnny Gibbons, N. Barney "Billy" Terwiliger, Charley Reeves, and Augustus "Gad" Moore.[68] Terwiliger and Moore were the only persons of these five on "Red" Yeager's list of road agents, at least as described by Nathaniel Langford.[69]

The five executions were harshly and publicly criticized by some of the attorneys who valued law and procedure. Detractors of vigilante-style executions endeavored to organize a counter society.[70] Members of the Vigilance Committee suppressed the nascent counter society by handing the attorneys in charge written notices banishing them from Idaho Territory, which at that time still included Alder Gulch, and threatening them with death if they were to return.[71] The attorneys who received the threatening notices were H. P. A. Smith and James M. Thurmond, both of whom had unsuccessfully defended George Ives at his trial.[72] Smith was not particularly well liked, having earned the nickname "Shenanigan Smith" from his occasional efforts to help his "rough clients" jump mining claims at the expense of others.[73] The threats behind the banishments of Smith and Thurmond were not taken lightly. When informed of his banishment, Smith struck a pose and melodramatically responded, "Banished from Rome! What's banished but set free from daily contact with the things I loathe?"[74] Smith moved to Gallatin City near the source of the Missouri River and then to Salt Lake City in Utah,[75] but he reestablished a law practice in Helena, Montana, in 1865.[76] Thurmond also relocated to Salt Lake City but, as will be seen, would be heard from again later.[77] Attorneys Alexander Davis and John D. Ritchie, who had also helped defend George Ives, were not selected for banishment. Ritchie would not be banished, perhaps because he was an early member of the Vigilance Committee, according to M. A. Leeson's list. Davis was tactful in his dealings with the Vigilance Committee and was too respected to be banished from the territory.

The most infamous day in Montana's vigilante history came to a close. Night fell, but the work of the Vigilance Committee was not completed as other road agents were still to be captured and executed. A posse of twenty-one vigilantes headed by James Williams left Virginia City in search of Steve Marshland, Cyrus Skinner, Aleck Carter, Johnny Cooper, George Shears, and Bob Zachary.[78]

Steve Marshland, like his counterpart, "Dutch John" Wagner, suffered severe frostbite to his extremities in the days following their unsuccessful robbery of Moody's stagecoach. Marshland's frostbite was worse than Wagner's. The frostbite was so severe that he lay incapacitated in a cabin at Clark's Ranch near the Big Hole River.[79] A vigilante posse led by Thomas Pitt split off from the main posse and had no difficulty apprehending Marshland at the cabin on the evening of January 16, 1864, as Marshland was in no condition to put up any resistance.[80] Both of Marshland's feet were so gangrenous that his boots had to be cut off.[81] His feet were afflicted with scabs, sores, and oozing pus.[82] Marshland tried to explain his gangrene by attributing it to the freezing of his feet while prospecting for gold at the head of Rattlesnake Creek.[83]

When Marshland was accused of having participated in the attempted robbery of Moody's stagecoach and was suspected of having been shot in the chest, he thumped his chest and denied any involvement in the crime.[84] Members of the posse responded by forcibly opening Marshland's shirt, whereupon they found evidence of a bullet wound, which tied him to the attempted robbery.[85] Marshland's incapacitation at the cabin may therefore have been from the gangrenous feet or from the bullet wound he had suffered to the chest or both. In any event, Marshland's name was among those on Yeager's road agent list. As with "Dutch John" Wagner, Marshland's presence in the vicinity of the stagecoach a day prior to the botched robbery, and the existence of a bullet wound on his person, were merely circumstantial pieces of evidence pointing to Marshland's complicity in the crime. Marshland's role in the attempted robbery of Moody's stagecoach had already been confessed by "Dutch John" Wagner. Whatever the strengths or weaknesses of the evidence against Marshland, it was more than enough for the vigilantes to feel comfortable in declaring his guilt.

The posse did not take Marshland to Virginia City for further proceedings before the Executive Committee of the organization. Indeed, Marshland's medical condition was such that it might have been impossible for him to survive a trip to Virginia City in the January cold. The posse chose instead to hang Marshland on the spot,[86] leaning a pole against a corral gate for height and borrowing a box taken from the cabin for a drop.[87] When told that he was to be hanged, Marshland questioned the authority of the vigilante posse, arguing that his hanging could not be legal.[88] Captain Williams responded, "It might not be legal, but it will be fatal."[89] Before his hanging, Marshland confessed to various crimes.[90] He begged that he not be killed, but as with others who had pleaded for their lives, his sentence of death would not be revoked.[91] Whatever human sympathy Marshland's physical condition might have engendered in his captors was not enough to save him from the noose.

Vigilante posses had a practice in some, though not all, cases of leaving road agents' corpses dangling from their nooses for days as a sign to others of the consequences people face for committing crimes. In Marshland's case, his lower extremities were so infected with gangrene that the stench of his corpse attracted dogs and wolves to the area.[92] The posse grew concerned that the wolves posed a risk to their horses.[93] The members of the posse might also have been concerned for their own nasal sensibilities. Accordingly, the posse cut Marshland's body down from his noose and buried him the same night in a grave that they managed to dig into the frozen ground.[94]

The following day Pitt's posse linked up again with the main posse that was headed by James Williams.[95] The vigilantes headed toward Cottonwood in search of Bill Bunton, who, it was believed, had opened a saloon there after winning it gambling with the former owner.[96] Bunton and a friend, Tex Crowell, were forcibly captured at Bunton's home the evening of January 18, 1864.[97] The following morning Bunton threatened that he would "get one of [the vigilantes] yet," and upon being searched, a Derringer was recovered on his person that he had somehow acquired after his arrest the previous evening.[98] Bunton was questioned about his role in the robbery of "Bummer Dan" McFadden's stagecoach, the sharing of proceeds realized from the crime, and about stealing cattle from a Jack Thomas.[99] The questioning was led by James Williams.[100] The evidence against Bunton appears to have been greatly dependent upon information that had been earlier provided by Bunton's cook at the Rattlesnake Ranch, "Red" Yeager. Yeager's confession had been particularly venomous about Bunton's criminal activities.[101] Bunton maintained his innocence at all times.[102] The vigilantes did not find Bunton's claims of innocence persuasive, as they unanimously voted him guilty and sentenced him to be hanged.[103]

A separate interrogation was undertaken of Tex Crowell at another location, resulting in Crowell being set free as a result of insufficient evidence against him.[104] Notably, Crowell's name did not appear on Yeager's list. Crowell ultimately fled the jurisdiction.[105] Dimsdale claims that Crowell was a guilty man who was set free, as evidence was later obtained that Crowell was a thief and highwayman.[106]

Bunton was taken to the nearby corral gate of Louis Demarest, which was made of two upright posts and a crossbeam.[107] He gave his gold watch to his business partner, Cooke.[108] The noose was hung from the crossbeam. Bunton was elevated on top of a board supported by two boxes.[109] He was very particular about the exact location of the knot at his neck.[110] Bunton wanted his neck to be broken and quipped that he wished for "a mountain three hundred feet high to jump off."[111] His last words, reminiscent of George Ives' last words, were "I am innocent."[112] On the count of three, Bunton jumped from the board to assure a good drop and died instantly when he fell.[113] Demarest's wife was so appalled that their corral posts had been used for the execution that she made her husband cut the posts down so that they could never again be used for any executions.[114]

Williams's vigilante posse pressed on to Hell Gate in the Bitter Root Valley, where it was believed that more road agents could be found.[115] The ninety-mile trip was made slower because of the snow.[116] By January 24, 1864, as the vigilante posse neared Hell Gate, Captain Williams divided his men, sending one contingent along with Clark Fork River to cut off an escape route through the mountain passes of the Mullan Road, while sending the second contingent directly into Hell Gate.[117] A scout, sent ahead into Hell Gate to identify locations that would be raided, reported back his findings.[118] The posse then rode into Hell Gate on a tight run and, after mistaking a house and correcting the error, found Cyrus Skinner and his wife at Skinner's saloon.[119] Skinner was ordered to throw up his hands, whereupon he was arrested, bound with rope, and taken down the road for a trial at the general store owned by C. P. Higgins and Frank Worden.[120]

Vigilantes then entered the Miller house next door, where they found Aleck Carter lying in a bed, half drunk.[121] Dan Harding was the vigilante who opened the door to the house and said, "Aleck, is that you?" When Carter replied "Yes," he saw that several guns were pointed at him.[122] Carter came to his senses and remarked, "These are rather tight papers, ain't they, boys?"[123] Upon further conversation that included the identities of the men already hanged by the vigilantes, Carter noted, "Not an innocent man hung yet."[124]

Carter was bound and taken to the Higgins and Worden store to be tried with Skinner.[125] During the trial, Skinner's wife, Nellie Skinner, tried to interfere with the process and was taken under guard back to Skinner's saloon, where Johnny Cooper was discovered in a back room suffering from three gunshots that he had received the previous day during a drunken quarrel with Aleck Carter.[126] Cooper was Skinner's nephew.[127] Cooper was brought to the Higgins and Worden store for interrogation but was tried separately from Skinner and Carter.[128]

The Skinner and Carter trial took three hours.[129] Skinner confessed to no crimes.[130] Carter was more compliant. He confessed that he had been an accessory after the fact to the murder of Nicholas Tiebolt, taking one of the stolen mules to the Irwin Ranch at Big Hole.[131] Both men were unanimously found guilty, sentenced to death, and taken to the corral behind the Higgins and Worden store for torchlight hangings shortly after midnight.[132] Two poles were placed over the corral fence and dry goods boxes were arranged for drops.[133] During his escort to the corral, Skinner ran off from his guard, shouting, "Shoot! Shoot!"[134] He was secured without bloodshed and then made a second effort to escape while standing upon the dry goods box before his execution.[135] The rope was adjusted around Skinner's neck as he struggled, and he was then told, "You may jump now, as soon as you please."[136] Carter was calmer and was granted a last wish of smoking a pipe while standing atop his dry goods box.[137] He denied to the end being the murderer of Nicholas Tiebolt.[138] The last words of both men were "I am innocent,"[139] similar to the last words of George Ives and Bill Bunton at their own hangings. Both Skinner and Carter died instantly upon their drops.[140]

Johnny Cooper denied having committed any robberies.[141] He was questioned during his trial about a murder in Idaho.[142] Evidence at his trial included the presence of his name upon Yeager's list and the testimonies of Hell Gate residents from whom he had allegedly stolen property, including a French fur trader named Brown whose daughter Cooper intended to marry.[143] Authors Mather and Boswell suggest that the fur trader did not much like Cooper for taking his best horses without permission and for repeatedly borrowing money.[144] Evidence was also discussed of Cooper's attempted robberies of C. A. Broadwater in the Deer Lodge Valley and of William Babcock near Virginia City.[145] Cooper was convicted and, because of his recently inflicted bullet wounds, was transported to the gallows upon a sleigh.[146] He was given time to write a letter to his parents in New York State and to enjoy a final smoke of a pipe before being hanged from the same dry goods box used earlier in the morning by his uncle, Cyrus Skinner.[147]

While Skinner, Carter, and Cooper were being detained, a team of eight vigilantes headed by Thomas Pitt rode from Hell Gate to the ranch of Barney "Baron" O'Keefe on a tip that a traveler, perhaps Bob Zachary, was staying there.[148] Zachary was wanted for the robbery of Leroy Southmayd, among other things.[149] Upon approach, O'Keefe readily admitted that Zachary was staying with him.[150] Zachary was found in a bedroom with a pistol and a knife but was forcibly secured and taken to Hell Gate.[151]

O'Keefe incidentally mentioned that a stranger had also stopped at Hezekiah Van Dorn's cabin in the Bitter Root Valley, and his description of that man seemed to match that of George Shears.[152] Three vigilantes therefore split off from Pitt's group and found Shears in an inner room of the cabin, knife in hand.[153] Shears offered no resistance, willingly identified for his captors the horses in the corral that he had recently stolen, confessed his guilt and said, "I knew that I should have to go up, some time; but I thought I could run another season."[154] When informed by the vigilantes that he would be hanged, Shears was indifferent to his fate, cool and complaisant.[155] He was taken to a nearby barn where a rope was thrown over a beam and he was requested to climb a ladder for height.[156] Shears climbed the ladder and, with a high degree of gentility under the circumstances, said, "Gentlemen, I am not used to this business, never having been hung before. Shall I jump off or slide off?"[157] When told that he should jump, Shears said, "All right. Good bye," and he jumped.[158] Both Dimsdale and Langford used remarkably similar descriptions of Shears's execution, suggesting that Langford borrowed language from Dimsdale in this instance. They both even wrote that the "drop was long and the rope tender."[159]

Meanwhile, Zachary's captors delivered him to the main vigilante group at Hell Gate between 7:00 and 8:00 a.m. on January 25, 1864.[160] Zachary made no confession.[161] He was declared guilty and sentenced to be hanged in the same corral where Skinner, Carter, and Cooper had been executed.[162] Zachary dictated a letter to his mother and warned his brother and sister to avoid whiskey, card playing, and bad company.[163] Zachary's last moments were spent praying that God would forgive the vigilantes for what they were doing, as it was the only way of ridding the territory of road agents.[164] With his death, the vigilantes thought that their work at Hell Gate was completed, and the entire posse prepared for its return to Virginia City.

As the posse left Hell Gate, it received word that "Whiskey Bill" Graves was at Fort Owen in the Bitteroot Valley.[165] Graves had previously vowed to shoot any vigilante who might come near him.[166] A company of three vigilantes separated from the main group, arrested Graves at the fort before he could offer any resistance, and took him to a tree at the present-day Lee Metcalf Wildlife Refuge to be hanged.[167] The capture might have been made easier by the fact that Graves was suffering from partial "snow blindness."[168] Snow blindness, also known as photokeratitis, is a burning of the cornea from ultraviolet UVB rays, which occurs when the person has prolonged exposure to highly reflective snow. To provide a drop for his hanging, Graves was seated upon a horse behind a rider, and when the animal bounded forward, Graves's neck was immediately broken from the fall.[169]

Williams's posse returned to Alder Gulch, and a separate posse was then organized to seek the only remaining road agent in the region whose name was on Yeager's list: Bill Hunter.[170]

Hunter had escaped arrest in Virginia City on the day that George "Clubfoot" Lane, Frank Parish, Boone Helm, Hayes Lyons, and Jack Gallagher were jointly hanged, January 14, 1864. He headed into the Madison Valley and sustained frostbite to both of his feet, making travel difficult.[171] Hunter survived by receiving charity from settlers along the Gallatin River.[172] On February 2, 1864, he reached Wesley P. Emery's cabin on the Gallatin River where a friend, Dennis Riordan, was staying.[173] Emery's cabin provided Hunter with shelter from a severe snowstorm.[174] He advised the occupants of the cabin that the vigilantes were pursuing him and that, while he knew the members of the criminal gang who had been captured and hanged, he was personally innocent of all wrongdoing except for having once carried a message on the gang's behalf.[175]

Events that transpired at the cabin are recounted in the reminiscences of Wesley P. Emery, which are archived at the Montana Historical Society and which, assuming their accuracy, provide a firsthand account from the cabin owner himself.[176] Hunter may have been seen approaching the cabin, as thirteen vigilantes who had braved the snowstorm surrounded the cabin the next morning, on February 3, 1864.[177] The vigilante posse was headed by Sheriff Adriel Davis of Junction City and included John Lott, John Bagg, Richard McLaren, and Charles Leyendecker.[178] The posse had spent a night during the search at the ranch of Joseph Slade, who will be seen later in this narrative.[179]

At the cabin, Emery answered their knock on the door unaware that guns were drawn on him.[180] Emery was asked whether he had seen a man in his midtwenties with a moustache, wearing a soldier's overcoat and pants fixed with buckskin.[181] The description matched that of Hunter, though Hunter had shaved his moustache and was showing only stubble.[182] Emery asked if the group was looking for a man named Hunter and was informed by the group's leader that they were.[183] Emery informed the group that Hunter was inside the cabin with a gun and did not intend to be taken alive.[184] Emery invited all thirteen vigilantes into the ten-by-twelve-foot cabin, while Hunter was under bedsheets in a bunk pretending to be asleep.[185] Adriel B. Davis removed the cover from Hunter's face and said, "Hello, Bill, wake up. I want to talk to you."[186] Hunter observed that he was the object of six aimed shotguns.[187] Upon being asked if he was armed, Hunter surrendered a revolver that he had kept under the bedclothes.[188] Hunter said, "If you take me to Virginia City for a fair trial I'll go, but if not, I won't go."[189] Hunter was assured by Davis that he would receive a fair trial.[190]

Hunter left Emery's cabin with the vigilante posse, protesting his innocence and trusting that he would receive a trial in Virginia City.[191] A total of thirteen horses and fourteen men were seen leaving the cabin—twelve vigilantes on horses, Hunter on a horse, and one man on foot, headed for an open snow-covered prairie two miles away adorned with cottonwood and willow trees around the perimeter.[192] Along the way, a vote was taken to administer vigilante punishment summarily.[193] According to Dimsdale, the man who had assured Hunter a fair trial in Virginia City—presumably a reference to Adriel Davis—protested the group's decision to perform the hanging.[194] In any event, a rope was thrown over a bough of one of the cottonwood trees and Hunter was hanged by being hoisted off the ground.[195] As he was dying, Hunter instinctively reached for his empty holster and used his trigger finger to fire imaginary bullets.[196] Thirteen men left the site of the cottonwood, each on his own horse.[197] The next day, Hunter's lifeless body was found hanging on the cottonwood tree, from a horizontal limb twelve feet off the ground.[198] The note pinned to the corpse said, "Bill Hunter, executed to satisfy the strict requirements of justice."[199]

James Henry Marley, a miner who lived in Alder Gulch for three years, noted in his diary the hangings of Sheriff Plummer and others in Bannack, five men in Virginia City, and additional hangings at Rattlesnake, Deer Lodge, and elsewhere.[200] He wrote that "such wholesale hangings [ought] to rid the country of these desperados who have rendered traveling dangerous. Weather warm and pleasant."[201]

The death of Bill Hunter marked the end of the executions of the members of the road agent syndicate who were initially known and captured. The further executions that would occur in Alder Gulch in 1864 would be responses to ad hoc crimes that did not involve crimes against travelers.

On February 17, 1864, there was hanging in Virginia City of a nineteen-year-old boy, name unknown, who had shot a man in the bowels while in a tavern.[202]

Three weeks later, on March 10, 1864, J. A. Slade was hanged by vigilantes in Virginia City. The circumstances of Slade's hanging are so unique that they are dealt with separately in a later chapter of this narrative.

James Brady was hanged in Nevada City on June 15, 1864, after a vigilante trial for having shot a personal enemy named Thomas Murphy, even though Murphy survived the wound.[203]

Jem Kelly was hanged from a balm of Gilead tree at the Snake River Ferry on September 5, 1864, for his alleged involvement in a series of petty theft crimes.[204] Jem Kelly was the first person hanged by the Montana vigilantes acting outside of Montana Territory, but would not be the last.

John "The Hat" Dolan was hanged in daylight before a large crowd on September 17, 1864, for having stolen $700 from a roommate. Many in the Nevada City crowd objected to Dolan's hanging as an excessive punishment for a mere property crime between roommates. James Williams felt the need to deliver a speech to the crowd at the site of the hanging, warning it to make no attempt to rescue the prisoner and declaring that the death sentence would be carried out regardless of the public's opposition. The vigilantes underscored the point by aiming their weapons at the crowd, the very commonfolk that the organization was originally formed to protect. Members of the crowd, fearing that they were about to be fired upon, turned and ran from the site in panic, upending a mule-drawn cart in the process and causing minor injuries. During the commotion, Dolan was hanged. To mollify the remaining or returning crowd, a prominent vigilante, who the *Montana Post* did not identify by name, delivered a further speech that such stern punishments were necessary to assure the security of society. If a modern-day public opinion poll were taken of the residents of Alder Gulch the day after Dolan's hanging, the Vigilance Committee would probably not have fared well.[205]

None of these crimes involving J. A. Slade, Jem Kelly, or John "The Hat" Dolan necessarily involved gold or the transportation of gold wealth, and none involved any organized criminal syndicate. The vigilante hangings of men like the nineteen-year-old boy, Slade, Brady, Kelly, and Dolan are significant, as they represented an expansion of the mission of the Vigilance Committee into the remedying of "social ills" such as unruly behavior, fights in taverns, drunken shootouts, and minor one-on-one thefts.

The spate of hangings at Alder Gulch in 1864 ran its course. The trial in absentia of J. C. Rawley and his subsequent capture and execution in Bannack on October 31, 1864, as will be described in a later chapter of this narrative, closed out the deadliest single year for vigilante executions in Montana history. Many of Plummer's road agent gang had been killed. Of the specific names on Yeager's infamous list of road agents, only two individuals—Augustus "Gad" Moore and Billy Terwiliger—avoided capture and death by successfully fleeing Montana Territory.[206] Other individuals whose names were not on Yeager's list, but who also fled the territory to avoid capture, included William Mitchell, Harvey Meade, "Rattlesnake Dick," "Cherokee Bob," Tex Crowell (after having been earlier captured and released), Jeff Perkins, Samuel Bunton, "Irwin of Big Hole,"[207] William Moore, and Charles Reeves.[208] Independent of Plummer's organization, H. G. Sessions and H. D. Moyer were specifically banished from the territory in 1864 for having circulated "bogus gold dust."[209] Still other persons who might have been inclined to engage in criminal activities were deterred from doing so for fear of receiving the ultimate penalty.

Less noted by history are the instances of banishing persons from the territory, far short of exacting the ultimate punishment of death. The concept of banishment was not universally approved, as there was a saying that "if a man ain't fit to live here after doing a crime, he ain't fit to live nowhere."[210] Lew Callaway nevertheless wrote that "[a] large number of men were banished from the Territory; Nobody knows how many."[211] Alexander Toponce was quoted as saying, "I don't think they [the vigilantes] made any mistake in hanging anybody. The only mistake they made was that about fifty percent of those whom they merely banished should have been hung instead, as quite a number of these men were finally hung."[212]

Conditions were ripe for territorial government to begin to take root. Much of the criminal element was dead or scattered. Significantly, Chief Judge Hezekiah Hosmer arrived in the territory and convened his first grand jury on December 5, 1864, and was determined to wrest full law enforcement responsibility from the Vigilance Committee.

Panning for Nuggets

The banishment of attorneys H. P. A. Smith and James M. Thurmond from Montana Territory, upon veiled threats of death, damaged not only the attorneys' law practices but also their personal reputations. Thurmond was embittered by his banishment and is the only person to have commenced a civil lawsuit arising out of his treatment by Alder Gulch vigilantes. In Utah Thurmond managed to obtain jurisdiction over an Alder Gulch vigilante named Jeremiah M. Fox for a lawsuit that sought damages from Fox for helping orchestrate his banishment and for defaming his character. The suit caused considerable consternation among the vigilantes in Alder Gulch. A hotly contested jury trial was conducted in Salt Lake City, resulting in a verdict of 11 to 1 in Thurmond's favor and an award of damages against Fox for the sum of approximately $3,000. Since the verdict was not unanimous, the presiding judge ordered a second trial, which resulted in a unanimous verdict in Thurmond's favor and a damages award of $8,000.[213]

Thurmond should have known that he would never be permitted to collect a dime of his jury award. The vigilantes, who, by definition, operated outside of legitimate judicial channels, refused to respect the civil judgment and would not allow Thurmond to collect the damages awarded to him by the Salt Lake City jury. Thurmond was *indicted in Montana for crimes for which he would assuredly be hanged, and a request was drawn up for his extradition from Utah—but Thurmond was also informed that he could remain safely in Utah if he "drie[d] up" his $8,000 damages award.*[214] *Dimsdale wrote of the suit that "[a]fter some peculiar developments of justice in Utah, [Thurmond] judiciously withdrew all proceedings and gave a receipt in full of all past and future claims on the Vigilance Committee."*[215] *According to Nathaniel Langford, Thurmond waived the collection of damages and released the vigilantes from future civil liability, as a result of "intimidation" that had been directed against him. The* Montana Post *blamed the Utah trial court for miscarrying justice and triumphantly described the post-trial settlement as one that would discourage further litigation against members of the Vigilance Committee.*[216] *Nothing ever came of Thurmond's indictment in Montana, in obvious exchange for the agreement that released all vigilantes, including Jeremiah M. Fox, from the payment of monetary damages. It appears that Thurmond valued his life more than he valued the award of $8,000.*

Notes

1. Dimsdale, *Vigilantes of Montana*, 142; Langford, *Vigilante Days*, 238; Allen, *Decent Orderly Lynching*, 246.
2. Dimsdale, *Vigilantes of Montana*, 136; Langford, *Vigilante Days*, 234; Gard, *Frontier Justice*, 180; Aaron T. Ford Reminiscences, 1903, Mont. Hist. Soc., SC-702, box 1-1, p. 6.
3. Dimsdale, *Vigilantes of Montana*, 137; Langford, *Vigilante Days*, 234.
4. Dimsdale, *Vigilantes of Montana*, 137–38; Langford, *Vigilante Days*, 234.
5. M. W. Anderson, "Notes on W. Y. Pemberton's Lecture before the Unity Club at Unitarian Church, May 12, 1868," William Y. Pemberton Papers, 1863–69, Mont. Hist. Soc., SC-629, p. 15.
6. Dimsdale, *Vigilantes of Montana*, 138; Langford, *Vigilante Days*, 234–35; Leeson, *History of Montana*, 297; Gard, *Frontier Justice*, 180–81.
7. Birney, *Vigilantes*, 268.
8. Dimsdale, *Vigilantes of Montana*, 138; Langford, *Vigilante Days*, 235; Leeson, *History of Montana*, 297; Thrapp, *Vengeance!*, 163.
9. Dimsdale, *Vigilantes of Montana*, 138; Langford, *Vigilante Days*, 235. Birney quotes the statement, identical in meaning, as "I am as innocent as a baby." Birney, *Vigilantes*, 292.
10. Dimsdale, *Vigilantes of Montana*, 138–39; Langford, *Vigilante Days*, 235; Birney, *Vigilantes*, 292; Thrapp, *Vengeance!*, 164.
11. Dimsdale, *Vigilantes of Montana*, 139; Langford, *Vigilante Days*, 236; Gard, *Frontier Justice*, 181.
12. Dimsdale, *Vigilantes of Montana*, 139; Langford, *Vigilante Days*, 236.
13. Dimsdale, *Vigilantes of Montana*, 139; Langford, *Vigilante Days*, 236.
14. Dimsdale, *Vigilantes of Montana*, 139.
15. Birney, *Vigilantes*, 270.
16. Ibid.
17. Dimsdale, *Vigilantes of Montana*, 141; Leeson, *History of Montana*, 297.
18. Dimsdale, *Vigilantes of Montana*, 139; Langford, *Vigilante Days*, 236.
19. Birney, *Vigilantes*, 271.
20. Ibid., 272.

21. Ibid.

22. Dimsdale, *Vigilantes of Montana*, 140; Langford, *Vigilante Days*, 236–37; Leeson, *History of Montana*, 297.

23. Dimsdale, *Vigilantes of Montana*, 140; Langford, *Vigilante Days*, 237.

24. Dimsdale, *Vigilantes of Montana*, 140; Langford, *Vigilante Days*, 237; Birney, *Vigilantes*, 271; Gard, *Frontier Justice*, 181.

25. Dimsdale, *Vigilantes of Montana*, 141; Langford, *Vigilante Days*, 237.

26. Sanders and Bertsche, *X. Beidler*, 89.

27. Dimsdale, *Vigilantes of Montana*, 136; Thompson, *Tenderfoot in Montana*, 186; Sanders and Bertsche, *X. Beidler*, 90; Barsness, *Gold Camp*, 48; Donovan, *Hanging around the Big Sky*, book 2, 103; Wesley P. Emery Reminiscences, 1907, Mont. Hist. Soc., SC-668, folder 1-1, p. 6.

28. Dimsdale, *Vigilantes of Montana*, 142; Leeson, *History of Montana*, 297; Thrapp, *Vengeance!*, 165; Barsness, *Gold Camp*, 48; Gard, *Frontier Justice*, 181.

29. Dimsdale, *Vigilantes of Montana*, 142; Langford, *Vigilante Days*, 238; Thrapp, *Vengeance!*, 165, 167; Gard, *Frontier Justice*, 181; Aaron T. Ford Reminiscences, 1903, Mont. Hist. Soc., SC-702, box 1-1, p. 6.

30. Dimsdale, *Vigilantes of Montana*, 143; Langford, *Vigilante Days*, 240.

31. Gard, *Frontier Justice*, 181.

32. Dimsdale, *Vigilantes of Montana*, 142; Gard, *Frontier Justice*, 181.

33. Thrapp, *Vengeance!*, 165.

34. Dimsdale, *Vigilantes of Montana*, 142; Langford, *Vigilante Days*, 238.

35. Dimsdale, *Vigilantes of Montana*, 143; Langford, *Vigilante Days*, 241; Thompson, *Tenderfoot in Montana*, 186.

36. Birney, *Vigilantes*, 275; Donovan, *Hanging around the Big Sky*, book 2, 77.

37. Langford, *Vigilante Days*, 238.

38. Dimsdale, *Vigilantes of Montana*, 143; Langford, *Vigilante Days*, 240; Thompson, *Tenderfoot in Montana*, 187; Thrapp, *Vengeance!*, 168; Gard, *Frontier Justice*, 181; Aaron T. Ford Reminiscences, 1903, Mont. Hist. Soc., SC-702, box 1-1, p. 6.

39. Langford, *Vigilante Days*, 240.

40. Anderson, "Notes on W. Y. Pemberton's Lecture," 14.

41. Birney, *Vigilantes*, 273.

42. Ibid.

43. Ibid.

44. Ibid.

45. Dimsdale, *Vigilantes of Montana*, 144; Gard, *Frontier Justice*, 181. Thompson reports Lane's last words as "Well good bye, old fellow, I'm off"; Thompson, *Tenderfoot in Montana*, 186. Tom Donovan recounts that Lane's rope stretched just enough for the toes of his good foot to reach the floor and that he spent several minutes strangling from the rope while trying to raise himself up on his toes. The manner of Lane's death, according to Donovan, is what prompted cursing and anger from the other condemned men. Donovan, *Hanging around the Big Sky*, book 2, 77. However, the version of Lane's death involving strangulation is not found in other texts.

46. Dimsdale, *Vigilantes of Montana*, 144; Barsness, *Gold Camp*, 48–49; Thompson, *Tenderfoot in Montana*, 186; Birney, *Vigilantes*, 276; Gard, *Frontier Justice*, 181.

47. Dimsdale, *Vigilantes of Montana*, 144; Thompson, *Tenderfoot in Montana*, 187; Birney, *Vigilantes*, 276; Bartholomew, *Henry Plummer*, 26; Thrapp, *Vengeance!*, 168; Gard, *Frontier Justice*, 181.

48. Langford, *Vigilante Days*, 240.

49. Ibid., 241; Anderson, "Notes on W. Y. Pemberton's Lecture," 14.

50. Thompson, *Tenderfoot in Montana*, 187; Gard, *Frontier Justice*, 181–82.

51. Dimsdale, *Vigilantes of Montana*, 144; Langford, *Vigilante Days*, 241; Thompson, *Tenderfoot in Montana*, 187; Thrapp, *Vengeance!*, 168; Bartholomew, *Henry Plummer*, 26; Gard, *Frontier Justice*, 182; Aaron T. Ford Reminiscences, 1903, Mont. Hist. Soc., SC-702, box 1-1, p. 6.

52. Dimsdale, *Vigilantes of Montana*, 144; Langford, *Vigilante Days*, 241; Barsness, *Gold Camp*, 49; Birney, *Vigilantes*, 276; Thompson, *Tenderfoot in Montana*, 187; Thrapp, *Vengeance!*, 199; Allen, *Decent Orderly Lynching*, 247; Milner and O'Connor, *As Big as the West*, 95; Bartholomew, *Henry Plummer*, 26; Convis, *Frontier Vigilantes*, 20; Donovan, *Hanging around the Big Sky*, book 2, 78; Anderson, "Notes on W. Y. Pemberton's Lecture," 14; undated note on Pemberton's stationery, William Y. Pemberton Papers, Mont. Hist. Soc., SC-629, folder 1-1; Aaron T. Ford Reminiscences, 1903, Mont. Hist. Soc., SC-702, box 1-1, p. 6.

53. Dimsdale, *Vigilantes of Montana*, 144: Bartholomew, *Henry Plummer*, 26; Gard, *Frontier Justice*, 182; Donovan, *Hanging around the Big Sky*, book 2, 78; Aaron T. Ford Reminiscences, 1903, Mont. Hist. Soc., SC-702, box 1-1, p. 6.

54. Dimsdale, *Vigilantes of Montana*, 144.

55. Ibid.; Langford, *Vigilante Days*, 241–42; Birney, *Vigilantes*, 276; Thrapp, *Vengeance!*, 199; Bartholomew, *Henry Plummer*, 26–27; Gard, *Frontier Justice*, 182; Convis, *Frontier Vigilantes*, 23; Donovan, *Hanging around the Big Sky*, book 2, 84–85.

56. Aaron T. Ford Reminiscences, 1903, Mont. Hist. Soc., SC-702, box 1-1, p. 6.

57. Dimsdale, *Vigilantes of Montana*, 143; Langford, *Vigilante Days*, 239; Birney, *Vigilantes*, 273–74; Gard, *Frontier Justice*, 181.

58. Dimsdale, *Vigilantes of Montana*, 144; Langford, *Vigilante Days*, 241; Thompson, *Tenderfoot in Montana*, 187; Gard, *Frontier Justice*, 182.

59. Sheehan was born in 1852. Her later married name was Mary "Mollie" Ronan. Baumler, *Girl from the Gulches*, ix.

60. Baumler, *Girl from the Gulches*, 39; Johnson, *Bloody Bozeman*, 103–4.

61. Baumler, *Girl from the Gulches*, 39; Johnson, *Bloody Bozeman*, 87–88.

62. Johnson, *Bloody Bozeman*, 104.

63. John W. Grannis Diaries, 1863–78, Mont. Hist. Soc., SC-301, folder 4-4.

64. Dimsdale, *Vigilantes of Montana*, 145; Barsness, *Gold Camp*, 49.

65. Dimsdale, *Vigilantes of Montana*, 145.

66. Fisher and Holmes, *Gold Rushes*, 335.

67. Ibid.

68. Mather and Boswell, "Epilogue"; Mather and Boswell, *Vigilante Victims*, 152–53.

69. Langford, *Vigilante Days*, 195.

70. Dimsdale, *Vigilantes of Montana*, 145.

71. Ibid.; Bancroft, *History*, 641. The region was still part of Idaho, as Montana Territory would not be formed until the following May.

72. Toponce, *Reminiscences*, 72; Allen, *Decent Orderly Lynching*, 250.

73. "Life and History of A. T. Ford," Aaron T. Ford Reminiscences, 1903, Mont. Hist. Soc., SC-702, folder 1-1, p. 13. Mining claims generated work for attorneys, who often took a share of the ground as their compensation in lieu of money payments. Bakken, *Mining Law of 1872*, 74–75. Indeed, of the twenty-three attorneys that Judge Hezekiah Hosmer swore into the Montana bar on October 5, 1864, nineteen held mineral claims in the territory. Safford, *Mechanics of Optimism*, 15.

74. Mather and Boswell, "Epilogue"; Mather and Boswell, *Vigilante Victims*, 151.

75. "Trial and Execution of George Ives," Wilbur Fisk Sanders Papers, Mont. Hist. Soc., MC-53, box 5, folder 5-1, p. 8; Allen, *Decent Orderly Lynching*, 268.

76. Mather and Boswell, "Epilogue."

77. Langford, *Vigilante Days*, 254; Allen, *Decent Orderly Lynching*, 268.

78. Thompson, *Tenderfoot in Montana*, 188.
79. Dimsdale, *Vigilantes of Montana*, 147; Langford, *Vigilante Days*, 243; Leeson, *History of Montana*, 290; Thompson, *Tenderfoot in Montana*, 188; Thrapp, *Vengeance!*, 173; Allen, *Decent Orderly Lynching*, 259.
80. Langford, *Vigilante Days*, 243; Allen, *Decent Orderly Lynching*, 259; Thompson, *Tenderfoot in Montana*, 189.
81. Cushman, *Montana*, 107.
82. Donovan, *Hanging around the Big Sky*, book 2, 87.
83. Ibid.
84. Ibid.
85. Dimsdale, *Vigilantes of Montana*, 148; Langford, *Vigilante Days*, 243; Allen, *Decent Orderly Lynching*, 259; Donovan, *Hanging around the Big Sky*, book 2, 87.
86. Allen, *Decent Orderly Lynching*, 259; Thrapp, *Vengeance!*, 173; Bartholomew, *Henry Plummer*, 27.
87. Dimsdale, *Vigilantes of Montana*, 148; Langford, *Vigilante Days*, 244; Gard, *Frontier Justice*, 182; Thompson, *Tenderfoot in Montana*, 189; Donovan, *Hanging around the Big Sky*, book 2, 88.
88. Donovan, *Hanging around the Big Sky*, book 2, 87.
89. Ibid.
90. Dimsdale, *Vigilantes of Montana*, 148; Langford, *Vigilante Days*, 244; Thrapp, *Vengeance!*, 173; Gard, *Frontier Justice*, 182; Donovan, *Hanging around the Big Sky*, book 2, 88.
91. Dimsdale, *Vigilantes of Montana*, 148.
92. Ibid.; Langford, *Vigilante Days*, 244; Cushman, *Montana*, 107; Allen, *Decent Orderly Lynching*, 259; Donovan, *Hanging around the Big Sky*, book 2, 88.
93. Langford, *Vigilante Days*, 244.
94. Ibid.; Allen, *Decent Orderly Lynching*, 259; Donovan, *Hanging around the Big Sky*, book 2, 88.
95. Langford, *Vigilante Days*, 244; Allen, *Decent Orderly Lynching*, 260.
96. Allen, *Decent Orderly Lynching*, 261; Dimsdale, *Vigilantes of Montana*, 150; Callaway, *Montana's Righteous Hangmen*, 66.
97. Leeson, *History of Montana*, 297.
98. Dimsdale, *Vigilantes of Montana*, 149–50; Langford, *Vigilante Days*, 245.
99. Dimsdale, *Vigilantes of Montana*, 149–50; Allen, *Decent Orderly Lynching*, 261; Leeson, *History of Montana*, 144 and 298.
100. Allen, *Decent Orderly Lynching*, 261.
101. Dimsdale, *Vigilantes of Montana*, 115.
102. Ibid., 150; Langford, *Vigilante Days*, 245; Leeson, *History of Montana*, 298; Allen, *Decent Orderly Lynching*, 261.
103. Dimsdale, *Vigilantes of Montana*, 150; Leeson, *History of Montana*, 298; Allen, *Decent Orderly Lynching*, 261.
104. Dimsdale, *Vigilantes of Montana*, 150; Leeson, *History of Montana*, 298; Callaway, *Montana's Righteous Hangmen*, 66; Allen, *Decent Orderly Lynching*, 262; Thompson, *Tenderfoot in Montana*, 189.
105. Leeson, *History of Montana*, 266.
106. Dimsdale, *Vigilantes of Montana*, 150; see also Callaway, *Montana's Righteous Hangmen*, 66; Allen, *Decent Orderly Lynching*, 262.
107. Dimsdale, *Vigilantes of Montana*, 150; Bartholomew, *Henry Plummer*, 27; Allen, *Decent Orderly Lynching*, 261; Gard, *Frontier Justice*, 182.
108. Leeson, *History of Montana*, 298.
109. Dimsdale, *Vigilantes of Montana*, 150; Bartholomew, *Henry Plummer*, 27.
110. Bartholomew, *Henry Plummer*, 27.

111. Dimsdale, *Vigilantes of Montana*, 151; Langford, *Vigilante Days*, 245; Leeson, *History of Montana*, 298; Callaway, *Montana's Righteous Hangmen*, 66; Thrapp, *Vengeance!*, 174; Thompson, *Tenderfoot in Montana*, 189.

112. Dimsdale, *Vigilantes of Montana*, 151.

113. Ibid.; Langford, *Vigilante Days*, 245; Leeson, *History of Montana*, 298; Callaway, *Montana's Righteous Hangmen*, 66; Thompson, *Tenderfoot in Montana*, 189; Bartholomew, *Henry Plummer*, 28; Gard, *Frontier Justice*, 182–83.

114. Dimsdale, *Vigilantes of Montana*, 151; Langford, *Vigilante Days*, 245–46.

115. Dimsdale, *Vigilantes of Montana*, 151; Langford, *Vigilante Days*, 246; Allen, *Decent Orderly Lynching*, 262; Callaway, *Montana's Righteous Hangmen*, 67.

116. Dimsdale, *Vigilantes of Montana*, 151–52; Langford, *Vigilante Days*, 246; Callaway, *Montana's Righteous Hangmen*, 67; Thompson, *Tenderfoot in Montana*, 189–90; Allen, *Decent Orderly Lynching*, 262.

117. Allen, *Decent Orderly Lynching*, 263.

118. Dimsdale, *Vigilantes of Montana*, 153; Langford, *Vigilante Days*, 246; Callaway, *Montana's Righteous Hangmen*, 68.

119. Dimsdale, *Vigilantes of Montana*, 153; Langford, *Vigilante Days*, 247; Callaway, *Montana's Righteous Hangmen*, 68; Allen, *Decent Orderly Lynching*, 263.

120. Dimsdale, *Vigilantes of Montana*, 153; Langford, *Vigilante Days*, 246–47; Allen, *Decent Orderly Lynching*, 263.

121. Dimsdale, *Vigilantes of Montana*, 153; Allen, *Decent Orderly Lynching*, 263; Thrapp, *Vengeance!*, 174.

122. Dimsdale, *Vigilantes of Montana*, 153; Donovan, *Hanging around the Big Sky*, book 2, 97.

123. Langford, *Vigilante Days*, 246; Allen, *Decent Orderly Lynching*, 263.

124. Dimsdale, *Vigilantes of Montana*, 153; Langford, *Vigilante Days*, 247; Allen, *Decent Orderly Lynching*, 263; Thrapp, *Vengeance!*, 174; Clampett, "Vigilantes," 451.

125. Dimsdale, *Vigilantes of Montana*, 153; Langford, *Vigilante Days*, 247; Allen, *Decent Orderly Lynching*, 263.

126. Dimsdale, *Vigilantes of Montana*, 153; Langford, *Vigilante Days*, 247; Allen, *Decent Orderly Lynching*, 263–64; Donovan, *Hanging around the Big Sky*, book 2, 93.

127. Mather and Boswell, *Vigilante Victims*, 140–41; Donovan, *Hanging around the Big Sky*, book 2, 93.

128. Allen, *Decent Orderly Lynching*, 264; Mather and Boswell, *Vigilante Victims*, 141; Dimsdale, *Vigilantes of Montana*, 157; Langford, *Vigilante Days*, 247.

129. Dimsdale, *Vigilantes of Montana*, 153; Langford, *Vigilante Days*, 247; Donovan, *Hanging around the Big Sky*, book 2, 93.

130. Dimsdale, *Vigilantes of Montana*, 154; Langford, *Vigilante Days*, 247.

131. Dimsdale, *Vigilantes of Montana*, 154; Langford, *Vigilante Days*, 247.

132. Dimsdale, *Vigilantes of Montana*, 157; Langford, *Vigilante Days*, 248; Bartholomew, *Henry Plummer*, 28; Mather and Boswell, *Vigilante Victims*, 134; Donovan, *Hanging around the Big Sky*, book 2, 94.

133. Dimsdale, *Vigilantes of Montana*, 157; Langford, *Vigilante Days*, 248; Callaway, *Montana's Righteous Hangmen*, 68; Bartholomew, *Henry Plummer*, 28; Donovan, *Hanging around the Big Sky*, book 2, 94.

134. Dimsdale, *Vigilantes of Montana*, 157; Langford, *Vigilante Days*, 248; Bartholomew, *Henry Plummer*, 28; Mather and Boswell, *Vigilante Victims*, 134; Donovan, *Hanging around the Big Sky*, book 2, 96.

135. Dimsdale, *Vigilantes of Montana*, 157; Langford, *Vigilante Days*, 248; Donovan, *Hanging around the Big Sky*, book 2, 96.

136. Dimsdale, *Vigilantes of Montana*, 157; Langford, *Vigilante Days*, 248.

137. Dimsdale, *Vigilantes of Montana*, 157; Langford, *Vigilante Days*, 249; Mather and Boswell, *Vigilante Victims*, 134–35.

138. Dimsdale, *Vigilantes of Montana*, 158; Langford, *Vigilante Days*, 248; Mather and Boswell, *Vigilante Victims*, 136.

139. Langford, *Vigilante Days*, 249; Bartholomew, *Henry Plummer*, 29; Mather and Boswell, *Vigilante Victims*, 137.

140. Langford, *Vigilante Days*, 249.

141. Mather and Boswell, *Vigilante Victims*, 141.

142. Langford, *Vigilante Days*, 247; Donovan, *Hanging around the Big Sky*, book 2, 97.

143. Dimsdale, *Vigilantes of Montana*, 157; Langford, *Vigilante Days*, 247; Allen, *Decent Orderly Lynching*, 265.

144. Mather and Boswell, *Vigilante Victims*, 142.

145. Donovan, *Hanging around the Big Sky*, book 2, 97.

146. Dimsdale, *Vigilantes of Montana*, 158; Langford, *Vigilante Days*, 249; Allen, *Decent Orderly Lynching*, 265; Mather and Boswell, *Vigilante Victims*, 142; Donovan, *Hanging around the Big Sky*, book 2, 94.

147. Dimsdale, *Vigilantes of Montana*, 158; Langford, *Vigilante Days*, 249: Donovan, *Hanging around the Big Sky*, book 2, 97.

148. Dimsdale, *Vigilantes of Montana*, 154; Langford, *Vigilante Days*, 247; Allen, *Decent Orderly Lynching*, 264; Callaway, *Montana's Righteous Hangmen*, 68; Thompson, *Tenderfoot in Montana*, 190.

149. Allen, *Decent Orderly Lynching*, 264.

150. Ibid.

151. Langford, *Vigilante Days*, 247; Bartholomew, *Henry Plummer*, 29; Callaway, *Montana's Righteous Hangmen*, 68; Thrapp, *Vengeance!*, 174; Allen, *Decent Orderly Lynching*, 264.

152. Dimsdale, *Vigilantes of Montana*, 155; Langford, *Vigilante Days*, 247; Callaway, *Montana's Righteous Hangmen*, 68; Thompson, *Tenderfoot in Montana*, 190; Allen, *Decent Orderly Lynching*, 264; Donovan, *Hanging around the Big Sky*, book 2, 99,

153. Dimsdale, *Vigilantes of Montana*, 155; Langford, *Vigilante Days*, 247; Callaway, *Montana's Righteous Hangmen*, 68; Thompson, *Tenderfoot in Montana*, 190; Donovan, *Hanging around the Big Sky*, book 2, 99.

154. Dimsdale, *Vigilantes of Montana*, 155; Langford, *Vigilante Days*, 247; Callaway, *Montana's Righteous Hangmen*, 68; Thrapp, *Vengeance!*, 174; Thompson, *Tenderfoot in Montana*, 190 (similarly quoting Shears as saying, "I knew I should come to this some time, but did not think it would be so soon."); Donovan, *Hanging around the Big Sky*, book 2, 99.

155. Dimsdale, *Vigilantes of Montana*, 155; Langford, *Vigilante Days*, 247; Callaway, *Montana's Righteous Hangmen*, 68; Thompson, *Tenderfoot in Montana*, 190; Allen, *Decent Orderly Lynching*, 265.

156. Dimsdale, *Vigilantes of Montana*, 155; Langford, *Vigilante Days*, 248; Callaway, *Montana's Righteous Hangmen*, 68; Thompson, *Tenderfoot in Montana*, 190; Allen, *Decent Orderly Lynching*, 265; Mather and Boswell, *Vigilante Victims*, 137; Donovan, *Hanging around the Big Sky*, book 2, 99.

157. Dimsdale, *Vigilantes of Montana*, 155; Langford, *Vigilante Days*, 248; Callaway, *Montana's Righteous Hangmen*, 68; Thompson, *Tenderfoot in Montana*, 190; Allen, *Decent Orderly Lynching*, 265; Mather and Boswell, *Vigilante Victims*, 137; Donovan, *Hanging around the Big Sky*, book 2, 99; Bartholomew, *Henry Plummer*, 30.

158. Dimsdale, *Vigilantes of Montana*, 155; Langford, *Vigilante Days*, 248; Callaway, *Montana's Righteous Hangmen*, 68; Thompson, *Tenderfoot in Montana*, 190; Allen, *Decent Orderly Lynching*, 265; Mather and Boswell, *Vigilante Victims*, 137; Donovan, *Hanging around the Big Sky*, book 2, 99; Bartholomew, *Henry Plummer*, 30.

159. Dimsdale, *Vigilantes of Montana*, 155; Langford, *Vigilante Days*, 248.

160. Dimsdale, *Vigilantes of Montana*, 158.

161. Ibid., 155.

162. Dimsdale, *Vigilantes of Montana*, 158; Callaway, *Montana's Righteous Hangmen*, 69.

163. Dimsdale, *Vigilantes of Montana*, 158; Langford, *Vigilante Days*, 249; Thompson, *Tenderfoot in Montana*, 191; Bartholomew, *Henry Plummer*, 30; Donovan, *Hanging around the Big Sky*, book 2, 98.

164. Langford, *Vigilante Days*, 249; Thompson, *Tenderfoot in Montana*, 191; Donovan, *Hanging around the Big Sky*, book 2, 98.

165. Dimsdale, *Vigilantes of Montana*, 155; Langford, *Vigilante Days*, 248; Donovan, *Hanging around the Big Sky*, book 2, 99.

166. Dimsdale, *Vigilantes of Montana*, 156; Langford, *Vigilante Days*, 248; Donovan, *Hanging around the Big Sky*, book 2, 100.

167. Dimsdale, *Vigilantes of Montana*, 156; Langford, *Vigilante Days*, 248; Donovan, *Hanging around the Big Sky*, book 2, 100.

168. Dimsdale, *Vigilantes of Montana*, 155; Langford, *Vigilante Days*, 248; Donovan, *Hanging around the Big Sky*, book 2, 100.

169. Dimsdale, *Vigilantes of Montana*, 156; Langford, *Vigilante Days*, 248; Donovan, *Hanging around the Big Sky*, book 2, 100.

170. Purple, *Perilous Passage*, 136.

171. Wesley P. Emery Reminiscences, 1907, Mont. Hist. Soc., SC-668, folder 1-1, p. 6.

172. Dimsdale, *Vigilantes of Montana*, 159; Langford, *Vigilante Days*, 250.

173. Wesley P. Emery Reminiscences, 1907, Mont. Hist. Soc., SC-668, folder 1-1, pp. 6–7.

174. Dimsdale, *Vigilantes of Montana*, 159.

175. Wesley P. Emery Reminiscences, 1907, Mont. Hist. Soc., SC-668, folder 1-1, p. 7.

176. Ibid.

177. Ibid.

178. Allen, *Decent Orderly Lynching*, 270; Mather and Boswell, *Vigilante Victims*, 146; Donovan, *Hanging around the Big Sky*, book 2, 101.

179. Mather and Boswell, *Vigilante Victims*, 147; Donovan, *Hanging around the Big Sky*, book 2, 101.

180. Wesley P. Emery Reminiscences, 1907, Mont. Hist. Soc., SC-668, folder 1-1, p. 9.

181. Ibid., p. 10.

182. Ibid.

183. Ibid.

184. Ibid.

185. Ibid.; Clampett, "Vigilantes," 451; Dimsdale, *Vigilantes of Montana*, 161; Langford, *Vigilante Days*, 251.

186. Wesley P. Emery Reminiscences, 1907, Mont. Hist. Soc., SC-668, folder 1-1, p. 10; Donovan, *Hanging around the Big Sky*, book 2, 101.

187. Dimsdale, *Vigilantes of Montana*, 162; Langford, *Vigilante Days*, 251; Leeson, *History of Montana*, 300.

188. Dimsdale, *Vigilantes of Montana*, 162; Leeson, *History of Montana*, 300; Mather and Boswell, *Vigilante Victims*, 148.

189. Wesley P. Emery Reminiscences, 1907, Mont. Hist. Soc., SC-668, folder 1-1, p. 10; Clampett, "Vigilantes," 451; Mather and Boswell, *Vigilante Victims*, 147 (recounting a slightly different quote).

190. Wesley P. Emery Reminiscences, 1907, Mont. Hist. Soc., SC-668, folder 1-1, p. 10; Mather and Boswell, *Vigilante Victims*, 147.

191. Wesley P. Emery Reminiscences, 1907, Mont. Hist. Soc., SC-668, folder 1-1, p. 10; Leeson, *History of Montana*, 300.

192. Wesley P. Emery Reminiscences, 1907, Mont. Hist. Soc., SC-668, folder 1-1, p. 10; Clampett, "Vigilantes," 451; Donovan, *Hanging around the Big Sky*, book 2, 102; Dimsdale, *Vigilantes of Montana*, 163; Leeson, *History of Montana*, 300.

193. Dimsdale, *Vigilantes of Montana*, 163; Langford, *Vigilante Days*, 252; Allen, *Decent Orderly Lynching*, 270.

194. Dimsdale, *Vigilantes of Montana*, 163.

195. Langford, *Vigilante Days*, 252; Mather and Boswell, *Vigilante Victims*, 148; Donovan, *Hanging around the Big Sky*, book 2, 103.

196. Dimsdale, *Vigilantes of Montana*, 164; Langford, *Vigilante Days*, 252; Donovan, *Hanging around the Big Sky*, book 2, 103.

197. Wesley P. Emery Reminiscences, 1907, Mont. Hist. Soc., SC-668, folder 1-1, p. 10.

198. Ibid.

199. Donovan, *Hanging around the Big Sky*, book 2, 103–4.

200. James Henry Marley Diary, 1862–65, Mont. Hist. Soc., SC-533, folder 1-2.

201. Ibid.

202. "Life and History of A. T. Ford," Aaron T. Ford Reminiscences, Mont. Hist. Soc., SC-702, folder 1-1, p. 13; see also Donovan, *Hanging around the Big Sky*, book 2, 28.

203. Dimsdale, *Vigilantes of Montana*, 179–81; Callaway, *Montana's Righteous Hangmen*, 114; Allen, *Decent Orderly Lynching*, 294.

204. Dimsdale, *Vigilantes of Montana*, 186–87; Callaway, *Montana's Righteous Hangmen*, 115; Milner and O'Connor, *As Big as the West*, 98; Allen, *Decent Orderly Lynching*, 298.

205. L. A. Fenner, "Remembrances of Pioneer Days," Laurence Abraham Fenner Reminiscences, 1898, Mont. Hist. Soc. SC-686, box 1-1; Donovan, *Hanging around the Big Sky*, book 2, 114; Dimsdale, *Vigilantes of Montana*, 187–88; Allen, *Decent Orderly Lynching*, 302; Olsen, "Lawlessness and Vigilantes," 171; Dimsdale, *Vigilantes of Montana*, 189; Allen, *Decent Orderly Lynching*, 302; *Montana Post*, Sept. 24, 1864, p. 2, col. 2; Allen, *Decent Orderly Lynching*, 302; "Execution at Nevada, M.T.," *Montana Post*, Sept. 24, 1864, p. 2, col. 2; Allen, *Decent Orderly Lynching*, 303.

206. Leeson, *History of Montana*, 267.

207. Ibid., 266–67.

208. Purple, *Perilous Passage*, 136.

209. Leeson, *History of Montana*, 266.

210. Donovan, *Hanging around the Big Sky*, book 2, 113.

211. Thrapp, *Vengeance!*, 175.

212. Thrapp, *Vengeance!*, 163.

213. Allen, *Decent Orderly Lynching*, 314–15, citing *Deseret News*, Feb. 8, 1865, and *Union Vedette*, Feb. 27, 1865.

214. Allen, *Decent Orderly Lynching*, 315, citing a letter from Langford to Samuel Hauser dated May 8, 1865.

215. Dimsdale, *Vigilantes of Montana*, 21.

216. "Local and Other Items—The Thurmond-Fox Case," *Montana Post*, June 3, 1865, p. 2, col. 1.

10

The Establishment of a
Territorial Court at Alder Gulch

Law now reigns supreme.

—*Montana Post*, January 28, 1865

A significant actor in the efforts to introduce lawful procedure to Montana Territory was its chief judge, Hezekiah L. Hosmer. To his friends, his nickname was "Hez."[1]

Hosmer had almost died in a house fire as a child.[2] He was born in Hudson, New York, on December 10, 1814, and when he was sixteen years old moved to Cleveland, Ohio, where he studied law under the tutelage of a relative.[3] The relative, a Mr. Allen, also gave instruction in the law to another student, Stephen A. Douglas,[4] who would later run against Abraham Lincoln for the presidency of the United States. Hosmer was admitted to the practice of law in Ohio in 1835.[5] After practicing law and engaging in some journalism, he devoted himself as the full-time editor of the *Toledo Daily Blade* from 1844 to 1855.[6] He also wrote plays, addressed learned societies, and gave temperance lectures.[7] He returned to the practice of law and dabbled in Whig Party politics until 1860, when he became an active Republican.[8]

Hosmer stated in his unpublished autobiography that "[i]n the Lincoln campaign I took a prominent part and won considerable reputation for my speeches."[9] In 1861 he traveled to Washington, DC, in the hope of securing the position of congressional librarian.[10] He was instead hired as the secretary to the House Committee on Territories, which was chaired by Ohio congressman James M. Ashley.[11] His work for the committee included the organization of the territory of Montana.[12] Through his familiarity with territorial issues and

DOI: 10.7330_9780874219203.c010

his newly formed connections in Washington, Hosmer was appointed during the summer of 1864 to the position of chief judge of the recently formed territory of Montana.[13] He arrived in Montana in October of that year.[14] Hosmer's biographical sketch described Montana as "further from the center of civilization than South Africa is today."[15] The same biographical sketch described the settlers of Bannack and Virginia City in 1863 and 1864 as being worse than "the convicts liberated on the approach of Napoleon on condition that they burn Moscow."[16] Miners' courts in Montana were arbitrary, law books were absent, no legislature had yet met, no municipal buildings had been erected, and the Organic Act made no provision for the procedures by which courts were to be organized and conducted.[17]

Hosmer did not necessarily accept the position of chief justice for the sole purpose of serving the law. Federal appointees often used their positions to advance private commercial interests, and Hosmer was no exception. Indeed, during his time in Montana, Judge Hosmer invested in mining, roads, financing, ranches, and in the manufacture of pottery and brick.[18] It was said that he "tried to get [his] fingers into every financial pie within reach."[19] Correspondence from Hosmer's territorial business partner, T. C. Everts, contained Everts's prediction that "we can make enough to satisfy us in two years, which is long enough to live in this country."[20] Hosmer's primary focus appears to have been directed at mining ventures. He invested in his own mining company within weeks of his arrival in Montana, maintaining operations at Norwegian Gulch.[21] He also invested in the Oro Fino Mining Company with such territorial luminaries as Attorney General Edward Nealley, attorney William Chumasero, Internal Revenue collector Nathaniel Langford, Madison County sheriff Robert C. Knox, county treasurer Andrew Leach, Virginia City treasurer Richard Leach, banker Joseph Mallard, and banker Samuel T. Hauser.[22] He wrote a letter to eastern investors in 1865 vouching for Edwin Reuthven Purple's New York and Montana Mining and Discovery Company, pitching that "I believe there never will be another time on this continent when opportunities so inviting will be presented for investment as are now open here."[23] Author Jeffrey Safford states that Hosmer's "thirst for profit at least equaled, if not exceeded, his passion for justice under the law."[24] However, there is no evidence that Hosmer or any of Montana's territorial judges ever decided court cases in a manner calculated to advance their personal commercial interests.

Upon Hosmer's arrival in the territory, there was not yet any written penal law or criminal procedure. Montana's First Territorial Legislature convened in Bannack on December 12, 1864.[25] It would be the only time that a session of the territorial legislature would be held in Bannack. The legislature remained in session until February 9, 1865.[26] The first legislature passed sweeping statutes that were largely borrowed from the "Field Code" of New York State and the statutes already on the books in Idaho, which, organizationally, were several steps ahead of Montana. The laws of the First Territorial Legislature are known as the Bannack Statutes. They included a Criminal Practice Act, which, despite its title suggestive of criminal procedure, was actually a penal law, and, separately, an Act to Regulate Proceedings in Criminal Cases, which defined the territory's criminal procedures.

Chief Judge Hosmer faced monumental challenges upon his arrival in Montana Territory. His first courtroom was established in the dining room of the Planters House Hotel at the corner of Idaho and Jackson Streets.[27] Court convened at the hotel after breakfast dishes were cleared, and an improvised bench was created by assembling tables close together with another table on top of the others.[28] Hotel guests were inconvenienced by the arrangement, so the courtroom was later moved to the Union League Room, which had one door at its rear and a floor covered with sawdust.[29] On another occasion, when Hosmer held court in Gallatin City, proceedings were held in a private home where mosquitoes were a problem. Court was conducted "in the midst of dense smoke created by burning pine boughs, which dispersed the mosquitoes and well nigh dispersed the court."[30] Hosmer did not wait for the legislature to pass civil and criminal codes before convening his first sessions of court and assembling a grand jury. Prior to the enactment of the Bannack Statutes, Hosmer recognized common law as controlling the substance of his cases and Idaho law as controlling the procedures.[31] The chief judge convened a grand jury on December 5, 1864, and informed its members that the vigilantes must give way to the courts.[32] His remarks were prepared, clear, and, at times, eloquent.

By design, grand juries today operate in secret, subject to very strict exceptions recognized by statute and court order.[33] Today a knowing violation of the grand jury secrecy rules subjects the violator to the punishments authorized for contempt of court.[34] A grand jury's function is to review evidence of alleged wrongdoing and determine whether particular individuals should be charged with particular crimes.[35] Grand juries provide a check upon the power of government to wrongfully, abusively, or vindictively accuse persons of crimes for which there is no reasonable cause for believing the defendant responsible. In Montana today the grand jury receives its charge from a judge who instructs its members of their duties and the matters they may consider.[36] Today indictments against Montana defendants, also known as "True Bills," cannot be returned unless at least eight members of the grand jury concur in the result.[37]

In sharp contrast with the procedures of today, the work of the grand jury that was convened by Chief Judge Hosmer on December 5, 1864, was not conducted in secret. In fact, Hosmer's introductory remarks to the grand jurors were on the center-front page of the *Montana Post* in its edition published on Saturday, December 10, 1864, under the headline "Court Proceedings."[38] By today's standards, the publication of a judge's remarks to a grand jury appears foreign and wholly unprecedented. Of course, since the territorial legislature had not yet enacted any procedural statutes governing grand juries and other matters, Judge Hosmer was free to conduct the proceeding however he wished.

Hosmer is quoted as observing that in the creation of new settlements, well-intentioned men are forced "to free themselves of that vile class of adventurers which infest all unorganized communities for the purposes of fraud, robbery and murder."[39] Hosmer noted that in Montana "[t]he sources of official power had been monopolized by the very class which preyed upon society" and that the "greatest villain of them all . . . was the principal ministerial officer of the Territory [who] had at his back a band of wretches who had become hardened in their bloody trade."[40] Judge Hosmer's mention of the "principal ministerial officer of the Territory" was an obvious but perhaps exaggerated reference to Sheriff Henry Plummer, without identifying Plummer by name.

Hosmer noted in his remarks that in responding to crime, the mining settlements in the region had faced two stark choices—either to "give the Territory over to misrule and murder or, alternatively, "to hang the offenders."[41] Hosmer commended the work of the vigilantes for temporarily serving the cause of justice and hanging the offenders.[42] He announced that the members of the Vigilance Committee would not face criminal charges for their past conduct. He said, "It is no part of the business of this court to find fault with what has been done; but rather, in common with all good citizens, to laud the transactions of an organization which in the absence of law, assumed the delicate and responsible office of purging society of all offenders against its peace, happiness and safety."[43] However, Hosmer then informed the grand jurors that the vigilantes had fulfilled their work and that "[t]o go farther is to commit crime," as the territorial court was now "clothed with ample power to investigate and punish all offence [*sic*] against the peace and good order of society."[44] With rhetorical flourish, Hosmer said, "Let us erect no more impromptu scaffolds. Let us inflict no more midnight executions."[45] Significantly and perhaps ominously, Judge Hosmer warned that if the vigilantes acted on their own again, he would call upon the grand jury to indict *them* for murder.[46]

Not only were Judge Hosmer's remarks to the grand jury made public, but the names of the seventeen grand jurors were published on the front page of the *Montana Post*. The grand jury consisted of J. J. Hull (designated foreman), John Ault, Thomas Baume, George Brandt, Joseph Brown, Lester Campbell, L. H. Davenport, William Decker, J. Hildebrand, B. R. Martin, J. W. Pattee, L. S. Peck, Samuel Russell, Henry Thompson, John Vanderbilt, W. P. Wheeler, and

Figure 10.1. Chief Judge Hezekiah Hosmer of the Montana Supreme Court. (Courtesy of the Montana Historical Society, image 942-877.)

James Williams.[47] Notably, two early members of the Vigilance Committee who signed the original vigilante oath, dated December 23, 1863, Thomas Baume and James Williams, were impaneled members of the grand jury.[48] It is not known whether the impanelment of Baume and Williams was coincidental or by deliberate forethought, and whether other less notable members of the Vigilance Committee may have also been impaneled. With a population in Alder Gulch numbering in the thousands by late 1864, the odds of both Baume and Williams being randomly impaneled on the grand jury appear to be statistically remote. More likely, at least some of the members of Hosmer's inaugural grand jury were drawn from the ranks of the Vigilance Committee by deliberate design. Judge Hosmer likely felt that his remarks needed to be heard directly by prominent members of the Vigilance Committee, as well as by the public at large, in order to effect a change in the recognized method of law enforcement going forward.

Hosmer's remarks were well received by the newly sworn members of the territorial bar.[49] Editorially, the *Montana Post* approved of Judge Hosmer's instructions to the grand jury with great flourish. It wrote, "Any one reading [Hosmer's] charge to the Grand Jury must be struck with admiration at the masterly manner in which the delicate subjects therein discussed are handled."[50] While also praising the vigilantes, the *Montana Post* urged that "we must rejoice that the day has arrived when the services which we so thankfully acknowledge are no longer necessary," as "the visitations of authorized justice are the only true remedy."[51]

The chief judge's published remarks to the grand jury were a shot across the bow of vigilantism. Tactically, and perhaps brilliantly, Hosmer's public grand jury remarks painted the Vigilance Committee into a corner, where further vigilante executions would be viewed by the public as a violation of the efforts that were underway to provide Montana with a lawful and judicial forum for punishing criminals. From December 5, 1864, forward, members of the Vigilance Committee were on notice that if they proceeded with further extrajudicial executions, they did so at their own peril. The reaction of the vigilantes was mixed. One person suggested to Judge Hosmer that he take care of civil matters while leaving criminal affairs to the vigilantes.[52] On the other hand, the vigilantes had little choice but to give Judge Hosmer's court a fair opportunity to demonstrate that it could capably adjudicate and punish criminals in the region.[53] To do so, and after some debate with local attorneys, Hosmer chose to apply the practice statutes of Idaho Territory until such time that a Montana legislature could enact its own procedural and penal statutes.[54] He also declared that "California Rules" would govern placer mining claims, that both gold dust and "greenbacks" could be used as legal tender in the territory, and that contracts could be enforced despite the absence of Internal Revenue stamps.[55]

The impanelment of a grand jury in Virginia City undermined a primary reason for the existence of vigilantism in Alder Gulch. As noted, vigilantism in the region grew from a confluence of three factors—the value and importance of gold, the insecure means of transporting wealth by horse or stagecoach upon trails in the region, and the absence of effective police, prosecutorial, and judicial resources. The three factors at Alder Gulch were akin to a three-legged stool: if one leg were to be removed, the stool could no longer stand. Hosmer's court removed one of the three primary reasons for vigilantism, which had the effect of deferring further vigilantism at least until the court system could prove its worth.

The gradual increased presence of federal law enforcement in Montana had the effect of significantly dampening vigilante activities. Judge Hosmer deserves historical credit for the artful manner in which he sought to transition the region from vigilantism to the rule of law. Even Dimsdale declared in the *Montana Post* that "[l]aw now reigns supreme."[56] Notably, vigilante executions virtually ceased in the area of Bannack and Alder Gulch, even though, as noted by author Frederick Allen, the Vigilance Committee remained intact as a veritable "shadow government"[57] monitoring events with a watchful eye. The patience of the vigilantes in Alder Gulch even endured through four early murder trials presided over by Judge Hosmer, which each resulted in acquittals of the defendants.[58]

The initial activities of the grand jury that convened in Virginia City were inauspicious at best. The grand jurors filed their first indictments on December 31, 1864, and then rushed to a local saloon.[59] Among the early criminal charges that were filed, five were for crimes of adultery. There were two indictments alleging assaults with a deadly weapon and two others for major thefts.[60] There was one indictment for fraud, and one for bigamy, incest, and mayhem. The only indictment for a potentially mortal crime was one for attempted murder.[61] The grand jury might not have been above political influence, favoritism, and abuse of its authority, as two of its initial indictments alleged "exhibiting deadly weapons,"[62] which was a daily and routine occurrence in western mining communities at that time and suggests that the unfortunate persons charged with those crimes might have been singled out for selective enforcement.

Weeks later, the first territorial legislature completed its work and enacted the Bannack Statutes, which included Montana's first codes of criminal law and procedure. The legislature defined a wide range of crimes, including murder in the first degree, murder in the second degree, voluntary manslaughter, involuntary manslaughter, and defenses such as justifiable homicide and excusable homicide. As will become relevant here, murder in the first degree was defined in the Bannack Statutes as "the unlawful killing of a human being, with malice aforethought, either express or implied."[63] Implied malice is an intent to take a life that can be proven from the circumstances of the killing, such as murders involving poison, lying in wait, torture, premeditation, or deaths incurred during the commission of the crimes of arson, rape, robbery, and burglary.[64] Express malice is a deliberate intention demonstrated by "external circumstances capable of proof," such as the making of a threat to kill that is later carried out by the defendant.[65] Any murder not qualifying under the definition of first degree was deemed in the Bannack Statutes to be murder in the second degree.[66] The only authorized punishment for murder in the first degree was death, whereas the punishment for murder in the second degree was a term of imprisonment of between ten years and life.[67] The mandated method for imposing the death penalty was "hanging by the neck."[68]

The Bannack Statutes also defined the lesser charge of manslaughter, which was the unlawful killing of a person in the absence of express or implied malice.[69] It was defined as having two forms. The first form was "voluntary manslaughter," whereby the defendant was provoked into taking another person's life through voluntary conduct prompted by an irresistible heat of passion.[70] The second form was "involuntary manslaughter," whereby the defendant did not intend for his actions to result in the death of another person, but whose conduct in the commission of another unlawful act might produce someone's death as its consequence.[71] The authorized punishment for manslaughter was a term of imprisonment not exceeding ten years, with no statutory distinction between voluntary and involuntary manslaughters.[72]

Under the Bannack Statutes, homicides could be excused under certain circumstances. One such circumstance was "justifiable homicide," also known as self-defense, whereby the defendant reasonably believes that there is an urgent and pressing threat to his own life or of great bodily harm.[73] A person may commit a killing in self-defense if a reasonable person would do so to save his own life or prevent great bodily harm.[74] An "excusable homicide," by contrast, included accidental deaths arising out of lawful activities, such as from the wielding of an axe when the blade flies off of its handle and strikes the victim.[75] Justifiable and excusable homicides were not punishable.

Procedurally, the Bannack Statutes established a twelve-person grand jury system, of which nine members needed to concur in order to render an indictment.[76] Grand jury proceedings under the Bannack Statutes were to be conducted in secret.[77] The legislature also enacted statutes of limitations and procedures regulating indictments, arraignments, bail, arrests, trials and retrials, and appeals.[78] The Bannack Statutes prohibited blacks, mulattos, Native American Indians, and Chinese from giving evidence against any white person.[79] It punished men for the "infamous crime against nature" involving another man or beast by imprisonment for not less than five years.[80] It imposed criminal culpability not only for accessories to crimes but also accessories after the fact.[81] Married women were exempted from criminal culpability if acting under the threat, command, or coercion of a husband, except for crimes punishable by death.[82] Otherwise, the criminal statutes were expressly applicable to females.[83] The courts of the territory were given jurisdiction over all offenses committed against the laws of Montana, to be punished, as a general rule, in the county where the offense was committed.[84] No person could be convicted of any crime after trial absent proof of guilt beyond a reasonable doubt,[85] which is the standard uniformly required for almost all crimes today.

The Bannack Statutes became effective when they were approved on February 9, 1865.[86] As a result, 1865 held out great promise for effective and consistent criminal prosecutions. During that year, four different persons were charged with murder and tried by juries in a courtroom presided over by Judge Hosmer. All four cases ended in acquittals, including the case against A. J. McCausland, who shot his business partner, J. M. Kenna, in a dry goods store in the presence of a dozen witnesses.[87] McCausland would not live for long, as after his acquittal he would be murdered on a trail during an ill-fated excursion to Missouri in the summer of 1865.[88]

Another early murder trial was that of John Thorburn for killing D. D. Chamberlain in Central City.[89] In that case William Chumasero acted as prosecutor while Wilbur Fisk Sanders and Thomas Thoroughman acted as defense counsel.[90] It was during Thorburn's trial that a prospective juror, who was a prominent vigilante, was asked during jury selection whether he had any conscientious opinions against the death penalty, to which the prospective juror replied, "In all cases where it is not done by a Vigilance Committee!"[91]

Despite the early poor track record of convictions, the vigilantes' deference to the fledgling court system in Alder Gulch continued to hold through much of 1865.

The tide of public opinion in Alder Gulch began to turn against continued vigilante activity as early as the latter half of 1864. On September 10, 1864, a mere five days after the vigilante trial and execution of Jem Kelly, a leading citizen named James Fergus published a letter in the *Montana Post* addressed to "the Gentlemen of the Vigilante Committee." In the letter, Fergus argued that "the time for vigilante justice" had passed and that American citizens had "the right to be tried [for crimes] by the laws of their country, in open court and by a jury of their country men."[92] In what can only be viewed as a full frontal assault against the continuing activities of the vigilantes, Fergus also wrote in his letter that "the power that deprives [persons accused of crimes] of that right is a tyrant and a usurper be it one or many."[93] The short-term impact of Fergus's letter was limited, as John "The Hat" Dolan was hanged by the vigilantes a mere seven days later, on September 17, 1864. Nevertheless, in the general and longer-term sense, vigilantism waned in Alder Gulch as a result of a confluence of factors that included the creation of Montana Territory on May 26, 1864, the operation of Chief Judge Hosmer's court from late 1864 and thereafter, the designation of Virginia City as the territory's capital in 1865,[94] and the enactment by the First Territorial Legislature of criminal codes of law and procedure, effective in February of 1865.

Vigilantism did not drop off altogether, however. Approximately one year after Fergus's letter, the Vigilance Committee posted a public notice dated

September 19, 1865, warning the public of further vigilante activity.[95] In its notice, the Vigilance Committee, citing the continuing failure of government authorities to adequately prevent crime and punish offenders, warned "all malefactors," including all person who might draw deadly weapons except in matters of self-defense, that they "will be summarily dealt with."[96] The notice also stated that the Vigilance Committee would "respect and sustain the action of the civil authorities,"[97] suggesting that vigilante action would be undertaken only in those instances when governmental law enforcement failed.

A very small number of further executions occurred at Alder Gulch despite the presence of an established court in the territory. The timing of the executions was spread over three years, and the executions were sporadic. These included a double hanging of John Morgan and John Jackson in Virginia City on September 27, 1865.[98] Morgan and Jackson were caught stealing horses from a corral and were taken into custody by vigilantes.[99] They were hanged together from a hay frame leaning over the corral of a slaughterhouse, with a note on Morgan's back that said, "Road Agents Beware."[100] In the diary written by James P. Miller, who observed Morgan's and Jackson's bodies, the signs on their backs instead said, "Hung by the Vigilance Committee for being road agents."[101]

In Alder Gulch 1866 was a quiet year for vigilante executions.

The following year, 1867, saw the executions of George Rosenbaum in Nevada City on either January 31 or February 1 of that year and Charles Wilson in Virginia City on September 25.[102] Rosenbaum had been whipped and banished from the territory by vigilantes during the fall of 1866, but according to the February 2, 1867, edition of the *Montana Post*, he was a "scoundrel" who was captured and hanged by vigilantes in Nevada City while in apparent violation of the prior banishment.[103] Wilson's body was found hanging from a pole at a quarry with a note pinned to his clothing that said "Vigilantes."[104] According to the *Montana Post*, it was believed that Wilson belonged to an organization that robbed and burglarized certain stores in Virginia City.[105] The hangings of Morgan, Jackson, Rosenbaum, and Wilson appear to have been isolated incidents in 1865 and 1867 and did not represent an orchestrated resurgence of muscular vigilantism in the Alder Gulch region. The persons responsible for those hangings were never arrested or prosecuted for their conduct, if their identities were even known to law enforcement authorities at all.

Criticism of further vigilante activity, which many people dared not utter during the first half of 1864, was more public in later years. Perhaps the best representation of the demise of vigilantism at Alder Gulch was a warning that was printed in the *Montana Post* on March 2, 1867. It read:

Figure 10.2. Nevada City as it appeared in 1866. (Courtesy of the Montana Historical Society, image 950-147.)

NOTICE!

We, now, as a sworn band of law-abiding citizens, do hereby solemnly swear that the first man that is hung by the Vigilantes of this place, we will retaliate five for one, unless it be done in broad daylight, so that all may know what it is for. We are all satisfied that in times past, you did some glorious work, but the time has come when law should be enforced. Old fellow-members, the time is not like it was. We had good men with us; but now, there is a great change. There is not a thief come to the country but what "rings" himself into the present committee. We know you all. You must not think you can do as you please. We are American citizens, and you shall not drive, and hang, whom you please.[106]

The notice was signed "Five For One."[107] A reading of the newspaper warning suggests that it was written by persons in the collective, likely five in number, and all onetime members of the Vigilance Committee. If so, the newspaper warning also suggests that a sharp division had developed within the ranks of the committee regarding its future as an organization. In the story that accompanied the warning, the *Montana Post*, which by then was edited by Henry Nichols Blake, described the vigilance movement as a "sleeping lion" that was facing a "crisis."[108] Blake further wrote that members of the organization who did not share its principles and mission needed to be removed from it, so that the Vigilance Committee "could continue honored by the good people, and feared by the bad."[109] In other words, the Vigilance Committee was challenged to purge itself of members who no longer shared the organization's mission of summarily punishing criminal offenders. If there had ever been any question about whether the *Montana Post* would continue its editorial support for the vigilantes after Thomas Dimsdale's death, Blake's article on the front page of the newspaper on March 2, 1867, dispelled all doubt.

In any event, the "Five For One" warning was published a month after the vigilante hanging of George Rosenbaum, perhaps suggesting a connection between the two events. If the newspaper notice was a reaction to the hanging of Rosenbaum, it apparently did not have a lasting effect as it did not deter the vigilante hanging of Wilson approximately six months later.

The production of gold in Virginia City began to decline, and with it, the mining communities of Alder Gulch began losing population to other areas of the territory, most notably Helena. The decline of Alder Gulch would be slow but steady over several years. Virginia City's decline is symbolized by a business decision of Benjamin R. Dittes, the owner of the weekly *Montana Post*. In 1868, Dittes moved his presses to Helena, where the *Montana Post* resumed publication as a daily newspaper on April 20 of that year.[110]

Vigilantism at Alder Gulch went on a hiatus after the establishment of Judge Hosmer's court, with limited exceptions in 1865 and 1867. It would not be long after the establishment of Hosmer's court before another vigilance committee would arise 120 miles to the north, in Helena. Vigilantism would continue to be a force in Montana Territory, though elsewhere than at Alder Gulch.

Panning for Nuggets

In 1864, Congressman James M. Ashley, chairman of the US House Committee on Territories, envisioned territorial borders that significantly differed from those that ultimately came into being. Ashley initially wished to place the eastern two-thirds of present-day Montana into a territory called Idaho; place the lower part of present-day Idaho and much of Wyoming into a territory called Montana; and enlarge Washington Territory to include the upper portion of modern-day Idaho and the western third of modern-day Montana. Ashley's plans were set aside in favor of the current configuration, as Idaho's Republican delegate to Congress, William Wallace, wished to separate Idaho and Montana along the Bitterroot Mountains to rid Idaho of predominantly Democrat voters who lived on the Montana side of the mountain range.[111] In other words, the location of the Idaho-Montana border is a product of crass gerrymandering.

Notes

1. T. C. Everts to Hosmer, January 6, 1865, Hezekiah Hosmer Papers, 1848–70, Mont. Hist. Soc. (hereafter Hosmer Papers), SC-104, folder 1-1.

2. "Hezekiah L. Hosmer Autobiography," Hosmer Papers, SC-104, folder 1-1, p. 14.

3. J. A. Hosmer, "Biographical Sketch of Hezekiah L. Hosmer," Hosmer Papers, SC-104, box 1-1, vol. 3, p. 1.

4. "Hezekiah L. Hosmer Autobiography," 16.

5. Hosmer, "Biographical Sketch," 2.

6. Ibid., 2–3; "Hezekiah L. Hosmer Autobiography," 16.

7. Guice, *Rocky Mountain Bench*, 67.

8. Hosmer, "Biographical Sketch," 3.

9. "Hezekiah L. Hosmer Autobiography," 22.

10. Hosmer, "Biographical Sketch," 3; "Hezekiah L. Hosmer Autobiography," 22; Guice, *Rocky Mountain Bench*, 67.

11. Hosmer, "Biographical Sketch," 3.

12. Ibid.

13. Ibid.

14. Allen, *Decent Orderly Lynching*, 304.

15. Hosmer, "Biographical Sketch," 3.

16. Ibid., 4.

17. Ibid., 6–8.

18. Guice, *Rocky Mountain Bench*, 147.

19. Ibid.

20. Ibid., 66, citing correspondence from T. C. Everts to Hezekiah L. Hosmer dated January 6, 1865, Western Americana Collection, Yale University.

21. Safford, *Mechanics of Optimism*, 15.

22. Ibid., 21–22.

23. Ibid., 26.

24. Ibid.

25. Laws 1865, First Terr. Legis.

26. Ibid.

27. Hosmer, "Biographical Sketch," 7–8; Bancroft, *History*, 655n25.

28. Hosmer, "Biographical Sketch," 8. Hosmer would not enjoy the trappings of a real courtroom in a dedicated courthouse until mid-February, 1868, when he presided over the trial of codefendants Hadzer, Ellis, and Ewing for their alleged murder of Frank Hanna. "New Court Room," *Virginia Tri-Weekly Post*, Feb. 18, 1868, p. 3, col. 2, and Feb. 20, 1868, p. 3, col. 1; "Judicial," *Montana Post*, Feb. 22, 1868, p. 8, col. 2.

29. Spence, "Territorial Bench in Montana," 29.

30. Spence, *Territorial Politics*, 29, quoting from Judge Hosmer.

31. E.g., "Decision and Order, Dec. 19, 1864," Hosmer Papers, SC-104, folder 1-1; Bancroft, *History*, 660–61; Spence, *Territorial Politics*, 29.

32. Allen, *Decent Orderly Lynching*, 309; Greever, *Bonanza West*, 228.

33. Mont. Code Ann. 46-11-317(2) (1991); Mont. Code Ann. 46-11-316 (1991).

34. Mont. Code Ann. 46-11-317(2) (1991).

35. Mont. Code Ann. 46-11-314 (1991).

36. Mont. Code Ann. 46-11-311 (1991).

37. Mont. Code Ann. 46-11-331 (2009).

38. "Court Proceedings," *Montana Post*, Dec. 10, 1864, p. 1, col. 4.

39. Ibid.

40. Ibid.

41. Ibid.

42. Ibid.; see also Hosmer, "Biographical Sketch," 7.

43. "Court Proceedings," *Montana Post*, Dec. 10, 1864, p. 1, col. 4.

44. Ibid.

45. Ibid.

46. Allen, *Decent Orderly Lynching*, 309.

47. "Court Proceedings," *Montana Post*, Dec. 10, 1864, p. 1, col. 6.

48. Ibid.

49. Hosmer, "Biographical Sketch," 8. On the same day, Hosmer swore in the attorneys who became authorized to practice law within the territory. Those attorneys consisted of Wilbur Fisk Sanders, Dr. Giles Gaylord Bissell, R. B. Parrott, R. H. Robertson, J. A. Spratt, Charles S. Bagg, L. W. Borton, A. E. Mayhew, E. B. Nealley, W. M. Stafford, Thos. Thoroughman, John C. Turk, William Chumasero, H. Burns, J. A. Johnston, William Y. Pemberton, J. Cook, Edward Sheffield, Alexander Davis, William L. McMath, William J. McCormick, G. W. Stapleton, and Sam Ward. Journal Entry, Monday, Dec. 5, 1864, William Y. Pemberton Papers, 1863–69, Mont. Hist. Soc, SC-629, box 1-1.

50. "Opening of the District Court," *Montana Post*, Dec. 10, 1864, p. 2, col. 1.

51. Ibid.

52. Hosmer, "Biographical Sketch," 8–9; Allen, *Decent Orderly Lynching*, 309.

53. Allen, *Decent Orderly Lynching*, 309.

54. Hosmer, "Biographical Sketch," 9.

55. Ibid., 10–13.

56. Allen, *Decent Orderly Lynching*, 314, citing the *Montana Post*, Jan. 28, 1865.

57. Ibid.

58. Ibid., 320.

59. Howard, *Montana High, Wide, and Handsome*, 46.

60. Ibid., 47.

61. Ibid.

62. Ibid.

63. Laws 1865, First Terr. Legis., C.P.A. ch. 4, sec. 15.

64. Ibid., sec. 17. In many states today, a death that occurs during the commission of a violent felony is referred to as "felony murder."

65. Ibid., sec. 16.

66. Ibid., sec. 17. The Bannack Statutes did a poor job defining the precise elements of murder in the second degree.

67. Ibid., sec. 17.

68. Laws 1865, First Terr. Legis., Proceedings Act, ch. 1, sec. 220.

69. Laws 1865, First Terr. Legis., C.P.A. ch. 4, sec. 18.

70. Ibid., secs. 18–20.

71. Ibid., sec. 21.

72. Ibid., sec. 22.

73. Ibid., secs. 25–28.

74. Ibid., secs. 26, 27.

75. Ibid., sec. 30.

76. Laws 1865, First Terr. Legis., Proceedings Act, ch . 1, secs. 53, 58.

77. Ibid., sec. 69.

78. Laws 1865, First Terr. Legis., C.P.A., ch. 1, secs. 20–23, 24–52, 110–16; Laws 1865, First Terr. Legis., Proceedings Act, ch . 1, secs. 79–105, 107, 118–27, 129–53, 154–94, 204–14, 242–57.

79. Laws 1865, First Terr. Legis., C.P.A. ch. 3, sec. 13.

80. Ibid, C.P.A. ch. 4, sec. 44.

81. Ibid., C.P.A, ch. 2, secs. 10–11.

82. Ibid., C.P.A, ch. 1, sec. 6.

83. Laws 1865, First Terr. Legis., Procedural Act, ch. 1, sec. 156.

84. Laws 1865, First Terr. Legis., Proceedings Act, ch . 1, sec. 12.

85. Ibid., ch . 1, sec. 186.

86. Laws 1865, First Terr. Legis., art. 8, p. 712.

87. Hosmer, "Biographical Sketch," 15; Bancroft, *History*, 658; Allen, *Decent Orderly Lynching*, 321.

88. Allen, *Decent Orderly Lynching*, 321. McCausland was killed a month after his acquittal, which Hosmer's biographical sketch attributes to criminal road agents, but it may also be plausible that McCausland met his death at the hands of vigilantes who took justice into their own hands. There is, however, no evidence of vigilante involvement.

89. Hosmer, "Biographical Sketch," 13–14.

90. Ibid.

91. Ibid., 14. The historical materials relied upon do not disclose the identity of the vigilante or whether he was placed upon the Thorburn jury.

92. Peavy and Smith, *Pioneer Women*, 281n 2.

93. Ibid.

94. Bakken, *Invitation to an Execution*, 341.

95. Vigilantes Records (Virginia City), 1863–84, Mont. Hist. Soc., SC-953, box 1-2, p. 215.

96. Ibid.

97. Ibid. The full text of the notice reads:

> Notice to all whom it may concern:
>
> Whereas, drivers [*sic*] foul crimes and outrages against the persons and property of the citizens of Montana have been lately committed, and
>
> Whereas, the power of the civil authorities, though exerted to its full extent, is frequently insufficient to prevent their commission, and to punish perpetrators thereof,
>
> Now this is to warn and notify all whom it may concern that the Vigilance Committee, composed of the citizens of the Territory, have determined to take these matters in their own hands, and to inflict summary punishment upon any and all malefactors, in every case where the civil authorities are unable to enforce the proper penalty of the law.
>
> The practice of drawing deadly weapons, except as a last resort for the defense of life, being dangerous to society, and in numerous instances leading to affrays and bloodshed,
>
> Notice is hereby given that the same is prohibited, and offenders against this regulation will be summarily dealt with. In all cases the committee will respect and sustain the action of the civil authorities. This notice will not be repealed, but will remain in full force and effect from this date.
>
> By order of the Vigilance Committee.
>
> September 19th, 1865.

98. "Local Items," *Montana Post*, Sept. 30, 1865, p. 3, col. 1; Leeson, *History of Montana*, 286; Birney, *Vigilantes*, 345.

99. "Local Items," *Montana Post*, Sept. 30, 1865, p. 3, col. 1; Leeson, *History of Montana*, 286; Birney, *Vigilantes*, 345.

100. "Local Items," *Montana Post*, Sept. 30, 1865, p. 3, col. 1; Leeson, *History of Montana*, 289; Birney, *Vigilantes*, 345.

101. Virginia City Chamber of Commerce, "Fun Facts."

102. "Vigilantes at Work," *Helena Weekly Herald*, Oct. 3, 1867, p. 7, col. 4; Allen, *Decent Orderly Lynching*, 348, 366; Bakken, *Invitation to an Execution*, 341 (attributing the execution to Wilson's act of informing road agents about the cargo and schedules of Wells Fargo stagecoaches).

103. "Gone to His Death," *Montana Post*, Feb. 2, 1867, p. 1, col. 2.

104. "Hung by the Vigilantes," *Montana Post*, Sept. 28, 1867, p. 8, col. 4.

105. Ibid.

106. "Vigilantes vs. Anti-Vigilantes," *Montana Post*, Mar. 2, 1867, p. 1, col. 6; Abrahams, *Vigilant Citizens*, 68; Barsness, *Gold Camp*, 53.

107. "Vigilantes vs. Anti-Vigilantes," *Montana Post*, Mar. 2, 1867, p. 1, col. 6.

108. Ibid.

109. Ibid.

110. Access Genealogy, "Montana Organization, Boundaries, Elections, 1864–1866."

111. Allen, *Decent Orderly Lynching*, 280.

11

Vigilantism Migrates North to Helena, 1865–70

[T]his is to notify all whom it may concern, that crime must and will be suppressed;
and, to that end, all offenders will be summarily dealt with, and punished as of old.

—Order of the Helena Vigilance Committee, summer 1865

H ezekiah Hosmer was Montana's first chief judge, having been appointed to the position by President Lincoln on June 30, 1864. Montana Territory was organized to have two additional associate judges. Those judges were Lorenzo P. Williston and Ammi Giddings, who were each appointed to their positions on the Supreme Court by President Lincoln on June 22, 1864.[1] Williston had been born in Binghamton, New York, practiced law in Pennsylvania, served in the Pennsylvania State House of Representatives from 1856 to 1860, and sat on the Dakota Supreme Court until his transfer to Montana at the behest of President Lincoln.[2] The judges' terms were each for four years.[3] Montana Territory was divided into three judicial districts, with each of the judges providing trial-level services in their individually assigned judicial districts.[4] Hosmer sat in Virginia City and Deer Lodge.[5] Williston initially sat in Bannack[6] and did not particularly distinguish himself, as Bannack was in decline during much of his term in office. Giddings was to sit in Helena.[7] There is some suggestion that Hosmer secured for himself the judicial district that included Virginia City, as it was the most commercially active area of Montana at the time and enabled Hosmer to pursue extrajudicial business ventures.[8]

Giddings decided not to serve in Montana at all due to the ill health of his wife, but he did not relinquish his initial commission until March 11, 1865.[9] Montana was therefore without one of its three Supreme Court justices for a

DOI: 10.7330_9780874219203.c011

number of months, at a time when the establishment of a territorial court system was very much needed. The vacant court seat was in the judicial district that was to be headquartered in Helena. Helena's judicial district would be without a court, and without a judge, until Giddings's seat on the Supreme Court could be filled by his replacement, Lyman E. Munson.[10] Even after Munson's appointment, it would be another four months before the judge would arrive in Helena to take up his duties.[11]

As Judge Hosmer swore in his first grand jury at Virginia City in December of 1864 and busied himself with civil and criminal cases in the many months that followed, the residents of Helena and its surrounding region awaited the replacement of Judge Giddings and the arrival of Judge Munson. In the meantime, Helena experienced a vacuum of effective law enforcement, similar to what had been experienced in Alder Gulch during the two preceding years. Many of the ingredients for vigilantism were initially present in Helena. Between June 9 and November 23, 1865, there were almost a dozen vigilante hangings in Helena or at other settlements in the greater Helena area.[12] As will be shown, almost one and a half dozen additional men would be executed in and around Helena, at a much slower rate, between June 9, 1865, and April 30, 1870.

The vigilantism that occurred in Helena from 1865 to 1870 appears to have received less attention from historians than that given to Bannack and Alder Gulch in 1863–64. While several autobiographies, biographies, and history books have been written about the events in Bannack and Alder Gulch in 1863 and 1864, which are acknowledged and cited here, considerably less has been written during the past 150 years about the development of Helena and the vigilantism that occurred there during its nascent history. Even the Internet contains far less of the history, focus, and romanticism of Helena's vigilante roots than it gives to the areas of Bannack and Alder Gulch in 1863–64.

There are perhaps different reasons why Helena has received less attention from historians than Bannack, Virginia City, and the other gold-mining communities of Alder Gulch. First, the number of vigilante executions in Helena was approximately the same as the number of vigilante executions in Bannack and Alder Gulch. However, the Helena executions were stretched over a period of several years whereas most of the Bannack and Alder Gulch executions occurred in a single year, 1864. The number of hangings in Helena, while significant, may not seem as shocking or as intense by comparison. If Helena was the tortoise, Bannack and Alder Gulch were the hare.

Second, vigilantism in Helena occurred on a criminal-by-criminal, ad hoc basis, unlike many of the executions in the region of Bannack and Alder Gulch, which were for the most part focused against members of a single organized criminal enterprise.

Third, there were no executions in Helena of law enforcement personnel such as the executions of Sheriff Henry Plummer and Deputy Sheriffs Buck Stinson and Ned Ray in Bannack. Nor did known Helena executions violate double jeopardy, as with the hanging of Buck Stinson in Bannack on January 10, 1864, or arise from extraterritorial bounty hunting, as will be shown with the execution of John "The Hat" Dolan on September 17, 1864. Nor did Helena vigilantes hang prisoners outside of Montana Territory, as with the execution of Jem Kelly by Alder Gulch vigilantes at the Snake River Ferry in Idaho on September 5, 1864.

Finally, vigilantism was not new to Montana Territory by the time it arose in Helena, as it had already received considerable notoriety from the activities in the south central portion of the territory in 1863–64. In other words, by the time Helena's so-called Committee of Safety became active, the presence of vigilantism in Montana was already well worn and, in the view of many persons, an acceptable practice.

Notwithstanding, the executions that occurred in the region of Helena from 1865 to 1870 are no less interesting, bloody, or compelling than their earlier counterparts. They were motivated by the same mix of serious criminal activities, the absence of credible law enforcement, and in some cases the connection to wealth, as had similarly motivated vigilantism in 1864. The execution of James Daniels in Helena on March 2, 1866 is particularly noteworthy. Daniels was hanged while in possession of an official reprieve from the territorial governor and morbidly personified a constitutional power struggle waged at the time between the executive and judicial branches of government, and between Republicans and Democrats, over the extent of the gubernatorial power to pardon and reprieve convicted prisoners. The Daniels execution is dealt with in detail in the next chapter.

Helena, which is Montana's current state capital, has a history of its own that is in some ways similar to, and in some ways distinct from, the history of Bannack and the mining communities of Alder Gulch.

Like Virginia City, Helena has its origins in prospecting in the mid-1860s. Four prospectors were down on their luck after several months of failing to find gold in other parts of Montana Territory.[13] The prospectors are sometimes referred to as the four Georgians, though in fact only two of the men were actually from Georgia—John S. Cowan and John Crab.[14] The other two men were Bob Staley from London, England, and Daniel Jackson "D. J." Miller from Albertville, Alabama.[15] The description of the prospectors as Georgians is accurate only if it is intended as a reference to the "Georgian method" of prospecting that they used in their work.[16] D. J. Miller's story is particularly compelling, as he wished to marry Mary Henry of Albertville but could not receive permission from her wealthy father unless, and until, Miller could provide the comfortable lifestyle to which Henry was deserving.[17] Miller therefore set out for California, and then to Montana, to earn his fortune as a prospector out of love for Mary Henry and the hope that some day he could marry her.[18]

In present-day Helena, the four "Georgian" prospectors struck gold on July 14, 1864, at a desolate creek that they named Last Chance Gulch.[19] The gulch received its name as its discoverers were prepared to declare defeat and return to their homes unless they could discover gold at this last digging.[20] The gulch was located northwest of the settlement at Montana City and southeast of Jefferson City and Silver City.[21] Cowan is credited as the prospector within the group who first discovered gold at the gulch.[22] Staley described in a letter how, on the same day of the group's discovery, he had dug into the gravel at the gulch and "[t]hree or four little flat, smooth nuggets and some fine gold was the result; nuggets that made the pan ring when dropped into it—and a very refreshing sound it was."[23]

The members of the discovery party established a mining district and, in order to maximize their anticipated profits, created rules that only the original discoverers could hold more than two claims at the site.[24] Staley was designated as the district's recorder.[25] Crab and Cowan traveled to Alder Gulch for tools and provisions, prompting an inevitable group of men to follow them back to the discovery site.[26] The good news of the discovery spread rapidly, and a settlement was established. The location of the first gold find is now covered by Wall Street and an adjoining blacktopped parking lot.[27] However, in a report of the Society of Montana Pioneers dated April 15, 1921, which was written to resolve controversy over the actual discovery location, the site was identified as being at the intersection of Fuller Avenue and Sixth Avenue West,[28] a conclusion that some historians now view as in error.[29]

Last Chance Gulch was known as Last Chance City by September of 1864.[30] The settlement initially consisted of only five cabins,[31] one of which still exists today and is open to tourism. The five cabins were constructed by the present-day West Main Street near its intersection with South Cruse Avenue in Helena. The settlement was also briefly known to some persons as Crabtown, named after one of the four miners of the discovery party, John Crab.[32] But the name "Crabtown" sounded demeaning to some of the earliest settlers, and during a town meeting conducted at the cabin of George J. Wood[33] on October 30, 1864, the name was changed, once again, to Helena.[34] Names that were proposed but not selected included Pumpkinville, Squashville, Rochester, Winona, and Tomah, the last being the name of a local Indian chief.[35] The name St. Helena had been proposed by a miner, John Somerville, who hailed from the Helena located in Scott County, Minnesota.[36] The proposed name was

Figure 11.1. Cabin at the original settlement site of Last Chance Gulch. (Photo by author.)

quickly shortened to the plainer sounding "Helena."[37] The Southerners at the settlement approved of the name as they likened it to Helena, Arkansas, a busy port city on the Mississippi River.[38] Just as the name of Virginia City emerged from Unionist and Confederate compromise and accommodation, Helena's name might not have been finalized without the mutual assent of those holding Unionist and Secessionist sympathies. Southerners pronounced the city's name "Hel-EE-na," consistent with the Arkansas pronunciation.[39] Later, however, the pronunciation morphed into HELL-ena,[40] as miners may have used the latter pronunciation as a means of acknowledging the area's rough living conditions at the time, particularly in the winter. The early settlers provided for a system of local taxation and performed a survey of the town.[41] Unlike Virginia City, no regular townsite could initially be established as none of its ground could be considered "non-mineral."[42] Nevertheless, business and residential districts gradually formed around the road that led to Dry Gulch.[43] The road to Dry Gulch included a bridge that extended over a mud-prone area, and the road came to be known as Bridge Street.[44] Bridge Street became Helena's main thoroughfare and was later renamed State Street,[45] by which it is still known today. A street one block away was called Broadway and still exists today.[46]

Helena grew rapidly. On October 30, 1864, 200 residents of Helena cast ballots in Montana's first territorial elections.[47] At that time, there were only three women in Helena, the wives of John Somerville, Abraham Mast, and P. B.

Anthony.[48] The first person to die in Helena of natural causes was Dr. Rodney L. Pococke.[49] The First Presbyterian Church was organized under the leadership of Reverend T. V. Moore.[50] A Masonic lodge was established, and Helena witnessed its first wedding ceremony on May 4, 1865.[51]

Newspapers often played a role in the mining boomtowns as they were the only formal means of mass communication at the time. A newspaper owned by Thomas J. Favorite and Bruce Smith, the *Montana Radiator*, commenced publication in Helena on December 17, 1865.[52] The newspaper was sold to two men named Posnainsky and House, who changed the name of the paper to the *Helena Herald* as of November 15, 1866, and who employed Robert Emmet Fisk as their editor.[53] The paper was resold to the Fisk brothers the following year.[54] It continued to be edited by Robert Emmet Fisk, became a daily in 1867, and editorially favored Republicans.[55] A second newspaper that favored Republicans, the *Tri-Weekly Republican*, published its first edition on July 7, 1866, but after a mere thirty-two issues was relocated by its owner to Virginia City and published there as the *Tri-Weekly Post* until 1867.[56] A Democratic-leaning newspaper, the *Rocky Mountain Gazette*, commenced publication in Helena on August 11, 1866.[57] Its owners were E. S. Wilkinson, C. H. Wilkinson, H. N. Maguire, and Peter Ronan, and the newspaper remained in business until its facilities were destroyed by a fire on August 23, 1872.[58] The *Rocky Mountain Gazette* rose from its ashes in 1873, but before another year passed, it was again destroyed by a fire, on January 9, 1874.[59] The *Montana Post* was relocated by its owner from Virginia City to Helena in March of 1868.[60] The *Montana Post* published its last issue in early 1869.[61] While the press today endeavors to maintain some measure of objectivity in reporting hard news, the newspapers in the western territories made no effort to conceal their political biases, which were openly revealed by the manner in which they wrote and emphasized the stories on which they reported.

Samuel T. Hauser founded and was president of S. T. Hauser and Company, later known as the First National Bank of Helena, to which federal and territorial banking licenses were issued on July 16 and August 15, 1866.[62] The bank employed a cashier named Theodore H. Kleinschmidt, who was so expert at weighing gold dust that he could identify the specific gulch from which the dust was obtained just by examining the color and quality of the sample.[63] By 1880, Helena's population had grown to 3,600 residents.[64] Many of the people who initially migrated to Helena came from Virginia City and Bannack. Mollie Sheehan, whose father was a storekeeper, moved with her family from Virginia City to Helena in mid-1865.[65] Wilbur Fisk Sanders, who had successfully prosecuted George Ives in December of 1863, relocated his interests there as well.[66] Sanders, a Republican, had already run for, and lost, the election during the

Figure 11.2. Samuel T. Hauser. (Courtesy of the Montana Historical Society, image 942-605.)

fall of 1864 to be Montana's nonvoting delegate in the US Congress.[67] Anton Holter expanded his lumber interests into Helena during 1865.[68] John X. Beidler, who had been a member of the posse that arrested Ives in the death of Nicholas Tiebolt, met "Dutch John" Wagner on a trail after the attempted robbery of Moody's stagecoach and placed more than his share of nooses around the necks of Alder Gulch road agents, moved to Helena, where he spent the rest of his days.[69] There Beidler became a deputy US marshal. John Fetherstun, who had been involved in the apprehension of Wagner on a trail from Bannack on January 6, 1864, and which led to Wagner's execution five days later, also relocated to Helena, where he became a deputy US marshal.[70]

It was at about that time that President Lincoln was shot and killed at Ford's Theater in Washington, DC. Lincoln was shot on April 14, 1865, and died the next day.[71] News of Lincoln's death did not reach Montana for several days and could not be reported in the *Montana Post* until its weekly edition published on April 29, 1865, a full two weeks after the president's death.[72] Mollie Sheehan recalled that when news of Lincoln's death reached her school at midday, most of the girls at the school, who were daughters of Southern parents, cheered and danced around the room.[73] She joined in with her classmates but later regretted the conduct.[74]

Helena was built of wood and was significantly damaged by great fires in 1869, 1872, and 1874.[75]

As with Virginia City, the discovery of gold attracted not just prospectors to the area, but various "roughs," gamblers, and criminals. The gamblers who arrived in Helena included, by small-world coincidence, two mortal enemies from Salt Lake City named Harry Slater and John Keene. On June 8, 1865, Keene spotted Slater at the front door of Sam Greer's saloon on Bridge Street.[76] The two men had an unresolved quarrel from their earlier days in Salt Lake City,[77] wherein Slater had placed a revolver into Keene's mouth and had run him out of town.[78] In Helena Keene walked up to Slater from behind, drew his Colt, and shot Slater in the head execution-style.[79] According to the *Montana Post*, Keene hurried from the scene but then gave himself up to Charley Curtis, who turned him over to Helena's sheriff, George Wood.[80] There was not yet any jail in Helena, so Wood confined Keene at his own private residence.[81] Members of the public forcibly took Keene from Wood's custody, but rather than conducting an impromptu lynching, they chose to organize a trial by jury.[82] The trial was conducted in the absence of Judge Lyman Munson, who had not yet arrived in Helena to begin his judicial services.

The jury was assembled in a lumber shed owned by William Vantelburg.[83] Stephen Reynolds was selected to act as the trial judge.[84] A potential juror for the trial was John Sweeney, who also happened to be the only carpenter living in Helena.[85] Sweeney was excused from jury service so that he could make the coffin that was needed for Slater's corpse,[86] which he worked on while the selected jurors heard the evidence and conducted their deliberations.[87] The jury consisted of B. B. Burchette (foreman), A. Jack Edwards, C. C. Fanner, S. M. Hall, Edward Houser, Major Charles Hutchinson, S. Kayser, John Nichols, Edward Porter, and a Mr. Shears.[88] Helena's *Weekly Herald* identified all of the selected jurors by name, and its list also included Zerah French.[89] Some members of the jury had been early members of the Vigilance Committee in Virginia City prior to the economic growth of Helena.

Several witnesses were sworn to testify later that day, which was the first day of a two-day trial. The witnesses included Dr. Palmer, Charles Greer, Sam Greer, Charles French, James Binns, James Parker, Jem Geero, and a Mr. Philips.[90] Dr. Palmer testified that Slater incurred a bullet wound over the right eye and died

Figure 11.3. Helena sheriff George Wood. (Courtesy of the
Montana Historical Society, image 945-670.)

within three minutes of the incident.[91] The defendant, Keene, interrupted Dr.
Palmer's testimony to explain that he had shot Slater in self-defense,[92] but as
other witnesses then testified on behalf of the prosecution, it may be assumed
that Keene was instructed that he would have a chance to testify later in the
trial. Dr Palmer told the jury that when he examined Slater's body, he found
no gun in the vicinity that could have been in the possession of Slater, which
undermined any claim by Keene that he had acted in self-defense.[93]

Some of the prosecution's witnesses saw or knew nothing of the event. Sam
Greer and Philips saw portions of the shooting and its immediate aftermath.[94]
James Parker testified that he rode to Helena with Keene and that during the
trip Keene wondered aloud whether Slater would be in town.[95] Charles French
observed portions of the shooting and identified Keene as the gunman.[96] The
hour must have been late by the time of Charles French's testimony, as a candle

Figure 11.4. Charles French. (Courtesy of the Montana Historical Society, image 942-279.)

needed to be brought to Keene for French to make his in-court identification of the accused.[97] French's testimony is particularly noteworthy as another individual with the same surname, Zerah French, was a member of the jury.[98] Assuming, given the relatively small population of Helena at the time, that Zerah French and Charles French were related in some manner, the circumstances would suggest that the participants of the trial perceived no particular conflict for a juror to be related to a key identification witness of the prosecution.

At least one historian suggests that juror French and witness French were one in the same person.[99] Certainly, it would be a significant commentary on the legal proceedings of the territory at the time if a juror at a trial was also called as a witness for the prosecution in the same case. By today's standards, such a conflict of fairness would never be tolerated or even imagined. No court records have survived that officially identify the jurors and witnesses at the Keene trial.[100]

Different newspaper accounts provide both men with different first names.[101] Records exist of Zerah French, who was born in New York State in 1827, lived in Virginia City and Helena during the 1860s, California in the 1870s, and Michigan in the 1880s.[102] Zerah French married Margaret Robinson, who predeceased him, and had five children including the eldest daughter, Cecily, whose reminiscences are archived at the Montana Historical Society.[103] Far fewer records exist of a Charles French, though a man identified as "C. French" appears on an election poll list in Virginia City drawn in 1864.[104] Moreover, a period photograph of Charles French exists in the Montana Historical Society photograph archives.[105] Different newspaper accounts separately naming both Zerah and Charles French, documents verifying the existence of Zerah French, and threadbare documents verifying the existence of a "C. French" in the same region of Montana at a time when miners freely migrated from boomtown to boomtown, suggest that the juror and the witness at the Keene trial with the surname of French were likely two different individuals.

Toward the end of the first trial session, Keene requested an adjournment of the proceedings in order to obtain two witnesses that he believed were necessary to his defense, "Walsh" and an Irishman named Mike.[106] Some persons opposed a trial adjournment on the ground that it would require a guarding of the prisoner overnight.[107] The court originally denied the adjournment, but upon reconsideration, it agreed to recess the trial in order for Keene to summon his witnesses on condition that the number of men guarding Keene overnight be raised to forty.[108] One potential witness who could attest to the blood feud that had apparently existed between Keene and Slater and who Keene believed would exonerate him of the crime was in Blackfoot City.[109] Blackfoot City was forty-five miles distant.[110] A messenger was dispatched to retrieve the witness.

The second day of the trial began the following morning at 8:00 a.m.[111] Most of the additional witnesses who testified did not observe the relevant events. One witness, Mr. Boyden, testified that immediately after the shooting he heard Keene say to Slater, "You damned son of a bitch, you have ruined me in Salt Lake City!"[112]

According to author Dan Cushman, the messenger located the witness that was sought in Blackfoot City but returned to Helena without him, as the messenger learned from the witness that Keene had merely once said that "whenever Slater and I meet one of us must die."[113] John X. Beidler wrote in his journal that the witness was actually brought to the trial and testified to the same statement.[114] Cushman's account may be the more plausible, given the failure of the *Montana Post* to report the testimony of any independent witness addressing the specific history of Keene and Slater, even though it detailed the testimonies of several other witnesses on other matters relating to the crime. Moreover, since the trial was completed by 9:50 a.m. of its second day,[115] time and distance might have proven an insurmountable problem for Keene to overcome in obtaining the testimony of any far-off witnesses. In any event, the information that the Blackfoot City witnesses might have provided was hardly evidence that Slater would have killed Keene without warning had the tables between the two men been turned.

Keene did not deny his involvement in the shooting.[116] Instead, he testified during his trial that he and Slater had a prior agreement that if their paths ever crossed again, one would shoot the other on sight.[117] "He'd have done it to me," Keene explained.[118]

Keene was convicted by a unanimous jury.[119] Judge Reynolds asked for those assembled to give "fair and decent expressions of public sentiment" on the issue of the sentence, and during the debate that followed, portions of the trial testimony were read back.[120] Eventually, a motion carried that Keene be executed.[121] He was the first person in newly formed Helena who was sentenced to be hanged. Keene was resigned to his fate, remarking that "[a]ll I wanted was a fair trial; I think I have got it, and death is my doom."[122] Keene was given an hour to settle his affairs.[123]

The carpenter, John Sweeney, who had not been placed on the jury, was still working on Slater's coffin when he received a message from the jurors that said, "Make that two."[124]

Finding a suitable place to hang Keene initially posed a problem. The area had been denuded of many of its trees, as wood was needed in the construction of buildings and sluice boxes and for use as fire wood during the previous winter. Over the crest of Bridge Street in the direction of Dry Gulch, woodcutters had left one old, large, weather-worn bull pine with a strong horizontal branch suitable for hangings.[125] The tree was approximately one mile from the location of the Last Chance gold discovery. Keene was taken to the tree and made to stand upon the endgate of a wagon that was to provide his drop.[126] His last request was for a drink of whiskey, which was honored.[127] The hanging was superintended by John X. Beidler.[128] It occurred a few minutes before noon.[129] Before the wagon gate was pulled from underfoot, Keene became defiant and said, "I killed the son of a bitch and would do the same thing over again and if you don't like that you can drive your damn old cart off as fast as you damn please."[130] Unfortunately for Keene, the cart was not pulled from underfoot fast enough or his drop was not long enough, as he experienced a "swinging drop" and strangled on the noose for twenty-three minutes before dying.[131]

The tree from which Keene was hanged became known as the Old Hangman's Tree, or the Hanging Tree for short.[132] It became a visible symbol of the region's rough-and-tumble frontier justice. The location of the tree is believed to have been at present-day Blake Street near its intersection with State Street.[133] The precise location of the tree is difficult to find today because of the later construction of roads and private homes in the area. Between 1865 and 1870, the Hanging Tree would be put to use on a number of mortal occasions.

Keene's conviction and hanging should not be viewed as vigilantism. Keene received a rudimentary trial with a jury of citizens consistent with the norms of the time, along with an adjournment intended to provide an opportunity for procuring potential defense witnesses. The jury may have simply and correctly believed that Slater's murder was unjustified despite Keene's explanation to the contrary. Indeed, under common law, a person may use deadly force in self-defense, but only when that person reasonably believes that *imminent* deadly force is about to be used. Montana's First Territorial Legislature had incorporated the principle into the Bannack Statutes in 1865.[134] Montana statutorily recognizes the same principle today.[135] Keene's explanation, if true, that both men had sworn to kill the other on sight, was not a persuasive defense under the law, as Slater was shot suddenly in the back of the head at a time when Slater apparently did not pose an "imminent" risk of death or serious physical harm to Keene.

The Keene conviction and sentence forced the fledgling community at Helena to consider how it would provide law enforcement moving forward. Although vigilantism was on hiatus in Bannack and Alder Gulch as a result of the establishment there of Judge Hezekiah Hosmer's territorial court, the judicial mechanisms that would eventually be established in Helena by Judge Lyman Munson were not yet in place. In the immediate aftermath of Keene's execution, leading residents of Helena formed a Committee of Safety that would act as the force of law at least until an effective court could be established.[136]

The name of Helena's newly created vigilante organization, Committee of Safety, presented a much more neutral and uncontroversial tone than that suggested by the title of the Alder Gulch Vigilance Committee. Its membership was secret, but Charles J. D. Curtis is believed to have been the "chief" of the organization.[137] Nathaniel Langford had been asked to be the organization's chief but declined the position on the ground that he did not have the time for such responsibilities and instead contented himself with merely being one of ten members of the organization's governing Executive Committee.[138] Any written oath or bylaws generated by the Helena Committee of Safety are not preserved.[139] Langford defined the crimes for which the committee would act as limited to horse stealing, highway robbery, and murder, and like the bylaws of the counterpart organization in Virginia City, the only authorized punishment for offenders was death.[140]

Helena's Committee on Safety did not have to wait long before acting. The month following Keene's trial and execution, Jack Silvie, also known as Jacob

Seachriest, was seized in Diamond City, a new mining camp in Confederate Gulch forty miles from Helena.[141] According to Dimsdale, Silvie was accused of "robbery, obtaining goods under false pretenses, and various other crimes of a kindred sort."[142] Upon his initial questioning in Diamond City, Silvie confessed to having joined the road agents in Virginia City.[143] James Williams, who had been a prominent figure in the Virginia City movement, John X. Beidler, and others traveled to Diamond City to take possession of the prisoner so that he could be more closely examined by Helena's Committee of Safety.[144]

At Helena, Silvie repeated his Diamond City statements, but then retracted them.[145] Upon further questioning by the Executive Committee of the Committee of Safety, he repeated his earlier confession but said that he had joined his band of robbers at the Columbia River and merely traveled with them to Virginia City via the Snake River.[146] By mentioning the Snake River, Silvie unwittingly implicated himself as belonging to a band of thieves and murderers that preyed upon freighters in that area.[147] Silvie confessed to the murder of one miner at the Snake River whose description matched the body of a man who had been found there shot in the back of the head.[148] Silvie described how he had shot the man and tied the corpse to a large rock that was then thrown into the river.[149] The corpse of that murder victim had nevertheless been found by the same posse that had tracked down and hanged Jem Kelly.[150]

The Executive Committee of the Committee of Safety unanimously voted that Silvie be executed at the Hanging Tree later that evening, at 1:00 a.m.[151] When Silvie was brought to the Hanging Tree for his execution and realized his end was near, he confessed to a dozen additional murders in gruesome detail.[152] He was not given a drop. Perhaps the executioners did not think he deserved one. Instead, the hangman's noose was placed around Silvie's neck, and Silvie was hoisted into the air to die by slow strangulation.[153]

Author Lew L. Callaway Jr. offers a more sinister explanation for how the Committee of Safety might have obtained a murder confession from Jack Silvie. He suggests that while the Executive Committee was not initially satisfied of Silvie's guilt, it arranged for a minister to speak with Silvie privately in the cabin where he was being held and to pray with him.[154] According to Callaway, Silvie confessed his misdeeds to the minister, who then conveyed the confessions to the Executive Committee, which determined Silvie's guilt and imposed a sentence of death.[155] If events unfolded in that manner, then the vigilantes did not respect any confidentiality to the communications between a penitent and a religious counselor. However, Callaway's description of events, while plausible, is not entirely convincing, as he offers a second, conflicting description of events that does not have Silvie confess to any crime until he was brought to the Hanging Tree.[156] The seeming inconsistency might be explained if crimes were confessed to the minister and then other crimes were confessed by him at the Hanging Tree.

When Judge Lyman Munson finally arrived in Helena, one of his first sights was that of a man's corpse suspended from the Hanging Tree.[157] Munson convened the first grand jury in the territory's Third Judicial District, which was centered in Helena, on August 12, 1865.[158] Unlike Hosmer's earlier grand jury charge in Virginia City, Munson made no direct reference to vigilantes. Munson instructed the grand jurors in a general sense that "while you are the right arm and sword power of the government, you are at the same time the shield of the citizen, to protect him from false accusations, and to see that he does not unjustly suffer from any action of yours."[159] Munson instructed that "[t]he speed and certainty with which offenders are brought to justice, and punished for their offences, are the surest preventive of crime, and the best guaranty that a citizen can have in the enjoyment of his inalienable rights."[160] He highlighted the right of an accused citizen to have allegations examined by a grand jury.[161] The judge made a point of assuring the grand jurors that no criminal charges would be brought against persons who had been in rebellion against the United States during the Civil War.[162] The closest Munson might have come in his remarks to referencing vigilantism, in the most subtle of ways, was during his pronouncement that the grand jurors "bring into requisition and activity all the energy of the government for the suppression of crime and the protection of virtue, without which no community or people can long prosper," and that the law "must . . . sanctify every action."[163] Notably, Munson made no direct or indirect threats that vigilantes would be prosecuted in the event that they continued taking the law into their own hands.

History can ponder whether, if Judge Munson's arrival in Montana had not been delayed for as long as it was, Helena could have avoided the initial formation of its Committee of Safety by tethering itself to a judicial form of justice that could have adjudicated the allegations against Keene, Silvie, and others. The likely answer is no. Munson appears to have taken no overt steps to stand up to vigilantism in Helena, a factor that may be of historical significance. Whereas the vigilantes ceased most of their activities in and around Virginia City in order to give the judicial system a fair chance to work at Alder Gulch, noticeably less respect was given to Munson and his court. Fourteen vigilante executions occurred within the eight months immediately following Munson's grand jury address. Author Tom Donovan suggests that Munson, new to Montana from Connecticut, might have been perceived as a carpetbagger whose Eastern style of Ivy League justice was too slow, too expensive, and inadequate for the demands and patience of Helena's Committee of Safety.[164] Many of the residents of Helena instead preferred a form of justice that was fast, firm, and fatal.[165]

Indeed, according to Donovan, Montana would not hang its first judicially convicted murderer for another eleven years.[166] Moreover, no indictment would be brought by Munson's grand juries against any member of Helena's Committee of Safety for the extrajudicial hanging of any suspected criminals.

Helena's Committee of Safety was busy throughout the fall of 1865 and the winter and spring of 1866. On September 11, 1865, a saloon keeper named J. Hineman was robbed of forty or fifty dollars while traveling on foot to Helena, and although Hineman was shot during the commission of the crime, he survived the wound.[167] A posse left from Helena in search of the criminal responsible.[168] On September 15, 1865, Jack Howard was hanged in Diamond City. A piece of paper pinned to his leg identified him as a "Robber."[169]

On September 18, 1865, Tommy Cooke was hanged by vigilantes from Helena's Hanging Tree. A note pinned to his body merely said, "Pick pocket."[170]

On October 3, 1865, Con Kirby was also hanged from the Hanging Tree. There was no note pinned to his body identifying his crime.[171]

On November 21, 1865, George Sanders was hanged by vigilantes on the Hanging Tree. A note pinned to his body said, "This man was hung for robbing A. Slane of $1,180 and for other small stealings."[172]

Two persons whose names are unknown were hanged at the Prickly Pear Tollgate, near Helena, in October of 1865.[173] An additional person, name unknown, was hanged at Confederate Gulch during the same month.[174]

On November 23, 1865, two additional unknown prisoners were hanged from the Hanging Tree.[175]

On February 5, 1866, a man named Charles Jewitt and an accomplice were hanged in Gallatin City. At a saloon in Diamond City, Jewitt drew his pistol to shoot a man with whom he had a disagreement.[176] Jewitt's bullet missed the intended target and instead struck a German man named Fisher as Fisher was entering the bar.[177] Jewitt was arrested by Sheriff Mendenhall and placed under guard, but local vigilantes seized Jewitt from the guards and hanged him from a tree overlooking Gallatin City.[178] Jewitt was not the only person to be forcibly seized from law enforcement and hanged by vigilantes. During the first week of January 1865, Zacharia Fogarty, who had been charged with a murder at Fort Owen, 270 miles southeast of Helena, had been taken by vigilantes while awaiting transport to Bannack for trial and was summarily hanged for his crime.[179]

On March 12, 1866, Leander W. Johnson was forcibly taken from a sheriff's custody and hanged by vigilantes in Deer Lodge, near Helena, for having stolen cattle from a rancher named Reese Anderson.[180] Disfigurement observed on Johnson's face and neck after the hanging suggested that his neck did not break upon his drop and that he instead died of slow strangulation.[181] According to a Dr. Hardenbrook, who later became the coroner for Deer Lodge County, the missing cattle eventually returned to Anderson's ranch in their own time.[182] The Johnson hanging is significant and deserving of more historical attention than it has received, as it may represent the hanging of an innocent man if the cattle in question merely wandered off from their owner's land on their own accord.

On April 20, 1866, a man named J. L. Goones was hanged after having been convicted by a miners' court in the stabbing of a mining partner, Hugh "Jack" Dowd, during an altercation.[183] Goones had pointed his rifle at Dowd and was about to shoot, but a third person knocked the muzzle at the last moment and the bullet fired into the roof.[184] Dowd responded by attempting to strangle Goones.[185] Goones took a butcher knife and stabbed Dowd between the fifth and sixth ribs, twisting the blade mercilessly before removing it and damaging one of Dowd's lungs.[186] Goones was hanged despite the fact that Dowd survived the wound. After Goones's death, it was observed that his forehead, which had always been concealed by a hat, had a scar-tissued brand that was a common punishment for petty crimes.[187]

During the first full year of prospecting at Helena, the gold discovery party employed approximately seventy men and paid them $6.00 to $10.00 per day.[188] After deducting all business costs and expenses, the discovery party cleared a profit of $170,000,[189] a sizable profit in the western territories during the 1860s. One of the prospectors employed by the discovery party was John "Frenchy" Crouchet, who was believed to have stolen sluice boxes during the late evening of June 4, 1866, or during the early hours of the following morning. The thief wore a pair of old boots that were left behind at the crime scene.[190] The next work day Crouchet was unable to work because of sore feet.[191] An inference was drawn that Crouchet's feet were sore the day after the sluice boxes were stolen because he had worn the ill-fitting boots to disguise his footsteps during his commission of the crime.[192] The evidence seemed plausible but was also entirely circumstantial. Crouchet was forcibly taken from his tent and hanged on June 5, 1866.[193]

An entirely different story surrounding Crouchet's hanging was offered in the 1915 reminiscences of H. Frank Adkins. Adkins observed Crouchet's corpse at the "old pine with its 'fruit' this time in the shape of Frenchy."[194] According to Adkins, Crouchet stole money from an elderly man, and upon his hanging for the crime, a note was pinned at the Hanging Tree that said, "This man, Frenchy, was hanged for stealing $800 from an old grey headed man and also for trying to swear away the lives of innocent men."[195] Adkins's account of Crouchet's crime is eerily similar in many respects to the $1,180 robbery of A. Slane by George Sanders, for which Sanders was separately hanged. The inconsistent versions of whether Crouchet was hanged for stealing sluice boxes from his employers or stealing money from an elderly man may indicate, though by no means conclusively, that Adkins's version written fifty years after the event confuses Crouchet's hanging with that of Sanders.

The spate of vigilante executions in the Helena region occurred despite the presence of Judge Lyman Munson. The events in the greater Helena area prompted grave concerns by the territorial lawyers and Chief Judge Hezekiah Hosmer that vigilantism could spread back to Virginia City. Hosmer could not have wanted the vigilantism in Helena to spark a revival of vigilantism in Alder Gulch. Hosmer determined that a further charge was warranted to a grand jury in Virginia City, which he delivered on August 7, 1866.[196] The idea for a further grand jury charge may have originated from a bipartisan roster of attorneys that included Alexander Davis, John D. Ritchie, and even Wilbur Fisk Sanders.[197] Sanders's involvement suggests that there were limits to the extent of vigilantism that even he could support. In his second charge to the grand jury, Hosmer noted the fact that the Vigilance Committee in Alder Gulch had not formally disbanded, and he urged its members to cooperate in the capturing of criminals so that the *courts* could handle the cases.[198] Hosmer charged the grand jury, as he did in December of 1864, that it should pursue its duties diligently to have a positive effect that would ward off further vigilantism.[199] Executions that later occurred at Alder Gulch between 1865 and 1867, limited and sporadic as they were, may be historically viewed as a "last gasp" of vigilantism in that immediate region. The greater amount of vigilante activity was occurring 120 miles to the north, in the general Helena area, during the same period,[200] where an even newer gold rush was attracting prospectors and others to such a degree that Helena would become Montana's territorial capital in 1875.[201]

There was a deadly and unfortunate shootout among prospectors at Cave Gulch, approximately thirty miles northeast of Helena, on December 14, 1866.[202] The shootout arose from a claim-jumping incident and resulted in the deaths of five men.[203] The original discoverers of Cave Gulch had decided to abandon their claims, believing them to be unprofitable, and they relocated their mining efforts to the Confederate Gulch.[204] Other men then reaped great profits at Cave Gulch, prompting the original discoverers to return to the camp to reclaim their placer tracts.[205] Disagreement over the rightful possession of the tracts resulted in a shootout between the competing groups of prospectors.[206] The prospectors who were killed were James Hassett, Thomas "Black Jack" Cheevers, Charles McLaughlin, Tim McCoy, and Patrick Considine.[207] The incident was unusual as it defied the cordiality and cooperation that often characterized the relationship between prospectors engaged in placer mining and, for reasons unknown, circumvented any miners' court that would normally have been used to resolve the competing claims. The Committee of Safety arrested several of the shooting suspects, returned them to Helena, and ultimately gave the prisoners over to law enforcement authorities for lawful trials.[208] Indictments were then filed against nine defendants, John Dimperson, George Rashaw, James Sigler, Joseph E. Cassell, Frederick Wichman, Jacob Hart, Robert M. Bateman, John Bowman, and James DeHaven.[209] Judge Lorenzo Williston changed the venue of the cases to Edgerton County and jointly tried the cases there.[210] Several witnesses testified at the trial,[211] and ultimately, all defendants were acquitted of the crimes charged and returned to Cave Gulch amid great celebration "over their escape from the perils of the law."[212]

Although Helena's Committee of Safety chose to treat the Cave Gulch incident as one suitable for official law enforcement, the incident provided further impetus for a vigilante presence in the region. Vigilante posters were printed and distributed in the same month as the nine defendants' arrests, and a full text of the poster's language was later republished in the *Montana Post* on January 5, 1867. It read:

> Read and Reflect
>
> In view of the fact that crime has run riot to such an alarming extent in the Territory of Montana (particularly east of the Missouri River) during the past six months, and that murders and high handed outrages have been of such frequent occurrence as to excite the just indignation of all good citizens, it is believed that now is the time that the good work should be re-commenced. Therefore, this is to notify all whom it may concern, that crime must and will be suppressed; and, to that end, all offenders will be summarily dealt with, and punished as of old.
>
> By Order of the Vigilance Committee.[213]

The next several months were quiet ones for vigilante activists in the region. Then on October 22, 1867, J. M. Douglas, a man in his mid-twenties, was arrested in Helena for stealing twenty-two head of cattle from men named Pelaux and LeBeau.[214] He escaped from custody later in the week but was recognized at Big Hole Station on November 9, 1867. A five-man posse that set out to locate Douglas found him along the Rattlesnake River and transported him the following day to the cattle ranch from which the cattle were allegedly stolen. Douglas offered to give the cattle owners whatever property he owned to "square accounts," but was instead hanged from a tree on November 13, 1867, at Red Mountain City.[215] Vigilantes on this and other occasions were uncompromising.

The year 1868 brought further vigilante executions in the region. A rancher named Ike Milner had hired two employees, one named Spaulding, who was approximately fifty years old, and another named Billy Wilson, who was in his early twenties.[216] There is some evidence suggesting that Billy Wilson was actually a runaway as young as sixteen years old.[217] Wilson's employment was terminated when it was discovered that he had stolen money from Milner's store.[218] Shortly thereafter, Spaulding set out to make some purchases, ostensibly at Helena, but in actuality he left with Wilson for Salt Lake City, Utah. At the same time, two horses were stolen from the nearby ranch of Thomas Reeves, and Reeves connected the departure of Spaulding and Wilson with his two missing horses. Through the use of telegraphed descriptions of Spaulding, Wilson, and the stolen horses, James C. O'Connor managed to locate and capture the two suspects at the point of his shotgun. The two horses in Spaulding's and Wilson's possession did not match the descriptions that had been provided, but it was ascertained that the suspects had exchanged the animals for others.[219]

According to the *Virginia Tri-County Post*, a two-day vigilante trial was conducted during which Spaulding blamed Wilson for inducing him to steal the horses.[220] Spaulding's defense was highly questionable, as Wilson was less than half of Spaulding's age and was not considered to be the more controlling personality. During the trial, Wilson feigned sickness and escaped custody but was later recaptured.[221] Spaulding was hanged at White Tail Deer Station on January 29 or 30, 1868. A butcher's hoist was used as the hanging mechanism.[222] Before his execution Spaulding was permitted to write to his son, urging him "to take warning by his father's fate and shun bad company and drink."[223] Wilson, as a result of his flight and recapture, was hanged in Jefferson Valley on January 30, 1868.[224] Wilson was hanged from a tripod of three corral poles erected at a roadside for all to see.[225] The earth was frozen so solid in January of 1868 that no grave could be dug for Wilson. The corpse therefore remained suspended from the makeshift gallows for several days.[226] Wilson's body eventually needed to be disposed. A hole was chopped through the ice of the Jefferson River and young Billy Wilson's remains were fed to the fish.[227]

On May 18, 1868, George Ballou was executed for taking part in the stabbing death of Johnny Gordon outside of Gordon's saloon.[228] The incident occurred while Ballou and his three friends were in a state of intoxication at approximately 9:00 p.m. the previous evening.[229] Ballou and his friends were looking for a man named Ned McGovern, with whom Ballou had come to blows earlier in the evening.[230] Gordon was stabbed by Ballou in the back, the arm, the abdomen, and near the throat and lived for approximately twenty minutes before dying from the wounds.[231] Ballou tried to escape the gulch but fell into a prospector's hole while running in the darkness and was captured.[232] An impromptu trial was conducted over two hours in a vacant building once used by the Lee & O'Connell Store, and testimony was heard from a number of witnesses.[233] Ballou's fate was determined by a jury, so his capital punishment should not be viewed as a product of vigilantism. Ballou was hanged from a

Figure 11.5. Helena as it appeared in 1867. (Courtesy of the Montana Historical Society, image 954-230.)

beam of a building while standing on boxes, a mere six hours after his commission of the crime.[234] Ballou's accomplices escaped capture.[235]

The execution of Jack Varley on August 13, 1868, provides another example of vigilantes forcibly seizing a defendant from official law enforcement. Varley robbed Julian Guezals of property at knife point,[236] and Guezals, who was born in Spain, swore out an arrest warrant that was given to Deputy Sheriff Kane.[237] Kane said that a white man did not deserve to be punished much for robbing a "greaser," though Guezals had lived in the United States and its territories for more than thirty years and had served in the US Navy.[238] Guezals was summoned to identify the prisoner.[239] Vigilantes located and captured Varley and refused to turn him over to Deputy Sheriff Kane.[240] Instead, they conducted their own impromptu trial, which appears to have consisted of Guezals's identification of the accused as the culprit and which resulted in Varley being hanging at Beartown.[241] Beartown is now a ghost town located west of Helena.[242] The *Montana Post* declared in reporting the hanging "[t]hat a strong and organized vigilance committee is now in existence in this vicinity there is but little doubt."[243]

William Hinson was hanged by vigilantes on August 20, 1868, from tripod gallows.[244] His crime was highway robbery.[245]

The public's attitude began turning away from vigilantism in Helena in 1870. In January of that year, there was a dispute between a Chinese man named Ah Chow and John R. Bitzer that resulted in the shooting death of Bitzer. The underlying facts of the dispute are murky. Chow may have caught Bitzer in Chow's cabin with a female member of his family.[246] Chow's wife, Jasmine, explained that Bitzer had attacked her and was shot when her husband and Bitzer struggled for control of the gun.[247] Dr. Enoch Shore, who had earlier treated Chow for a right-arm injury, was of the opinion that Chow's arm was too disabled to engage in the shooting of Bitzer.[248] Bitzer, before succumbing to death, said that he had entered Chow's cabin to assist a women that Chow was beating in a domestic dispute.[249] Despite the conflicting versions of events, Chow disappeared after the shooting and a $600 reward was posted for his capture.[250] Helena's Chinese community agreed to aid in the search for Chow,[251] as a result of pressure received from members of the broader Helena population or, perhaps, out of fear of potential retribution against them if they withheld their cooperation.

The incident between Chow and Bitzer must be viewed in the broader context of the relationship between whites and Chinese that existed at the time. In 1870 nearly 2,000 persons of Chinese origin resided in Montana, representing roughly 10 percent of the territory's total population.[252] The migration was eastward from China to California, and then from California to Montana. The Chinese were not particularly liked by the white majority, but they were tolerated so long as they primarily confined themselves to work in menial and servient tasks such as operating laundries, groceries, and restaurants.[253] The Chinese typically lived in segregated "Chinatown" districts in Alder Gulch and later, in Helena.[254] In at least one locale, Chinese businesses were required to pay a special $15.00 quarterly tax that was not imposed upon white-owned businesses.[255]

Some Chinese were prospectors, but they were excluded from the prime placer tracts and instead mined abandoned placer claims and worn-out drift mines.[256] Many white miners refused to hire Chinese men as laborers.[257] Those who did generally paid Chinese workers lower than prevailing wages, which forced some white men out of the job market and which occasionally caused tensions.[258] In 1872 the territorial legislature passed a statute that prohibited the Chinese from owning their own placer claims.[259] The statute was struck down two years later in a decision of 2 to 1 by the Montana Supreme Court in the case of *Territory v. Lee*.[260] By 1874, the Montana Supreme Court consisted of Chief Judge Decius Wade II and Justice Francis G. Servis, who were both appointees of President Grant, and Justice Hiram Knowles, a holdover appointee of President Johnson. Judge Wade, writing for the majority in *Territory v. Lee*, reasoned that since mineral lands were owned by the federal government rather than by the territory, the territory had no sovereignty to regulate the ownership of placer claims.[261] In a separate concurring majority opinion, Justice

Servis reasoned that the unequal treatment of the Chinese under the Montana statute violated the terms of the Burlingame-Seward Treaty, which had been entered into between the United States and Empire of China on February 5, 1870.[262] Both lines of reasoning appear from their legal merits to be equally valid, though the two judges in the majority must not have thought so, as they failed to render a single majority opinion adopting either or both of the two alternative grounds for striking down the exclusionary Chinese placer mine law.

Only Justice Knowles voted to uphold the discriminatory statute, arguing in dissent that Montana Territory had superior possessory powers over its lands than the federal government, which could devolve to individual miners but not to noncitizens. Knowles wrote in his dissent that he was "unable to see how such legislation interferes with the Constitution of the United States, its laws, or the Organic Act of our Territory, or is not a rightful subject of legislation."[263] Knowles's dissent is not legally persuasive, as he entirely overlooked the right of any naturalized Chinese citizens to the equal protection of the law as guaranteed by the Fourteenth Amendment, which had become effective in 1868, and did not even address Justice Servis's arguments regarding the supremacy of the Burlingame-Seward Treaty with China. Article 4 of the US Constitution renders treaties with any foreign nation the supreme law of the land,[264] and since the territory of Montana was a creation of the federal government, the Sino-American treaty was supreme in Montana as well.[265]

The Bannack Statutes rendered any "Chinaman" incompetent to testify in courts except against other Chinese, Negroes, and Native American Indians.[266] Whites sometimes took advantage of the Chinese in business transactions, knowing that the Chinese could not later testify in court to establish their claims.[267] Chinese men were sometimes beaten or shot when they sought to collect their bills or wages.[268] In many local court cases involving only Chinese litigants and witnesses, little attempt was made to understand the actual facts on which decisions would be made.[269] Chinese laborers pursuing their tasks were occasionally tripped, stoned, and pelted with snowballs, rocks, and broken bottles, much to the amusement of white bystanders.[270] A song dismissive to the Chinese took root with the lyrics

> *In spite of what ancients or moderns have said,*
> *Of whirlpools so deep and volcanoes so red;*
> *Of all things on earth the one I most dread*
> *Is the Mongolian locust, John Chinamen.*[271]

The Montana Chinese lived separately and unequally from the white men and women, not just because of cultural differences and ethnic prejudices against them, but because of pronounced religious differences as well.[272] The Chinese worked on the Sunday Sabbath,[273] which the Fourth Montana Territorial Legislature set aside in 1867 as the Lord's Day,[274] and their religious observances were, on occasion, mocked. Indeed, the *Montanian* newspaper reported that the Chinese "will buy idols of the oldest style, and then these heathens will then bow down to wood and stone. People who worship gold cannot see much sense in adoring cheap articles like these."[275] Despite being surrounded by an alien culture, the Chinese never abandoned their religious beliefs.[276]

The irony of the discrimination against the territorial Chinese was that it occurred during the immediate aftermath of the Civil War and its statement about ethnic and cultural equality under the law, at the time of the passage of the Thirteenth Amendment in 1865, which prohibited slavery, the Fourteenth Amendment in 1868, which guaranteed all citizens equal protection under the law, and the Fifteenth Amendment in 1870, which guaranteed citizens the right to vote regardless of race or color. The constitutional protections afforded by the Fourteenth, Fifteenth, and Sixteenth Amendments held little practical meaning for Montana's territorial Chinese.

Given this backdrop of the relationship between Montana's whites and Chinese, the ethnic prejudices of the time might have held Ah Chow guilty of the murder of John R. Bitzer regardless of the actual underlying facts of Bitzer's death. Indeed, had the crime been Asian-on-Asian, the broader Helena community might have taken little notice. In this instance, however, the crime was allegedly committed by a Chinese man against a white man, which required that the matter be taken seriously. Anti-Chinese prejudice and distrust was reflected by the tenor of an article published about the crime by the *Daily Rocky Mountain Gazette*. The newspaper, reporting on the cooperation of the Chinese community in searching for Chow, advised in the same news column that "the friends of the deceased not place their entire reliance in the proffered aid of the Mongolians, but at the same time to do all that they can to keep up the hunt and catch the murderer."[277]

Within days, Chow was caught by the infamous lawman John X. Beidler, who gave him over to the Committee of Safety, which in turn hanged Chow from the bough of the Hanging Tree on January 24, 1870.[278] A sign was pinned to his back that said, "Ah Chow, the murderer of John R. Bitzer. Beware! The Vigilantes still live!"[279] Crowds came to the Hanging Tree to view Chow's body dressed, as it was, in an old soldier's overcoat, with his boots off.[280]

Editorial opinion of the execution was mixed. The *Daily Rocky Mountain Gazette* declared that "[t]he verdict of the public is that Ah Chow justly deserved to die for the murder of John R. Bitzer."[281] The *Helena Herald* wrote that "[t]he miserable, abandoned wretch . . . has, at last, been brought to dreadful accountability . . . His worthless body now dangles in the air . . . That his awful fate is a just one none can deny."[282] However, notwithstanding the ethnic prejudices that were prevalent, other newspapers such as the *New North-West* of Deer Lodge contained language that was openly critical of the execution, as serious doubts surfaced about whether Chow was an unfortunate victim in the sordid affair.[283] The apprehension and execution of Ah Chow called vigilantism into open question, at least among those who feared that an innocent man might have been hanged for having acted in self-defense or in the chivalrous defense of a family member.

Beidler's conduct in Chow's apprehension was itself a controversial issue. He collected the $600 reward money that had been offered for Chow's capture. Vigilantes had not previously profited financially from their activities. While Beidler may have viewed the reward as well deserved, others viewed it negatively as blood money, and it earned Beidler considerable resentment.[284] Beidler soon received a note, signed "200 Anti-Vigilantes," that threatened him with death.[285] The vigilante arrest and execution of Chow reflected the impatience of some to abide by the slower, more methodical procedures of official judicial process. The *Daily Rocky Mountain Gazette* wrote that "[i]f Ah Chow had fallen into the hands of the constituted authorities when the murder was first committed he doubtless would not have been hung without all the forms of law."[286] The newspaper continued, "It would have been better, perhaps, that he should have been dealt with by the authorities; but it is better that summary justice should have been dealt out to him than to have let him escape [justice]."[287] Put another way, it was, in the newspaper's view, preferable to execute Chow without a trial than to afford him the legal process by which Chow might have been acquitted.

The public's reservations about the execution of Ah Chow did not eliminate further vigilante executions. On March 12, 1870, W. C. Patrick was arrested for the murder of John Benser.[288] While in custody in Diamond City, Patrick was seized by vigilantes and hanged.[289]

Tolerance for vigilante executions in Helena further waned with the "double hangings" of Joseph Wilson and Arthur Compton. Both men, acting in concert, attempted to kill George Leonard and steal money from him.[290] Leonard owned a ranch on the Missouri River near Beaver Creek.[291] He had been drinking heavily at Joe Reed's saloon, located on present-day Rodney Street in Helena.[292] When Leonard left the saloon he was pursued by Compton and Wilson on horseback, catching up to him at Spokane Creek.[293] Compton and Wilson fired seven shots at Leonard, striking him once in the thigh.[294] Leonard fell from his horse and was beaten, robbed, and left for dead.[295] He was found alive the next morning by George Ammerman and was taken to Peter Greenishe's ranch nearby, where he gave a detailed description of the two horses that his assailants had ridden.[296]

An investigation was undertaken by Sheriff Steele. According to the *Daily Rocky Mountain Gazette*, "two suspicious characters had hired horses at the Pacific stables late in the afternoon Wednesday which exactly corresponded with the wounded man's description, and did not return them to the stable until twelve o'clock the same night."[297] With that information, Joseph Wilson was arrested at the home of James Wood and was then taken by Sheriff Steele to Leonard for identification.[298] Leonard was unable to specifically identify Wilson as one of his assailants.[299] By then, Arthur Compton was in custody and was also taken to Leonard for identification.[300] Leonard identified Compton as the man who fired the initial shot at him,[301] which, apparently, was sufficient evidence for holding Wilson as well. At the courthouse square in Helena, a crowd debated whether to try Compton and Wilson immediately or the next day, with the majority determining that the trial be held the next day.[302] Judge Robert Lawrence, who sought prompt retribution, described the crime as the worst in the territory since the days of Henry Plummer.[303] District attorney John H. Shober urged the crowd to permit a fair trial.[304] When Shober's arguments prevailed, Harvey H. English was chosen to act as trial judge.[305] In the meantime, the prisoners remained in the custody of Sheriff Steele.[306]

There appears to be disagreement in the historical literature about whether Compton and Wilson ever received their judicial trials. According to the *Daily Rocky Mountain Gazette*, Compton and Wilson received no trial, as a vigilante mob seized the prisoners from the sheriff, pronounced them guilty of attempted murder, and took them on a wagon to the Hanging Tree in the direction of Dry Gulch.[307]

According to author Tom Donovan, Compton and Wilson received a one-day trial that included a full jury and testimony from George Ammerman, A. K. Kingsbury, J. Thomas Lowery, and Reverend S. G. Lathrop of the Methodist Episcopal Church, to whom Wilson confessed his crime while in custody the night before.[308] W. B. Morris (or Morrison) testified to his witnessing of George Leonard's positive identification of Compton as one of the culprits.[309] Leonard apparently did not testify, perhaps due to the gravity of his medical condition. Both defendants confessed to their involvement in the shooting, though Compton maintained that he never intended to kill anyone.[310] Compton's testimony may have seemed incredible to the jury, as he had inconsistently admitted to having fired a total of four shots at Leonard.[311] The jury returned a verdict during the mid-afternoon finding both defendants guilty of assault with intent to kill and robbery.[312] Interpretive historian Dr. Ellen Baumler has likewise written that a Compton-Wilson trial was conducted by a group of twelve vigilantes at a warehouse, only steps away from the county courthouse.[313] The issue of the sentence was offered to the crowd that had assembled. Over the objections of

District Attorney Shober and local judge George Symes, the crowd declared by voice vote that the defendants each be hanged.[314]

A Compton-Wilson trial was most likely held, as photographic evidence of the hangings depicts a large crowd at the event during daylight. Had Compton and Wilson been seized by vigilantes and denied trials, it would likely have occurred at night when vigilantes preferred to conduct their extrajudicial executions, as darkness generally helped vigilantes maintain their anonymity and lessened the possibility of attempts to rescue the prisoners. For the photograph to depict executions that had occurred on an earlier evening, it would mean that a large crowd had malingered or assembled at the site of the hanging bodies into the next day. More likely, the photograph was taken contemporaneous with the events after an open trial and executions during daytime.

In any event, on April 27, 1870, nooses were adjusted around Compton's and Wilson's necks by Jesse Armitage, who also tied the prisoners' arms and legs.[315] The two condemned men stood upon dry goods boxes at the rear of the wagon, and when the wagon was driven forward, the men dropped.[316] Compton's neck broke instantly from the fall.[317] Wilson was not so fortunate, as the noose knots turned toward the back of his neck and he died from an eight-minute strangulation at the end of the rope.[318]

Photography was becoming more and more common at the time. The photograph of Wilson's and Compton's executions was widely circulated throughout the region, showing their bodies hanging side by side from the tree, their necks bent at the noose, amid of a crowd of men and boy onlookers. The photograph was surreal and had the effect of further eroding public support for vigilantism in the region.[319]

During the decade of the 1870s, vigilante executions, though not unheard of, became rare throughout the whole of Montana Territory. Executions included those of John W. "Steamboat Bill" St. Clair on February 1, 1873, for the murder of a woman in Bozeman, Jack "Old Man" Triplett on February 1, 1873, for the drunken murder of a restaurateur in Bozeman, and a Chinese "John Doe" in October of 1875 for improper behavior around young girls in Beaverhead County.[320]

Unlike most of the vigilante executions in Bannack and Alder Gulch against organized murderers and robbers of travelers, the vigilante executions in and around Helena from 1865 to 1870 were directed at a more assorted and broad-based criminal element. The vigilantes in and around Helena operated against murderers like Jack Silvie, attempted murderers and robbers like Joseph Wilson and Arthur Compton, thieves of significant sums of money such as George Sanders, alleged cattle thieves like Leander Johnson, and horse thieves such as Sanders and Charles Wilson. They took on petty crooks like Tommy Cooke

Figure 11.6. The double hanging of Joseph Wilson and Arthur Compton on April 27, 1870, for their shooting and robbery of George Leonard at Spokane Creek. (Courtesy of the Montana Historical Society, image 948-121.)

and John "Frenchy" Crouchet. They also settled scores with persons involved in saloon brawls and shootouts like Charles Jewett, his unnamed accomplice, and George Ballou. Gold wealth was not always a prime motivator of the crimes that caught vigilantes' attention in and around Helena, nor was the insecurity of travel a factor in all cases. Wealth and property in a more general sense, the absence of credible law enforcement, and the unwillingness of the grand jury to investigate vigilantes continued to be prominent factors in Helena's protracted vigilante violence, as they had been in earlier years at Bannack and Alder Gulch.

Panning for Nuggets

The infamous photograph taken of the double hanging of Joseph Wilson and Arthur Compton on April 27, 1870, for the shooting and robbery of George Leonard shows a young boy standing prominently at the forefront of the assembled crowd. The boy in the photograph is David H. Hilger, who lived until 1939 and who, during his adult life, served as secretary to the Montana Historical Society.[321] Hilger was twelve years old at the time the photograph was taken.[322] He does not appear to be the youngest member of the crowd. The town of Hilger, in Fergus County, Montana, today bears his name.[323]

Notes

1. Bancroft, *History*, 643–44; mt.gov, "Judicial Branch: Brief History."
2. Cameron, "Bar of Tioga County," 126.
3. Organic Act for the Territory of Montana, Act May 26, 1864, ch. 95, sec. 9, 13 Stat. 85.
4. Ibid., ; Spence, *Territorial Politics*, 2, 26.
5. Donovan, *Hanging around the Big Sky*, book 1, 1.
6. Ibid.
7. Ibid.
8. Guice, *Rocky Mountain Bench*, 66.
9. Ibid., 67; mt.gov, "Judicial Branch: Brief History."
10. Bancroft, *History*, 644; Allen, *Decent Orderly Lynching*, 323; mt.gov, "Judicial Branch: Brief History."
11. Allen, *Decent Orderly Lynching*, 323.
12. Ibid., 366; Greever, *Bonanza West*, 228.
13. Hello Helena, "Helena History."
14. Axline et al., *More from the Quarries*, 157–58.
15. Ibid., 154–55.
16. Georgia on my Mind, "The Four Georgians."
17. Axline et al., *More from the Quarries*, 154.
18. Ibid.
19. Ibid. Frederick Allen identifies the date of the discovery as July 17, 1864. Allen, *Decent Orderly Lynching*, 296. A plaque near the discovery site identifies July 14, 1864, as the discovery date.
20. Axline et al., *More from the Quarries*, 154.
21. Burlingame, *Montana Frontier*, 90.
22. Campbell, *From the Quarries*, 11.
23. Wolle, *Montana Pay Dirt*, 68.
24. Ibid.
25. Burlingame, *Montana Frontier*, 90.
26. Ibid.
27. Axline et al., *More from the Quarries*, 156; "History Proves That No One Is Infallible," 5.
28. Axline et al., *More from the Quarries*, 163.

29. Ibid., 157; "History Proves That No One Is Infallible," 5.

30. Cushman, *Montana*, 195–96.

31. Campbell, *From the Quarries*, 12.

32. Hello Helena, "Helena History."

33. Axline et al., *More from the Quarries*, 122.

34. Ibid., 158; Greever, *Bonanza West*, 220; Graf, *Land of Liberty*, 22. However, Dan Cushman identifies the date of the meeting as October 1, 1864. Cushman, *Montana*, 197. The date of October 30, 1864, is likely the correct one, as it is reflected on a plaque near the discovery site.

35. Leeson, *History of Montana*, 694; Wolle, *Montana Pay Dirt*, 68; Axline et al., *More from the Quarries*, 123.

36. Leeson, *History of Montana*, 694; Cushman, *Montana*, 197.

37. Leeson, *History of Montana*, 694.

38. Cushman, *Montana*, 197.

39. Helena Board of Trade, *Helena Illustrated*, 5; Axline et al., *More from the Quarries*, 126; Cushman, *Montana*, 197.

40. Helena Board of Trade, *Helena Illustrated*, 5.

41. Cushman, *Montana*, 198.

42. Ibid.

43. Ibid.

44. Ibid.

45. Ibid.

46. Ibid.

47. Campbell, *From the Quarries*, 12.

48. Helena Board of Trade, *Helena Illustrated*, 5.

49. Axline et al., *More from the Quarries*, 76.

50. Ibid., 26.

51. Campbell, *From the Quarries*, 13.

52. Leeson, *History of Montana*, 327; Bancroft, *History*, 652n22 (identifying the time of initial publication as March of 1866).

53. Bancroft, *History*, 652n22.

54. Leeson, *History of Montana*, 327; Bancroft, *History*, 652n22; Axline et al., *More from the Quarries*, 175; Library of Congress / National Endowment for the Humanities, "Chronicling America: About the *Helena Herald*"; Access Genealogy, "Montana Organization, Boundaries, and Elections."

55. Leeson, *History of Montana*, 327; Access Genealogy, "Montana Organization, Boundaries, and Elections."

56. Bancroft, *History*, 652n22; Leeson, *History of Montana*, 322; Access Genealogy, "Montana Organization, Boundaries, and Elections," n. 2.

57. Ibid.

58. Bancroft, *History*, 652n22; Leeson, *History of Montana*, 327; Baumler, *Girl from the Gulches*, 78, 112–13; Access Genealogy, "Montana Organization, Boundaries, and Elections," n. 2.

59. Leeson, *History of Montana*, 327.

60. Bancroft, *History*, 652n22; Library of Congress / National Endowment for the Humanities, "Chronicling America: About the *Montana Post*."

61. Library of Congress / National Endowment for the Humanities, "Chronicling America: About the *Montana Post*.".

62. "Legal Documents 1859–1899," First National Bank of Helena Records, Mont. Hist. Soc., MC-116, folder 38-1. Hauser became a leading citizen in the territory as a shrewd and successful banker and was a future governor of Montana. See, generally, Lingenfelter, *Bonanzas & Borrascas*.

63. "Guide to the First National Bank," First National Bank of Helena Records, MC-116, Folder 38-11.
64. Helena Board of Trade, *Helena Illustrated*, 6.
65. Baumler, *Girl from the Gulches*, 52.
66. Axline et al., *More from the Quarries*, 175.
67. Allen, *Decent Orderly Lynching*, 304.
68. Holter Family Papers, Mont. Hist. Soc., MC-80, box 1, folders 5, 6, 7, 8.
69. Langford, *Vigilante Days*, 218.
70. Sanders and Bertsche, *X. Beidler*, 147.
71. Bishop, *Day Lincoln Was Shot*.
72. "Horrible Assassination of President Lincoln," *Montana Post*, Apr. 29, 1865, p. 1, col. 3.
73. Baumler, *Girl from the Gulches*, 48.
74. Ibid.
75. Mendenhall, *Gold and Silver Mining*, 10.
76. Sanders and Bertsche, *X. Beidler*, 114; Allen, *Decent Orderly Lynching*, 321; Cushman, *Montana*, 201.
77. Allen, *Decent Orderly Lynching*, 321; Cushman, *Montana*, 202.
78. Donovan, *Hanging around the Big Sky*, book 2, 31.
79. Cushman, *Montana*, 202; Wolle, *Montana Pay Dirt*, 72.
80. "Murder of Harry Slater," *Montana Post*, June 7, 1865, p. 2, col. 3.
81. Leeson, *History of Montana*, 302; Birney, *Vigilantes*, 343; Donovan, *Hanging around the Big Sky*, book 2, 31.
82. "Murder of Harry Slater," *Montana Post*, June 7, 1865, p. 2, col. 3.
83. Leeson, *History of Montana*, 302; Sanders and Bertsche, *X. Beidler*, 114–15.
84. "Local History," *Helena Weekly Herald*, Oct. 3, 1867, p. 8, col 4; "Murder of Harry Slater," *Montana Post*, June 17, 1865, p. 2, col. 3; Leeson, *History of Montana*, 302.
85. Sanders and Bertsche, *X. Beidler*, 114.
86. Ibid.
87. Cushman, *Montana*, 203.
88. Leeson, *History of Montana*, 302; Donovan, *Hanging around the Big Sky*, book 2, 31;. "Murder of Harry Slater," *Montana Post*, June 17, 1865, p. 2, col. 3.
89. "Murder of Harry Slater," *Montana Post*, June 17, 1865, p. 2, col. 3; "Local History," *Helena Weekly Herald*, Oct. 3, 1867, p. 8, col. 4. The *Montana Post* article does not provide juror French's first name, but the full name is provided in the later article by the *Helena Weekly Herald*.
90. "Murder of Harry Slater," *Montana Post*, June 17, 1865, p. 2, col. 3.
91. Ibid.
92. Ibid.; Donovan, *Hanging around the Big Sky*, book 2, 31.
93. Donovan, *Hanging around the Big Sky*, book 2, 32.
94. "Murder of Harry Slater," *Montana Post*, June 17, 1865, p. 2, col. 3.
95. Ibid.
96. Ibid.; Donovan, *Hanging around the Big Sky*, book 2, 32.
97. "Murder of Harry Slater," *Montana Post*, June 17, 1865, p. 2, col. 3; Donovan, *Hanging around the Big Sky*, book 2, 32.
98. "Local History," *Helena Weekly Herald*, Oct. 3, 1867, p. 8, col. 4.
99. Donovan, *Hanging around the Big Sky*, book 2, 31–32.
100. Author's correspondence with Ellie Arguimbau of the Montana Historical Society, Nov. 15, 2011.
101. Cf. "Murder of Harry Slater," *Montana Post*, June 17, 1865, p. 2, col. 3, with "Local History," *Helena Weekly Herald*, Oct. 3, 1867, p. 8, col. 4.
102. Author's correspondence with Ellie Arguimbau of the Montana Historical Society, Nov. 15, 2011.
103. Ibid.; Cicily Adelia French Reminiscences, Mont. Hist. Soc., SC-782.

104. Author's correspondence with Ellie Arguimbau of the Montana Historical Society, Nov. 15, 2011, citing 1864 Poll List, Virginia City, p. 43.

105. "French, Charles," Photograph Archives, Mont. Hist. Soc., 942-279.

106. Donovan, *Hanging around the Big Sky*, book 2, 32.

107. "Local History," *Helena Weekly Herald*, Oct. 3, 1867, p. 8, col. 4.

108. Ibid.; Donovan, *Hanging around the Big Sky*, book 2, 32.

109. Sanders and Bertsche, *X. Beidler*, 114; Cushman, *Montana*, 202.

110. Sanders and Bertsche, *X. Beidler*, 114; Cushman, *Montana*, 203.

111. "Murder of Harry Slater," *Montana Post*, June 17, 1865, p. 2, col. 3.

112. Ibid.

113. Cushman, *Montana*, 203.

114. Sanders and Bertsche, *X. Beidler*, 114.

115. "Murder of Harry Slater," *Montana Post*, June 17, 1865, p. 2, col. 3.

116. Cushman, *Montana*, 202.

117. Campbell, *From the Quarries*, 9; Cushman, *Montana*, 202.

118. Cushman, *Montana*, 202; Birney, *Vigilantes*, 344.

119. Sanders and Bertsche, *X. Beidler*, 115; Birney, *Vigilantes*, 344.

120. Donovan, *Hanging around the Big Sky*, book 2, 33.

121. Ibid.

122. Ibid.

123. Ibid.

124. Cushman, *Montana*, 203.

125. Ibid.; "Local History," *Helena Weekly Herald*, Oct. 3, 1867, p. 8, col. 4.

126. Cushman, *Montana*, 203.

127. Sanders and Bertsche, *X. Beidler*, 116 (Beidler's journal merely referred to the drink as "the desired liquid"); Cushman, *Montana*, 203. The *Montana Post* reported that the last request was for a glass of water. "Murder of Harry Slater," *Montana Post*, June 17, 1865, p. 2, col. 4.

128. Leeson, *History of Montana*, 302; Callaway, *Montana's Righteous Hangmen*, 117; Birney, *Vigilantes*, 344; Donovan, *Hanging around the Big Sky*, book 2, 33.

129. "Murder of Harry Slater," *Montana Post*, June 17, 1865, p. 2, col. 3.

130. Sanders and Bertsche, *X. Beidler*, 116; Cushman, *Montana*, 203 (quoting slightly different verbiage).

131. Sanders and Bertsche, *X. Beidler*, 116; Cushman, *Montana*, 203. Another source says that Keene strangled for only three or four minutes before dying. Donovan, *Hanging around the Big Sky*, book 2, 34.

132. Campbell, *From the Quarries*, 9; Cushman, *Montana*, 204; Allen, *Decent Orderly Lynching*, 321.

133. Helena As She Was, "The Hanging Tree."

134. Laws 1865, First Terr. Legis., C.P.A. ch. 4, secs. 25–27.

135. Mont. Stat. Ann. 45-3-102 (2009); see also *State v. Miller*, 290 Mont. 97 (1998).

136. Campbell, *From the Quarries*, 9; Allen, *Decent Orderly Lynching*, 322.

137. Allen, *Decent Orderly Lynching*, 338.

138. Ibid., 343, citing correspondence from Langford to his grandfather dated Jan. 16, 1867.

139. Author's correspondence with Ellie Arguimbau of the Montana Historical Society, Nov. 15, 2011.

140. Allen, *Decent Orderly Lynching*, 343, citing correspondence from Langford to his grandfather dated Jan. 16, 1867.

141. Donovan, *Hanging around the Big Sky*, book 2, 136.

142. Dimsdale, *Vigilantes of Montana*, 208; Callaway, *Montana's Righteous Hangmen*, 117; see also Donovan, *Hanging around the Big Sky*, book 2, 136–37.

143. Dimsdale, *Vigilantes of Montana*, 209.
144. Allen, *Decent Orderly Lynching*, 323; Callaway, *Montana's Righteous Hangmen*, 117; Donovan, *Hanging around the Big Sky*, book 2, 137.
145. Dimsdale, *Vigilantes of Montana*, 210.
146. Ibid.
147. Leeson, *History of Montana*, 302; Dimsdale, *Vigilantes of Montana*, 210; Allen, *Decent Orderly Lynching*, 323.
148. Dimsdale, *Vigilantes of Montana*, 207, 208, 210; Callaway, *Montana's Righteous Hangmen*, 119.
149. Donovan, *Hanging around the Big Sky*, book 2, 137.
150. Dimsdale, *Vigilantes of Montana*, 207.
151. Leeson, *History of Montana*, 303; Dimsdale, *Vigilantes of Montana*, 210; Donovan, *Hanging around the Big Sky*, book 2, 137 (identifying the time for the hanging as midnight).
152. Dimsdale, *Vigilantes of Montana*, 212–13; Donovan, *Hanging around the Big Sky*, book 2, 138.
153. Dimsdale, *Vigilantes of Montana*, 213; Birney, *Vigilantes*, 345; Allen, *Decent Orderly Lynching*, 323; Donovan, *Hanging around the Big Sky*, book 2, 138.
154. Callaway, *Montana's Righteous Hangmen*, 119.
155. Ibid.
156. Ibid.
157. Spence, *Territorial Politics*, 30.
158. "Judge L. E. Munson's Charge to the Grand Jury of the Third Judicial District," Lyman Ezra Munson Papers, 1866–99, Mont. Hist. Soc., SC-553, folder 1.
159. Ibid.
160. Ibid.
161. Olsen, "Lawlessness and Vigilantes," 182.
162. Judge L. E. Munson's Charge to the Grand Jury of the Third Judicial District, Mont. Hist. Soc., SC-553, folder 1.
163. Ibid.
164. Donovan, *Hanging around the Big Sky*, book 1, 3.
165. Bakken, *Practicing Law*, 100 (referring to vigilantism as offering mining camps and cattle towns "simplicity, certainty, and severity of punishment").
166. Donovan, *Hanging around the Big Sky*, book 1, 3.
167. Ibid., book 2, 139.
168. Ibid.
169. "Diamond City Items," *Montana Post*, Sept. 30, 1865, p. 3, col. 3; Allen, *Decent Orderly Lynching*, 326. Diamond City was southeast of Helena and northeast of Virginia City, and roughly equidistant from each.
170. "Helena Items," *Montana Post*, Sept. 23, 1865, p. 3, col. 2; Kidston, "Tree of Death"; Donovan, *Hanging around the Big Sky*, book 2, 140.
171. "Still Another," *Montana Post*, Oct. 7, 1865, p. 3, col. 2; Kidston, "Tree of Death"; Donovan, *Hanging around the Big Sky*, book 2, 140.
172. Allen, "Montana Vigilantes and the Origins of the 3-7-77"; Donovan, *Hanging around the Big Sky*, book 2, 140.
173. "Helena Items," *Montana Post*, Oct. 7, 1865, p. 3, col. 2; Donovan, *Hanging around the Big Sky*, book 2, 140 (speculating that the men might have been involved in the shooting robbery of J. Hineman).
174. "Helena Items," *Montana Post*, Oct. 7, 1865, p. 3, col. 2.
175. Allen, *Decent Orderly Lynching*, 366; Donovan, *Hanging around the Big Sky*, book 2, 141.
176. Donovan, *Hanging around the Big Sky*, book 2, 141.

177. "Gallatin Valley," *Montana Post*, Feb. 17, 1866, p. 2, col. 1; Allen, *Decent Orderly Lynching*, 338; Donovan, *Hanging around the Big Sky*, book 2, 141. Gallatin City was located where the Gallatin, Jefferson, and Madison Rivers converge, in what is now Gallatin County.

178. Donovan, *Hanging around the Big Sky*, book 2, 141.

179. Leeson, *History of Montana*, 223, 302.

180. "Hanged," *Montana Post*, Mar. 24, 1866, p. 3, col. 1; "Letter from German Gulch—Murder and Retribution," *Montana Post*, May 12, 1866, p. 1, col. 6; Allen, *Decent Orderly Lynching*, 339; Olsen, "Lawlessness and Vigilantes," 173. Donovan's account of the Johnson hanging is different. He writes that Johnson was convicted by a miners' court and transported to the jail in Virginia City, where the county sheriff refused to hold the prisoner and returned him to Deer Lodge. Because guarding Johnson in custody in Deer Lodge would have cost ten dollars per day, a decision was made to hang Johnson instead. Donovan, *Hanging around the Big Sky*, book 2, 35–36.

181. Donovan, *Hanging around the Big Sky*, book 2, 36.

182. Ibid.

183. "Letter From German Gulch—Murder and Retribution," *Montana Post*, May 12, 1866, p. 1, col. 6; Donovan, *Hanging around the Big Sky*, book 2, 36.

184. Donovan, *Hanging around the Big Sky*, book 2, 36.

185. Ibid.

186. Ibid., 36–37.

187. Ibid., 37–38.

188. Campbell, *From the Quarries*, 10.

189. Ibid.

190. Ibid.

191. Ibid.

192. Ibid.

193. Ibid. The *Montana Post* ran a different account of Crouchet's crime, that he stole $700 from Captain John Rogers while Rogers was intoxicated. "Helena Letter," *Montana Post*, June 9, 1866, p. 3, col. 2.

194. H. Frank Adkins Réminiscences, 1915, Mont. Hist. Soc., SC-350, box 1-1, p. 1.

195. Ibid.

196. Allen, *Decent Orderly Lynching*, 340.

197. Ibid., 341.

198. Olsen, "Lawlessness and Vigilantes," 177, 179.

199. Allen, *Decent Orderly Lynching*, 340.

200. Ibid., 366.

201. Malone, Roeder, and Lang, *Montana*, 110; Helena Travel Guide, "History of Helena, MT."; Virginia City Chamber of Commerce, "A Brief Virginia City History."

202. "Savage Affray in Cave Gulch," *Montana Post*, Dec. 22, 1866, p. 8, col. 4; Allen, *Decent Orderly Lynching*, 342.

203. Allen, *Decent Orderly Lynching*, 342.

204. "Savage Affray in Cave Gulch," *Montana Post*, Dec. 22, 1866, p. 8, col. 4.

205. Ibid.

206. Ibid.

207. "District Court—Second and Third Days of the Trial of the Cave Gulch Prisoners," *Montana Post*, Mar. 23, 1867, p. 8, col. 4; "Cave Gulch Trial—Continued," *Montana Post*, Mar. 23, 1867, p. 8, col. 5; "District Court," *Montana Post*, Mar. 16, 1867, p. 8, col. 5; "Savage Affray in Cave Gulch," *Montana Post*, Dec. 22, 1866, p. 8, col. 4.

208. "Brought Back," *Montana Post*, Dec. 29, 1866, p. 8, col. 4; Allen, *Decent Orderly Lynching*, 342–43.

209. "District Court," *Montana Post*, Mar. 16, 1867, p. 8, col. 5.

210. "Court Adjourned," *Montana Post*, Jan. 26, 1867, p. 8, col. 3.
211. "District Court—Second and Third Days of the Trial of the Cave Gulch Prisoners," *Montana Post*, Mar. 23, 1867, p. 8, col. 4; "Cave Gulch Trial—Continued," *Montana Post*, Mar. 23, 1867, p. 8, col. 5; "District Court," *Montana Post*, Mar. 16, 1867, p. 8, col. 5.
212. "A Jubilee," *Montana Post*, Mar. 30, 1867, p. 8, col. 4.
213. "A Caution to the Desperate," *Montana Post*, Jan. 5, 1867, p. 8, col. 4.
214. "Met His Fate," *Montana Post*, Nov. 23, 1867, p. 3, col. 2; Donovan, *Hanging around the Big Sky*, book 2, 187.
215. "Met His Fate," *Montana Post*, Nov. 23, 1867, p. 3, col. 2; Donovan, *Hanging around the Big Sky*, book 2, 187.
216. "The Spaulding-Wilson Affair," *Virginia Weekly Post*, Feb. 1, 1868, p. 2, col. 2.
217. Donovan, *Hanging around the Big Sky*, book 2, 150.
218. "The Spaulding-Wilson Affair," *Virginia Weekly Post*, Feb. 1, 1868, p. 2, col. 3.
219. Ibid.
220. Ibid.
221. Ibid.
222. Donovan, *Hanging around the Big Sky*, book 2, 148.
223. "The Spaulding-Wilson Affair," *Virginia Weekly Post*, Feb. 1, 1868, p. 2, col. 3.
224. Ibid.
225. Ibid.
226. Donovan, *Hanging around the Big Sky*, book 2, 150.
227. Ibid.
228. "Murder at Reynolds City," *Montana Post*, May 20, 1868, p. 3, col. 1.
229. Ibid.
230. Donovan, *Hanging around the Big Sky*, book 2, 38.
231. Ibid., 39.
232. Ibid.
233. Ibid.
234. Ibid.
235. "Murder at Reynolds City," *Montana Post*, May 20, 1868, p. 3, col. 1.
236. "The Consequences," *Montana Post*, Aug. 28, 1868, p. 5, col. 3.
237. Donovan, *Hanging around the Big Sky*, book 2, 40.
238. Ibid.
239. "The Execution at Beartown," *Montana Post*, Aug. 21, 1868, p. 1, col. 5.
240. Donovan, *Hanging around the Big Sky*, book 2, 40.
241. "The Execution at Beartown," *Montana Post*, Aug. 21, 1868, p. 1, col. 6; Donovan, *Hanging around the Big Sky*, book 2, 40.
242. Garnet Preservation Society, "Garnet Ghost Town."
243. "The Execution at Beartown," *Montana Post*, Aug. 21, 1868, p. 1, col. 6.
244. "Hanging of Col. Geo. Hynson for Highway Robbery," *Helena Weekly Herald*, Aug. 27, 1868, p. 7, col. 1. The article misidentified the prisoner's name, confusing him with a Colonel Hynson. The newspaper corrected its misidentification of the prisoner's name in a later issue. "Important from Benton, An Erroneous Statement," *Helena Weekly Herald*, Sept. 3, 1868, p. 7, col. 3.
245. "Hanging of Col. Geo. Hynson for Highway Robbery," *Helena Weekly Herald*, Aug. 27, 1868, p. 7, col. 1.
246. Allen, *Decent Orderly Lynching*, 349.
247. Donovan, *Hanging around the Big Sky*, book 2, 153–54.
248. Ibid., 153.
249. Allen, *Decent Orderly Lynching*, 349.
250. Ibid.

251. "Search for Murderer," *Daily Rocky Mountain Gazette*, Jan. 21, 1870, p. 3, col. 1.

252. Malone, Roeder, and Lang, *Montana*, 85.

253. Ibid.; Milner and O'Connor, *As Big as the West*, 25; McConnell and Reynolds, *Idaho's Vigilantes*, 235; Magnaghi, "Virginia City's Chinese Community," 125; Fifer, *Montana Ghost Towns*, 10.

254. Fifer, *Montana Ghost Towns*, 10.

255. Greever, *Bonanza West*, 235; McConnell and Reynolds, *Idaho's Vigilantes*, 235.

256. Malone, Roeder, and Lang, *Montana*, 85; Milner and O'Connor, *As Big as the West*, 25; McConnell and Reynolds, *Idaho's Vigilantes*, 235.

257. Barsness, *Gold Camp*, 240.

258. Liping Zhu, "'Chinaman's Chance,'" 237.

259. Laws 1872, Seventh Terr. Legis., Mining Law, ch. 82, p. 593; Barsness, *Gold Camp*, 244–45; Malone, Roeder, and Lang, *Montana*, 85; see, generally, Bakken, *Mining Law of 1872*.

260. *Territory v. Lee*, 2 Mont. 124 (1874); Barsness, *Gold Camp*, 245.

261. *Territory v. Lee*, 2 Mont. 124 (1874); Barsness, *Gold Camp*, 245.

262. *Territory v. Lee*, 2 Mont. 124 (1874); Barsness, *Gold Camp*, 245. The Burlingame-Seward Treaty gave China full diplomatic status as an equal among nations and gave Chinese individuals the same rights as people from other nations to migrate freely to the United States. Gyory, *Closing the Gate*, 26. The terms of the Burlingame-Seward Treaty were later abrogated by the United States' Chinese Exclusion Act of 1882, which banned practically all Chinese migration to the United States for ten years and which was then renewed in 1892, 1902, and 1904. Gyory, *Closing the Gate*, 26.

263. *Territory v. Lee*, 2 Mont. 124.

264. US Const., art. 6, clause 2.

265. *Virgin Islands v. Milosavljevic*, 2010 WL 3746176, *2 (V.I. Super. 2010); *Territory of Hawaii v. Ho*, 41 Haw. 565 (Haw. Terr. 1957). Justice Servis's concurrence, that treaties with foreign nations were controlling in the territories, was actually ahead of its time, as the concept did not develop in full for approximately another seventy years.

266. Laws 1865, First Terr. Legis., Title XII, ch. 1, sec. 320, and ch. 3, sec. 13. Similar statutes existed in other western territories, including California. Judge Ogden Hoffman of the US District Court for the Northern District of California refused to follow California statutory and case law that prohibited Chinese testimony against whites, and instead accepted their testimony in civil and criminal cases. Fritz, *Federal Justice in California*, 211.

267. Magnaghi, "Virginia City's Chinese Community," 138.

268. Ibid.

269. Barsness, *Gold Camp*, 242.

270. Magnaghi, "Virginia City's Chinese Community," 138.

271. "John Chinamen," *Helena Daily Herald*, July 7, 1870.

272. Malone, Roeder, and Lang, *Montana*, 85.

273. Barsness, *Gold Camp*, 241.

274. "An Act for the Better Observance of the Lord's Day," Laws 1867, Fourth Terr. Legis., sec. 1.

275. Barsness, *Gold Camp*, 212, citing the *Montanian*, Apr. 22, 1875, p. 5.

276. Magnaghi, "Virginia City's Chinese Community," 132.

277. "Search for Murderer," *Daily Rocky Mountain Gazette*, Jan. 21, 1870, p. 3, col. 1.

278. Allen, *Decent Orderly Lynching*, 349.

279. Campbell, *From the Quarries*, 32; Donovan, *Hanging around the Big Sky*, book 2, 153.

280. "Ah Chow Executed," *Daily Rocky Mountain Gazette*, Jan. 26, 1870, col. 1.

281. Ibid.

282. Wolle, *Montana Pay Dirt*, 72, citing *Helena Herald*, Jan. 25, 1870.

283. Allen, *Decent Orderly Lynching*, 349, citing *New North-West*, Jan. 28, 1870.

284. Allen, *Decent Orderly Lynching*, 350.
285. Ibid.
286. "Ah Chow Executed," *Daily Rocky Mountain Gazette*, Jan. 26, 1870, col. 1.
287. Ibid.
288. Donovan, *Hanging around the Big Sky*, book 2, 154.
289. Ibid.
290. Helena As She Was, "The Hanging Tree"; Donovan, *Hanging around the Big Sky*, book 2, 155–56 (identifying the victim's name as George Lenharth).
291. "Shooting of George Leonard by Two Highwaymen," *Daily Rocky Mountain Gazette*, Apr. 29, 1870, p. 3, col. 1.
292. Kidston, "Tree of Death."
293. Ibid.
294. Ibid.; "Shooting of George Leonard by Two Highwaymen," *Daily Rocky Mountain Gazette*, Apr. 29, 1870, p. 3, col. 1.
295. Kidston, "Tree of Death"; "Shooting of George Leonard by Two Highwaymen," *Daily Rocky Mountain Gazette*, Apr. 29, 1870, p. 3, col. 1.
296. "Shooting of George Leonard by Two Highwaymen," *Daily Rocky Mountain Gazette*, Apr. 29, 1870, p. 3, col. 1; Donovan, *Hanging around the Big Sky*, book 2, 156.
297. "Shooting of George Leonard by Two Highwaymen," *Daily Rocky Mountain Gazette*, Apr. 29, 1870, p. 3, col. 1.
298. Ibid.
299. "The Highway Robbery," *Daily Rocky Mountain Gazette*, Apr. 30, 1870, p. 3, col. 1.
300. Ibid.
301. Ibid.
302. Ibid.
303. Donovan, *Hanging around the Big Sky*, book 2, 157.
304. Ibid.
305. Ibid.
306. "The Highway Robbery," *Daily Rocky Mountain Gazette*, Apr. 30, 1870, p. 3, col. 1.
307. Ibid.
308. Donovan, *Hanging around the Big Sky*, book 2, 157–59.
309. Ibid., 159.
310. Ibid.
311. Ibid.
312. Ibid.
313. Bakken, *Invitation to an Execution*, 341.
314. Ibid.; Donovan, *Hanging around the Big Sky*, book 2, 159.
315. Donovan, *Hanging around the Big Sky*, book 2, 159.
316. Ibid.
317. Ibid.
318. Bakken, *Invitation to an Execution*, 341; Donovan, *Hanging around the Big Sky*, book 2, 159.
319. Allen, *Decent Orderly Lynching*, 350.
320. Donovan, *Hanging around the Big Sky*, book 2, 163–66. Although the crimes committed by St. Clair and Triplett were unrelated, both men were forcibly taken from the same jail by vigilantes and hanged together from a crossbeam at an abandoned slaughterhouse. Ibid.
321. "Hangman's Tree Was Gallows First 10 Cases," *Montana Record Herald*, July 12, 1939, p. 1, col. 2; Donovan, *Hanging around the Big Sky*, book 2, 154 (as to Hilger's position with the Montana Historical Society).
322. Hilger, "My Roots Run Deep."
323. Central Montana, "Hilger, Montana Community Information."

12

The Power of Reprieve and the
Execution of James Daniels

*When escaped murderers utter threats of murder against peaceable citizens, mountain
law is apt to be administered without much regard to technicalities.*

—Thomas Dimsdale, March 17, 1866

*It don't take a bigger rope to hang the Governor of Montana than it does to hang a
horse thief or a murderer.*

—Anonymous threat delivered to Acting Governor Thomas Meagher

Thomas Dimsdale, the editor of the *Montana Post*, died of tuberculosis on September 22, 1866.[1] Dimsdale's bellwether book, *The Vigilantes of Montana*, was first published in Virginia City earlier that same year. Individual chapters of the book were published in the *Montana Post* as a periodic series under the same headline as the title of the book. According to author Frederick Allen, the newspaper used the chapters as a promotional tool to boost its circulation, offering a free copy of the book as an incentive bonus to persons who purchased a one-year $10.00 subscription to the newspaper.[2] Since the newspaper did not exist for the first half of 1864 when the majority of vigilante executions occurred in Bannack and Alder Gulch, the *Montana Post's* publication of the chapter series enabled the newspaper to capitalized on Dimsdale's writings after the fact.

The *Montana Post* ran its series with one additional chapter-length summary of vigilante tales that is not contained in the published book. The additional chapter sequentially continued the chapter numbers where Dimsdale's book left off. Chapter 24, as published on March 17, 1866, in newspaper form, has as its

DOI: 10.7330_9780874219203.c012

title "A Full and Complete History of the Chase, Capture, Trial and Execution of All the Outlaws Who Figured in the Bloody Drama."[3] The piece reads like a summary of prior chapters with an early description of events involving Sheriff Plummer and of other persons and events promised for later editions of the newspaper.[4] The newspaper chapter describes, among other things, the arrest and execution of James Daniels in Helena.[5] Chapter 24 is excellent source material about the arrest and execution of James Daniels. The Daniels execution may be the most interesting of the Helena executions because in addition to being part of the history of vigilantism at the time, it is the only execution that arose in the context of a political struggle between Montana's territorial governor, the territorial court, and Helena vigilantes over the power of the executive pardon and reprieve. Daniels, it will be shown, was unwittingly caught up in disputes between executive and judicial authorities over the extent of their constitutional powers, ultimately losing his life in the process at the hands of Helena vigilantes. The story of James Daniels is worthy of its own chapter here, even if a separate chapter is necessarily absent from Dimsdale's book.

Some background is first in order as to Governor Thomas Francis Meagher.[6] Montana's first territorial governor, Sidney Edgerton, was a refined Ohioan who harbored no long-term plans of living with his family in the "uncivilized" hinterland of Montana. Mining claims that he had purchased and then sold proved to be very profitable and provided a further incentive for him to return to "the States." Meanwhile, President Lincoln, while he was preoccupied by the Civil War, never filled the position of Montana's territorial secretary of state. Two persons that President Andrew Johnson later appointed to the post, Dr. Henry P. Torsey of the Wesleyan Seminary and Female College in Maine and Brigadier General John Coburn of Indiana, each declined the job.[7] The third appointment was the charm. Meagher was appointed by President Johnson as Montana's secretary of state in early August of 1865 and arrived in Bannack, Montana, on September 23 of the same year.[8] The appointment suited Meagher's interests at the time, as it provided him with a steady salary and offered the opportunity for further political advancement.[9]

There was no office of lieutenant governor in territorial Montana. Under the laws of succession, if the office of governor were to become vacant for any reason, the secretary of state would become acting governor until such time that a new gubernatorial appointment was made by the president of the United States.[10] The arrival of Meagher in the territory was Sidney Edgerton's cue to return to Ohio. Edgerton left for Ohio within days of Meagher's arrival in Bannack,[11] and upon his departure, Meagher automatically became the acting governor. At the time, Meagher anticipated that Edgerton would eventually return to Montana Territory and resume his duties as governor, but Edgerton actually had no such plans.[12] Edgerton remained outside of Montana for several months before officials in Washington, DC, learned of his prolonged absence and ultimately removed him from office,[13] but the process had the effect of lengthening the time that Meagher would serve as acting governor. Edgerton's removal from office did not become official until April of 1866.[14] Henceforth, this text will refer to Meagher as governor even though it was merely an acting title. The appointment of Edgerton's successor was in the hands of President Andrew Johnson, who ultimately selected Green Clay Smith, a congressman from Kentucky, for a term that began on July 13, 1866.[15]

Meagher succeeded to executive authority in Montana during what would prove to be tumultuous political times. He was, if anything, colorful and came to Montana with an unusual past. He was born in Waterford, on the southern coast of Ireland, in 1823, the son of a successful merchant.[16] In 1828 Daniel O'Connell, a Catholic, was elected president of the Board of Trade, which led to the passage of the Catholic Emancipation Act in 1829.[17] As a result of the act, Catholics could, for the first time, be elected to many public offices and become members of the British Parliament.[18] Thomas Meagher's father, Thomas Meagher Sr., became mayor of Waterford and a member of the British Parliament,[19] which had the effect of introducing Meagher, the son, to politics. Meagher was educated at a Jesuit boarding school, which provided a rigorous education but which, in Meagher's view, taught little of Irish history.[20] He later studied law in Dublin.[21]

During the 1840s, Irish leaders, including particularly O'Connell, peacefully lobbied for a repeal of the Act of the Union of 1800, which had transferred law-making authority from the Irish Parliament in Dublin to the British Parliament in London.[22] Meagher, who was a firebrand on the issue of Irish home rule, joined the Young Ireland group, which also sought repeal of the Act of the Union, and became one of its most prominent spokesmen.[23] The initial affiliation of O'Connell's Repeal Association and Meagher's Young Ireland group was doomed to fail, as O'Connell stressed the need for peaceful political change while Meagher used the rhetoric of violence. On July 26, 1846, Meagher delivered a speech that distinguished himself for masterful oratory, repeating the phrases "Abhor the sword? Stigmatize the sword? No, my lord," in describing instances where violence in Europe had led to constructive political change.[24] Meagher's rhetoric was so incendiary that he was not permitted to finish his speech, and the Young Ireland group was expelled from the O'Connell-controlled Repeal Association.[25]

In 1848 Meagher and his colleagues organized an uprising against the British rule of Ireland during which one man died and another man was wounded.[26] The uprising failed from the lack of adequate arms, planning, money, discipline, and support.[27] One rebel organizer, John Blake Dillon, successfully avoided the British authorities by fleeing to New York disguised as a Catholic priest.[28] Meagher and three other rebel organizers, Patrick O'Donoghue, William Smith O'Brien, and Terence MacManus, were captured by the British authorities, tried by a court, and condemned to death by hanging.[29] Meagher was at all times unrepentant and courageous, telling the English court, "I am here to regret nothing I have ever done—to retract nothing I have ever said . . . Judged by the law of England, I know this crime entails the penalty of death; but the history of Ireland explains this crime, and justifies it."[30]

The death sentence also included a directive that after Meagher's death from hanging, his head was to be decapitated and the remainder of the corpse was to be divided into four quarters, to be disposed of in whatever manner Queen Victoria would think fit.[31]

Although the appeals of the sentences by Meagher, O'Donoghue, Smith O'Brien, and MacManus were unsuccessful, an act of Parliament reprieved them from their death sentences in favor of lifetime banishments to Tasmania, at which Meagher and his colleagues arrived in October of 1849.[32] The death sentences were commuted as the British government feared that the death sentences were against public opinion and would prompt an even greater Irish rebellion.[33]

In Tasmania Meagher married Catherine Bennett and then fathered a daughter.[34] In January of 1852, Meagher escaped Tasmania by ship.[35] He arrived in New York on May 26, 1852 where, by virtue of his Irish rebellion and escape from exile, he became an instant celebrity as "Meagher of the Sword" and "the Irish Patriot."[36] He was awarded an honorary degree by Fordham University and earned a comfortable living as a lecturer throughout the United States as his fame as a leading Irish citizen in America continued to grow.[37] His fame and credibility with Irish Americans gave him access in 1853 to Senator James Shields and President Franklin Pierce.[38] All was not well, however, as Meagher's wife, Catherine, and their daughter had both separately died of natural causes by 1854.[39] Catherine died in Ireland from complications that arose during the birth of the couple's second child, Bennett, who remained with his paternal grandfather in Waterford and who never saw his father.[40]

Meagher met his second wife, Elizabeth "Libby" Townsend, and married her at the residence of Catholic archbishop John J. Hughes on November 14, 1855.[41] Townsend was the daughter of a wealthy New York merchant.[42] The relationship between Meagher and his father-in-law was very strained.[43] Meagher continued his lecturing and launched and edited a New York weekly newspaper, the *Irish News*.[44] He also became a member of the New York State bar in 1855.[45]

Meagher believed by the outbreak of the Civil War that it was in the interests of Irish independence for the Union to be preserved and that military experience gained in the war could be put to good use in future Irish uprisings against the British.[46] Although after becoming a naturalized US citizen he had enrolled as a Democrat, Meagher's views on the Civil War favored the Union. The recruiting system at the time gave higher rank to officers who could raise large numbers of troops and Meagher, with his fame, initially became a captain by raising a company that was incorporated into the Sixty-Ninth New York Militia.[47] The company became known as the Irish Brigade. The New York militia was federalized and fought in Virginia at the First and Second Battles of Bull Run, the Peninsula, Antietam, and Fredericksburg as part of General George McClellan's army.[48] Along the way, Meagher was promoted to the rank of brigadier general.[49] From its battles, the brigade earned another nickname, "the Bloody Irish."[50] Meagher later resigned as a general of the Irish Brigade in a principled belief that the brigade was not receiving the men and materiel that it deserved.[51] The resignation was accepted by President Lincoln, effective May 14, 1863.[52] He was not reassigned to any new army responsibilities until the spring of 1864 and, even then, never regained a command.[53] Meagher's hopes of receiving a further promotion and a command were thwarted by staff of the regular army who viewed him as a "political" general rather than a "military" one, and he was accused in the final days of the war of drunken incompetence while moving a battalion from Tennessee to Maryland.[54]

Nevertheless, had it not been for his role in the Civil War, Meagher may never have earned an appointment as secretary of Montana Territory. He also owed his appointment to the fortuity that two earlier appointees, Henry P. Torsey and John Coburn, had each declined their appointments.[55] Meagher's appointment was issued on August 4, 1865.[56] By the time Meagher arrived in Montana's territorial capital, which was still Bannack at the time, the first session of the territorial legislature had already convened several months earlier, in December of 1864. The Organic Act had established a procedure for a census, the apportionment of election districts based upon the census results, and the election of representatives to the two-house territorial legislature.[57] As a result of the initial Montana elections, the Republicans, identified at the time as Unionists, controlled the upper legislative house known as the Council while the Democrats controlled the lower house known as the Assembly.[58] Republicans attained a majority of the Council only through a sleight of hand that was engineered by Governor Sydney Edgerton, by which all legislators were required to take an oath that depicted Democrats as betrayers of the Union.[59]

The laws of Montana's First Territorial Legislature are sometimes referred to in historical literature as the Bannack Statutes, as Bannack was the territory's capital when the legislature initially sat. The First Territorial Legislature had adopted without much controversy many of the routine laws that were already on the books in neighboring Idaho, from which the territory of Montana had been carved.[60] Among the laws enacted by Montana's first legislature was the adoption of "hanging by the neck" as the official form of death penalty within the territory.[61] The death penalty law provided that judicial hangings be conducted in the presence of the judge, prosecutor, court clerk, two physicians, a minister or priest selected by the defendant, a maximum of two friends or relatives of the defendant, and twelve "respectable citizens."[62] Laws that were specific to private interests, such as those giving exclusive rights to mining companies, ditch companies, railroads, townsites, toll bridges, and ferries, were also adopted by the first legislature.[63] It was an open secret that the territorial legislature was corrupted by special interests, as a result of which it earned the uncomplimentary moniker as "the toll road legislature."[64]

At the time Meagher arrived in Montana, a political controversy was swirling about the possible reapportionment of the legislature. The Organic Act, which had created Montana Territory, contained no provision for reapportionment, which was an unfortunate flaw of its draftsmanship. A reapportionment bill had been introduced to the first legislature that would have increased the size of the upper Council from seven members to fourteen and the Assembly from thirteen members to twenty-six.[65] Certain Republicans and a small number of Democrats opposed reapportionment, claiming that a doubling of the size of the legislature would be unnecessarily costly.[66] The true reason for Republican opposition may have been their concern that new elections might cause them to lose their majority in the one house of the legislature that they already controlled,[67] since a significant portion of Montana's population consisted of emigrants from the southern United States that favored the Confederacy in the Civil War and that decidedly leaned Democrat. Nevertheless, the reapportionment bill passed both houses of the First Territorial Legislature, only to be vetoed by Republican Governor Edgerton on the forty-seventh day of the forty-eight-day legislative session.[68] Edgerton explained his veto based upon the bill's cost.[69] An effort to override the governor's veto fell short by one vote in the Assembly.[70] Edgerton adjourned the legislature the next day.[71] Thereafter, there was no longer any mechanism on the books for the election of any future territorial legislature, and without a legislature, certain territorial offices that required legislative approval, such as those of treasurer, auditor, and superintendent of public instruction, could not be filled.[72]

In the confusion that followed during the summer of 1865, the Democrats nominated candidates for the next legislature's seats using the election districts of the original legislature, while the Republicans nominated almost no candidates

THOMAS FRANCIS MEAGHER.*

Figure 12.1. Acting Governor Thomas Francis Meagher. (Courtesy of the Montana Historical Society, image 943-820.)

based on their belief that the reapportionment issue was still legislatively unresolved.[73] Candidates were also nominated for territorial offices that were supposed to be filled by the appointment of the governor with the advice and consent of the Council.[74] The elections were held on September 4, 1865, and the Democrats naturally won large majorities as well as the seat of the territory's delegate to the US Congress.[75] However, the legitimacy of the territorial elections was questionable as the first legislature had earlier adjourned without resolving the issue of the reapportionment on which the elections were to be based.

Meagher arrived in Bannack a mere nineteen days after the 1865 territorial elections. He was a registered Democrat but was not initially viewed as being motivated by partisan loyalties. The primary differences between Democrats and Republicans at the time, nationally and in Montana Territory, were defined by the issues of the Civil War. Meagher, though a Democrat, had fought for the Union in the Civil War and might therefore have felt more naturally aligned upon his arrival with Montana Republicans than with local Democrats.[76] However, Meagher was alienated from the Montana Republicans on the basis of subtle religious differences. The territorial Republicans tended to be Protestant and Masonic, whereas Meagher was a staunch Roman Catholic.[77] No doubt partisan Democrats were hopeful that Meagher, a fellow Democrat, would convene the newly elected legislature that their party would handily control. Partisan Republicans had an opposite agenda and argued that a new legislature could not be called into session, as the first legislature had adjourned improperly and could not meet again without new enabling authority from the US Congress.[78]

Initially, Meagher refused to convene a second legislature.[79] He might have been content to run the territory by executive fiat, without the check and balance that a constituted legislature would provide. Meagher had the additional governing advantage of commanding the territorial militia.[80] Meagher asked that Montana Supreme Court justice Lyman Munson, a Republican who had accepted a federal judicial appointment, to provide an opinion as to whether a second legislature, if convened, would be legitimate.[81] Predictably, and perhaps even by prearrangement, Munson rendered an opinion that a second legislature would not be valid.[82] Based on Munson's advisory opinion, Meagher published an announcement in the *Montana Post* on December 23, 1865, that "[i]t is clearly my conviction that the Legislative functions of the Territory have temporarily lapsed."[83] Meagher further announced that in his view, enabling legislation was required from Congress to authorize him to redistrict the territory, reapportion the representatives, and convene a legislature for the people's business.[84] He solicited the support of Montana's representative in the Congress, Samuel McLean, to lobby for federal legislation that would address the problem.[85] Initially, Meagher's stance ingratiated himself to the territory's Republicans and its judiciary and alienated him from his fellow Democrats.

Approximately six weeks later, Meagher did a complete backflip on the issue.[86] On February 1, 1866, he called into session the Republican-controlled Council elected in 1864 and the Democrat-controlled Assembly elected in 1865, ostensibly to deal with the issue of the territory's growing debt.[87] The calling of one house controlled by Republicans and the other house controlled by the Democrats might have been a well-intentioned effort on Meagher's part to chart a bipartisan course and to legitimize the acts that the second legislature would produce. The session was scheduled for March 5, 1866, in Virginia

City.[88] A full copy of Meagher's proclamation calling forth the second legislature was published in the *Montana Post* for two consecutive weeks, in the
newspaper's editions of February 3 and February 10, 1866.[89] Meagher asserted
in the proclamation that "the power is vested in me to convene the Legislature,
notwithstanding the Apportionment Bill . . . moreover, a Legislative [*sic*] does
lawfully and constitutionally exist, and that it only awaits the summons of the
executive to give it full life and action."[90]

Democrats welcomed Meagher into their political fold like a prodigal son.
The amends that Meagher had made with his fellow Democrats were clear from
his public remarks about them. He said, "I can truly and safely say, that these
Southerners and Southern sympathizers are now as heartily to be relied upon by
the Administration and its friends, as any other men in the Territory."[91]

One theory behind Meagher's changed position was that prominent
Democrats succeeded in persuading him that the first legislature had passed significant laws providing for successive legislatures and that reapportionment was
the only piece missing from the broader legislative mosaic.[92] Democrats argued
that the Bannack Statutes evidenced an intent that there be a continuation
of the legislature's work in successive years. Another theory behind Meagher's
changed position was that providing for legislative democracy was consistent
with his views of home rule in his native Ireland.[93]

Yet another more intriguing theory for Meagher's changed position is that
Meagher was motivated by longer-term ambitions of eventually being appointed
to a seat in the US Senate in the event that Montana were to become a state and
that he would need Democratic friends in Montana and Washington to further
the territory's hopes of statehood.[94] Indeed, it was about at this time, on January
20, 1866, that Meagher penned a letter to President Andrew Johnson proposing Montana's admission as a state of the United States.[95] Democrats favored
statehood in the belief that they could gain control of the state government and
the jobs and power that would flow from it; Republicans opposed statehood for
that same partisan reason.[96] Territories hoping for statehood were required to
submit a state constitution to the Congress for its approval, and another reason
that Meagher may have had for calling of the second legislature, beyond dealing
with government debt, was for the legislature to sanction a state constitutional
convention that Meagher wished to convene in Helena on March 26, 1866.[97]
Montana did not have a population sufficient for the territory's admission as a
state, but that rule had been waived by the Congress two years earlier when the
thinly populated but silver-rich territory of Nevada was admitted as a state.[98] An
important piece of business that Meagher demanded of the second legislature
was a bill to authorize the anticipated constitutional convention and to appropriate the funding necessary to enable it. To underscore the point, Meagher

may have threatened to use his militia to keep all food and, more important, all whiskey from the territorial legislators until they accomplished his bidding.[99]

Governor Meagher may have correctly assessed that the odds of his becoming a future senator from Democratic Montana were greater than the odds of his ever being appointed governor by a future US president. President Andrew Johnson, though a Democrat, was embattled during his term in office, which included defending himself from impeachment proceedings in 1868. Meagher's eventual successor as governor, Green Clay Smith, would serve from the time of his appointment through the end of Johnson's presidential term. National elections after the Civil War then favored Republicans in every four-year cycle for almost a generation until the election of Grover Cleveland in 1884. Meagher had displayed political ambition and daring throughout his life, during his participation in a rebellion in Ireland, his escape from Tasmania, and during the Civil War. It is entirely plausible that Meagher's decision to call a second territorial legislature, after having publicly declared that he lacked the authority to do so, is explained by the governor's continuing political ambitions aimed at becoming a US senator.

The Republicans, of course, were furious. Meagher was mocked by Republicans who referred to him by the diminishing nickname of "the Acting One."[100] Judge Munson was particularly angry at Meagher, having earlier provided the governor with an informal legal opinion that the second legislature would not be valid, which Meagher had initially and publicly adopted. Munson repeated his legal opinion that the calling of a second legislative session was illegal under the language of the Organic Act.[101] Governor Meagher publicly rebuked Judge Munson for doing so, telling him through the pages of the *Montana Democrat*, "I do not and shall not hold myself in the least accountable to you for my official acts."[102] Attorney Wilbur Fisk Sanders, who by then was the head of the Union (Republican) Party in the territory, declared that the second legislature would be squelched by the courts.[103] Governor Meagher threatened that he would enforce the will of the legislature, if necessary, by calling forth his militia.[104]

The issue played out on the pages of the *Montana Post* for weeks. Meagher was repeatedly excoriated by the newspaper for calling the second legislature into session. The fact that he recalled the Republican-controlled 1864 Council was not viewed as having particular bipartisan significance. The edition of the *Montana Post* published on February 3, 1866, described Governor Meagher's flip-flop on the issue by noting that "the Executive mind has undergone a complete revolution within the past few weeks."[105] Dimsdale's newspaper adopted the Republican Party's position that since Governor Edgerton's veto of the Apportionment Bill had not been overridden by the first legislature, all legislative authority of Montana Territory lapsed until such time that the US Congress could pass an act enabling a new territorial legislature.[106] In the edition of the *Montana Post* published on February 17, 1866, the newspaper editorially mocked the illogic of Meagher's call for both a legislature and a constitutional convention: that a constitutional convention could somehow remedy the absence of a duly apportioned legislature, while a legislature not yet duly appointed could call for a constitutional convention.[107] The newspaper accused Meagher, in essence, of circular reasoning. In the same edition, under the headline "A Queer Legislature," the newspaper questioned the second legislature's legality and cost and predicted a "repeal of genuine laws, and the enactment of bogus ones [as] another consequence of this absurd scheme of the needy demagogues of the Territory."[108]

To respond to the controversy, Meagher delivered an address to Montana Democrats on February 17, 1866. He was once again in the good graces of his own political party. He took particular aim at the Republican judiciary, vowing that he "would take care that no judge, whatever his powers or consequence, should dispute or disobey" any laws to be passed by the second legislature.[109] Soon the Republican judiciary would be punished. Meagher would take revenge upon Thomas Dimsdale and the *Montana Post* as well.

Meagher had a serious drinking problem. A Republican lawyer, William Chumasero, bitterly complained in a letter to Senator Lyman Trumbull of Illinois that Meagher had been drunk nearly every day since his arrival in the territory.[110] Chumasero described Meagher's habits as "beastly and filthy" and stated that Meagher remained intoxicated for days on end "polluting his bed and person in the most indecent and disgusting manner."[111] The animosity between the governor and the Republicans prompted the Republicans to frequently and publicly criticize Meagher for his apparent alcoholism. The public references to Meagher's drinking became more and more common.

Republicans were nevertheless powerless to prevent the new legislature from meeting. The Second Montana Territorial Legislature convened on March 5, 1866, and remained in session until April 14, 1866.[112] Neil Howie remarked in his diary that Governor Meagher was drunk on the first day of the legislative session.[113] During its session, the legislature engaged in substantive and necessary law making. It created and amended the boundaries of certain counties.[114] It chartered a public school system.[115] It provided procedures for qualifying, calling, and exempting jurors.[116] It created territory-wide positions of superintendent of public instruction, auditor, and treasurer, which were to be initially filled by appointment of the governor pending the next scheduled election for the commencement of two-year terms.[117] It delineated the authority of county assessors to collect revenue and county surveyors to execute surveys and maintain proper land records.[118] It created district attorney positions.[119] It enacted legislation regarding inheritance, licensure, divorce, and dower.[120] The second legislature apportioned the legislative districts of the territory, established two-year terms for its Council and one-year terms for its Assembly, and scheduled territorial elections for September of 1866 based upon the new legislative districts.[121] The second legislature formalized three judicial districts within the territory, the first consisting of Madison, Gallatin, and Big Horn Counties, the second consisting of Deer Lodge, Beaverhead, and Missoula Counties, and the third consisting of Edgerton, Jefferson, Chouteau, Meagher, and Musselshell Counties.[122] The judges who were administratively assigned to the three judicial districts were Hezekiah Hosmer (First Judicial District), Lorenzo Williston (Second Judicial District), and Lyman Munson (Third Judicial District).[123]

While the main stated purposes of the Second Territorial Legislature were to pass a reapportionment bill, authorize a constitutional convention, and address territorial debt, the legislature also undertook partisan and other measures that catered to special interests.[124] No doubt most of the newly created governmental offices were awarded to Democrats. The second legislature passed a joint resolution tendering "profound regard and esteem to his Excellency, Andrew Johnson, President of the United States."[125] An assembly resolution endorsed President Johnson's plan for the reconstruction of the Southern states.[126] The second legislature named a new county after Governor Meagher,[127] which still bears his name to this day. Meagher County is located just east of Helena, with a county seat located at White Sulphur Springs.

The refusal of Judges Hosmer and Munson to recognize the legitimacy of the second legislative session also "occasioned personal enmities on the part of legislative members which prompted them to indulge in petty spite" against the judiciary.[128] It denied the Montana judges, all Republican, a wage increase over the base federal wage and, in fact, rescinded payment to the judges of a $2,500 salary supplement that had been approved for the judges by the Bannack legislature.[129] The *Montana Post* described the rescission as giving the territorial judges the "privilege to starve or steal."[130] The rescission of the salary supplement was a significant blow to the judges given the inadequacy of their federal wages and the high cost of living in the territory. Viewed in that light, the judges cannot be blamed for earning additional money from private commercial ventures such as the mining, ranching, and financing businesses of Chief Judge Hosmer. The second legislature also passed into law an unusual bill requiring the territorial judges to recuse themselves and reassign cases in any instance in which a party merely filed an affidavit of bias against them, regardless of whether any bias actually existed.[131] The effect of such legislation was significant, as it allowed any party in any case to file an affidavit of bias as a means of "judge shopping," thereby weakening the ability of the judiciary to bring contested matters to proper conclusions. The Democratic commissioners in Madison County refused Hosmer stationery and even refused to make any provisions for the judge to hold court.[132] During winter, Hosmer was the subject of a "freeze out," whereby he was denied firewood for the heating of his temporary workplace.[133]

Revenge was also taken against the *Montana Post* and its editor, Thomas Dimsdale. Dimsdale, a former schoolteacher, had been acting as the territory's temporary superintendent of public instruction.[134] The position had likely been a patronage appointment, either as a reward for the *Montana Post*'s editorial support of the Republican Party, or as a means of assuring that the newspaper would continue its support of Republicans going forward. Without particular fanfare, the *Montana Post* reported in its edition of March 24, 1866, that Governor Meagher had relieved Dimsdale of his duties as superintendent of public instruction and appointed Peter Ronan in his place.[135] The *Montana Post* was also the territory's official public printer. On March 30, 1866, Governor Meagher appointed Thomas J. Favorite, the editor and publisher of the Democratic-leaning *Montana Register* as the territory's new public printer.[136] The *Montana Post* reported its loss of business and stature with no fanfare by burying the item within a long list of bills that were under consideration by the second legislature.[137] The timing of these events occurring, as they did, within a few days of each other in March of 1866 can only suggest that the appointments of Ronan and Favorite were motivated as a means of targeted political retribution against Dimsdale and the *Montana Post*. The punishment that Dimsdale received would not sting for long, as he would die of tuberculosis within six months, on September 22, 1866.[138]

Montana's constitutional convention commenced on April 9, 1866.[139] It lasted six days and produced a proposed constitution that was necessary if Montana had any immediate hopes of gaining statehood.[140] The convention delegates were frequently unable to reach a quorum, so those who were present voted on behalf of those who were not.[141] Attendance by delegates was spotty, and no official records of its proceedings were kept.[142] Amazingly, the document was never reviewed by the US Congress as, according to one account, its only copy was lost by delegate Thomas E. Tutt while transporting it to a printer.[143] Another account explains that the sole copy of Montana's proposed constitution was destroyed in a fire.[144] In either event, all of the work of the constitutional convention was rendered meaningless since the proposed constitution was never reconstructed after the fact.

True to his word, Judge Munson heard a case in mid-1866 by which he was able to pass judgment on the legitimacy of the Second Territorial Legislature. The

Figure 12.2. Montana Supreme Court justice Lyman Munson. (Courtesy of the Montana Historical Society, image 944-038.)

case, *Townsend & Baker v. Laird*, involved an attachment of property permissible under a statute enacted by the second legislature, and defendant Laird raised the invalidity of the attachment law as a defense.[145] A full copy of Munson's decision in the case was published in the *Montana Post* on June 9, 1866.[146] In his decision Judge Munson acknowledged that it was a "delicate responsibility for courts to interfere with legislative enactments," but also recognized that his court was empowered to pass judgment upon whether the attachment law underlying the case was enacted in conformity with the requirements of the territory's Organic Act.[147] Munson noted that the Organic Act required that there be a census of the territorial population, an apportionment by the first legislature of election districts, and legislative elections in those districts and that "thereafter" the second legislature could convene and enact laws.[148] He concluded that the first legislature's failure to apportion election districts, which was a necessary condition to the assemblage of successive legislatures, rendered the enactments of the second legislature illegal.[149] Munson's decision did not merely grant defendant Laird's motion to vacate the attachment and nullify the second legislature's attachment law, but also declared that "*all* the public acts and doings of the so-called [second] Legislature are null and void."[150] Taking what can only be viewed as a public swipe at Governor Meagher, Munson reminded the public in his decision that the court's view on the illegality of the Second Territorial Legislature was consistent with the view initially shared by Meagher in December of 1865, when Meagher had declared that the legislative functions of the territory had lapsed when the first legislature recessed without enacting an apportionment bill.[151]

Legally, Munson's interpretation of Montana's Organic Act and his nullification of the enactments of the territory's second legislature appear to be correct. Section 4 of Montana's Organic Act did, in fact, set forth the sequencing of events that were plainly required to lawfully convene a legislature after the initial Bannack session had recessed, which consisted of the taking of a census, the apportionment of legislative districts, and the conduct of the elections themselves.[152] Munson properly concluded that the failure of the territory to perform all of those acts in their proper sequence, including in particular the territory's failure to enact an apportionment bill at the conclusion of the first legislative session in Bannack, rendered the second legislative session illegal and void. Munson's decision was consistent with governmental checks and balances that permit the judicial branch to declare statutes, under certain circumstances, void and unenforceable.[153]

The political and legal back-and-forth continued between the Democratic governor and the Republican judiciary. In September the *Montana Democrat* urged that Montana's three Supreme Court judges be removed from office and replaced by "new and friendly judges."[154] Governor Meagher wrote a letter to Secretary of State William Seward asking that Judges Hosmer and Munson be removed from their positions in the territory, though nothing ever came of the effort.[155] Other than that, Democrats in the territory simply ignored Munson's judicial pronouncement and acted as if the accomplishments of the Second Territorial Legislature were in full force and effect.

As a result of the second legislature's reapportionment of election districts, new elections were held in the territory on September 3, 1866.[156] Democrats did well, and based on those election results, Meagher called for a Third Territorial Legislature to convene for the winter of 1866–67.[157]

Meanwhile, 1,800 miles to the east, developments in Montana were being monitored by Republicans that held clear majorities in the US Congress. Although the federal Treasury Department was a function of the executive branch of government, the Treasury denied Montana reimbursement of the expenses it had incurred in convening the territory's second legislature.[158] The denial of the payment should have been viewed as an ominous warning that the territorial government could not do whatever its leaders pleased. The plans for a Third Territorial Legislature nevertheless proceeded undeterred. By the time the third session was actually convened on November 5, 1866, Green Clay Smith had assumed the duties of governor, having arrived in the territory on October 3, 1866.[159] Governor Smith agreed with Meagher and the Democrats that continued legislative functions were lawful.[160]

After the Third Territorial Legislature had convened, Chief Judge Hosmer, a Republican, who had been away on travel during the fall, returned to Montana and publicly weighed in on the controversy surrounding the successive legislative sessions.[161] On December 8, 1866, Hosmer issued a written advisory opinion that the Second Territorial Legislature was illegal under section 4 of the Organic Act and declared that any challenged acts of that legislature would be struck down by the court.[162] Hosmer's opinion *in extenso* was published in full in the December 22, 1866, edition of the *Montana Post*.[163] Hosmer's reasoning was essentially the same as that of Judge Munson's in the case of *Townsend & Baker v. Laird*, but Hosmer provided a deeper analysis of the plain language of section 4 of the Organic Act.[164] Hosmer's opinion, rendered as it was in December of 1866, necessarily targeted the Third Territorial Legislature as well, as the legal arguments that existed against the legality of the second legislature applied equally to the third. Montana Democrats once again simply ignored the judicial opinion, and its publication did not impede the continuing work of the Third Territorial Legislature.

To Governor Meagher, the judges on Montana's territorial Supreme Court had become a nuisance. The judges did not resign their offices. Meagher hoped to deal with the problem by reassigning the judges to areas of the territory that were inhabited mainly by buffalo and Native American Indians. "Let the judges read Blackstone to the Aborigines!" he wrote.[165] Soon the governor's wish of banishing the judiciary to the far reaches of the territory would be granted as to one of the three Supreme Court judges.

While much of the work of the Third Territorial Legislature dealt with legitimate issues of taxes and spending, the Democrat-controlled legislature specifically targeted and punished Republican judge Lyman Munson. The legislature did so by redrawing the boundaries of the territory's three judicial districts, scheduling the terms of the court in each district, and designating which judge would sit in which district, which the governor and the legislature had the authority to exercise under section 15 of Montana's Organic Act.[166] In doing so, they denied the judiciary any input in the process. The First Judicial District, which had earlier consisted of Madison, Gallatin, and Big Horn Counties, was reorganized by the third legislature to consist of Madison, Gallatin, and Beaverhead Counties,[167] which were, and still are, contiguous to one another in the southwestern portion of Montana and included the cities of Virginia City, Bannack, and Dillon. Chief Judge Hezekiah Hosmer was assigned by statute to continue presiding in the First Judicial District.[168] The Second Judicial District, which had earlier consisted of the noncontiguous counties of Deer Lodge, Beaverhead, and Missoula, was reorganized to consist of Deer Lodge, Missoula, Edgerton, Meagher, and Jefferson Counties,[169] which were contiguous to one another in the west central portion of Montana. The Second Judicial District included vibrant mining communities such as Helena, Anaconda, Missoula, and Whitehall and became the most attractive of the three judicial assignments.[170] Judge Lorenzo Williston was assigned by the third legislature to preside in the Second Judicial District.[171] The Third Judicial District, which had earlier consisted of Edgerton, Jefferson, Chouteau, Meagher, and Musselshell Counties, was significantly downsized to consist of only Chouteau, Big Horn, and Vivion Counties.[172] While Chouteau and Big Horn Counties still exist today, Vivion County does not, though it was located at the time in central Montana in present-day Musselshell County.[173] Judge Lyman Munson was assigned to preside in the Third Judicial District.[174]

The reason that the reorganization of the judicial districts was a punishment to Judge Munson becomes apparent when his district's counties are viewed on a map. Munson's district consisted of three far-flung counties, with none adjacent to any other, in rural areas well north and southeast of the political and economic developments taking place in the main of the territory. Chouteau County was, and is, located in the north central portion of the territory only seventy-five miles south of the Canadian border. Vivion County was in the central portion of the territory. Big Horn County was, and is, in the Yellowstone region toward the southeast quadrant of the territory. Munson's assignment to such a "sagebrush" district punished him in three distinct ways. First, close to 300 miles of rugged terrain separated Fort Benton, the county seat of Chouteau County, from Hardin, the county seat of Big Horn County. The Third Judicial District could not have been designed to be more inconvenient for Judge Munson's access and travel. The third legislature specified that the terms of court were to commence on the first Monday of both June and December each year at the county seat of northernmost Chouteau County and on the first Monday of April at the county seat of southernmost Big Horn

County, which subjected Munson to a rigorous year-round travel schedule.[175] The requirement that Munson hold court in Chouteau County for a term commencing every December forced him to travel long round-trip distances in the dead of winter each year.

The second reason that Munson's assignment to a sagebrush district was a deliberate punishment was that it represented a considerable loss of prestige. The assignment removed the judge from Edgerton County, which included Helena, at a time when the same legislature voted to temporarily relocate the territorial capital from Virginia City to Helena, though subject to an anticipated public referendum on the relocation issue.[176] As a result, Munson, who had become a vocal thorn in the side of territorial Democrats, was evicted from his proximity to a territorial seat of Montana's political power and was replaced there by Judge Williston, whose political temperament was considerably more reserved.

The third reason, adding further insult to injury, was that section 9 of the Organic Act required territorial judges to live within the judicial district to which they were assigned. As a result, if Munson chose to remain on the bench, he had to move his personal residence to one of the far-flung sagebrush counties.[177] There can be no doubt that the new design of the territory's judicial districts and the schedule for its terms of court were specifically intended to target Judge Munson for punitive treatment.

Munson could not have been pleased with the turn of events. If, as appears to be the case, the third legislature singled him out for punitive treatment in the hope that it would prompt his resignation from the bench, the plan did not succeed. Munson dutifully continued to serve on the territorial Supreme Court to the end of his four-year term in 1869, though his tenure on the bench during the remainder of his term appears to have been quiet and unremarkable.

Montana Republicans were so desperate over their powerlessness that their party leader, Wilbur Fisk Sanders, traveled to Washington, DC, in early 1867 with a plea that Congress void the enactments of the territory's second and third legislatures.[178] He may have been accompanied to Washington by Judge Munson, as Munson was notably absent from the territory between October of 1866 and January of 1867.[179] Sanders found sympathetic friends in the Republican-controlled Congress, including the chairman of the House Committee on Territories, Congressman James M. Ashley. The sense in Washington by the time the third legislature had completed its work was that Governor Meagher and the Democratic legislators had overplayed their hands. Indeed, the punitive measures taken against the Republican judiciary in December of 1866 may have been the political straw that ultimately broke the camel's back during the early weeks of 1867.

Figure 12.3. Congressman James Ashley (R-OH), chairman of the US House Committee on Territories. (Courtesy of the Montana Historical Society, image 940-620.)

Figure 12.4. Congressman Samuel McLean (D-MT), who warned that if Montana's second and third legislatures were nullified, the territory could break with the United States and affiliate instead with Canada. (Courtesy of the National Archives and Records Administration, Brady Collection, image 111-B-2989.)

The US Congress took the highly unusual step of proposing an amendment to Montana's Organic Act that, if passed, would declare the territory's second and third legislatures "null and void."[180] The legislation was opposed by certain congressional Democrats. Montana's elected nonvoting delegate to Congress, Samuel McLean, opposed the legislation and openly suggested that Montana consider seceding from its affiliation with the United States and affiliate instead with Canada.[181] On the floor of the Congress, McLean warned fellow congressmen, "Do not by unwise and oppressive legislation drive us over the border, while our love of country would actuate us to stand upon its outer edge, a living wall of strength in the defense of the land."[182] It was a bold secessionist statement to make on the House floor in the wake of the recently concluded Civil War, but it perhaps represents the level of political passion that had been reached by the persons intimately associated with Montana's partisan divide. McLean also openly criticized Montana's laws and judiciary and, in so doing, expressly rationalized vigilantism as a natural consequence of the territory's shortcomings.[183]

The Senate Committee on Territories, comprised of three Republicans and two Democrats, conducted a hearing on the proposed amendment to Montana's Organic Act and then voted 5 to 0 to recommend its passage.[184] On March 2, 1867, despite McLean's opposition and threats, the bill voiding

Montana's second and third legislatures passed both houses of Congress, with the unanimous support of Democrats, and was thereafter signed into law by the Democratic president, Andrew Johnson.[185] It authorized Governor Smith to call a "fourth" territorial legislature to enact an apportionment bill that the original Bannack legislature had failed to complete.[186]

The amended Organic Act also granted the territorial judges a long-overdue pay raise from $2,500 per year to $3,500 per year, but without any pay raise for the territory's governor, legislators, or other officials.[187] The grant of a pay raise to the judges, who were Republican, without any parallel pay raise to the territory's executive and legislative branch officers, who were overwhelmingly Democrats, was likely a deliberate slap at the Montana Democratic Party. It resulted in the judges prospectively receiving the highest federal salaries of all elected and appointed officials in the territory. Indeed, the Montana judges received an even greater windfall than the $1,000 of extra compensation conferred by the Congress. The invalidation of the second legislature necessarily voided the rescission of the $2,500 pay supplement that had earlier been authorized by the Bannack legislature at a time when the relationship between the three branches of territorial government was more constructive. The amendment of the Organic Act therefore resulted in the Montana judges receiving $3,500 of boosted federal pay plus entitlement to a $2,500 territorial pay supplement, for a total of $6,000 per annum, representing an immediate 140 percent hike in total compensation.

By its amendments to Montana's Organic Act, Congress also vested Montana's judiciary with the exclusive authority to define its judicial districts and to fix the times and places for the terms of court as a clear means of protecting the territorial judges from further abuse by the Montana legislature.[188] Vesting the judges with control over their own district boundaries, terms of court, and judicial assignments was a tremendous victory for the judiciary as it prevented any future "sagebrushing" of judges for political reasons and helped assure the independence of the judicial branch of territorial government. Private "vested" interests that had stakes in the acts of the nullified legislatures, such as toll roads, bridges, and mining companies, were specifically protected in the amendments to the Organic Act, as parties that had benefitted from the nullified enactments were expressly permitted to make claims for damages in the territorial courts.[189]

Montana's Republican judges, who rendered opinions that the second and third legislatures had not been lawfully convened, claimed vindication by the congressional amendment of the Organic Act, though in reality the nullification of both legislatures may have been prompted as much by party politics as by law. The act of Congress that nullified the two territorial legislatures was interpreted as merely suspending the enactments of the second and third sessions, so future legitimate legislatures could enact the same or similar pieces of legislation if they so chose.[190] Indeed, many of the substantive laws enacted by Montana's second and third legislatures, though voided, were easily and readily restored by the Fourth Montana Territorial Legislature, which, like its predecessor legislatures, was firmly controlled by Democrats.[191] At a minimum, the primary accomplishment of the congressional nullification of the acts of the two territorial legislatures was the protection it afforded to the independence of Montana's judiciary going forward, which might otherwise have been further eroded so long as the territory was controlled by one political party and its judiciary controlled by another.

The invalidation of Montana's second and third legislatures did not abate partisan animosities; if anything, it made them even worse.[192] Governor Meagher described Wilbur Fisk Sanders as "an unrelenting and unscrupulous extremist" and a vicious enemy who would "plunge this most beautiful and promising territory into the bitterest and the blackest hot water."[193] When the Fourth Montana Territorial Legislature convened for a legal session that ran from December 11 to December 24, 1867, it specifically passed a resolution calling upon Judges Hosmer and Munson to resign from Montana's Supreme Court.[194] Perhaps predictably, the Fourth Montana Territorial Legislature also rescinded the $2,500 judicial pay supplement that had been enacted by the original Bannack legislature, while at the same time conferring upon the governor a new additional pay supplement in the same amount.[195] The judges' 1867 financial windfall, consisting of their original $2,500 salary, a $1,000 federal raise, and a $2,500 territorial pay supplement, was therefore fairly short-lived, at least to the extent that the $2,500 pay supplement did not survive more than nine months of continuing partisan animosities.

The nullification of the second and third legislatures made clear to Montana Democrats, at least by implication, that the territory would not be granted quick or easy statehood so long as Democrats held the majority in Montana and so long as the Republicans controlled the US Congress. In fact, Montana would not be admitted as a state of the Union for another two decades, on November 8, 1889. The loss of the document reflecting Montana's proposed 1866 Constitution was therefore less significant to the participants than it might have initially seemed, as the document would not have been of any practical assistance at that time in furthering Montana's admission to the Union.

Against this unpleasant and highly charged partisan backdrop, there was a shooting incident at a saloon in Grizzly Gulch during the late evening or early morning hours of November 29–30, 1865.[196] Grizzly Gulch was a mining camp approximately half a mile north of Helena.[197] The shooting, as will be shown, set into motion a series of additional events that would render the political atmosphere even more toxic than it already was and would spur action by local vigilantes.

James B. Daniels and Andrew J. Gartley were playing in a card game at Con Prince's Belmont Saloon on Main Street.[198] While the game was in progress, an argument broke out concerning a particular poker hand.[199] No doubt some alcohol was also involved. Daniels jumped from his seat and was pushed by Gartley into a red-hot stove.[200] Gartley may have raised a large stool as a weapon.[201] Daniels responded by drawing his gun with one hand and an eight-inch knife with the other.[202] Gartley grabbed Daniels's gun but was then stabbed by Daniels once in the chest and once in the groin.[203] Gartley ran into the street, bleeding profusely, followed by Daniels, gun in hand.[204]

Daniels soon fled into the hills but was unsuccessful in escaping capture.[205] He was turned over to Neil Howie, who, by that time, was serving as a US marshal.[206] Gartley lingered several hours before dying from the stab wounds, and by fantastic odds Gartley's wife then died of what was said to have been a broken heart.[207] The circumstances naturally caught the public's attention. While certain public opinion ran against Daniels for the killing, he was not without a significant number of supporters. Helena's Committee of Safety took no action in deference to the legal process that was promised by Judge Lyman Munson, who had not yet been reassigned to his "sagebrush" judicial district.[208]

On December 8, 1865, a grand jury indicted Daniels for the intentional murder of Andrew Gartley.[209] Because public opinion in and around Helena was inflamed, the venue of the trial was changed from Edgerton County,[210] which included Helena, to Madison County, which included Virginia City, to assure a fair jury selection and trial.[211] The jury trial began in Virginia City on December 19, 1865.[212] The eleven-day period between the date of the indictment and the commencement of the trial underscores the limited nature of pretrial proceedings and trial preparation in the early legal courts of Montana Territory, and necessarily included the participants' travel time, on horseback, for the mountainous 120-mile distance from Helena to Virginia City.

The trial of James Daniels was not particularly noteworthy in and of itself. The prosecution sought to prove that Daniels had intentionally murdered Gartley as a result of the dispute that arose between them during their card game. The defense was that Daniels had acted in self-defense. A conviction to the "down charge" of manslaughter was also a possibility. Judge Lyman Munson presided over the trial, even though it was held outside of his district in Virginia City.[213] The prosecutors were William Chumasero and John H. Shober.[214] William Y. Pemberton, who had acted as the stenographer at the trial of George Ives, and Warren Toole were Daniels's defense attorneys.[215] The prosecution and the defense each had its witnesses.

Figure 12.5. Attorney William Chumasero, who prosecuted James Daniels for the barroom murder of Andrew
J. Gartley. (Courtesy of the Montana Historical Society,
image 941-506.)

Daniels was apparently no saint. It was believed that he had earlier committed a murder and an attempted murder at a gold camp in Tuolumne County,
California.[216] Langford described Daniels as "hardened to vice and crimes, and,
possibly, one of the worst of all ruffians whose careers I have passed under
review."[217] According to the *Montana Post* and author Tom Donovan, Daniels
threatened during his Virginia City trial to get revenge on the witnesses who
would testify against him.[218] In contrast, an Idaho City editor who had known
Daniels for years described him as "an enterprising, honest citizen, leading an
industrious, irreproachable life."[219]

For Daniels to be convicted of murder in the first degree under the Bannack
Statutes, the prosecution needed to prove that Daniels had killed Gartley
with the deliberate intention of doing so, out of express or implied malice

aforethought.[220] A prominent factual issue at the trial must have been Daniels's alleged chase of Gartley across the street, after the stabbing had already occurred, and any inference that a jury could reasonably draw of Daniels's state of mind by virtue of the chase. For voluntary manslaughter, evidence was needed that Daniels received a serious injury from Gartley that reasonably provoked Daniels to kill his victim in the heat of passion.[221] For that crime, a significant issue at trial must have necessarily included Gartley's conduct of knocking Daniels into a hot stove, raising a stool in a threatening manner, and the seriousness of any bodily injury that Daniels received in the altercation. To render a verdict of involuntary manslaughter, the jury would have had to find that Daniels never intended for Gartley to die but that during Daniels's commission of an unlawful act, such as an assault with a knife, Gartley's death was an unintended consequence.[222] Daniels's defense of justifiable homicide required evidence on his own part that his killing of Gartley was reasonably necessary to save himself from imminent death or serious bodily harm.[223] As to that defense, key factual issues must have included Gartley's knocking Daniels into a hot stove, Gartley's wielding of a stool as a weapon, whether Gartley was independently armed with a weapon, and the degree of control, if any, that Gartley was able to wield over Daniels's gun during the altercation at the stove. The defense included evidence that Gartley was physically larger than Daniels and witnesses who testified to Daniels's good character.[224]

After the attorneys delivered their closing arguments, Judge Munson gave the jury instructions on the law that was to guide their deliberations. For reasons unknown, Munson charged the jury under the laws of Nebraska Territory.[225] A possible reason for a jury charge under Nebraska law might be that printed copies of the Bannack Statutes were not yet available to Judge Munson, as the acts of the Bannack legislature had been sent to the state of Maine for printing and were not distributed within Montana Territory until they were paid for two years later.[226] A copy of Nebraska law might have been the only available or best guidance for Munson to follow.

If Judge Munson used the criminal code of Nebraska in his murder and manslaughter instructions to Daniels's jury, there is still a question of what law was actually given, as Nebraska enacted new sets of criminal codes in 1855, 1857, and 1859. Nebraska's First Territorial Legislature, which sat in Omaha from January 16 to March 16, 1855, replaced the common law specified by the territory's Organic Act with the criminal and civil codes of the state of Iowa, which were incorporated into Nebraska's law by reference.[227] Later Nebraska's Third Territorial Legislature, which convened on January 5, 1857, repealed the provision of the 1855 legislation that had adopted the criminal and civil codes of Iowa.[228] The repeal was vetoed by Nebraska governor Mark W. Izard, but the veto was then overridden by a vote of 12 to 1 in Nebraska's upper Council and a vote of 24 to 2 in its lower House.[229] Amazingly, Nebraska's Third Territorial Legislature, having successfully repealed the criminal and civil codes by its veto override, did not immediately replace those codes with any new indigenous Nebraska statutes, leaving the territory lawless until the issue could be subsequently addressed.

The problem that the Nebraska legislature had created for itself and the territory was readily perceived. Criminal and civil codes that were identical to the earlier Iowa versions were reenacted by Nebraska's legislature fairly quickly, but with an effective date of June 1, 1857. The Nebraska Supreme Court later held in the case of *Benet v. Hargus* that there could be no redress in the courts for any matters that arose during the first half of 1857 when Nebraska had no codes on its books.[230] The criminal and civil statutes of Nebraska that had become effective on June 1, 1857 were, in turn, repealed and replaced by a later legislative enactment that became effective on February 1, 1859.[231] The scarcity of law books on the western frontier calls into question whether Judge Munson used at the Daniels trial the Nebraska's criminal code of 1855, or 1857, or 1859. In any event, a court charging a jury with the "wrong law" is normally a basis for a defendant to appeal a criminal conviction, though as this narrative will show, no judicial appeal was ever pursued by Daniels in this instance. With the benefit of twenty-twenty hindsight, Munson's use of Nebraska's law at the Daniels trial, for a matter decided by a jury in Montana, could have been, and should have been, point one in Daniels's brief submitted on any appeal of his criminal conviction.

The jury rendered its verdict in the Daniels case on Christmas Eve, 1865.[232] Trial lawyers are often wary of verdicts rendered on the eve of a major holiday, for fear that the jurors might rush their deliberations in order to be finished with their court business before the holiday is to commence. In any event, the jury sorted through the evidence presented during the trial and acquitted Daniels of intentional murder, but convicted him of a lesser manslaughter offense.[233] The historical record is unclear whether the manslaughter conviction was of the voluntary or involuntary variety, though either form of manslaughter could fit the facts of the Daniels case. Conceivably, the jury's determination might be a classic example of a "compromise verdict," since it represents the middle ground between murder in the first degree on the one hand and an outright acquittal based upon self-defense on the other. Any compromise verdict might have been a product of a genuinely divided jury or perhaps merely a desire by the jury to complete its deliberations immediately ahead of the Christmas holiday.

The jury's verdict, whether for voluntary or involuntary manslaughter, subjected Daniels to a sentence of imprisonment that could not exceed ten years.[234]

Judge Munson imposed upon Daniels a sentence of three years of hard labor, to be served in the territorial prison that had been built, by that time, in Virginia City as well as the payment of a $1,000 fine.[235] At first blush, the three-year sentence, being toward the lower end of what was statutorily authorized, might suggest that Munson was attempting to conclude the case in a manner that was measured. A more practical reason that Munson imposed a three-year sentence may have been that sentences up to three years in length were to be served at a county jail within Montana, whereas lengthier prison sentences were to be served at a federal penitentiary in Detroit, Michigan.[236] The cost of transporting a prisoner under guard to Detroit, and the possibility that a prisoner might escape during any such trips, made the imposition of jail sentences greater than three years less than desirable or satisfactory.[237] In capital cases the imposition of judicial death sentences might have seemed more certain and conclusive than lengthy prison terms served in a far-off penitentiary and, in that light, might have encouraged judicial hangings over the lesser option of extended incarcerations.[238] Daniels, however, was not convicted of any capital crime, so the imposition of a jail sentence and a fine was Judge Munson's only authorized choice. The sentence requirement that Daniels perform hard labor while in prison might have been Munson's way of compensating for the seemingly "light" three-year sentence, when a sentence more than triple that length was permitted under Montana law. The same might be said for the $1,000 fine, which represented a considerable sum of money in Montana in 1865. Daniels's conviction and sentence received a scant three-sentence report in the edition of the *Montana Post* published on December 30, 1865,[239] perhaps given the absence of a murder conviction, the impossibility of a death sentence, and the distance between Grizzly Gulch—where the crime was committed—and Virginia City, where the newspaper was still then being published.

Daniels commenced his term of incarceration. The January 6, 1866, edition of the *Montana Post* included a short story about Daniels's placement in jail, not because there was still anything particularly notorious about the prisoner or his conviction at the time, but because of a decision by the sheriff of Madison County to release Daniels from custody in the absence of any assurance that his boarding costs would be paid.[240] Ultimately, the problem was resolved when Deputy Marshal John Fetherstun, who had transported Daniels to Virginia City, personally backed the full faith and creditworthiness of his "Uncle Sam," and the prisoner was forced to return to his cell.[241]

Daniels's legal strategy while in prison was to seek a pardon for the manslaughter offense from President Andrew Johnson and to seek a release from prison pending consideration of the pardon application. Attorney William Y. Pemberton prepared the necessary papers, including a petition that was to be presented to Governor Meagher.

The entire petition for the release of Daniels was published in the *Montana Radiator*.[242] The full text is reproduced here as Appendix C. The petition maintained that Daniels had been acting in self-defense when he killed James Gartley.[243] The petition attested to Daniels's good character without mentioning any aspects of his alleged sordid and violent past.[244] It requested Governor Meagher "to reprieve and pardon" Daniels in the belief that such a remedy "would result in universal satisfaction to all unbiased persons in this community acquainted with the facts and circumstances connected with said homicide and trial."[245] It was signed by Daniels's attorneys, the law firm of Pemberton & Toole, and by thirty-one additional individual supporters, including some of the jurors who had rendered the manslaughter verdict.[246] Significantly, the petition requested that Daniels receive a "reprieve and pardon," written in the conjunctive rather than in the disjointive. By its plain language, the petition requested of Governor Meagher the issuance of two independent forms of relief, those of a reprieve and a pardon.

The legal distinction between a pardon and a reprieve is legally significant and was particularly so in this instance. A pardon is an act of grace that completely forgives an individual for criminal conduct and releases the person from any punishment imposed for the crime committed.[247] A reprieve or "respite" is a withholding of a sentence for an interval of time, without affecting the underlying criminal conviction for which the sentence was imposed.[248] The Organic Act of 1864, by which the US Congress created the territory of Montana, provided in section 2 that the territorial governor "may grant pardons and respites for offences against the laws of said Territory, and reprieve for offences against the laws of the United States, until the decision of the President of the United States can be made known."[249] A fair reading of the Organic Act suggests, therefore, that Governor Meagher possessed the authority to "pardon" offenders for violations of purely territorial laws and to merely "reprieve" offenders for violations of federal laws pending a determination of a full pardon application to the president of the United States. Such a construction of the law is consistent with the US Constitution, which provides, in article 2, section 2, that the president "shall have the Power to grant Reprieves and Pardons for Offenses against the United States, except in Cases of Impeachment." The Organic Act could not bestow upon a territorial governor any authority that would conflict with or usurp powers expressly granted to the president of the United States.

The authority of a territory's executive officer to grant pardons has been interpreted by courts on various occasions and under different circumstances to be unrestricted and not subject to legislative or judicial review.[250] Nevertheless, before any such legal determinations were rendered by territorial courts,

Montana's first legislature enacted statutes that tinkered with the circumstances under which sentences could be modified postjudgment. Those circumstances were limited to the grant of judicial authority to suspend the execution of judgments for capital offenders who were found to be insane and for women who appeared to be pregnant.[251] Daniels's conviction was not a capital offense, his sanity was never an issue at trial, and, clearly, he was not a pregnant woman. Therefore, if Daniels entertained any hopes of being relieved of his manslaughter conviction or sentence, his immediate remedy resided in the petition that his attorneys presented to Governor Meagher and in Meagher's discretionary power under the Organic Act to grant it.

A crucial legal question in determining the scope of Governor Meagher's authority with respect to the petition was whether Daniels's conviction for manslaughter was under federal or territorial law. If the conviction was federal, then Meagher had no authority to pardon Daniels for the crime since such pardon power resided exclusively with the president of the United States. Under those circumstances, Meagher's power as defined by the Organic Act was limited to the issuance of a "reprieve" of Daniels's sentence until a full pardon application could be heard by the president in Washington, DC. By contrast, if Daniels's manslaughter conviction was under territorial law, then Meagher's authority extended to a full pardon for the criminal offense itself.

Daniels had been tried and convicted before Judge Lyman Munson, an appointee of the late President Lincoln. Under the US Constitution, federal courts are vested with jurisdiction to handle cases that fall into a number of subject categories, including questions of federal constitutional law, international treaties, maritime controversies, claims under federal statutes, claims between states, claims between citizens of different states, and land claims between citizens and another state.[252] Section 9 of the Organic Act specifically vested the three federally appointed judges in Montana Territory with the same jurisdiction as that of the federal district and appellate circuit courts of the United States.[253] By the same token, the federal judges in Montana, though appointed by the president of the United States, constituted the only superior court in Montana Territory, and they naturally consulted and were to generally rely upon the penal law as contained within the Bannack Statutes.

At the time, federal courts did not necessarily bind themselves to the substantive laws of the states or territories in which they sat. For example, an 1810 case from the US Supreme Court, *Fletcher v. Peck*, recognized a "general common law" that was superior to the substantive law of the individual states or territories.[254] An 1842 case from the US Supreme Court, *Swift v. Tyson*, repeated the principle, which continued unaffected in American jurisprudence for several decades.[255] An 1873 case, *Hornbuckle v. Toombs*, which arose in Montana, held that federal courts sitting within the territories were to follow the practices, pleadings, forms, and modes of proceeding as set by the territorial legislatures.[256] It was not until 1938, in *Erie R.R. v. Tompkins*,[257] that the Supreme Court reversed the principle and held that except for matters involving the federal constitution and federal statutes, the US courts were required to apply to cases the substantive laws of the individual states in which they sat while adhering to federal law in matters of procedure. The *Erie R.R. v. Tompkins* case marked a significant shift in the relationship between federal and state laws in American courts. In the 1860s, however, when the former principles were controlling, matters handled by territorial courts were viewed as "federal," so any full pardon sought by a convicted criminal such as James Daniels would naturally fall to the president of the United States to decide. Neither side to the controversy that arose over Daniels's reprieve made the argument that his conviction was a matter of purely territorial law that would vest the governor with the power to grant both a reprieve and a pardon.

The petition that was submitted to Governor Meagher on James Daniels's behalf was granted, in part, by an executive order dated February 22, 1866.[258] Meagher's order, citing authority under section 2 of the Organic Act, granted a "reprieve [to] the said James B. Daniels, for the said offence of Manslaughter . . . until the decision of the President of the United States is made known thereon."[259] The order directed the sheriff of Madison County to immediately release Daniels from custody.[260] Whereas the Daniels's petition had requested both a "reprieve and pardon" from Meagher, the governor was careful to grant the petition only to the limited extent of a "reprieve." Meagher appears to have closely followed the limits of his authority under section 2 of the Organic Act. The plain language of Meagher's executive order granted absolutely no "pardon" to Daniels for the underlying manslaughter offense. A full text of the reprieve is contained in Appendix D.

Notably, the reprieve conferred by Governor Meagher was granted on February 22, 1866, which was only three weeks after Meagher had announced that he was calling Montana's second legislature into session and only two weeks before the second legislature actually convened. The reprieve, which released a prisoner who had been sentenced to incarceration by Judge Munson, was therefore issued at the height of the animosity that had erupted between Governor Meagher and Judge Munson over the convening of the territory's second legislature. The timing of Daniels's attorneys in presenting the petition could not have been better for their client. Moreover, Daniels's political stars were favorably aligned as his attorney, William Y. Pemberton, and Governor Meagher were both Democrats at a time when partisan passions were at a zenith.[261] Conversely, the prosecutor of Daniels's case, William Chumasero, was an active Republican.[262]

In addition to the political animosities that were burning at the time, the prospects for Daniels's reprieve may have benefitted from a more subtle factor that was unique to Governor Meagher. People are a product of their backgrounds and experiences. Earlier in life, Meagher had been condemned by an English court to be hanged for his rebellious Irish activities, and he directly benefited from a reprieve of the death sentence by an act of the British Parliament that included his banishment to Tasmania instead. The odds were astronomical that Daniels's petition would be presented to a presidentially appointed acting governor who, earlier in life, had been reprieved from an onerous criminal sentence himself. Meagher's own experiences could not have been lost upon him and may have been the most singularly significant factor motivating him to show James Daniels mercy. In that light, politics might have had nothing to do with the grant of Daniels's reprieve, or at least politics may have merely dovetailed with the governor's personal desires, which were influenced by his own life story. The public's perception, however, was much different.

By virtue of the reprieve, Daniels was released from prison a free man, pending his further application for a pardon from the president of the United States. Persons who believed Daniels guilty of murder and who considered his manslaughter conviction and sentence as too lenient in the first place were both incensed and disappointed. Their feelings may be understandable. The vigilantes in Helena had, in this instance, stepped aside and allowed Daniels's fate to be adjudicated in a court of law. They respected the jury's verdict and Judge Munson's three-year prison sentence and fine.[263] Those who were disappointed by the verdict and sentence could at least take solace from the knowledge that Daniels was confined at a jail in Virginia City and subject to daily hard labor for an extended period of time. Then, for the first time in the territory's young history, an acting governor stepped in and released the prisoner from jail, which seemingly undermined the judicial process that the vigilantes had chosen to respect. The fact that section 2 of the Organic Act granted the governor the authority to issue the reprieve was of no particular importance to those who disagreed with Daniels's release. Events suggested, at least to those who wished to see Daniels severely punished, that their confidence in Helena's fledgling legal system had been misplaced.

The reprieve may represent excellent lawyering by William Y. Pemberton on Daniels's behalf, but predictably the result was unpopular for Meagher. Meagher became the target of anger, frustration, and likely political revenge. Meagher might not have cared much about public opinion as, technically, he served as the territorial secretary of state by appointment of the president and was merely an acting governor pending the arrival of a new gubernatorial appointee. He was therefore not accountable to any electorate. The invectives that were hurled at Meagher included the accusation that he had signed Daniels's release while in a state of intoxication, having no appreciation of what he was doing.[264] The *Montana Post*, apparently assuming that Meagher had acted in sobriety, wrote that the governor was "mislead by evil counselors."[265] The newspaper criticized Meagher for "not seeking good and disinterested advice."[266] It also belittled Meagher, claiming that "a moment's reflection [would] have convinced him of the injustice and impolicy of letting loose a murderer . . . where the criminal had bitterly sworn to be revenged on the witnesses for the prosecution, if he should get free."[267]

Most residents of Montana Territory in 1866 were not interested in, or did not necessarily understand, the fine legal distinction between an executive "reprieve" on the one hand and a full "pardon" on the other. What people did know was that Daniels had been convicted of a crime and sentenced to three years of hard labor and a fine and that, as a result of an order signed by their territorial governor, Daniels had become a free man. Daniels's freedom looked and sounded much like a pardon even though, from a legal standpoint, it was nothing of the sort. The *Montana Post* repeatedly and mistakenly referred to Meagher's order as a "pardon,"[268] notwithstanding the plain language of Meagher's directive that Daniels was granted merely a "reprieve." Meagher's political enemies might have deliberately chosen to frame the issue as an executive grant of a pardon to embarrass Meagher, by making it appear that he had granted relief that he was not authorized under the Organic Act to provide.

Among the many people that were disturbed by Daniels's reprieve was Judge Munson. Munson's opposition to the reprieve might have been fueled by a combination of two factors. The obvious factor is that Munson, having been the judge that presided over Daniels's trial and imposed his sentence, may have felt that his judicial authority had been undermined by the reprieve. A strong stance against Daniels's release might have appeared necessary to maintain a proper separation and balance between the executive and judicial branches of territorial government, not only as to the Daniels matter but for future criminal matters as well. Of course, if Governor Meagher was possessed of authority to reprieve Daniels from his sentence, Munson had no legitimate constitutional complaint, since the power of reprieve is *part* of the checks and balances between the executive and judicial branches of government recognized by the US Constitution and by the Organic Act that created Montana Territory.

A second factor that might have motivated Munson's efforts to reincarcerate Daniels was the highly charged climate of territorial politics at the time. Republicans, including Munson, were angry with Meagher over his convening of the territorial legislature for its second session. Meagher had aligned himself politically with Montana Democrats and no longer enjoyed the protection and collegiality of Republicans who were eager to exact political revenge. While judges today are required to scrupulously avoid involvements in politics except when running in elections for their own judicial offices, Judge Munson had no qualms about involving himself in the partisan controversy surrounding the governor's call for a second legislative session. Munson and other Republicans might have believed that the Democratic Party generally, and their governor specifically, could be politically damaged if a convincing argument could be made that Meagher released a convicted criminal from prison without any authority to do so under the Organic Act.

Munson responded to Daniels's release in a visible way, by making a 120-mile trip from Helena to Virginia City to personally request that Meagher rescind his order.[269] According to the *Montana Post*, Munson found the governor intoxicated, "still in his debauch," and the release order was not rescinded.[270]

Munson further responded by sending a pointed letter to Governor Meagher, dated March 1, 1866. The letter was written a mere four days prior to the convening of the Montana's Second Territorial Legislature. In the letter Munson argued that the governor's authority under section 2 of the Organic Act was limited to only capital cases, such as murder, in which the defendant faced death by hanging and did not extend to less serious offenses, such as manslaughter, which carried noncapital sentences.[271] Munson argued that even the power of reprieve did not allow the governor to release Daniels from custody during the time that his pardon application might be pending before the president.[272] A full copy of Munson's letter was published in the *Montana Post*.[273] Editorially, the newspaper described the letter as reflecting "sound principles" and "manly independence and firmness."[274] Since, in Munson's view, Governor Meagher had exceeded his authority in releasing Daniels from imprisonment, Munson issued a new order to the US marshal for the rearrest of Daniels.[275] Munson advised in his letter that a US marshal, John Fetherstun, would obey the court's order.[276]

A constitutional crisis had erupted. By executive order, the governor of Montana Territory had ordered the release of a prisoner from incarceration. By counter order, a Supreme Court justice of Montana Territory directed the rearrest and reincarceration of the same person, with the presumed backing of the US marshal. The executive and judicial branches of the newly minted Montana Territory were at loggerheads. The territorial government, which in some ways was already dysfunctional, had become even more so.

Notably, neither Meagher or Munson cited any specific legal authority in support of their interpretations of section 2 of the Organic Act. The reason is that there was none at the time. A resolution of the issue on its merits requires reliance upon the plain language of the Organic Act to determine its meaning.

As already shown, the plain language of section 2 of the Organic Act provided that the territorial governor could grant pardons and respites for violations of territorial laws, and reprieves for offenses against federal laws until such time that the president could render a decision on the matter. In granting a reprieve, Meagher found that Daniels's conviction was based upon circumstances that were "to a great extent, justifiable on the part of the said Daniels."[277] Meagher also noted that the petition was supported by "numerous good citizens of the County of Edgerton . . . including several jurymen, who, by their verdict, contributed to the aforesaid conviction."[278] The fact that certain jurors signed Daniels's petition, which seemingly undercut their own verdict, may further suggest that the manslaughter conviction had been a "compromise verdict" between divided jurors facing an imminent Christmas holiday.

In any event, there appears to be no evidence that Meagher's grant of Daniels's reprieve was a product of inappropriate influences. Certainly, as governor, Meagher was vested with the discretion to grant or deny the petition as he saw fit. Here, the grant of Daniels's petition does not appear to have been an abusive or improvident exercise of that discretion, given the witnesses who testified for the prosecution, the defense during the trial of the matter, and the colorable claim of self-defense raised at trial, which enabled Daniels to avoid a conviction for the higher charge of intentional murder.

Munson's argument, that Meagher's authority to issue reprieves existed only in more serious matters involving capital punishment, is not supported by the plain language of section 2 of the Organic Act. Section 2 grants the territorial governor authority to grant pardons, respites, and reprieves for territorial and federal "offenses," without any language limiting the scope of such offenses to only those involving a death penalty. Under the legal concept of *expressio unius est exclusio alterius*,[279] the failure of a legislature to place certain language in a statute is presumed to be intentional. By application of *expressio unius est exclusio alterius*, the failure of the US Congress to expressly limit reprieve authority in the Organic Act to capital offenses, rather than to all offenses generally, requires an interpretation of the law as applying to *all* offenses, regardless of the measures of punishment authorized for them under the law. Any contrary interpretation would read into the Organic Act a meaning that the Congress chose not to express in the statute.

Moreover, Munson's interpretation of the Organic Act strains logic. If, as Munson argued in his letter of March 1, 1866, the governor would have had authority to reprieve a prisoner facing a death sentence, the obvious purpose of such a reprieve is to prevent the sentence from being carried out before the president can have the opportunity to decide a petition for a full pardon. Here, however, Daniels was sentenced merely to a period of imprisonment, hard labor, and the payment of a fine, so the issuance of a reprieve, without Daniels's release from prison, would have represented a continuation of his punishment while any pardon application was pending before the president. The pardon process would necessarily take time, given the distance between Montana and Washington and the inefficiencies of transportation and communication at the time. Accordingly, under Munson's view for noncapital cases, there would never be any need for reprieves in noncapital cases, and the authority in the Organic Act that a governor may issue a reprieve would, under these circumstances, have no practical effect or meaning. Therefore, regardless of whether Daniels was found guilty of manslaughter under a territorial or federal law, it appears that Governor Meagher acted within the scope of his authority under the Organic Act in ordering at least a reprieve of Daniels's sentence. Those who criticized the reprieve could have legitimately taken issue with whether it was warranted on the merits of the case, but they had no credible basis for attacking the legal *authority* of the governor to entertain and grant the petition. Paradoxically, the position taken by Governor Meagher, a lawyer with limited legal experience, was correct on the law, while the position taken by Lyman Munson, an experienced Yale-educated attorney and appointed Supreme Court justice, was not correct. Munson's failure to correctly interpret the Organic Act suggests that his opposition to Daniels's release was motivated more by partisan politics, or by the protection of judicial turf, than by sound legal principles.

The legal dispute between the executive and judicial branches of the territorial government over the propriety of Daniels's release did not fester long. The issue was soon rendered academic, though not by the orderly mechanisms of government nor by any artful compromise of the participants. Rather, the dispute was rendered academic by the conduct of James Daniels and the vigilantes of Helena.

Upon his release from prison, Daniels was heard in Virginia City saloons disparaging the Helena vigilantes and threatening to return to Helena to avenge himself on the three witnesses who had testified against him at his trial.[280]

Return to Helena he did.

Fifteen miles from Helena, Daniels stopped at Duston's Hot Springs Ranch, where he repeated his threats against the witnesses who had testified against him.[281] According to the *Montana Post*, news of his threats "arrived in town almost as soon as he did."[282]

William Chumasero, who had prosecuted Daniels, wrote a letter to Wilbur Fisk Sanders on March 4, 1866, which mentioned Daniels's release and which contained an ominous prediction. He wrote, "Daniels has gone to Helena and it is very much to be hoped that the Vigilantes have performed the last said offices for him—I know they will if they get hold of him."[283] In other words, prior to learning of Daniels's ultimate fate, Chumasero wrote that he would be hanged by the Helena vigilantes if he were to be captured by them. Perhaps Chumasero possessed inside knowledge of vigilante intentions. More likely, Chumasero, an attorney closely involved with the criminal prosecution, merely understood the temperament and predispositions of vigilante activists and the manner in which Daniels's release would be viewed by them.

Chumasero was not aware that at the time his letter was posted, his prediction about Daniels's fate had already proven true.

Daniels arrived in Helena by stagecoach on the evening of March 2, 1866, in what was reported to be "fine spirits."[284] With Munson arriving in Virginia City from Helena by March 1, the timing of the two men's travels suggests that they likely passed one another in opposite directions at some point in late February 1866, if not literally, then at least generally. Upon his arrival at Helena, Daniels quickly developed misgivings about his own personal safety.[285] He was astute enough to realize, by direct warnings or by inference, that his own life had slipped into immediate danger. Of course, Daniels had created his own problem by returning to Helena as he did, vowing to avenge himself on the witnesses who had earlier testified against him. Daniels dealt with the problem by seeking out deputy US marshal John Fetherstun to request, and receive, protective federal custody.[286] Fetherstun had not yet received a copy of Judge Munson's order for Daniels's rearrest, since it had been signed by Munson only the day before in Virginia City, 120 miles south of Helena.[287] The order was still with Munson, who was separately hastening back to Helena from Virginia City but who had not yet arrived.[288] Fetherstun kept Daniels at his own office, an express office, and thereafter, at the D. L. Coleman Store, where he was to spend the night.[289] Fetherstun then left Daniels to see what he could learn about vigilante intentions by speaking with various men at several Helena-area saloons.[290] He learned nothing of value,[291] though there was no assurance that the persons he spoke with were inclined to divulge to Fetherstun any meaningful information. Indeed, Fetherstun's approach to known or suspected vigilantes may have unwittingly revealed to them Daniels's specific whereabouts at the D. L. Coleman Store.

However vigilantes learned of Daniels's location, a group of masked men stormed the Coleman store at approximately 9:00 p.m., seized Daniels, and took him to the Hanging Tree before 10:00 p.m. the same evening.[292] The events suggest that the circumstances of Daniels's capture were not pleasant. After arriving at the Hanging Tree, Daniels was hanged.[293] The only trial Daniels ever received was the one that had been conducted the previous December before Judge Munson on the underlying criminal charge.

The reprieve that was signed by Governor Meagher authorizing Daniels's release from prison was present in Daniels's coat pocket when he was hanged.[294] The reprieve was taken from the corpse the following day.[295] The Helena Committee of Safety viewed its extralegal authority to impose the ultimate punishment upon Daniels as superior to the authority of the territory's acting governor to release the prisoner from jail.

Also the next day a photograph was taken of Daniels's corpse hanging from the noose several feet off the ground. The photograph is maintained in the archives of the Montana Historical Society in Helena. The absence in the photograph of any visible object beneath Daniels's feet, and the rather high distance between the bottom of his boots and the ground below, might suggest that his hanging was performed by hoisting rather than by a drop. In keeping with vigilante tradition, a note was pinned to his clothing. However, in breaking with vigilante tradition, the pinned note did not merely identify the condemned man's crime, but instead announced a threat to a specific third person—Governor Meagher. Ominously, the note read, "If an acting Governor does this again, we'll hang him too."[296]

To underscore the vigilantes' dissatisfaction with Meagher, a six-inch slice of the rope used in the execution of James Daniels was then delivered to the governor via Pony Express with a message that warned, "It don't take a bigger rope to hang the Governor of Montana than it does to hang a horse thief or a murderer."[297]

If Meagher were a cautious man, he might have feared that he was marked for death. But it was never in Meagher's character to be fearful of anything. At a minimum, Meagher was placed on notice that he was not beyond the reach of Helena's vigilantes if, in their view, future circumstances warranted their further action against him. The members of Helena's Committee of Safety, or at least its rogue members, must truly have felt invincible to have issued threats against the life of the acting governor of their territory.

History can only wonder whether Daniels's fate would have been different if Judge Munson had arrived in Helena before Daniels in the beginning of March, with his signed order for Daniels's rearrest. Had Daniels been formally rearrested, it is conceivable that he could have been returned to the jail at Virginia City before any harm could befall the trial witnesses who had testified against him, and the vigilantes might have seen no need to intervene.

The deputy US marshal from whom Daniels sought protective custody, John Fetherstun, was so embarrassed by the action of the vigilantes that he felt compelled to pen a letter to the public that was published in the edition of the *Montana Post* of March 10, 1866. Fetherstun explained in the letter that at the time Daniels was captured and hanged, he was not actually under Fetherstun's custody or protection.[298]

Figure 12.6. The body of James Daniels, after being hanged by vigilantes on March 2, 1866, with the governor's reprieve in his pocket. (Courtesy of the Montana Historical Society, image 948-124.)

Opinion of the Daniels hanging was mixed and, in some respects, heated. The *Montana Post* accused Governor Meagher of issuing the "pardon" to "win favor at the hands of a certain class," making reference to Irish voters and Democrats who could provide Meagher with support if the question of a US senatorship were to be brought up in the future.[299] The newspaper praised Judge Munson's handling of the Daniels trial, his personal appeal to Governor Meagher that the post-trial "pardon" be rescinded, and his opposition to vigilantism.[300] The *Montana Post* reiterated its view that Daniels's release was a pardon rather than a reprieve and that the governor lacked the authority to issue the "pardon" that led to Daniels' death.[301] The newspaper also conceded, however, that the Daniels hanging was motivated not because of the "pardon" itself but because Daniels had uttered mortal threats against trial witnesses, which made him "unfit to live in the community."[302] Dimsdale wrote in the *Montana Post*:

> When escaped murderers utter threats of murder against peaceable citizens, mountain law is apt to be administered without much regard to technicalities, and when a man says he is going to kill anyone, in a mining community, it is understood that he means what he says, and must abide the consequences. Two human beings had fallen victim to his thirst for blood—the husband and his wife. Three more were threatened; but the action of the Vigilantes prevented the commission of the contemplated atrocities.[303]

By contrast, the *Montana Radiator*, a Helena newspaper more favorably disposed to Governor Meagher,[304] aimed its criticisms of the hanging at the vigilantes and at Judge Munson. The *Montana Radiator* argued to its readers that "it was wrong to hang the man notwithstanding he was illegally released" and that Judge Munson contributed to the hanging by "the excitement that he manifested."[305] Nathaniel Langford criticized Daniels's hanging in his book. Langford believed that the execution "did not have the official sanction of the Executive Committee of Helena" and described the hanging as "an unauthorized act of certain irresponsible members of the organization at Helena."[306] According to Langford, if Daniels had been wrongfully released, he could just as easily have been rearrested.[307] Langford condemned the Daniels execution as the "one case where the Vigilantes exceeded the boundaries of right and justice, and became themselves the violators of law and propriety."[308] Langford also wrote that the Daniels's hanging prompted a meeting of the Executive Committee of the separate vigilance organization in Virginia City, which expressed its disapproval of the actions of their vigilante counterparts in Helena.[309] One Montana historian summed up Daniels's unfortunate circumstances by observing that Daniels was "indicted for a crime he did not commit [charged with murder but convicted of manslaughter]; tried by a court without jurisdiction [adjudicating a purely territorial, rather than federal, crime]; reprieved by a governor by mistake [regarding the question of the governor's authority to release the prisoner]; and lynched by a mob."[310]

The harshest public criticism of Daniels's hanging appears to have come from his attorney, William Y. Pemberton. A meeting was held in Central Hall where speeches were made about the Daniels matter. Pemberton described Daniels's hanging not only as a deliberate "murder" but as "a political thing" in furtherance of a partisan agenda aimed at Governor Meagher and the Montana Democrats.[311] In other words, Pemberton attributed Daniels's death to rank political partisanship waged by Republicans against Meagher and the Democratic Party, with his client, James Daniels, caught in between.

For their part, the vigilantes were unrepentant and rejected the suggestion that Daniels's hanging was in any way influenced by the politics of the time. A vigilante who identified himself with the nom de plume of "Index" published a letter in the *Montana Post* on March 17, 1866, attributing Daniels's death solely to the threats he had made to the lives of three witnesses who had testified for the prosecution at the trial.[312] "Index" stated that he was "glad that we have men among us who know how to meet the emergency" and that "very few good men regret this action."[313] Public letters from vigilante activists were uncommon. The fact that Index's letter was written in this instance suggests that some vigilante members might have felt stung by the accusations that they had killed a man out of political partisanship and that a public response was required.

Whatever the controversy over Daniels's execution, there was no further fallout. The members of Helena's Committee of Safety who had hanged Daniels were not identified, and no persons were ever prosecuted for any crimes related to his death. Nor were there political ramifications for Governor Meagher, as his appointed successor, Green Clay Smith, arrived to assume the gubernatorial duties in the normal course of events approximately six months later.

Ironically, Daniels might have survived the crisis had he not petitioned the governor for a reprieve and a pardon in the first place. Had he served his full prison term, he could have performed three years of hard labor and paid a fine, and would eventually have been released from custody at the conclusion of his sentence with a new lease on life.

Governor Meagher's tenure in Montana was at best bold, and at worst politically inept. He came to the Montana governorship without any American governmental, administrative, or political experience.[314] He responded to the normal checks and balances of tripartite government by acting dictatorially, ignoring the territory's judiciary, and bullying the territory's legislators when it suited his purposes. Nevertheless, he has been lionized by Montana history. He endeavored to be a strong leader in Montana as he had in Ireland two decades before. Outside the scope of this book, he raised, as governor, a contingent of troops to fight an ineffective war against Native American Indians in the territory, costing almost a million dollars for militia expenses and supplies, which the Congress settled in 1871 for roughly half the amount billed.[315] He is remembered for his flip-flop on whether to call the Second Territorial Legislature into session and receives much of the blame for calling two legislatures that were ultimately nullified by the US Congress. Historian Paul R. Wylie complains, perhaps rightly so, that placing all of the blame on Meagher for the two "bogus" legislatures is not entirely fair, as Governor Edgerton could share blame for allowing the first legislature to recess without completing work on an acceptable reapportionment bill and as Governor Smith could share blame for proceeding with the third legislature during his appointed term in office.[316] As for James Daniels, Meagher's grant of a reprieve was, with the benefit of hindsight, a deadly mistake, and one that might conceivably have been avoided had the governor provided Daniels's prosecutor with an opportunity to respond to the petition before granting the reprieve.[317] Historians who have characterized Daniels's release as an unauthorized pardon are mistaken, perhaps caused by their reliance upon newspaper articles and other original source materials that mischaracterized the release as a "pardon" because of the political biases that they reflected at the time. Any criticisms of Meagher's tenure should be tempered by the tumultuous, challenging, and unorganized time in which he performed the chief executive functions within the territory.

There is a curious postscript to the Daniels execution that is worth noting. During the evening of July 1, 1867, roughly sixteen months after James Daniels's execution, Thomas Francis Meagher died under circumstances that were unusual.[318] He was a guest on a docked steamboat named the *G. A. Thompson*.[319] At the time, he was once again the acting governor of Montana Territory, as Governor Smith, who by then had been appointed by President Johnson, was away from the territory on an extended trip to Washington, DC.[320] Meagher drowned when he fell from the steamboat into the Missouri River.[321] He was forty-four years old.[322] Meagher's wife, Libby, arranged for patrols of the Missouri downriver, but all efforts to locate Meagher proved fruitless and his body was never recovered.[323]

The *Montana Post*, with whom Meagher had had a most difficult relationship, chose to run its initial story about the governor's death on page 5 of the edition published July 6, 1867.[324] The paper chose to fill much of the front page of that same edition with a story demystifying the beliefs and history of the Mormon religion.[325] A well-attended meeting of citizens was assembled on

July 4, 1867, at a theater on Wood Street in Helena in tribute to Governor Meagher.[326] The persons present passed various resolutions of regret and admiration, as well as condolences to Meagher's "immediate relatives and friends throughout the world, and most especially Mrs. Elizabeth Meagher, his disconsolate and bereaved widow."[327] Similar resolutions were issued by Governor Smith and by the Fenian Brotherhood of Red Mountain City, Montana.[328] Judge Munson was surprisingly generous to Meagher in a public eulogy delivered in Helena, saying that he "was a gentleman of most extraordinary mental endowments, of intellectual culture, of social attainments, of generous impulses, and of patriotic emotions."[329] In Virginia City, Chief Judge Hosmer was also effusive, saying that Meagher "possessed a noble heart—a generous and manly spirit, and a most genial disposition. There was nothing in his faults to extinguish the fire of great virtues."[330]

There have been many speculations about the manner in which Meagher died. One theory is that Meagher fell overboard while in a state of intoxication and was too drunk to swim from the river to safety.[331] Drunkenness was still not out of the ordinary for the acting governor of Montana Territory. Wilbur Fisk Sanders who, despite political differences, spent much of the fateful day with Meagher, reported that the governor had not been drinking that afternoon.[332] Sanders did not claim that he remained with Meagher into the evening and, therefore, did not exclude the possibility that Meagher consumed alcohol closer to the time of his death. Another theory is that Meagher committed suicide, as he was suffering from certain uncomfortable physical ailments and was in serious financial debt.[333] However, history provides no credible evidence that Meagher's demise was by his own hand. Still other people speculated that Meagher's death involved foul play, whether motivated by partisan political resentments, Native American Indian animosity, enmity between the British and the Irish, or by vigilante revenge.[334] Once again, hard evidence of foul play in the death of Thomas Francis Meagher was lacking for many years.

The unresolved circumstances of Meagher's death might have been forgotten to all but historians. Then, in 1913, a man named Frank Diamond, aka Pat Miller, claimed on his deathbed that he had been hired by the vigilantes to help murder Meagher in exchange for a payment to him of $8,000.[335] Diamond claimed that he had murdered Meagher on the deck of the steamship on the Missouri River, threw the body overboard, and escaped by jumping into the water and swimming ashore.[336] The confession was made to a saloon proprietor named Jack Thompson while Diamond was suffering from an apparent heart attack.[337] The confession caused quite a stir as Meagher had remained a titanic figure in the history of Montana Territory. Diamond did not die from his heart attack, but instead recovered and was then imprisoned in the Missoula

County jail by authorities who were seriously considering bringing him to trial for Meagher's murder.[338]

Thereafter, another man, named David McMillan Billingsly, aka Dave Mack, stepped forward and confirmed that Governor Meagher had been murdered by vigilantes,[339] but Mack was inconsistent in important respects with Diamond's description of how the crime was committed. According to Mack, Meagher was kidnapped from the boat and was then hanged and secretly buried.[340] Mack's version of the crime was initially published in the *Anaconda Standard* on June 2, 1913.[341] Meagher's pardon of James Daniels was identified as the sole motivating reason for the vigilante murder of Meagher.[342] Former vigilantes and some of their descendants immediately denied the accusations.[343]

The vigilantes' involvement in Meagher's death was called into question when Diamond, facing potential criminal charges from the event, recanted his confession by claiming that he was drunk at the time he uttered the confession.[344] Diamond may very well have been drunk when he confessed to the murder of Governor Meagher and other serious crimes, as his heart attack occurred during a round of heavy drinking at Jack Thompson's saloon.[345] The recanted confession of one potentially intoxicated person, three and a half decades after the event, inconsistent with a description of the event by another person, fails to adequately rebut the weight of statements by eyewitnesses who were proximate to the actual events surrounding Meagher's late-evening demise, that Meagher simply fell overboard and died an accidental death.

If Meagher died an accidental death, there is an unfortunate irony to his demise. During his life, he faced the death penalty for his rebellion against the English but survived. Like all soldiers, he also faced death during the Civil War but survived all of his battles in that conflict as well. In Montana he garnered more than his fair share of enemies, but no harm came to him. An accidental death was not befitting of the life Meagher lived, prompting fellow Young Irelander Richard O'Gorman to lament after the fact, "Would that he had died on the battlefield."[346]

Meagher was eulogized by various persons in various ways inside and outside of Montana. There were many tributes to him published in American and Irish newspapers at the time. On June 28, 1963, President John F. Kennedy honored Meagher and the Irish Brigade in an address he delivered to the Irish Parliament.[347] Meagher's most lasting tribute is not reflected by any words stated but by the erection of his statue, upon a horse, clutching a raised sword, which to this day dominates the lawn of the Montana State Capitol in front of its main entrance. The statue was unveiled in a well-attended ceremony held on July 4, 1905.[348] The sword ties his life in Montana to the "sword speech" that Meagher delivered in 1846 that launched his fame.

Figure 12.7. Statue of Governor Thomas Francis Meagher on the lawn of the Montana Capitol. (Photo by author.)

Panning for Nuggets

The skeletal remains of James Daniels were discovered in his coffin during excavation for a new school building on Davis Street, in Helena, in July 1931.[349] *Daniels's skeleton was identified by the boots on the foot bones and the stitching on clothing material that matched those on the corpse depicted in the preserved photograph of Daniels's hanging. Daniels's skull was part of a vigilante display at the Montana Historical Society until 1991, when a change in the state's law regarding human remains, known as the Human Skeletal Remains and Burial Site Protection Act, required that the remains be sent to the Montana Preservation Burial Board for interment.*[350]

Notes

1. Bancroft, *History*, 641n31; "Died," *Montana Post*, Sept. 22, 1866, p. 5, col 3; "Thomas J. Dimsdale," *Montana Post*, Sept. 29, 1866, p. 4, col. 2.
2. Allen, *Decent Orderly Lynching*, 349.
3. "A Full and Complete History of the Chase, Capture, Trial and Execution of All the Outlaws Who Figured in the Bloody Drama," *Montana Post*, Mar. 17, 1866, p. 4, col. 1. Chapter 29 of the Dimsdale book, which involved the capture and execution of Jack Silvie,

began in the edition of the *Montana Post* published on March 10, 1866, and continued with its description of James Daniels's conviction, release, and execution the following week.

4. Ibid.

5. Ibid.

6. Meagher, pronounced as "Mar."

7. Wylie, *Irish General*, 226; Spence, *Territorial Politics*, 18.

8. Wylie, *Irish General*, 329.

9. Ibid., 226.

10. Organic Act for the Territory of Montana, Act May 26, 1864, ch. 95, sec. 3, 13 Stat. 85.

11. Wylie, *Irish General*, 231; Keneally, *Great Shame*, 401. Keneally notes that Edgerton began his journey using the same coach in which Meagher had arrived.

12. Wylie, *Irish General*, 232.

13. Ibid.

14. Ibid., n. 34.

15. Keneally, *Great Shame*, 446. Meagher would become acting governor of the territory a second time during the first few months of 1867, when Governor Smith was in Washington lobbying for greater protection against Native American Indian tribes. Wylie, *Irish General*, 285.

16. Jones, *Irish Brigade*, 19; Burlingame, *Montana Frontier*, 160.

17. Jones, *Irish Brigade*, 19.

18. Ibid.

19. Ibid.; Keneally, *Great Shame*, 72; see also Wylie, *Irish General*, 88.

20. Jones, *Irish Brigade*, 19.

21. Wylie, *Irish General*, 29.

22. Jones, *Irish Brigade*, 24.

23. Ibid., 25.

24. Wylie, *Irish General*, 39–40; Keneally, *Great Shame*, 119.

25. Jones, *Irish Brigade*, 27; Wylie, *Irish General*, 40.

26. Jones, *Irish Brigade*, 28–30.

27. Ibid., 30.

28. Wylie, *Irish General*, 86; Keneally, *Great Shame*, 171.

29. Jones, *Irish Brigade*, 32; Wylie, *Irish General*, 58; Keneally, *Great Shame*, 169, 177–79; Burlingame, *Montana Frontier*, 160.

30. Wylie, *Irish General*, 60.

31. Ibid., 58, citing the *London Times*, Oct. 25, 1848.

32. Jones, *Irish Brigade*, 32; Wylie, *Irish General*, 67; Burlingame, *Montana Frontier*, 160.

33. Wylie, *Irish General*, 61.

34. Jones, *Irish Brigade*, 32; Keneally, *Great Shame*, 232, 246 (identifying the child as a son named Henry); Burlingame, *Montana Frontier*, 160.

35. Jones, *Irish Brigade*, 33.

36. Ibid., 33–34.

37. Ibid., 34.

38. Wylie, *Irish General*, 87–88; Keneally, *Great Shame*, 258.

39. Jones, *Irish Brigade*, 34; Keneally, *Great Shame*, 250–51, 274.

40. Wylie, *Irish General*, 91; Keneally, *Great Shame*, 274 (identifying the child by the name of Thomas Francis Meagher III). Bennett came to the United States when he was eighteen years old and enrolled at the US Military Academy at West Point, but was expelled because of deficient grades in mathematics and French. He later worked for the Fellowship of Eagles in Manila, Philippines, where he died on November 9, 1909. Find a Grave, "Thomas Bennett Meagher."

41. Jones, *Irish Brigade*, 12; Wylie, *Irish General*, 97; Keneally, *Great Shame*, 284; Burlingame, *Montana Frontier*, 161.

42. Jones, *Irish Brigade*, 11.

43. Ibid.

44. Jones, *Irish Brigade*, 14; Wylie, *Irish General*, 98; Keneally, *Great Shame*, 284, 296; Burlingame, *Montana Frontier*, 161.

45. Burlingame, *Montana Frontier*, 160.

46. Jones, *Irish Brigade*, 16–17.

47. Ibid., 17–18; Wylie, *Irish General*, 120; Keneally, *Great Shame*, 321; Burlingame, *Montana Frontier*, 161.

48. Jones, *Irish Brigade*, 93–94, 104.

49. Keneally, *Great Shame*, 339–40; Burlingame, *Montana Frontier*, 161.

50. Howard, *Montana High, Wide, and Handsome*, 44.

51. Jones, *Irish Brigade*, 175–76; Wylie, *Irish General*, 190; Keneally, *Great Shame*, 382–83.

52. Jones, *Irish Brigade*, 177.

53. Wylie, *Irish General*, 209.

54. Allen, *Decent Orderly Lynching*, 331.

55. Bancroft, *History*, 643n3.

56. Ibid., 643.

57. Organic Act of the Territory of Montana, Act May 26, 1864, ch. 95, sec. 4, 13 Stat. 85.

58. Wylie, *Irish General*, 248–49.

59. Keneally, *Great Shame*, 431.

60. Wylie, *Irish General*, 249.

61. Laws 1865, First Terr. Legis., Procedure Act, ch. 1, sec. 220; see also Donovan, *Hanging around the Big Sky*, book 1, 5.

62. Laws 1865, First Terr. Legis., Procedure Act, ch. 1, sec. 222; see also Donovan, *Hanging around the Big Sky*, book 1, 5.

63. Wylie, *Irish General*, 249.

64. Ibid.

65. Ibid.

66. Ibid.

67. Allen, *Decent Orderly Lynching*, 331.

68. Wylie, *Irish General*, 250, citing First Legislative Assembly of the Territory of Montana, *House Journal of the First Session of the Legislative Assembly of Montana* (Bannack, 1864–65), 178; Bancroft, *History*, 647; Burlingame, *Montana Frontier*, 161; Spence, *Territorial Politics*, 31.

69. Wylie, *Irish General*, 250, citing First Legislative Assembly of the Territory of Montana, *House Journal of the First Session of the Legislative Assembly of Montana* (Bannack, 1864–65), 200.

70. Ibid.

71. Ibid., citing First Legislative Assembly of the Territory of Montana, *House Journal of the First Session of the Legislative Assembly of Montana* (Bannack, 1864–65), 205.

72. Wylie, *Irish General*, 250.

73. Ibid., 251.

74. Ibid., 250–51.

75. Ibid., 251.

76. Burlingame, *Montana Frontier*, 159; Spence, *Territorial Politics*, 36.

77. Howard, *Montana High, Wide, and Handsome*, 42.

78. Wylie, *Irish General*, 252; Burlingame, *Montana Frontier*, 162; Spence, *Territorial Politics*, 36–37; Allen, *Decent Orderly Lynching*, 331–32.

79. Bancroft, *History*, 647.

80. Howard, *Montana High, Wide, and Handsome*, 43.

81. Wylie, *Irish General*, 252.

82. Ibid.

83. Ibid., 252, citing "Local and Other Items," *Montana Post*, Dec. 23, 1985. Arguably, an announcement of such importance to the territory should not have been headlined by the newspaper merely as an "other item."

84. Wylie, *Irish General*, 252; Bancroft, *History*, 647.

85. Spence, *Territorial Politics*, 37.

86. Howard, *Montana High, Wide, and Handsome*, 42–43; Bancroft, *History*, 647; Burlingame, *Montana Frontier*, 162.

87. Wylie, *Irish General*, 254; Bancroft, *History*, 647; Spence, *Territorial Politics*, 38.

88. Wylie, *Irish General*, 254; Bancroft, *History*, 647; Spence, *Territorial Politics*, 38.

89. "Calling the Legislature," *Montana Post*, Feb. 3, 1866, p. 2, col. 1; "Proclamation," *Montana Post*, Feb. 10, 1866, p. 3, col. 2.

90. "Calling the Legislature," *Montana Post*, Feb. 3, 1866, p. 2, col. 1; "Proclamation," *Montana Post*, Feb. 10, 1866, p. 3, col. 2.

91. Spence, *Territorial Politics*, 37.

92. Wylie, *Irish General*, 253.

93. Ibid.

94. Keneally, *Great Shame*, 446–47; Burlingame, *Montana Frontier*, 160; Allen, *Decent Orderly Lynching*, 332.

95. Keneally, *Great Shame*, 446–47; Burlingame, *Montana Frontier*, 160; Allen, *Decent Orderly Lynching*, 332.

96. Malone, Roeder, and Lang, *Montana*, 102.

97. "Calling the Legislature," *Montana Post*, Feb. 17, 1866, p. 1, col. 4; Malone, Roeder, and Lang, *Montana*, 102. The constitutional convention that was initially contemplated for March 26, 1866, was not actually convened until April 9, 1866 (see Bancroft, *History*, 649) as a result of bad weather that impeded delegates' travel.

98. Malone, Roeder, and Lang, *Montana* 102.

99. Howard, *Montana High, Wide, and Handsome*, 43.

100. Allen, *Decent Orderly Lynching*, 333; Malone, Roeder, and Lang, *Montana*, 102.

101. Opinion *in extenso* of Hon. Hezekiah Hosmer, Dec. 8, 1866, Wilbur Fisk Sanders Papers, Mont. Hist. Soc., MC-53, box 3, folder 3-14; Wylie, *Irish General*, 254.

102. Keneally, *Great Shame*, 432.

103. Opinion *in extenso* of Hon. Hezekiah Hosmer, Dec. 8, 1866, Wilbur Fisk Sanders Papers, Mont. Hist. Soc., MC-53, box 3, folder 3-14; Wylie, *Irish General*, 254.

104. Allen, *Decent Orderly Lynching*, 334.

105. "Calling the Legislature," *Montana Post*, Feb. 3, 1866, p. 2, col. 1.

106. Ibid.

107. "Calling the Legislature," *Montana Post*, Feb. 17, 1866, p. 1, col. 4.

108. "A Queer Legislature," *Montana Post*, Feb. 17, 1866, p. 2, col. 2.

109. "Acting Governor Meagher's Address," *Montana Post*, Feb. 24, 1866, p. 2, col. 1.

110. Allen, *Decent Orderly Lynching*, 334; Barsness, *Gold Camp*, 146.

111. Athearn, *Thomas Francis Meagher*, 154; Allen, *Decent Orderly Lynching*, 334.

112. Laws 1866, Second Terr. Legis., p. 1.

113. Spence, *Territorial Politics*, 38.

114. Laws 1866, Second Terr. Legis., chs. 4, 10, 19, 22.

115. Laws 1866, Second Terr. Legis., ch. 13.

116. Laws 1866, Second Terr. Legis., ch. 24. Section 10 of chapter 24 exempted from jury service the following persons: priests and ministers, physicians, attorneys, active firemen, government officers, and "all idiots and insane persons."

117. Laws 1866, Second Terr. Legis., ch. 12, sec. 1; ch. 14, secs. 1–13, 14–23, ch. 32, secs. 3, 11.

118. Laws 1866, Second Terr. Legis., chs. 26, 34.

119. Laws 1866, Second Terr. Legis., ch. 32, sec. 6.

120. Laws 1866, Second Terr. Legis., chs. 3, 11, 30, 36.

121. Laws 1866, Second Terr. Legis., ch. 7, secs. 3, 4, ch. 32, secs. 4, 5, ch. 13, sec. 2.

122. Laws 1866, Second Terr. Legis., ch. 29, sec. 1.

123. Ibid., sec. 2.

124. Legislative enactments were reported upon in detail. See, e.g., "Legislative Proceedings," *Montana Post*, Apr. 7, 1866, p. 2, col. 3.

125. Laws 1866, Second Terr. Legis., Joint Resolution No. 11 (April 13, 1866).

126. Spence, *Territorial Politics*, 38–39.

127. Wylie, *Irish General*, 257.

128. J. A. Hosmer, "Biographical Sketch of Hezekiah L. Hosmer," Hezekiah Hosmer Papers, 1848–70, Mont. Hist. Soc., SC-104, box 1-1, vol. 3, p. 18.

129. Wylie, *Irish General*, 255; Bancroft, *History*, 648; Spence, *Territorial Politics*, 28, 41; Keneally, *Great Shame*, 432; Allen, *Decent Orderly Lynching*, 340.

130. "Fatal Mercy," *Montana Post*, Mar. 10, 1866, p. 2, col. 1; Spence, *Territorial Politics*, 41.

131. Wylie, *Irish General*, 257. The authority of the territorial legislature to restrict the discretion of the judiciary was later litigated in a matter wherein Chief Judge Hosmer refused to remove himself from an action despite the defendant's filing of an affidavit of bias. The litigation resulted in a determination that legislatures have the right to deprive courts of discretion such as in matters of disqualification, which had the effect of upholding the law. *Godbe v. McCormick*, 1 Mont. 105 (1868).

132. Hosmer, "Biographical Sketch," 18.

133. Spence, *Territorial Politics*, 44.

134. Bancroft, *History*, 641n31.

135. "Local Items," *Montana Post*, Mar. 24, 1866, p. 3, col. 1. The office of superintendent of public instruction was created by Montana's First Territorial Legislature in 1865, and the salary for the position was set and funded by the Second Territorial Legislature in 1866. The law that set the salary was repealed by an act of the US Congress on March 2, 1867. However, on April 10, 1867, a later territorial legislature, elected as a result of proper apportionment and redistricting, restored the office and its salary, though with a slightly different salary. As a result of litigation, it was determined that the salary authorized by the controversial Second Territorial Legislature was earned by its then occupant. *Carpenter v. Rodgers*, 1 Mont. 90 (1868). Peter Ronan, by small-world coincidence, later became the husband of young Mollie Sheehan, who was several years younger than he. Baumler, *Girl from the Gulches*, 117.

136. "Legislative Proceedings," *Montana Post*, Apr. 7, 1866, p. 2, col. 3.

137. Ibid.

138. Dimsdale was replaced as editor by an attorney, Henry Nichols Blake, who joined the Vigilance Committee and continued the newspaper's editorial support of vigilante activities. Allen, *Decent Orderly Lynching*, 339.

139. A detailed text on the making of western state constitutions is Bakken, *Rocky Mountain Constitution Making*.

140. Malone, Roeder, and Lang, *Montana*, 102.

141. Bancroft, *History*, 649.

142. Burlingame, *Montana Frontier*, 162; Malone, Roeder, and Lang, *Montana* 102.

143. Burlingame, *Montana Frontier*, 162; Malone, Roeder, and Lang, *Montana* 102.

144. Ibid.

145. Bancroft, *History*, 650.

146. "Illegality of the Acts of the Legislature—Judge Munson's Decision," *Montana Post*, June 9, 1866, p. 2, col. 4; Bancroft, *History*, 650. Arrangements for publication of Montana

Supreme Court decisions in official case books had not yet been made, so there is no legal citation for *Baker v. Laird*.

147. "Illegality of the Acts of the Legislature—Judge Munson's Decision," *Montana Post*, June 9, 1866, p. 2, col. 4; Bancroft, *History*, 650.

148. Ibid.

149. Ibid.

150. "Illegality of the Acts of the Legislature—Judge Munson's Decision," *Montana Post*, June 9, 1866, p. 2, col. 4 (emphasis added); Bancroft, *History*, 650; Spence, *Territorial Politics*, 40–41; Keneally, *Great Shame*, 432.

151. "Illegality of the Acts of the Legislature—Judge Munson's Decision," *Montana Post*, June 9, 1866, p. 2, col. 4.

152. Organic Act for the Territory of Montana, Act May 26, 1864, ch. 95, sec. 4, 13 Stat. 85.

153. The authority of courts to strike down legislation as unconstitutional was first pronounced in the landmark case of *Marbury v. Madison*, 1 Cranch 137 (1803).

154. Spence, *Territorial Politics*, 41, citing *Montana Democrat*, Sept. 6, 1866.

155. Keneally, *Great Shame*, 432. Seward had earlier survived an attempt on his life at his home the evening of April 14, 1865, at the hands of Lewis Powell, a coconspirator of John Wilkes Booth. Seward is perhaps best known for his purchase of Alaska from Russia in 1867 for $7,200,000.

156. Bancroft, *History*, 650.

157. Malone, Roeder, and Lang, *Montana*, 102.

158. Bancroft, *History*, 650; Spence, *Territorial Politics*, 43.

159. Wylie, *Irish General*, 262; Malone, Roeder, and Lang, *Montana*, 103.

160. Wylie, *Irish General*, 262; Malone, Roeder, and Lang, *Montana*, 103.

161. "Opinion," *Montana Post*, Dec. 22, 1866, p. 2, col. 3.

162. Hosmer, "Biographical Sketch," 17–18; Opinion *in extenso* of Hon. Hezekiah Hosmer, Dec. 8, 1866, Wilbur Fisk Sanders Papers, Mont. Hist. Soc., MC-53, box 3, folder 3-14; Allen, *Decent Orderly Lynching*, 334; Spence, *Territorial Politics*, 44; Malone, Roeder, and Lang, *Montana*, 102. By today's rules of conduct, judges may not announce in advance that laws will be declared null and void, and it is ethically improper for any judge today to do so.

163. "Opinion," *Montana Post*, Dec. 22, 1866, p. 2, col. 3.

164. Cf. "Opinion," *Montana Post*, Dec. 22, 1866, p. 2, col. 3, with "Illegality of the Acts of the Legislature—Judge Munson's Decision," *Montana Post*, June 9, 1866, p. 2, col. 4.

165. Keneally, *Great Shame*, 432 (letter to Secretary of State William Seward).

166. Organic Act of the Territory of Montana, Act May 26, 1864, ch. 95, sec. 15, 13 Stat. 85 et seq.; Spence, *Territorial Politics*, 44.

167. Laws 1866, Second Terr. Legis., ch. 29, sec. 3; Laws 1866, Third Terr. Legis., ch. 5, sec. 1.

168. Laws 1866, Third Terr. Legis., ch. 5, sec. 2.

169. Laws 1866, Second Terr. Legis., ch. 29, sec. 3; Laws 1866, Third Terr. Legis., ch. 5, sec. 1.

170. Spence, *Territorial Politics*, 44.

171. Laws 1866, Third Terr. Legis., ch. 5, sec. 1; Spence, *Territorial Politics*, 44.

172. Laws 1866, Third Terr. Legis., ch. 5, sec. 1.

173. Laws 1866, Third Terr. Legis., ch. 25, sec. 1 (changing the name of Musselshell County to Vivion County); Mtgenweb Project, "Montana: Individual County Chronologies," "Musselshell (original)."

174. Laws 1866, Third Terr. Legis., ch. 5, sec. 1.

175. Laws 1866, Third Terr. Legis., ch. 5, sec. 6. Court sessions for Vivion County were to be "attached" to those of Big Horn County and not separately scheduled.

176. Ibid., ch. 27, sec. 1. The third legislature designated Helena as the territory's new capital, subject to a statewide vote of the public that would be held in September of 1867. Ibid., sec. 2. The legislation was vetoed, but the issue resurfaced in successive years, and the capital

was not moved to Helena until 1875. Access Genealogy, "Montana, Politics, Legislation, and Reform."

177. Organic Act of the Territory of Montana, Act May 26, 1864, ch. 95, sec. 9, 13 Stat. 85; Malone, Roeder, and Lang, *Montana*, 102.

178. Notes on Sanders Address at Virginia City on May 21, 1867, Wilbur Fisk Sanders Papers, Mont. Hist. Soc., MC-53, box 4, folder 4-1; Malone, Roeder, and Lang, *Montana*, 102; Burlingame, *Montana Frontier*, 163.

179. Spence, *Territorial Politics*, 44.

180. Act, March 2, 1867, 14 Stat. 426, ch. 150, sec. 5.

181. Allen, *Decent Orderly Lynching*, 340.

182. Bancroft, *History*, 651; Access Genealogy, "Montana Organization, Boundaries, and Elections"; see also Allen, *Decent Orderly Lynching*, 340.

183. Allen, *Decent Orderly Lynching*, 340–41.

184. "Remember This," *Montana Post*, Aug. 17, 1867, p. 1, col. 4.

185. Ibid.

186. Act, March 2, 1867, 14 Stat. 426, ch. 150, sec. 5.

187. Ibid., sec. 3; Bancroft, *History*, 668; Spence, *Territorial Politics*, 45. The *Montana Post* had editorially favored pay raises for a variety of Montana government officials. "Give, Give, Give," *Montana Post*, Aug. 17, 1867, p. 5, col. 2.

188. Act, March 2, 1867, 14 Stat. 426, ch. 150, sec. 4; Bancroft, *History*, 668; Spence, *Territorial Politics*, 45; Guice, *Rocky Mountain Bench*, 59; Keneally, *Great Shame*, 426.

189. Act, March 2, 1867, 14 Stat. 426, ch. 150, sec. 6; Wylie, *Irish General*, 262.

190. *Carpenter v. Rodgers*, 1 Mont. 90 (1868); Bancroft, *History*, 668.

191. Laws 1867, Fourth Terr. Legis.; Spence, *Territorial Politics*, 47.

192. Hosmer, "Biographical Sketch," 18–19.

193. Wylie, *Irish General*, 313–14; Spence, *Territorial Politics*, 37–38.

194. Bancroft, *History*, 671.

195. Laws 1867, Fourth Terr. Legis., "An Act to amend an act entitled 'An Act to provide increased compensation to the officers of the Territory,'" approved January 24, 1865, secs. 1 and 4.

196. Donovan, *Hanging around the Big Sky*, book 2, 142; Allen, *Decent Orderly Lynching*, 334.

197. Bancroft, *History*, 722n7.

198. Leeson, *History of Montana*, 303; Axline et al., *More from the Quarries*, 12. The book identifies the date of the event as December 29, rather than November 29, of 1865.

199. Donovan, *Hanging around the Big Sky*, book 2, 142; "The Virginia Vigilantes," *Montana Post*, Mar. 17, 1866, p. 4, col. 1.

200. Donovan, *Hanging around the Big Sky*, book 2, 142; Axline et al., *More from the Quarries*, 12.

201. See Appendix C, Petition for the Reprieve and Pardon of James Daniels.

202. Donovan, *Hanging around the Big Sky*, book 2, 142.

203. Ibid.; Axline et al., *More from the Quarries*, 12.

204. Donovan, *Hanging around the Big Sky*, book 2, 142.

205. Ibid.

206. Allen, *Decent Orderly Lynching*, 334; Axline et al., *More from the Quarries*, 13.

207. Leeson, *History of Montana*, 303; Donovan, *Hanging around the Big Sky*, book 2, 142; Keneally, *Great Shame*, 435; "James Daniels," *Montana Post*, Mar. 24, 1866, p. 4, col. 2.

208. Keneally, *Great Shame*, 435.

209. Donovan, *Hanging around the Big Sky*, book 2, 142.

210. Edgerton County was renamed Lewis and Clark County in 1867, by which it is known today.

211. Donovan, *Hanging around the Big Sky*, book 2, 143.

212. Ibid.

213. Ibid.

214. Ibid.

215. Ibid.

216. Ibid., 142; Langford, *Vigilante Days*, 296; Axline et al., *More from the Quarries*, 12; "Fatal Mercy," *Montana Post*, Mar. 10, 1866, p. 2, col. 1; "James Daniels," *Montana Post*, Mar. 24, 1866, p. 4, col. 2.

217. Langford, *Vigilante Days*, 296; Axline et al., *More from the Quarries*, 12.

218. Donovan, *Hanging around the Big Sky*, book 2, 143; "Fatal Mercy," *Montana Post*, Mar. 10, 1866, p. 2, col. 1.

219. Mather and Boswell, *Vigilante Victims*, 154.

220. Laws 1864, First Terr. Legis., C.P.A. ch. 4, secs. 15–17. Today in Montana intentional murder is referred to as "deliberate homicide" and is defined in Mont. Code Ann. 45-5-102 (1999). Montana's definition is somewhat different from that of most states, as a person may be convicted of deliberate homicide in Montana for knowing and purposeful conduct, without actually intending to cause another person's death, so long as there is a high probability that death will result from such conduct. E.g., *State v. Ballenger*, 227 Mont. 308, 312 (1987). In most other states today, intentional murder requires an intent that death of the victim be the conscious objective.

221. Laws 1865, First Terr. Legis., C.P.A. ch. 4, secs. 18–20.

222. Ibid., sec. 21.

223. Ibid., secs. 25–27.

224. See Appendix C, Petition for the Reprieve and Pardon of James Daniels.

225. Axline et al., *More from the Quarries*, 13.

226. Guice, *Rocky Mountain Bench*, 25.

227. Nebraska State Historical Society, "First Territorial Legislature."

228. Laws 1857, Third Terr. Legis., p. 137. The reason for the repeal is attributed to a unique circumstance. A lawyer-legislator happened to be defense counsel to a defendant accused of murdering another man over a land claim. The legislator sought repeal of Nebraska criminal statutes in an effort to prevent the client's arrest and conviction for murder. Despite the repeal of Nebraska's criminal code the client was arrested and convicted anyway, but ultimately the Nebraska Supreme Court reversed the judgment of conviction because of the absent of a criminal code at the time of the adjudication. Reportedly, the widow of the murdered man commenced a civil suit for damages and met the similar difficulty that the underlying law had been repealed, but it is reported that counsel for the widow ultimately secured for his client title to the land that led to her husband's murder in the first place. Cutler, "Repeal of the Criminal Code."

229. Cutler, "Repeal of the Criminal Code."

230. *Benet v. Hargus*, 1 Neb. 419 (1871).

231. Ibid.

232. Donovan, *Hanging around the Big Sky*, book 2, 143.

233. Langford, *Vigilante Days*, 296; Leeson, *History of Montana*, 303; Keneally, *Great Shame*, 434; Donovan, *Hanging around the Big Sky*, book 2, 143; Axline et al., *More from the Quarries*, 13; Allen, *Decent Orderly Lynching*, 334.

234. Laws 1865, First Terr. Legis., C.P.A. ch. 4, sec. 22. The ten-year maximum sentence applies to both voluntary and involuntary manslaughter, even though, arguably, involuntary manslaughter is a less serious offense.

235. Langford, *Vigilante Days*, 296; Leeson, *History of Montana*, 303; Keneally, *Great Shame*, 434; Donovan, *Hanging around the Big Sky*, book 2, 143; Axline et al., *More from the Quarries*, 13; Allen, *Decent Orderly Lynching*, 334.

236. Access Genealogy, "Montana Organization, Boundaries, and Elections." Ground was not broken for the construction of a federal penitentiary in Montana, at Deer Lodge, until

1870, and the facility was not ready for housing prisoners until 1871. Bancroft, *History*, 670n10; Spence, *Territorial Politics*, 31.

237. Access Genealogy, "Montana Organization, Boundaries, and Elections"; Bancroft, *History*, 654, 670n10; Spence, *Territorial Politics*, 31.

238. Access Genealogy, "Montana Organization, Boundaries, and Elections"; Bancroft, *History*, 654, 670n10; Spence, *Territorial Politics*, 31.

239. "Helena Items," *Montana Post*, Dec. 30, 1865, p. 3, col. 2.

240. "A Commercial Transaction," *Montana Post*, Jan. 6, 1866, p. 2, col. 2.

241. Ibid.

242. "Hanging of Daniels, Again," *Montana Radiator*, Mar. 17, 1866, p. 3, col. 1. The article lists the date of the petition as March 6, 1866, but that date must be incorrect as it had already been acted upon by Governor Meagher on February 22, 1866.

243. Ibid.

244. Ibid.

245. Ibid.

246. Ibid.; Leeson, *History of Montana*, 303; Keneally, *Great Shame*, 435 (misnumbering the signatories by one).

247. *State v. District Court of Eighteenth Judicial Dist. in and for Blaine County*, 73 Mont. 541 (Mont. 1925).

248. Ibid. A variation of the reprieve concept is a "commutation," which is a remission of part of a sentence and a substitution of a lesser penalty for the one originally imposed.

249. Organic Act for the Territory of Montana, Act May 26, 1864, ch. 95, sec. 2, 13 Stat. 85.

250. *Goo v. Hee Fat*, 35 Haw. 827, 1941 WL 7951, *5 (Haw. Terr. 1941); *In Re* Crimmins, 20 Haw. 518, 1911 WL 1780, *8 (Haw. Terr. 1911)(concurrence by Perry, J.); *Territory v. Richardson*, 9 Okla. 579, 60 P. 244 (Okla. Terr. 1900); *In Re* Moore, 4 Wyo. 98, 31 P. 980 (Wyo. 1893).

251. *State v. District Court of Eighteenth Judicial Dist. in and for Blaine County*, 73 Mont. 541 (Mont. 1925), citing Bannack Statutes, CPA, secs. 223, 226, 239.

252. US Const., art. 3, sec. 2.

253. Organic Act for the Territory of Montana, Act May 26, 1864, ch. 95, sec. 9, 13 Stat. 85.

254. 6 Cranch 87 (1810).

255. 41 U.S. 1, 5 (1842). *Swift* held that federal courts were not required to follow the decisions of state courts in matters of commercial or general jurisprudence, but were to do so on issues of purely local law; see also Purcell, *Brandeis*, 51.

256. 85 U.S. 648 (1873).

257. 304 U.S. 64 (1938).

258. "James B. Daniels Release, 1866," Mont. Hist. Soc., SC-1634; Axline et al., *More from the Quarries*, 13; Olsen, "Lawlessness and Vigilantes," 173; Bancroft, *History*, 648; Leeson, *History of Montana*, 303.

259. "James B. Daniels Release, 1866," Mont. Hist. Soc., SC-1634; Axline et al., *More from the Quarries*, 13; Olsen, "Lawlessness and Vigilantes," 173; Bancroft, *History*, 648; Leeson, *History of Montana*, 303.

260. "James B. Daniels Release, 1866," Mont. Hist. Soc., SC-1634; Axline et al., *More from the Quarries*, 13; Olsen, "Lawlessness and Vigilantes," 173; Bancroft, *History*, 648; Leeson, *History of Montana*, 303; Langford, *Vigilante Days*, 296; Keneally, *Great Shame*, 435; Allen, *Decent Orderly Lynching*, 334.

261. Burlingame, *Montana Frontier*, 156; "Montana," *American Annual Cyclopedia and Register of Important Events of the Year*, 7:476.

262. Keneally, *Great Shame*, 431.

263. "Miscellaneous Items," *Montana Post*, Mar. 17, 1866, p. 1, col. 5.

264. Axline et al., *More from the Quarries*, 13; Allen, *Decent Orderly Lynching*, 335.

265. "Fatal Mercy," *Montana Post*, Mar. 10, 1866, p. 2, col. 1.

266. Ibid.

267. Ibid.

268. "The Discharge of Daniels," *Montana Post*, Mar. 3, 1866, p. 2, col. 1; "Fatal Mercy," *Montana Post*, Mar. 10, 1866, p. 2, col. 1; "Miscellaneous Items," *Montana Post*, Mar. 17, 1866, p. 1, col. 5; "The Legislature and Judge Munson," *Montana Post*, Mar. 31, 1866, p. 2, col. 1. Editorially, the newspaper adopted critics' viewpoint that the release of a prisoner for any offense less than a capital crime was a pardon rather than a reprieve.

269. Lyman E. Munson, biographical materials, Lyman Ezra Munson Papers, 1866–99, Mont. Hist. Soc. SC-553, folder 1; Langford, *Vigilante Days*, 296; Allen, *Decent Orderly Lynching*, 336; "The Discharge of Daniels," *Montana Post*, Mar. 3, 1866, p. 2, col. 1; "The Legislature and Judge Munson," *Montana Post*, Mar. 31, 1866, p. 2, col. 1.

270. "Local Items," *Montana Post*, Mar. 3, 1866, p. 2, col. 1.

271. Lyman E. Munson, biographical materials, Lyman Ezra Munson Papers, 1866–99, Mont. Hist. Soc. SC-553, folder 1; Axline et al., *More from the Quarries*, 14; Leeson, *History of Montana*, 303.

272. Lyman E. Munson, biographical materials, Lyman Ezra Munson Papers, 1866–99, Mont. Hist. Soc. SC-553, folder 1; Axline et al., *More from the Quarries*, 14; Leeson, *History of Montana*, 303.

273. "Local Items," *Montana Post*, Mar. 3, 1866, p. 2, col. 1.

274. "The Discharge of Daniels," *Montana Post*, Mar. 3, 1866, p. 2, col. 1.

275. Ibid.; Axline et al., *More from the Quarries*, 14; Olsen, "Lawlessness and Vigilantes," 173.

276. "The Discharge of Daniels," *Montana Post*, Mar. 3, 1866, p. 2, col. 1; Axline et al., *More from the Quarries*, 14; Olsen, "Lawlessness and Vigilantes," 173.

277. "James B. Daniels Release, 1866," Mont. Hist. Soc. SC-1634.

278. Ibid.

279. *Expressio unius est exclusio alterius* is a Latin phrase meaning that an expression or inclusion of one thing in a statute implies the exclusion of other things not expressed or included. Garner, *Black's Law Dictionary*, 661.

280. Bancroft, *History*, 648; Donovan, *Hanging around the Big Sky*, book 2, 143.

281. "Fatal Mercy," *Montana Post*, Mar. 10, 1866, p. 2, col. 1.

282. Ibid.

283. Wilbur Fisk Sanders Papers, Mont. Hist. Soc., MC-53, folder 2-6.

284. Donovan, *Hanging around the Big Sky*, book 2, 143; Axline et al., *More from the Quarries*, 14; "Helena Newsletter," *Montana Post*, Mar. 10, 1866, p. 3, col. 2.

285. "Helena Newsletter," *Montana Post*, Mar. 10, 1866, p. 3, col. 2.

286. Donovan, *Hanging around the Big Sky*, book 2, 143; Allen, *Decent Orderly Lynching*, 336.

287. "Fatal Mercy," *Montana Post*, Mar. 10, 1866, p. 2, col. 1.

288. "The Virginia Vigilantes," *Montana Post*, Mar. 17, 1866, p. 4, col. 1.

289. "Fatal Mercy," *Montana Post*, Mar. 10, 1866, p. 2, col. 1.

290. Ibid.

291. Ibid.

292. Ibid.

293. Langford, *Vigilante Days*, 296; Axline et al., *More from the Quarries*, 15; Birney, *Vigilantes*, 345; Allen, *Decent Orderly Lynching*, 336; Olsen, "Lawlessness and Vigilantes," 173; "Fatal Mercy," *Montana Post*, Mar. 10, 1866, p. 2, col. 1; "Helena Newsletter," *Montana Post*, Mar. 10, 1866, p. 3, col. 2.

294. Allen, *Decent Orderly Lynching*, 336. The reprieve document was removed from Daniels's pocket the following day. "Helena Newsletter," *Montana Post*, Mar. 10, 1866, p. 3, col. 2.

295. "Helena Newsletter," *Montana Post*, Mar. 10, 1866, p. 3, col. 2.

296. Donovan, *Hanging around the Big Sky*, book 2, 144; Barsness, *Gold Camp*, 146. Howard, *Montana High, Wide, and Handsome*, 44 (reflecting words that differ in form but not substance: "Do this again and you'll meet the same fate").

297. Keneally, *Great Shame*, 458.

298. "Execution of Daniels: Letter from Deputy Marshal Fetherstun," *Montana Post*, Mar. 10, 1866, p. 2, col. 2.

299. "Miscellaneous Items," *Montana Post*, Mar. 17, 1866, p. 1, col. 5.

300. "The Legislature and Judge Munson," *Montana Post*, Mar. 31, 1866, p. 2, col. 1.

301. Ibid.

302. "James Daniels," *Montana Post*, Mar. 24, 1866, p. 4, col. 2.

303. "The Virginia Vigilantes," *Montana Post*, Mar. 17, 1866, p. 4, col. 1.

304. The *Montana Radiator* was owned by Thomas Favorite, Bruce Smith, and others, but it ceased publication in July of 1866. By the fall of 1866, a new newspaper, the *Weekly Herald*, began publishing from the *Montana Radiator*'s former office and was favorably regarded. Leeson, *History of Montana*, 327.

305. "Hanging of Daniels, Again," *Montana Radiator*, Mar. 17, 1866, p. 2, col. 2.

306. Langford, *Vigilante Days*, 297.

307. Ibid., 296.

308. Ibid.

309. Ibid., 296–97.

310. Howard, *Montana High, Wide, and Handsome*, 44.

311. "Pardon of Daniels," *Montana Post*, Mar. 17, 1866, p. 1, col. 5.

312. Ibid.

313. Ibid.

314. Barsness, *Gold Camp*, 146.

315. Wylie, *Irish General*, 301.

316. Wylie, *Irish General*, 262.

317. "Pardon of Daniels," *Montana Post*, Mar. 17, 1866, p. 1, col. 5.

318. Wylie, *Irish General*, 304–5.

319. Keneally, *Great Shame*, 454.

320. Malone, Roeder, and Lang, *Montana*, 103.

321. "Died," *Montana Post*, July 6, 1867, p. 5, col. 3; Wylie, *Irish General*, 305; Howard, *Montana High, Wide, and Handsome*, 44; Keneally, *Great Shame*, 455; Allen, *Decent Orderly Lynching*, 348; Barsness, *Gold Camp*, 149–50.

322. Wylie, *Irish General*, 304.

323. Keneally, *Great Shame*, 456.

324. "Died," *Montana Post*, July 6, 1867, p. 5, col. 3.

325. "Mormonism Defined," *Montana Post*, July 6, 1867, p. 1, col. 1.

326. "Citizen's Meeting," *Montana Post*, July 13, 1867, p. 8, col. 4.

327. Ibid.

328. "Proclamation by the Governor," *Montana Post*, July 6, 1867, p. 5, col. 2; "Resolutions," *Montana Post*, July 27, 1867, p. 4, col. 6.

329. "Resolutions of the Helena Bar," *Montana Post*, July 6, 1867, p. 5, cols. 3–4.

330. "Meeting in Virginia," *Montana Post*, July 6, 1867, p. 5, col. 4.

331. Wylie, *Irish General*, 305.

332. Ibid., 313.

333. Ibid., 305–6.

334. Ibid., 309; Howard, *Montana High, Wide, and Handsome*, 44–45.

335. Howard, *Montana High, Wide, and Handsome*, 44; "Meagher Murdered, Enemy Confesses," *New York Tribune*, May 30, 1913, p. 1, col. 6; "Old Indian Fighter May Be Tried

for Murder of Man Who Died 46 Years Ago," *The Day Book*, June 11, 1913, pp. 22–23; Keneally, *Great Shame*, 457 (identifying the confessor as "Millar.")

336. "Battleflag of the Irish Brigade," *The Sun*, June 8, 1913, p. 1, col. 2.

337. "Did Old Indian Fighter Slay Governor 46 Yrs. Ago?," *Tacoma Times*, June 13, 1913, p. 1, col. 2; "Old Indian Fighter May Be Tried for Murder of Man Who Died 46 Years Ago," *The Day Book*, June 11, 1913, pp. 22–23.

338. "Did Old Indian Fighter Slay Governor 46 Yrs. Ago?," *Tacoma Times*, June 13, 1913, p. 1, col. 2.

339. Wylie, *Irish General*, 313, citing "General Meagher Executed by Vigilantes, Dave Mack Says," *Anaconda Standard*, June 2, 1913; Howard, *Montana High, Wide, and Handsome*, 45.

340. Keneally, *Great Shame*, 457; "Battleflag of the Irish Brigade," *The Sun*, June 8, 1913, p. 1, col. 2.

341. Wylie, *Irish General*, 309; see also "Battleflag of the Irish Brigade," *The Sun*, June 8, 1913, p. 1, col. 2.

342. Wylie, *Irish General*, 313.

343. Howard, *Montana High, Wide, and Handsome*, 45; Keneally, *Great Shame*, 458.

344. Wylie, *Irish General*, 313.

345. "Old Indian Fighter May Be Tried for Murder of Man Who Died 46 Years Ago," *The Day Book*, June 11, 1913, p. 22.

346. Wylie, *Irish General*, 330.

347. Ibid., 329; John F. Kennedy Presidential Library and Museum, "Address before the Irish Parliament."

348. Keneally, *Great Shame*, 457.

349. Donovan, *Hanging around the Big Sky*, book 2, 144; Axline et al., *More from the Quarries*, 15. The two books differ as to whether Daniels's remains were discovered in 1931 or 1933.

350. Donovan, *Hanging around the Big Sky*, book 2, 144; Axline et al., *More from the Quarries*, 15; see also Mont. Stat. Ann. 22-3-804(3) (1991).

13

Normative Due Process and Trial Procedure in the Criminal Cases of 1860s Montana

Why should there not be a patient confidence in the ultimate justice of the people? Is there any better or equal hope in the world?

—President Abraham Lincoln, First Inaugural Address, March 4, 1861

Whatever due process vigilantes did or did not provide prisoners must be examined in the context of due process expectations and practices of 1860s America and its territories.

During the years following the American Revolutionary War, the idea of using English common law was out of favor, compounded by Anglophobia, American independence and patriotism, and the spirit of reform.[1] In fact, statutes were passed by state legislatures in New Jersey, Delaware, Pennsylvania, Kentucky, and New Hampshire specifically prohibiting the precedential citation of cases decided by English courts, and Ohio in 1806 repealed an act that had declared English common law to be in force within the state.[2] Over time, however, outside of a few uniquely formed American legal precedents reported in a handful of books, the development of law in the United States and in the territorial frontier had few indigenous sources.[3] The resolution of disputed cases often defaulted to recognized English law books that ultimately revived the use and acceptability of the common law.[4]

As territories were created in the American West, the US Congress typically included a civil and criminal code in each of the territory's Organic Acts, or at least vested the territorial courts with the authority to apply the common

DOI: 10.7330_9780874219203.c013

law to all cases. Wisconsin was organized on April 20, 1836, Iowa on June 12, 1838, Oregon on August 14, 1848, Minnesota on March 3, 1849, New Mexico and Utah on September 9, 1850, Washington on March 2, 1853, Nebraska and Kansas on May 30, 1854, Colorado on February 28, 1861, Nevada and Dakota on March 2, 1861, Arizona on February 24, 1863, Idaho on March 3, 1863, and Montana on May 26, 1864.[5] Later territories were organized for Wyoming on July 25, 1868,[6] Hawaii on July 7, 1879,[7] Oklahoma on May 2, 1890,[8] Puerto Rico on April 12, 1900,[9] and Alaska on August 24, 1912.[10] Territories would then set their own legal paths upon the later drafting of their individual constitutions.[11]

Idaho Territory was created when Congress pieced together portions of land taken from the existing territories of Washington, Dakota, Nebraska, and Utah.[12] In creating Idaho Territory, of which Montana was initially a part, the US Congress, preoccupied by the Civil War, failed to provide Idaho with any civil or criminal code.[13] Clever attorneys therefore argued that there were no actual laws on the books that persons could be charged with violating.[14] Indeed, legal precedent developed in Idaho that there could be no criminal prosecutions and convictions absent the existence of a criminal code defining unlawful behaviors. In the 1866 case of *People v. Williams*, the Idaho Territorial Supreme Court held, on appeal for defendant Williams, that at the time he was initially charged with his crime, there were no laws on the books for him to have violated and hence the charge against him could not stand.[15] A similar holding had been rendered by the Nebraska Territorial Supreme Court in *Benet v. Hargus*, which the reader has already encountered and which related to the first half of 1857 when there were no criminal or civil codes on the books in that territory as well.[16] The effect of the *Williams* decision was that it released all persons incarcerated in Idaho for crimes committed between the establishment of Idaho Territory on March 3, 1863, and the enactment of its criminal code on January 4, 1864, a period of approximately ten months.[17] Wilbur Fisk Sanders lamented the reality that "neither the constitution nor the laws were present to assert themselves or to secure to the citizens of this region that protection which they meant to supply."[18] On January 4, 1864, Idaho's First Territorial Legislature rectified the problem by adopting English common law as the basis for all legal proceedings in the territory.[19]

When Montana was created as a separate territory on May 26, 1864, the US Congress, having not learned from its Idaho mistake, again failed to provide the new territory with any controlling criminal or civil code.[20] Case law from neighboring Idaho provided that a newly created territory did not carry forward the criminal laws of the territory from whence it came, absent a provision in the new territory's Organic Act expressly saying so.[21] There was no provision in Montana's Organic Act that expressly or impliedly carried over Idaho law into

Montana. Montana's territorial courts appear to have never addressed the question that was raised in the *Williams* case in Idaho of how to treat criminal defendants arrested for unlawful conduct before the enactment of any formal territorial criminal code. Montana's earliest territorial courts borrowed Idaho statutes and the common law as nonbinding guides during that period,[22] although the authority to do so appears to have been legally questionable at best.

In January of 1865 Montana's First Territorial Legislature enacted the Bannack Statutes, which codified criminal conduct and formally adopted English common law "so far as the same is applicable and of a general nature, and not in conflict with special enactments of this territory."[23] In 1867 Montana adopted a comprehensive Civil Practice Act, modeled after the California Civil Code.[24] Trials in the settled regions of Montana in the mid-1860s were therefore greatly influenced, if not actually governed by, the English common law.

The constitutional aspects of criminal law in the United States were undeveloped in certain significant respects in the 1860s. The US Constitution contained then, as it does now, a number of significant provisions that greatly impact criminal jurisprudence. The Fourth Amendment contains the right against unreasonable searches and seizures. The Fifth Amendment requires that charges of "capital, or otherwise infamous" crimes be presented by a grand jury, assures due process, and protects all persons from double jeopardy and compulsory self-incrimination. The Sixth Amendment assures all persons the right to a speedy trial, the confrontation of witnesses, a trial by jury, and the representation of counsel. The Eighth Amendment prohibits cruel and unusual punishments. The first ten amendments to the US Constitution were ratified by most of the original thirteen states on various dates between 1789 and 1791. The Thirteenth Amendment, prohibiting slavery, did not become effective until December 6, 1865. The Fourteenth Amendment, which was later interpreted as requiring that the states abide by certain federally recognized constitutional guarantees, did not become effective until July 9, 1868. The Fifteenth Amendment, which guaranteed all men the right to vote regardless of race or color, did not become effective until February 3, 1870. Montana's Organic Act prohibited the territory's legislature from enacting any laws that would conflict with the rights, protections, and privileges of the US Constitution and, by extension, the constitutional amendments.[25]

Although the first ten amendments to the Constitution were part of the law of the land in the United States in the 1860s, though not necessarily applicable to the states until after the 1868 enactment of the Fourteenth Amendment, most of the landmark decisions of the US Supreme Court that interpreted the meaning and application of those amendments had not yet been rendered. Five well-known cases from the Supreme Court illustrate the point. *Mapp v. Ohio,* which interprets the Fourth and Fifth Amendments to the US Constitution, requires the suppression of evidence seized as a result of a warrantless search of a premises.[26] *Gideon v. Wainwright* interpreted the Sixth and Fourteenth Amendments by requiring that indigent defendants be entitled to appointed counsel in order for the right to counsel to be meaningful and effective.[27] *Brady v. Maryland* interpreted the Fifth and Fourteenth Amendments by requiring that prosecutors disclose exculpatory information that favors the accused, a rule made applicable to all of the states.[28] *Escobedo v. Illinois,* interpreting the Sixth and Fourteenth Amendments, requires the suppression from evidence of statements made by a defendant when the defendant requested, and was then denied, the assistance of counsel during police interrogation.[29] *Miranda v. Arizona* requires the issuance of "Miranda rights" to an accused during a custodial interrogation—advising that the defendant has the right to remain silent, that any statements may be used against the defendant in a court of law, that the defendant has the right to counsel, and that an indigent defendant may have counsel appointed to act on his or her behalf.[30] The *Miranda* case interprets the Fifth, Sixth, and Fourteenth Amendments to the Constitution. Later cases decided by the Supreme Court have refined the circumstances and narrow exceptions to the rules set forth in *Mapp, Gideon, Brady, Escobedo*, and *Miranda*.

Cases such as *Mapp v. Ohio, Gideon v. Wainwright, Brady v. Maryland, Escobedo v. Illinois*, and *Miranda v. Arizona* are arguably among the most significant cases decided by the US Supreme Court on the subject of constitutional criminal law. Doubtless, there are others. But notably *Mapp* was decided in 1961. *Gideon* and *Brady* were each decided in 1963. *Escobedo* was decided in 1964. *Miranda* was decided in 1966. The most significant cases of constitutional criminal law in US history were not decided until a full 100 years after the incidences of vigilantism in Bannack, Virginia City, and Helena in Montana Territory. Accordingly, in 1860s America, the rights set forth in the Fourth, Fifth, Sixth, Eighth, and Fourteenth Amendments had significantly less impact and meaning than they did a century later. The constitutional amendments provided the bones that framed the rights of defendants when dealing with police, prosecutors, and courts in criminal matters. Flesh was not put on the bones until landmark cases were rendered by the US Supreme Court generations later. The rendering of those decisions helped fulfill a prediction uttered by President Lincoln in rhetorical form during his first inaugural address on March 4, 1861: "Why should there not be a patient confidence in the ultimate justice of the people? Is there any better or equal hope in the world?"

But in the 1860s in the western territories, during the time of Lincoln, criminal investigations, trials, and sentences were crudely thought of in some ways similar, and in other ways dissimilar, to how they are thought of today, and without the benefit of the developments in constitutional law that came the following century. Trials at the mining communities in the western frontier reflected a mix of due process values imported from the eastern United States, while at the same time they reflected vigilante values in the swiftness and fatality of sentences.[31] In terms of similarities, the legal trials conducted in south central Montana in the mid-1860s followed rudimentary procedural outlines that included the presiding guidance of one or more judges, the selection of impartial jurors, opening statements by the prosecutor and the defense, the presentation of direct evidence that could be cross-examined or impeached by the defense, the right of the defendant to present evidence in his own defense that could in turn be cross-examined or impeached, closing statements, instructions to the jurors, and a deliberative verdict. Residents of mining communities in the western territories attempted to mimic, as best as possible, the procedures of justice that they knew existed in the eastern United States.[32] Certain general evidentiary rules were sometimes acknowledged, such as the rule against the use of hearsay. Many of the foregoing procedures were followed during the previgilante public trial of George Ives in Nevada City. Similarly, during the trial of John Keene in a Helena "people's court," the trial included a judge, the presentation of prosecution and defense evidence and arguments, cross-examinations, and a deliberative verdict as to both the defendant's guilt and sentence.

There were also many differences from the procedures that are commonly recognized today. While the defendants had the acknowledged right to counsel, there was not yet any right for counsel to be appointed for a defendant unable to afford one.[33] There was not yet any federally recognized right to remain silent, which, if violated by an uncounseled or a coerced confession, would render post-arrest statements inadmissible as evidence.[34] The most compelling example in Montana history might be that of John A. Jessrang of Dillon, Montana, in 1883, when a mob placed a noose around his neck and repeatedly pulled him off the ground, nearly strangling him each time, in an effort to obtain a confession to the murder that he was believed to have committed.[35] There was also no developed legal authority against unauthorized searches and seizures.[36] Upon arrest, a defendant's trial was typically commenced within mere hours, or at least within days, thereby limiting opportunities for pretrial preparation and the investigation of evidence.[37] Without the protections of the Fifth Amendment and Montana's criminal procedural requirements today,[38] extrajudicial proceedings such as vigilante trials did not afford the convening of a grand jury or any written indictment specifying the charges and the date and time of the underlying alleged conduct.[39] Any formal advisement to the defendant of the nature of charges was merely oral, delivered before or at the commencement of the trial, unlike the formal arraignment procedures uniformly required today.[40]

Also unlike Montana's law today, there was in judicial and extrajudicial proceedings no plea bargaining and no dispositions by means of *nolo contendere*.[41] There was no pretrial discovery such as the exchange of witness identities and statements,[42] statements of the accused,[43] expert witness information,[44] tangible evidence,[45] documents,[46] or potentially exculpatory material in the possession of the prosecutor.[47] The imposition of the death penalty by means of hanging, even for property crimes such as horse stealing,[48] was so second nature in the territory that no one gave any thought to whether the punishment was unconstitutionally cruel or unusual.

Judges presiding over criminal trials were not always attorneys and sometimes acted not singularly, but as members of judicial panels. The trials of Buck Stinson, Hayes Lyons, and Charley Forbes for the killing of D. H. Dillingham, for instance, were presided over by a three-man panel consisting entirely of medical doctors, Dr. Giles Gaylord Bissell, Dr. William L. Steel, and Dr. Samuel Rutar.[49] Likewise, the trial of John Keene in Helena was presided over by a layman, Stephen Reynolds. Prosecutors and defense counsel were also not necessarily attorneys. The trials of Buck Stinson, Hayes Lyons, and Charley Forbes provide yet another example, as the person appointed to act as prosecutor was a blacksmith named E. R. Cutler.[50] There were few if any law books available in the territory,[51] and certainly no law library or electronic Westlaw, so that trial rulings would often be made based merely on what the judges believed to be correct after hearing arguments from counsel.

The role of a presiding judge was not as well defined as it is today. In the trial of John Keene in Helena, spectators and perhaps jurors had a say in the heated debate over whether to grant Keene an adjournment of his trial so that he could procure the attendance of defense witnesses. In the trial of George Ives, it was the prosecutor, Wilbur Fisk Sanders, and not the presiding judges who ultimately determined the timing of Ives's execution.

Some cases in the territory would be tried before a jury of twelve after a quick and rudimentary jury selection process. Other trials, such as those of Stinson, Lyons, and Forbes, used whatever citizenry was in attendance as a "jury of the whole," passing judgment on the ultimate question of guilt and, when relevant, determining the sentence to be imposed. In such instances, the gathered citizenry would simply make its majority wish known by voice vote, or, alternatively, they would divide into two groups, with one group representing a vote for guilt and the other for acquittal, or in matters of sentence, to hang the accused or not. In the trial of George Ives, the impaneled jury was twenty-four jurors rather than twelve, and the jury merely rendered an "advisory" verdict of guilt, which was then subject to acceptance or rejection by the assembled spectators as a jury of the whole.[52] In the Ives trial, the recommended verdict of guilt did not need to be unanimous, as it was recorded as 23-1.[53] The jury as a whole adopted the verdict and then separately voted by an overwhelming voice vote for the execution of Ives by hanging.[54]

The quantum of evidence sufficient to meet a standard of reasonable doubt may have been influenced on a trial-by-trial basis by the whims and passions of the crowds determining the ultimate questions of guilt. The Ives trial, for instance, may provide an example of the extent to which various forms of evidence offered by the prosecutor, and alibi evidence offered by the defense, was or was not actually weighed and evaluated in a deliberative manner before the quick verdict of guilt was reached by the crowd.

By today's standards, the conduct of trials by an en masse jury raises a host of nightmarish due process problems. There was no telling whether particular spectators voting on guilt, acquittal, or sentence were present for the entirety of a trial. There was also no telling whether, in the absence of courthouse-style seating and microphones, all the evidence could even be seen and heard by the entirety of the crowd.[55] There could be no assurance that all spectators were fair and impartial arbiters of the case and that they were not influenced by information, rumor, or innuendo outside of the developed evidence. Since there was not yet a courthouse in the region in 1864, trials would be held in a public place, such as on a main street where the judges, attorneys, and witnesses would be positioned atop wagons or other elevated surfaces. Verdicts and sentences by voice acclamation could be influenced by matters unrelated to the trial evidence, such as whether a particular defendant was popular or unpopular with the local citizenry or related to members of the crowd by blood, marriage, or commerce. In addition, verdicts and sentences determined by immediate group action provided, by nature and definition, no opportunity for discussion and deliberation upon the evidence and instead called for instant decision making amid the passions of the crowd and the immediacy of the moment.

Spectators at such trials were common. Between 1,000 and 1,500 people were estimated to be in attendance at the trial of George Ives, consisting of miners, freighters, merchants, butchers, gamblers, and criminals.[56] If the estimate of the size of the crowd is accurate, such a large number of open-air spectators underscores the question of whether all of the testimony and arguments could possibly have been heard by those who were later called upon to determine Ives's guilt and sentence. In any event, trials were a form of rare entertainment at the time.[57] Organized communal entertainment was limited to occasional boxing matches, foot races, and pie-eating contests. Trials on the western frontier were usually conducted with speed, typically lasting no more than a day or two, as the participants and the spectators needed before too long to return to their daily commercial or other activities. As shown in the trial of

George Ives, the presentation of evidence and the attorneys' summations on the final day of the trial had to be completed by 3:00 p.m. so that the jury's deliberation and any sentence that might be imposed could be completed by the end of the day.[58]

Sentences were also significantly different than they are in modern-day Montana and other jurisdictions. Today the state of Montana has a defined statutory scheme that differentiates misdemeanors and felonies based upon the potential penalties of each.[59] In Montana Territory in 1863–64, there were not yet jail sentences as there were no jails.[60] Secure locations were used only on an ad hoc basis to hold defendants during the brief interval of time between their arrests and their trials.[61] There were no presentence reports providing the court with wide-ranging information about the defendant for use in determining an appropriate sentence.[62] Unlike Montana's law today, there was no broad menu of penalties such as deferred sentences,[63] suspended sentences[64] with probationary conditions,[65] community-based placement programs,[66] community service,[67] defined fines,[68] license suspensions,[69] youth placements,[70] statutory financial restitution,[71] home arrest,[72] rehabilitative treatment programs,[73] prerelease programs,[74] work release programs,[75] and early-release parole.[76] The usual menu of criminal sentence options in the mid-1860s, before the territory's adoption of a statutory criminal code, was quite limited to hanging, or perhaps whipping,[77] or banishment from the territory. In one unusual jury case tried at a miners' court at Biven's Gulch, near Alder Gulch, a defendant who had stolen a horse was sentenced to be beaten by the plaintiff, with the jury standing by to assure that the sentence was carried out.[78] The execution of defendants by hanging was usually a well-attended public spectacle, observed by men, women, and even children alike.[79] The Montana Historical Society has photographs depicting certain condemned criminals hanging from their nooses. On those rare occasions when photographs were taken and are preserved, they depict large crowds of persons gathered about the site.[80] Dimsdale reports that 5,000 persons attended the execution of James Brady in Nevada City and that "thousands" later assembled at the same locale for the execution of John "The Hat" Dolan.[81]

Criminal justice in the territory in 1863–64 afforded defendants no practical appellate remedies either. A legal sentence could be avoided if the accused were to obtain a pardon or reprieve from the governor of the territory, but usually a sentence of death by hanging, or public whipping, was carried out the same day as the conviction or on the next. Vigilantism was, by definition, extrajudicial and immediate. There was therefore no true opportunity for seeking, much less obtaining, either an appeal to a higher court or a gubernatorial pardon or reprieve.[82] Even in the case of James Daniels, who, while in prison after a formal court case, petitioned for and obtained a reprieve of his sentence from Governor Meagher, Helena vigilantes dissatisfied with the outcome seized and hanged him while the governor's reprieve was still lodged in his pocket.[83] The highly charged circumstances were recounted in detail in the previous chapter.

The legislation that created Montana Territory on May 26, 1864, also created a system of territorial courts, though the courts were fraught with systemic weaknesses. A chief judge and two additional judges for Montana Territory were appointed for four-year terms by the president of the United States with the advice and consent of the US Senate.[84] Each judge acted as a district judge with the same jurisdiction as any judge in the district courts of the United States.[85] But unlike in the United States, the territorial judges also collectively formed a three-judge appellate panel, meaning that the trial judge was among the judges hearing the appeal, which naturally raised concerns about appellate fairness and impartiality.[86] The appellate system later changed when the US Congress provided for the appointment in Montana of a fourth Supreme Court justice and required the automatic disqualification from the appellate panel of the particular trial judge.[87] Today, the court systems of the federal government and of all fifty states are arranged so that judges do not sit on the appeals of their own trial-level cases.

Life as a Montana judge was not just challenging but tough. Despite whatever little attention the Montana judicial branch received from Congress, there were at first no formal court facilities, meaning that proceedings were relegated to saloons, hotels, and public streets. Law books were scarce.[88] Geographically, Montana was large and rural, consisting of 143,776 square miles.[89] It was difficult, if not unrealistic, for three or four judges to cover the entirety of the territory by horseback.[90] Montana was simply too vast for a very small cadre of judges to provide the entire territory with a fully credible, meaningful system of justice. The Montana judges were paid $2,500 per year between 1864 and March 2, 1867, an amount that was deemed inadequate given the high cost of living at the time in the West and that was less than what attorneys could typically earn in private practices.[91] The inadequacy of salaries for territorial judges was recognized by everyone during that time except for the members of the US Congress, which set and kept the base amount.[92] The judiciary did not receive its $1,000 federal raise in 1867 except by the fortuity that its district boundaries, terms of court, judicial assignments, and general independence, was abused by the Second and Third Territorial Legislatures to such a degree that the Republicans in Congress felt compelled to come to the judges' aid and restore a balance between the branches of Montana's government. Until that time, their district boundaries, assignments, and the timing of their terms

Figure 12.8. Reverend W. C. Shippen, who cut down Helena's infamous Hanging Tree. (Courtesy of the Montana Historical Society, image 944-944.)

of court were used by the territorial legislature as political footballs to punish the judges, particularly Lyman Munson, for rendering opinions and taking stands on issues of which the legislature did not approve. Even after the nullification of Montana's Second and Third Territorial Legislatures, judicial pay continued to be used as a political weapon, as the $2,500 pay supplement authorized by the Bannack legislature was rescinded by the Fourth Territorial Legislature in December of 1867.[93] The collective difficulties of being a member of Montana's early territorial Supreme Court lessened only with time and territorial development.

Accordingly, criminal trials in south central Montana in 1863–64 were at best rudimentary forerunners of what has become procedurally commonplace and significantly lacked the level of due process and judicial predictability that is familiar and understood as fair and necessary today.

Panning for Nuggets

Helena's infamous Hanging Tree came to be viewed negatively and forebodingly with the passage of time. Methodist minister W. C. Shippen formed a committee that cut it down in 1875.[94] *Some residents of Helena were indignant that the tree was cut down.*[95] *Officially, the tree was cut down because flooding had undermined its roots and made it a danger to people and property.*[96] *Unofficially, the tree's removal symbolized Helena's rejection of further vigilantism, which might have been the true reason for its removal.*

Notes

1. Hamilton, *Anglo-American Law*, 117.
2. Ibid.
3. Ibid., 122.
4. Ibid.
5. *Clinton v. Englebrecht*, 80 U.S. 434, 445 (1871).
6. Wyoming Territory Organic Act.
7. P.L. 56-331, 31 Stat. 141.
8. Oklahoma Organic Act.
9. P.L. 56-191, 31 Stat. 77.
10. Organic Act of 1912.
11. See, generally, Bakken, *Rocky Mountain Constitution Making*.
12. *People v. Williams*, 1 Idaho 85 (1866); see also Wells, "Notable Idaho Nineteenth-Century Judicial Cases."
13. Organic Act of the Territory of Idaho, 12 U.S. Stat. 808, ch. 117 (1863).
14. Allen, *Decent Orderly Lynching*, 240.
15. 1 Idaho 85 (1866)
16. 1 Neb. 419 (1871).
17. Buchanan, " "Gold."
18. Ibid., citing William Fisk Sanders Papers, Mont. Hist. Soc., MC-53, box 5, folders 7–8.
19. Allen, *Decent Orderly Lynching*, 240.
20. Organic Act of the Territory of Montana, Act May 26, 1864, ch. 95, 13 Stat. 85 (1864); Guice, *Rocky Mountain Bench*, 21.
21. *People v. Williams*, 1 Idaho 85 (1866).
22. Guice, *Rocky Mountain Bench*, 21.
23. Ibid., 21–22.
24. Ibid., 22. According to Guice, Montana's Civil Practice Act of 1867 was actually published in Maine and was not distributed within the Territory until two years after its enactment, due to an absence of funding for the publication. Ibid., 25.
25. Organic Act of the Territory of Montana, Act May 26, 1864, ch. 95, sec. 6, 13 Stat. 85 et seq.
26. *Mapp v. Ohio*, 367 U.S. 643, 655 (1961).
27. *Gideon v. Wainwright*, 372 U.S. 335, 344 (1963).
28. *Brady v. Maryland*, 373 U.S. 83, 87 (1963).
29. *Escobedo v. Illinois*, 378 U.S. 478, 490–91 (1964).
30. *Miranda v. Arizona*, 384 U.S. 436, 444 (1966).
31. Andrea McDowell, "Criminal Law," 327, 329.
32. Reid, *Policing the Elephant*, 120.
33. The leading federal case on this concept is *Gideon v. Wainwright*, 372 U.S. 335, 343–44 (1963). The adoption of the concept by Montana is reflected in many state cases: e.g., *State*

v. Dethman, 358 Mont. 384 (2010); *Halley v. State*, 344 Mont. 37 (2008); *State v. Walker*, 344 Mont. 477 (2008); *State v. Browning*, 333 Mont. 132 (2006); *Hendricks v. State*, 331 Mont. 47 (2006); *State v. Mann*, 331 Mont. 137 (2006); *State v. Buck*, 331 Mont. 517 (2006); *State v. Weldele*, 315 Mont. 452 (2003); *State v. Howard*, 312 Mont. 359 (2002); *State v. Johnson*, 302 Mont. 544 (2000); *State v. LaMere*, 298 Mont. 358 (2000); *State v. Okland*, 283 Mont. 10 (1997); *State v. Craig*, 274 Mont. 140 (1995); *State v. Swan*, 199 Mont. 459 (1982); *State v. Pepperling*, 177 Mont. 464 (1978); *State v. Forsness*, 159 Mont. 105 (1972); Petition of Brittingham, 155 Mont. 525 (1970); Petition of Hunsinger, 153 Mont. 445 (1969); *Lewis v. State*, 152 Mont. 460 (1969); *State ex rel Berger v. District Court of Thirteenth Judicial Dist. in and for Big Horn County*, 150 Mont. 128 (1967); *Harding v. State*, 149 Mont. 147 (1967); *Nelson v. State*, 144 Mont. 439 (1964).

34. The leading federal cases on this concept are *Miranda v. Arizona*, 384 U.S. 436, 444–45 (1966) and *Escobedo v. State of Illinois*, 378 U.S. 478, 485 (1964). The adoption of the concept by Montana is reflected in many its state cases: e.g., *State v. Hurlbert*, 351 Mont. 316 (2009); *State v. Morrisey*, 351 Mont. 144 (2009); *State v. Lacey*, 349 Mont. 371 (2009); *State v. Munson*, 339 Mont. 68 (2007); *State v. Buck*, 331 Mont. 517; *State v. Reavley*, 318 Mont. 150 (2003); *State v. Lawrence*, 285 Mont. 140 (1997); *State v. Woods*, 283 Mont. 359 (1997); *State v. Cassell*, 280 Mont. 397 (1996); *State v. Fuller*, 276 Mont. 155 (1996); *State v. Finley*, 173 Mont. 162 (1977).

35. Allen, *Decent Orderly Lynching*, 357. Jessrang survived the ordeal, but three weeks later a mob, believing him guilty despite the absence of any confession, broke into the jail cell where he was being held and hanged him summarily.

36. US Const., Fifth Amend., and Mont. Const., art. 2, sec. 11. The leading federal case on this concept is *Mapp v. Ohio*, 367 U.S. 643, 655 (1961). The adoption of the concept by Montana is reflected in many state cases: e.g., *State v. Pipkin*, 289 Mont. 240 (1998); *State v. Anderson*, 258 Mont. 510 (1993); *State v. Sundberg*, 235 Mont. 115 (1988); *City of Helena v. Lamping*, 221 Mont. 370 (1986); *State v. Kao*, 215 Mont. 277 (1985); *State v. Ribera*, 183 Mont. 1 (1979); *State v. Briner*, 173 Mont. 185 (1977); *State v. Thorsness*, 165 Mont. 321 (1974); *State v. Hull*, 158 Mont. 6 (1971); Application of Gray, 155 Mont. 510 (1970); *State v. Dess*, 154 Mont. 231 (1969); *State v. Williams*, 153 Mont. 262 (1969); *State v. Langan*, 151 Mont. 558 (1968).

37. Examples include the trials of Deputy Buck Stinson, Hayes Lyons, Charley Forbes, George Ives, and George Hilderman; see also Reid, *Policing the Elephant*, 127–28.

38. Mont. Code Ann. 46-11-301 (1991) through 46-11-332 (1991). See, generally, *U.S. v. Boggs*, 493 F. Supp. 1050, 1051–52 (D.C. Mont. 1980); Matter of Secret Grand Jury Inquiry, John and Jane Does Thirty Through Thirty-Nine, 170 Mont. 354 (1976); *State ex rel Woodahl v. District Court of First Judicial Dist., in and for Lewis and Clark County*, 166 Mont. 31, 39–40 (1975).

39. US Const., Fifth Amend.; Mont. Code Ann. 46-11-401 (2009) and 46-11-331 (1991). See, generally, *State v. Wilson*, 340 Mont. 191, 197 (2007); *State v. Little*, 260 Mont. 460, 470 (1993); *State v. Sanderson*, 214 Mont. 437, 453 (1985); *State v. Clark*, 209 Mont. 473, 481 (1984); *State v. Coleman*, 177 Mont. 1, 22–23 (1978); *State v. Hall*, 171 Mont. 33, 35 (1976).

40. Mont. Code Ann. 46-12-102 (1991) and 46-2-201 (2005). See, generally, *State v. Schneiderhan*, 261 Mont. 161, 166 (1993); *State v. Longneck*, 201 Mont. 367, 372–72 (1982); *State v. Rodriguez*, 192 Mont. 411, 418 (1981); Petition of Hunsinger, 152 Mont. 446–47; *State ex rel Biebinger v. Ellsworth*, 147 Mont. 512, 517-18 (1966); see also Mont. Const., art. 2, sec. 24.

41. Mont. Code Ann. 46-12-204(1) (2002). See, generally, *State v. Keys*, 293 Mont. 81, 85 (1999); *Yother v. State*, 182 Mont. 351, 358 (1979); *State v. White*, 321 Mont. 45, 49 (1994). *Nolo contendere* is a plea by a criminal defendant that disposes of the case and subjects the defendant to a sentence, but which does not rise to the level of an actual admission of guilt to the crime.

42. Mont. Code Ann. 46-15-322(1)(a) (1993). See, generally, *State v. Golder*, 301 Mont. 368, 369–70 (2000); *State v. Sol*, 282 Mont. 69, 78–79 (1997); *State v. Sage*, 221 Mont. 192, 195–97 1986); *State v. Haag*, 176 Mont. 395, 400–1 (1978).

43. Mont. Code Ann. 46-15-322(1) (1993). See, generally, *State v. Elliott*, 308 Mont. 227, 237–38 (2002), denial of postconviction relief affirmed, 325 Mont. 345 (2005); *State v. Santos*, 273 Mont. 125, 136–37 (1995); *State v. Bauer*, 210 Mont. 298, 308–9 (1984); *State v. Weinberger*, 204 Mont. 278, 293–94 (1983).

44. Mont. Code Ann. 46-15-322(1)(c) (1993). See, generally, *State v. Morrissey*, 351 Mont. 144, 174–77 (2009); *State v. Normandy*, 347 Mont. 505, 507–9 (2008); *State v. Boettiger*, 324 Mont. 20 (2004); *State v. Bailey*, 320 Mont. 501, 503–6 (2004); *State v. Ray*, 267 Mont. 128, 140 (1994); *State v. Smith*, 220 Mont. 364, 373–74 (1986).

45. Mont. Code Ann. 46-15-322(1)(d) (1993).

46. Ibid. See, generally, *City of Billings v. Peterson*, 322 Mont. 444, 452–53 (2004); *State v. Romero*, 279 Mont. 58, 73–74 (1996); *State v. Hatfield*, 269 Mont. 307, 312 (1995).

47. Mont. Code Ann. 46-15-322(1)(e) (1993). See, generally, *Brady v. Maryland*, 373 U.S. 83 (1963); *Gollehon v. State*, 296 Mont. 6, 9–11 (1999), reh. denied, cert. denied, 529 U.S. 1041 (2000); *State v. Field*, 328 Mont. 26, 30 (2005); *Kills on Top v. State*, 303 Mont. 164, 172–73 (2000); *State v. Baker*, 301 Mont. 323, 326–28 (2000); *State v. Ellenburg*, 301 Mont. 289, 302–3 (2000), habeas corpus dism'd. in part, 2007 WL 295224 (D. Mont. 2007), habeas corpus denied, 2007 WL 710195 (D. Mont. 2007); *State v. Duffy*, 300 Mont. 381, 386–87 (2000); *State v. Stewart*, 253 Mont. 475, 480–81 (1992); *State v. Palmer*, 207 Mont. 152, 156 (1983); *State v. Patterson*, 203 Mont. 509, 513 (1983).

48. Bakken, *Invitation to an Execution*, 393–94.

49. Dimsdale, *Vigilantes of Montana*, 66; Langford, *Vigilante Days*, 131; Birney, *Vigilantes*, 111. Bissell was educated at Yale and had presided over miners' courts. Allen, *Decent Orderly Lynching*, 157. His name appeared earlier in this article as the man who changed the proposed name of Varina City to Virginia City on account of his Unionist sympathies.

50. Dimsdale, *Vigilantes of Montana*, 67; Langford, *Vigilante Days*, 131; Birney, *Vigilantes*, 111. Dimsdale identifies defense counsel at those trials as Judge Harry Percival Adams Smith, whom Langford and Allen describe as a well-known frontier attorney. Langford, *Vigilante Days*, 131; Allen, *Decent Orderly Lynching*, 105.

51. Guice, *Rocky Mountain Bench*, 25.

52. Allen, *Decent Orderly Lynching*, 187.

53. Langford, *Vigilante Days*, 186; Allen, *Decent Orderly Lynching*, 187; Johnson, *Bloody Bozeman*, 92–93. In Montana today guilt must be established by a unanimous verdict of jurors. Mont. Const., art. 2, sec. 26.

54. Langford, *Vigilante Days*, 186; Allen, *Decent Orderly Lynching*, 187.

55. Sanders and Bertsche, *X. Beidler*, 56. For instance, Wilbur Fisk Sanders, who successfully prosecuted George Ives, wrote that "[i]t was very evident that the men who were to try the defendants, would not, all of them, hear the testimony"; ibid.

56. Ibid., 60; Johnson, *Bloody Bozeman*, 92; Birney, *Vigilantes*, 196; Allen, *Decent Orderly Lynching*, 177; Milner and O'Connor, *As Big as the West*, 90; Barsness, *Gold Camp*, 39; Mather and Boswell, *Hanging the Sheriff*, 77 (limiting the number to 1,000); Hamilton, *From Wilderness to Statehood*, 248.

57. Trials have been a form of high-profile interest and entertainment throughout American history including, for instance, the trials of Aaron Burr, John Brown, Mary Surratt, Julius and Ethel Rosenberg, Ted Kaczynski (see Ferguson, *Trial in American Life*), and, more recently, O. J. Simpson. The trial of George Ives was significant for its local place and time but did not command any national importance.

58. John W. Grannis Diaries, 1863–78, Mont. Hist. Soc., SC-301, folder 1-1; Dimsdale, *Vigilantes of Montana*, 91; Allen, *Decent Orderly Lynching*, 186.

59. Mont. Code Ann. 45-1-201 (1977). Misdemeanors are defined in MCA 45-2-101(42) (2009) as offenses punishable by fines or imprisonment, or both, and where the authorized sentence of imprisonment is one year or less. Felonies are defined in MCA 45-2-1-1(23) as offenses for which the authorized punishment is imprisonment for more than one year or death.

60. Johnson, *Bloody Bozeman*, 93n17.

61. For instance, when Buck Stinson, Hayes Lyons, and Charley Forbes were arrested for shooting D. H. Dillingham, they were held in a log building, under guard, pending the conduct of their trials. Dimsdale, *Vigilantes of Montana*, 65.

62. Mont. Code Ann. 46-18-111(1) (2009) (for felony offenses). See, generally, *State v. Smith*, 261 Mont. 419, 423 (1993), after new hearing, 280 Mont. 158 (1996), cert. denied, 522 U.S. 965 (1997), dismissal of postconviction relief, 303 Mont. 47 (2000), cert. denied, 533 U.S. 917 (2001).

63. Mont. Code Ann. 46-18-201(1)(a) (2009); 45-9-102(2) (2005). See, generally, *State v. Brinson*, 351 Mont. 136, 141–42 (2009); *State v. Essig*, 353 Mont. 99, 103–4 (2009); *State v. Sadowsky*, 347 Mont. 192, 194 (2008); *State v. Teets*, 343 Mont. 73, 75 (2008); *State v. Deshazo*, 343 Mont. 77, 79 (2008); *State v. Seals*, 336 Mont. 416, 421 (2007); *Smith v. County of Missoula*, 297 Mont. 368, 374 (1999); *Gonzales v. Blodgett*, 193 Mont. 504, 505 (1981).

64. Mont. Code Ann. 46-18-201(2) (2009). See, generally, *State v. Brinson*, 351 Mont. 141–42; *State v. Bullman*, 349 Mont. 228, 236 (2009); *State v. Rogers*, 239 Mont. 327, 329 (1989); *State v. Simpson*, 296 Mont. 335, 338 (1999); *State v. Drew*, 158 Mont. 214, 217 (1971).

65. Mont. Code Ann. 46-18-201(4)(o). See, generally, *State v. Stiles*, 347 Mont. 95, 98 (2008); *State v. Hunter*, 347 Mont. 155, 157 (2008); *State v. Heddings*, 347 Mont. 169, 173 (2008); *State v. Greeson*, 336 Mont. 1, 4 (2007); *State v. Simpson*, 296 Mont. 338; *State v. Drew*, 158 Mont. 217; *State v. Rogers*, 239 Mont. 329.

66. Mont. Code Ann. 46-18-201(3)(a)(v) (2009); 53-20-101 (1995); 53-20-148(5) (1997); 53-30-321 (1997). See, generally, *In re* T.P., 345 Mont. 152, 156–57 (2008); *State v. Lamb*, 307 Mont. 54, 58 (2001); Matter of W.M., 252 Mont. 225, 229 (1992); Matter of M.J.P., 226 Mont. 183, 186 (1987).

67. Mont. Code Ann. 46-18-201(4)(j) (2009); 7-32-2302 (2001). See, generally, *State v. Grindheim*, 323 Mont. 519, 531–33 (2004); *Christian v. Sixth Judicial Dist. Court*, 319 Mont. 162, 167 (2004).

68. Mont. Code Ann. 46-18-201(3)(a)(i) (2009); 46-18-231 (2007). See, generally, *Voerding v. State*, 332 Mont. 262, 268 (2006); *State v. George*, 313 Mont. 11, 13 (2002); *State v. Cripps*, 177 Mont. 410, 425 (1978); *State v. Babbit*, 175 Mont. 433, 438–39 (1978).

69. Mont. Code Ann. 46-18-201(6) (2009); 46-18-202(1)(e) (1994); 61-5-208(2) (2009). See, generally, *Parpart v. State*, 319 Mont. 182, 184 (2004); *Anderson v. Department of Justice*, 284 Mont. 109, 110–12 (1997); *Dewart v. State*, 254 Mont. 216, 217 (1992); *Horton v. State*, 221 Mont. 233, 236 (1986).

70. Mont. Code Ann. 46-18-201(3)(a)(iv)(A) (2009); 41-5-206 (2007); 41-5-2503 (1999); 52-5-111 (1997). See, generally, *State v. M.J.V., III*, 355 Mont. 547 (2009); *State v. Quesnel*, 353 Mont. 317, 321–22 (2009); *State v. Mainwaring*, 335 Mont. 322, 325–27 (2007); *State ex rel Elliot v. District Court of Sixth Judicial Dist., in and for Sweet Grass County*, 211 Mont. 1, 4–7 (1984);

71. Mont. Code Ann. 46-18-201(5) (2009). See, generally, *State v. Ness*, 352 Mont. 317, 320–21 (2009); *State v. Perkins*, 350 Mont. 387, 389–90 (2009); *State v. Borsberry*, 322 Mont. 271, 277 (2006); *State v. McIntire*, 322 Mont. 496, 499 (2004); *State v. Pritchett*, 302 Mont. 1, 4 (2000); *State v. Morgan*, 198 Mont. 391, 400 (1982).

72. Mont. Code Ann. 46-18-201(4)(k) (2009); 41-5-321(1)(c) (2001); 41-5-347(2) (1999); 41-5-346(2) (1997); 41-5-1304(1)(e) (2009); 46-18-1001(2) (1997); 46-18-1002 (1997); 46-18-734(3) (2005). See, generally, *State v. Clark*, 342 Mont. 461, 466 (2008); Matter of C.S., 210 Mont. 144, 145–47 (1984).

73. Mont. Code Ann. 46-18-201(3)(a)(vii); 46-18-201(4)(o) (2009). See, generally, *State v. Pease*, 233 Mont. 65, 71 (1988), cert. denied, 48 U.S. 1033 (1989); *State v. Larson*, 266 Mont. 28, 33 (1994).

74. Mont. Code Ann. 46-18-201(3)(a)(vi); 46-18-201(4)(i) and (n) (2009): Mont. Code Ann. 53-1-103(c) (2007). See, generally, *State v. Hastings*, 340 Mont. 1 (2007).

75. Mont. Code Ann. 46-18-201(4)(a) (2009); 46-18-701 (1997). See, generally, Petition of Williams, 145 Mont. 45, 54 (1965).

76. Mont. Code Ann. 46-23-201 (2003); 46-23-202 (2003). See, generally, *McDermott v. McDonald*, 305 Mont. 166, 170–71 (2001); *Sage v. Gamble*, 279 Mont. 459, 465 (1996).

77. Dimsdale, *Vigilantes of Montana*, 180 (describing a sentence imposed upon defendant Jem Kelly consisting of fifty lashes on the bare back).

78. Johnson, *Bloody Bozeman*, 93n17.

79. Ibid., 87–88, 103–4.

80. E.g., Allen, *Decent Orderly Lynching*, 351.

81. Dimsdale, *Vigilantes of Montana*, 181, 188.

82. Bakken, "Death for Grand Larceny, 46. Even where appellate remedies were available, such as in California, justice was swift from the date of arrest to the date of execution. George Tanner was arrested on April 3, 1852, for the theft of significant foodstuffs. His trial was conducted of April 14, his appeal was denied April 24, a rehearing on the appeal was denied July 16, and his execution was fulfilled on July 23, 1852, all within the span of three and a half months. Ibid., 47; *People v. Tanner*, 2 Cal. 257, 260–61 (Cal. 1852).

83. Allen, *Decent Orderly Lynching*, 336, citing the *Montana Post*, Mar. 10, 1866.

84. Guice, *Rocky Mountain Bench*, 11; Spence, *Territorial Politics*, 26.

85. Guice, *Rocky Mountain Bench*, 11.

86. Ibid., 11–12; Spence, *Territorial Politics*, 26.

87. Guice, *Rocky Mountain Bench*, 13, citing Statutes at Large 24:138; mt.gov., "Judicial Branch."

88. Guice, *Rocky Mountain Bench*, 25.

89. Lanman, *Biographical Annals*, 561.

90. Guice, *Rocky Mountain Bench*, 13–14.

91. Ibid., 38–39.

92. Ibid., 39.

93. Laws 1867. Fourth Terr. Legis., "An Act to amend an act entitled 'An Act to provide increased compensation to the officers of the Territory,'" approved January 24, 1865, sec. 4.

94. Cushman, *Montana*, 204.

95. Wolle, *Montana Pay Dirt*, 72.

96. Axline et al., *More from the Quarries*, 15.

14

Due Process and Procedure
Vigilante Arrests and Trials

"The evidences of their guilt were too patent to require much time for investigation, so that the [Vigilance] Committee decided unanimously on their execution."

—M. A. Leeson, 1885

"Boys, if I hadn't been so fat I would have died sure."

—Jem Kelly, June 15, 1864

Following the description of many of the vigilante events of Bannack, Alder Gulch, and Helena and also trial procedures that were generally used in the 1860s, some observations and conclusions can now be drawn about vigilante investigations, arrests, and sentences. Vigilante arrests and procedures will be discussed in this chapter. Observations about vigilante sentences are the subject of the next chapter. There are important incidences of Montana vigilantism yet to be discussed, as this and successive chapters will show.

An understanding of the standards and expectations for trials in 1863–64 allows critical analysis of whether the investigations and trials conducted by the vigilantes met, or failed to meet, at least the due process standards of the time. It is submitted here that the summary proceedings afforded by vigilantes fell below the general procedural standards of the time, both as to the trials discussed in this chapter and the sentences discussed in the next. Any judgment on the procedural standards used by the Vigilance Committee is necessarily restricted to the available historical record of the summary trials of those accused, to the extent such information has survived.

DOI: 10.7330_9780874219203.c014

The historical record suggests that when an accused was captured by the Vigilance Committee, there was no trial conducted in the sense of the public trials that were otherwise commonplace in the 1860s.[1] There were, in effect, no independent prosecutors, no defense attorneys,[2] no grand jury, no particular rules of evidence, no jury of peers, no public spectators, no stenographic record, and no right of appeal. The bylaws of the Vigilance Committee provided that its members were authorized to make arrests of men suspected of crimes and to then "report the same with proof to the Chief who will thereupon call a meeting of the Executive Committee and the judgment of such Executive Committee shall be final."[3] An accused's capture may have been on some occasions more an opportunity for the vigilantes to obtain a confession, and to obtain information about other criminals who were also to be arrested, than it was to adjudicate the merits of criminal charges. Members of the Vigilante Committee acted as both accusers and judges, a concept foreign to our understanding of due process today.[4]

In some instances it was a foregone conclusion that the capture of road agent conspirators was for the sole purpose of immediately hanging them, without trial, and with no contemplated procedure besides the arrest of the accused and the march to the gallows. This appears from the historical literature to have been the case with the arrests and executions of Henry Plummer, Hank Stinson, and Ned Ray on January 10, 1864, and Bill Hunter on February 3, 1864.[5]

As for other arrests, Dimsdale describes impromptu closed "trials" for Steve Marshland in one instance, Cyrus Skinner in another instance,[6] James Brady in another, Jem Kelly in yet another, and John "The Hat" Dolan, and R. C. Rawley, where witnesses were called or evidence was examined and discussed before verdicts were reached.[7] The trial of Cyrus Skinner lasted approximately three hours[8] and the trial of John "The Hat" Dolan was described by Dimsdale as "patient and lengthened."[9]

The trial of James Brady, accused of having shot and wounded saloon keeper Thomas Murphy in Nevada City,[10] included an identification of Brady by the victim, testimony from witnesses of the event, and, ultimately, testimony from Brady himself wherein he attributed the shooting to his state of intoxication.[11] For much of the past century, Montana law allowed for intoxication to be taken into account in determining a defendant's mental state as an element of the crime charged.[12] In 1987 Montana law was changed so that intoxication is no longer a defense to criminal conduct.[13] Similarly, intoxication was not a persuasive defense at vigilante trials, and Brady's trial resulted in his being convicted and sentenced to death by hanging, despite Brady's claimed drunkenness at the time his crime was committed.[14]

Brady was permitted prior to his execution to write a letter to his daughter. He wrote that he had "been arrested, tried and sentenced to be hanged by the

Vigilance Committee," for having "tried to take the life of my fellow-man" by "shoot[ing] him through a window."[15] He added that in his dying hour, "I entreat you to be a good girl. Walk in the ways of the Lord. Keep Heaven, God and the interest of your soul, before your eyes."[16] A butcher's hoist was used for Brady's hanging with a box and a plank rigged for his drop.[17] The execution occurred in front of spectators at approximately 4:00 p.m. on June 15, 1864, at a location on the outskirts of Nevada City.[18] If Brady's captors executed him in anticipation that the shooting victim, Thomas Murphy, would die from the gunshot, they were mistaken, as Murphy unexpectedly survived the wound.[19] The execution of Brady for the shooting of Murphy, despite Murphy's survival of the wound, was criticized by Professor J. W. Smurr of Montana State University in a historically significant article published by him in 1958 in *Montana: The Magazine of Western History.*[20]

The intoxication defense was also unpersuasive in the trial and execution of John "The Hat" Dolan, who was convicted of stealing money from a miner, and George Ballou, who was hanged for the stabbing death of Johnny Gordon outside of a saloon. Immediately before his execution, Dolan confessed to the crime and sought to excuse his behavior on the ground of intoxication, but the excuse was insufficient to save his life.[21]

The trial of R. C. Rawley, who was accused of spying for the road agent gang, was conducted in Rawley's absence and resulted in his arrest and summary execution that same night, without the opportunity to be represented by counsel or to present any defense at the trial.[22] Rawley's trial and execution is somewhat controversial. He had either fled or been banished from Alder Gulch during the initial days of vigilantism in early 1864, and lost both feet to frostbite during his absence, but in a display of poor judgment he had returned to the area by the fall of the same year.[23] He complained about the vigilantes in a letter that fell into the hands of the Vigilance Committee members, and the next day Rawley was dead.[24] Dimsdale makes a cryptic reference in his discussion of the trial to Rawley's "present line of action and speech,"[25] suggesting that his oral or written utterances were among the evidence raised against him at his trial. Dr. Ellen Baumler, a historian at the Montana Historical Society, attributes the trial and execution of Rawley to his threat "to expose the identities of the vigilantes,"[26] further suggesting that Rawley's utterances were causing him trouble with the Vigilance Committee and were an apparent factor in his trial and death. Rawley was hanged from the same gallows where Sheriff Plummer had been hanged, his two bony foot stumps exposed to the chilly air.[27] Rawley's execution may be among the most condemnable of the vigilante hangings, for it may represent the hanging of a man for having exercised the First Amendment right to free speech. His execution was performed on October 31, 1864, and was the last vigilante execution in what proved to be the deadliest single year for vigilante executions in Montana.[28]

The trials of "Dutch John" Wagner and Steve Marshland were unique among vigilante proceedings in that they relied upon the existence of physical evidence of the alleged crime. Both men were suspected of having been involved in the robbery of Moody's stagecoach, bound for Salt Lake City. During the incident the masked robbers had both been shot before their escapes, one in the chest and one in the shoulder.[29] Both men were named on "Red" Yeager's list of road agents. When Wagner was questioned by Neil Howie and John Fetherstun, and later by members of the vigilante posse in Bannack in early January 1864, he was forced to expose his shoulder, which revealed a bullet-wound injury. The inspection of Wagner's shoulder was akin to a warrantless search. Wagner's explanation for the wound, that it was accidentally self-inflicted, lacked all credibility. There appears to be no historical evidence that while Wagner was in custody, he was specifically identified by any member of Moody's party as a participant in the crime. Information that one of the masked robbers had been shot in the shoulder and another shot in the chest may have been pure word-of-mouth hearsay. Absent an identification of Wagner's person by a member of Moody's party, the existence of the bullet wound to his shoulder was merely circumstantial evidence, likely based upon a hearsay version of the criminal events. However, it was very strong circumstantial evidence, as a rational fact finder could readily draw the connection between the existence of the shoulder wound and the Moody's stagecoach robbery. The physical evidence of Wagner's bullet wound, coupled with Wagner's name on the Yeager list, were all the vigilantes felt they needed to convict him of the attempted robbery of the stagecoach and the attempted murder of its drivers when he fired his shotgun at them.

Similarly, when Marshland was arrested by the Vigilance Committee on January 15, 1864,[30] his "trial" consisted of being questioned about a chest wound, which Marshland denied.[31] An immediate examination of Marshland's chest, again equivalent to a warrantless search, revealed the mark of a recent bullet wound, which was deemed sufficient evidence to justify a sentence of death by hanging,[32] even though, by today's standards, all of the evidence against Marshland might also appear to have been merely circumstantial. Of course, the case against Marshland was stronger than the case against Wagner. Both men had bullet-wound injuries on their bodies that matched the description of events that had transpired during the stagecoach robbery. Both men were named on "Red" Yeager's list. However, Wagner, after being informed that he was to be hanged, confessed his role in the attempted robbery and implicated Marshland as his accomplice. By the time Marshland was captured, the vigilantes had Wagner's confession for use against Marshland, notwithstanding the fact that Wagner was dead and unavailable for any cross-examination on Marshland's behalf. Such procedural and evidentiary issues were of no particular concern to the vigilantes, possessed as they were of two suspects named on Yeager's list, with bullet wounds to Wagner's shoulder and Marshland's chest, and Wagner's identification of Marshland as a coconspirator just before Wagner's own death.

In Helena, Arthur Compton and Joseph Wilson, who were jointly arrested and tried for the robbery and attempted murder of George Leonard, received a one-day evidentiary trial before their convictions and executions on April 30, 1870.[33] In the greater Helena region, Billy Wilson and Spaulding, who were jointly arrested for horse stealing, received a trial that lasted two days in January of 1868, suggesting that it was in some way meaningful.[34] George Ballou, who was arrested for the murder of John Gordon on May 17, 1868, and Jack Varley, who was accused of separately robbing Julian Guezals on August 12, 1868, each received impromptu "show up" trials that led to their convictions and executions.[35] Leander Johnson also received an impromptu trial for cattle stealing that resulted in his death by hanging on March 12, 1866.[36] The Johnson trial and hanging is notable for likely being a miscarriage of justice, as the missing cattle reportedly returned to its owner after Johnson was dead.[37]

The Wilson-Spaulding trial in 1868 and the Compton-Wilson trial in 1870 are the two instances in which defendants were tried jointly. The 1864 hangings in Virginia City of five road agents, George "Clubfoot" Lane, Frank Parish, Hayes Lyons, Jack Gallagher, and Boone Helm, do not qualify as joint trials as the accused men were never formally tried. The conduct of joint trials raises peculiar legal issues that are of some relevance here. Under Montana law today, two or more defendants may be charged in a single indictment if they are alleged to have been involved in the same criminal transaction.[38] Similarly, two or more defendants may be tried jointly if the defendants could be charged by a single indictment and "the interests of justice require" the joinder.[39] Joint trials will be conducted of related defendants to advance the administration of justice, the conservation of judicial resources, and the minimization of the burdens upon jurors and witnesses.[40] An exception to the statutory preference for joint trials is when a defendant makes a statement prior to trial, out of the presence of the codefendant, that inculpates the codefendant in the charged crime and that will be introduced at the trial. In such instances, separate trials will normally be required to assure that the inculpatory statement of the defendant is not used against the codefendant in violation of the codefendant's right to confrontation as guaranteed by the Sixth Amendment.[41] The rule for conducting separate trials in such instances makes perfect sense today, where there is typically a clear temporal demarcation between the investigatory stage of a case on the one hand and the formal prosecutorial stage on the other. In the impromptu trials of 1860s and 1870s Montana, however, the investigatory stage of an alleged crime and the prosecuted trial of the accused were often one in the same proceeding, as was the case with defendants Billy Wilson and Spaulding in 1868 and defendants Arthur Compton and Joseph Wilson in 1870. In those instances, where one defendant implicates a codefendant in the crime, as with the testimony of Spaulding that the alleged horse thievery was Billy Wilson's idea, the presence of the codefendant at the trial might require separate trials under the standards of today. In stark contrast, they were certainly deemed unnecessary under the standards used in the western territories in the 1860s and 1870s.

Some of the vigilante "trials" of road agents consisted only of conversation with the prisoner resulting in a confession to alleged criminal conduct. Confessions were deemed to be sufficient evidence, standing alone, to warrant a suspect's execution,[42] as in the arrests and hangings of "Red" Yeager on January 4, 1864,[43] Frank Parish,[44] Boone Helm,[45] and Hayes Lyons[46] on January 14, 1864,[47] Alex Carter on January 25, 1864,[48] and Jack Silvie on July 9, 1865.[49] In other cases, confessions were volunteered only after the prisoner had been informed that he was to be hanged, as with the arrest of "Dutch John" Wagner[50] and John "The Hat" Dolan.[51] According to Dimsdale, Wagner's admissions corroborated the details of Yeager's extensive confession, and he implicated himself and Steve Marshland in the attempted robbery of the Moody's stagecoach that resulted in their being shot at in early December 1863.[52] Jack Silvie, who may have confessed to the murder of a single miner at the Snake River before his fate was determined by the Executive Committee of Helena's Committee of Safety,[53] confessed to almost a dozen other murders after he had been brought to the place of his execution.[54]

The confession by Billy Page to Hill Beachy in Lewiston, Idaho, was unique and notable. Page admitted to involvement in the Magruder Trail murders as a result of being tricked into believing that his companions had confessed to their crimes and that he and they were facing imminent death by hanging. He had even seen four nooses suspended from a rafter. Today a detective's or prosecutor's express or implied threat to a suspect of imminent death is not permitted. Such intimidating and coercive conduct is prohibited, as the right against self-incrimination is constitutionally guaranteed by federal and state constitutions, and the waiver of the right to remain silent is only valid where it is done by the suspect knowingly and voluntarily.[55] Conduct akin to the interrogation techniques of Hill Beachy would today result in the suppression from evidence of the suspect's confession and any information derived from the confession as "fruit of the poisonous tree."[56]

Some vigilante "trials" amounted to little more than some discussion among members of the Vigilance Committee as to their satisfaction of defendants' guilt and the time and location of the planned execution of the prisoner. As described by M. A. Leeson in his *History of Montana* regarding the arrests and joint executions of Helm, Parish, Lyons, Gallagher, and Lane on January 14, 1864, "[t]he evidences of their guilt were too patent to require much time for investigation, so that the [Vigilance] Committee decided unanimously on their execution."[57] In other words, using questionable logic, knowledge of the prisoners' guilt was so clear that no trials were deemed necessary for them.

The execution of Hayes Lyons occurred after his confession to the murder of Sheriff Plummer's honest chief deputy, D. H. Dillingham.[58] As earlier noted, Hayes Lyons and Buck Stinson had been convicted of the killing by a jury en masse and sentenced to death by hanging, but the sentences were then rescinded after the acquittal of their colleague in crime, Charley Forbes. While Lyons may have been suspected by the Vigilance Committee of other road agent behavior, his later arrest and execution specific to the Dillingham murder violated the constitutional Fifth Amendment right to be free from double jeopardy.[59]

Lew L. Callaway Jr. writes that when Jack Silvie was brought to Helena for questioning, his confession to the murder of a miner on the Snake River might have been acquired through a minister, who spoke to Silvie in furtherance of contrition, prayer, and penance.[60] Today, the confidentiality of communications between an accused and his clergyman is a privilege that is universally accepted. Indeed, Montana law today excludes from evidence confessions that are made by an accused while seeking or receiving religious guidance, admonishment or advice and when the cleric is acting within his or her religious role in furtherance of the practices and discipline of a church.[61] The privilege means that absent the consent of the accused, no member of the clergy may be compelled to testify about matters made in religious confidence.[62] The privilege is limited only to statements that qualify as confessions to crimes.[63] Privileged communications, such as those commonly applied to clergy and penitents, doctors and patients, attorneys and clients, and husbands and wives, are not rooted in common law and are in fact in derogation of the common law. The earliest predecessor of the Montana statute recognizing a clergy-penitent privilege was enacted in 1867,[64] two years after the questioning of Jack Silvie by the Executive Committee of Helena's Committee of Safety. Therefore, under the laws in existence at the time of Silvie's execution, nothing would have prevented the vigilantes from using a minister as a pretext to obtain a confession, if in fact they did so. However, statutory law would not permit the use of any such evidence today.

In one instance, the Vigilance Committee engaged in extraterritorial kidnapping to apprehend a suspected thief. John "The Hat" Dolan was believed to have stolen $700 from a miner, and not long after the crime, he left town in the direction of Salt Lake City, Utah.[65] The vigilantes hired a private investigator, John McGrath, who learned that Dolan was living in Springville, south of Salt Lake City, under the alias John Coyle.[66] A local marshal did not permit McGrath to arrest Dolan, or Coyle, in Utah Territory in the absence of an arrest warrant or formal charges.[67] Undeterred, McGrath kidnapped Dolan, acting, in effect, as a bounty hunter, and returned him to the Vigilance Committee for his trial and execution.[68] Dolan admitted his $700 theft prior to his execution.[69] The execution was performed on September 17, 1864, in Nevada City, with the assistance of 500 armed vigilantes who guarded against any rescue attempt that might have been contemplated by persons within the large crowd of spectators that had gathered for the unusual daylight execution.[70]

Vigilante punishment was also exacted extraterritorially in the case of Frank Williams, who was captured and executed near Denver in January of 1866. Williams had been employed as a stagecoach driver during the summer of 1865, at which time he drove several successful merchants from Virginia City to St. Joseph, Missouri, with $60,000 in gold dust in their possession.[71] The merchants included Parker and McCausland of Virginia City, Mers and David Dinan from Nevada City, and Brown and Carpenter, who were added to the party before the Snake River Bridge.[72] The gold dust in their possession was hidden in buckskin bags concealed on their persons and in sacks hidden under seats of the coach.[73] As the stagecoach neared Pontneuf Canyon, it was besieged by road agents, who shot and killed McCausland, Mers, and Dinan.[74] Carpenter was also shot but managed to survive by pretending that he was already dead.[75] Brown escaped the ambush by successfully absconding into a nearby thicket.[76] Parker received a gunshot wound that ultimately required the amputation of his leg at the thigh.[77] The road agents rummaged through the bodies and the coach and stole whatever they could find.[78] The coach driver, Williams, was unharmed and returned to Virginia City with the dead and wounded in tow.[79] Vigilante posses were dispatched to capture the road agents and recover the stolen treasure, but despite a generous financial reward offered by the stage company for the capture of the culprits, no efforts to capture them proved immediately successful.[80]

Williams soon left his employment as a stagecoach driver.[81] Given the nightmarish events that he had experienced, no one could blame him. He relocated to Salt Lake City, whereupon he spent money beyond what he could have honestly earned, which aroused the suspicions of those who were determined to avenge the robbers.[82] A vigilante posse from Montana later caught up with Williams at Godfrey's Station, near Denver, and arrested him.[83] Williams confessed that he had driven the stagecoach into the ambush to aid the thieves and, like "Red" Yeager before him, provided a detailed account of the names and

residences of eleven other persons involved in the robbery and murder conspiracy.[84] Williams's account was corroborated, at least circumstantially, by the fact
that he had been left unharmed by the road agents at the time that the bloody
crimes were committed. The prisoner claimed that he did not know beforehand
that the robberies would also involve murder,[85] but there is no way of knowing
whether that was ignorant truth or a self-serving statement intended to exonerate himself or, at least, to assuage a guilty conscience. Williams was summarily
hanged near Denver, well outside of Montana Territory.[86] Some of the persons
that Williams implicated in the plot were later captured and also executed.[87]
The Williams execution is a further example of vigilantes extending their lethal
reach beyond Montana's borders.

During the same month, January of 1866, the vigilantes engaged in yet
another instance of extraterritorial arrest and execution. A bounty hunter named
George Hurst was in pursuit of Michael Duffy for crimes unspecified.[88] Hurst
found Duffy in Utah and delivered him to a Utah court but was informed by
the court that it had no legal jurisdiction over the matter.[89] In fact, the court
placed Hurst, rather than Duffy, into custody for contempt of court.[90] Hurst
escaped his captors, located Duffy a second time, and rather than making the
effort to return Duffy to Montana, killed Duffy instead in Salt Lake City.[91]

The Vigilance Committee professed to adhere to a standard that no man
would be put to death unless there was no doubt of his guilt.[92] On paper, the
"no doubt" standard sounds higher than today's criminal standard of requiring proof beyond a reasonable doubt.[93] However, in the absence of meaningful
trials, or in some instances any trials at all, there is reason to be skeptical that
the "no doubt" standard was followed in actual practice. Indeed, trials involving the presentation of evidence, the cross-examination and impeachment of
witnesses, and the determination of witnesses' credibility, are typically required
for any triers of fact to determine whether a defined standard of guilt has been
established. The absence of such due process, even when measured by the norm
of the time, suggests that vigilantism in the region of Bannack and Alder Gulch
in 1963–64 and Helena from 1865 to 1870 was a development peculiar to their
places and times. The Virginia City vigilantes appear to have been confident of
their evidence, as they convicted and hanged most of the men they captured
between January 4 and October 31, 1864.[94] The Helena Committee of Safety
exuded similar confidence in its efforts during the latter half of the 1860s.

History also suggests that evidence sufficient to meet some credible standard of proof was not entirely lacking when the vigilance committees made
their arrests. In certain limited instances, persons captured by vigilance committees for investigation and trial were found not guilty or, if implicated in
wrongdoing, were not hanged. An example of this includes the circumstances

of Tex Crowell, who was arrested with road agent conspirator Bill Bunton but who was acquitted by the Vigilance Committee after a short trial on the basis of insufficient evidence against him.[95]

Another person who avoided a vigilante hanging, at least initially, was Jem Kelly, who was tried with James Brady for the shooting of a saloon keeper named Thomas Murphy.[96] Kelly was believed to be a member of the same criminal band as Jack Silvie, who had been hanged in Helena, and John "The Hat" Dolan, who had been hanged in Nevada City.[97] In any event, while Brady was convicted and hanged for having shot Murphy, Kelly was determined to have merely been an accessory after the fact and was sentenced to fifty lashes on his bare back, administered the same day as the sentence.[98] Kelly's hands were tied together and then fastened to an overhead beam of an unfinished building in Nevada City, and five men administered the lashes using a rawhide whip.[99] Kelly screamed with every lash of the whip and later told bystanders, "Boys, if I hadn't been so fat I would have died sure."[100] Kelly did not avoid the noose for long, as he was later arrested for horse thievery allegedly perpetrated at Portneuf Canyon in Idaho, outside of Montana Territory,[101] and was hanged on a balm of Gilead tree by vigilantes that had tracked him down on September 5, 1864.[102] Just as the vigilantes had no apparent concerns about kidnapping John "The Hat" Doyle outside of any procedures governing extraterritorial extraditions, they also had no concerns about arresting and executing Jem Kelly in Idaho, outside of Montana's defined territorial boundaries.

Yet another person who was spared the noose after his vigilante arrest was a man named Henry Brent. According to John X. Beidler's journal, there was circumstantial evidence that Brent was a road agent, though he steadfastly maintained his innocence throughout his interrogation and trial.[103] Brent was convicted by the vigilantes but was inexplicably banished from the territory instead of being hanged.[104] Later that night, John X. Beidler, John Stuart, James Arneaux, and J. J. Healy were riding home when they stumbled into a skirmish with local Native American Indians.[105] According to Beidler, Brent was in the area and was supposedly shot by Indians.[106] Brent said he was prepared to die, but not until the vigilante party that tended to him believed his claim of innocence.[107] When the vigilante party accepted Brent's claim of innocence, Brent drew his pistol and shot himself so that the others could escape the Indian skirmish unharmed.[108] Perhaps the account is true. But perhaps not, if hawkish members of the Vigilance Committee took issue with Brent's sentence of banishment and then took matters into their own hands with a convenient cover story of an Indian attack that happened to result in Brent's death. History will never know. Henry Brent, like Jem Kelly, avoided a death sentence at the conclusion of his trial, but neither lived long after being set free.

The historians most critical of the vigilantes' activities and defensive of Sheriff Plummer and others have been R. E. Mather and F. E. Boswell.[109] They argue that Yeager's confession, on which the vigilantes acted in arresting and executing the sheriff, was made under duress and that there is no evidence that Yeager spoke from any direct knowledge of the facts.[110] To the extent that Yeager's confession was later corroborated by "Dutch John" Wagner before his own execution, Mather and Boswell note that Wagner's confession was also made under duress and was never documented in any writing.[111] However, Mather and Boswell possess no actual evidence that the Yeager and Wagner confessions were fabricated, inaccurate, or unreliable and instead reach their conclusions on the basis of speculations rendered more than a century after the events. Mather and Boswell, upon minimizing the rate of crime at Alder Gulch in 1863–64,[112] attribute to the members of the Vigilance Committee a sinister profit motive behind their activities.[113] The supposed smoking-gun evidence of profit motive was the postexecution impoundment by the vigilantes of deceased prisoners' property to pay burial expenses and debts, which included somewhat well-to-do arrestees such as Sheriff Plummer and Cyrus Skinner.[114]

However, Mather and Boswell ignore that most of the persons executed were not particularly well-heeled. Mather and Boswell note that as sheriff, Henry Plummer received no set salary but rather mere "piece rate" payments of 25¢ for summoning witnesses and jurors, $1.00 for serving warrants, $2.50 for attending trials, and 25¢ per mile for travel expenses.[115] Plummer apparently did not spend much of his time as a gold prospector while in Montana. The revisionist theory that the Vigilance Committee was motivated by financial profit, rather than by frustration over the nature and rate of crime and the desire to protect lives and property, raises the question of how Plummer managed to obtain any wealth in the first place in the limited time span between his arrival in Bannack in the fall of 1862 and his execution on January 10, 1864. Far more likely, the vigilantes were bound together by a mixture "of courage, duty, and also a large dose of skepticism about the ability of frontier democracy to police itself"[116] at the time. The financial implications of vigilante executions arose in a stark way in the case of John "The Hat" Dolan. One of the provisions of the bylaws of the Vigilance Committee was the postexecution payment of both burial costs and debts owed to creditors of the persons executed. Dolan was sentenced to death for having stolen $700 from the trouser pocket of a miner who was his roommate.[117] Immediately prior to his execution, Dolan, who was in possession of gold nuggets worth $300, offered to pay that amount in restitution for his crime with a promise that he would repay the remaining $400 if he were freed.[118] Once again, last-minute negotiation by the condemned man proved fruitless as the vigilantes refused the offer.[119] After the execution, the

Vigilance Committee paid to the crime victim[120] the amount lost by the refusal of Dolan's offer.[121] It may be presumed that the $300 in gold nuggets that Dolan possessed at the time of his execution was among the assets that were used to reimburse the crime victim. If that was the case, Dolan had little to bargain with in exchange for his life, since the nuggets would have been paid to the robbery victim whether Dolan were to live or die. While the balance of the restitution to the crime victim was not necessarily paid by Dolan, the vigilantes' willingness to arrange for a payment of the $400 balance reflects an adherence to the letter, or at least spirit, of their organizational bylaws, at least on that occasion.

Having examined vigilante procedures for arresting and adjudicating suspected criminals, attention next turns to the sentences imposed upon those who were convicted.

Panning for Nuggets

The hanging of an elected sheriff, such as that of Henry Plummer, was newsworthy beyond Montana Territory. Reports of Sheriff Plummer's hanging appeared in newspapers in California, Colorado, Idaho, Oregon, and Utah. Prior to his death, Henry Plummer had written to his relatives that his life was in danger for having been a staunch supporter of the Union in the Civil War. Later Plummer's brother and sister learned of their sibling's death, and in 1869 they prepared to leave New York City to avenge their sibling's execution, which they attributed to his loyalty to the Union. Nathaniel Langford reports in his book that he and Edwin Reuthven Purple met with Plummer's brother and sister while they were in New York to persuade them not to travel to Montana, but to no avail. Langford and Purple therefore gave the brother and sister a copy of Thomas Dimsdale's book, The Vigilantes of Montana, *to help convince them "of the utter fruitlessness of their contemplated journey."[122] Plummer's brother and sister were grieved by the revelations contained in Dimsdale's book but were grateful to Langford and Purple for saving them an unnecessary trip to Montana Territory.[123]*

Notes

1. The trial of George Ives, conducted between December 19 and December 21, 1863, and the trial of George Hilderman, conducted on December 22, 1863, preceded the formation of the Vigilance Committee.
2. Greever, *Bonanza West*, 228.
3. Allen, *Decent Orderly Lynching*, 262.
4. Indeed, article 3, section 2, of the US Constitution guarantees defendants accused of crimes the right to a trial by jury. This provision existed in the Constitution in 1863–64 and applied to the territories.
5. Langford, *Vigilante Days*, 224–26; Dimsdale, *Vigilantes of Montana*, 126–29, 162–64; Allen, *Decent Orderly Lynching*, 228–29, 250. According to Allen, Plummer was told that

he would be hanged during the same minute of his arrest by the Vigilance Committee. Allen, *Decent Orderly Lynching*, 227..

6. Dimsdale, *Vigilantes of Montana*, 153. According to Dimsdale, the Skinner trial lasted approximately three hours.

7. Dimsdale, *Vigilantes of Montana*, 147–48 (as to Steve Marshland), 153–54 (as to Cyrus Skinner), 179–80 (as to James Brady), 186 (as to Jem Kelly on the occasion he was convicted and hanged), 187–88 (as to John "The Hat" Dolan), and 193–94 (as to R. C. Rawley).

8. Ibid., 153.

9. Ibid., 188; Donovan, *Hanging around the Big Sky*, book 2, 112; see also Callaway, *Montana's Righteous Hangmen*, 116.

10. Leeson, *History of Montana*, 301; Birney, *Vigilantes*, 340; Milner and O'Connor, *As Big as the West*, 97–98.

11. Dimsdale, *Vigilantes of Montana*, 179–80; Callaway, *Montana's Righteous Hangmen*, 114.

12. Former MCA 45-2-203 and its predecessor statutes, MCA 94-2-109 and 94-2-119(1); *Montana v. Egelhoff*, 518 U.S. at 51; *State v. Bingman*, 229 Mont. 101, 106 (1987); *State v. Ostwald*, 180 Mont. 530, 536 (1979); *State v. Lukus*, 149 Mont. 45, 55 (1967); *State v. Laughlin*, 105 Mont. 490 (1937); *State v. Reagin*, 64 Mont. 481 (1922).

13. Mont. Stat. Ann. 45-2-203 (1987); *Montana v. Egelhoff*, 518 U.S. 37, 56 (1996) (applying Montana state law); *State v. Smith*, 329 Mont. 526, 532–33 (2005), den. of postconviction relief aff'd., 337 Mont. 532 (2007); *State v. Strauss*, 317 Mont. 1, 15–16 (2003).

14. Dimsdale, *Vigilantes of Montana*, 180.

15. Ibid., 181.

16. Ibid.

17. Ibid.

18. Ibid.

19. Birney, *Vigilantes*, 340; Milner and O'Connor, *As Big as the West*, 97–98.

20. Smurr, "Some Afterthoughts on the Vigilantes."

21. "Execution at Nevada, M.T.," *Montana Post*, Sept. 24, 1864, p. 2, col. 2; Dimsdale, *Vigilantes of Montana*, 188; Allen, *Decent Orderly Lynching*, 302.

22. Dimsdale, *Vigilantes of Montana*, 193–94; see also Abrahams, *Vigilant Citizens*, 65.

23. Dimsdale, *Vigilantes of Montana*, 192; Leeson, *History of Montana*, 302; Birney, *Vigilantes*, 342; Allen, *Decent Orderly Lynching*, 305–6.

24. Allen, *Decent Orderly Lynching*, 306.

25. Dimsdale, *Vigilantes of Montana*, 193.

26. Bakken, *Invitation to an Execution*, 341.

27. Leeson, *History of Montana*, 301; Birney, *Vigilantes*, 342; Allen, *Decent Orderly Lynching*, 307.

28. Birney, *Vigilantes*, 342; Allen, *Decent Orderly Lynching*, 307 (referring to Rawley's body found hanging the early morning of October 31, 1864); Donovan, *Hanging around the Big Sky*, book 2, 116.

29. Dimsdale, *Vigilantes of Montana*, 53; Langford, *Vigilante Days*, 174; Allen, *Decent Orderly Lynching*, 162; Birney, *Vigilantes*, 177–78; Johnson, *Bloody Bozeman*, 91.

30. Dimsdale, *Vigilantes of Montana*, 147.

31. Ibid., 148.

32. Ibid.; Birney, *Vigilantes*, 300.

33. Donovan, *Hanging around the Big Sky*, book 2, 157–59.

34. "The Spaulding-Wilson Affair," *Virginia Weekly Post*, Feb. 1, 1868, p. 2, col. 2.

35. Donovan, *Hanging around the Big Sky*, book 2, 38–40; "The Execution at Beartown," *Montana Post*, Aug. 21, 1868, p. 1, col. 6.

36. Donovan, *Hanging around the Big Sky*, book 2, 35–36.

37. Ibid., 36.

38. Mont. Code Ann. 46-11-404(4) (1991).

39. Mont. Code Ann. 46-13-210 (1993).

40. *State v. Dess*, 207 Mont. 468, 474 (1984).

41. *Bruton v. United States*, 391 U.S. 123 (1968); *State v. Fitzpatrick*, 174 Mont. 174 (1977) (criticized on other grounds).

42. Today Montana law is more stringent. A defendant may not be convicted of a crime solely on the strength of an admission of fact or a confession to committing the crime. *State v. Campbell*, 278 Mont. 236, 244 (1996); *State v. Taufer*, 109 Mont. 275 (1939). Before an extrajudicial confession may be admitted into evidence, the prosecution must introduce evidence tending to independently establish the commission of the crime charged. Mont. Code Ann. 46-16-215 (1999); *State v. McGarvey*, 329 Mont. 439, 445–46 (2005), cert. denied, 547 U.S. 1083 (2006); *State v. Martinosky*, 294 Mont. 426, 431 (1999); *State v. Hayworth*, 289 Mont. 433, 446–47 (1998); *State v. Campbell*, 278 Mont. at 244–45; *State v. Gould*, 216 Mont. 455, 471 (1985); *State v. Ratkovich*, 111 Mont. 19, 25 (1940); *State v. Taufer*, 109 Mont. 275. The independent evidence need not necessarily establish that the crime was committed by the defendant. *State v. Campbell*, 278 Mont. 245 (1996).

43. Dimsdale, *Vigilantes of Montana*, 114–15.

44. Allen, *Decent Orderly Lynching*, 245 (confessing to participation in the recent crime wave and, in particular, the stagecoach robbery of "Bummer Dan" McFadden); Langford, *Vigilante Days*, 234; Gard, *Frontier Justice*, 180.

45. Langford, *Vigilante Days*, 236; Allen, *Decent Orderly Lynching*, 245 (confessing to the murder of two men in Missouri and California, but denying participation in the road agent gang); Gard, *Frontier Justice*, 181.

46. Dimsdale, *Vigilantes of Montana*, 141; Langford, *Vigilante Days*, 237; Allen, *Decent Orderly Lynching*, 245–46 (confessing to the earlier murder of D. H. Dillingham); Gard, *Frontier Justice*, 181.

47. Allen, *Decent Orderly Lynching*, 244; Gard, *Frontier Justice*, 180–81.

48. Dimsdale, *Vigilantes of Montana*, 154. According to Dimsdale, Carter did not confess to the murder of Nicholas Tiebolt, but did admit to being an accessory before and after the fact to the theft of the mules that had been in Tiebolt's charge at the time of his murder.

49. Ibid., 212–13; Donovan, *Hanging around the Big Sky*, book 2, 138.

50. Dimsdale, *Vigilantes of Montana*, 134–35; Thompson, *Tenderfoot in Montana*, 184; Birney, *Vigilantes*, 261.

51. "Execution at Nevada, M.T.," *Montana Post*, Sept. 24, 1864, p. 2, col. 2; Dimsdale, *Vigilantes of Montana*, 186; Allen, *Decent Orderly Lynching*, 302; Callaway, *Montana's Righteous Hangmen*, 116.

52. Dimsdale, *Vigilantes of Montana*, 125.

53. Ibid., 210.

54. Ibid., 212–13.

55. See, e.g., *North Carolina v. Butler*, 441 U.S. 369, 374–75 (1979); *Brewer v. Williams*, 430 U.S. 387, 404 (1977); *State v. Main*, 360 Mont. 470, 477–78 (2011); *State v. Blakney*, 197 Mont. 131, 138 (1982).

56. See, e.g., *Harrison v. United States*, 392 U.S. 219, 222 (1968); *State v. Olson*, 311 Mont. 270, 279 (2002). An exception to the suppression of evidence obtained as fruit of the poisonous tree exists when the prosecution can demonstrate to the satisfaction of the court that the same evidence would have been independently or inevitably discovered. *State v. Lacey*, 349 Mont. 371, 388 (2009); *State v. Therriault*, 302 Mont. 189, 206 (2000).

57. Leeson, *History of Montana*, 297.

58. Dimsdale, *Vigilantes of Montana*, 141; Langford, *Vigilante Days*, 237; Allen, *Decent Orderly Lynching*, 245–46; Gard, *Frontier Justice*, 181.

59. US Const., Fifth Amend.

60. Callaway, *Montana's Righteous Hangmen*, 119.
61. Mont. Stat. Ann. 26-1-804 (2009).
62. *State v. MacKinnon*, 288 Mont. 329 (1998).
63. Bergman, Hollander, and Duncan, *Wharton's Criminal Evidence*, sec. 39:28.
64. Laws 1867, Fourth Terr. Legis., pp. 210–11, secs. 373–77 (1867).
65. Leeson, *History of Montana*, 301; Allen, *Decent Orderly Lynching*, 301; Birney, *Vigilantes*, 342.
66. Allen, *Decent Orderly Lynching*, 301; Leeson, *History of Montana*, 301.
67. "In Transit," *Montana Post*, Sept. 17, 1864, p. 3, col. 3; Allen, *Decent Orderly Lynching*, 301.
68. Allen, *Decent Orderly Lynching*, 301; Leeson, *History of Montana*, 301; Birney, *Vigilantes*, 342; Milner and O'Connor, *As Big as the West*, 98; Olsen, "Lawlessness and Vigilantes," 171.
69. Birney, *Vigilantes*, 342; Allen, *Decent Orderly Lynching*, 302; Donovan, *Hanging around the Big Sky*, book 2, 315.
70. L. A. Fenner, "Remembrances of Pioneer Days," Laurence Abraham Fenner Reminiscences, 1898, Mont. Hist. Soc. SC-686, box 1-1; Donovan, *Hanging around the Big Sky*, book 2, 114; Olsen, "Lawlessness and Vigilantes," 171.
71. Langford, *Vigilante Days*, 331.
72. Ibid.
73. Ibid.
74. Ibid., 332.
75. Ibid.
76. Ibid.
77. Ibid.
78. Ibid.
79. Ibid.
80. Ibid.
81. Ibid.
82. Ibid.
83. Ibid. Colorado had become a separate territory by an act of Congress on February 28, 1861.
84. Ibid.
85. Ibid.
86. "Arrest of a Suspicious Character," *Montana Post*, Jan. 27, 1866, p. 3, col. 1 (relying on a news account published by the *Salt Lake City Telegraph*); Langford, *Vigilante Days*, 332; Allen, *Decent Orderly Lynching*, 338.
87. Langford, *Vigilante Days*, 332.
88. Allen, *Decent Orderly Lynching*, 338.
89. Ibid.
90. "Arrest of a Suspicious Character," *Montana Post*, Jan. 27, 1866, p. 3, col. 1 (relying on a news account published by the *Salt Lake City Telegraph*); Allen, *Decent Orderly Lynching*, 338.
91. Allen, *Decent Orderly Lynching*, 338.
92. Callaway, *Montana's Righteous Hangmen*, 111.
93. *In Re* Winship, 397 U.S. 358, 364 (1970); *Adams v. State*, 336 Mont. 63, 77 (2007); *State v. Clark*, 290 Mont. 479 (1998); *State v. Lucero*, 214 Mont. 334, 342 (1984); *State v. Korell*, 213 Mont. 316, 330 (1984).
94. Dimsdale, *Vigilantes of Montana*, 116, 117, 128, 129, 135, 136, 144, 145, 155, 158, 165, 176, 186, 194.
95. Ibid. 150; Allen, *Decent Orderly Lynching*, 262; Leeson, *History of Montana*, 298.
96. Dimsdale, *Vigilantes of Montana*, 179–80; Allen, *Decent Orderly Lynching*, 294.
97. Leeson, *History of Montana*, 302.

98. Dimsdale, *Vigilantes of Montana*, 180; Leeson, *History of Montana*, 301; Allen, *Decent Orderly Lynching*, 294; Birney, *Vigilantes*, 340–41.

99. Donovan, *Hanging around the Big Sky*, book 2, 113.

100. Leeson, *History of Montana*, 301; Birney, *Vigilantes*, 341.

101. Allen, *Decent Orderly Lynching*, 298; Callaway, *Montana's Righteous Hangmen*, 115; Milner and O'Connor, *As Big as the West*, 98. The extraterritorial nature of Kelly's trial and sentence may have been of little or no concern to the Vigilance Committee, and the vigilantes admittedly took law into their own hands. Allen, *Decent Orderly Lynching*, 298–99.

102. Dimsdale, *Vigilantes of Montana*, 186; Birney, *Vigilantes*, 341; Allen, *Decent Orderly Lynching*, 298; Callaway, *Montana's Righteous Hangmen*, 115–16.

103. Sanders and Bertsche, *X. Beidler*, 95.

104. Ibid.

105. Ibid.

106. Ibid.

107. Ibid.

108. Ibid.

109. E.g., Mather and Boswell, *Vigilante Victims*; see also Mather and Boswell, *Hanging the Sheriff*.

110. Mather and Boswell, *Hanging the Sheriff*, 110.

111. Ibid., 114.

112. Ibid., 100; see also Abrahams, *Vigilant Citizens*, 71.

113. Mather and Boswell, *Hanging the Sheriff*, 97; see also Abrahams, *Vigilant Citizens*, 69–70.

114. Mather and Boswell, *Hanging the Sheriff*, 97–98.

115. Ibid., 36.

116. Allen, *Decent Orderly Lynching*, 184.

117. Dimsdale, *Vigilantes of Montana*, 187; Allen, *Decent Orderly Lynching*, 301; Callaway, *Montana's Righteous Hangmen*, 116.

118. "Execution at Nevada, M.T.," *Montana Post*, Sept. 24, 1864, p. 2, col. 2; Dimsdale, *Vigilantes of Montana*, 188; Allen, *Decent Orderly Lynching*, 301; Callaway, *Montana's Righteous Hangmen*, 116.

119. "Execution at Nevada, M.T.," *Montana Post*, Sept. 24, 1864, p. 2, col. 2; Dimsdale, *Vigilantes of Montana*, 188; Allen, *Decent Orderly Lynching*, 301; Callaway, *Montana's Righteous Hangmen*, 116.

120. The crime victim is identified as James Brady by Dimsdale and Callaway (see Dimsdale, *Vigilantes of Montana*, 187; Callaway, *Montana's Righteous Hangmen*, 116), but as James Redmond Allen (Allen, *Decent Orderly Lynching*, 301).

121. Dimsdale, *Vigilantes of Montana*, 188. Dimsdale's narrative does not make clear whether money paid was the $300 that Dolan could have paid immediately, or $700 that Dolan offered to eventually pay in full.

122. Langford, *Vigilante Days*, 227.

123. Ibid.

15

Due Process and Procedure
Vigilante Sentences

For God's sake, let me see my dear beloved wife!

—J. A. Slade, March 10, 1864

The regulations and bylaws of the Vigilance Committee specifically provided that "[t]he only punishment that shall be inflicted by this Committee is death."[1] Thus, Jem Kelly's first sentence of fifty lashes and Henry Brent's banishment notwithstanding, the bylaws of the Vigilance Committee left no room for due process once a prisoner had been determined to be guilty of a crime against life or property. The imposition of a death penalty by hanging was the almost certain outcome when arrestees were determined to be guilty of the crimes of which they were accused. Executions on the western frontier were commonplace not only for persons who committed murder, but also for persons who committed attempted murder and theft.[2] An 1851 statute in California conferred upon jurors sentencing options for nonlethal robbery and grand larceny that included the imposition of death, subject to its review by a judge.[3]

The Eighth Amendment to the US Constitution prohibits cruel and unusual punishment.[4] The US Supreme Court has never invalidated on Eighth Amendment grounds any state's chosen *method* for carrying out a sentence of death.[5] Although the Supreme Court has expressly found capital punishment constitutional by means of firing squad,[6] electrocution,[7] and lethal injection,[8] it has merely denied *certiorari* to challenges of capital punishment by means of hanging[9] and lethal gas.[10] *Certiorari* is the procedure by which the US Supreme Court may accept or reject an application to hear a proposed appeal.[11] Today the death penalty is a permitted form of punishment in thirty-four states and

DOI: 10.7330_9780874219203.c015

is not permitted in the remainder.[12] The death penalty is permitted by federal law under more than three dozen criminal statutes regarding specified capital offenses.[13] It is also permitted by the US military for certain designated offenses under the Uniform Code of Military Justice.[14] Death by hanging is still a recognized form of judicial execution in the states of Washington,[15] New Hampshire (if lethal injection is impractical in a given case),[16] and Delaware (as an alternative means of execution if lethal injection is ever held there to be unconstitutional).[17] The last execution in Montana by means of a legal hanging was that of Philip J. Coleman Jr. on September 10, 1943, as punishment for Coleman's commission of murder.[18] Montana ceased using hanging as form of judicial execution in 1997, when lethal injection became the sole permitted means of execution within the state.[19]

A complete discussion of the Montana vigilantes requires an examination of the death penalty they imposed by means of hanging. The Bannack Statutes required hanging as the sole means of performing legal executions in Montana Territory.[20] Hanging was a standard method of execution used in the United States in the 1860s and continued to be the standard until the 1890s when death by electrocution gained more favor.[21] Indeed, the persons convicted of being involved in the conspiracy to assassinate President Abraham Lincoln were executed by hanging in the yard of the Old Penitentiary at the Washington Arsenal in Washington, DC, on July 7, 1865.[22] Death by hanging was by no means a penalty confined at the time to the western territorial frontier.

The method of judicial hanging as a means of execution is sometimes referred to as the "long drop."[23] Executioners are to calculate the length of the drop based on the subject's weight, height, and build.[24] The prisoner's hands are pinioned, usually in the back, using handcuffs, rope, or a strap.[25] The goal is for the subject's body to accelerate downward in order to produce between 1,000 and 1,250 foot-pounds of torque on the neck when the noose jerks tight along the slip knots.[26] A rope with a thickness of between ¾ inch and 1¼ inches is less likely to break upon the drop than a thinner rope.[27] A rope that is treated to reduce surface friction better tightens around the neck than one that is not.[28] When the slip knots of the noose are positioned on the left side of the neck, under the jaw, the jolt at the end of the drop breaks the axis bone at the neck, which then severs the spinal cord.[29] The result is that the prisoner loses consciousness almost immediately.[30] Death results in the minutes that follow from the lack of blood and oxygen to the brain.[31]

A key element to an execution by hanging is the length of the prisoner's drop. If the drop distance is too long, the subject may be decapitated.[32] If the drop distance is too short, there is not enough force of gravity to break the subject's neck, and, as a result, the subject will suffer a slow, excruciating, and ultimately fatal strangulation.[33] No decapitations are known to have occurred during the Montana executions in the latter 1800s, but one did occur during the judicial hanging of "Black Jack" Tom Ketchum in New Mexico on April 1, 1901.[34] Vigilante and judicial hangings in Montana included drop distances that were apparently too short, where the accused strangled to death while on the noose, as with the executions of Buck Stinson and Ned Ray on January 10, 1864, John Keene on June 9, 1865, Leander Johnson on March 12, 1866, and Joseph Wilson on April 27, 1870.

In 1892 the British Home Office developed "drop tables" to be used for precisely calculating the proper distances based upon the prisoner's weight; the tables were refined in 1913.[35] *Procedures for Military Executions*, published by the Department of the Army in December 1947, used similar grim computations as those developed by the British; they remained in effect until January 17, 2006, when lethal injection replaced hanging as the designated means of military executions.[36] The drop table adopted by the US military and related procedures are reproduced in Appendix E. The drop tables reveal that the lighter a person, the longer the drop needs to be. Conversely, the heavier a person, the shorter the drop should be. For full-grown men between 120 and 220 pounds, a drop is to be between a maximum of 8 feet 1 inch and a minimum of 5 feet, respectively (Appendix E).

According to the drop tables, a typical grown man weighing 170 pounds should have a drop distance of six feet. However, the sophisticated mathematical computations set forth by the British in 1892 and by the US military in 1947 were not known or necessarily employed in Montana in the 1860s, as hangings instead typically used a "standard" drop distance of four to six feet.[37] According to Langford, the drop used during the collective executions of George "Clubfoot" Lane, Frank Parish, Hayes Lyons, Jack Gallagher, and Boone Helm on January 14, 1864, was only three feet, significantly less than the distance called for by the later drop tables,[38] but apparently sufficient in each of those instances to accomplish the results intended.[39] Dimsdale's description of the hanging of Sheriff Plummer was that Plummer's frame was hoisted into the air by his executioners and then dropped manually. There is no historical record that Plummer's executioners were themselves elevated above the gallows platform to gain additional drop height. Plummer's drop may therefore have been of limited distance, though sufficient. Buck Stinson was hanged just before Plummer upon the same gallows, and, according to Dimsdale, "he was some minutes dying" because of a slipped knot on the noose.[40] One may surmise whether insufficient drop height might have been the real reason for Stinson's slow strangulation, if his frame was lifted by his executioners similar to the execution of Plummer, and whether Dimsdale chose not to reveal the failure of the vigilantes to perform the hanging properly.

In describing the executions of various road agent conspirators, Dimsdale sometimes specifically mentions the pinioning of the hands behind the prisoner's back, as in the executions of "Red" Yeager and George Brown,[41] George "Clubfoot" Lane,[42] John "The Hat" Dolan,[43] and Jem Kelly.[44] Mollie Sheehan recalled that when she observed the hanging of Joseph A. Slade, which is discussed in greater detail later in this chapter, she observed that Slade's arms were pinioned as he was marched to the site of his execution.[45]

The historical record suggests that other than the use of standard rope, there was no uniformity in the actual devices that were used in the performance of the executions, as vigilante executions occurred in several different locales in the area of Bannack and Alder Gulch. The same was true for some of the hangings that later occurred near Helena. The vigilantes therefore improvised with whatever materials were available for each execution, as reflected by the varied means and methods that were employed for the hangings performed during the period. "Red" Yeager and George Brown were each hanged from a tree limb, after standing on stools, at a ranch in the Stinking Water Valley.[46] Sheriff Plummer, Deputy Sheriff Buck Stinson, and Ned Ray were hanged from gallows,[47] which, ironically, had been constructed earlier by Henry Plummer after his election as sheriff of Bannack.[48] R. C. Rawley was also hanged from the same gallows on a later date.[49] The gallows at Bannack apparently were not constructed with any trap door for the drop, as the accounts of Plummer's hanging describe that his frame was lifted in his executioners' arms as high as possible, and his body was then suddenly and unceremoniously dropped.[50] "Dutch John" Wagner was hanged from a crossbeam of a building in Bannack, having been elevated for his drop by a barrel.[51] George "Clubfoot" Lane, Frank Parish, Hayes Lyons, Deputy Jack Gallagher, and Boone Helm were hanged together from a beam of a building in Virginia City, having been elevated upon dry goods boxes.[52] Steve Marshland was hanged from a pole at Big Hole Valley, his body elevated moments before the execution by a box.[53] Bill Bunton was hanged from a horizontal crossbeam connecting the vertical posts of a corral gate of a ranch, after standing on a board placed between two boxes.[54] George Shears was hanged from the crossbeam of a barn in Frenchtown after climbing a ladder for height.[55] Cyrus Skinner, Alex Carter, Johnny Cooper, and Robert Zachary were hanged from two poles that leaned over a corral fence at Hell Gate, and each of the prisoners was provided a store box for drop height.[56] Bill Hunter was hanged from a limb of a cottonwood tree[57] near Emery's Cabin in the Gallatin Valley, using the "hoisting" method.[58] "Whiskey Bill" Graves was also hanged from a tree limb, but a horse was used to elevate him above the ground and to produce his drop when the horse was caused to gallop forward.[59] James Brady was executed on gallows at Nevada City, with a plank and a box used as a drop.[60] Jem Kelly was hanged from a balm of Gilead tree, standing on a wagon plank that had been wedged through a notch of the tree until it was suddenly withdrawn from beneath his feet.[61] John "The Hat" Dolan's drop was also brought about when a plank was withdrawn from under his feet.[62]

In Helena John Keene was hanged from the infamous Hanging Tree and stood upon the endgate of a wagon that was withdrawn from under his feet.[63] The other hangings in Helena were from the same Hanging Tree. Outside of Helena, Jack Silvie was hanged from a tree via the "hoisting" method, as he was too despised by his executioners to be given the benefit of a drop.[64] George Ballou was hanged from the beam of a building, using boxes to create a drop.[65] William Hinson and Billy Williams were separately hanged from gallows made of tripod poles.[66] Williams's alleged partner in crime, Spaulding, was hanged from a butcher's hoist.[67]

The improvised nature of the executions, using whatever devices and materials were available at the moment, might have caused some of the prisoners concern that their deaths would not be quick and painless. Dimsdale and Langford recount that some of the condemned men chose to jump off their elevated platforms to assure a more powerful drop. Those conspirators included George "Clubfoot" Lane,[68] George Shears,[69] and Bill Bunton,[70] as well as James Brady[71] after having been convicted of a crime unrelated to the road agent conspiracy. Whether any of the individuals who jumped from a height actually saved themselves from a slow strangulation is a matter of pure speculation.

The hangings carried out by the vigilance committees were not always flawless in their performance. Dimsdale states that the noose knot slipped under the chin of Buck Stinson, if that explanation is accepted, as a result of which "he was some minutes dying."[72] Ned Ray may have placed his fingers between his neck and the noose at the last moment, which prevented his neck from breaking and which caused him to slowly strangle for several minutes before expiring.[73] In Helena John Keene, though not hanged by vigilantes per se, had a three and a half foot "swinging drop" off of the back of a wagon, and it took twenty-three minutes for him to die.[74] The body of Leander Johnson exhibited signs that he had suffered a slow strangulation at the end of his noose.[75] Similarly, when Joseph Wilson was hanged at Helena's Hanging Tree, the noose knots turned to the back of the neck and Wilson died by slow strangulation.[76] When hangings were "botched" in such fashion, there was apparently never any effort made to remove the prisoner from the end of the rope and redo the execution more properly. Any argument that death by hanging is cruel and unusual is more easily made regarding those instances when the hangings were botched and where defendants were caused to strangle over several minutes at the end of their ropes.

"Greaser Joe" Pizanthia's death occurred in a more unusual way. As previously noted, Pizanthia fought his capture on January 11, 1864. While fighting, he wounded one member of the vigilante posse, Smith Ball, and killed another member, George Copley. The vigilantes responded by not only capturing Pizanthia but also shooting him several times in the back while he lay on the ground. They then hung his body by a clothesline on a pole, shot rounds into Pizanthia's corpse while raised, and burned his body to ashes.[77] There was no trial. There was no deliberation. There was no consideration of any sentence. In all likelihood, Pizanthia's fate was sealed before the vigilante posse even arrived at his cabin to apprehend him, with only the exact manner of his death to be determined. While it is understandable that passions were raised by the unfortunate shootings of Ball and Copley during the effort to capture Pizanthia, the punishment administered to him was entirely without due process and resembled mob violence more than the staid and perfunctory procedures followed by the vigilantes during the majority of their other arrests and executions.

The circumstances of the apprehension and execution of Joe Pizanthia, however disturbing, were exceeded by the arrest and execution of J. A. Slade. The moral authority claimed by the Vigilance Committee, if any, was derived from its desire to rid the region of violent criminals who were terrorizing the community, particularly its travelers. Indeed, the oath of the Vigilance Committee signed by its members on December 23, 1863, defined the committee's purpose as "arresting thievs [*sic*] & murderers & recovering stollen [*sic*] property."[78] Any arrests and executions of persons other than thieves, murderers, or possessors of stolen property, undermined the de facto authority of the organization as a whole. This appears to have occurred in the case of J. A. Slade.

"Captain" Slade was never accused, nor even suspected, of having committed any robberies or "unauthorized" murders in the immediate region.[79] In fact, Slade was a supporter of the vigilantes,[80] having housed a vigilante posse at his cabin during the search for road agent Bill Hunter.[81] By many accounts, when Slade was sober, he was a most personable, hospitable, and respectful individual.[82] Mark Twain once met Slade and described him as "so friendly and so gentle spoken that I warmed to him in spite of his awful history."[83]

In the early 1860s Slade worked as a freighter superintendent for the Overland Stage Company and earned a reputation for protecting his cargo at all costs, even if it meant killing outlaws along the way.[84] Jules Reni had been Overland's freighter superintendent before Slade.[85] While in the job, Reni allegedly conspired with his Indian wife and her tribe to steal Overland's horses, for which Overland paid a reward for their return.[86] Reni allegedly split the reward money with the thieves until the plot was uncovered by Slade, whom Overland rewarded with Reni's job.[87] As a result, Slade and Reni became mutual, sworn

Figure 15.1. Homestead of J. A. and Maria Slade. (Courtesy of the Montana Historical Society, image 951-092.)

enemies. Reni responded by preying upon freighters as an outlaw. Slade got the best of the mutual enmity by eventually capturing Reni, shooting him to death, and cutting off Reni's ears, which he then continuously kept in his pocket as souvenirs.[88] With time, the ears became leathery and were often displayed by Slade to friends and acquaintances as a conversation piece. Alexander Toponce knew Slade personally, and in his autobiography Toponce described the manner in which Reni was killed. According to Toponce, Slade tied Reni to a corral gate, drank alcohol, and occasionally fired a bullet at Reni, shooting him in an arm, and then in a leg, and then in another part of the body until eventually one of the many gunshot wounds to Reni proved fatal.[89]

Slade and his wife, Maria, established a ranch that they called Ravenswood on the banks of the Madison River.[90] Slade also built a passable trail that provided travelers with access through the Tobacco Root Mountains, for which he charged a toll.[91] He was a particular friend and drinking buddy of William Fairweather, who had made the initial discovery of gold at Alder Gulch.[92]

According to author Lew L. Callaway Jr., Slade engaged in extraordinary acts of generosity. One example involved the shooting death of Dr. Bartholomew, who was married and had two small children. Bartholomew was killed during a dispute with Charley Bacon and Harry Smith over the amount of a bill for the construction of a chimney.[93] Slade and a friend, moved by the Bartholomew family's loss, caught Bacon and Smith and hanged them in retribution for their crime.[94] Slade paid Mrs. Bartholomew the money that was taken from Bacon and Smith at the time of their deaths, and took the Bartholomew family into his home for a month until arrangements could be made for the family to move to Omaha to live with Mrs. Bartholomew's parents.[95] There was another instance of uncommon charity involving J. A. Slade. Two of Slade's freight drivers killed a saloon keeper named Jules Savoie and his squaw and burned down their home; in the process, a young daughter who had fled the event then froze to death while in hiding.[96] The Slades took in Savoie's son Jemmy, who had survived the melee, and raised him as their own.[97]

Slade was not a model citizen, however, as he had committed several frontier murders earlier in his life, though not necessarily in Montana, and was a fugitive from justice in Illinois.[98] When taken to drink, which occurred frequently, Slade was a dangerous hellion known to ride up and down Virginia City's main street on a horse yelling, shooting his pistol, entering stores and saloons breaking glass, and committing other acts of property destruction.[99] Shopkeepers learned to lock up their stores when Slade was known to be in town.[100] During one drunken rampage, he entered a Virginia City theater and insulted the actresses and members of the audience, ruining the show.[101] On another occasion, he dumped a pail of milk onto a milkman and threatened several men with his gun.[102] On another occasion, in the Dorris store, he pulled a gun on a man who had requested he leave the premises.[103] His reckless, drunken excursions through Virginia City and other settlements were well known and feared. People grew tired of his behavior, even with his later apologies and offers to pay for the damages he caused.[104] Despite warnings that he cease his dangerous and antisocial conduct, it persisted.[105] On March 10, 1864, Slade and his friend, William Fairweather, while intoxicated, were brought to Judge Alexander Davis's People's Court for arraignment on charges arising from their drunken mischief the night before.[106] In open court Slade tore up the warrant that had been issued by Judge Davis for his arrest and left on horseback.[107]

Wilbur Fisk Sanders saw Slade in Virginia City and implored him to go home, but Slade refused.[108] James Williams, who had earned his stripes with the vigilantes, asked Alexander Toponce to find Slade and tell him to leave Virginia City.[109] Dutifully, Toponce found Slade in the process of shooting up one of the local saloons.[110] Slade refused to comply, and when Toponce reported back to Williams that he was unsuccessful in convincing Slade to leave town, Williams asked John X. Beidler to retrieve Slade.[111]

A little later in the day, while still drunk, Slade found Judge Davis at Pfouts and Russell's store and took him hostage at gunpoint using a cocked derringer.[112] Davis remained calm and stoic throughout the unfortunate episode.[113] A bystander, Bill Hunt, came into the store and, seeing what was transpiring between Slade and Davis, drew two revolvers in both hands, aimed them at Slade's head, and told Slade to drop his gun or be killed.[114] In his diary, John X. Beidler claimed that the standoff lasted for a while.[115] Dimsdale and Langford suggest that the standoff ended rather quickly. Davis recognized that Slade was in danger of being arrested

Figure 15.2. William Fairweather, who first discovered gold at Virginia
City and who later became a good friend and drinking partner of J. A.
Slade. (Courtesy of the Montana Historical Society, image 942-132.)

and hanged and urged Slade to flee Virginia City.[116] Slade left the store but continued to refuse suggestions that he leave Virginia City altogether.[117]

Word of the day's antics spread and apparently angered many people who
had already lost patience with Slade. Six hundred miners marched into town
demanding that Slade be punished by death.[118] When Slade realized that he was
in jeopardy, he returned to Judge Davis and asked for his help.[119] Accounts differ
as to what happened next. According to Alexander Toponce, Slade was seized by
John X. Beidler and brought to Williams.[120] According to other accounts, Slade
was seized by a mob and dragged down Jackson Street.[121] Over the objection of
Judge Davis and others who attempted to intercede on Slade's behalf, the vigilante Executive Committee voted to execute Slade as a means of maintaining
the social order.[122] According to historian Dorothy M. Johnson, the Executive

Committee was initially reluctant to impose a sentence of death but decided to do so if the miners agreed unanimously upon that punishment, which they did.[123]

The die was cast. Alexander Toponce claims to have been an intimate witness to these events. Slade was brought to Captain Williams, who said, "You will find a pen, ink and paper on that table, Mr. Slade, if you wish to write anything."[124] Slade responded, "I don't understand. Why should I write anything?"[125] Williams answered, "Because you will be hung in just thirty minutes."[126]

Slade finally grasped the full gravity of the situation. He sobered quickly and begged for his life.[127] He apologized to Judge Davis for his conduct and also appealed to him specifically.[128] The appeal to the judge made sense, as he was the person with the right to feel most aggrieved by the day's episodes, and a call for leniency from him might have gone a long way to diffuse the passions of the crowd. Indeed, Davis asked Captain Williams, who was a leader of the crowd, to merely banish Slade from the territory.[129] Captain Williams was unmoved and described the decision to execute Slade as final.[130] Davis then asked for permission to address the crowd to make a further appeal on Slade's behalf, and stories differ as to whether he then did so. Williams warned Davis that while he had a right to address the crowd if he wished, he might place himself into physical jeopardy by doing so.[131] According to Nathaniel Langford, Davis addressed the crowd on Slade's behalf anyway in a last-ditch effort to save his life, but his pleas fell upon deaf ears.[132] According to author Hoffman Birney, Davis did not address the crowd, telling Slade, "All that I could do would be to repeat your own words, Slade. I have no influence."[133]

Slade also appealed to Paris Pfouts.[134] The appeal to Pfouts made sense as well, as Pfouts was the elected president of the Vigilance Committee. Slade could not have begged for his life from any higher member of the Vigilance Committee. The approach to Pfouts suggests that while membership in the Vigilance Committee was a secret, it might have been an open secret. Moreover, Slade had been a supporter of the Vigilance Committee, and through those personal contacts he might have been keenly aware of the identities of the vigilante leadership. Nevertheless, all further efforts at persuasion with vigilante leaders proved to be fruitless.[135] As with other vigilante executions, such as the execution of Sheriff Plummer, the sentence of death, once decided upon, was simply not negotiable.

As Slade was led to the site of his execution in the corral behind the Pfouts and Russell store,[136] a friend, Naylor Thompson, declared to the crowd that Slade could not be hanged unless he was himself killed first.[137] Thompson backed off when guns were raised and pointed at him.[138]

When informed of the developments, Slade's wife, Maria, left her home immediately on horseback and without waiting for a saddle.[139] Slade implored

Figure 15.3. Alexander Davis, the judge of the short-
lived People's Court. (Courtesy of the Montana
Historical Society, image 941-900.)

the crowd that he be permitted to see his wife before his execution, "For God's
sake, let me see my dear beloved wife!"[140] Certain members of the crowd,
including Albert M. Hart, chanted that Slade be allowed to see his wife before
being hanged, but, in Hart's words, "the mob turned their guns upon us and
commanded us to shut up."[141] Young Mollie Sheehan, whose school day had
just ended, was in the crowd and heard Slade plead to see his wife.[142] Sheehan
recalled that preparations for the hanging had been deliberately hastened to
complete the task before the expected imminent arrival of Maria Slade.[143]

J. A. Slade was placed upon a dry goods box and hanged from a crossbeam
of a gated corral behind a store at Virginia City.[144] His execution was arranged
for and conducted with dispatch, as it was feared that the arrival of Maria Slade,
crying and pleading for her husband's life, would change the sentiment of the
crowd and prompt a public demand for a rescission of the death sentence.[145]

Maria Slade arrived at the site of the execution only minutes too late to affect the outcome.[146] She fainted from her horse when told of the news of her husband's death.[147] The twelve-mile ride of Maria Slade on her black horse, named Billy Bay, with her long black hair flowing in the wind, screaming to save the life of her husband, became legendary.[148]

Maria Slade was inconsolable. She said, "He should never have died by the rope of a hangman. No dog's death should have come to such a man."[149] Maria Slade made such a ruckus that James Williams threatened her with the same fate as her husband if she did not quiet down.[150] It would be hours before she would be sufficiently composed to give directions regarding the disposition of the body.[151] During that time, Mollie Sheehan slipped away from her home to find Maria Slade sobbing and moaning, and told her how sorry she felt for her.[152]

If Slade always carried Jules Reni's leathery severed ears in his pocket, as is believed, then the ears were likely on Slade's person at the time he was hanged.

Dimsdale, a consistent supporter of the vigilantes, rationalized Slade's execution as having "had a most wonderful effect upon society . . . , that no one man could domineer or rule over the community."[153] Langford was also unsympathetic to Slade, writing that he had become "so reckless and regardless of human life that . . . he was at times a most dangerous character, and [that] by his defiance of the authority and wholesome discipline of the Vigilantes, brought upon himself the calamity which he suffered."[154] Langford's approval of Slade's execution is difficult to reconcile with his criticism of the vigilante execution of James Daniels, as Daniels's manslaughter conviction in a court of law would appear to justify a greater punishment than the misbehaviors of Slade. Aside from Dimsdale and Langford, opinion on Slade's execution by the residents of Virginia City was mixed.[155] Mollie Sheehan reminisced that she and her family, and many other "good citizens," disapproved of the execution. She wrote that although Slade was a braggart and a brawler who went on many rowdy sprees, he had committed no serious crimes in Montana worthy of death.[156] It has been said that Slade was the only man ever hanged by the vigilantes for having committed a mere misdemeanor.[157]

The group executions of George "Clubfoot" Lane, Frank Parish, Hayes Lyons, Jack Gallagher, and Boone Helm on January 14, 1864, had prompted earlier discussions among members of the Vigilance Committee as to whether a more open form of criminal justice should be implemented involving attorneys, juries, rules of procedure, and public scrutiny.[158] The arguments in favor of an open form of criminal justice were made to them by attorneys in the region such as H. P. A. Smith, James M. Thurmond, and Alexander Davis, despite threats made to their personal safety by vigilantes who did not welcome any criticism

Figure 15.4. Nathaniel P. Langford. (Courtesy of the Montana Historical Society, image 943-405.)

of their activities.[159] All three attorneys had been part of the defense team during the earlier public trial of George Ives.[160] Alexander Davis was particularly effective in ultimately persuading the president of the Vigilance Committee, Paris Pfouts, and the organization's Executive Committee to create a People's Court, to which Davis was named the judge.[161]

The People's Court had begun to operate in public sometime in mid-February 1864 after the vigilante hanging of Bill Hunter.[162] However, the People's Court was ignored during the arrest and execution of J. A. Slade on March 10, 1864,[163] prompting Davis's resignation from its bench as a matter of principle.[164] Thereafter, the People's Court was not a factor in the vigilante arrests and executions of James Brady, Jem Kelly, John "The Hat" Dolan, and R. C. Rawley, which all occurred between June and October of 1864,[165] nor did the concept of a People's Court regain traction in Virginia City in later years. The creation of Davis's People's Court was an excellent idea, and one that, if taken seriously, might have transitioned Alder Gulch away from continuing vigilantism. However, the arrest and execution of Slade destroyed whatever effectiveness that the People's Court might have had. Davis's efforts stood little chance in the face of the vigilante executions that extended in the latter months of 1864 beyond the members of the road agent syndicate, to the executions of others who engaged in personal, reckless, or one-on-one behaviors that rose to the level of social ills.

Prior to J. A. Slade's execution, the vigilantes had not usually or seriously considered imposing remedies less harsh than death, such as public whippings or banishments from the territory. The execution of Slade has been condemned by history, as it was a departure from the stated and limited purpose of the Vigilance Committee for punishing robbers and murderers.[166] Slade was not hanged for robbery or murder. Authors Lew L. Callaway Jr. and Tom Donovan both note that the vigilantes have been harshly condemned for Slade's execution.[167] Author Andrew P. Morriss classifies Slade's execution as a "mistake."[168] Hoffman Birney wrote that capital punishment was deserved by all persons hanged by the vigilantes except for Slade.[169] Author Dorothy Johnson called Slade's execution for disorderly conduct "shameful."[170] The severity and finality of the event caused the Vigilance Committee to thereafter consider two other potential punishment options for persons guilty of "lesser" offenses, as circumstances might warrant—banishment from the territory and whipping. Of the remaining vigilante arrests in Alder Gulch in 1864, only Jem Kelly appears to have received the lesser punishment of a public whipping for his role as an accomplice after the fact in the nonfatal shooting of Thomas Murphy by James Brady on June 15, 1864.[171] Yet even in Kelly's case, he was hanged two months later at the Snake River Ferry for a series of unrelated crimes.[172]

One theme that is consistent throughout many of the vigilante hangings in Montana is the respectfulness that the executioners usually demonstrated toward the men who were condemned to death as well as the eerie acquiescence to death of the persons sentenced to be hanged. Frequently, as seen in this narrative, men who were condemned to death were given an opportunity to pray, as in the executions of Henry Plummer and "Dutch John" Wagner, to have a last drink, as in the executions of Jack Gallagher and John Keene, to enjoy a smoke of a pipe, as in the case of Aleck Carter, or to write distant relatives, as in the executions of George Ives, "Dutch John" Wagner, Bob Zachary, and Spaulding. The circumstances of the executions followed an unwritten code: that although prisoners were condemned to die, their hangings would be conducted in a manner that was respectful and cooperative.[173] Orderliness was maintained, in some instances, even by deliberately keeping wives and girlfriends away from the execution sites, as in the cases of Ned Ray and his girlfriend Madam Hall, Hayes Lyons and his girlfriend Cora, Cyrus Skinner and his wife, Nellie, and J. A. Slade and his wife, Maria.

For the most part, persons informed that they would be hanged accepted their fate immediately and then cooperated in the manner of their deaths, which contributed to the orderliness of the procedures. The most striking example is that of George Shears, who, upon climbing the ladder for his hanging, referred to his executioners as "Gentlemen" and politely asked them whether he should slide or jump off of the rungs, as he was unfamiliar with the particulars of the process.[174] There were some mild and limited exceptions to the solemnity of vigilante hangings, which perhaps are to be expected in human nature. Some condemned men attempted to bargain for their lives, such as Sheriff Plummer, "Dutch John" Wagner, J. M. Douglas, and John "The Hat" Dolan. Other condemned men verbally expressed anger to their captors moments prior to their hangings, such as Jack Gallagher and John Keene. Two persons attempted to physically escape their captors, those being George Ives prior to his trial and Billy Wilson during his trial, but both were caught and ultimately executed. Only Joe Pizanthia fought the vigilantes to his death while killing George Copley in the process. In the vast majority of cases, the attitude and behavior of the condemned men was overwhelmingly that of resignation, perhaps part of an unwritten mountain code that when a vigilance committee determined that an accused must die, there was to be a brave acceptance of death rather than any physical resistance to it.

Vigilante executions are woven into the fabric of Montana history. As will be shown in the next chapter, Montana has not escaped its vigilante past, as its vigilantism has reverberated, in various ways, during the century and a half that has followed.

Panning for Nuggets

The origin of the phrase "kick the bucket" could be associated with hangings, as the kicking of a bucket would provide a drop for anyone being hanged. However, the true origin of the phrase has nothing to do with the hanging of humans. The wooden frame used to hang animals by the feet during slaughter is called a bucket, and if an animal struggles or spasms while being slaughtered, the bucket is kicked before death.[175]

Notes

1. Callaway, *Montana's Righteous Hangmen*, 49; Allen, *Decent Orderly Lynching*, 197. Despite the severity of the bylaws, Jem Kelly escaped death and received fifty lashes after having been found to be a mere accomplice after the fact in the nonfatal saloon shooting of Thomas Murphy.
2. Bakken, *Invitation to an Execution*, 393–94.
3. Bakken, "Death for Grand Larceny," 47. George Tanner became the first person sentenced to death under the California statute. He appealed his sentence on the ground that during jury selection, a prospective juror was not seated who had voiced a conscientious objection to the death penalty. An appellate court held that the courts were obligated to uphold the public policies expressed by the legislature in statutes and that the allowance of a juror opposed in all circumstances to the death penalty would defeat the legislative intent and, in effect, repeal the law. Ibid., 47; *People v. Tanner*, 2 Cal. 257, 259–60 (Cal. 1852).
4. US Const., Eighth Amend. It reads: "Excessive bail shall not be required, nor excessive fines imposed, nor cruel and unusual punishment inflicted."
5. *Baze v. Rees*, 553 U.S. 35, 48 (2008).
6. *Wilkerson v. Utah*, 99 U.S. 130, 134–35 (1879).
7. *In Re* Kemmler, 136 U.S. 436, 448–49 (1890). The continuing viability of *Kemmler* has been called into question as to its factual assumptions and the legal standard utilized by the court in deciding the appeal. Denno, "Adieu to Electrocution," 665, 670–71.
8. *Gregg v. Georgia*, 428 U.S. 153, 175 (1976); Cf. *Nelson v. Campbell*, 541 U.S. 637, 645–46 (2004).
9. *Campbell v. Blodgett*, 18 F.3d 662, 683 (9th Cir. 1994), reh. and reh. en banc denied, 20 F.3d 1050 (9th Cir. 1994), cert. denied, 511 U.S. 1119 (1994).
10. *Gray v. Lucas*, 710 F.2d 1048, 1061 (5th Cir. 1983), reh. denied, 714 F.2d 137 (1983), cert. denied, 463 U.S. 1237 (1983). In the case of *Stewart v. LeGrand*, 526 U.S. 115, 119 (1999), the Supreme Court held that the defendant waived any Eighth Amendment challenge to his capital sentence by lethal gas, as he had chosen that method of execution over that of lethal injection. In the case of *Gomez v. U.S. Dist. Court for the Northern Dist. of California*, 503 U.S. 653, 753–54 (1992), the majority of the court did not reach the issue of the constitutionality of lethal injection, as the issue had not been raised in prior appeals.
11. Garner, *Black's Law Dictionary*, 258. *Certiorari* is a Latin term meaning "to be informed of; to be made certain in regard to." The grant of *certiorari* directs a lower appellate court to deliver its file to the Supreme Court for the latter's review.
12. Death Penalty Information Center, "Facts about the Death Penalty." The states that permit the death penalty in at least one form are Alabama (see Ala. Stat. Ann. 13A-5-40[a][1]-[18]), Arizona (see Ariz. Rev. Stat. 13-703[F]), Arkansas (see Ark. Code Ann. 5-10-101), California (see Cal. Penal Code 3604), Colorado (see Colo. Rev. Stat. Ann. 18-1.3-1202), Connecticut (see Conn. Gen. Stat. Ann. 53a–54b), Delaware (see Del. Code Ann. tit. 11, sec. 4209), Florida (see Fla. Stat. Ann. 922.105), Georgia (see Ga. Code Ann. 17-10-38), Idaho (see Idaho Code Ann. 19-2716), Indiana (see Ind. Code 35-50-2-9), Kansas (see Kan. Stat. Ann. secs. 21-3439, 21-4625, and 21-4636), Kentucky (see KRS 532.025), Louisiana (see La. R.S. 14:30 and 14:113), Maryland (see Md. Code, Corr. Servs. 3-905), Mississippi (see Miss. Code Ann. 97-3-19[2] and 97-25-55[1]), Missouri (see V.A.M.S. 565.020), Montana (see Mont. Code Ann. secs. 46-18-303 and 45-5-503), Nebraska (see Neb. Rev. Stat. 29-2543), Nevada (see Nev. Rev. Stat. secs. 200.030, 200.033, and 200.035), New Hampshire (see N.H. Rev. Stat. 630:1[III]), North Carolina (see N.C. Gen. Stat. Ann. 14-17), Ohio (see O.R.C. secs. 2903.1, 2929.02, and 2929.04), Oklahoma (see Okl. Stat. Ann. tit. 22, sec. 1014), Oregon (see Ohio Rev. Code Ann. 163.095), Pennsylvania (see 61. Pa. C.S.A. 4304), South Carolina (see S.C. Code Ann. 16-3-20[C][a]), South Dakota (see

S.D. Codified Laws 23A-27A-32), Tennessee (see Tenn. Code Ann. 39-13-204), Texas (see Texas Penal Code 19.03), Utah (see Utah Code Ann. 76-5-202), Virginia (see Va. Code Ann. 18.2–31), Washington (see Wash Rev. Code Ann. 10.95.180), and Wyoming (see Wyo. Stat. Ann. 7-13-904).

13. 8 U.S.C. 1342 (murder related to the smuggling of aliens); 18 U.S.C. 32–34 (destruction of aircraft, motor vehicles and other equipment resulting in death); 18 U.S.C. 36 (murder committed during a drive-by shooting); 18 U.S.C. 37 (murder committed at an international airport); 18 U.S.C. 115(b)(3) (retaliatory murder of a family member of a law enforcement official); 18 U.S.C. 241, 242, 245, and 247 (civil rights offenses resulting in death); 18 U.S.C. 351 (murder of defined federal officials); 18 U.S.C. 794 (espionage); 18 U.S.C. 844(d), (f), and (i) (death or destruction resulting from the interstate transportation of explosives); 18 U.S.C. 924(i) (drug-trafficking murder using a firearm); 18 U.S.C 930 (murder committed in a federal facility); 18 U.S.C. 1091 (genocide); 18 U.S.C. 1111 (first degree murder); 18 U.S.C. 1114 (murder of a federal judge or law enforcement official); 18 U.S.C. 1118 (murder by a federal prisoner); 18 U.S.C. 1119 (murder of a US citizen in a foreign country); 18 U.S.C. 1120 (murder of an escaped federal prisoner already sentenced to life in prison); 18 U.S.C. 1121 (murder of a state or local law enforcement official or corrections officer assisting a federal investigation); 18 U.S.C. 1201 (murder during a kidnapping); 18 U.S.C. 1203 (murder during a hostage taking); 18 U.S.C. 1503 (murder of a court officer or juror); 18 U.S.C. 1512 (murder with intent to prevent testimony of a witness or informant); 18 U.S.C. 1513 (retaliatory murder of a witness, victim, or informant); 18 U.S.C. 1716 (mailing an article with intent to kill the recipient or resulting in death); 18 U.S.C. 1751 (assassination or kidnapping resulting in the death of the president or vice president); 18 U.S.C. 1958 (murder for hire); 18 U.S.C. 1959 (murder involved in a racketeering offense); 18 U.S.C. 1992 (wilfully wrecking a train resulting in death); 18 U.S.C. 2113 (murder in connection with bank robbery); 18 U.S.C. 2119 (murder related to carjacking); 18 U.S.C. 2245 (murder related to rape or child molestation); 18 U.S.C. 2251 (murder related to the sexual exploitation of children); 18 U.S.C. 2280 (murder committed during an offense against maritime navigation); 18 U.S.C. 2281 (murder related to an offense against a fixed maritime platform); 18 U.S.C. 2332 (terrorist murder of a US citizen in another country); 18 U.S.C. 2332a (murder by means of a weapon of mass destruction); 18 U.S.C. 2w340 (murder related to torture); 18 U.S.C. 2381 (treason); 21 U.S.C. 848(e) (murder related to a continuing criminal enterprise or related murder of a federal, state, or local law enforcement officer); and 49 U.S.C. 1472–73 (death resulting from an aircraft hijacking); see also Death Penalty Information Center, "Federal Laws providing for the Death Penalty."

14. 10 U.S.C. 886–934.

15. Wash. Rev. Code Ann. 10.95.180(1) (1996). The statute provides that lethal injection is the presumptive form of execution within the state, except that the defendant may elect hanging instead. See also *Rupe v. Wood*, 93 F.3d 1434, 1443 (9th Cir. 1996) (holding that a prisoner weighing over 400 pounds did not face unconstitutional cruel and unusual punishment under Washington State's death penalty statute, where weight created a risk of decapitation during hanging, as the 1996 amendment to the statute identifies lethal injection as the presumptive method for imposing the sentence), cert. den, 519 U.S. 1142 (1997).

16. N.H. Rev. Stat. Ann. 630:5 (XIV) (1990).

17. Del. Code Ann. tit. 11, sec. 4209(f) (2009). However, it appears that Delaware's statutory methodology of lethal injunction has withstood constitutional challenge. *State v. Deputy*, 644 A.2d 411, 418 (Del. Supr. 1994), aff'd, 648 A.2d 423 (Del. Supr. 1994); see also Death Penalty Information Center, "Methods of Execution"; Layton, "How Does Death by Hanging Work?"; Clark County Prosecuting Attorney, "Methods of Execution."

18. Bakken, *Invitation to an Execution*, 348.

19. Mont. Code Ann. 46-19-103(3) (1997). Predecessor statutes in Montana permitted the imposition of the death penalty by hanging, and hanging under that Montana statute was found by both federal and state courts to not violate the constitutional prohibition against cruel and unusual punishment. *Langford v. Day*, 110 F.3d 1380, 1393 (9th Cir. 1996), cert. den, 522 U.S. 881 (1997); *State v. Coleman*, 185 Mont. 299, 406 (Mont. 1979), cert. den, 446 U.S. 970 (1980), reh. den, 448 U.S. 914 (1980); see also Death Penalty Information Center, "Methods of Execution," specifically, "Authorized Methods by State—Montana." Between 1983 to 1997, Montana death row inmates could be executed by means of hanging or lethal injection. Mont. Code Ann. 46-19-103 (1983).
20. Laws 1865, First Terr. Legis., Proceedings Act, ch. 1, sec. 220.
21. Death Penalty Information Center, "Descriptions of Execution Methods—Hanging."
22. Ward, *Civil War*, 392.
23. Layton, "How Does Death By Hanging Work?"
24. Ibid.
25. Capital Punishment U.K., "Hanged by the Neck Until Dead!"
26. Ibid.
27. *Campbell v. Blodgett*, 18 F.3d at 685.
28. Ibid.
29. Capital Punishment U.K., "Hanged by the Neck Until Dead!"
30. Ibid.
31. Ibid.
32. Layton, "How Does Death by Hanging Work?"
33. Ibid.; see also Caughey, *Their Majesties the Mob*, 15.
34. Ketchum, who weighed 200 pounds, had been convicted in a territorial court of an attempted train robbery. While the drop length was originally calculated for him to be 5 feet 9 inches, the executioner increased the length to 7 feet and had soaked and stretched the rope to reduce its elasticity. The Ketchum hanging is viewed as the worst bungled execution in the history of the western frontier. Wilson, *Frontier Justice*, 138–40; see also Bartholomew, *Black Jack Ketchum*.
35. Capital Punishment U.K., "Hanged by the Neck Until Dead!"
36. Department of the Army, *U.S. Army Corrections System*, ch. 3, sec. 3-1; see also Death Penalty Information Center, "Execution in the Military—Overview."
37. Capital Punishment U.K., "Hanged by the Neck Until Dead!"
38. Department of the Army, *Procedure for Military Executions*, sec. 3, para. 16.
39. Langford, *Vigilante Days*, 241; see also Dimsdale, *Vigilantes of Montana*, 143–44.
40. Dimsdale, *Vigilantes of Montana*, 128.
41. Ibid., 116; see also Gard, *Frontier Justice*, 178.
42. Dimsdale, *Vigilantes of Montana*, 143.
43. Ibid., 188.
44. Ibid., 186. Additionally, Caughey mentions the pinioning of the hands of Ned Ray leading up to his execution. Caughey, *Their Majesties the Mob*, 84.
45. Baumler, *Girl from the Gulches*, 40.
46. Dimsdale, *Vigilantes of Montana*, 116; Langford, *Vigilante Days*, 195–96; Mather and Boswell, *Hanging the Sheriff*, 82–83; Gard, *Frontier Justice*, 178; Donovan, *Hanging around the Big Sky*, book 2, 54.
47. Dimsdale, *Vigilantes of Montana*, 128; Sanders and Bertsche, *X. Beidler*, 93.
48. Langford, *Vigilante Days*, 225; Thompson, *Tenderfoot in Montana*, 181; Pace, *Golden Gulch*, 36; Caughey, *Their Majesties the Mob*, 83–84; Bakken, *Invitation to an Execution*, 341; Bartholomew, *Black Jack Ketchum*, 46–47; Barsness, *Gold Camp*, 47; Crutchfield, *It Happened in Montana*, 39; Olsen, "Lawlessness and Vigilantes," 162.
49. Birney, *Vigilantes*, 342; Leeson, *History of Montana*, 301.

50. Dimsdale, *Vigilantes of Montana*, 128; Langford, *Vigilante Days*, 226; Thompson, *Tenderfoot in Montana*, 181; Caughey, *Their Majesties the Mob*, 85; Taylor, *Roaring in the Wind*, 215; Barsness, *Gold Camp*, 47.

51. Dimsdale, *Vigilantes of Montana*, 135; Langford, *Vigilante Days*, 232; Thompson, *Tenderfoot in Montana*, 185; Gard, *Frontier Justice*, 180.

52. Langford, *Vigilante Days*, 241; Thompson, *Tenderfoot in Montana*, 186–87; see also Pace, *Golden Gulch*, 36; Mather and Boswell, *Hanging the Sheriff*, 91; Johnson, *Bloody Bozeman*, 99; Gard, *Frontier Justice*, 181; Bartholomew, *Black Jack Ketchum*, 25.; Barsness, *Gold Camp*, 48.

53. Dimsdale, *Vigilantes of Montana*, 148; Donovan, *Hanging around the Big Sky*, book 2, 88.

54. Dimsdale, *Vigilantes of Montana*, 150; Gard, *Frontier Justice*, 182; Leeson, *History of Montana*, 298.

55. Allen, *Decent Orderly Lynching*, appendix; Dimsdale, *Vigilantes of Montana*, 155; Thompson, *Tenderfoot in Montana*, 190; Birney, *Vigilantes*, 306. According to Allen, the location of Shears's execution might instead have been the Bitterroot Valley.

56. Dimsdale, *Vigilantes of Montana*, 157–58; see also Bartholomew, *Black Jack Ketchum*, 28 (as to the hanging of Cyrus Skinner).

57. Dimsdale, *Vigilantes of Montana*, 164; Langford, *Vigilante Days*, 252; Gard, *Frontier Justice*, 183.

58. Allen, *Decent Orderly Lynching*, appendix; Donovan, *Hanging around the Big Sky*, book 2, 103.

59. Dimsdale, *Vigilantes of Montana*, 156; Gard, *Frontier Justice*, 183.

60. Dimsdale, *Vigilantes of Montana*, 181; Thompson, *Tenderfoot in Montana*, 191.

61. Dimsdale, *Vigilantes of Montana*, 186–87; Allen, *Decent Orderly Lynching*, 298.

62. "Execution at Nevada, M.T.," *Montana Post*, Sept. 24, 1864, p. 2, col. 2.

63. Sanders and Bertsche, *X. Beidler*, 116; Cushman, *Montana*, 203.

64. Dimsdale, *Vigilantes of Montana*, 213; Birney, *Vigilantes*, 345; Allen, *Decent Orderly Lynching*, 323; Donovan, *Hanging around the Big Sky*, book 2, 138.

65. Donovan, *Hanging around the Big Sky*, book 2, 38.

66. "Hanging of Col. Geo. Hynson for Highway Robbery," *Helena Weekly Herald*, Aug. 27, 1868, p. 7, col. 1; "The Spaulding-Wilson Affair," *Virginia Tri-Weekly Post*, Feb. 1, 1868, p. 3, col. 2.

67. Donovan, *Hanging around the Big Sky*, book 2, 148.

68. Dimsdale, *Vigilantes of Montana*, 144; Birney, *Vigilantes*, 276; Milner and O'Connor, *As Big as the West*, 95; Gard, *Frontier Justice*, 181; see also Thompson, *Tenderfoot in Montana*, 186; Bartholomew, *Black Jack Ketchum*, 26; Barsness, *Gold Camp*, 48–49.

69. Dimsdale, *Vigilantes of Montana*, 155; Bartholomew, *Black Jack Ketchum*, 30.

70. Dimsdale, *Vigilantes of Montana*, 151; Langford, *Vigilante Days*, 245; Gard, *Frontier Justice*, 182–83.

71. Dimsdale, *Vigilantes of Montana*, 181.

72. Ibid., 128.

73. Ibid., 129; Langford, *Vigilante Days*, 226; Bakken, *Invitation to an Execution*, 341; Allen, *Decent Orderly Lynching*, 228; Birney, *Vigilantes*, 253; Caughey, *Their Majesties the Mob*, 84; Gard, *Frontier Justice*, 179; Bartholomew, *Black Jack Ketchum*, 20; see also Barsness, *Gold Camp*, 47.

74. "Murder of Harry Slater," *Montana Post*, June 17, 1865, p. 2, col. 4; Sanders and Bertsche, *X. Beidler*, 116; Cushman, *Montana*, 203.

75. Donovan, *Hanging around the Big Sky*, book 2, 36.

76. Kidston, "Tree of Death."

77. Dimsdale, *Vigilantes of Montana*, 131–32; Langford, *Vigilante Days*, 229; Sanders and Bertsche, *X. Beidler*, 94; Allen, *Decent Orderly Lynching*, 231; Mather and Boswell, *Hanging the Sheriff*, 90; Taylor, *Roaring in the Wind*, 217.

78. Langford, *Vigilante Days*, 6; Callaway, *Montana's Righteous Hangmen*, 45; Allen, *Decent Orderly Lynching*, 195.

79. Dimsdale, *Vigilantes of Montana*, 168.
80. Langford, *Vigilante Days*, 287; Dimsdale, *Vigilantes of Montana*, 168; Allen, *Decent Orderly Lynching*, 275; Johnson, *Bloody Bozeman*, 101.
81. Allen, *Decent Orderly Lynching*, 275; Donovan, *Hanging around the Big Sky*, book 2, 107. According to Allen, Slade did not ride with the vigilante posses.
82. Dimsdale, *Vigilantes of Montana*, 167; Allen, *Decent Orderly Lynching*, 274; Johnson, *Bloody Bozeman*, 56n13.
83. Allen, *Decent Orderly Lynching*, 274.
84. Callaway, *Montana's Righteous Hangmen*, 81, 92, 96.
85. Donovan, *Hanging around the Big Sky*, book 2, 108.
86. Ibid.
87. Ibid.
88. Toponce, *Reminiscences*, 149; Callaway, *Montana's Righteous Hangmen*, 88–89; Donovan, *Hanging around the Big Sky*, book 2, 109; Aaron T. Ford Reminiscences, 1903, Mont. Hist. Soc., SC-702, box 1-1, p. 6.
89. Toponce, *Reminiscences*, 148.
90. Callaway, *Montana's Righteous Hangmen*, 101.
91. Ibid., 102.
92. Ibid.
93. Ibid., 93.
94. Ibid., 94.
95. Ibid., 94–95.
96. Ibid., 92–93.
97. Ibid., 93.
98. Dimsdale, *Vigilantes of Montana*, 173, 176; Johnson, *Bloody Bozeman*, 101; Donovan, *Hanging around the Big Sky*, book 2, 109.
99. Langford, *Vigilante Days*, 286; Toponce, *Reminiscences*, 149; Allen, *Decent Orderly Lynching*, 274; Abrahams, *Vigilant Citizens*, 64; M. W. Anderson, "Notes on W. Y. Pemberton's Lecture before the Unity Club at Unitarian Church, May 12, 1868," William Y. Pemberton Papers, 1863–69, Mont. Hist. Soc., SC-629, p. 16.
100. Dimsdale, *Vigilantes of Montana*, 168.
101. Callaway, *Montana's Righteous Hangmen*, 104; Sanders and Bertsche, *X. Beidler*, 98.
102. Callaway, *Montana's Righteous Hangmen*, 105; Birney, *Vigilantes*, 329–30.
103. Dimsdale, *Vigilantes of Montana*, 170.
104. Langford, *Vigilante Days*, 286.
105. Ibid.; Dimsdale, *Vigilantes of Montana*, 169; Allen, *Decent Orderly Lynching*, 275.
106. Langford, *Vigilante Days*, 286; Dimsdale, *Vigilantes of Montana*, 169; Leeson, *History of Montana*, 300; Allen, *Decent Orderly Lynching*, 275–76; Birney, *Vigilantes*, 329.
107. Langford, *Vigilante Days*, 286; Dimsdale, *Vigilantes of Montana*, 170; Donovan, *Hanging around the Big Sky*, book 2, 105; M. W. Anderson, "Notes on W. Y. Pemberton's Lecture before the Unity Club at Unitarian Church, May 12, 1868," William Y. Pemberton Papers, 1863–69, Mont. Hist. Soc., SC-629, p. 16.
108. Albert M. Hart Reminiscences, 1908, Mont. Hist. Soc., SC-802.
109. Toponce, *Reminiscences*, 149.
110. Ibid., 149–50.
111. Ibid., 151.
112. Langford, *Vigilante Days*, 287; Allen, *Decent Orderly Lynching*, 276; Leeson, *History of Montana*, 301; Abrahams, *Vigilant Citizens*, 65; Donovan, *Hanging around the Big Sky*, book 2, 105; see also Johnson, *Bloody Bozeman*, 101.
113. Allen, *Decent Orderly Lynching*, 276.
114. Ibid.

115. Birney, *Vigilantes*, 333.
116. Allen, *Decent Orderly Lynching*, 276.
117. Birney, *Vigilantes*, 333.
118. Johnson, *Bloody Bozeman*, 101; Donovan, *Hanging around the Big Sky*, book 2, 106.
119. Birney, *Vigilantes*, 333.
120. Toponce, *Reminiscences*, 151.
121. Albert M. Hart Reminiscences, 1908, Mont. Hist. Soc., SC-802.
122. Langford, *Vigilante Days*, 289; Dimsdale, *Vigilantes of Montana*, 171; Pace, *Golden Gulch*, 50; Allen, *Decent Orderly Lynching*, 276–77.
123. Johnson, *Bloody Bozeman*, 101.
124. Toponce, *Reminiscences*, 151.
125. Ibid.
126. Ibid.
127. Dimsdale, *Vigilantes of Montana*, 171; Langford, *Vigilante Days*, 288; Allen, *Decent Orderly Lynching*, 276.
128. Dimsdale, *Vigilantes of Montana*, 171; Langford, *Vigilante Days*, 288; Allen, *Decent Orderly Lynching*, 276, 278; Donovan, *Hanging around the Big Sky*, book 2, 106.
129. Allen, *Decent Orderly Lynching*, 277.
130. Ibid.
131. Ibid., 277–78.
132. Langford, *Vigilante Days*, 288.
133. Birney, *Vigilantes*, 335.
134. Langford, *Vigilante Days*, 287.
135. Ibid., 287; Allen, *Decent Orderly Lynching*, 277–78.
136. Leeson, *History of Montana*, 301; Allen, *Decent Orderly Lynching*, 278.
137. Dimsdale, *Vigilantes of Montana*, 172–73; Birney, *Vigilantes*, 334; Donovan, *Hanging around the Big Sky*, book 2, 106.
138. Ibid.
139. Harriet Peck Fenn Sanders, "Diary of a Journey across the Plains in 1863 and Reminiscences of Early Life in Montana," Wilbur Fisk Sanders Papers, Mont. Hist. Soc., MC-53, box 6, folder 6-13, p. 99; Taylor, *Roaring in the Wind*, 261.
140. Johnson, *Bloody Bozeman*, 104; Baumler *Girl from the Gulches*, 40; see also Abrahams, *Vigilant Citizens*, 65; Langford, *Vigilante Days*, 289.
141. Albert M. Hart Reminiscences, 1908, Mont. Hist. Soc., SC-802.
142. Baumler, *Girl from the Gulches*, 40; Johnson, *Bloody Bozeman*, 104.
143. Baumler, *Girl from the Gulches*, 41; Johnson, *Bloody Bozeman*, 104.
144. Langford, *Vigilante Days*, 289; Dimsdale, *Vigilantes of Montana*, 172–73; Toponce, *Reminiscences*, 152; Sanders and Bertsche, *X. Beidler*, 100; Allen, *Decent Orderly Lynching*, 279; Callaway, *Montana's Righteous Hangmen*, 107–8; Taylor, *Roaring in the Wind*, 261; Johnson, *Bloody Bozeman*, 101; see also Milner and O'Connor, *As Big as the West*, 97.
145. Baumler, *Girl from the Gulches*, 41; Allen, *Decent Orderly Lynching*, 278.
146. Harriet Peck Fenn Sanders, "Diary of a Journey across the Plains in 1863 and Reminiscences of Early Life in Montana," Wilbur Fisk Sanders Papers, Mont. Hist. Soc., MC-53, box 6, folder 6-13, p. 99; Taylor, *Roaring in the Wind*, 261.
147. M. W. Anderson, "Notes on W. Y. Pemberton's Lecture before the Unity Club at Unitarian Church, May 12, 1868," William Y. Pemberton Papers, 1863–69, Mont. Hist. Soc., SC-629, p. 17.
148. Johnson, *Bloody Bozeman*, 101–2 (using the name Molly Slade rather than Maria Slade and identifying the horse as Billie Ray); see also Allen, *Decent Orderly Lynching*, 278; Birney, *Vigilantes*, 334.
149. Langford, *Vigilante Days*, 289.
150. Mather and Boswell, *Hanging the Sheriff*, 96.

151. Langford, *Vigilante Days*, 289.

152. Baumler, *Girl from the Gulches*, 41.

153. Dimsdale, *Vigilantes of Montana*, 176.

154. Langford, *Vigilante Days*, 289.

155. Ibid., 288; Allen, *Decent Orderly Lynching*, 278–79; Olsen, "Lawlessness and Vigilantes," 168.

156. Baumler, *Girl from the Gulches*, 41; Allen, *Decent Orderly Lynching*, 278.

157. Donovan, *Hanging around the Big Sky*, book 2, 107.

158. Allen, *Decent Orderly Lynching*, 251.

159. Ibid., 250–51.

160. Ibid.

161. Ibid., 251; see also Dimsdale, *Vigilantes of Montana*, 167–68.

162. Allen, *Decent Orderly Lynching*, 275.

163. Langford, *Vigilante Days*, 288–89; Leeson, *History of Montana*, 301; Allen, *Decent Orderly Lynching*, 292; Birney, *Vigilantes*, 334–35; Abrahams, *Vigilant Citizens*, 64–65; Gard, *Frontier Justice*, 184.

164. Allen, *Decent Orderly Lynching*, 292.

165. Ibid. The People's Court also appears to have played no role in the trial of Jem Kelly over the murder of Thomas Murphy, which resulted in punishing Kelly with fifty lashes and the execution of James Brady on June 15, 1864 (see Dimsdale, *Vigilantes of Montana*, 179–80); Allen, *Decent Orderly Lynching*, 294–95), prior to Kelly's later arrest and execution on September 15, 1864, for unrelated crimes.

166. Vigilante Oath, dated Dec. 23, 1963.

167. Callaway, *Montana's Righteous Hangmen*, 109; Donovan, *Hanging around the Big Sky*, book 2, 107.

168. Morriss, "Private Actors," 129n51.

169. Birney, *Vigilantes*, 223.

170. Johnson, *Bloody Bozeman*, 101. Of course, taking a judge hostage at gunpoint while intoxicated is a more serious offense than mere "disorderly conduct," though not an offense warranting the imposition of capital punishment.

171. Dimsdale, *Vigilantes of Montana*, 180; Leeson, *History of Montana*, 301; Allen, *Decent Orderly Lynching*, 294; Birney, *Vigilantes*, 340–41.

172. Dimsdale, *Vigilantes of Montana*, 186–87; Callaway, *Montana's Righteous Hangmen*, 115; Milner and O'Connor, *As Big as the West*, 98; Allen, *Decent Orderly Lynching*, 298.

173. Reid, *Policing the Elephant*, 192. Reid's book demonstrates that executions by hanging were conducted in an orderly manner in various western territories other than Montana, including particularly California.

174. Dimsdale, *Vigilantes of Montana*, 155; Langford, *Vigilante Days*, 248; Callaway, *Montana's Righteous Hangmen*, 68; Thompson, *Tenderfoot in Montana*, 190; Bartholomew, *Black Jack Ketchum*, 30; Allen, *Decent Orderly Lynching*, 265; Donovan, *Hanging around the Big Sky*, book 2, 99.

175. Martin, "Kick the Bucket."

16

Postmortem Echoes of Times Past

Some more cold lead and twisted hemp is badly needed on the Musselshell.

—*Fort Benton River Press*, July 9, 1884

I request that the State of Montana grant Sheriff Henry Plummer a pardon.

—Frederick J. Morgan, May 21, 1993

Gold was found at Bannack, Alder Gulch, Helena, and many other less notorious locations of Montana in the latter half of the 1860s. It was dug. It was panned. It was sluiced. It was mined. It was found in various forms such as gold dust, flakes, and nuggets. The problem was that as a natural resource near the surface of the Montana earth, its supply was finite. Gold was discovered, extracted, and sold to the point where its better and easier finds were eventually exhausted.

By the early 1880s, the price of gold was still $20.67 an ounce. Gold continued to be sluiced and mined, but the easiest finds were depleted and the territory's production of the yellow metal was in decline.[1] While precious metal production totaled $18,000,000 in 1865, it steadily declined during the 1870s and totaled only $4,702,636 in 1880.[2] By the 1880s, however, vast areas of Montana that had previously been accessible only by horse and stagecoach became more readily accessible by trains. While trains made Montana accessible to persons and goods, the converse was equally true—trains also permitted western territorial products to be exported to other regions of the continent. Trains would have a profound effect upon the nature of Montana's economy.

Americans were an enterprising people. The Protestant work ethic, rugged individualism, and the limitless opportunities of free-market capitalism enabled

338

DOI: 10.7330_9780874219203.c016

Figure 16.1. Montana cattle range in the 1880s. (Courtesy of the Montana Historical Society, image 981-676.)

the country to expand westward and, in the process, to construct farms, towns, and cities from virgin land. Settlers in the western territories were aided by abundant natural resources. Along the way, people were also ingeniously innovative. Factories in the East relied more and more upon the use of machinery and assembly-line labor to mass-produce products. Homestead farms also benefitted from innovation, such as improved iron plows for planting, mechanical twine-binders for reaping wheat, and barbed wire for the fencing of acreage.[3]

In this climate of expansion, innovation, and entrepreneurship, persons interested in cattle ranching on the open plains were poised to reap considerable financial rewards. Cattle could be raised and fed on the open range. The plains were seemingly limitless, open, and available for use. Montana grasses were plentiful and nutritious, and raising cattle was easier than agriculture and more certain than mining.[4] Cattle could be raised and slaughtered to feed prospectors in the mining territories, railroad workers in the states and territories where railroads were under construction, and army soldiers protecting the frontier. Cattle products could also be shipped by train to places like Chicago, Illinois, and Abilene and Wichita, Kansas.[5] Cattle ranching romanticized the proverbial "cowpoke" who worked eighteen-hour days and drove herds great distances for sale, adorned with long boots, spurs, chaps, gloves, and a western-style hat for protection against the sun, on a horse with a saddle containing limited provisions.

The economics of cattle ranching made sense. During the 1860s, the population of the United States grew by 22 percent while the number of cattle in the country decreased by 7 percent.[6] By the end of the Civil War, cattle that could be sold in Texas for $3.00 to $5.00 per head could be sold in the northern markets for $30.00 to $50.00 per head.[7] By 1880, cattle ranches had spread throughout the American plains from the Rio Grande at the south to the Canadian border at the north.[8] Cattle ranching extended into Montana, where there were wide-open prairies, unlimited grass for grazing, and a proximity to the Northern Pacific Railroad upon its completion in 1883.[9]

Cattle became Montana's "new gold." Cattle presented a compelling advantage that gold could not, in that it was a resource that was seemingly and forever renewable. While the "beef bonanza" would eventually crash as a result of falling prices in 1885, a severe drought that left the animals in poor condition in 1886, and an unusually fierce winter in 1886–87, the years prior to 1885 were boom times for cattle ranchers in the western territories.[10]

Just as gold discoveries attracted criminals and "roughs" to mining communities, large cattle ranches were targeted by poachers. Theft, it seems, was always one step behind financial success in Montana in the latter half of the 1800s. On one level, cattle theft was a local, unorganized problem. Granville Stuart noted that the cows of a neighboring rancher frequently had twin and triplet calves while Stuart's own cows were, by fantastic odds, nearly all barren.[11] Localized problems like these were resolvable, as, in that instance, Stuart threatened to hang the neighbor if his cows had any more "twins."[12] On a broader level, however, the cattlemen had $35 million worth of property scattered over 75,000 square miles of virtually uninhabited countryside, which were conditions that were ideal for large-scale and concerted cattle thievery.[13] Organized bands of rustlers had fortified hideouts and worked with coconspirators in Canada and elsewhere to dispose of the stolen cattle.[14] The bands operated not only in eastern Montana but additionally in western Dakota and northeastern Wyoming.[15]

Horse stealing was also a problem in the region. Horses were a primary means of individual transportation in the wide open regions of the unsettled American West. The theft of a horse was a serious crime, akin to how car theft is considered today. The theft of multiple horses by organized rings was similar to modern-day car theft rings and chop shops. In Montana in the 1880s horse stealing was a very serious crime that commanded special attention.[16] Granville Stuart wrote that "[i]t had come to be almost impossible to keep a team or saddle horse on a ranch unless one slept in the manger with a rifle."[17] Horse and cattle stealing grew to epidemic proportions the early 1880s.[18] A single robbery in 1884 reportedly involved the theft of 200 horses.[19] The circumstances prompted the *Fort Benton River Press* to comment in its edition of July 9, 1884 that "[s]ome more cold lead and twisted hemp is badly needed on the Musselshell."[20] The vigilante movement of 1884 known as Stuart's Stranglers became the first echo of the territory's vigilantism of the 1860s and arose out of the incessant theft of cattle and horses.

While historians have written less of Helena vigilantism than that of Bannack and Alder Gulch, even less has been published regarding the activities of Stuart's Stranglers in the Musselshell Valley region of Montana in 1884. One reason may be that the members of Stuart's Stranglers said less of their activities years after the fact than had their earlier counterparts in Bannack, Virginia City, and Helena.[21] Granville Stuart, who organized the Stranglers, had been a young man who prospected for gold in the areas of Bannack, Virginia City, and Deer Lodge during the early 1860s, and he and his brother James were peripheral participants in vigilante activities that occurred during that time.[22]

A meeting of the Montana Stock Growers Association was held in Miles City, Montana, on April 17, 1883, and attended by 279 of its members.[23] Chief among the subjects discussed was the problem of rustlers, whose activities had become so rampant in the region that it threatened the success of the cattle industry overall.[24] A decision was made at the meeting that a detective be hired by the association for each county, whose duties would be to investigate and arrest horse and cattle rustlers so that they could be brought to trial.[25] The association's 1883 plan did not succeed in resolving the problem.

Some cattle kings encouraged their ranch employees to purchase cattle that were mingled into the employers' herds in the belief that the employees would then have a stake in protecting the herds from theft. The concept had some success, but not enough to resolve the broader problem.[26]

At the association's next meeting in the spring of 1884 there was a consensus, as described by Granville Stuart, that the only way to deal with the problem of horse and cattle rustling "was to make the penalty for stealing so severe that it would lose its attractions."[27] Some members of the association argued in favor of raising a small army of cowboys.[28] Future president Teddy Roosevelt, who owned a ranch in neighboring Dakota Territory and who was a member of the Montana Stock Growers Association, was among those in favor of raising an army.[29] Others, including Granville Stuart, opposed the idea in the belief that the rustlers were fortified and armed and that many of their own lives would be lost and their own survivors might face trial for murder.[30] In the end, the association authorized that no action be taken, which had the effect of emboldening the rustlers.[31] What was apparently less known was that Granville Stuart, drawing upon his earlier life experiences as a young man in Bannack, Virginia City, and the Deer Lodge Valley, organized a fourteen-member vigilance committee that would address the problem of horse and cattle rustling instead.[32] While the number of Stranglers might have been limited, the organization had the backing of influential ranchers with ties to the Montana Stock

Growers Association.[33] In his reminiscences, Oscar O. Mueller wrote, quoting a local newspaper, that "[t]he law was powerless to deal with [the thieves], and it was left for exasperated and determined stockmen to put an end to their career of lawlessness."[34]

Rancher money was paid to informants who provided the vigilantes with details about the identities and whereabouts of horse and cattle thieves in the region.[35] One of the informants relied upon by the Stranglers was Pete "Prickly Pear" Proctor, also known as one of the "river rats," who would prove to be a player in a vigilante raid at Bates Point on July 20, 1884.[36]

On July 3, 1884, Sam McKenzie was hanged by Reece Anderson and his assistants at Fort Maginnis for stealing seven horses from H. P. Brooks of Andersonville, Montana.[37] A woman of French Canadian and Indian heritage, Isabelle Larocque, later recalled that McKenzie spent the night playing a violin at a dance, not aware that some of the guests were vigilantes intending to hang him by morning.[38]

On July 7, 1884, a vigilante posse set out from the DHS Ranch, which was partially owned by Granville Stuart, and captured four men for having stolen fifty horses from a rancher.[39] The posse consisted of Bill Burnett, Reece Anderson, A. W. "Gus" Adams, and Lynn Patterson.[40] The thieves were pursued to a cabin near the convergence of the Musselshell and Missouri Rivers, where the horses were identified by their owners despite having had their brand marks burned out.[41] Three of the four culprits were shot to death in their cabin.[42] A fourth man, named "California Jack," was captured. One of the Stranglers, Gus Adams, wished to keep "California Jack" alive as there was an outstanding $10,000 reward for his capture, but he was overruled by Bill Burnett.[43] "California Jack" was hanged from a Cottonwood tree while seated on a horse that was caused to bolt forward at the sound of a pistol shot and the crack of a whip.[44]

The same evening, Burnett's posse appeared at the home of Billy Downes, who admitted that he and "California Ed" had stolen horses from local Indians but insisted that they had never stolen property from white men.[45] The protestations of Downes and "California Ed," who was also present, were not believed, as there were twenty-six horses in the corral bearing the brands of well-known area ranches.[46] Downes and "California Ed" were taken to nearby grove of trees and hanged.[47] Their hangings are believed to be the only time that vigilantes' activities in 1884 were deemed by other vigilantes to have been unjustified.[48] The hangings were condemned by Granville Stuart himself, as Downes was a family man and may have only had a few horses that were of little value.[49] Teddy Roosevelt wrote in the February 1888 edition of *Century Magazine* that persons had been executed in Montana, "not, however, with the best judgment in all cases."[50]

On the same day as the Downes and "California Ed" executions, "Rattle-snake Jake" Fallon and Charles "Long Hair" Owen were killed during an infa-mous gun battle with private citizens in Lewistown.[51]

On or about July 9, 1884, vigilantes hanged Leo and Narcossa Laverdure north of the Missouri River, near Clagget, at the mouth of the Judith River.[52]

At about the same time another vigilante posse set out to find three other suspected horse thieves, "Red Mike," Brocky Gallagher, and "Dutch" Louis Meyers in the vicinity of Rocky Point.[53] The three men were captured and pled guilty to horse stealing, but Granville Stuart is unclear in his book about whether the men were actually hanged.[54] M. A. Leeson wrote that "Dutch" Louis Meyers and one or two other men in his party had been lynched.[55] Oscar O. Mueller states that the three men actually escaped capture as the vigilante posse was diverted to another location and as efforts to locate the three men continued into October of 1884 in the Little Rockies.[56] Given the ambiguity of Stuart's writing, Leeson's failure to name all of the persons supposedly hanged, and Mueller's insistence that the men had escaped capture, the evidence appears to tilt in favor of the conclusion that "Red Mike," Brocky Gallagher, and "Dutch" Louis Meyers were not actually hanged.

Another band of outlaws was believed to be operating in the region headed by John Stringer, also known as "Stringer Jack."[57] Stringer often stayed at an abandoned wood yard owned by "Old Man" Jack James and his two sons at Bates Point, a well-known gathering place for thieves.[58] "Old Man" Jack is referred to by some sources with the surname of James and as a relative of the infamous Missouri outlaw Jesse James.[59] Other sources suggest that the fam-ily connection to Jesse James is unsubstantiated.[60] A vigilante posse was orga-nized consisting of Granville Stuart, "Floppin' Bill" Cantrell, Jim Hibbs, Lynn Patterson, Bill Clark, Jack Ludich (or Ludwig), Charley Pettit, Butch Starley, John Single, J. L. Stuart, Andrew Fergus, A. W. "Gus" Adams, Jack Tabor, Bill Burnett, and Pete "Prickly Pear" Proctor.[61]

The vigilante posse raided the Bates Point property on July 20, 1884.[62] "Old Man" Jack, his two sons, Frank Hanson, and Bill Williams were in a dirt-roofed cabin on the property while a pole tent nearby was occupied by "Stringer Jack," Paddy Rose, "Swift Bill," Dixie Burr, Orville Edwards, Silas Nickerson, Phelps, Eugene Burr, and Johnnie Owens.[63] The vigilante posse divided itself into three parts, with one assigned to the cabin, one assigned to the pole tent, and a third guarding the posse's own encampment and equipment.[64] When the contingent assigned to the cabin ordered "Old Man" Jack to open his corral and release his horses, he released the horses but then returned to the cabin and opened rifle fire upon the vigilantes, who fired back.[65] "Old Man" Jack might have correctly surmised that the vigilante contingent intended to hang him and his colleagues regardless of his actions. The vigilantes also responded to the gunfire by setting fire to the cabin, and all of the cabin's occupants died either from gunshots or from the fire itself.[66] In the words of Oscar O. Mueller, the fire was set amid gunfire by "two of the most daring members of the Vigilantes, Lynn Patterson and Jack Tabor."[67] The assault on the compound lasted for a total of two hours.[68] In his reminiscences, Harold Rash wrote, based upon his information, that the cabin fire became so intense that two of the men inside came outside with their hands up, whereupon they were summarily shot and killed.[69]

Meanwhile, there was a vigilante assault upon the pole tent. The tent's occupants fled in different directions, and all were wounded at the site with the exception of Edwards and Nickerson.[70] Stringer was shot to death in a dense clump of willows.[71] Burr managed to successfully hide from the melee within a dry well.[72] Rose escaped the area altogether.[73] The remainder of the party regrouped and took a raft down the Missouri River where, on or about July 22, 1884, they were discovered and arrested by soldiers stationed at Fort Maginnis.[74] The prisoners were transferred to the custody of Deputy US Marshal Samuel Fischel, who transferred custody to the vigilante posse, which then hanged the prisoners from a pole placed between two cabins located near the mouth of the river.[75] Paddy Rose was fortunate that he did not accompany the others downriver. Instead, he escaped Bates Point by himself and ultimately fled to the safety of Canada.[76] The vigilantes inventoried 165 stolen horses at Bates Point after the event.[77] The vigilantes' informant, Pete "Prickly Pear" Proctor, was shipped out of the region by steamboat to protect him from potential retribution by the local criminal element.[78]

The actions of the vigilantes in July of 1884 received support from local newspapers, including the *Fort Benton River Press,* which described the conduct as "the only way to put a quietus on this business," and the *Mineral Argus,* which stated editorially that "[t]he most speedy and safe cure is to hang [the thieves] as fast as they are captured."[79] The *Rocky Mountain Husbandman* published articles by James Fergus defending the vigilantes, and its editors, John Vrooman and R. H. Sutherlin, gave their editorial support.[80] The August 1884 edition of the *Montana Stock & Mining Journal* summarized the vigilante activities of the prior month: "at least twenty outlaws have been made to fill unhonored graves in the Lower Judith and Musselshell region."[81] The *Journal* declared that there was no question about the guilt of the persons killed.[82] The *Journal* blamed the need for vigilantism on the ineffectiveness of government law enforcement. It stated that "[i]t is a sad commentary on common justice as administered by law, when the rough exterior of a cowboy can be said in truth to cover a mind and heart capable of better discerning and punishing crime."[83]

Figure 16.2. Granville Stuart, also known as "Mr. Montana." (Courtesy of the Montana Historical Society, image 945-174.)

Nevertheless, the activities of Stuart's Stranglers were not roundly popular with the general citizenry. Oscar O. Mueller described the public's reaction to the deaths as a "storm of protest."[84] Relatives and friends of the men who were killed did not passively accept what had happened, and for many years Granville Stuart remained cautious about discussing the Stranglers for fear of potential retribution.[85] Unsubstantiated rumors circulated over the course of months and years that the Stranglers killed scores of men, oftentimes for ulterior motives having nothing to do with fighting crime.[86]

Moreover, the spate of killings during the summer of 1884 did not apparently end horse and cattle thievery in the region. The *Daily Yellowstone Journal* cryptically mentioned that in mid-November 1884 four men were "lynched" for horse and cattle thievery.[87] A letter from Granville Stuart to James Fergus, written a year later, suggests that the issue of horse thievery was a problem that was continuing. Stuart wrote on July 26, 1885, that "[o]ur safety lies in keeping close watch of our horses and if enough are taken so that the trail can be followed to pursue as quickly as possible."[88]

History can speculate whether Stuart's Stranglers would have been formed at all had the views of Granville Stuart, and like-minded cattlemen, not been influenced by their experiences in the Montana mining communities twenty years earlier.

The methods used by Stuart's Stranglers for suppressing animal rustling sharply contrasts with the methods used by the Wyoming Stock Growers Association in 1892 for dealing with similar problems. In Johnson County toward the northeastern quadrant of the state, the rustling problem was defined by the large cattle interests as persistent poaching by smaller homesteaders. Wealthy cattle owners financed and organized an army of local and Texas invaders, whose mission was to assassinate seventy elected officials, community leaders, and owners of small cattle ranches in mid-April of 1892.[89] The army of invaders met strong resistance from the local citizenry, which surrounded the invaders at the TA Ranch near Buffalo, Wyoming.[90] A two-day shooting standoff ended only upon the arrival of federal troops dispatched from nearby Fort McKinney.[91] Criminal charges against the members of the invading army were withdrawn by the prosecutor on January 21, 1893, as a series of clever legal maneuvers by defense attorneys made the conviction of any defendant virtually impossible.[92] Despite the dismissal of the criminal charges, the Johnson County War was a loss for the monied cattle interests in eastern Wyoming.

In Montana there were some ad hoc executions by vigilantes after events had quieted in Helena in 1870 and before the appearance of Stuart's Stranglers in 1884. M. A. Leeson makes reference to some of the executions for crimes such as murder, robbery, and arson between 1871 and early 1884.[93] One set of vigilante hangings were of Milford Coomes and William Henry Smith on March 18, 1883, for the alleged arson of a stable owned by H. H. McNally.[94] Eight horses, three cows, and a large supply of hay and grain were lost in the fire.[95] The two men were hanged from the limbs of aspen trees at Greenhorn, roughly twelve miles west of Helena.[96] Another ad hoc vigilante hanging was of William Rigney from a train trestle in Miles City on July 25, 1883, as a result of Rigney having assaulted two daughters of a prominent local resident while drunk.[97] The numbers "3–7–77" were attached to Rigney's shirt when his body was found.[98] The significance of these numbers will be discussed later in this chapter. Charley Brown, who had been a member of various vigilante posses operating out of Virginia City in 1864, is believed to have orchestrated Rigney's hanging.[99] The Coomes, Smith, and Rigney hangings, however, were incidents defined by their unique and limited facts. What makes Stuart's Stranglers historically significant by comparison is the planned organization of its efforts against a broad criminal element in the region, as opposed to merely operating on an ad hoc basis when a particular crime arose.

The vigilantism of 1884 caught the attention of Montana's territorial government. Governor John Schuyler Crosby noted that the criminal element operating in thinly populated areas needed to be confronted by extralegal means until the cattlemen could be protected by the federal government.[100] The territorial legislature that convened in 1885, known as the "Cowboy Legislature," enacted several bills favorable to ranchers, including one that regulated the registration of brands and another that established a Board of Livestock Commissioners with authority to hire livestock inspectors and detectives.[101] One of the earliest persons hired by the Commissioners was "Floppin' Bill" Cantrell,[102] a member of Stuart's Stranglers, who was described in that capacity as "very reliable, efficient, and fearless."[103]

*   *

The persons involved with vigilantism in Montana in the 1860s and 1880s are now long gone. One might believe, after so many years have passed since the relevant events, that the history of Montana vigilantism was closed. But it was not. Montana's vigilante history has produced additional continuing echoes.

A second echo of the territory's vigilantism took the form of the mock trial of Sheriff Henry Plummer that was sponsored by the Twin Bridges Public School System at the Madison County Courthouse in Virginia City on May 7, 1993, 129 years after the initial wave of vigilante executions at Bannack and Alder Gulch.[104] The idea for the trial arose from teacher Mark Weber's assignment of term papers on Sheriff Plummer, based upon Thomas Dimsdale's *The Vigilantes of Montana* as well as Ruth Mather and F. E. Boswell's *Hanging the Sheriff*, which presented opposite viewpoints of Plummer's role in crime and his hanging for it.[105] Judge Barbara Brook presided over the trial, with twelve adult jurors comprised of four men and eight women who heard three and a half hours of testimony.[106]

As a matter of trial strategy, Plummer's defense team sought to support its claim that Plummer had been framed by political adversaries, by showing inconsistencies between "Red" Yeager's list of road agents as described at different times by Dimsdale, Langford, and Beidler.[107] Judge Brook permitted into evidence only the Beidler list of road agents, as no students were playing the roles of Dimsdale or Langford by which their lists could be evidentially authenticated.[108] In any event, Sheriff Plummer's name appears on all of the lists described by Dimsdale, Langford, and Beidler. As a fallback position, the defense summation focused upon the lack of direct evidence tying Plummer to criminal activities capable of meeting the standard of guilt,[109] which might actually have been the strongest of the available defense arguments.

The mock jury deliberated about the evidence for an hour and a half.[110] The jury then reported a 6-6 deadlock which, ironically, is colloquially known as "hung jury," and the student playing the role of Henry Plummer was told that he was "free to go."[111] A total of seventy-two newspapers, historical journals, and television and radio stations from ten western states covered the story.[112] The 1993 mock trial is the only actual trial that Henry Plummer ever received in connection with his alleged road agent activities in Montana.

*   *   *

A third echo arises from the mock trial and regards the continuing historical controversy of whether Sheriff Plummer was wrongfully executed by the vigilantes. On July 1, 1993, a petition was filed seeking an official pardon for Sheriff Plummer. The pardon petition, dated May 21, 1993, was filed by Frederick J. Morgan, the publisher of History West Publishing, and by Professor Jack Burrows of the San Jose City College History Department. The petitioners argued that Plummer's pardon was warranted by the results of the mock trial at the Twin Bridges School and by the published opinion of Montana State University professor J. W. Smurr questioning the uncritical acceptance of the writings of Thomas Dimsdale and Nathaniel P. Langford. The petitioners also relied upon the historical research of Ruth Mather and F. E. Boswell, authors of various books on vigilantism, including *Hanging the Sheriff, Vigilante Victims*, and *Gold Camp Desperados*, which consistently present a sympathetic view of Henry Plummer and which represent, in their own ways, serious historical research and thought-provoking hypotheses.[113] The petition was supported by letters submitted by author-historians Frederick Morgan and Jack Burrows and by several other persons interested in the application residing in such varied states as California, Florida, Idaho, New York, Oregon, and Montana.[114] Support for the pardon application was clearly orchestrated. The petition, signed by Morgan, stated in its concluding paragraph that "[o]n behalf of my staff and the individual readers and scholars who have prodded our company to help correct a historical injustice, I request that the State of Montana grant Sheriff Henry Plummer a pardon."[115] The full text of the petition for the pardon of Henry Plummer is reproduced in Appendix F.

The petition was referred in the normal course to the Montana Board of Pardons and Parole, and Republican governor Marc Racicot promised that the application would receive prompt attention.[116]

In August of 1993, the Montana Board of Pardons and Parole declined to review the petition for the pardon of Sheriff Plummer. The board found that since Plummer had not been convicted in any official court of law, it was therefore without jurisdiction to act upon the petition on its merits.[117] The denial of the petition, for lack of jurisdiction, appears to be a procedurally correct determination. There have been no further efforts made for a pardon of Sheriff Plummer.

The 1993 petition that sought the pardon of Sheriff Plummer visibly represents the continuing historical controversy over whether Plummer was, in fact, the head of a criminal enterprise. Was Plummer an innocent man wrongfully hanged by the vigilantes?

The weight of the evidence supports the conclusion that Henry Plummer was a generally violent man and that he was involved in the criminal enterprise that led to his death. The 1993 petition for Plummer's pardon was not the first time that a petition had been filed to exonerate him for crime, but the second. California governor John Weller had already pardoned Plummer for the adjudicated murder of John Vedder, which resulted in Plummer's release from San Quentin prison in August of 1859.[118] Apologists for Henry Plummer fail to acknowledge that he had been convicted of murder in California by two juries prior to the establishment of his residency in Montana and that he would not have been present in Montana at all but for Governor Weller's political favor or mercy that pardoned him from his adjudicated California homicide. While Plummer's murder conviction in California is not evidence that he later committed any crimes in Montana Territory, it may speak indirectly and negatively of his general character, tendency for violence, and the placement of his own interests ahead of others in society. Indeed, Plummer's violent tendencies, which were revealed on several other occasions, appear to be sufficiently documented.

Authors Ruth E. Mather and F. E. Boswell have argued in their books that many of the people who were hanged by the vigilantes in Alder Gulch came from good family backgrounds, such as Buck Stinson,[119] while some of the vigilante leaders gambled, drank, and married unusually young girls.[120] However, the good upbringing of some of the persons hanged is not evidence that they were law-abiding during their rough-and-tumble years on the Montana gold-mining frontier. Henry Plummer's friend Cyrus Skinner was a known escapee from San Quentin prison prior to his own execution by Montana vigilantes.[121] To the extent that any of the vigilantes may have drunk heavily or gambled frequently, such activities were commonplace for grown men at that place and time and also cast no light on the guilt of the individual conspirators identified by "Red" Yeager in January of 1864. While the accounts of the days' history by Dimsdale and Langford, standing alone, may or may not be sufficient to definitively say who was guilty of what, the details of those accounts are corroborated in many respects by other authors in letters, diaries, reminiscences, and additional writings independent of Dimsdale and Langford and by confessions of some of the condemned men prior to their own executions. Conrad Kohrs is an example, who wrote in his autobiography of his belief that robbery attempts against him by George Ives and "Dutch John" Wagner had been at the instigation of Sheriff Plummer.[122] Henry Tilden is another example, who recounted that he had been robbed at gunpoint on November 14, 1863, by three men that included Sheriff Plummer.[123] Tilden's revelation is what caused the vigilantes assembled in Bannack to decide upon executing Plummer the next day.[124] There is no reason to doubt Wilbur Fisk Sanders's expressed belief in Tilden's honesty, and on the evening in question, Plummer never arrived at the Rattlesnake Ranch, where he had earlier announced he would be. The extent to which Dimsdale and Langford are independently corroborated in their details by other independent writings bolsters the traditional accounts of Montana vigilante history and undermines the revisionist accounts. Under the traditional view, Sheriff Plummer and his associates were guilty of the crimes for which they were hanged. People at the time, though living lives far different from ours today, nevertheless had the common sense to connect dots, at least with respect to the major actors of the criminal conspiracy that plagued Bannack and Alder Gulch in 1863–64.

*   *   *   *

A fourth echo of times past concerns the remains of George "Clubfoot" Lane. Lane was hanged in Virginia City on January 14, 1864, with four other members of the road agent gang, Frank Parish, Hayes Lyons, Jack Gallagher, and Boone Helm. Years later, in 1907, some of the aged ex-vigilantes disputed who was buried where along the row of graves on Boot Hill.[125] One account states that the dispute was between Wilbur Fisk Sanders and Adriel Davis,[126] but that account cannot be entirely accurate as Sanders had indisputably died two years earlier, in 1905.[127] The account can be accurate only if the date in question preceded Sanders's death. In any event, one of the aged ex-vigilantes insisted he knew where Lane was buried, so they dug up the grave and found Lane's remains, identifiable by the deformed bones of his foot.[128] Lane's foot bones can be viewed today as an exhibit at the Thompson-Hickman Museum and Library on Idaho Street in Virginia City, Montana.[129]

*   *   *   *   *

A fifth echo is the numerical sequence "3–7–77." The numbers frequently appeared at the sites of vigilante activities, both in San Francisco in the 1850s and in Montana in the 1860s, and are uniquely associated with vigilantism. The mere

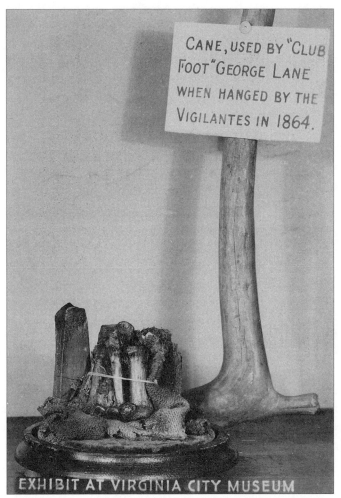

Figure 16.3. The exhumed and deformed foot bones of George "Clubfoot" Lane. (Courtesy of the Montana Historical Society, image 956-267.)

appearance of the numbers in a public location was a warning sign to criminals that they leave town. The numerical sequence could mysteriously appear anywhere on posters, tent flaps, and sidewalks. As communities grew in Montana in the late 1800s at places like Butte, Billings, Bozeman, Helena, and Missoula, the appearance of "3–7–77" announced the presence of a band of vigilantes prepared to impose summary punishment upon wrongdoers. No book on Montana vigilantism could be complete without an acknowledgment of the numbers and their meaning to law and order in the vast expanses of the state's boundaries.

What do the numbers symbolize? The meaning of the "mystic numbers" has befuddled many. One explanation is that they refer to the size of a grave that must typically be dug for persons executed; namely, three feet wide, seven feet long, and seventy-seven inches deep.[130] This explanation, while perhaps plausible, fails to account for the differences in the heights and sizes of vigilante victims' corpses and the sizes of their graves.

Another explanation is that it refers to the amount of time that vigilantes gave someone to get out of town—three hours, seven minutes, and seventy-seven seconds.[131] This alternate explanation is not persuasive, as vigilantes imposed executions rather than banishments in the vast majority of instances and as there is no logical reason why, with sixty-second minutes and sixty-minute hours, the numbers would also refer to seventy-seven seconds.[132] A related explanation, that a criminal could flee Helena for Butte in 1879 for three dollars on a seven o'clock stagecoach, with the significance of "77" uncertain,[133] fails to acknowledge that "3–7–77" preceded the rise of vigilantism in Helena.

A further explanation is that the numbers refer to the professions of the earliest members of the Alder Gulch Vigilance Committee: namely, three lawyers, seven merchants, and seventy-seven miners.[134] This explanation is also unsatisfactory. The first known meeting for the formation of a Vigilance Committee at Alder Gulch on December 20, 1863, on the eve of the George Ives verdict, was attended by five men rather than three—Wilbur Fisk Sanders, Major Alvin W. Brockie, John Nye, Captain Nick Wall, and Paris Pfouts.[135] Odds are, of the first eighty-seven committee members, more professions were represented than merely lawyers, merchants, and miners. The theory excludes ranchers, coachmen, assayers, doctors, teachers, farmers, freighters, newspapermen, and all other remaining professions.

Yet another explanation is Masonic in origin. It posits that a dying man gave a Masonic sign to two friends and discovered that they, too, were Masons. The three men discussed finding enough other Masons to give the dying man a funeral with full Masonic rites. Additional Masons were enlisted, bringing the total to seven. When the funeral was held, seventy-six Masons were in attendance, plus the decedent, bringing the total to seventy-seven.[136] But this explanation is as unsatisfactory as the others. It recognizes the bond that Masons had for one another in the western territories, which enabled them to trust one another with the life-and-death issues associated with vigilantism. However, the linking of "3–7–77" to Masonic fraternity is based upon no documentable facts and appears to be nothing more than unsubstantiated lore.

The most plausible explanation of "3–7–77" is that it traces its origin to the San Francisco vigilantes who had earlier used the same numerical symbols and that the numbers were merely borrowed by the various Montana vigilance organizations that formed later.[137] In San Francisco vigilante members were each assigned a number, and the numbers 3, 7, and 77 represented executive positions that were authorized to impose death sentences upon captured crimi-nals.[138] The numerical sequence appeared during later incidences of vigilantism in Denver.[139] The true origin and meaning of the numbers must therefore be sought in California rather than in Montana. Predictably, the mystic numbers will continue to confound students of western territorial vigilantism.

Irrespective of the numbers' hidden meaning, they have appeared, on occa-sion, at certain unpleasant events during the last century. In 1917 the controver-sial leader of the leftist Industrial Workers of the World, Frank Little, was seized by masked men and hanged from a bridge with a sign on his back bearing the numbers "3–7–77." During a portion of 1973, Madison County police were temporarily assigned to Helena and left the Virginia City area without police protection. Signs depicting "3–7–77" appeared in their absence, including five signs that were prominently displayed on the day that a murder suspect was arraigned in a Madison County court.[140]

Since 1956, the "3–7–77" sequence has been depicted on the shoulder patch of the uniforms of the Montana State Highway Patrol as a symbol of aggres-sive law enforcement.[141] The "3–7–77" moniker is understood in the unpopu-lated, rural expanses of Montana. The state, after all, had no specific statewide speed limit until 1999.[142] In 2009 Montana enacted its Firearms Freedom Act, signed into law by Democratic governor Brian Schweitzer, providing that guns, gun accessories, and ammunition manufactured and used exclusively within Montana are not part of interstate commerce and, therefore, are exempt from federal gun control regulation.[143] The absence of a state speed limit for so many years, and the state's efforts to be exempted from federal gun laws, fit the inde-pendence of the "3–7–77" patch on the state's highway patrol uniforms. Similar symbolism would appear out of place in many other states such as those on the east and west coasts and in the industrial Midwest.

*   *   *   *   *   *

A sixth echo of Montana vigilante past is found in the sixty ghost towns that dot the map of the former territory. Ghost towns may be found at Alton, Argo, Bannack, Barker, Bean, Bear Creek, Bearmouth, Bowler, Cable, Carter, Castle City, Coloma, Comet, Coolidge, Copper Cliff, Elkhorn, Ewing, Exeter, Fort Benton, Fox, Garnet, Gilt Edge, Maiden, Gold Creek, Granite, Hassel, Hecla, Hillsboro, Hughsville, Independence, Kendall, Keystone, Landusky, Lauren, Lion City, Lockhart Ranch, Maiden, Mammoth, Marysville, Melrose, Montana City, Nevada City, Old Chico, Pardee, Pioneer in Beaverhead County, Pioneer in Powell County, Pony, Red Lion, Rimini, Rockvale, Ruby Gulch, Silesia, Silver Bow, Southern Cross, Storrs, Taft, Virginia City, Washoe, Wicks, and Zortman.[144] The overwhelming majority of Montana ghost towns consist, at best, of some old buildings or cabins, abandoned mineshafts, and other ruins. Most of the remnants of Alton, in Glacier County, are now at the bottom of a lake.[145]

Bannack is one of Montana's more famous ghost towns for reasons that are obvious to the reader. After Sheriff Plummer's hanging in 1864, gold hunters have searched the area for decades for whatever treasure Plummer might have left hidden there.[146] There is no credible evidence that any treasure was ever found, and the lore that Plummer's treasure existed might actually exceed the reality.

The most famous of Montana's ghost towns are Virginia City and Nevada City in Madison County, which offer organized tours, activities, museums, cemeteries, gift stores, re-creations, and historic sites. Virginia City and Nevada City declined in the 1870s and 1880s from a combination of three irreparable economic factors: the gradual depletion of their gold resources, the relocation of Montana's territorial capital to Helena, and the absence of a railroad line connecting the cities to any centers of commerce. Virginia City, the territory's former capital, has been a continuously operating municipality since its founding in 1863, with approximately 150 year-round present-day residents,[147] and it has been preserved with the assistance of the Montana Heritage Commission.[148] To this day, the scars of extensive placer mining activity are visible along the rocky banks of Alder Gulch, and the historic cemeteries of Virginia City continue to look down at the town from their crests high above.

*   *   *   *   *   *   *

The reader might wonder what eventually happened to some of the major actors in Montana vigilantism of the 1860s, to the extent that information about them is known.

John Bozeman, who blazed the Bozeman Trail, which helped facilitate access to the region, met an unfortunate and ironic fate on April 18, 1866, when he was killed by Blackfeet Indians a few miles east of present-day Livingston, Montana, on the south side of the Yellowstone River.[149] He was traveling at the time with Tom Cover,[150] who had been with William Fairweather when gold was discovered in Alder Gulch on May 26, 1863. Bozeman was initially buried at the site of his death, but his body was later exhumed and reburied in the Sunset Hills Cemetery in the city that bears his name.[151]

William Fairweather, the initial discoverer of gold at Alder Gulch and the drinking partner of J. A. Slade, mismanaged the money he had earned from his placer mining until he was broke; he died of natural causes at Pete Daly's ranch at the age of thirty-nine.[152]

Barney Hughes, another member of the Virginia City discovery party, invested much of his mining wealth in San Francisco real estate, only to learn that the man who sold it to him did not actually own it in the first place.[153]

Figure 16.4. Virginia City today. (Photo by author.)

Hughes returned to prospecting and died of natural causes at age ninety-one in Wisdom, Montana, on October 15, 1909.[154] Hughes had the longest known lifespan of any individual recounted in this narrative.

Tom Cover, another member of the Alder Gulch discovery party, used his gold wealth to make even more money in milling and then in real estate in San Bernardino, California.[155] He mysteriously disappeared in the 1880s, his fate unknown.[156]

James "Bill" Sweeney of the discovery party took his gold wealth to North Dakota and died there in the 1920s.[157]

The details of Henry Rodgers's life after leaving Alder Gulch are uncertain.

Henry Edgar, the final member of the party that discovered gold at Alder Gulch, lived to an old age.[158] A copy of a journal that he maintained in 1863 was transcribed by Israel Clem, a member of Montana's Seventh Territorial Legislature.[159] The transcription was given to the Montana Historical Society, which included the material in its 1900 publication entitled *Contributions to the Historical Society of Montana.* During his later years he earned his living as a farmer, and his wife's letters suggest that money was tight in their old age.[160] Edgar died on November 12, 1910, at the age of eighty-two.[161] The town of Edgar, Montana, located approximately twenty-five miles southwest of Billings, is named after him.[162]

Hill Beachy, who was most instrumental in Lewistown, Idaho, for bringing to justice the perpetrators of the particularly gruesome Magruder Trail murders, made a living operating a stage line between Nevada and Idaho.[163] While his date of birth is uncertain, he died of a stroke in San Francisco on May 24, 1875, at the estimated age of fifty-three.[164] He outlived his wife and six of his seven children and was buried with his family at the Marysville Cemetery near Yuba City, California, just north of Sacramento.[165]

Billy Page, who had been part of the Magruder Trail robbery but who saved his life in Lewiston, Idaho, by testifying against "Doc" Howard, Chris Lowrie, and James Romaine, worked for Hill Beachy for approximately one year, during which time he was the subject of continued public scorn.[166] He was then shot and killed by an adversary during a drunken brawl.[167]

Anton Holter, who was shot at during a trail robbery on December 8, 1863, by two men believed to be George Ives and Aleck Carter, made a fortune in lumber and in the wholesaling and retailing of hardware, mining equipment, and machinery.[168] One of his companies, A. M. Holter Hardware Company, became the oldest continuously operated business in Montana until its liquidation in 1958.[169] Holter died on July 16, 1921, at the age of ninety.[170]

Although "Bummer Dan" McFadden slipped into obscurity after his days at Alder Gulch, his caricature inspired a printed cartoon strip in 1947 called *Loafer's Reward*.[171]

Captain James Williams, who led vigilante posses, met an unfortunate end. Williams, a cattleman, faced financial ruin when the harsh winter of 1887 killed untold head of cattle in Montana.[172] He had traveled into Virginia City to discuss a bank loan and, upon leaving the bank, purchased an ounce of laudanum at a drugstore.[173] He may also have been depressed over having lost an election for the office of county sheriff.[174] During the early morning hours of February 21, 1887, he wandered through a snowstorm to a field at the lower portion of his ranch and committed suicide by poisoning himself with the laudanum.[175] Williams's frozen corpse was not discovered for two days by those who searched for him.[176] His body was located on its side in the snow, with a scarf and mittens used as a pillow, next to the empty laudanum bottle.[177] He died at age fifty-three.[178] In an undated letter Williams's son, John M. Williams, described his deceased father as "a true leader of men [who] excelled as an organizer and his control of turbulent men was perfect . . . The Montana Vigilance Committee was irresistible[,] absolutely fearless[.] [H]e was at no time arrogant[,] he was a kindly father and an honorable Gentleman."[179] Williams was honored by the Montana State Legislature in 1907 by the placement of a bronze plaque in the main hall of the Capitol.[180] A plaque in his honor also adorns the wall of a historic building at the corner of Wallace and Van Buren Streets in Virginia City, the same site where George "Clubfoot" Lane, Frank Parish, Boone Helm, Hayes Lyons, and Jack Gallagher were hanged on January 14, 1864.

Figure 16.5. Plaque in honor of James Williams in a preserved building near the corner of Wallace and Van Buren Streets, Virginia City. (Photo by author.)

Adriel Davis, the sheriff of Junction City who headed the vigilante posse that captured William Hunter, among others, died in Montana of natural causes on January 21, 1915, roughly half a century after the events.[181]

George Hilderman, who was tried immediately after George Ives for the murder of Nicholas Tiebolt, went to California upon his banishment from Montana, where he later died.[182]

Attorney H. P. A. Smith, a member of the defense team at the trial of George Ives, had been banished from the territory by the Vigilance Committee in 1864. He lived briefly in Utah and Arizona; in a display of great courage he returned to Montana in 1865 to meet any charge that the vigilantes believed could be made against him.[183] The vigilantes left him alone. He established a law practice in Helena and died there of natural causes in 1870 at the age of fifty.[184] Smith's obituary in the *Rocky Mountain News* described him as "a man of much more than ordinary ability, but ruined himself and doubtless shortened his life by dissipation and irregular habits."[185]

Attorney James M. Thurmond, who had also been banished by the Alder Gulch vigilantes to Salt Lake City in 1864, later relocated to Dallas, Texas, where he served as mayor in 1879 and 1880.[186] According to the *Waco Daily Examiner*, Thurmond "had many narrow escapes from serious personal violence, on account of his bitter, venomous sentiments and his violent expressions of hatred for his enemies and his opponents."[187] He was ousted as mayor by a vote of the city council but two years later sought to resurrect his political career by running for the position of city alderman from Dallas's Second Ward.[188] On March 14, 1882, at the age of forty-four, he was shot and killed in a courtroom during a quarrel with a fellow lawyer and political rival, Robert E. Cowart.[189] Witnesses described Thurmond as the initial aggressor of the two, and according to one newspaper account, "both men almost simultaneously drew their pistols."[190] Cowart's bullet struck Thurmond in the head, "blowing out his brain and causing instant death."[191] Cowart was indicted and tried for murder in the second degree. The jury selection for Cowart's trial proved difficult, as many people in the Dallas community had formed strong opinions about the case prior to the trial.[192] The jury's deliberations also proved difficult, as the jurors were initially unable to reach a verdict, but after further discussions that continued through an entire night, Cowart was convicted of murder and sentenced to seven years of imprisonment.[193] The conviction was a surprise to many in the community who knew of Thurmond's temperament and who believed that Cowart had acted in self-defense.[194] Fortunately for Cowart, he was granted a new trial a year later and was acquitted.[195] Notably, Thurmond's killing was dealt with from beginning to end through the Texas court system and not through vigilantism. Thurmond probably would have approved.

William Y. Pemberton, who acted as the court reporter during the trial of George Ives and who provided legal representation to James B. Daniels in Helena, had a distinguished career as an attorney, public servant, judge, and historian. In 1887 he helped successfully prosecute Thomas Harding for a murder in Dillon, Montana, and Harding's execution was the first "legal" hanging performed in Beaverhead County in southwest Montana.[196] He served as a delegate to Montana's 1866 and 1884 constitutional conventions, was a judge in the Second District from 1890 to 1893, and was then elected chief judge of the state of Montana in November of 1892, a position in which he served from 1893 to 1899.[197] Later in his life, Pemberton wrote an essay on the early history of Montana courts.[198]

Wilbur Fisk Sanders achieved lifetime notoriety for his successful prosecution of George Ives. He went on to a successful and well-rounded career in law and politics. He served as the head of Montana's Republican Party. He was elected to four terms in the Montana Territorial Legislature and in 1890 became a US senator for Montana, serving in that capacity until 1893.[199] He also served as the first president of the Montana Historical Society.[200] In February of 1905, the Montana State Legislature created Sanders County, named for him a few months before his death.[201] Sanders County is located in the northwest quadrant of the state, inclusive of the Cabinet Mountains and the Clark Fork River, with a county seat at Thompson Falls. Sanders died in Helena of cancer on July 8, 1905.[202] After Sanders's death, Anton Holter, a staunch Republican, headed the Wilbur F. Sanders Memorial Association, which raised money for the erection of Sanders's statue, which was placed in the Montana Capitol rotunda in 1913, but which was later moved to the second floor near the building's side parking lot.[203] The base of the statue has three lines under Sanders's name, the last of which is a reference to the command that is given the moment before a defendant facing execution is caused to drop:

PIONEER SOLDIER
LAWYER STATESMAN
MEN DO YOUR DUTY

Thomas Dimsdale's newspaper articles on vigilante exploits proved so popular with the public that appreciative vigilantes honored him at an award ceremony in early October of 1865, at which he was presented with an ivory-handled silver-mounted pistol and coordinating leather belt.[204] Dimsdale married thirty-year-old Annette Hotchkiss in May of 1866.[205] He died of tuberculosis on September 22, 1866, at the young age of thirty-five, only four months after the marriage.[206] His book, *The Vigilantes of Montana*, which is still available today, is his life's legacy. It is the single most detailed account, written contemporaneously with the events in question, of the vigilante activities of the region in 1864 and 1865. From the standpoint of historians, Dimsdale's death was devastatingly unfortunate, as it prevented his continuing narrative of vigilante events in the months and years that followed.

Nathaniel Langford had a distinguished career in public service as a tax collector for the US Internal Revenue Service, with his jurisdiction being the territory of Montana.[207] As noted in the preface, he was nominated by outgoing President Andrew Johnson to be governor of Montana Territory in 1868, but the lame-duck Senate refused to act upon the nomination.[208] In 1870 Langford became the first superintendent of the Yellowstone Reserve and from 1872 to 1876 was the bank examiner for the western territories.[209] Langford's book, *Vigilante Days and Ways,* was first published in 1890. Langford died of natural causes in St. Paul, Minnesota, on October 18, 1911, at the age of seventy-nine.[210]

Alexander Toponce lived a long life as a miner, rancher, freighter, and businessman in various western territories and states, dying of natural causes on

Figure 16.6. Statue of Wilbur Fisk Sanders, Montana Capitol Building. (Photo by author.)

May 13, 1923, at the age of eighty-three.[211] On May 10, 1869, he was present for the driving of the "Golden Spike" in Promontory, Utah, which connected the Union Pacific and Central Pacific Railroads.[212] His reminiscences were published by his family after his death.[213]

Edwin Ruthven Purple died of pneumonia in New York on January 20, 1879, at the age of forty-eight.[214] He is buried not in Madison County, Montana, but, ironically, in Madison County, New York.[215]

Paris Pfouts left a manuscript describing his life that included the organization and earliest days of the Alder Gulch Vigilance Committee. However, only three and a half pages of the one-hundred-page manuscript address the formation and work of the Vigilance Committee, as most of the manuscript is instead devoted to Pfouts's family roots and his broader life and accomplishments outside of Montana.[216] This suggests that either Pfouts did not consider vigilante events as particularly significant in his life, or, alternatively, he continued to downplay the details of those events to protect the persons involved. Pfouts was elected mayor of Virginia City in 1865, defeating John J. Hull in the election by only one vote.[217] His win was attributed to the fact that Pfouts had been a supporter of the Confederacy whereas Hull had been a supporter of the Union, even though the Civil War had ended the same year.[218] Pfouts returned to his native St. Louis in 1867 to establish a wholesale grocery business there.[219] He died of natural causes at the home of his son in Dallas, Texas, in 1910, at the age of eighty-one.[220]

Sydney Edgerton returned to Ohio after serving as Montana's first territorial governor and practiced law there until his death on July 19, 1900, at the age of eighty-one.[221] According to the *Akron Daily Democrat*, Edgerton's death was not attributed to any one malady but to "a general breaking down of an unusually strong constitution."[222]

Three of the women described in this narrative, Electa Plummer, Maria Slade, and Mollie Sheehan, each later married husbands and lived to old ages. Sheriff Plummer's widow, Electa Plummer, had actually left him on September 2, 1863, two months after their marriage and three months before her husband's death.[223] She had moved to Salt Lake City complaining of loneliness because her husband was so preoccupied with his work.[224] It is uncertain whether Electa Plummer had learned that her husband was living life on both sides of the law and whether that information, if known, contributed to her decision to leave the marriage.[225] On January 19, 1874, she remarried a widowed South Dakota rancher named James Maxwell, who already had six children, and bore two sons of her own.[226] She never spoke out against the men who had executed her first husband.[227] A letter from one of her step-daughters, Mrs. John Slattery, addressed to the Montana Historical Society on July 1, 1930, assured that Electa

Maxwell never returned to Montana, which belied any rumors that she bore a son with Henry Plummer or that she had ever found a large sum of money that Plummer had hidden away.[228] Electa Maxwell died in South Dakota on May 5, 1912, from complications of a fractured hip sustained from a fall, three days short of her seventieth birthday.[229] She is buried at Wakonda, South Dakota.[230]

Maria Slade sold the house and ranch where she and her husband, J. A. Slade, had lived in exchange for the sum of $7,000.[231] She probated her husband's will, which had the distinction of being the first probate proceeding in the history of Montana Territory, as most persons who died in the western mining communities did not make wills.[232] One year and twelve days after the hanging of her husband, Maria Slade remarried a local store owner, James Kiskadden, on March 22, 1865.[233] She was regarded as an exceptionally beautiful woman, the best dancer, the best horsewoman, the best female gun shooter in all of the Northwest.[234] According to the *Montana Post,* which reported the story of Maria and James Kiskadden's nuptials, the wedding was performed by Chief Judge Hezekiah Hosmer and two gold "V's" were imbedded upon two wedding cakes at the couple's Virginia City reception.[235] The couple moved to Salt Lake City.[236] Although the newspaper extended well wishes to the bride and groom—"May you and your amiable bride enjoy many long years of happiness and content"[237]—the marriage did not last, as there were frequent arguments and violent quarrels between them.[238] Maria and James Kiskadden received a divorce almost three years later, on March 12, 1868.[239] It was said that Maria Slade Kiskadden had become too embittered and violent from the execution of her first husband.[240] James Kiskadden later married a Salt Lake City dancer named Annie Adams, and their child, Maude Adams, became a nationally renowned actress during the years before and after the turn of the twentieth century.[241] Maria Slade Kiskadden next married Elhener Crosby, but that marriage also did not work, and she eventually returned to her native Missouri.[242] During the last years of her life, she made her living as the madam of a brothel, though historians dispute whether its location was in Omaha or Chicago.[243]

Mollie Sheehan and other young children at Alder Gulch made a practice of cleaning prospectors' sluice boxes at the end of each workday. There was an innocuous incident of Mollie's childhood that she remembered for years to come. One day she cleaned a sluice box that belonged to Peter Ronan, but was careful to place her new bonnet on a crosspiece of the box to protect it from getting dirty.[244] Ronan was not aware of the child's presence and lifted the gate of the box, which splattered Sheehan's bonnet with mud.[245] Young Mollie was indignant, yelling at Ronan, "I'll never, never, never again, Mister, take gold from your sluice boxes!"[246] The incident was Sheehan's first memory of Ronan, who was many years her senior.[247] The Sheehan family followed Montana's gold rush from Virginia City to Helena. In 1869, as a teenager, Sheehan moved with her family from Helena to California, where she toiled on her father's farm and, thereafter, on June 14, 1872, graduated from the Academy of the Sisters of St. Vincent de Paul.[248] While in California, she maintained correspondence with Peter Ronan, who had remained in Helena and Blackfoot City, and married him in February of 1873.[249] At the time of her marriage, Mollie wore her hair so long that it extended below her hips.[250] The couple lived happily in Helena and had nine children.[251] Ronan gave up his careers as a prospector and newspaperman and made a living as a federal government agent to the Indian tribes at the Flathead Reservation from 1877 until his death on August 20, 1893.[252] Mollie Sheehan, known as an adult as Mary Ronan, was widowed for a total of forty-seven years. In 1929 she dictated her reminiscences to her daughter, Margaret, who used the reminiscences, entitled *Memoirs of a Frontiers Woman*, as a master's thesis at Montana State University, now the University of Montana. The thesis became the basis of two books, *Frontier Woman: The Story of Mary Ronan as Told to Margaret Ronan*, by H. G. Merriam of the University of Montana,[253] and *Girl from the Gulches: The Story of Mary Ronan*, by interpretive historian Dr. Ellen Baumler of the Montana Historical Society.[254] Mary Ronan outlived five of her children and died in 1940 of natural causes at the approximate age of eighty-eight.[255] Mollie Sheehan is the youngest person to appear in this narrative and, given her long lifespan, is apparently the only individual personally familiar with the events of Alder Gulch who survived to the year 1940.

D. J. Miller of Albertville, Alabama, was one of the "last chance" prospectors who discovered gold at Helena and who the reader will recall sought gold wealth so that he would be permitted to marry Mary Henry of his home state. Miller became so wealthy as a result of the gold discovery at Last Chance Gulch that he did, in fact, marry Mary Henry, with the blessing of Mary Henry's father.[256] The couple had three children and moved to Waco, Texas, where Mary died in 1895.[257] Miller returned to his native Alabama and died there in 1914 of natural causes at the approximate age of eighty-three.[258]

Another member of the discovery party at Last Chance Gulch was John Cowan. Cowan cashed out his gold holdings early and returned to his native Georgia, where he built a sawmill.[259] He died on March 3, 1900, at the age of eighty-seven.[260]

Neil Howie worked as a US marshal and deputy US marshal in Helena until 1870, when he left for Wyoming to help defend his brother in a murder trial.[261] Howie remained in the Wyoming, Colorado, and Utah territories until 1874, when he moved to South America to prospect for gold; he died there of malaria in the spring after his arrival, near French Guyana.[262]

Figure 16.7. Mollie Sheehan, known in her adult years as Mary
Ronan, on her wedding day in 1873. (Courtesy of the Maureen
and Mike Mansfield Library, University of Montana, K. Ross Toole
Archives, image 83.0138.)

Howie's diaries for the years 1864 through 1869 are archived at the Montana
Historical Society.[263]

Although Governor Thomas Francis Meagher is believed to have died at the
Missouri River on July 1, 1867, his body was never recovered and his cause of
death was never definitively ascertained. In 1898 a trapper named Tom Dunbar
found the preserved, ossified remains of a middle-aged man in the water of the

Missouri River south of Fort Benton.[264] The hands of the body were bound together with rawhide, and there was a bullet hole in the center of the forehead.[265] The body measured 5 feet 10 inches and was clean-shaven except for a moustache.[266] The figure greatly resembled that of Governor Meagher.[267] Dunbar sold the petrified body to R. A. Fraser of Helena, who organized the Montana Petrified Man Company and exhibited the ossified body of "Governor Meagher" for almost twenty years at fairs in Montana and the greater United States.[268] It mattered little that no account of Meagher's death ever included a gunshot wound to the head. "Petrified Man" was thereafter exhibited at shows in Australia and New South Wales, near to where Meagher had earlier been banished by Great Britain.[269]

Elizabeth "Libby" Meagher, the wife of Governor Meagher, returned to New York in the autumn of 1867 after her husband's death, settled in the town of Rye, and lived there as a widow for thirty-nine years.[270] There was no reason for her to stay in Montana after her husband's death. She lived off a small annual income derived from mineral leases that she and her husband had acquired during their brief time in Montana.[271] Elizabeth Meagher died on July 5, 1906, at the age of seventy-five and is buried at Green-Wood Cemetery in Brooklyn, New York.[272] Although the body of her husband was never located by the patrols that searched the Missouri River during the summer of 1867, a gravestone for her husband was placed beside her own gravestone in 2008.[273]

Green Clay Smith, who succeeded Thomas Meagher as governor of Montana, resigned from his gubernatorial position on April 9, 1869, as he had become an ordained Baptist minister the same year and was assigned by his superiors to a church in Frankfort, Kentucky.[274] He was a strong advocate of temperance and was nominated for the US presidency in 1876 by the National Prohibition Party, receiving 9,522 votes in the election.[275] The election was won by Republican Rutherford B. Hayes of Ohio over Democrat Samuel J. Tilden of New York, in what was one of the closest and most controversial presidential elections in American history. Votes received by third-party candidates in close states were therefore of political significance. Smith served as pastor of the Metropolitan Baptist Church in Washington, DC, from 1890 until his death from natural causes on June 29, 1895, at the age of seventy-nine.[276]

Ohio Congressman James M. Ashley, chairman of the House Committee on Territories, who was influential in naming Montana, drawing its boundaries, and pushing the legislation that voided the acts of the territory's second and third legislatures, lost his bid for reelection to the US House of Representatives in 1868.[277] He was then appointed by President Ulysses S. Grant as Montana's third governor, the successor of Green Clay Smith.[278] Ashley had an excellent working knowledge of the territory, but his appointment was approved by the

US Senate by a mere one-vote margin.[279] Ashley served as Montana's governor only briefly, from April 9, 1869, to July 12, 1870, as he was removed from office for his public criticisms of the same president who had appointed him.[280] Ashley thereafter served as president of the Toledo, Ann Arbor & Northern Railroad from 1877 to 1893.[281] He died of heart failure at a Michigan sanitarium on September 16, 1896, at the age of seventy-one.[282]

Democratic congressman Samuel McLean, who upon the nullification of Montana's second and third legislatures warned on the floor of the US House of Representatives that Montana could disassociate with the United States and affiliate instead with Canada, did not run for reelection after completing his second term in office in 1867.[283] In 1870 he formed the McLean Silver Mining Company and relocated his residence to Burkeville, Virginia, where he lived until his death from natural causes on July 16, 1877.[284] He was always quite obese and died at the relatively young age of fifty.[285]

Samuel T. Hauser made substantial money in banking and later became the seventh governor of Montana, serving in office by appointment of President Grover Cleveland from July 14, 1885, until February 7, 1887.[286] He died of natural causes on November 10, 1914, at the age of eighty-one.[287]

John X. Beidler was renowned for his enthusiastic vigilantism. Of the small number of portrait photographs taken of him, he is almost always posed, whether standing or seated, holding a long-barreled rifle. Beidler was not much taller than the length of his rifles,[288] but his short height was belied by an indisputable inner toughness and courage. He spent several years as a deputy US marshal in Helena and demonstrated a continuing knack for apprehending suspected criminals. Beidler arrested hundreds of men during his lifetime, often in distant regions of the territory and without the assistance of others, and personally hanged some of the men that he captured.[289] Later in life he became embittered and destitute, living off of the charity of others who fondly remembered his legendary law enforcement accomplishments. He died in Helena of natural causes on January 22, 1890, at the age of fifty-eight.[290] Helen Fitzgerald Sanders, who was the daughter-in-law of Wilbur Fisk Sanders, and William H. Bertsche Jr. assembled Beidler's journals into a book entitled *X. Beidler: Vigilante*, which was published in 1957. Beidler might have been quite amazed that his journals ever merited publication.

William Chumasero had a long and lucrative career as an attorney in Montana Territory. He had prosecuted James Daniels at trial for the murder of Andrew Gartley, which resulted in Daniels's conviction to the lesser included charge of manslaughter. He is less known for the crucial role he played as an attorney in matters that resulted in the removal of Montana's capital from Virginia City to Helena, which was approved by the Eighth Montana

Territorial Legislature on February 11, 1874, subject to a public referendum.[291] It was not the first time that the location of Montana's capital was put to a public referendum, nor would it be the last. The vote of the legislature must have pleased Chumasero, as his law office was located in Helena and it could only be of benefit for a lawyer to be proximate to a state or territorial capital. But when the public referendum was conducted on the issue on August 3, 1874, the majority of the voters in the territory were reported to have favored retaining the seat of government in Virginia City. The vote results were close but controversial. Chumasero commenced a case in the Montana Supreme Court, *Chumasero v. Potts*, alleging that the votes of two counties—Meagher County and Gallatin County—had not been properly counted in determining the referendum and that a correction would tip the final tally in favor of Helena.[292] In Meagher County in particular, Chumasero claimed that the public had voted 561 to 29 to move the territorial capital to Helena but that the voting results had been recorded by the territorial secretary in reverse order, 29 in favor to 561 opposed.[293] Chumasero's suit successfully resulted in the issuance of a court order in early 1875 that compelled the inclusion of the correct votes of the two disputed counties.[294] *Chumasero v. Potts* was the first case in the young Montana territory to stand for the proposition that courts could compel governmental officers to perform ministerial acts, a legal concept known as *mandamus*.[295] Chumasero's adversaries took the matter to the US Supreme Court, which, in October 1875, dismissed the appeal on the ground that Chumasero's adversaries would not be damaged by a proper counting of the counties' ballots.[296] The final vote tally, determined after the lawsuit had been decided by Montana's Supreme Court, resulted in the reversal of the election results and the relocation of the territorial capital to Helena,[297] which hastened the continuing economic and population decline of Virginia City. The result of the case has had lasting political and economic effects, as Helena remains Montana's capital to this day.[298] Chumasero died of pneumonia at Redondo Beach, California, on February 23, 1893, at the age of seventy-four.[299] His body was returned to Helena for interment.

Montana Supreme Court justice Lorenzo P. Williston was not a particularly notable player in the territory's legal history or its story of vigilantism, perhaps because he spent much of his judicial tenure traveling outside of Montana rather than judging cases.[300] He completed his full term on the Montana Supreme Court in July of 1868 and was replaced by Hiram Knowles of Iowa.[301] Williston resumed the practice of law in Pennsylvania and died there of a stroke in 1887 at the age of seventy-two.[302]

Chief Judge Hezekiah Hosmer also completed his four-year term on the Montana Supreme Court in July of 1868, when Henry L. Warren became

Hosmer's successor.[303] Hosmer stayed in the region for several years by serving as postmaster general of Virginia City, an appointment made by President Ulysses S. Grant.[304] The appointment might have been a consolation prize if Hosmer wished to stay in Virginia City to mind his various business interests there, and if President Grant had a competing interest in naming his own appointees to high judicial offices. Hosmer later moved to San Francisco and held government positions there in the US Custom House from 1879 to 1887 and in the California State Mining Department from 1887 until his natural death on October 31, 1893, at the age of seventy-eight.[305]

Judge Lyman Munson returned to his native Connecticut after the completion of his appointed four-year judicial term in April of 1869.[306] He was replaced on the Montana Supreme Court by George G. Symes of Kentucky.[307] Munson practiced law into his advanced years and died of natural causes in New Haven on February 7, 1908, at the age of eighty-seven.[308] One month after Munson's death, a tribute was published in his honor in the *Yale Law Review*.[309]

Conrad Kohrs, who escaped robbery attempts by George Ives and "Dutch John" Wagner, became Montana's "Cattle King" with control of ten million acres of land for grazing in four American states and Canada.[310] He won election to Montana's infamous "Cowboy Legislature" in 1885 and to the Montana State Legislature in 1902.[311] In 1883 he became a cattle partner of Granville Stuart.[312] While active in the Montana Stock Growers Association during the 1880s, Kohrs became friends with Theodore Roosevelt, and the two men maintained their friendship for at least three decades.[313] He was a delegate to the 1904 National Republican Convention in Chicago, which nominated Theodore Roosevelt for the presidency of the United States.[314] Roosevelt stayed at Kohrs's home in Helena for a day in 1912 while Roosevelt again campaigned for the White House that year as the Bull Moose candidate.[315] Kohrs completed his autobiography in 1900,[316] and many of his property holdings are today titled to the federal government as national parks.[317] He died in Helena of natural causes on July 23, 1920, at the age of eighty-five.[318]

Granville Stuart, who is also sometimes referred to today as "Mr. Montana," was the general manager of the DHS cattle ranch, which he initially owned in partnership with Andrew Davis, Erwin Davis, and Samuel T. Hauser.[319] His elder brother James had died unexpectedly on September 30, 1873, at the age of forty-two.[320] The loss of his sibling affected him deeply, as he wrote that "[w]e had been together all our lives and his death leaves a gap in my life that will never close."[321] Stuart married a woman from the Snake Indian tribe named Awbonnie, and together they raised nine children.[322] Mather and Boswell point out that Stuart married his Indian wife in 1863 when she was merely twelve years old,[323] though the marriage was apparently successful and certainly of a long term. Awbonnie died a few days after a childbirth in 1889 and Stuart remarried a schoolteacher a year later.[324] Stuart served several terms in the Montana legislature in the 1870s and in 1883 and was president of both the Montana Stock Growers Association and the Montana Board of Livestock Commissioners.[325] His election as president of the Montana Stock Growers Association occurred only days after his successful vigilante raid upon "Old Man" Jack's encampment at Bates Point, suggesting that the second event was a reward for the first.[326] Stuart was the president of the Society of Montana Pioneers in 1886–87, the first secretary of the Montana Historical Society, and president of the society between 1890 and 1895.[327] He served as the US ambassador to Uruguay and Paraguay between 1894 and 1898.[328] His book, *Forty Years on the Frontier*, was intended to document the history of Montana Territory, but Stuart died before the work was fully completed. He died of natural causes in Missoula on October 2, 1918, at the age of eighty-four.[329]

Today streets in Helena are named after John Bozeman, Wilbur Fisk Sanders, Samuel T. Hauser, Anton Holter, and Granville Stuart.

Some of the men who played prominent roles in the early history of Virginia City and Helena are buried at the Forestvale Cemetery in Helena. Marked graves can be found within easy strolling distances of one another for Wilbur Fisk Sanders, Samuel T. Hauser, Anton Holter, William Chumasero, and John X. Beidler, among others. The monument at the gravesite of John X. Beidler was donated by the Society of Montana Pioneers and reads:

> JOHN X. BEIDLER
> BORN AUG. 14, 1831
> DIED JAN. 22, 1890
> 3 - 7 - 77
> PUBLIC BENEFACTOR
> BRAVE PIONEER
> TO TRUE OCCASION TRUE
> ERECTED BY THE
> SOCIETY OF MONTANA PIONEERS

Of course, many of the persons involved in the story of Montana vigilantism were the very persons who were executed by hanging, after the infamous trial of George Ives that launched the cascade of vigilante arrests and punishments in the subsequent months and years. The following is a summary of the persons arrested, convicted, and executed in this narrative, primarily by the vigilantes in Bannack, Alder Gulch, the area of greater Helena between 1864 and 1875, and the area of the Musselshell Valley in 1883 and 1884.

Figure 16.8. Tombstone of John X. Beidler at the Forestvale
Cemetery in Helena. (Photo by author.)

Name	Place of Execution	Date
George Ives	Nevada City	December 21, 1863
Erastus "Red" Yeager	Stinking Water Valley	January 4, 1864
George W. Brown	Stinking Water Valley	January 4, 1864
Sheriff Henry Plummer	Bannack City	January 10, 1864
Deputy Sheriff Ned Ray	Bannack City	January 10, 1864
Deputy Sheriff Buck Stinson	Bannack City	January 10, 1864
"Dutch John" Wagner	Bannack City	January 11, 1864
"Greaser Joe" Pizanthia	Bannack City	January 11, 1864
George "Clubfoot" Lane	Virginia City	January 14, 1864
Frank Parish	Virginia City	January 14, 1864

continued on next page

Name	Place of Execution	Date
Hayes Lyons	Virginia City	January 14, 1864
Deputy Sheriff Jack Gallagher	Virginia City	January 14, 1864
Boone Helm	Virginia City	January 14, 1864
Steven Marshland	Big Hole Ranch	January 16, 1864
William Bunton	Deer Lodge Valley	January 19, 1864
George Shears	Frenchtown	January 24, 1864
Cyrus Skinner	Hell Gate	January 25, 1864
Aleck Carter	Hell Gate	January 25, 1864
John Cooper	Hell Gate	January 25, 1864
Robert Zachary	Hell Gate	January 25, 1864
William "Whiskey Bill" Graves	Fort Owens	January 26, 1864
William Hunter	Gallatin Valley	February 3, 1864
Unknown	Virginia City	February 17, 1864
"Doc" Howard	Lewiston, Idaho	March 4, 1864
Chris Lowery	Lewiston, Idaho	March 4, 1864
Jim Romaine	Lewiston, Idaho	March 4, 1864
J. A. Slade	Virginia City	March 10, 1864
James Brady	Nevada City (Montana)	June 15, 1864
Jem Kelly	Snake River Ferry, Idaho	September 5, 1864
John "The Hat" Dolan	Nevada City (Montana)	September 17, 1864
R. C. Rawley	Bannack City	October 31, 1864
Zacharia Fogarty	Fort Owen	Early January, 1865
John Keene	Helena	June 9, 1865
Jack Silvie	Helena	July 29, 1865
Jack Howard	Diamond City	September 15, 1865
Tommy Cooke	Helena	September 18, 1865
John Morgan	Virginia City	September 27, 1865
John Jackson	Virginia City	September 27, 1865
Con Kirby	Helena	October 3, 1865
Unknown	Prickly Pear Tollgate	October 1865
Unknown	Prickly Pear Tollgate	October 1865
Unknown	Confederate Gulch	October 1865
George Sanders	Helena	November 21, 1865
Unknown	Helena	November 23, 1865

continued on next page

Name	Place of Execution	Date
Unknown	Helena	November 23, 1865
Frank Williams	Denver, Colorado	January 1866
Michael Duffy	Salt Lake City, Utah	January 1866
Charles Jewett	East Gallatin	February 5, 1866
Unknown	East Gallatin	February 5, 1866
James Daniels	Helena	March 2, 1866
Leander Johnson	Deer Lodge	March 12, 1866
J. L. Goones	German Gulch	April 20, 1866
John "Frenchy" Crouchet	Helena	June 5, 1866
George Rosenbaum	Nevada City	February 1, 1867
Charles Wilson	Virginia City	September 25, 1867
James M. Douglas	Red Mountain City	November 13, 1867
[First name unknown] Spaulding	White Tail Deer Station	Jan. 29 or 30, 1868
Billy Wilson	Jefferson Valley	January 30, 1868
George Blue (or Ballou)	Reynolds City	May 18, 1868
Jack Varley	Beartown	August 13, 1868
William Hinson	Fort Benton	August 20, 1868
Ah Chow	Helena	January 24, 1870
W. C. Patrick	Diamond City	March 12, 1870
Arthur Compton	Helena	April 27, 1870
Joseph Wilson	Helena	April 27, 1870
[First name unknown] Baker	Radersburg	1871
[First name unknown] Hunt	West Gallatin	1871
Jack "Old Man" Triplett	Bozeman	February 1, 1873
John W. "Steamboat Bill" St. Clair	Bozeman	February 1, 1873
Jack Shuster	[Unknown]	July 1, 1873
Unknown	Beaverhead County	October 1875
Milford Coomes	Greenhorn	March 18, 1883
William Henry Smith	Greenhorn	March 18, 1883
William Rigney	Miles City	July 22, 1883
Sam McKenzie	Near Fort Maginnis	July 3, 1884
Unknown	Convergence of Missouri and Musselshell Rivers	July 7, 1884

continued on next page

Name	Place of Execution	Date
Unknown	Convergence of Missouri and Musselshell Rivers	July 7, 1884
Unknown	Convergence of Missouri and Musselshell Rivers	July 7, 1884
"California Jack"	Convergence of Missouri and Musselshell Rivers	July 7, 1884
Billy Downes	Near the mouth of the Musselshell River	July 7, 1884
"California Ed"	Near the mouth of the Musselshell River	July 7, 1884
Leo Laverdure	Clagget	July 9, 1884
Narcossa Lavdure	Clagget	July 9, 1884
"Old Man" Jack James	Bates Point	July 20, 1884
[First name unknown] James	Bates Point	July 20, 1884
[First name unknown] James	Bates Point	July 20, 1884
Frank Hanson	Bates Point	July 20, 1884
Bill Williams	Bates Point	July 20, 1884
"Stringer Jack"	Bates Point	July 20, 1884
"Swift Bill"	Near Fort Maginnis	July 22, 1884
Orville Edwards	Near Fort Maginnis	July 22, 1884
[First name unknown] Phelps	Near Fort Maginnis	July 22, 1884
Silas Nickerson	Near Fort Maginnis	July 22, 1884
Johnnie Owens	Near Fort Maginnis	July 22, 1884

The foregoing vigilante executions were not Montana's last. They continued on a sporadic basis even after Montana gained its statehood in 1889. Later vigilante hangings were less notorious since, as years wore on, the "Wild West" became less wild, the Montana gold rush was over, and effective law enforcement continued to take root.

Panning for Nuggets

A long-running social tradition in Helena is its annual Vigilante Parade. The parade was held for the first time in May of 1924. It was organized by Helena High School principal Albert J. Roberts to celebrate the adventurous lives and customs of Montana pioneers, particularly those who first settled the Last Chance Gulch. Work on the 1924 parade was intended to unify the junior and senior classes of the local high school and to channel students' efforts into productive and worthwhile activities. The parade comprises displays and floats representing different aspects of early Montana history. The parade that was held in 1939 was attended by Norway's Crown Prince Olaf and Princess Martha. The high school takes a leading role in its organization each year.[331] *Principal Roberts became mayor of Helena in 1937, and the parade is his enduring personal legacy.*

Notes

1. Leeson, *History of Montana*, 223.
2. Ibid.
3. Blum et al., *National Experience*, 415–16.
4. Bancroft, *History*, 734–35.
5. Blum et al., *National Experience*, 408–9.
6. Ibid., 415–16.
7. Ibid., 408.
8. Ibid., 409.
9. Northern Pacific Railway Historical Association, "Home."
10. Blum et al., *National Experience*, 410.
11. Stuart, *Forty Years on the Frontier*, 2:195.
12. Ibid.
13. Morriss, "Miners, Vigilantes, and Cattlemen," 664.
14. Hamilton, *From Wilderness to Statehood*, 398; Morriss, "Miners, Vigilantes, and Cattlemen," 664.
15. Hagedorn, *Roosevelt in the Badlands*, 139.
16. Milner and O'Connor, *As Big as the West*, 220.
17. Stuart, *Forty Years on the Frontier*, 2:176.
18. Bakken, *Invitation to an Execution*, 342.
19. Mueller, "Central Montana Vigilante Raids," 23.
20. Ibid., citing *Fort Benton River Press*, July 9, 1884.
21. Morriss, "Miners, Vigilantes, and Cattlemen," 664.
22. Stuart, *Forty Years on the Frontier*, 2:157, 231, 257.
23. Ibid., 175.
24. Ibid., 176.
25. Ibid., 177.
26. Smith, *War on the Powder River*, 29; Morriss, "Miners, Vigilantes, and Cattlemen," 663.
27. Stuart, *Forty Years on the Frontier*, 2:196. Granville Stuart's less notable brother, James, was a successful miner and merchant in the area of Deer Lodge until his death in 1873. James Stuart had a penchant for young girls. Milner and O'Connor, *As Big as the West*, 144–46. Today he would likely face jail as a pedophile.
28. Stuart, *Forty Years on the Frontier*, 2:196.
29. Ibid., 197; Milner and O'Connor, *As Big as the West*, 239.
30. Stuart, *Forty Years on the Frontier*, 2:196.
31. Ibid., 197.
32. Ibid., 209; Harold Rash Reminiscences, Mont. Hist. Soc. SC-677, box 1-1, p. 5.
33. Stuart, *Forty Years on the Frontier*, 2:221.
34. "The Central Montana Vigilante Raids of 1884," Oscar O. Mueller Collection, Mont. Hist. Soc., MC-93, box 1, folder 1-11, p. 2 (hereafter cited as "Vigilante Raids of 1884," Mueller Collection). Montana was not the only territory to experience organized violence related to the cattle industry. See, e.g., Davis, *Wyoming Range War*; Smith, *War on the Powder River*.

35. Milner and O'Connor, *As Big as the West*, 221.
36. "Vigilante Raids of 1884," Mueller Collection, 13.
37. Ibid., 5; Milner and O'Connor, *As Big as the West*, 222.
38. Milner and O'Connor, *As Big as the West*, 223.
39. "Vigilante Raids of 1884," Mueller Collection, 8.
40. Milner and O'Connor, *As Big as the West*, 227.
41. "Vigilante Raids of 1884," Mueller Collection, 8; Milner and O'Connor, *As Big as the West*, 227.
42. "Vigilante Raids of 1884," Mueller Collection, 9. The culprits may have consisted of five men instead of four. Milner and O'Connor, *As Big as the West*, 227.
43. Milner and O'Connor, *As Big as the West*, 227.
44. "Vigilante Raids of 1884," Mueller Collection, 9.
45. Stuart, *Forty Years on the Frontier*, 2: 206.
46. Ibid.
47. Ibid.
48. "Vigilante Raids of 1884," Mueller Collection, 10.
49. Ibid.; Milner and O'Connor, *As Big as the West*, 232.
50. Milner and O'Connor, *As Big as the West*, 239, citing Theodore Roosevelt, "In Cattle Country," *Century Magazine* (Feb. 1888). The article became part of a book by Roosevelt titled *Ranch Life and the Hunting Trail*.
51. "Vigilante Raids of 1884," Mueller Collection, 5–6.
52. Ibid., 2.
53. Stuart, *Forty Years on the Frontier*, 2:206; "Vigilante Raids of 1884," Mueller Collection, 7. Stuart's account does not specifically mention "Dutch" Louis Meyers.
54. Stuart, *Forty Years on the Frontier*, 2:206.
55. Leeson, *History of Montana*, 315.
56. "Vigilante Raids of 1884," Mueller Collection, 7–8.
57. Stuart, *Forty Years on the Frontier*, 2:197.
58. "The Central Montana Raids of 1884," Oscar O. Mueller Collection, Mont. Hist. Soc., MC-93, box 1, folder 1-14.
59. "Vigilante Raids of 1884," Mueller Collection, 11.
60. Milner and O'Connor, *As Big as the West*, 231.
61. "Vigilante Raids of 1884," Mueller Collection, 12–13. This same source identifies Ludich, Pettit, and Starley as employees of Stuart at the DHS Ranch. Reece Anderson was not among the group headed for Bates Point, as he had been "benched" as a result of the questionable executions of Billy Downes and "California Ed"; ibid., 10.
62. "The Central Montana Raids of 1884," Oscar O. Mueller Collection, Mont. Hist. Soc., MC-93, box 1, folder 1-14; "Vigilante Raids of 1884," Mueller Collection, 12–13; Milner and O'Connor, *As Big as the West*, 232. However, Granville Stuart identified the date of the raid as July 8. Stuart, *Forty Years on the Frontier*, 2:207. The date identified by Mueller appears to be more accurate as his narrative is based upon multiple third-party sources.
63. Stuart, *Forty Years on the Frontier*, 2:207; "Central Montana Raids," Mueller Collection. There is a dispute as to whether Bill Williams was, in fact, present at Bates Point at the time of the vigilante raid. "Vigilante Raids of 1884," Mueller Collection, 15; Milner and O'Connor, *As Big as the West*, 232.
64. Stuart, *Forty Years on the Frontier*, 2:207; Milner and O'Connor, *As Big as the West*, 232.
65. Stuart, *Forty Years on the Frontier*, 2:207; Milner and O'Connor, *As Big as the West*, 234.
66. Stuart, *Forty Years on the Frontier*, 2:207; "The Central Montana Raids of 1884," Oscar O. Mueller Collection, Mont. Hist. Soc., MC-93, box 1, folder 1-14; Milner and O'Connor, *As Big as the West*, 234.
67. "Vigilante Raids of 1884," Mueller Collection, 11.

68. "The Central Montana Raids of 1884," Oscar O. Mueller Collection, Mont. Hist. Soc., MC-93, box 1, folder 1-14.

69. Harold Rash Reminiscences, Mont. Hist. Soc., SC-677, box 1-1, p. 5.

70. Stuart, *Forty Years on the Frontier*, 2:208–9; "Vigilante Raids of 1884," Mueller Collection, 11.

71. Stuart, *Forty Years on the Frontier*, 2:208.

72. Ibid.

73. Ibid., 208–9.

74. The date is "on or about" July 22 because members of the Stranglers returned to the DHS Ranch on July 23, 1884. If the Stranglers split into separate parties after the assault on Bates Point, the date of the arrests at Fort Maginnis might not be accurate. "Vigilante Raids of 1884," Mueller Collection, 11–12.

75. Stuart, *Forty Years on the Frontier*, 2:208; Milner and O'Connor, *As Big as the West*, 237; "Vigilante Raids of 1884," Mueller Collection, 12. The last source disputes that the men were hanged by vigilantes, instead suggesting that Fischel and his deputies undertook the hangings.

76. Stuart, *Forty Years on the Frontier*, 2:208–9.

77. Ibid., 209.

78. "Vigilante Raids of 1884," Mueller Collection, 13, citing a letter from Granville Stuart to T. J. Bryan dated Oct. 22, 1886.

79. Ibid., 2.

80. Ibid.

81. "Judge, Jury and Justice," *Montana Stock & Mining Journal*, Aug. 1884, p. 63, col 2.

82. Ibid.

83. Ibid.

84. "Vigilante Raids of 1884," Mueller Collection, 13.

85. Milner and O'Connor, *As Big as the West*, 242.

86. "Vigilante Raids of 1884," Mueller Collection, 14.

87. *Daily Yellowstone Journal*, Nov. 23, 1884, p. 1, col. 6.

88. Letter to James Fergus from Granville Stuart, July 26, 1885, James Fergus Family Papers, Mont. Hist. Soc., MC-28, box 2, folder 2-7.

89. Davis, *Wyoming Range War*, 165.

90. Ibid., 161–73.

91. Ibid., 179.

92. Ibid., 253. The Texans who were charged had been released on bond pending the trial and did not return to Wyoming for the trial itself. Twenty-three of twenty-five Wyoming defendants appeared for their trial. Ibid., 247. The trial judge, Richard H. Scott, had ruled that all of the defendants were to be tried jointly, meaning that, collectively, 414 peremptory challenges were available to the defendants during jury selection, in addition to an unlimited number of challenges to potential jurors for cause. Ibid., 250. Criminal convictions were not possible, as the jury selection process could not yield the required number of fair and impartial jurors given the number of juror challenges and the limited population of Laramie County where the matter had been venued for trial. Ibid., 252–53.

93. Leeson, *History of Montana*, 303–4.

94. Donovan, *Hanging around the Big Sky*, book 2, 174.

95. Leeson, *History of Montana*, 304.

96. Donovan, *Hanging around the Big Sky*, book 2, 174.

97. Bakken, *Invitation to an Execution*, 342; Donovan, *Hanging around the Big Sky*, book 2, 177.

98. Donovan, *Hanging around the Big Sky*, book 2, 179.

99. Ibid., 179.

100. Milner and O'Connor, *As Big as the West*, 240, citing Report of the Governor of Montana, 48th Cong., 2nd sess, 1884, H. Ex. Doc. 1, serial 2287, p. 559.

101. Milner and O'Connor, *As Big as the West*, 240; Morriss, "Miners, Vigilantes, and Cattlemen," 666.

102. Milner and O'Connor, *As Big as the West*, 240.

103. "Vigilante Raids of 1884," Mueller Collection, 14.

104. "Mock Trial Set for Infamous Old West Sheriff," *Moscow-Pullman Daily*, May 6, 1993, p. 4C, col. 1; Weber, "Trial of Henry Plummer."

105. "Henry Plummer Freed Second Time Around," *Montana Standard*, May 8, 1993, p. 1, col. 1; "Mock Trial of Infamous 19th Century Sheriff Ends in Mistrial," *Moscow-Pullman Daily*, May 13, 1993, p. 4C, col. 1.

106. "Henry Plummer Freed Second Time Around," *Montana Standard*, May 8, 1993, p. 1, col. 1; Weber, "Trial of Henry Plummer."

107. Weber, "Trial of Henry Plummer."

108. Ibid.

109. Ibid.

110. Ibid.

111. Ibid.; Pryor, *Lawmen*, 50.

112. Weber, "Trial of Henry Plummer"; Pryor, *Lawmen*, 50.

113. Mather and Boswell, *Gold Camp Desperados*.

114. Pryor, *Lawmen*, 50; Appendix F, Petition for Pardon of Henry Plummer dated May 21, 1993.

115. Appendix F, Petition for Pardon of Henry Plummer dated May 21, 1993.

116. Pryor, *Lawmen*, 50.

117. "No Pardon for Plummer," *Dillon Tribune*, Sept. 15, 1993; "No Pardon for Outlaw Sheriff," *Independent Record*, Sept. 9, 1993, p. 11A, col. 1.

118. Pryor, *Lawmen*, 46; Pace, *Golden Gulch*, 29; Allen, *Decent Orderly Lynching*, 50; Gard, *Frontier Justice*, 169; Birney, *Vigilantes*, 64; Anonymous, *Banditti of the Rocky Mountains*, 22; Cushman, *Montana*, 114.

119. Mather and Boswell, *Vigilante Victims*, 36.

120. Ibid., 173 (Granville Stuart's marriage to twelve-year-old Awbonnie).

121. Allen, *Decent Orderly Lynching*, 90.

122. Kohrs, *Conrad Kohrs*, 29.

123. Langford, *Vigilante Days*, 170.

124. Allen, *Decent Orderly Lynching*, 224.

125. Thrapp, *Vengeance!*, 168–69; Johnson, *Bloody Bozeman*, 99n19.

126. Birney, *Vigilantes*, 277.

127. "Wilbur Fisk Sanders Dead," *Times Dispatch*, July 8, 1905, p. 1, col. 4; "Death of Colonel Saunders [*sic*], Pioneer Lawyer of Montana, " *Intermountain and Colorado Catholic*, July 15, 1905, p. 6, col. 3.

128. Birney, *Vigilantes*, 278; Johnson, *Bloody Bozeman*, 99n19. The graves of all five men have since been marked by tombstones for posterity.

129. The author has personally viewed the exhibit; see also Pace, *Golden Gulch*, 86; Johnson, *Bloody Bozeman*, 99n19; Roadside America, "Club Foot George's Club Foot."

130. Callaway, *Montana's Righteous Hangmen*, 124; Birney, *Vigilantes*, 296.

131. Callaway, *Montana's Righteous Hangmen*, 123; Birney, *Vigilantes*, 296.

132. Birney, *Vigilantes*, 296. Callaway notes that, on occasion, the numbers were depicted as "3-11-77," with the difference jokingly explained as meaning that sometimes the vigilantes gave their targets an additional four minutes to flee. Callaway, *Montana's Righteous Hangmen*, 123.

133. Allen, "Montana Vigilantes and the Origin of 3-7-77," 54.

134. Association of Montana Troopers, "3-7-77."

135. Allen, *Decent Orderly Lynching*, 182–83; Thrapp, *Vengeance!*, 150.

136. Morriss, "Miners, Vigilantes, and Cattlemen: Property Rights," 57; Ellen Baumler, *Montana Moments*, 188.

137. Callaway, *Montana's Righteous Hangmen*, 122–23; Thrapp, *Vengeance!*, 175; Birney, *Vigilantes*, 296.

138. Birney, *Vigilantes*, 297.

139. Callaway, *Montana's Righteous Hangmen*, 123.

140. "3-7-77," *Montana Standard*, Mar. 16, 1975.

141. Allen, *Decent Orderly Lynching*, 360.

142. Montana Highways, "Montana Speed."

143. Mont. Stat. Ann. 30-20-104 et seq. (2009). As of this writing, the only court case addressing the Firearms Freedom Act was a declaratory judgment action brought by a gun manufacturer and retailer, which was dismissed for the court's lack of subject matter jurisdiction and the plaintiffs' failure to state a claim upon which the requested relief could be granted. *Montana Shooting Sports Ass'n. v. Holder*, 2010 WL 4102940 (D.Mont. 2010).

144. Montana Ghost Towns, http://www.ghosttowns.com/states/mt/moalpha.html (accessed Jan. 22, 2012).

145. Ghost Towns, "Montana Ghost Towns," "Alton."

146. Pryor, *Lawmen*, 48; Fisher and Holmes, *Gold Rushes*, 337.

147. Montana Heritage Commission, "Virginia City."

148. Montana Department of Commerce, "Montana Heritage Commission."

149. Doyle, *Journeys to the Land of Gold*, 742. However, discrepancies in Cover's story has led some historians to question whether murdered by someone other than Indians. Montana History, "Bozeman."

150. Doyle, *Journeys to the Land of Gold*, 742.

151. Ibid.; Thrapp, *Vengeance!*, 232.

152. Pace, *Golden Gulch*, 85; Johnson, *Bloody Bozeman*, 328.

153. Pace, *Golden Gulch*, 85; Johnson, *Bloody Bozeman*, 328.

154. Ibid.; Montana State Genealogy Society, "Montana State Death Index."

155. Pace, *Golden Gulch*, 85.

156. Ibid.

157. Ibid.

158. Ibid.

159. Edgar, "Journal," 124.

160. Ibid.

161. Montana State Genealogy Society, "Montana State Death Index."

162. Travel Montana, "Edgar, Montana."

163. Find a Grave, "Hill Beachy."

164. Ibid.; "Death of Hill Beachy," *Los Angeles Daily Herald*, May 25, 1875, p. 2, col. 4.

165. Find a Grave, "Hill Beachy"; "Death of Hill Beachy," *Los Angeles Daily Herald*, May 25, 1875, p. 2, col. 4.

166. Langford, *Vigilante Days*, 201; Thompson, *Tenderfoot in Montana*, 157; Birney, *Vigilantes*, 159.

167. Langford, *Vigilante Days*, 201; Thompson, *Tenderfoot in Montana*, 157; Birney, *Vigilantes*, 159.

168. E.g., Holter Family Papers, Mont. Hist. Soc., MC-80, box 12, folders 7, 9, 10.

169. Ibid., box 86, folder 1-8.

170. GenForum, "Anton Holter."

171. Michigan State University Libraries, Special Collections Division, "Loafer's Reward."

172. Callaway, *Montana's Righteous Hangmen*, 180; Allen, *Decent Orderly Lynching*, 361.

173. Mather and Boswell, *Vigilante Victims*, 157.

174. Ibid.

175. Callaway, *Montana's Righteous Hangmen*, 182; Mather and Boswell, *Vigilante Victims*, 157–58; Allen, *Decent Orderly Lynching*, 362.

176. Mather and Boswell, *Vigilante Victims*, 158.

177. Ibid.

178. Ibid., 157.

179. Letter by John M. Williams, James "Cap" Williams Papers, 1886, Mont. Hist. Soc., SC-1418.

180. Mather and Boswell, *Vigilante Victims*, 158.

181. RootsWeb, "Montana Death Records 1910–1919—D: Davis, Adriel B."

182. Donovan, *Hanging around the Big Sky*, book 2, 26.

183. Mather and Boswell, *Vigilante Victims*, 151.

184. Mather and Boswell, "Epilogue"; Mather and Boswell, *Vigilante Victims*, 151.

185. "Obituary," *Rocky Mountain News*, Dec. 7, 1870.

186. Evi.com, "Dallas Mayors."

187. "J. M. Thurmond, Ex-Judge, Ex-Mayor, Etc., Dies with His Boots On," *Waco Daily Examiner*, Mar. 15, 1882, p. 1, col. 3.

188. Ibid.

189. Langford, *Vigilante Days*, 254; "J. M. Thurmond, Ex-Judge, Ex-Mayor, Etc., Dies with His Boots On," *Waco Daily Examiner*, Mar. 15, 1882, p. 1, col. 3.

190. "J. M. Thurmond, Ex-Judge, Ex-Mayor, Etc., Dies with His Boots On," *Waco Daily Examiner*, Mar. 15, 1882, p. 1, col. 3.

191. Ibid.

192. "Progress of Cowart's Trial," *Waco Daily Examiner*, May 4, 1882, p. 1, col. 6.

193. "The Verdict of a Dallas Jury," *Waco Daily Examiner*, May 9, 1882, p. 2, col. 1; "Weekly Banner," *Brenham Weekly Banner*, May 11, 1882, p. 2, col. 2.

194. "Weekly Banner," *Brenham Weekly Banner*, May 11, 1882, p. 2, col. 2; "The Verdict of a Dallas Jury," *Waco Daily Examiner*, May 9, 1882, p. 2, col. 1.

195. University of North Texas Digital Library, "The WPA Dallas Guide and History," 72.

196. Donovan, *Hanging around the Big Sky*, book 2, 302–3.

197. Bakken, *Invitation to an Execution*, 340; Allen, *Decent Orderly Lynching*, 177. mt.gov, "Judicial Branch: Chief Justices of Montana"; "Montana: Government," *American Annual Cyclopedia and Register of Important Events*, 17:476.

198. Pemberton, "Montana's Pioneer Courts."

199. Allen, *Decent Orderly Lynching*, 362; Mather and Boswell, *Vigilante Victims*, 152.

200. Mather and Boswell, *Vigilante Victims*, 152. Mather and Boswell attribute to Sanders nefarious motives in becoming president of the Montana Historical Society, as its presidency gave him control over the records of the events of 1864.

201. Axline et al., *More from the Quarries*, 16.

202. "Wilbur Fisk Sanders Dead," *Times Dispatch*, July 8, 1905, p. 1, col. 4; "Death of Colonel Saunders [*sic*], Pioneer Lawyer of Montana, " *Intermountain and Colorado Catholic*, July 15, 1905, p. 6, col. 3.

203. Wilbur Fisk Sanders Dead," *Times Dispatch*, July 8, 1905, p. 1, col. 4; "Death of Colonel Saunders [*sic*], Pioneer Lawyer of Montana, " *Intermountain and Colorado Catholic*, July 15, 1905, p. 6, col. 3.

204. Mather and Boswell, *Vigilante Victims*, 176; Allen, *Decent Orderly Lynching*, 327.

205. Mather and Boswell, *Vigilante Victims*, 176.

206. Bancroft, *History*, 641n31; "Died," *Montana Post*, Sept. 22, 1866, p. 5, col 3; "Thomas J. Dimsdale," *Montana Post*, Sept. 29, 1866, p. 4, col. 2.

207. Langford, *Vigilante Days*, 7.

208. Spence, *Territorial Politics*, 57; Allen, *Decent Orderly Lynching*, 362.

209. Ibid.

210. Ibid.; "Outside News Condensed," *Bemidji Daily Pioneer*, Oct. 19, 1911, p. 1, col. 2.

211. Toponce, *Reminiscences*, 4 (publisher's preface).

212. Ibid., 177.

213. Ibid., 4 (publisher's preface).

214. Find A Grave, "Edwin Ruthven Purple."

215. Ibid.

216. Pfouts, *Four Firsts*, 98–100.

217. Ibid., 5.

218. Ibid.

219. Allen, *Decent Orderly Lynching*, 314; Sargent, "Journal of Paris Pfouts."

220. Allen, *Decent Orderly Lynching*, 363.

221. "Death of Venerable Ex-Governor Sydney Edgerton," *Akron Daily Democrat*, July 19, 1900, p. 1, col. 1; Allen, *Decent Orderly Lynching*, 362; RootsWeb, "Biography of Sydney Edgerton."

222. "Death of Venerable Ex-Governor Sydney Edgerton," *Akron Daily Democrat*, July 19, 1900, p. 1, col. 1.

223. Allen, *Decent Orderly Lynching*, 120–21.

224. Ibid.

225. Towle, *Vigilante Woman*, 30.

226. Mather and Boswell, *Hanging the Sheriff*, 184–85 (identifying the number of Electa Maxwell's children as three); Towle, *Vigilante Woman*, 44; Allen, *Decent Orderly Lynching*, 361; University of Montana Western, "Epilogue." Towle states that James and Electa Maxwell had three children of their own, though the letter from Mrs. John Slattery identifies only two children, named Vernon and Clarence.

227. Allen, *Decent Orderly Lynching*, 361.

228. Towle, *Vigilante Woman*, 43–44.

229. Allen, *Decent Orderly Lynching*, 361; University of Montana Western, "Epilogue"; Towle, *Vigilante Woman*, 44.

230. Mather and Boswell, *Hanging the Sheriff*, 185; Towle, *Vigilante Woman*, 44; Allen, *Decent Orderly Lynching*, 361.

231. Towle, *Vigilante Woman*, 148.

232. Ibid.

233. Donovan, *Hanging around the Big Sky*, book 2, 110; Towle, *Vigilante Woman*, 148.

234. Towle, *Vigilante Woman*, 149.

235. "Married," *Montana Post*, Mar. 25, 1865, p. 3, col. 2; Towle, *Vigilante Woman*, 148.

236. Towle, *Vigilante Woman*, 148.

237. "Married," *Montana Post*, Mar. 25, 1865, p. 3, col. 2.

238. Towle, *Vigilante Woman*, 148.

239. Donovan, *Hanging around the Big Sky*, book 2, 110; Towle, *Vigilante Woman*, 149.

240. Towle, *Vigilante Woman*, 149.

241. Ibid.

242. Donovan, *Hanging around the Big Sky*, book 2, 110.

243. Towle, *Vigilante Woman*, 149.

244. Baumler, *Girl from the Gulches*, 37.

245. Ibid.

246. Ibid.

247. Ibid.

248. Ibid., 88, 110.

249. Ibid., 123.

250. Ibid., ii.

251. Ibid., xv.

252. Ibid., xv, 220.

253. Published by the University of Montana in 1973.

254. Baumler, *Girl from the Gulches*, xvii, xviii. The difference between the two books is that Merriam's deliberately omitted personal information and correspondences, which was not omitted in Baumler's book because of the passage of time by its publication in 2003.

255. Ibid., xviii.

256. Axline et al., *More from the Quarries*, 154.

257. Find a Grave, "Daniel Jackson 'D. J.' Miller."

258. Ibid.

259. Bancroft, *History*, 721.

260. Find A Grave, "John F. Cowan."

261. US Marshals Service, "Neil Howie." The murder trial is noteworthy as it was the first trial in US history at which a woman served as a juror. The brother was convicted of the crime but was ultimately paroled from the prison in Detroit, Michigan, where he had been incarcerated.

262. Ibid.

263. Neil Howie Diaries, Mont. Hist. Soc., SC-302.

264. "May Be General Meagher's Body," *St. Paul Globe*, Jan. 7, 1900, p. 20, col. 4; Keneally, *Great Shame*, 457.

265. "May Be General Meagher's Body," *St. Paul Globe*, Jan. 7, 1900, p. 20, col. 4; Keneally, *Great Shame*, 457.

266. "May Be General Meagher's Body," *St. Paul Globe*, Jan. 7, 1900, p. 20, col. 4.

267. Ibid.; Keneally, *Great Shame*, 457.

268. "May Be General Meagher's Body," *St. Paul Globe*, Jan. 7, 1900, p. 20, col. 4; Keneally, *Great Shame*, 457 (identifying the purchaser of the body as Arthur Miles).

269. Keneally, *Great Shame*, 457.

270. Ibid., 456.

271. Ibid., 456–57.

272. Civil War Women Blog, "Elizabeth Meagher."

273. Ibid.

274. Arlington National Cemetery Website, "Green Clay Smith."

275. Ibid.

276. Ibid.

277. "Well Known Attorney and Politician, of Toledo, Dies in a Michigan Sanitarium," *Marietta Daily Leader*, Sept. 17, 1896, p. 1, col. 5 (the obituary appears to contain a typographical error extending Ashley's congressional career to 1886 instead of 1868); Allen, *Decent Orderly Lynching*, 362–63.

278. Spence, "Spoilsman in Montana," 24–35.

279. Spence, *Territorial Politics*, 60.

280. Ibid.; Ward M. Canaday Center for Special Collections, University of Toledo, "Finding Aid: James M. Ashley Papers, 1860–1960," biographical sketch.

281. Ward M. Canaday Center for Special Collections, University of Toledo, "Finding Aid: James M. Ashley Papers, 1860–1960," biographical sketch.

282. Ohio History Central, "James Ashley."

283. Find a Grave. "Samuel McLean."

284. Ibid.

285. Ibid.

286. Genealogy Trails History Group, "List of Governors of Montana."

287. Haines, "Biographical Appendix: Samuel T. Hauser."

288. Mather and Boswell, *Vigilante Victims*, 29.

289. Bancroft, *History*, 659n28. Bancroft identifies the number of men hanged by Beidler to be as many as thirty. The estimate may be high.

290. "Death of X. Beidler," *Daily Yellowstone Journal*, Jan. 24, 1890, p. 1, col. 4.

291. Laws 1874, Eighth Terr. Legis., p. 43.

292. 2 Mont. 242, *2 (1875).

293. Ibid.

294. *Chumasero v. Potts*, 2 Mont. 242, *10 (1875).

295. Ibid.

296. *Potts v. Chumasero*, 92 U.S. 358, 360 (1875).

297. "News of the Week," *Hartford Herald*, Jan. 20, 1875, p. 2, col. 2; "News in Brief," *Andrew County Republican*, Jan. 22, 1875, p. 2, col. 2.

298. A public referendum also concluded in 1894 on the question of whether the Montana state capital should be retained in Helena or moved to Anaconda. Helena was favored by a copper baron, William A. Clark, while Anaconda was favored by a competing copper baron, Marcus Daly. Each man spent considerable sums of money in support of his favored city. The results of the public referendum were controversial but in the end favored Helena.

299. "Montana News," *Fergus County Argus*, Mar. 2, 1893, p. 3, col. 2; GenForum, "William Chumasero."

300. Bancroft, *History*, 648–49.

301. Morriss, "Legal Argument," 87.

302. Cameron, "Bar of Tioga County," 126.

303. Morriss, "Legal Argument," 87.

304. "Hezekiah L. Hosmer Autobiography," Hezekiah Hosmer Papers, 1848–70, Mont. Hist. Soc., SC-104, folder 1-1, p. 23.

305. Ibid.; "Died," *San Francisco Morning Call*, Nov. 1, 1893, p. 10, col. 4.

306. Morriss, "Legal Argument," 87.

307. Ibid.

308. Herringshaw, *Herringshaw's National Library of American Biography*, 263; "Obituary Notes," *New York Sun*, Feb. 15, 1908, p. 3, col. 3.

309. "School and Alumni Notes," 410.

310. National Park Service, "Grant-Kohrs Ranch."

311. Kohrs, *Conrad Kohrs*, 80, 100.

312. Ibid., 76. The partnership resulted from Kohrs's purchase of A. J. and Erwin Davis's share of the DHS Ranch.

313. Ibid., 100.

314. Ibid.

315. Ibid.

316. Ibid.

317. National Park Service, "Grant-Kohrs Ranch."

318. Kohrs, *Conrad Kohrs*, 101.

319. The DHS Ranch is sometimes also referred to as the D-H Ranch. Its name appears to reflect the surname initials of its owners.

320. Kittredge and Krauzer, "'Mr. Montana' Revised," 20.

321. Remley, "Granville Stuart, Cowman," 39.

322. The spelling of Awbonnie's name varies from text to text.

323. Mather and Boswell, *Vigilante Victims*, 173; Remley, "Granville Stuart, Cowman," 33.

324. Remley, "Granville Stuart, Cowman," 33; Kittredge and Krauzer, "'Mr. Montana' Revised," 18, 20.

325. Milner and O'Connor, *As Big as the West*, 257.

326. "Vigilante Raids of 1884," Mueller Collection, 12.

327. Ibid., 17.

328. Milner and O'Connor, *As Big as the West*, 291, 305.

329. Ibid., 340; "Granville Stuart Is Dead," *North Platte Semi-Weekly Tribune*, Oct. 11, 1918, p. 9, col. 1.

330. There are conflicting accounts of whether Williams was present at Bates Point and killed as reported by Granville Stuart.

331. Vigilante Parade, "History."

17

Conclusion

No freeman shall be taken or imprisoned or disseised or exiled or in any
way destroyed, nor will we go upon him nor send upon him, except by
the lawful judgment of his peers or by the law of the land.

—Magna Carta, June 15, 1215

T his book has endeavored to avoid use of the term "vigilante justice."
Vigilantism, by definition, deprives or at least curtails an accused's
due process. The denial or curtailment of due process is not a form of
justice. The term "vigilante justice" is therefore a misnomer, a contradiction
in terms. The vigilantism that occurred in Montana in the 1860s and beyond
cannot be fully understood without discussing its history in the context of
due process.

"Due process" is a concept that holds great importance in American jurisprudence. It has its origin in the Magna Carta, which provided, in clause 39,
that "No freeman shall be taken or imprisoned or disseised or exiled or in any
way destroyed, nor will we go upon him nor send upon him, except by the
lawful judgment of his peers or by the law of the land." The concept was raised
for the first time in the United States when the State of New York proposed
a due process amendment to the Constitution at the time its ratification was
being considered by the individual states. The New York amendment read, "No
person ought to be taken imprisoned or disseised of his freehold, or be exiled
or deprived of his Privileges, Franchises, Liberty or Property but by due process
of Law.[1] James Madison studied the amendments proposed by the various states
and included due process language in the Fifth Amendment in the form that
we are familiar with today.[2] The Fifth Amendment to the US Constitution provides that no person shall "be deprived of life, liberty, or property, without due

DOI: 10.7330_9780874219203.c017

process of law," which is a simpler, streamlined version of the language found in the Magna Carta and in the New York proposal.

Courts have filled volumes of legal texts with decisions interpreting the meaning and extent of due process. Some decisions have assumed landmark importance and have been referenced in this narrative, such as *Miranda v. Arizona, Mapp v. Ohio, Gideon v. Wainwright, Escobedo v. Illinois,* and *Brady v. Maryland.*

Why is due process important? Many explanations can be given. The most basic explanation, however, is that if government cannot deprive a citizen of life, liberty, or property without due process of law, the absence of due process means that government may act unchecked in taking a citizen's life, liberty, and property. In criminal cases property is at stake if a defendant may be compelled to pay fines or restitution as part of a sentence. Liberty is at stake if a defendant may be incarcerated while unable to make bail pending trial, or as part of sentence upon a plea of guilty or a trial conviction. A defendant's life is at stake in capital cases in which the death penalty is authorized by law and sought by the prosecution. In Montana in the 1860s vigilante activity could affect in every case the prisoner's life, liberty, and property. Any absence of due process by the vigilantes rendered their own powers unchecked. Unchecked power at the hands of a vigilance committee should be as much of a concern as, or of more concern than, unchecked power at the hands of a government.

Because due process is a cornerstone of American jurisprudence, it is a subject that is of importance. Its importance is not just present-day. Due process is a concept that is important to our past and to what it says about our national history.

Due process has two essential components. One component is the process and procedures that guide the investigation, arrest, prosecution, conviction, sentence, and appellate remedies associated with an individual's legal cases. The second component addresses the amount of process that is due and owing to the individual. Defining the process is *qualitative*. The amount of process that is due is *quantitative*. The merger of the qualitative and quantitative aspects of due process in court proceedings assures that the system of justice followed in our country is constitutionally legitimate and fair to all parties. For generations, when Americans have had civil disputes among themselves, they have not resolved the disputes by means of knives, guns, or fights in the street, where one party forces his or her will upon another. Courts have been used to resolve civil disputes in a civilized fashion, as due process protections assure that litigants will have a level and fair playing field that includes an impartial judge and jury, the presentation of evidence that is subject to well-defined rules of admissibility and cross-examination, and the opportunity for parties to make persuasive argument to the trier of fact. Similarly, in criminal matters, our society has not, for the most part, relied upon mob violence or self-help to promote the deterrent and retributive purposes of criminal justice. To the contrary, our courts are guided by well-accepted rules and procedures designed to assure that any convictions are warranted on the evidence, and acquittals, when occurring, are required where the burden of proving guilt is not satisfied. Vigilantism has been an exception to that societal practice.

The system of civil and criminal justice in the United States depends upon its recognized legitimacy, which is derived in great measure from its centurion enforcement of due process. Key to any quantitative and qualitative assessment of due process is the defendant's opportunity to be heard at the judicial proceeding through competent counsel, to challenge evidence that is presented, and to assure that rules of evidence and procedure are followed by the court.[3] Without due process, the judicial system cannot function as a credible arbiter of the criminal and civil disputes that inevitably arise in society. Without a judicial system rooted in due process, people may respond to their baser instincts, where self-appointed persons or groups take law into their own hands and exact justice in whatever manner is determined to be appropriate at the moment.

How should the Montana vigilantes be viewed today? The answer may differ depending upon whether their conduct is judged against the legal standards of our time, or theirs.

The vigilante movements in Montana in the 1860s seem entirely foreign to us today, even though they occurred upon land that is part of our own country, under the same federal Constitution and its first fourteen amendments that still guide us today,[4] and involved our forebears of only five or six generations ago. The concept of arresting and summarily hanging individuals, as occurred in the cases of many of the persons who received the ultimate form of retribution, is repulsive when measured against the notions of due process that we recognize today. For that reason, we may not be able to understand how the men enforcing criminal law could treat other human beings in such a cruel, barbaric, and summary manner.

If we overlook judging the vigilantes' behavior by our current standards, which were not known to them, and critique them instead upon the less-developed due process standards that were known and understood during their own time, the vigilantes still fell short of affording basic legal protections to their prisoners in the vast majority of circumstances. The vigilantes in Bannack, Alder Gulch, and the greater Helena region, particularly, overran in particular cases the rights of the accused to probable cause as a condition of arrest, non-self-incrimination, indictments, counsel, public trials, juries, warranted searches and seizures, compulsory process for obtaining witnesses for the defense, the protection against double jeopardy, and, some might argue, the protection against cruel and unusual punishments, all of which were constitutionally protected to some degree by the language of article 3, section 2, and the Fourth, Fifth, Sixth, Eighth, and Fourteenth Amendments of the US Constitution. The fact that so many constitutional rights were violated, in so many instances and over so many years, underscores the extent to which the concept of due process, as understood at the time, was not well developed in the 1860s and was certainly not as sacrosanct as it is today.

Some persons during the time of vigilantism differentiated between mob violence, which was unacceptable, and a "decent, orderly lynching," whereby the crime was atrocious and there could be no mistake about the identity of the criminal, which was considered acceptable.[5] In fact, the two forms of criminal punishment raise a distinction without a difference to the extent that either form violates the constitutional rights of the accused. The "decency" and "orderliness" of an execution does not excuse flagrant violations of generally accepted principles of due process.

What makes vigilantism in Montana in the 1860s historically noteworthy is that the vigilante movements represented a marked and significant departure, to a lethal degree, from the legal norms that governed criminal justice in the courts of the United States and its territories. That is especially true when measured against the due process norms of today, but is also true when measured against the lesser due process norms of earlier times. The vigilantes in Montana were persons united in purpose who took the law into their own hands, for reasons they deemed necessary under the circumstances they faced, and exacted justice as they deemed fit. Vigilantism represents an unusual period of Montana history specifically and of United States history as a whole. It happened in part because of the value that humankind placed upon gold, at a time when gold was worth only $20.67 an ounce.

In keeping with the nonjudgmental historical tone of this manuscript, the vigilance committees that operated from Alder Gulch in 1863–64 and in the region of greater Helena in 1865–70 can be critiqued in two ways. On the one hand, its members acted out of desperation to save themselves, their families, and their friends from robbery or murder that was threatened by ruthless criminals operating in the area. They were forced to take the law into their own hands as there were no effective or credible police, prosecutorial, or judicial mechanisms provided by any government to perform the task on their behalf. For them, their ends justified their means.[6] They compromised due process for an immediate, temporal gain of security. Certainly, no one wishes that anyone ever be in such desperate circumstances, where the resort to vigilantism becomes a seeming necessity in the minds of otherwise law-abiding individuals.

According to Dimsdale, "[t]he question of the propriety of establishing a Vigilance Committee depends upon the answers which ought to be given to the following questions: Is it lawful for citizens to slay robbers or murderers, when they catch them; or ought they wait for policemen where there are none, or put them in penitentiaries not yet erected?"[7] Dimsdale answered his own question by observing that under such circumstances it was necessary for "good, law-abiding, and order-sustaining men [to] unite for mutual protection, and for the salvation of the community" and that "nothing but severe and summary punishment would be of any avail to prevent crime, in a place where life and gold were so much exposed."[8] Paris Pfouts claimed in his autobiography that the Vigilance Committee "gave peace to the Territory for a long time" and that "the people enjoyed the most perfect safety from depredations by outlaws which no milder means could have accomplished."[9]

On the other hand, the vigilance committees took significant and arguably unjustifiable shortcuts from the rudimentary norms of due process otherwise in effect at the time. They lost sight of the fact that where due process is concerned, the means and the ends are one in the same thing.[10] In addition to rights that were deprived to persons accused of crimes, the quantum of evidence relied upon in pronouncing convictions and sentences was sometimes suspect. In some instances the vigilantes departed from the expressed purpose of their bylaws of routing out murderers and robbers, as in the tragic case of J. A. Slade, where no robbery or murder had occurred as a precursor to Slade's pronounced sentence of death. The organization's bylaws were sometimes ignored in other ways, as with the decision to hang Erastus "Red" Yeager and George W. Brown at the Stinking Water Valley rather than return them to Virginia City for action by the Executive Committee. The execution of Hayes Lyons, if predicated upon Lyons's confessed murder of D. H. Dillingham, violated notions of double jeopardy as he had already been tried and convicted for the same offense. The vigilantes were unconcerned about geographic limitations and the procedures for lawful extradition, as with the arrest of Jem Kelly at Pontneuf Canyon and execution at the Snake River ferry in Idaho Territory, the bounty hunting of John "The Hat" Dolan from Utah Territory, and the extraterritorial executions of Frank Williams in Denver, Colorado, and Michael Duffy in Salt Lake City, Utah. The execution of Leander W. Johnson at Deer Lodge, for the theft of cattle that may have wandered off on their own accord, appears to represent the hanging of an innocent man and a life that might have been saved had there been a modicum of due process used during the procedures that led to Johnson's death. The execution of James Daniels in Helena, despite Daniels's possession of a lawful reprieve, issued by the territorial governor, should also be harshly criticized to the extent that Daniels had already placed himself into the custody of a deputy US marshal by the time he was captured and hanged.

There is less historical excuse for vigilantism in Helena between 1865 and 1870 than there is for Bannack and Alder Gulch in 1864. Chief Judge Hezekiah Hosmer did not arrive in the territory to set up court in Virginia City until the fall of 1864. Before Hosmer's arrival, there was truly no formal, effective, or reliable law enforcement in place at a time when persons were transporting gold wealth through remote trails from the region. The factors giving rise to vigilantism were all present. In Helena, by contrast, Judge Lyman Munson arrived during the summer of 1865, after the peoples' court execution of John Keene and the vigilante execution of Jack Silvie. Once Munson arrived, respect should have been given to the mechanisms of Judge Munson's court, as had been the case earlier in Virginia City upon the establishment of Judge Hosmer's court. Once Hosmer's court was operating in Virginia City, vigilante executions became the exception to the rule. This was in sharp contrast to Helena, where vigilante executions continued at a brisk pace from 1865 to 1870, despite the presence of Munson's territorial court. The conditions that gave rise to vigilantism in Alder Gulch were not all present in Helena in the late 1860s, yet vigilante executions continued there unabated for several years. Moreover, whereas Virginia City vigilantism was for the most part confined to defendants who were known or believed to be part of a single ongoing criminal enterprise, the vigilantism in the greater Helena area from 1865 to 1870 was prompted by the commission of a variety of unrelated ad hoc crimes.

Perhaps, in comparing the events of Alder Gulch with those of Helena, we can conclude that Chief Judge Hosmer was simply more forceful and persuasive than Judge Munson in credibly instructing grand juries that vigilantism needed to stop and in persuading active vigilantes to heed the judiciary's call. Or, perhaps, the personalities and attributes of the two judges contributed to a differing sense of whether, and when, vigilantism needed to finally give way to the territorial courts. Or, perhaps, all of the factors that contributed to vigilantism in Bannack and Alder Gulch did not need to be present to prompt vigilantism in and around Helena, as the mere existence of a vigilance committee in Alder Gulch in 1864 "legitimized" the role of ordinary people taking law into their own hands elsewhere. There is unfortunately no objective method for determining the answers to these questions.

And what of the attorneys that were prominent during vigilante days? Should not the attorneys trained in the law be judged against a higher standard of assuring respect for even baseline notions of due process? Virtually no critiques have been written about the role of attorneys in Montana's vigilante history. Historical opinion of the role of attorneys should not be monolithic.

Some attorneys in this narrative, such as Sydney Edgerton and Wilbur Fisk Sanders, were members and strong supporters of vigilante organizations. Other attorneys, such as H. P. A. Smith and James M. Thurmond, were so vocal in their opposition to vigilante activities that they were banished from Montana Territory upon threats of death. Yet other attorneys, such as Alexander Davis and John Ritchie, tempered their public criticisms of vigilante activities and made a decent living representing clients without meaningful threat to their lives and livelihoods. Attorneys, as a group, deserve at least some credit for prevailing upon Chief Judge Hosmer to give a second charge to the grand jury in Virginia City on August 7, 1866, in a deliberate effort to prevent a resurgence of vigilantism that was feared for Alder Gulch by many lawyers at the time, Wilbur Fisk Sanders included. History's judgment of the role played by attorneys in Montana's vigilante history is therefore mixed and depends upon the reader's sympathies, perspectives, and temporal focus.

The judges, however, should pass the scrutiny of history. They arrived in an untamed territory, without the benefit of indigenous legal precedents, and faced the challenge of establishing a credible judicial system necessary to stem the tide of vigilante executions.[11] Chief Judge Hosmer, in particular, used his role as a public bulwark against vigilantism and in favor of judicial processes. He publicly charged his grand juries in both 1864 and 1866 that vigilantism needed to give way to formal law enforcement and courts. Hosmer did so in the absence of a courthouse, law books, supplies, and Montana legal precedent. He delivered a system of criminal and civil justice which, by its mere existence, offered a stark and civilized alternative to vigilante ways. His colleague, Lyman Munson, while perhaps less vocal and persuasive than Hosmer in his opposition to vigilantism, also sought to introduce "Eastern-style" judicial procedures for the adjudication of criminal and civil disputes in the territory to supplant the vigilante system that existed in the previous judicial vacuum. Both men, along with their other early colleague, Judge Lorenzo P. Williston, created a judicial system that foundationally set Montana Territory, and the state, on a path of longer-term judicial legitimacy. However rough were the earliest days of Montana's territorial court system, the decades that followed have been distinguished.

To say that the vigilantes acted completely without due process is an exaggeration. Certainly, they did not provide due process in the sense that we understand the concept today. Nor should they be held to today's standards, which have taken many court cases and several generations to develop. Even today's constitutional and statutory standards of justice are not perfect. While the significant bulk of current criminal and civil cases reach results that are just and proper, there are undoubtedly some instances in which persons who have committed crimes are nevertheless acquitted by juries, and, conversely, there are persons innocent of crimes who are wrongly convicted. The best example of the latter may be found among the defendants who years after their convictions are exonerated from crimes based upon today's DNA technology, which was not available at the times of their earlier criminal trials.[12] Therefore, were we to measure the level of vigilante due process against the due process standards of today, we should recognize that even today's expectations do not represent a standard of perfection.

Measured by due process concepts that were understood at the time, the Montana vigilantes oftentimes acted in violation of their own bylaws and hanged persons precipitously and without trials. For the most part, the vigilantes performed investigations and hanged those individuals when they were satisfied of the person's guilt. The instances in which the vigilantes acted outside of their own defined bounds, and outside of the crude concepts of due process that existed in their time, detracts considerably from history's judgment of their overall activities, as with the particular executions of J. A. Slade in Virginia City, James Daniels in Helena, and Leander Johnson in Deer Lodge.

All of the foregoing arose, ultimately, from man's pursuit of gold worth $20.67 per ounce. The price of gold was a compelling incentive for the criminal element to take advantage of both the absence of effective law enforcement in the pioneer West and the opportunities for theft in the desolate and unprotected overland trails of Montana Territory. Nevertheless, as written by Sir Thomas More, the patron saint of lawyers,

> They wonder much to hear that gold, which in itself is so useless a thing, should be everywhere so much esteemed, that even man, for whom it was made, and by whom it has its value, should yet be thought of less value than this metal.[13]

Panning for Nuggets

Montana's number one industry today is agriculture, particularly its grains and livestock. Within the state's mining sector, coal now provides Montana's largest production value, followed by precious metals such as palladium, gold, and platinum. Shale oil under the eastern regions of Montana, near its border with Canada and North Dakota, may present Montana with its greatest future natural resource potential.

Since 1862, the volume of gold production in Montana has ranked seventh among all of the states in the nation. Since roughly the same time, the territory and state of Montana ranks first in the nation in its number of vigilante executions.

No persons who engaged in vigilante executions in Montana, and the related executions in neighboring Idaho, Colorado, and Utah as described in this narrative, were ever charged with any crimes arising out of their vigilante conduct.

Notes

1. "Ratification of the Constitution by the State of New York."
2. Revolutionary War and Beyond, "James Madison Speech to Congress—June 8, 1789."
3. *Armstrong v. Manzo*, 380 U.S. 545, 552 (1965); *Grannis v. Ordean*, 234 U.S. 385, 394 (1914).
4. The Thirteenth Amendment, which abolished slavery, was ratified in 1865. The Fourteenth Amendment, which prohibits the states from abridging the privileges and immunities of citizens guaranteed under the federal Constitution, was ratified in 1868.
5. Allen, *Decent Orderly Lynching*, 358; Kelley, "Hanging Tree and the Pillory," 8, both citing an editorial by Robert Fisk published in the *Helena Daily Herald* on August 27, 1883, in regard to the mob hanging of John A. Jessrang in Dillon, Montana.
6. Kelley, "Hanging Tree and the Pillory," 8. The same article was reproduced in the *Vermont Bar Journal* 35, no. 1 (Spring 2009): 38–41.
7. Dimsdale, *Vigilantes of Montana*, 16.
8. Ibid., 15. 225.
9. Pfouts, *Four Firsts*, 100.
10. Kelley, "Hanging Tree and the Pillory," 8.
11. Bancroft, *History*, 655.
12. A joint project between the Michigan Law School and Northwestern University School of Law's Center for Wrongful Convictions reveals that between 1989 and 2012, the number of postconviction criminal exonerations exceeded 2,000. Stigile, "New Exoneration Registry Shows at Least 2,000 Convicts Cleared."
13. Thomas More, *Utopia* (1516), quoted in Bartlett, *Bartlett's Familiar Quotations*, 155.

Appendix A

Organic Act of the Territory of Montana, with Amendment

A N ACT to provide a temporary government for the Territory of Montana.

Be it enacted by the Senate and House of Representatives of the United States of America in Congress assembled:

That all that part of the territory of the United States included within the limits, to wit: commencing at the point formed by the intersection of the twenty-seventh degree of longitude west from Washington and the forty-fifth degree of north latitude; thence due west of said forty-fifth degree of latitude to a point formed by its intersection with the thirty-fourth degree of longitude west from Washington; thence due south along said thirty-fourth degree of longitude to its intersection with the forty-fourth degree and thirty minutes of north latitude to a point formed by its intersection with the crest of the Rocky mountains; thence following the crest of the Rocky mountains northward till its intersection with the Bitter Root mountains; thence northward along the crest of said Bitter Root mountains to its intersection with the thirty-ninth degree of longitude west from Washington; thence along said thirty-ninth degree of longitude northward to the boundary line of the British possessions; thence eastward along said boundary line to the twenty-seventh degree of longitude west from Washington; thence southward along said twenty-seventh degree of longitude to the place of beginning, be, and the same is, hereby created into a temporary government by the name of the Territory of Montana: *Provided,* That nothing in this act contained shall be construed to inhibit the government of the United States from dividing said Territory or changing its boundaries in such manner and at such time as Congress shall deem convenient and proper, or from attaching any portion of said Territory to another State or Territory of the United States: *Provided, further,* That nothing in this act contained shall be construed to impair the rights of persons or property now pertaining to the Indians in said Territory so long as such rights shall remain unextinguished by treaty between the United States and such Indians, or to include any territory which, by treaty with any Indian tribes, is not, without the consent of said tribe, to be included within the territorial limits or jurisdiction of any State or Territory; but all such territory shall be excepted out of the boundaries, and constitute no part of the Territory of Montana, until said tribe shall signify their assent to the President of the United States to be included within said Territory, or to affect the authority of the government of the United States to make any regulations respecting such Indians, their lands, property, or other rights, by treaty, law, or otherwise, which it would have been competent for the government to make if this act had never passed.

Sec. 2. *And be it further enacted,* That the executive power and authority in and over said Territory of Montana shall be vested in a governor, who shall hold his office for four years, and until his successor shall be appointed and qualified, unless sooner removed by the President of the United States. The governor shall reside within said Territory, and shall be commander-in-chief of the militia and superintendent of Indian affairs thereof. He may grant pardons and respites for offences against the laws of said Territory, and reprieve for offences against the laws of the United States, until the decision of the President of the United States can be made known thereon; he shall commission all officers who shall be appointed to the office under the laws of the said Territory, and shall take care that the laws be faithfully executed.

Sec. 3. *And be it further enacted,* That there shall be a secretary of said Territory, who shall reside therein, and hold his office for four years, unless sooner removed by the President of the United States; he shall record and preserve all laws and proceedings of the legislative assembly hereinafter constituted, and all the acts and proceedings of the governor in his executive department; he shall transmit one copy of the laws and journals of the legislative assembly within thirty days after the end of each session, and one copy of the executive proceedings and official correspondence semi-annually, on the first days of January and July in each year, to the President of the United States, and two copies of the laws to the President of the Senate and the Speaker of the House of Representatives, for the use of Congress. And in case of the death, removal, resignation, or absence of the governor from the Territory, the secretary shall be, and he is hereby, authorized and required to execute and perform all the powers and duties of the governor, during such vacancy or absence, or until another governor shall be duly appointed and qualified to fill such vacancy.

Sec. 4. *And be it further enacted*, That the legislative power and authority of the said Territory shall be vested in the governor and a legislative assembly. The legislative assembly shall consist of a council and house of representatives. The council shall consist of seven members having the qualifications of voters, and hereinafter prescribed, whose term of office shall continue two years. The houses of representatives shall, at its first session, consist of thirteen members, possessing the same qualifications as prescribed for the members of the council, and whose term of service shall continue one year. The number of representatives may be increased by the legislative assembly, from time to time, to twenty-six, in proportion to the increase in qualified voters; and the council, in like manner, to thirteen. An apportionment shall be made, as nearly equal as practicable, among the several counties or districts for the election of the council and representatives, giving to each section of the territory representation in the ratio of qualified voters as nearly as may be. And the members of the council and the house of representatives shall reside in, and be inhabitants of, the district, or county, or counties for which they may be elected, respectively. Previous to the first election, the governor shall cause a census or enumeration of the inhabitants and qualified voters of the several counties and districts of the territory to be taken by such persons and in such mode as the governor shall designate and appoint, and the person so appointed shall receive a reasonable compensation therefor, And the first election shall be held at such time and places, and be conducted in such manner, both as to the persons who shall superintend such election and the returns thereof, as the governor shall appoint and direct; and he shall at the same time declare the number of members of the council and house of representatives to which each of the counties or districts shall be entitled under this act. The persons having the highest number of legal votes in each of said council districts, respectively, for members of the council, shall be declared by the governor to be duly elected to the council; and the persons having the highest number of legal votes for the house of representatives in each of said representative districts, respectively, shall be declared by the governor to be duly elected members of said house. *Provided*, That in case two or more persons voted for shall have an equal number of votes, and in case a vacancy shall occur in either branch of the legislative assembly, the governor shall order a new election. And the persons thus elected to the legislative assembly shall meet at such place and on such day as the governor shall appoint; but thereafter the time, place and manner of holding and conducting all elections by the people, and the apportioning the representation in the several counties or districts to the council and house or representatives, according to the number of qualified voters, shall be prescribed by law, as well as the day of commencement of the regular sessions of the legislative assembly: *Provided,* That no session in any one year shall exceed the term of forty days, except the first session, which may continue sixty days.

Sec. 5. *And be it further enacted,* That all citizens of the United States, and those who have declared their intentions to become such, and who are otherwise described and qualified under the fifth section of the act of Congress providing for a temporary government for the Territory of Idaho, approved March third, eighteen hundred sixty-three, shall be entitled to vote at said first election, and shall be eligible to any office within the said Territory; but the qualifications of voters, and of holding office, at all subsequent elections, shall be such as shall be prescribed by the legislative assembly.

Sec. 6. *And be it further enacted,* That the legislative powers of the Territory shall extend to all rightful subjects of legislation consistent with the Constitution of the United States and the provisions of this act; but no law shall be passed interfering with the primary disposal of the soil; no tax shall be imposed upon the property of the United States. Nor shall the lands or other property of non-residents be taxed higher than the lands or other property of residents. Every bill that shall have passed the council and the houses of representatives of the said Territory shall, before it becomes a law, be presented to the governor of the Territory. If he approve, he shall sign it; but if not, he shall return it, with his objections, to the house in which it originated, who shall enter the objections at large upon their journal and proceed to reconsider it. If, after such reconsideration, two-thirds of that house shall agree to pass the bill, it shall be sent, together with the objections, to the other house, by which it shall likewise be reconsidered, and, if approved by two-thirds of that house, it shall become a law. But in all such cases the votes of both houses shall be determined by yeas and nays, to be entered on the journal of each house, respectively. If any bill shall not be returned by the governor within three days (Sundays excepted) after it shall have been presented to him, the same shall be a law, in like manner as if he had signed it, unless the assembly, by adjournment, prevent its return; in which case it shall not be a law: *Provided,* That whereas slavery is prohibited in said Territory by act of Congress of June nineteenth, eighteen hundred and sixty-two, nothing herein contained shall be construed to authorize or permit its existence therein.

Sec. 7. *And be it further enacted,* That all township, district, and county officers, not herein otherwise provided for, shall be appointed or elected, as the case may be, in such manner as shall be provided by the governor and legislative assembly of the Territory of Montana. The governor shall nominate and, by and with the advice and consent of the legislative council, appoint all officers not herein otherwise provided for; and in the first instance the governor alone may appoint all said officers, who shall hold their offices until the end of the first session of the legislative assembly, and shall lay off the necessary districts for members of the council and house of representatives, and all other officers.

Sec. 8. *And be it further enacted*, That no member of the legislative assembly shall hold or be appointed to any office which shall have been created, or the salary or emoluments of which shall have been increased while he was a member, during the term for which he was elected, and for one year after the expiration of such term; but this restriction shall not be applicable to members of the first legislative assembly. And no person holding a commission or appointments under the United States, except postmasters, shall be a member of the legislative assembly, or shall hold any office under the government of said Territory.

Sec. 9. *And be it further enacted*, That the judicial power of said Territory shall be vested in a supreme court, district courts, probate courts, and in justices of the peace. The supreme court shall consist of a chief justice and two associate justices, any two of whom shall constitute a quorum, and who shall hold a term at the seat of government of said territory annually; and they shall hold their offices during the period of four years, and until their successors shall be appointed and qualified. The said Territory shall be divided into three judicial districts, and a district court shall be held in each of said districts by one of the justices of the supreme court at such times and places as may be prescribed by law; and the said judges shall, after their appointments, respectively, reside in the district which shall be assigned them. The jurisdiction of the several courts herein provided for, both appellate and original, and that of the probate courts and the justices of the peace, shall be limited by law: *Provided*, That justices of the peace shall not have jurisdiction of any matter in controversy when the title of land may be in dispute, or where the debt or sum claimed shall exceed one hundred dollars; and the said supreme and district courts, respectively, shall possess chancery as well as common law jurisdiction. Each district court, or the judge thereof, shall appoint its clerk, who shall also be the register in chancery, and shall keep his office at the place where the court may be held. Writs of error, bills of exceptions, and appeals, shall be allowed in all cases from the final decisions of said districts courts to the supreme court under such regulations as may be prescribed by law. The supreme court, or the justices thereof, shall appoint its own clerk; and every clerk shall hold his office at the pleasure of the court for which he shall have been appointed. Writs of error and appeals from the final decisions of said supreme court shall be allowed, and may be taken to the Supreme Court of the United States, in the same manner and under the same regulations as from the circuit courts of the United States, where the value of the property, or the amount in controversy, to be ascertained by the oath or affirmation of either party, or other competent witnesses, shall exceed one thousand dollars, except that a writ of error or appeal shall be allowed to the Supreme Court of the United States from the decision of the said supreme court created by this act, or of any judge thereof, or of the district courts created by this act, or of any judge thereof, upon any writs of habeas corpus involving the question of personal freedom. And each of the said district courts shall have and exercise the same jurisdiction, in all cases arising under the Constitution and laws of the United States, as is vested in the circuit and district courts of the United States; and the first six days of every term of said courts, or so much thereof as shall be necessary, shall be appropriated to the trial of causes arising under the said Constitution and laws; and writs of error and appeal in all such cases shall be made to the supreme court of said Territory the same as in other cases. The said clerks shall receive, in all such cases, the same fees which the clerks of the district courts of Washington Territory now receive for similar services.

Sec. 10. *And be it further enacted*, That there shall be appointed an attorney for the said Territory, who shall continue in office four years, and until his successor shall be appointed and qualified, unless sooner removed by the President of the United States, and who shall receive the same fees and salary as the attorney of the United States for the present Territory of Washington. There shall also be a marshal for the Territory appointed, who shall hold his office for four years, and until his successor shall be appointed and qualified, unless sooner removed by the President of the United States, and who shall execute all processes issuing from the said courts when exercising their jurisdiction as circuit and district courts of the United States. He shall perform the duties, be subject to the same regulations and penalties, and be entitled to the same fees as the marshal of the district court of the United States for the present Territory of Washington, and shall, in addition, be paid two hundred dollars annually as a compensation for extra services. There shall also be appointed by the President of the United States, by and with the advice and consent of the Senate, a surveyor general for said Territory, who shall locate his office at such place as the Secretary of the Interior shall from time to time direct, and whose duties, powers, obligations, responsibilities, compensation, and allowances for clerk hire, office rent, fuel, and incidental expenses, shall be the same as those of the surveyor general of New Mexico, under the direction of the Secretary of the Interior, and such instructions as he may from time to time deem it advisable.

Sec. 11. *And be it further enacted*, That the governor, secretary, chief justice, and associate justices, attorney, and marshal, shall be appointed by the President of the United States, by and with the advice and consent of the Senate. The governor and secretary to be appointed as aforesaid shall, before they act as such, respectively, take an oath or affirmation before the district judge, or some justice of the peace in the limits of said Territory, duly authorized to administer oaths and affirmations by the laws now in force therein, or before the chief justice or some associate justice of the Supreme Court of the United States, to support the Constitution of the United States, and faithfully discharge the duties of their respective offices; which said oaths, when so taken, shall be certified by the person by whom the same shall be taken; and such certificates shall be received and recorded by the said secretary among the executive proceedings; and the chief justice and associate justices, and all civil officers in said Territory, before they act as such, shall take a like oath or affirmation before the said governor, secretary, or some judge or justice of the peace of the Territory who may be duly commissioned or qualified, or before the chief justice or some associate justice of the Supreme Court of the United States, which said oath or affirmation shall be certified and transmitted by the person taking the same to the secretary, to be by him recorded as aforesaid; and afterwards the like oath or affirmation shall be taken, certified, and recorded in such manner and form as may be prescribed by law. And any person who has heretofore been appointed chief justice or associate justice of the Territory of Idaho, who has not yet taken the oath of office, as prescribed by the act organizing said Territory, may take said oath or affirmation before the chief judge or associate justice of the Supreme Court of the United States. The governor shall receive an annual salary of two thousand five hundred dollars; the chief justice and associate justices shall receive an annual salary of two thousand five hundred dollars; the secretary shall receive an annual salary of two thousand dollars. The said salaries shall be paid quarter yearly from the dates of the respective appointments at the treasury of the United States; but no payment shall be made until said officers shall have entered upon the duties of their respective appointments. The members of the legislative assembly shall be entitled to receive four dollars each day during their attendance at the sessions thereof, and four dollars each for every twenty miles' travel in going to and returning from said sessions, estimated according to the nearest usually traveled route; and an additional allowance of four dollars per day shall be paid to the presiding officer of each house for each day he shall so preside. And a chief clerk, one assistant clerk, one engrossing and one enrolling clerk, a sergeant-at-arms and doorkeeper may be chosen for each house; and the chief clerk shall receive four dollars per day, and the other officers three dollars per day during the session of the legislative assembly; but no other officers shall be paid by the United States; *Provided*, that there shall be but one session of the legislative assembly annually, unless, on an extraordinary occasion, the governor shall think proper to call the legislative assembly together. There shall be appropriated annually the usual sum, to be expended by the governor, to defray the contingent expenses of the Territory, including the salary of the clerk of the executive department. And there shall also be appropriated annually a sufficient sum, to be expended by the secretary of the Territory, and upon an estimate to be made by the Secretary of the Treasury of the United States, to defray the expenses of the legislative assembly, the printing of the laws, and other incidental expenses. And the governor and secretary of the Territory shall, in the disbursement of all moneys intrusted to them, be governed solely by the instructions of the Secretary of the Treasury of the United States, and shall semi-annually account to the said Secretary for the manner in which the aforesaid moneys shall have been expended; and no expenditure shall be made by said legislative assembly for objects not specially authorized by the acts of Congress making appropriations, nor beyond the sums thus appropriated for such objects.

Sec. 12. *And be it further enacted,* That the legislative assembly of the Territory of Montana shall hold its first session at such time and place in said Territory as the governor thereof shall appoint and direct; and at said first session, or as soon thereafter as they shall deem expedient, the governor and legislative assembly shall proceed to locate and establish the seat of government for said Territory at such place as they may deem eligible: *Provided,* That the seat of government fixed by the governor and legislative assembly shall not be at any time changed except by an act of the said assembly, duly passed, and which shall be approved, after due notice, at the first general election thereafter, by a majority of the legal votes cast on that question.

Sec. 13. *And be it further enacted,* That a delegate to the House of Representatives of the United States, to serve for the term of two years, who shall be a citizen of the United States, may be elected by the voters qualified to elect members of the legislative assembly, who shall be entitled to the same rights and privileges as are exercised and enjoyed by the delegates from the several other Territories of the United States to the said House of representatives; but the delegate first elected shall hold the seat only during the term of Congress to which he shall be elected. The first election shall be held at such time and places, and be conducted in such manner, as the governor shall appoint and direct, and at all subsequent elections the times and places, and the manner of holding the elections, shall be prescribed by law. The person having the greatest number of legal votes shall be declared by the governor to be duly elected, and a certificate thereof shall be given accordingly. That the Constitution and all laws of the United States, which are not locally inapplicable, shall have the same force and effect within the said Territory of Montana as elsewhere within the United States.

Sec. 14. *And be it further provided,* That when the lands in the said Territory shall be surveyed under the direction of the government of the United States, preparatory to bringing the same into market, sections numbered sixteen and thirty-six in each township in said Territory shall be, and the same are hereby, reserved for the purpose of being applied to schools in said Territory and in the States and Territories hereafter to be erected out of the same.

Sec. 15. *And be it further enacted,* That, until otherwise provided by law, the governor of said Territory may define the judicial districts of said Territory, and assign the judges who may be appointed for said Territory to the several districts, and also appoint the times and places for holding courts in several counties or sub-divisions in each of said judicial districts, by proclamation to be issued by him; but the legislative assembly, at their first or any subsequent session, may organize, alter, or modify such judicial districts, and assign the judges, and alter the times and places of holding the courts, as to them shall seem proper and convenient.

Sec. 16. *And it be further enacted,* That all officers to be appointed by the President of the United Sates, by and with the advice and consent of the Senate, for the Territory of Montana, who, by virtue of the provisions of any law now existing, or which may be enacted by Congress, are required to give security for moneys that may be intrusted with them for disbursement, shall give such security at such time and in such manner as the secretary of the Treasury may prescribe.

Sec. 17. *And be it further enacted,* That all treaties, laws, and other engagements made by the government of the United States with the Indian tribes inhabiting the Territory embraced within the provisions of this act, shall be faithfully and rigidly observed, anything contained in this act to the contrary notwithstanding; and that the existing agencies and superintendencies of said Indians be continued, with the same powers and duties which are now prescribed by law, except that the President of the United States may, at his discretion, change the location of the office of said agencies or superintendents.

Sec. 18. *And be it further enacted,* That, until Congress shall otherwise direct, all that part of the Territory of Idaho included within the following boundaries, to wit: Commencing at a point formed by the intersection of the thirty-third degree of longitude west from Washington with the forty-first degree of north latitude; thence along said thirty-third degree of longitude to the crest of the Rocky mountains; thence northward along the said crest of the Rocky mountains to its intersection with the forty-fourth degree and thirty minutes of north latitude; thence eastward along the forty-fourth degree thirty minutes north latitude to the thirty-fourth degree of longitude west from Washington; thence northward along the thirty-fourth degree of longitude to its intersection with the forty-fifth degree north latitude; thence eastward along the forty-fifth degree of north latitude to its intersection with the twenty-seventh degree of longitude west from Washington; thence south along said twenty-seventh degree of longitude west from Washington to the forty-first degree north latitude; thence west along said forty-first degree of latitude to the place of beginning, shall be, and is hereby, incorporated temporarily into and made part of the Territory of Dakota. [Approved May 26, 1864, 13 Stat. 85]

Amendment to the Organic Act That Nullified Montana's Second and Third Territorial Legislatures

AN ACT Amendatory of "An Act to provide a temporary government for the Territory of Montana," approved May 26, 1864.

Be it enacted by the Senate and House of representatives of the United States of America in Congress assembled:

That the legislative assemblies of the several territories of the United States shall not, after the passage of this act, grant private charters or special privileges, but they may, by general incorporation acts, permit persons to associate themselves together as bodies corporate for mining, manufacturing, and other individual pursuits.

Sec. 2. *And be it further enacted,* That the probate courts of the Territory of Montana, in their respective counties, in addition to their probate jurisdiction, are hereby authorized to hear and determine civil causes wherein the damage or debt claimed does not exceed five hundred dollars, and such criminal cases arising under the laws of the Territory as do not require the intervention of a grand jury; *Provided,* That they shall not have jurisdiction in any matter in controversy when the title or right to the peaceable possession of land may be in dispute, or chancery, or divorce causes; *And provided further,* That in all cases an appeal may be taken from any order, judgment, or decree of said probate court to the district court.

Sec. 3 *And be it further enacted,* That the chief justice and associate justices of said Territory and the Territory of Idaho shall each receive an annual salary of thirty-five hundred dollars.

Sec. 4. *And be it further enacted,* That the judges of the supreme court of said territory, or a majority of them, shall, when assembled at the seat of government of said Territory, define the judicial districts of said Territory, and assign the judges who may be appointed for said territory to the several districts, and shall also fix and appoint the times and places for holding the courts in the several counties or sub-divisions in each of said judicial districts, and alter the times and places of holding the courts as to them shall seem proper and convenient, but not less than two terms shall be held at each place of holding court each year.

Sec. 5. *And be it further enacted,* That for the purpose of reviving the legislative functions of the Territory of Montana, which have been adjudged therein to have lapsed, the governor of said Territory be, and is hereby, authorized, on or before the first day of July, eighteen hundred and sixty-seven, to divide said territory into legislative districts for the election of members of the council and house of representatives, and to apportion among said districts the number of members of the legislative assembly provided for in the Organic Act of said Territory, and the election of said members of the legislative assembly shall be held at such time and shall be conducted in the manner prescribed by the legislative assembly of the territory at the session thereof, begun and holden at the city of Bannack, in eighteen hundred and sixty-four and eighteen hundred and sixty-five, and the qualifications of voters shall be the same as that prescribed by said Organic Act, saving and excepting the distinction therein made on account of race and color, and the legislative assembly, so elected, shall convene at the time prescribed by said legislative assembly at the session last aforesaid. The apportionment provided for in this section shall be based upon such an enumeration of the qualified electors of the said several legislative districts as shall appear from the election returns in the office of the secretary of said territory, and from such other sources of information as will enable the governor, without taking a new census, to make an apportionment which shall fairly represent the people of the several districts in both houses of the legislative assembly, but the legislature may at any time change the legislative districts of the Territory as fixed by the governor.

Sec. 6. *And be it further enacted,* That all acts passed at the two sessions of the so-called legislative assembly of the Territory of Montana, held in eighteen hundred and sixty-six, are hereby disapproved and declared null and void, except such acts as the legislative assembly herein authorized to be elected, shall by special act, in each case, re-enact: *Provided, however,* That in all the claims of vested rights thereunder, the party claiming the same shall not, by reason of anything in this section contained, be precluded from making and testing said claim in the courts of said Territory: *And provided further,* That no legislation or pretended legislation in said territory since the adjournment of the first legislative assembly shall be deemed valid until the election of the legislative assembly herein provided for shall take place.

Sec. 7. And be it further enacted, That from and after the first day of April next, the salary of each of the judges of the several supreme courts in each of the organized territories (except Montana and Idaho) shall be two thousand five hundred dollars.

Sec. 8. *And be it further enacted,* That all acts and parts of acts inconsistent with this act are hereby repealed. [Approved March 2, 1867, 14 Stat. 426]

Appendix B

Bylaws of the Vigilance Committee

This Committee shall consist of a President or Chief, an Executive Officer, Secretary, Treasurer, Executive Committee, Captains and Lieutenants of Companies and such gentlemen of known worth and integrity as the Captains, Lieutenants, and other officers enumerated above may deem worthy of being members.

The President shall be the supreme ruler of the Committee, shall reside in Virginia City, and shall have the power to appoint Captains to raise Companies wherever and whenever he deems the interest of the Committee require the same, to call together the Executive Committee whenever the same should be convened to order the arrest of any suspicious or guilty person, to preside at all meetings whenever present, and to have such other powers as would naturally devolve upon one occupying his position.

A majority of votes of the Executive Committee shall constitute an election for President, and he shall hold his office until his successor is appointed and accepts the position.

The Executive Officer shall have the government and control of all Captains, Lieutenants, and Companies, shall see that all orders of the Chief and Executive Committee are duly executed, shall have the selection of all persons sent out upon any expedition by the Executive Committee and choose a leader for the same and in case of the death or absence of the chief shall assume the duties of the office of President, until a new President is chosen.

The Secretary shall keep a correct record of all things proper to be written, the names of the Chief, Executive Officer, Secretary, Treasurer, Executive Committee, and the names of Captains and Lieutenants of Companies.

DOI: 10.7330_9780874219203.c019

The Treasurer shall receive all monies belonging to the Committee, keep a true account of the same and pay them out again upon orders of the Executive Committee attested by the Secretary.

The Executive Committee shall consist of seventeen members, to wit: The President, Executive Officer, Treasurer, Secretary of the Committee, four persons to be selected from Virginia City, three from Nevada [City], one from Junction, one from Highland, one from Pine Grove, two from Summit, and one from Bivins Gulch, any eight of whom shall constitute a quorum.

It shall be the duty of the Executive Committee to legislate for the good of the whole Committee—to try all criminals that may be arrested, to pass upon all accounts that may be presented, and if just to order the same paid by the Treasurer and to take general supervision of all criminal acts that may be committed within this Territory or come under their notice.

The Captains of Companies may be appointed by the President or the Executive Officer, who shall hold their offices until elected by the Companies themselves, every Captain shall have power to appoint one or more Lieutenants— the Captains and Lieutenants shall have the power to recruit their companies from men of integrity living in their midst, and when any one Company outside of Virginia City numbers over fifty effective men a division should be made and two companies formed from the same and officers elected from each.

It shall be the duty of members to attach themselves to some company and whenever any criminal act shall come to their knowledge to inform his Captain or Lieutenant of the same, when the officers so informed shall call together the members of his Company, (unless the Company has chosen a committee for such purpose) when they shall proceed to investigate the case, and elicit the facts and should the said company conclude that the person charged with any offense should be punished by the committee, the Captain or Lieutenant will first take steps to arrest the Criminal and then report the same with proof to the Chief who will thereupon call a meeting of the Executive Committee and the judgment of such Executive Committee shall be final.

The only punishment that shall be inflicted by this Committee is death.

The property of any person executed by this Committee shall be immediately seized upon and disposed of by the Executive Committee for the purpose of paying the Expenses of the Committee, and should the persons executed have creditors living in this Territory it shall be the duty of the Committee to first pay the Expenses of the Committee and Execution & Funeral Expenses, afterwards to pay the residue over to some one for the benefit of said creditors.

Vigilantes Records (Virginia City), 1863–84, Mont. Hist. Soc., SC-953.

Appendix C

Petition for the Reprieve and Pardon of James Daniels

To his Excellency, T. F. Meagher, Acting Governor of Montana:

The undersigned, your fellow citizens and petitioners, would respectfully represent to your Excellency, that at the last term of the United States District Court, for the 3rd Judicial District of the Territory of Montana, one James B. Daniels, who was indicted by the grand jury for said District, and tried before said indictment on said indictment on the charge of murder in the first degree, was convicted of the crime of manslaughter, and sentenced by the Judge of said court to three years imprisonment at hard labor, and to pay a fine of one thousand dollars, and that under said sentence said Daniels was and is now imprisoned, in the county jail of Madison County. Your petitioners believe that the circumstances under which the homicide alleged to have been committed in said indictment, by said Daniels upon the person of the deceased, James Gartley, were most provoking and outrageous, placing said Daniels, in the affray, which ended in the death of said Gartley, in great danger of receiving great bodily harm, or loosing [sic] his life from the assault commenced and prosecuted by said Gartley upon the person of said Daniels, with a large heavy stool, and that said Daniels had every reason to apprehend, by having been stricken down into a burning box-stove by said Gartley, and that said Gartley being very much [the] larger and stronger man while Gartley's friends were doing everything to urge him to inflict serious bodily injury and harm upon said Daniels, that said Daniels inflicted the fatal wounds with every reason and circumstance tending to establish to the satisfaction of any reasonable man, of the great and immediate danger that surrounded him. Believing, also, that the charge of the Judge was illiberal to said Daniels, to which we refer your Excellency, as published in the Territory; and believing also, that said Daniels established at said trial, a

DOI: 10.7330_9780874219203.c020

good and enviable character as a good peaceable, law abiding citizen, and that he is a most proper subject and person on whom to bestow executive clemency, would most respectfully request and pray your Excellency to reprieve and pardon the said James B. Daniels, as we are convinced that such an exercise of Executive clemency, would result in universal satisfaction to all unbiased persons in this community acquainted with the facts and circumstances connected with said homicide, and said trial. And your petitioners will ever pray, etc.

Pemberton & Toole, R. B. Parrott, J. B. Bernard, E. B. Waterbury, H. H. Snow, W. Scott, J. E. Vinton, G. Plummer, G. B. Whitson, G. M. Dorsey, J. G. Wilson, Ed. J. Zimmerman, Jess Brant, Westly Alexander, Mark A. Moore, H. T. Wilson, Jas. B. Prather, P. H. Rea, E. S. Wilkinson, E. D. Little, O. S. Brigs, J. G. Siebe, Thos. E. Tutt, S. H. Carls, Jr., W. T. Tutt, L. Huggins, Ed. House, Jr., W. C. Logan, R. C. Ewing, J. C. Hutchinson, B. B. Burchette.

"Hanging of Daniels, Again," Montana Radiator, Mar. 17, 1866, p. 3, col. 1.

Appendix D

Reprieve of James Daniels

EXECUTIVE OFFICE
TERRITORY OF MONTANA
Virginia City, February 22nd, 1866

Know all men, that whereas, at a late term of the United States District Court for the Third Judicial District of the Territory of Montana, one James B. Daniels was convicted of the crime of Manslaughter, and sentenced by the Judge of said Court, to three years of imprisonment and hard labor, and to pay a fine of One Thousand Dollars, And whereas, it appearing clearly from the petition of numerous good citizens of the County of Edgerton, where said conviction occurred, including several jurymen, who, by their verdict, contributed to the aforesaid conviction, that the circumstances under which the aforesaid offence was committed, was most provoking on the part of the deceased of the parties in conflict, and, to a great extent, justifiable on the part of the said Daniels

Now therefore, I, Thomas Francis Meagher, Acting Governor of the Territory of Montana, by virtue of the authority vested in me, as Governor of said Territory, by the second section of the Organic Act of Montana Territory, aforesaid, do hereby reprieve the said James B. Daniels, for the said offence of Manslaughter, committed, and of which he is convicted, as aforesaid, until the decision of the President of the United States, is made known thereon.

And, I do hereby order and direct the Sheriff of Madison County, or other person having charge of the prisoner wherein the said Daniels is confined, to immediately release and discharge the said James B. Daniels from custody.

In witness thereof, I have hereunto set my hand, and the seal of said Territory, this 22nd day of February, A.D. 1866.
Thomas Francis Meagher
Acting Governor,
Territory of Montana

"James B. Daniels Release, 1866," Mont. Hist. Soc., SC-1634.

DOI: 10.7330_9780874219203.c021

Appendix E

Military Procedures for Execution by Hanging

The officer charged with the execution will command the escort and make the necessary arrangements for the conduct of the execution. He will—

a. Instruct components of the escort in their duties.

b. Arrange for the receipt of the prisoner by the prisoner guard.

c. Arrange for the chaplain to accompany the prisoner.

d. Arrange for the presence of a medical officer at the scene of the execution.

e. Provide a proper gallows.

f. Provide a black hood to cover the head of the prisoner.

g. Provide a collapse board for use if necessary.

h. Cause the prisoner's arms to be secured before or immediately upon his receipt by the prisoner guard. The arms may be secured either behind the back or in front, fastened to the belt . . .

i. Arrange for a burial party as prescribed in paragraph 13k.

j. Determine the proper amount of drop of the prisoner through the trap door. A standard drop chart for normal men of given weights is given below. Variation of the drop because of physical condition may be necessary. A medical officer should be consulted to determine whether any factors, such as age, health, or muscular condition will affect the amount of drop necessary for a proper execution.

120 lbs. or less	8' 1"	170 lbs.	6' 0"
125 lbs.	7' 10"	175 lbs.	5' 11"
130 lbs.	7' 7"	180 lbs.	5' 9"
135 lbs.	7' 4"	185 lbs.	5' 7"
140 lbs.	7' 1"	190 lbs.	5' 6"
145 lbs.	6' 9"	195 lbs.	5' 5"

DOI: 10.7330_9780874219203.c022

150 lbs.	6' 7"	200 lbs.	5' 4"
155 lbs.	6' 6"	205 lbs.	5' 2"
160 lbs.	6' 4"	210 lbs.	5' 1"
165 lbs.	6' 2"	210 lbs and over	5' 0"

k. Rehearse the execution within 24 hours prior to the scheduled time for the execution. A sandbag or similar object approximating the prisoner's weight may be used to insure proper functioning of the gallows, trap door, and hangman's noose."

Department of the Army, Procedure for Military Executions, Pamphlet 27–4 (December 1947), sec. 3, "Execution by Hanging," para. 16.

Appendix F

Petition for Pardon of Henry Plummer, May 21, 1993

To: The Honorable Marc Racicot
Governor of the State of Montana
State Capitol Building
Helena, Montana 59620–0801

SUBJECT: Request for a Pardon

FROM: History West Publishing Company
P.O. Box 612066
San Jose, California 95161
and
Professor Jack Burrows
History Department
San Jose City College
2100 Moorpark Avenue
San Jose, California 95128–2799

CC: The Senate of the State of Montana
C/O The Honorable Fred Van Valkenburg, President
112 University
Missoula, Montana 59801

CC: The House of the State of Montana
C/O The Honorable John Mercer, Speaker
P.O. Box 450
Polson, Montana 59680

DOI: 10.7330_9780874219203.c023

CC: List of news media who have been following the Plummer trial and are awaiting a report on the pardon plea: 72 newspapers, historical journals, radio, and television of ten western states; the *New York Times*; national magazines; and television networks.

NOTE: The media is expecting our next news release on 30 June 1993. That release will include the two attached letters along with the replies from the Montana Governor and legislative bodies. If Montana officials have not yet replied by 30 June, the release will note that fact.

Dear Governor Racicot:

On 7 May 1993, the sixth grade of Twin Bridges Schools initiated a posthumous trial for Sheriff Henry Plummer in the Madison County courthouse. Students who had spent months researching took the roles of lawyers and witnesses, and The Honorable Barbara Brook presided. The jury was selected from registered voters of Madison County. Though the prosecution team presented a well researched and historically accurate case, they failed to obtain a conviction. After heated discussion and three votes, the jury remained at a six-to-six deadlock, and Judge Brook declared a mistrial and ordered the defendant released. Thus the headline of the *Montana Standard* for 8 May 1993 read, "Henry Plummer Freed."

The trial was more than a school activity to offer direct experience in the judicial system. It reflects the students' hesitance to presume the guilt of an untried law officer of early Montana. The fact that six jurors entertained reasonable doubt suggests that adults also are troubled by the long-accepted account of Plummer's alleged crimes. In light of 129 years of prejudgment of Plummer's guilt, the six jurors' doubt is astounding.

As early as 1958, J. W. Smurr, of the History Department of Montana State University, warned of the danger of uncritical acceptance of the writings of Nathaniel Langford and Thomas Dimsdale. Not only was Langford a vigilante, but as authors R. E. Mather and F. E. Boswell point out in their recent book *Vigilante Victims*, in all probability Dimsdale's name was also on the vigilante membership roll. Thus for twelve decades, historians have recorded as true fact a version of events prepared by the very men responsible for the assassination of the miners' democratically elected sheriff and three [*sic*] of his deputies. Yet the Governor's File of the State of California contains a document signed in 1859 by more than 100 officials of two counties stating that Henry Plummer was a man of "excellent character," and diaries and reminiscences of numerous Montana pioneers confirm this evaluation of Plummer's character.

The students of Twin Bridges have initiated a landmark trial. This trial is an eloquent appeal for textbooks that contain accurate information, that conforms to our justice system's tenet of the accused being innocent until proven guilty, and that respect our Constitutional amendments guaranteeing that guilt be determined only by due process of law.

On behalf of my staff and the individual readers and scholars who have prodded our company to help correct a historical injustice, I request that the State of Montana grant Sheriff Henry Plummer a pardon. Since Western history books uniformly declare Plummer guilty of conducting a huge band of murderous robbers, the Montana sheriff has in reality been *convicted*, and therefore a pardon is necessary. Until such time as Montana takes the lead in issuing an official statement, the historical inaccuracy written into our present school texts will prevail; and Montana students from grade school through university—as well as all other Western history students throughout the nation—will continue to be taught the counterproductive lesson that passing historical judgment on an untried individual is acceptable in America.

Respectfully,
Frederick J. Morgan, President

Pardon Application for Sheriff Henry Plummer, May 21, 1993, State of Montana Board of Pardons and Parole.

Acknowledgments

Truth be told, this writing was originally intended to be a law review article comparing Montana's vigilantism in the 1860s against the level of due process recognized by the law at the time. No law review article on that topic has yet been written, and the idea for it seemed to be both fresh and intriguing. As the research and writing grew larger and more involved, I eventually realized that the topic was too expansive to fit within a mere article to be published by a law school. The project took on a life of its own far beyond the initial expectations for it. Had the enormity of this project been known at the outset, it might somehow have been contained as a mere article focused narrowly upon the events of Bannack and Virginia City. Nevertheless, a book-length analysis does the subject matter far more justice than a limited article ever could.

The research and writing of any history book requires a significant commitment of time and effort by any author. It is a lonely endeavor much of the time. In my case, the responsibilities of a heavy caseload at the Appellate Division of the New York State Supreme Court, and of teaching as an adjunct professor at the Fordham University School of Law, meant that the research and writing of this book could be accomplished only on late nights, weekends, and during vacations. Internet technology makes research much more accessible today than it may have been in years past, reducing the number of individuals that a researcher must consult for assistance in locating relevant materials and in exploring ideas. There were nevertheless persons along the way who made my research tasks easier or who helped make the book more interesting than it might otherwise have been for myself and its readers. The following individuals deserve words of thanks for their assistance, ideas, or willingness to educate me in the subject, all without any expectation on their parts of any acknowledgment here.

Interpretive historian Dr. Ellen Baumler of the Montana Historical Society, upon being contacted in connection with this book, sent me unsolicited material that proved valuable to my research, particularly material on the role played by Masons in Virginia City.

Ellie Arguimbau of the Montana Historical Society proved to be invaluable in providing a research trail on the existence and whereabouts of "C. French" or Charles French. Her assistance enabled me to conclude, with some degree of historical confidence, that French did not act simultaneously as both a juror and a prosecution witness at the trial of John Keene in Helena, a conclusion that may differ from current popular belief. It represents one of the areas of the book where my analysis and conclusions are contrary to the conventional historical wisdom.

I also thank Brian Shovers, library manager at the Montana Historical Society, and Zoe Ann Stoltz, reference historian at the Montana Historical Society. They each aided my research of materials in the MHS stacks and the archived articles of *Montana: The Magazine of Western History* and educated me about a variety of electronic research sources such as Montana History, Chronicling America, and the Northwest Digital Archives, as well as the options available from MHS's own Internet site.

The selection of photographs of historic people, places, and things was an important aspect of this project since the photographs add visual texture and dimension to the subject. Thanks to Becca Kohl of the Montana Historical Society's Photograph Archive for her patience, thoroughness, and sunny demeanor in helping locate and provide many of the photographs used in this book. I also thank Lynn Giles of the Beaverhead County Museum, Holly Reed of the National Archives and Records Administration, and Mark Fritch of the University of Montana's Maureen and Mike Mansfield Library for their roles in locating relevant photographs and granting permission for their use.

Christine Slaughter of the State of Montana Board of Pardons and Parole acquired for me from dusty storage the petition that had been filed in May of 1993 seeking the pardon of Sheriff Henry Plummer. The documents she provided that were related to the petition added texture to the book's discussion of the mock trial at the Twin Bridges School and to the contents of the petition itself.

Bruce Bosso, the librarian at the Appellate Division of the New York State Supreme Court, Second Judicial Department, was gracious in helping electronically locate certain "old" federal legislation used in this manuscript.

Kevin Marsh, the editor of *Idaho Yesterdays* and a member of the History Department at Idaho State University, was helpful in directing me to publications related to the Magruder trail murders in Idaho.

Research would not have been possible without the capabilities also afforded by the staffs of the Dutchess County Library System, the Westchester County Library System, the Brooklyn Public Library, and, most significantly, the New York Public Library.

Thanks to Andrea Adovasio for her patient role in producing the manuscript in its various forms and at various times.

I am eternally grateful to Michael Spooner, director of Utah State University Press, for believing in the value of this book project and in navigating it to publication at USU Press. Publication by any university press is an academic achievement, but to be included among the thought-provoking titles that USU Press has published over the years is, for me, a particular honor for which I am humbly thankful.

This manuscript was much improved by the editing expertise of Alison Tartt and managing editor Laura Furney of the University Press of Colorado. Their efforts resulted in a more precise and readable book, both grammatically and historically, and reminded me of certain all-important English lessons from school, with which they, but not I, have greater familiarity.

I owe a debt of gratitude to those individuals close to me who proofread the draft manuscript during its various incarnations and who found errors in spelling or style, asked questions about the historical narrative, and offered helpful suggestions. These individuals include Michele, Phyllis, and Laura Dillon. I also thank and acknowledge two colleagues in the legal profession who allowed me to impose upon them for proofreading and for their trusted insights on issues of law raised in the book: Joel Aurnou, a former judge of the Westchester County Court who has spent a lifetime in criminal law and who is currently counsel to McCarthy Fingar LLP in White Plains, New York, and former Yorktown town justice Marc Oxman, who heads the law firm of Oxman Tulis Kirkpatrick Whyatt & Geiger LLP in White Plains, New York, and who has a particular appreciation for the intersecting legal and political issues discussed in this narrative.

Original-source research required two extended research trips to Montana. I am grateful to my wife and best friend, Michele, who stepped away from her vacation as a teacher during a summer to assist with the research in Montana, acquiring and reviewing 150-year-old newspaper articles that were available only on microfiche and helping to locate and select photographs used in the book. I am also grateful to my entire immediate family generally, as the time given to this book project could have been, and deservedly should have been, spent instead as quality time with them. For each of them, I am truly and forever blessed.

Bibliography

Historical Collections and Photograph Archives

    Beaverhead County Museum, Dillon, MT

    LegendsOfAmerica.com, Warsaw, MO

    Montana Historical Society, Helena, MT

Aaron T. Ford Reminiscences, 1903.
Albert M. Hart Reminiscences, 1908.
Alice E. and Martin Barret Reminiscences.
Andrew J. Smith Letter, 1867.
Carolyn Abbott Tyler Reminiscences, 1862–65.
Cicily Adelia French Reminiscences.
First National Bank of Helena Records, 1859–99.
Granville Stuart Papers.
H. Frank Adkins Reminiscences, 1915.
Harold Rash Reminiscences.
Helen Fitzgerald Sanders Collection, 1886–1955.
Henry Plummer Collection.
Hezekiah Hosmer Papers, 1848–70.
Holter Family Papers.
J. J. and W. J. Boyer Reminiscences, 1905.
James "Bill" Sweeney Reminiscences, 1921.
James "Cap" Williams Papers, 1886.
"James B. Daniels Release, 1866."
James Fergus Family Papers.
James Henry Marley Diary, 1862–65.
John F. Forgey Reminiscences.
John S. Lott Records, 1886.
John W. Grannis Diaries, 1863–78.
Joseph Alfred Slade Estate Papers.
Laurence Abraham Fenner Reminiscences, 1898.
Lyman Ezra Munson Papers, 1866–99.
Neil Howie Diaries.
Oscar O. Mueller Collection.
Photograph Archives.
Samuel T. Hauser and Granville Stuart Papers.
Sidney Edgerton Family Papers.
Thomas Conrad Papers, 1857–99.
Vigilantes Records (Virginia City), 1863–84.

Wesley P. Emery Reminiscences, 1907.
Wilbur Fisk Sanders Papers.
William Y. Pemberton Papers, 1863–69.

National Archives and Records Administration, College Park, MD

Brady Collection.

State of Montana Board of Pardons and Parole

Pardon Application for Sheriff Henry Plummer, May 21, 1993.

University of Montana, Maureen and Mike Mansfield Library, Missoula, MT

K. Ross Toole Archives.

Books, Articles, Internet Sources, Theses, and Dissertations

Abrahams, Ray. *Vigilant Citizens: Vigilantism and the State.* Malden, MA: Polity Press / Blackwell Publishers, 1998.

Access Genealogy. "Montana Organization, Boundaries, and Elections, 1864–1866." Accessed December 24 and 26, 2011. http://www.accessgenealogy.com/montana/montana_organization_boundaries_elections.htm.

Access Genealogy. "Montana Politics, Legislation, and Reform." Accessed October 17, 2011. http://www.accessgenealogy.com/montana/montana_politics_legislation_reform.htm.

Agency for Toxic Substances and Disease Registry. *Toxic Substances Portal.* Accessed March 4, 2012. http://www.atsdr.cdc.gov/substances/toxsubstance .asp?toxid=64.

Allen, Frederick. *A Decent Orderly Lynching.* Norman: University of Oklahoma Press, 2004.

Allen, Frederick. "Montana Vigilantes and the Origin of 3-7-77." *Montana: The Magazine of Western History* 51 (Spring 2001): 2–19.

Allen, Frederick. "Montana Vigilantes and the Origins of the 3-7-77." Accessed May 28, 2011. http://www.visitmt.com/history/montana_the_magazine_of_western_history /montanavigilantes1.htm.

The American Annual Cyclopedia and Register of Important Events of the Year. Accessed October 2, 2011. http://books.google.com/books?id=a0_AAAAYAAJ&pg=PA496&lpg=PA496&dq=American+Annual+Cyclopedia+william+pemberton+elected+chief+judge&source=bl&ots=M-kaCOXnl_&sig=gZadaKhdyPOUIoaIYglgkT2MwyE&hl=en&sa=X&ei=pQbFUeGnMuXn0wH0z4HwDQ&ved=0CC8Q6AEwAA#v=onepage&q=American%20Annual%20Cyclopedia%20william%20pemberton%20elected%20chief%20judge&f=false.

America's Library. "Lincoln Created the Montana Territory, May 26, 1864." Accessed November 23, 2010. http://www.americaslibrary.gov/jb/civil/jb_civil_montana_1.html.

Anonymous. *Banditti of the Rocky Mountains and the Vigilance Committee in Idaho.* Minneapolis: Ross & Haines, 1964.

Arlington National Cemetery Website. "Green Clay Smith, Major General, United States Army." Accessed June 9, 2012. http://www.arlingtoncemetery.net/gcsmith.htm.

Association of Montana Troopers. "3-7-77." Accessed January 26, 2012. http://www.montanatrooper.com/3-7-77/.

Athearn, Robert G. *Thomas Francis Meagher: An Irish Revolutionary in America.* Boulder: University of Colorado Press, 1949.

Axline, John, Ellen Baumler, Chere Jiusto, Leanne Kurtz, Harriett C. Meloy, Kimberly Morrison, Vivian A. Paladin, Richard B. Roeder, and Dave Walter. *More from the Quarries of Last Chance Gulch.* Vol. 2. Helena, MT: Helena Independent Record, 1996.

Bakken, Gordon Morris, ed. *Invitation to an Execution: A History of the Death Penalty in the United States.* Albuquerque: University of New Mexico Press, 2010.

Bakken, Gordon Morris. "Death for Grand Larceny." In *Historic U.S. Court Cases, An Encyclopedia.* 2nd ed. Vol. 1, ed. John W. Johnson. New York: Routledge, 2001.

Bakken, Gordon Morris. "Law and Legal Tender in California and the West." *Southern California Quarterly* 62, no. 3 (Fall 1980): 239–59. http://dx.doi.org/10.2307/41170887.

Bakken, Gordon Morris. *Practicing Law in Frontier California.* Lincoln: University of Nebraska Press, 1991.

Bakken, Gordon Morris. *Rocky Mountain Constitution Making, 1850–1912.* New York: Greenwood Press, 1987.

Bakken, Gordon Morris. *The Mining Law of 1872: Past, Politics, and Prospects.* Albuquerque: University of New Mexico Press, 2008.

Bakken, Morris Gordon, and Brenda Farrington. *Women Who Kill Men.* Lincoln: University of Nebraska Press, 2009.

Bancroft, Hubert Howe. *History of Washington, Idaho, and Montana, 1845–1889.* Vol. 31 of *The Works of Hubert Howe Bancroft.* San Francisco: History Company Publishers, 1887.

Bancroft, Hubert Howe. *Popular Tribunals.* Vols. 36 and 37 of *The Works of Hubert Howe Bancroft.* San Francisco: The History Company, 1887.

Barsness, Larry. *Gold Camp: Alder Gulch and Virginia City, Montana.* New York: Hastings House Publishers, 1962.

Bartholomew, Ed Ellsworth. *Black Jack Ketchum: Last of the Holdup Kings.* Houston: Frontier Press of Texas, 1955.

Bartholomew, Ed. *Henry Plummer, Montana Outlaw Boss.* Ruidoso, NM: Frontier Book Company, 1960.

Bartlett, John. *Bartlett's Familiar Quotations.* 15th ed. Boston: Little, Brown, 1980.

Baumler, Ellen, ed. *Girl from the Gulches: The Story of Mary Ronan.* Helena: Montana Historical Society Press, 2003.

Baumler, Ellen. *Montana Moments.* Helena: Montana Historical Society Press, 2010.

Bayoumi, Tamim, Barry Eichengreen, and Mark P. Taylor, eds. *Modern Perspectives on the Gold Standard.* Cambridge: Cambridge University Press, 1996.

Benson, Chris. *The Periodic Table of the Elements and Their Chemical Properties.* Mindmelder.com, 2009.

Bentor, Yinon. Periodic Table. Accessed March 4 and 22, 2012. http://www.chemicalelements.com.

Bergman, Barbara E., Nancy Hollander, and Theresa M. Duncan. *Wharton's Criminal Evidence.* 15th ed. New York: Thomson Reuters, 2011.

Big Hole Tourism Association. "History [of Big Hole Valley]." Accessed November 20, 2010. http://bigholevalley.com/History.html.

Birney, Hoffman. *Vigilantes.* Philadelphia: Penn Publishing Company, 1929.

Bishop, Jim. *The Day Lincoln Was Shot.* New York: Harper & Brothers Publishers, 1955.

Blum, John M., Edmund S. Morgan, Willie Lee Rose, Arthur M. Schlesinger Jr., Kenneth M. Stampp, and C. Vann Woodward. *The National Experience: A History of the United States.* 4th ed. New York: Harcourt Brace Jovanovich, 1977.

Boessenecker, John. *Gold Dust & Gunsmoke: Tales of Gold Rush Outlaws, Gunfighters, Lawmen, and Vigilantes.* New York: John Wiley & Sons, 1999.

Breining, Greg. *Super Volcano: The Ticking Time Bomb Beneath Yellowstone National Park.* St. Paul: Voyager Press, 2007.

Brown, Jonathan A. *Portraits of the States: Montana.* Milwaukee: Gareth Stevens Publishing, 2007.

Brown, Richard Maxwell. *Strain of Violence: Historical Studies of American Violence and Vigilantism.* New York: Oxford University Press, 1975.

Buchanan, Carol. *God's Thunderbolt: The Vigilantes of Montana.* N.p.: BookSurge, 2008.

Buchanan, Carol. "Gold, Greed, and a Vacuum of Law." Cleveland Civil War Roundtable. Accessed December 24, 2011. http://www.clevelandcivilwarroundtable.com/articles /society/gold_greed_law.htm.

Buchanan, Carol. "Dr. Jerome Glick: Surgeon to Murderers." Accessed May 20, 2012. http:// www.swanrange.com/blog/2011/06/07/dr-jerome-glick-surgeon-to-murderers/.

Burlingame, Merrill. *The Montana Frontier.* Helena, MT: State Publishing Company, 1942.

Butler, Chuck. "Bernanke Defends QE II . . ." *Daily Pfennig,* November 19, 2010. Accessed November 21, 2010. http://www.kitco.com/ind/Butler/printerfriendly/nov192010.html.

BuyCoin.com. "Platinum Coin History." Accessed November 21, 2010. http://www.buycoin .com/Platinum_Coin_History.php.

Callaway, Lew L., Jr., ed. *Montana's Righteous Hangmen: The Vigilantes in Action.* Norman: University of Oklahoma Press, 1982.

Cameron, David. "The Bar of Tioga County." In *Papers and Proceedings of the Tioga County Historical Society.* Vol. 1, 123–44. Wellsboro, PA: Tioga County Historical Society, 1906.

Campbell, William C. *From the Quarries of Last Chance Gulch.* Helena: Montana Record Publishing Company, 1951.

Capital Punishment U.K. "Hanged by the Neck Until Dead! The Process and Physiology of Judicial Hanging." Accessed December 29, 2010. http://www.capitalpunishmentuk.org /hanging2.html#table.

Caughey, John W. *Their Majesties the Mob: The Vigilante Impulse in America.* Chicago: University of Chicago Press, 1960.

Central Montana. "Hilger, Montana Community Information." Accessed December 23, 2011. http://centralmontana.com/communities/Hilger.htm.

Chronicling America. "About the Montana Post 1864–1869." Accessed January 8, 2012. http:// chroniclingamerica.loc.gov/lccn/sn83025293/.

Civil War Women Blog. "Elizabeth Meagher." Accessed May 19, 2012. http://www.civil warwomenblog.com/search?q=Elizabeth+Townsend+Meagher.

Clampett, J. W. "The Vigilantes of California, Idaho, and Montana." Montana Historical Society Pamphlet 780. Helena: Montana Historical Society, 1891.

Clark County Prosecuting Attorney. "Methods of Execution." Accessed December 29, 2010. http://www.clarkprosecutor.org/html/death/methods.htm.

CoinResource. "United States Coins History and Mint Information." Accessed December 23, 2010. http://www.coinresource.com/articles/frb_united_states_coins.htm.

The Coin Site. "1866–83 Nickel Five Cents Shield." Accessed December 23, 2010. http://www .coinsite.com/coinsite-pf/pparticles/05cshield.asp.

Collins, Ronald K. L. "Reliance on State Constitutions—The Montana Disaster." *Texas Law Review* 63 (March/April 1985): 1095–1139.

Convis, Charles L. *Frontier Vigilantes.* True Tales of the Old West, 17. Anaheim, CA: KNI, Incorporated, 2001.

Crutchfield, James Andrew. *It Happened in Montana.* Helena, MT: Morris Book Publishing, 2008.

Cuddihy, William. *The Fourth Amendment: Origins and Original Meaning, 602–1791.* New York: Oxford University Press, 2009. http://dx.doi.org/10.1093/acprof: oso/9780195367195.001.0001

Curry, Tom. *The Montana Vigilantes.* Waterville, ME: Wheeler Pub, 2007.

Cushman, Dan. *Montana, The Gold Frontier.* Great Falls, MT: Stay Away, Joe Publishers, 1973.

Cutler, William G. "Repeal of the Criminal Code." Part 4 of "Nebraska as a Territory." Transcribed by Ted and Carole Miller. *Andreas' History of the State of Nebraska.* Chicago: A. T.

Andreas / Western Historical Publishing Company, 1882. Accessed March 25, 2012. http://www.kancoll.org/books/andreas_ne/territory/territory-p4.html#repeal.

Dary, David. *The Oregon Trail: An American Saga.* New York: Alfred A. Knopf, 2004.

Davis, John W. *Wyoming Range War: The Infamous Invasion of Johnson County.* Norman: University of Oklahoma Press, 2012.

Death Penalty Information Center. "Descriptions of Execution Methods—Hanging." Accessed January 8, 2011. http://www.deathpenaltyinfo.org/descriptions-execution-methods.

Death Penalty Information Center. "Execution in the Military—Overview." Accessed January 8, 2011. http:// www.deathpenaltyinfo.org/us-military-death-penalty.

Death Penalty Information Center. "Facts about the Death Penalty." Accessed March 24, 2011. http://www.deathpenaltyinfo.org/documents/FactSheet.pdf.

Death Penalty Information Center. "Federal Laws Providing for the Death Penalty." Accessed April 3, 2011. http://www.deathpenaltyinfo.org/federal-laws-providing-death-penalty.

Death Penalty Information Center. "Methods of Execution." Accessed December 29, 2010. http://www.deathpenaltyinfo.org/methods-execution.

Denno, Deborah W. "Adieu to Electrocution." *Ohio Northern University Law Review* 2 (2000): 665–71.

Department of the Army. *Procedure for Military Executions.* Pamphlet 27–4 (December 1947). Accessed January 8, 2011. http://www.loc.gov/rr/frd/Military_Law/pdf/procedure_dec-1947.pdf.

Department of the Army. *U.S. Army Corrections System: Procedures for Military Executions.* Army Regulation 190-55. Washington, DC: Department of the Army, January 17, 2006. Accessed January 8, 2011. http://www.fas.org/irp/doddir/army/r190_55.pdf.

DiLorenzo, Thomas J. *The Real Lincoln.* Roseville, CA: Prima Publishing, 2002.

Dimsdale, Thomas J. *The Vigilantes of Montana.* Ann Arbor: D. W. Tilton & Co, 1866.

Donovan, Tom. *Hanging around the Big Sky, Book 1: Legal Hangings.* Great Falls, MT: Portage Meadows Publishing, 2007.

Donovan, Tom. *Hanging around the Big Sky, Book 2: The Unofficial Guide to Lynching, Strangling, and Legal Hangings of Montana.* Great Falls, MT: Portage Meadows Publishing, 2008.

Doyle, Susan Badger, ed. *Journeys to the Land of Gold.* Helena: Montana Historical Society Press, 2000.

Drabelle, Dennis. *Silver Mines, Boom Towns, and High Living on the Comstock Lode.* New York: St. Martin's Press, 2009.

Edgar, Henry. "Journal of Henry Edgar—1863." In *Contributions to the Historical Society of Montana.* Vol. 3, 124–42. Helena, MT: State Publishing Company, 1900.

Eichengreen, Barry, ed. *The Gold Standard in Theory and History.* New York: Methuen, 1985.

Elements Database. "Periodic Table." Accessed March 4, 2012. http://www.elementsdatabase.com.

Ellingsen, John D. "History of Virginia City Masonic Temple." Paul Bessel's Website: Virginia City Lodge #1. Accessed November 21, 2010. http://www.bessel.org/vacitylg.htm.

Ellingsen, John D., and John N. DeHaas. *If These Walls Could Talk: The History of the Buildings of Virginia City.* Bozeman: Montana Ghost Town Preservation Society, 1977.

Elliott, Diane. *Strength of Stone: The Pioneer Journal of Electa Bryan Plumer 1862–1864.* Guilford, CT: Twodot Publishing, 2002.

Ellison, Joseph. "The Mineral Land Question in California, 1848–1866." In *The Public Lands: Studies in the History of the Public Domain,* ed. Vernon Carstensen. Madison: University of Wisconsin Press, 1963.

Evi.com. "Dallas Mayors." Accessed March 16, 2012. http://www.evi.com/q/dallas_mayors.

Fazio, John C. "How the Civil War Was Won in Virginia City, Montana." *Montana Pioneer.* Accessed November 22, 2010. http://www.mtpioneer.com/2010-Nov-cover-civilwar.html.

Ferguson, Robert A. *The Trial in American Life*. Chicago: University of Chicago Press, 2007.

Fifer, Barbara. *Montana Ghost Towns*. Helena, MT: Farcounty Press, 2002.

Financial Sense. "Silver Still Consolidating: Update on Metals with David Morgan and Chris Vermeulen." Interview by Jim Puplava (digital audio recording). Accessed May 21, 2011. http://www.financialsense.com/financial-sense-newshour/guest-expert/2011/05/20/david-morgan-chris-vermeulen/silver-still-consolidating

Find a Grave. "Daniel Jackson 'D. J.' Miller." Accessed April 26, 2012. http://www.findagrave.com/cgi-bin/fg.cgi?page=gr&GRid=62660789.

Find a Grave. "Edwin Ruthven Purple." Accessed December 30, 2011. http://www.findagrave.com/cgi-bin/fg.cgi?page=gr&GRid=47796241.

Find a Grave. "Hill Beachy." Accessed March 11, 2012. http://www.findagrave.com/cgi-bin/fg.cgi?page=gr&GRid=65839368.

Find a Grave. "John F. Cowan." Accessed December 30, 2011. http://www.findagrave.com/cgi-bin/fg.cgi?page=gr&GSln=Cowan&GSiman=1&GSst=12&GSsr=201&GRid=36387346&.

Find a Grave. "Samuel McLean." Accessed June 12, 2012. http://www.findagrave.com/cgi-bin/fg.cgi?page=gr&GRid=15551691.

Find a Grave. "Thomas Bennett Meagher." Accessed October 25, 2011.http://www.findagrave.com/cgi-bin/fg.cgi?page=gr&GRid=59005961.

Fisher, Vardis, and Opal Laurel Holmes. *Gold Rushes and Mining Camps of the Early American West*. Caldwell, ID: Caxton Printers, 1968.

Freund, Paul A., and Arthur E. Sutherland. *Mark DeWolfe Howe, and Ernest J. Brown. Constitutional Law, Cases, and Other Problems*. 4th ed. Boston: Little, Brown and Company, 1977.

Fritz, Christian. *Federal Justice in California: The Court of Ogden Hoffman, 1851–1891*. Lincoln: University of Nebraska Press, 1991.

Funda-Mental. "The History behind the Nickel Coin." Accessed December 23, 2010. http://www.funda-mental.net/info/the-history-behind-the-nickel-coin.html.

Gard, Wayne. *Frontier Justice*. Norman: University of Oklahoma Press, 1949.

Garner, Bryan A., ed. *Black's Law Dictionary*. 9th ed. St. Paul, MN: West Publishing, 2009.

Garnet Preservation Society. "Garnet Ghost Town." Accessed June 3, 2012. http://www.garnetghosttown.net/directions.html.

Genealogy Trails History Group. "List of Governors of Montana." Accessed March 16, 2012. http://www.genealogytrails.com/mon/govenors.html.

GenForum. "Anton Holter." Accessed December 31, 2011. http://www.genforum.genealogy.com/holter/messages/5.html.

GenForum. "William Chumasero." Accessed June 14, 2012. http://genforum.genealogy.com/mt/lewisandclark/messages/76.html.

Georgia on My Mind (blog). "The Four Georgians." Accessed March 22, 2012. http://mymindisongeorgia.blogspot.com/2010/05/four-georgians.html.

Ghost Towns. "Montana Ghost Towns." Accessed January 22, 2012. http://www.ghosttowns.com/states/mt/moalpha.html.

Golden Eagle Coins. "American Gold Eagles." Accessed December 23, 2010. http://www.goldeneaglecoin.com/Buy_Gold/American_Gold_Eagles.

Golden Eagle Coins. "Silver American Eagles." Accessed December 23, 2010. http://www.goldeneaglecoin.com/buy_silver/silver_american_eagles.

Graf, Mike. *Land of Liberty: Montana*. Mankato, MN: Capstone Press, 2004.

Gray, Theodore. *The Elements: A Visual Exploration of Every Known Atom in the Universe*. New York: Black Dog & Leventhal Publishers, 2009.

Greever, William S. *The Bonanza West: The Story of the Western Mining Rushes 1848–1900*. Norman: University of Oklahoma Press, 1963.

Guice, John D. W. *The Rocky Mountain Bench: The Territorial Supreme Courts of Colorado, Montana and Wyoming 1861–1890*. New Haven: Yale University Press, 1972.

Gutherie, A. B., Jr. *The Big Sky*. New York: Houghton Mifflin, 1947.

Gyory, Andrew. *Closing the Gate: Race, Politics, and the Chinese Exclusion Act*. Chapel Hill: University of North Carolina Press, 1998.

Hagedorn, Herman. *Roosevelt in the Badlands*. New York: Houghton Mifflin, 1921.

Haines, Aubrey L. "Biographical Appendix, A–E: Samuel T. Hauser." In *Yellowstone National Park: Its Exploration and Establishment*. Washington, DC: US Department of the Interior, National Park Service, 1974. Accessed March 16, 2012. http://www.cr.nps.gov/history /online_books/haines1/iee4.htm.

Hamilton, James McClellan. *From Wilderness to Statehood: A History of Montana 1805–1900*. Portland, OR: Binford & Mort, 1957.

Hamilton, William Baskerville. *Anglo-American Law on the Frontier: Thomas Rodney and His Territorial Cases*. Durham, NC: Duke University Press, 1953.

Harris, Yvonne L. *The Vigilante's Bride*. Minneapolis: Bethany House, 2010.

Helena As She Was. "The Hanging Tree." Accessed May 28, 2011. http://www.helenahistory. org/hanging_tree.htm.

Helena Board of Trade. *Helena Illustrated: A History of the Early Settlement and the Helena Trade*. Minneapolis: Frank L. Thresher Publishers, 1890.

Helena Travel Guide. "The History of Helena, MT." Accessed March 6, 2011. http://bigsky fishing.com/Montana-Info/helena-mt-2.shtml.

Hello Helena. "Helena History: National Register of Historic Places for Helena, Montana." Accessed May 20, 2011. http://www.hellohelena.com/history.cfm.

Herringshaw, Thomas William. *Herringshaw's National Library of American Biography*. Vol. 4. Chicago: American Publishers' Association, 1914.

Hilger, David Henderson. "My Roots Run Deep." RootsWeb WorldConnect Program. Accessed December 23, 2011. http://wc.rootsweb.ancestry.com/cgi-bin/igm.cgi?op=GET &db=ahealydsnine1&id=I2421.

Hine, Kelly D. "Vigilantism Revisited: An Economic Analysis of the Extra-Judicial Self-Help or Why Can't Dick Shoot Henry for Stealing Jane's Truck." *American University Law Review* 47 (1998): 1221–43.

"History Proves That No One Is Infallible." *Society Star: A Publication of the Montana Historical Society.* Summer 2012

Hoggatt, Stan. "Western Treasures, Bannack, Montana: Impact on Native American Life and the Nez Perce Connection." Accessed November 22, 2010. http://www.nezperce.com /banack.html.

Holmes, Krys. *Montana: Stories of the Land*. Helena: Montana Historical Society Press, 2008.

Holmes, Oliver Wendell. *The Common Law*. Cambridge, MA: Belknap Press of Harvard University Press, 1963.

Howard, Joseph Kinsey. *Montana High, Wide, and Handsome*. New Haven: Yale University Press, 1943.

Hurst, James Willard. *A Legal History of Money in the United States, 1774–1970*. Lincoln: University of Nebraska Press, 1973.

Israel Science and Technology Homepage. "List of Periodic Table Elements Sorted by Abundance in Earth's Crust." Accesssed March 4, 2012. http://www.science.co.il/PTelements .asp?s=Earth.

Israel, Fred L. *Major Presidential Decisions: Roosevelt's Decision, the United States Leaves the Gold Standard*. New York: Chelsea House Publishers, 1980.

John F. Kennedy Presidential Library and Museum. "Address before the Irish Parliament, June 28, 1963." Accessed February 2, 2012. http://www.jfklibrary.org/Asset-Viewer /lPAi7jx2s0i7kePPdJnUXA.aspx.

Johnson, Dorothy M., John M. Crowley, and Gregory Lewis McNamee. "Montana: Statehood and Beyond." In *Encyclopedia Britannica*. Accessed November 23, 2010. http://www .britannica.com/EBchecked/topic/390518/Montana/279743/Statehood-and-beyond.

Johnson, Dorothy. *The Bloody Bozeman: The Perilous Trail to Montana's Gold*. New York: McGraw Hill, 1971.

Johnson, John W., ed. *Historic U.S. Court Cases, An Encyclopedia*. 2nd ed., 2 vols. New York: Routledge, 2001.

Jones, Paul. *The Irish Brigade*. Washington, DC: Robert B. Luce, 1969.

Jordan, Philip D. *Frontier Law and Order*. Lincoln: University of Nebraska Press, 1970.

Kadish, Sanford H., and Monrad Paulsen. *Criminal Law and its Processes*. 3rd ed. Boston: Little, Brown and Company, 1975.

Kidston, Martin J. "The Tree of Death." Accessed May 28, 2011. http://helenair.com/lifestyles /article_17972c78-76a5-11df-aea1-001cc4c002e0.html.

Kelley, David F. "The Hanging Tree and the Pillory: How the Roots of Criminal Law Differ in Vermont and Montana." *Montana Law Review* 34 (May 2009): 6.

Keneally, Thomas. *The Great Shame and the Triumph of the Irish in the English-Speaking World*. New York: Doubleday, 1999.

Kittredge, William, and Steven M. Krauzer. "'Mr. Montana' Revised: Another Look at Granville Stuart." *Montana: The Magazine of Western History* 36 (Autumn 1986): 14–23.

Kohrs, Conrad. *Conrad Kohrs: An Autobiography of a Pioneer Cattleman*. Polson, MT: Gull Printing, 1977.

Langford, Nathaniel P. *Vigilante Days and Ways*. 1890; repr., Helena, MT: American & World Geographic Publishing, 1996.

Lanman, Charles. *Biographical Annals of the Civil Governance of the United States*. Washington, DC: James Anglim, 1876.

Layton, Julia. "How Does Death by Hanging Work?" HowStuff Works. Accessed December 29, 2010. http://science.howstuffworks.com/life/human-biology/death-by-hanging.htm.

Lee, Richard. *Nuggets of History from Virginia City: Historic Articles from the* Virginia City Nugget, *1995–2005*. Virginia City, MT: Virginia City Preservation Alliance, n.d.

Leeson, M. A. *History of Montana 1739–1885*. Chicago: Warner, Beers & Company, 1885.

Legends of America. "Montana Legends: Bannack—Gold to Ghost." Accessed November 20, 2010. http://www.legendsofamerica.com/mt-bannack.html.

Legends of America. "Montana Legends: Virginia City—A Lively Ghost Town." Accessed November 21, 2010. http://www.legendsofamerica.com/mt-virginiacity.html.

Library of Congress / National Endowment for the Humanities. "Chronicling America: About the *Helena Herald*." Accessed June 1, 2011. http://chroniclingamerica.loc.gov/lccn /sn83025299/.

Library of Congress / National Endowment for the Humanities. "Chronicling America: About the *Montana Democrat*." Accessed January 28, 2012.http://chroniclingamerica.loc.gov /lccn/sn84036217/.

Library of Congress / National Endowment for the Humanities. "Chronicling America: About the *Montana Post*." Accessed November 21, 2010, and January 8, 2012. http:// chroniclingamerica.loc.gov/lccn/sn83025293/.

Life's Little Mysteries Staff. "Why Did Gold Become the Best Element for Money?" Accessed December 18, 2010. http://www.lifeslittlemysteries.com/gold-best-element-money-1167/.

Lingenfelter, Richard. *Bonanzas & Borrascas: Gold Lust and Silver Sharks, 1848–1884*. Norman, OK: Arthur H. Clark Company, 2012.

Little, Michael Edward. *Twelve Quiet Men*. Bloomington, IN: Michael Edward Little, 2003.

Los Alamos National Laboratory. Periodic Table of Elements. Accessed March 4, 2012. http:// periodic.lanl.gov/index.shtml.

Lowe, James A. *The Bridger Trail*. Spokane, WA: Arthur H. Clark Company, 1999.

Madison, Arnold. *Vigilantism in America*. New York: Seabury Press, 1973.

Magnaghi, Russell M. "Virginia City's Chinese Community." In *Chinese on the American Frontier*, ed. Arif Dirlik, 123–48. Lanham, MD: Rowman & Littlefield Publishers, 2001.

Malone, Michael P., Richard B. Roeder, and William L. Lang. *Montana: A History of Two Centuries*. Seattle: University of Washington Press, 1976.

Martin, Gary. "Kick the Bucket." The Phrase Finder. Accessed October 25, 2011. http://www.phrases.org.uk/meanings/218800.html.

Martin, Gary. "Riding Shotgun." The Phrase Finder.Accessed October 7, 2011. http://www.phrases.org/ukmeanings/riding-shotgun.html.

Marx, Jennifer. *The Magic of Gold*. New York: Doubleday, 1978.

Mather, R. E. "Was Dimsdale a Vigilante?" Vigilantes of Montana: Secret Trials and Midnight Hangings, 1863–1864. Accessed April 30, 2011, and May 1, 2012. http://www.yanoun.org/mont_vigi/articles/dimsmjr.html.

Mather, R. E., and F. E. Boswell. "Epilogue." Ch. 10 of *Hanging the Sheriff*. Vigilantes of Montana: Secret Trials and Midnight Hangings, 1863–1864. Accessed December 31, 2011. http://yanoun.org/mont_vigi/victims/epilog.html.

Mather, R. E., and F. E. Boswell. "First Witness for the Prosecution." In *Hanging the Sheriff*. Accessed July 30, 2012. http://my.umwestern.edu/Academics/library/libroth/MHD/vigilantes/HTS/mont6.htm.

Mather, R. E., and F. E. Boswell. *Gold Camp Desperados: Violence, Crimes, and Punishment on the Mining Frontier on the Mining Frontier*. San Jose, CA: History West Publishing, 1990.

Mather, R. E., and F. E. Boswell. *Hanging the Sheriff: A Biography of Henry Plummer*. Salt Lake City: University of Utah Press, 1987.

Mather, R. E., and F. E. Boswell. *Vigilante Victims: Montana's 1864 Hanging Spree*. San Jose, CA: History West Publishing, 1991.

McClure, Alexander K. *Three Thousand Miles through the Rocky Mountains*. Philadelphia: J. B. Lippincott & Co, 1869.

McConnell, W. J. *Early History of Idaho*. Glendale, CA: Arthur H. Clark Company, 1913.

McConnell, William J., and James S. Reynolds. *Idaho's Vigilantes*. Moscow: University of Idaho Press, 1984.

McDowell, Andrea. "Criminal Law beyond the State: Popular Trials on the Frontier." *B.Y.U.L. Rev.* 2 (2007): 327–86.

McGrath, Roger D. *Gunfighters, Highwaymen, and Vigilantes: Violence on the Frontier*. Berkeley: University of California Press, 1984.

McPherson, James M. *Battle Cry of Freedom: The Civil War Era*. New York: Oxford University Press, 1988.

MeasuringWorth. "Choosing the Best Indicator to Measure Relative Worth." Accessed December 24, 2010. http://www.measuringworth.com/indicator.html.

Mendenhall, W. T. *Gold and Silver Mining in Montana*. Boston: Collins Press, 1890.

MendonUtah.Net."Utah Northern Railroad." Accessed February 25, 2011. http://www.mendonutah.net/history/utah_northern_railroad.htm.

Merriam, H. G., ed. *Frontier Woman: The Story of Mary Ronan as Told to Margaret R. Ronan*. Bozeman: University of Montana Press, 1973.

Michigan State University Libraries. Special Collections Division. "Loafer's Reward." Accessed April 15, 2012. http://comics.lib.msu.edu/rri/lrri/lo.htm.

Milner, Clyde A., II, and Carol A. O'Connor. *As Big as the West: The Pioneer Life of Granville Stuart*. New York: Oxford University Press, 2009.

Montana Department of Commerce. "Montana Heritage Commission." Accessed January 22, 2012. http://www.montanaheritagecommission.mt.gov/default.mcpx.

Montana Heritage Commission. "Virginia City: The Discovery." Accessed November 20, 2010, and January 22, 2012. http://www.virginiacitymt.com/discovery.asp.

Montana Highways. "Montana Speed." Accessed February 3, 2012. http://www.us-highways
.com/montana/mtspeed.htm.

Montana History. "Bozeman." Accessed December 31, 2011.http://www.montanahistory.net
/placenames/bozeman.htm.

Montana State Genealogical Society. "Montana State Death Index." Accessed May 14, 2012.
http://montanamsgs.org/earlydeath/1900h2.html.

Montana Yesterday. "Montana's First Newspaper, the Montana Post, Began Publication This
Day in Virginia City in 1864." Accessed November 22, 2010. http://montanayesterday
.com/?page_id=775.

Morriss, Andrew P. "Hayek and Cowboys: Customary Law in the American West." *N.Y.U. J.L
& Liberty* 1 (2005): 35–64.

Morriss, Andrew P. "Legal Argument in the Opinions of Montana Territorial Chief Justice
Decius S. Wade." *Nevada Law Journal* 1 (Spring 2001): 38–80.

Morriss, Andrew P. "Miners, Vigilantes, and Cattlemen: Overcoming Free Rider Problems in
the Private Provision of Law." *Land and Water Law Review* 33 (1998): 581–695.

Morriss, Andrew P. "Miners, Vigilantes, and Cattlemen: Property Rights on the Western Frontier." *The Freeman* 57 (April 2007): 25–30.

Morriss, Andrew P. "Private Actors and Structural Balance: Militia and the Free Rider Problem
in Private Provision of Law." *Montana Law Review* 58 (1997): 115–66.

Morriss, Andrew P. "Returning Justice to Its Private Roots." *University of Chicago Law Review*
68, no. 2 (Spring 2001): 551–78. Accessed January 22, 2012. http://dx.doi.org/10.2307
/1600381.

Mtgenweb Project. "Montana: Individual County Chronologies." Accessed October 16, 2011.
http://www.rootsweb.ancestry.com/~mtbighrn/mtcountychronology.html.

mt.gov. "Judicial Branch: Brief History of the Montana Judicial Branch." Accessed June 3, 2011.
http://courts.mt.gov/history.mcpx.

mt.gov. "Judicial Branch: Chief Justices of Montana." Accessed October 26, 2011. http://www
.courts.mt.gov/supreme/chief_justices.mcpx.

Mueller, Oscar O. "The Central Montana Vigilante Raids of 1884." *Montana: The Magazine of
Western History* 1 (January 1951): 23–25.

Mueller, Richard K. "Granville Stuart and the Montana Vigilantes of 1884." Master's thesis,
University of Oregon, Eugene, 1980.

Mullan, John. *Report on the Construction of a Military Road from Fort Walla Walla to Fort Benton.*
Washington, DC: Government Printing Office, 1863.

National Park Service. "Grant-Kohrs Ranch, National Historic Site." Accessed July 29, 2012.
http://www.nps.gov/grko/index.htm.

NCR Retirement Fellowship. "James Ritty." Accessed March 26, 2012.http://www.ncr.org.uk
/page110.html.

Nebraska State Historical Society. "First Territorial Legislature." Accessed March 25, 2012.
http://www.nebraskahistory.org/publish/publicat/timeline/first_terr_legislature.htm.

"Neil Howie, Second U.S. Marshal of Montana Territory." Accessed December 30, 2011. http://
www.usMarshals.gov/district/mt/profiles/howie.html.

Netstate.com. "The State of Montana: The State Nicknames." Accessed December 18, 2011.
http://www.netstate.com/states/intro/mt_intro.htm.

New York City Department of City Planning. "Population." Accessed June 6, 2011. http://www
.nyc.gov/html/dcp/html/census/popcur.shtml.

Northern Pacific Railway Historical Association. "A Brief Introduction to the Northern Pacific
Railway." Accessed December 5, 2010. http://research.nprha.org/Help%20Files
/Northern%20Pacific%20Railway%20History.htm.

Northern Pacific Railway Historical Association. "Home." Accessed December 5 and 10, 2010.
http://www.nprha.org.

O'Neal, Bill. *The Johnson County War*. Waco, TX: Eakin Press, 2004.

Officer, Lawrence H., and Samuel H. Williamson. "The Price of Gold, 1257–2009." MeasuringWorth. Accessed November 19, 2010. http://www.measuringworth.com/datasets/gold/result.php.

Ohio History Central. "James Ashley." Accessed March 16, 2012. http://www.ohiohistorycentral.org/entry.php?rec=129.

Olsen, Barton Clark. "Lawlessness and Vigilantes in America: An Historical Analysis Emphasizing California and Montana." PhD diss., University of Utah, Salt Lake City, 1968.

Olson, Steven P. *The Oregon Trail: A Primary Source History of the Route to the American West*. New York: Rosen Publishing Group, 2004.

Oracle ThinkQuest. "Placer Mining." Accessed May 21, 2011. http://library.thinkquest.org/05aug/00461/placer.htm.

Owens, Kenneth N., ed. *Riches for All: The California Gold Rush and the World*. Lincoln: University of Nebraska Press, 2002.

Pace, Dick. *Golden Gulch: The Story of Montana's Fabulous Alder Gulch*. Virginia City, MT: Virginia City Trading Company, 1962.

Paul, Rodman W. *California Gold: The Beginning of Mining in the Far West*. Cambridge, MA: Harvard University Press, 1947.

Peavy, Linda, and Ursula Smith. *Pioneer Women: The Lives of Women on the Frontier*. New York: Smithmark, 1996.

Pemberton, W. Y. "Montana's Pioneer Courts." In *Contributions to the Historical Society of Montana*. Vol. 8, 99–104. Helena: Montana Historical and Miscellaneous Library, 1917.

Pfouts, Paris Swazy. *Four Firsts of a Modest Hero: The Autobiography of Paris Swazy Pfouts*. Ed. Harold Axford. Portland, OR: Dunham Printing, 1968.

Phillips, Paul C., ed. *Forty Years on the Frontier as Seen in the Journals and Reminiscences of Granville Stuart, Gold-Miner, Trader, Merchant, Rancher, and Politician*. Cleveland, OH: Arthur H. Clark Company, 1925.

Prince, Jerome. *Richardson on Evidence*. 10th ed. Brooklyn: Brooklyn Law School, 1973.

Pryor, Alton. *The Lawmen*. Roseville, CA: Stagecoach Publishing, 2006.

Purcell, Edward A. *Brandeis and the Progressive Constitution: Erie, the Judicial Power, and the Politics of the Federal Courts in Twentieth-Century America*. New Haven: Yale University Press, 2000.

Purple, Edwin Ruthven. *Perilous Passage: A Narrative of the Montana Gold Rush, 1862–1863*. Helena: Montana Historical Society Press, 1995.

Ralph, Chris. "Basic Placer Mining for Gold." Prospecting Encyclopedia. Accessed May 20, 2011. http://nevada-outback-gems.com/basic_prospecting/Basic_placer.htm.

Ransom, Roger L. "The Economics of the Civil War." EH.Net Encyclopedia. Accessed October 27, 2011. http://www.eh.net/encyclopedia/ article/ransom.civil.war.us.

"Ratification of the Constitution by the State of New York, July 26, 1788." Accessed April 30, 2012. http://constitution.org/rc/rat_decl-ny.htm.

Reid, John Phillip. *Policing the Elephant: Crime, Punishment, and Social Behavior on the Overland Trail*. San Marino, CA: Huntington Library Press, 1997.

Remley, David. "Granville Stuart, Cowman: To Surrender against an Adverse Fate." *Montana: The Magazine of Western History* 31 (Summer 1981): 28–41.

Revolutionary War and Beyond. "James Madison Speech to Congress—June 8, 1789." Accessed December 27, 2011. http://www.revolutionary-war-and-beyond.com/james-madison-speech-june-8-1789.html.

Roadside America. "Club Foot George's Club Foot." Accessed January 3, 2011. http://www.roadsideamerica.com/story/6169.

Rolle, Andrew F., ed. *The Road to Virginia City: The Diary of James Knox Polk Miller*. Norman: University of Oklahoma Press, 1960. http://dx.doi.org/10.2307/1891763

Roots, Roger. "Are Cops Constitutional?" *Seton Hall Constitutional Law Journal* 11, no. 192 (2001): 685–714.

RootsWeb. "Biography of Sydney Edgerton." Accessed March 16, 2012. http://www.rootsweb.ancestry.com/~nyccazen/Biographies/EdgertonS.html.

RootsWeb. "Montana Death Records 1910–1919—D: Davis, Adriel B." Accessed May 12, 2012. http://www.rootsweb.ancestry.com/~mtlcgs/mtmsgs/mtdeath10D.htm.

Ryan, Peter. *How the Gold Standard Works.* New York: Rosen Publishing, 2011.

Safford, Jeffrey J. *The Mechanics of Optimism: Mining Companies, Technology, and the Hot Springs Gold Rush, Montana Territory, 1864–1868.* Boulder: University Press of Colorado, 2004.

Sanders, Helen Fitzgerald, and William H. Bertsche Jr., eds. *X. Beidler: Vigilante.* Norman: University of Oklahoma Press, 1957.

Sanderson, Wayne T., Elizabeth M. Ward, Kyle Steenland, and M. R. Petersen. "Lung Cancer Case-Control Study of Beryllium Workers." *American Journal of Industrial Medicine* 39, no. 2 (February 2001): 133–44.

Sargent, Thomas. "The Journal of Paris Pfouts." Accessed December 30, 2011. http://www.yanoun.org/mont_vigi/contrib/pfouts.html.

"School and Alumni Notes." *Yale Law Journal* 17 (March 1908): 410

Schlichter, Detlev S. "Forty Years of Paper Money." *Wall Street Journal*, August 15, 2011. Acessed April 9, 2012. http://online.wsj.com/article/SB10001424053111903918104576500811399421094.html.

Shinn, Charles H. *Mining Camps: A Study in Frontier Government.* New York: Charles Scribner's Sons, 1885.

Shovers, Brian. "From Treasure State to Big Sky: Montana's Naturally Inviting and EZ 2 LUV State Nicknames and Mottos." Accessed December 18, 2011. http://www.visitmt.com/history/Montana_the_Magazine_of_Western_History/Spring03/treasurestate.htm.

Sievert, Ken, and Ellen Sievert. *Virginia City and the Alder Gulch.* Helena, MT: American & World, 1993.

Skousen, Mark. *Economics of a Pure Gold Standard: Irvington-on-Hudson.* New York: Foundation for Economic Education, 1977.

Smith, Helena Huntington. *The War on the Powder River.* Lincoln: University of Nebraska Press, 1967.

Smurr, J. W. "Some Afterthoughts on the Vigilantes." *Montana: The Magazine of Western History* 8, no. 2 (April 1958): 8–20.

Spence, Clark C. ""Spoilsman in Montana: James M. Ashley." *Montana: The Magazine of Western History* 18 (Spring 1968): 24–35.

Spence, Clark C. "The Territorial Bench in Montana: 1864–1889." *Montana: The Magazine of Western History* 13 (Spring 1963): 25–32, 57–65.

Spence, Clark C. *Territorial Politics and Government in Montana, 1864–1889.* Urbana: University of Illinois Press, 1975.

Stigile, Rob. "New Exoneration Registry Shows at Least 2,000 Convicts Cleared of Crimes Since 1989." *National Law Journal.* May 21, 2012. Accessed May 2, 2012. http://www.law.com/jsp/nlj/PubArticleNLJ.jsp?id=1202555386241&New_exoneration_registry_shows_at_least_2000_convicts_cleared_of_crimes_since_1989&slreturn=20130415151506.

Stillwater Palladium. Palladium, Metal of the 21st Century. "History of Palladium: Part 3—Wollaston's Contribution." Accessed November 21, 2010. http://www.Palladiumcoins.com/history3.html.

Stout, Tom. *Montana: Its Story and Biography.* Chicago: American Historical Society, 1921.

Stuart, Granville. *Forty Years on the Frontier.* 2 vols. Lincoln: University of Nebraska Press, 1977.

This edition combines the two volumes of the original edition, *Prospecting for Gold* (formerly vol. 1) and *Pioneering in Montana* (formerly vol. 2). Page numbering for the two volumes remains separate.

Stwertka, Albert. *A Guide to the Elements*. 2nd ed. New York: Oxford University Press, 2002.

Taylor, Robert Lewis. *A Roaring in the Wind*. New York: G. P. Putnam's Sons, 1978.

Thane, James L., Jr. "Montana Territory: The Formative Years, 1862–1870." Master's thesis, University of Iowa, 1972.

Thomasma, Melissa Poindexter. "'The Lawmen Faced the Outlaws No Badge Upon a Breast': Historical Memory and the Legacy of Henry Plummer and the Montana Vigilantes." Master's thesis, University of Montana, 2010.

Thompson, Francis M. *Tenderfoot in Montana: Reminiscences of the Gold Rush, the Vigilantes, and the Birth of Montana Territory*. Helena: Montana Historical Society Press, 2004.

Thrapp, Dan L. *Vengeance! The Saga of Poor Tom Cover*. El Segundo, CA: Upton & Sons Publishers, 1989.

Toole, Ross K. *Montana: An Uncommon Land*. Norman: University of Oklahoma Press, 1959.

Toponce, Alexander. *Reminiscences of Alexander Toponce*. Salt Lake City: Century Printing Company, 1923.

Towle, Virginia Rowe. *Vigilante Woman*. New Brunswick, NJ: A. S. Barnes & Co, 1966.

Travel Montana. "Edgar, Montana." Accessed December 30, 2011. http://www.travelmt.com/mt-cities-Edgar.html.

Treece, Paul Robert. *Mr. Montana: The Life of Granville Stuart*. Columbus: Ohio State University Press, 1974.

United States Census 2010. "Montana." Accessed June 6, 2011. http://www.census.gov/2010census/data/apportionment-dens-text.php.

United States Department of Agriculture. Forest Service. "Custer National Forest: Absaroka-Beartooth Wilderness." Accessed May 15, 2013. http://www.fs.usda.gov/detail/custer/specialplaces/?cid=stelprdb5345521.

United States Department of Labor. Occupational Safety and Health Administration. "Occupational Safety and Health Guidelines for Yttrium and Compounds." Accessed March 4, 2012. http://www.osha.gov/SLTC/healthguidelines/yttriumandcompounds/recognition.html.

United States History. "Idaho." Accessed January 1, 2011. http://www.u-s-history.com/pages/h1935.html.

United States Mint. "American Eagles." Accessed December 23, 2010.http://www.usmint.gov/mint_programs/?action=american_eagles.

United States Mint. "Nickel." Accessed March 22, 2012. http://www.usmint.gov/mint_programs/circulatingCoins/?action=CircNickel.

US Marshals Service. "Neil Howie, Second U.S. Marshal of Montana Territory." Accessed December 30, 2011. http://www.justice.gov/marshals/district/mt/profiles/howie.html

University of Montana Western. "Epilogue." Accessed December 30, 2011. http://www.my.umwestern.edu/Academics/library/libroth/MHD/vigilantes/HTS/epilog/htm.

University of North Texas Digital Library. "The WPA Dallas Guide and History." Accessed May 12, 2012. http://digital.library.unt.edu/ark:/67531/metadc28336/m1/96.

Uschan, Michael V. *The Oregon Trail: Landmark Events in American History*. Milwaukee: World Almanac Library, 2004.

Valentine, Alan. *Vigilante Justice*. New York: Reynal & Company, 1956.

The Vigilante Parade. "History." Accessed October 9, 2011. http://www.chs.helena.k12.mt/olyb/vigilante00/history.htm.

Virginia City Chamber of Commerce. "A Brief Virginia City History and the Virginia City Preservation Alliance." Accessed November 21, 2010. http://www.virginiacity.com/#history.

Virginia City Chamber of Commerce. "Fun Facts and Quotes." Accessed December 18, 2011. http://www.virginiacity.com/#fun_facts.

Virginia City Chamber of Commerce. "Virginia City Firsts." Accessed December 18, 2011. http://www.virginiacity.com/#fun_facts.

Wahl, Jenny. "Give Lincoln Credit: How Paying for the Civil War Transformed the United States Financial System." *Albany Government Law Review* 3 (2010): 700–18.

Ward, Geoffrey C. *The Civil War: An Illustrated History*. New York: Alfred A. Knopf, 1990.

Ward M. Canaday Center for Special Collections, University of Toledo. "Finding Aid: James M. Ashley Papers, 1860–1960." Accessed May 13, 2012. http://www.utoledo.edu/library/canaday/HTML_findingaids/MSS-002.html.

Webelements. "Arsenic." The Periodic Table on the Web. Accessed March 4, 2012. http://www.webelements.com/arsenic/.

Weber, Mark. "The Trial of Henry Plummer: May 7th, 1993." Vigilantes of Montana: Secret Trials and Midnight Hangings, 1863–1864. Accessed December 10, 2011. http://www.yanoun.org/mont_vigi/revisit/trial1.html.

Wells, Merle W. "The Idaho-Montana Boundary." *Idaho Yesterdays* 12 (Spring 1981): 13.

Wells, Merle. "Notable Idaho Nineteenth-Century Judicial Cases." *The Advocate (Boise, ID)* 43 (March 2000): 22.

Williamson, Samuel H. "Seven Ways to Compute the Relative Value of a U.S. Dollar Amount, 1774 to Present." MeasuringWorth. Accessed March 8, 2012 http://www.measuringworth.com/uscompare/.

Wilson, Gary A. *Outlaw Tales of Montana*. Guilford, CT: Morris Book Publishing, 2003.

Wilson, R. Michael. *Frontier Justice in the Wild West: Bungled, Bizarre, and Fascinating Executions*. Guilford, CT: TwoDot Publishing, 2007.

Wolle, Muriel Sibell. *Montana Pay Dirt: A Guide to the Mining Camps of the Treasure State*. Denver: Sage Books, 1963.

Wylie, Paul R. *The Irish General Thomas Francis Meagher*. Norman: University of Oklahoma Press, 2007.

Zhu, Liping. "'A Chinaman's Chance' on the Rocky Mountain Frontier." In *Chinese on the American Frontier*, ed. Arif Dirlik, 231–52. Lanham, MD: Rowman & Littlefield Publishers, 2001.

Newspapers

Akron (OH) Daily Democrat
Anaconda (MT) Standard
Andrew County Republican (Savannah, MO)
Bemidji (MN) Daily Pioneer
Big Horn County News (Hardin, MT)
Bozeman (MT) Daily Chronicle
Brenham (TX) Weekly Banner
Daily Rocky Mountain Gazette (Helena, MT)
Daily Yellowstone Journal (Miles City, MT)
Day Book (Chicago, IL)
Dillon (MT) Tribune
Fergus County Argus (Lewistown, MT)
Great Falls (MT) Tribune
Hartford (KY) Herald
Helena (MT) Daily Herald
Helena (MT) Weekly Herald
Independent Record (Helena, MT)
Intermountain and Colorado Catholic (Salt Lake City, UT)
Los Angeles Daily Herald

Madisonian (Ennis, MT)
Marietta (OH) Daily Leader
Montana Post (Virginia City, MT)
Montana Radiator (Helena, MT)
Montana Record Herald (Helena, MT)
Montana Standard (Butte, MT)
Montana Stock & Mining Journal (Helena, MT)
Moscow-Pullman (ID) Daily
National Law Journal
New York Sun
New York Times
New York Tribune
North Platte (NE) Semi-Weekly Tribune
Rocky Mountain News
San Francisco Morning Call
St. Paul (MN) Globe
Sun (London)
Tacoma (WA) Times
Times Dispatch (Richmond, VA)
Virginia Tri-Weekly Post (Virginia City and Helena, MT)
Virginia Weekly Post (Virginia City and Helena, MT)
Waco (TX) Daily Examiner

Government/Legal Sources

Constitutions

United States Constitution
Montana Constitution

Treaties

Burlingame-Seward Treaty between the United States of America and the Empire of China, entered into Februrary 5, 1870.
Fort Laramie Treaty of September 17, 1851, 11 Stat. 749 (1851).
Fort Laramie Treaty of February 16, 1868, 15 Stat. 635 (1868).

United States Statutes

Acts of the Second Congress, Sess. Law 1792, ch. 16, secs. 9, 11, and 16.
Acts of the Twenty-Fourth Congress, sess. 2, P.L. 24, 5 Stat. 136.
The Chinese Exclusion Act, Forty-Seventh Cong., sess. 1, ch. 126, approved May 6, 1882.
Act of February 25, 1862, ch. 33, secs. 3, 5, 12 Stat. 345, 346.
Act of June 3, 1864, ch. 106, 13 Stat. 99.
Act, March 2, 1867, 14 Stat. 426 (1867).
The Enabling Act of the State of Montana, February 22, 1889, 25 Stat. 676 (1889).
Federal Reserve Act of 1913, 12 U.S.C. ch. 3 (1913).
National Banking Act, ch. 58, 12 Stat. 665 (1863).
Organic Act of the Territory of Alaska, Act of August 24, 1912, ch. 387, 37 Stat. 512 (1912).
Organic Act of the Territory of Hawaii, P.L. 56-331, 31 Stat. 141 (1879).
Organic Act of the Territory of Idaho, Act of March 4, 1863, ch. 117, 12 Stat. 808 (1863).

Organic Act of the Territory of Montana, Act May 26, 1864, ch. 95, sec. 6, 13 Stat. 85 et seq. (1864).
Organic Act of the Territory of Oklahoma, Act May 2, 1890, ch. 182, 26 Stat. 81 (1890).
Organic Act of the Territory of Puerto Rico, P.L. 56-191, 31 Stat. 77 (1900).
Organic Act of the Territory of Wyoming, Act July 25, 1868, ch. 235, sec. 1, 16 Stat. 183 (1868).
P.L. 737, 48 Stat. 337.
P.L. 4231, 17 Stat. 424.
Trading with the Enemy Act, 40 Stat. 411, 415 (1917).

Montana Statutes

Laws 1865, First Terr. Legis., with Resolutions.
Laws 1866, Second Terr. Legis., with Resolutions.
Laws 1866, Third Terr. Legis., with Resolutions.
Laws 1867, Fourth Terr. Legis., with Resolutions.
Laws 1869, Fifth Terr. Legis., with Resolutions.
Laws 1870, Sixth Terr. Legis., with Resolutions.
Laws 1872, Seventh Terr. Legis., Mining Law, ch. 82, p. 593.
Laws 1874, Eighth Terr. Legis., with Resolutions.
Mont. Code Ann. 7-32-2302 (2001).
Mont. Code Ann. 22-3-804 (1991).
Mont. Code Ann. 26-1-102 (1983), 26-1-804 (2009).
Mont. Code Ann. 30-20-104 (2009).
Mont. Code Ann. 41-5-206 (2007), 41-5-2503 (1999).
Mont. Code Ann. 45-1-201 (1977), 45-2-101 (2009), 45-5-102 (1999), 45-2-203 (1987), 45-3-102 (2009), 45-7-303 (2009).
Mont. Code Ann. 46-2-201 (2005), 46-11-311 (1991), 46-11-314 (1991), 46-11-316 (1991), 46-11-317 (1991), 46-11-404 (1991), 46-11-331 (2009), 46-12-102 (1991), 46-12-204 (2002), 46-13-210 (1993), 46-15-322 (1993), 46-18-111 (2009), 46-18-201 (2009), 46-18-202 (1994), 46-18-231 (2007), 46-23-201 (2003), 46-23-202 (2003).
Mont. Stat. Ann. 52-5-111 (1997).
Mont. Stat. Ann. 53-20-101 (1995), 53-20-148 (1997), 53-30-321 (1997).
Mont. Stat. Ann. 61-5-208 (2009), later amended in 2013.
Former Mont. Stat. Ann. 45-2-203, 94-2-109, and 94-2-119.

Court Rules

Fed. Rule Evidence 804.
Mont. Rules of Evidence 404.
Mont. Code Ann. Rules 801, 802, 804.

Presidential Executive Orders

Executive Order 6102—Forbidding the Hoarding of Gold Coin, Gold Bullion, and Gold Certificates within the Continental United States (1933).
Executive Order 11825—Revocation of Executive Orders Pertaining to the Regulation of the Acquisition of, Holding of, or Other Transactions in Gold (1974).

About the Author

MARK C. DILLON is an associate justice in the Appellate Division of the New York State Supreme Court and an adjunct professor of law at Fordham Law School in New York City, and has a special interest in the history of law-making, law enforcement, and "unauthorized justice" in the Montana Territory of the 1860s.

Judge Mark C. Dillon at a historical marker in Virginia City, Montana.

Index